Midwest Studies in Philosophy
Volume VI

MIDWEST STUDIES IN PHILOSOPHY

EDITED BY PETER A. FRENCH, THEODORE E. UEHLING, JR., HOWARD K. WETTSTEIN
ASSOCIATE EDITOR JEFFERY JOHNSON

EDITORIAL ADVISORY BOARD:
  ROBERT AUDI (UNIVERSITY OF NEBRASKA)
  JONATHAN BENNETT (SYRACUSE UNIVERSITY)
  PANAYOT BUTCHVAROV (UNIVERSITY OF IOWA)
  DONALD DAVIDSON (UNIVERSITY OF CHICAGO)
  KEITH DONNELLAN (UNIVERSITY OF CALIFORNIA, LOS ANGELES)
  FRED I. DRETSKE (UNIVERSITY OF CALIFORNIA, LOS ANGELES)
  GILBERT HARMAN (PRINCETON UNIVERSITY)
  HERBERT HEIDELBERGER (UNIVERSITY OF MASSACHUSETTS)
  J. L. MACKIE (UNIVERSITY COLLEGE, OXFORD)
  DAVID ROSENTHAL (LEHMAN COLLEGE, CUNY)
  STEPHEN SCHIFFER (UNIVERSITY OF SOUTHERN CALIFORNIA)

Virtually all papers in MIDWEST STUDIES IN PHILOSOPHY are invited and previously unpublished. The editors will, however, consider unsolicited manuscripts that are received by January of the year preceding the appearance of a volume. All manuscripts must be pertinent to the topic area of the volume for which they are submitted. Address manuscripts to The Editors, MIDWEST STUDIES IN PHILOSOPHY, University of Minnesota, Morris; Morris, MN 56267.

The articles in MIDWEST STUDIES IN PHILOSOPHY are indexed in THE PHILOSOPHER'S INDEX.

Forthcoming Volumes
  Volume VII   February 1982 Social and Political Philosophy
  Volume VIII   February 1983 Contemporary Perspectives on the History of
                Philosophy

Previously Published Volumes:
  Volume I   February 1976 Studies in the History of Philosophy . . . . . out of print
  Volume II   February 1977 Studies in the Philosophy of Language . . . .in print
                Rev. Ed., Contemporary Perspectives in the Philosophy of Language
  Volume III   February 1978 Studies in Ethical Theory. . . . . .in print
  Volume IV   February 1979 Studies in Metaphysics. . . . . .in print
  Volume V   February 1980 Studies in Epistemology. . . . . .in print

Midwest Studies in Philosophy
Volume VI
The Foundations of Analytic Philosophy

Editors
PETER A. FRENCH
THEODORE E. UEHLING, JR.
HOWARD K. WETTSTEIN

Associate Editor
JEFFERY JOHNSON

University of Minnesota Press • Minneapolis

Copyright © 1981 by the University of Minnesota
All rights reserved.
Published by the University of Minnesota Press,
2037 University Avenue Southeast, Minneapolis MN 55414
Printed in the United States of America

Library of Congress Cataloging in Publication Data
Main entry under title:

The Foundations of analytic philosophy.

   (Midwest studies in philosophy; v. 6)
    1. Analysis (Philosophy)—Addresses, essays,
lectures. I. French, Peter A. II. Uehling,
Theodore Edward. III. Wettstein, Howard K.
IV. Series.
B808.5.F68   190   81-4722
ISBN 0-8166-1033-9   AACR2
ISBN 0-8166-1036-3 pbk.

The University of Minnesota
is an equal-opportunity
educator and employer.

Midwest Studies in Philosophy
Volume VI
The Foundations of Analytic Philosophy

Brentano's Analysis of the Consciousness of Time	Roderick M. Chisholm	3
Frege: The Last Logicist	Paul Benacerraf	17
Frege's Hierarchies of Indirect Senses and the Paradox of Analysis	Terence D. Parsons	37
Are There Atomic Propositions?	Fred Sommers	59
Frege on Predication	Richard L. Mendelsohn	69
Frege and Analytic Philosophy: Facts and Speculations	Michael D. Resnik	83
Frege and Chomsky on Thought and Language	J. M. Moravcsik	105
Russell's 1913 Map of the Mind	Douglas Lackey	125
What *Was* Russell's Neutral Monism?	Michael Lockwood	143
Knowledge, Acquaintance, and Awareness	A. R. White	159
The Vienna Circle	A. J. Ayer	173
Notes on the Ontology of Minds	Gustav Bergmann	189
Logical Form, Existence, and Relational Predication	Herbert Hochberg	215
Popper's Criticisms of Wittgenstein's *Tractatus*	E. D. Klemke	239
Peirce, Wittgenstein, and Systematic Philosophy	Renford Bambrough	263
The Light Wittgenstein Sheds on Religion	W. D. Hudson	275
The Discovery of Nonsense	Irving Thalberg	293
The Informativeness of Philosophical Analysis	Diana F. Ackerman	313
Ryle's Theories of Concepts	Morris Weitz	321

Ryle's Thoughts on Thinking. Zeno Vendler	335
Austin's Theory of Illocutionary Force . . . . Graham Bird	345
Illusions and Sense-Data . . . . David H. Sanford	371
Semantic Innocence and Uncompromising Situations . . . . Jon Barwise and John Perry	387
Analytic Philosophy and Mental Phenomena. . . . . John R. Searle	405
Quine and the Confirmational Paradoxes . . . . Charles Chihara	425
Reply to Chihara. . . . . W. V. Quine	453
The Significance of Naturalized Epistemology. . . . . Barry Stroud	455
Reply to Stroud . . . . W. V. Quine	473
The Metaphysic of Abstract Particulars . . . . Keith Campbell	477
The Fallacy behind Fallacies . . . . Gerald J. Massey	489
A Proposed Solution to a Puzzle about Belief . . . . . Ruth Barcan Marcus	501
Donnellan's Distinction . . . . Michael Devitt	511
Notes on Contributors	527

Midwest Studies in Philosophy
Volume VI

Brentano's Analysis of the Consciousness of Time

RODERICK M. CHISHOLM

Franz Brentano's conception of philosophical analysis is illustrated by his analysis of our consciousness of time. The analysandum is not a linguistic expression or a concept; it is an experience of a certain sort. Hence the analysis might be called "phenomenological," but Brentano prefers to say it is a matter of "descriptive psychology."

An analysis of our consciousness of time is not, or course, an analysis of time. Hence Brentano's analysis is consistent with a number of different conceptions of time. But it does presuppose that tense is to be taken seriously. In other words, Brentano does not accept the philosophical view, advocated by many contemporary philosophers of science, according to which distinctions of tense are merely "subjective" or otherwise "illusory." Nor does he believe that all truths can be expressed in untensed sentences.

I shall begin by formulating what Brentano takes to be a fundamental problem of descriptive psychology—that of accurately describing our awareness of temporal succession. Then I shall set forth the development of his views with respect to this problem.

THE SOURCE OF OUR CONCEPT OF TIME

The source of our concept of time, according to Brentano, is the intuitive experience he calls 'proteraesthesis" *[Proterästhese]* or "original association" *[ursprüngliche Association]*. This experience, he insists, is to be distinguished from sensation. Examples are the hearing of a melody, the seeing of something in motion, and the seeing of something at rest. In each case, we experience a succession *[Nacheinander]*: in the first case one note preceding another note; in the second case the moving object being now in one place and now in another; and in the third case one and the same thing remaining exactly where it was. The experience of any such succession involves what may be called an experience of the past *[Verganenheitsempfindung]*. The duration of such proteraesthesis is very brief. For example, in a single experience we "see" part of the circular motion of the second-hand of a clock, but we do not see the entire circular motion and if the motion were not sufficiently swift we would not see it at all. Yet brief as such experiences are, they enable us to acquire the concepts of past, present, and future, the concepts of before and after, and the concept of a temporal continuum extending indefinitely in two directions.

A PROBLEM OF DESCRIPTIVE PSYCHOLOGY

Consider now the proteraesthesis involved in the hearing of the first four notes of a melody, say *a, b, c,* and *d.* This provides us with a paradigm case of the experience of a succession.

In his lectures in Würzburg in 1873, Brentano depicted the hearing of such a melody by means of the accompanying diagram.[1]

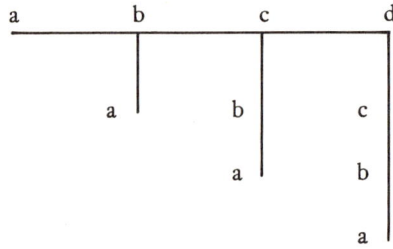

The horizontal line represents the actual temporal succession of the four notes that are heard, the direction from past to future being that from left to right: the line depicts the auditory *sensations* that the subject has at four different moments. The vertical lines depict the subject's *proteraesthesis* at three of these moments. The first vertical line illustrates the proteraesthesis that occurs during a moment that *b* occurs, the second during a moment that *c* occurs, and the third during a moment that *d* occurs.

The experience is not adequately described by saying this: "We experience *a* and then we experience *b* and then we experience *c.*" For such a statement would be a report only of a succession of experiences and not a report of an experience of succession. It could be true on occasions when it would be false to say that what we experience is *a* followed by *b* and then *b* followed by *c.* For example, if we had experienced *c* yesterday, *b* the day before, and *a* the day before that, we could say that we had experienced *a* and then experienced *b* and then experienced *c.* But we would not thereby have experienced a succession.

Some have said that the field of consciousness is temporally extended in the way in which, say, the visual field may be said to be spatially extended. According to this view, just as a red spot can be at the left side of the visual field and a blue spot at the right, so, too, the note *c* can be in the present part of the visual field while *b* is in a part that is past and *c* is in a part that is even more past. But does it make sense to say of the note *b* that it *is* past? If *b* is no longer in the present, we cannot say that it *is* in a part that is past. If we take tense seriously, as Brentano does, we cannot say of the field of consciousness or of the objects of sensation that they (now) *have* a temporal extension.[2]

Upon hearing the first three notes of the melody, we are aware of all three in a single experience, as depicted in the third vertical line. Yet the experience of a succession is not the experience we have when we are aware of three notes sounding together as in hearing a chord. The three notes *a*, *b*, and *c*, if heard all at once, would provide a discord and not the beginning of a melody. And therefore it will not do to say that the experience is a matter of hearing the three notes in such a way that the earlier notes are presented simply as being fainter than those that follow them. After all, what if the melody were a *descresendo*? When we hear the third note, the first and the second are presented with their original intensity.

It is tempting, but hardly adequate to the facts of the matter, to describe the experience of proteraesthesis by appeal to memory. Thus one might say: "First we hear the *a*, then we hear the *b* and at the same time remember having heard the *a*, and then, after that, we hear the *c* and remember having heard the *b*." Realizing that such a description still seems to leave something out, one may add: "On hearing the *c*, we remember not only having heard the *b* but also having heard the *b* *while* remembering having heard the *a*." The experience of the melody would thus be described as a combination of a present perception with the memory of a past perception and with the memory of a perception that is even more past. But this is hardly successful as a description of the experience of hearing a melody. The conclusion may seem inescapable, therefore, that we experience *c* as preceded by *a* and by *b*, and hence that, in experiencing *c*, we experience both *a* and *b* as past. But if we experience *a* and *b* now, how can we be said to be experiencing them as *not* now and as such that one of them is *before* the other?

We have, then, a problem for descriptive psychology. But the problem is more than this. If proteraesthesis is the source of our concept of time, then, if we cannot give a coherent account of proteraesthesis, it may be questioned whether we can give a coherent account of time. And so it was obvious to Brentano that the solution to the problem of proteraesthesis should also provide us with what is necessary for understanding time itself.

In his early lectures on the consciousness of time, Brentano attempted to solve the problem by saying that the temporal distinctions to be found within experience may be traced to the nature of the *objects* that are experienced. Then he revised his opinion and held that temporal distinctions are to be traced, not to the nature of the objects, but to the nature of the *act* — to the *way* in which they are experienced.

Before we examine this development of Brentano's conception, let us consider briefly the general theory of consciousness that he presupposes in these investigations.

THE GENERAL THEORY OF CONSCIOUSNESS

Brentano's general theory of consciousness may be set forth briefly as follows.

(1) Every psychical act involves the thinking of *[Vorstellung]* — or presentation of — an object. In Brentano's later writings he insists that the objects of thought or presentation are restricted to individual things or *entia realia* (e.g., to such things as horses, trees, unicorns). What we think of is always an individual thing, or concretum, as qualified in some way or other.

(2) Thinking-of is *intentional*. This means that, from the fact that an object is thus thought of, or presented, it does not follow that the object exists.

(3) *Judgment* is a matter of accepting or rejecting an object of thinking (an object of presentation). Hence judgments are either affirmative or negative. And since the object of judgment is the same as the object of the presentation that underlies the judgment, the object of judgment — according to Brentano's later view — is always an individual thing or *ens reale*. The object of judgment, therefore, is not the kind of propositional entity designated by means of such expressions as "that there are horses" or "that there are no unicorns." For example, if a person believes that there are horses, then *horse* constitutes the object of an affirmative judgment, and if he believes that there are no unicorns, then *unicorn* constitutes the object of a negative judgment.

(4) There are different *modes* of mudgment. In particular, one may distinguish judgments that are assertoric from judgments that are apodictic. For example, if a person can be said to judge that round squares are impossible, then he apodictically rejects round squares.

(5) No act of thinking, or presentation, occurs without the subject *ipso facto* judging with evidence that that act of thinking, or presentation, occurs. Brentano puts this by saying that the act of presentation has *itself* as its "secondary object." If I think of a unicorn, the unicorn is the "primary object" of my thinking; and my thinking of a unicorn is the "secondary object" of my thinking. Brentano would also put the latter point by saying that my thinking of the unicorn is an object of my "inner perception."

(6) *Inner perception* is always a matter of judging with evidence about one's own intentional acts. To say that I innerly perceive that I am thinking about a unicorn is to say that I judge with evidence — and therefore with truth — that I am thinking about a unicorn.

(7) *Sensation* is a matter of: (a) being presented with a certain sense-content, or sense-object, and (b) "blindly" accepting that content (i.e., making it an object of an affirmative judgment, but a judgment that is not evident). The sensation is accompanied by the evident judgment — the inner perception — that one is presented with that content.

Brentano also holds that the *objects* of sensation — for example, the patch of color one is said to sense — do not exist. (We have noted that presentation does not imply the existence of its object.) From the fact that I sense a red patch, it will follow that it is evident to me that I sense a red patch, but it will not follow that the red patch exists.

Brentano sometimes calls sensation "external perception" in order to contrast it with inner perception. One should note that this is not the contemporary philosophical use of "perception." Thus Brentano uses "see" and "hear," respectively, to refer to the sensing of a visual content and to the sensing of an auditory content. Hence, given his assumption about the existence of sensory content, he can say that, from the fact that I *see* a patch of color or *hear* a certain note, it does not follow that the patch of color or the note exists.

(8) *Proteraesthesis* is to be distinguished from sensation—for the objects of sensation, in the strict sense of the term "sensation," are not in any way presented as being past. But, as we have said, it is a necessary accompaniment of every sensation. Indeed, Brentano says that sensation exists only as the *boundary [Grenze]* of an experience of proteraesthesis.[3]

If a sense-content is the primary object of sensation, what is the primary object of proteraesthesis? We shall see that Brentano's views about the way to answer this question change in a very significant way.

PAST AND FUTURE AS "MODIFYING" ATTRIBUTES

We cannot say, of the earlier notes in the experience of proteraesthesis, that "they exist in the present with the attribute of being past." For nothing *has* the attribute of being past. If anything *has* a given attribute, that thing exists now and cannot be said merely to exist in the past. How, then, are we using the word "past" when we say that the note is presented as past?

When Brentano lectured on descriptive psychology at the University of Vienna between the years 1888 and 1891, he proposed the following account of the meaning of the word "past." The adjective "past" should not be thought of as expressing a genuine attribute at all. Rather, it may express what Brentano called "a modifying attribute *[ein modifizierendes Attribut]*."[4]

If we say of something that it is a "tall King" or a "wise King," we imply that the thing *is* a King, and our adjectives express genuine attributes. The adjectives "tall" and "wise" in the expressions "tall King" and "wise King" could be said to *add to* what is suggested by the noun "King." But if we say of something that it is an "apparent King" or a "supposed King," we do not imply that the thing *is* a King and our adjectives, therefore, are only "modifying."[5] Other English adjectives that may thus be modifying are: "deposed," "departed," "so-called," "former," "apparent." Such adjectives *subtract from* what is suggested by the noun "King." And if we speak of "*imagined* King" or of an "*imaginary* King," the adjectives may so modify the subject that the entire expression no longer designates an *ens reale* at all.

One way of characterizing such modifying adjectives is this. If the locution "There is an A B" is one wherein the word replacing "A" is a modifying adjective and one wherein the expression replacing "B" is a concrete term, the locution does not imply "There is a B." Now it is clear that "past" functions as such a modifying adjective. If we say of someone that he is "a past King," we do not imply that he *is* a king.

According to Brentano's early view, then, the adjectives "past" and "future" serve to modify their subjects in this way. Hence *past Kings* and *future Kings* are not genuine things but are merely *entia irrelia*. In other words, from the fact that something is true of a past King, or of a future King, we may not draw any particular conclusion about what exists now. (We can say only that present individuals are such that there *was* such-and-such a past King or there *will be* such-and-such a future King.) The experience of time, then, involves nonexistent things to which such modifying attributes may be applied.

Consider again the situation depicted in Brentano's diagram and, in particular, the experience the subject has when sensing the *second* note b. What is the status of the proteraesthesis that he then has with respect to the *first* note a? It is not as though he had one sensation having a present b as its object and another sensation having a past a as its object. The proteraesthesis involving the note a is comparable, rather, to the *secondary object* of the sensing of b. The secondary object of the sensing of b is, not b, but the *sensing of b*. And the proteraesthesis that accompanies the sensing of b is, not a sensing of a past a, but the past sensing of an a. Thus, where the *secondary* object of the sensation is a present sensation, the *primary* object of the proteraesthesis is a past sensation.[6] This means that the primary object of the proteraesthesis is a *modified intentional relation* — an intentional relation that is past. The modifying attribute of pastness was thought to be quantitative and capable of degrees.

But Brentano was to reject this "modification theory."

One problem was this. The past experiences that are involved in proteraesthesis are *entia irrelia*. And yet they form a continuum bounded by *entia realia* — by actual things that have no such modifying attributes. Writing to Anton Marty in 1894, Brentano expressed these misgivings about the earlier view: Past, present, and future form a continuum. But how can things so heterogeneous as *entia realia* and *entia irrelia* form a continuum? "There would be less difference between a non-thing and a thing than there would be between two non-things; indeed there would be infinitesimally little difference between them!"[7] Colors and sounds cannot form a continuum, for they are of different species. How, then, can things and nonthings form a continuum?

Moreover, the "modification theory" really leaves us with our problem, as Brentano came to see. Sentences containing such modifying expressions as "supposed king" and "false gold" can be rephrased in sentences that do not contain such expressions. Thus "He is a supposed king" tells us that the person in question is thought to be a king, and "That is false gold" tells us that the thing in question, though it may be thought to be gold, is not in fact gold. If "past" and "future" are thought to be modifying expressions, then, Brentano suggests, we should try to make a similar paraphrase of the sentences in which *they* appear. We will find we cannot succeed.[8]

He concluded that the only way to understand the source of our apprehension of temporal predicates is to think of them, not as being derived from the *objects* of our experience, but as being derived from *the ways in which we experience*.

To find the solution to our problem, then, we should look to the nature of the psychical act itself.

THE THEORY OF TEMPORAL MODES OF JUDGMENT

We consider, then, this possibility. Temporal differences within experience are to be thought of, not as differences in the objects that we are conscious of, but as differences in the ways in which we are conscious of the objects.[9] It is presupposed, then, that there are *temporal modes* of consciousness. Brentano first thought that such temporal modes apply primarily to judgment.

As we have noted, Brentano thought of differences of the quality of judgment—the distinction between affirmative and negative—as applying primarily to the *act* of judgment and not to the *object* of judgment. It is one thing to affirm or accept the object of judgment, and it is another thing to deny or reject it. Here, then, we have two modes of judgment—affirmative and negative. It was not difficult for Brentano, then, to suppose that differences of tense are comparable to differences of quality. And so in the 1890s when he first gave up the "modification theory," i.e., the doctrine according to which past and future are modifying attributes, he first replaced it by this view: the fact that there are temporal differences within experience is a matter of different modes of *affirmation*. It is one thing to affirm an object as now (i.e., to affirm the object *simpliciter*); it is another thing to affirm the object as past; and it is still another to affirm the object as future.[10]

The nature of this move is easy to illustrate, given a propositional theory of judgment. Thus if differences of tense are differences with respect to the *object* of judgment, we may distinguish the three objects: *Socrates is walking, Socrates was walking,* and *Socrates will be walking.* And each of these objects may be accepted or denied *simpliciter.* But if differences of tense are differences with respect to the *act* of judgment and not differences with respect to the object of judgment, then there is the single object of judgment—*Socrates walking*—which may be judged-present, judged-past, or judged-future. This theory is readily adaptable, of course, to Brentano's nonpropositional theory of judgment.

But Brentano did not hold that there are only three modes of temporal judgment. He held, rather, that there can be a continuum of temporal judgments. This continuum could be illustrated crudely by means of such expressions as "judged-past," "judged-more-past," and "judged-still-more-past." According to the earlier "modification theory," there could be said to be a continuum of nonthings bounded by things. But according to the later view there could be said to be, rather, a continuum of different species of judgment.

Brentano's description of the hearing of the melody would now become this: At the time of the hearing of the third note *c,* one accepts *c* in the mode of the present, one accepts *b* in a mode of the past, and one accepts *a* in the mode of a more distant past. The *object* of the acceptance of *b* in the past is now said to be the same as the object of the original sensation of *b* in the mode of the present. And similarly for *a.* Marty summarized this view as follows.

Here, too, the act of intuition incorporates the affirmative judgment as well; and now it is not too far-fetched to say that instead of thinking of the objects of proteraesthesis as being modified in a continual way, we transfer this modification to the corresponding affirmation while the object remains unchanged. The object of proteraesthesis is the same as that of sensation, but it is connected with a modified form of the affirmation. For example, red is always seen and affirmed, but this affirmation is subject to a continual transformation and it is this transformation that, as it were, makes the object temporally remote and that constitutes the source of our knowledge of time.[11]

But surely there is more to proteraesthesis than the fact that we *judge* or *accept* the relevant object in different temporal modes. Moreover, as Brentano came to realize, our consciousness of time cannot be explicated merely by reference to such differences of *judgment*. For judgment is not the only intentional attitude that may be directed toward the past and the future. What we call past things and future things may also be emotional objects—objects of love or hate—without thereby being judged. And they may be simply objects of thought, without being loved or hated, accepted or negated.

Brentano now makes a further revision.

TEMPORAL MODES OF PRESENTATION

According to Brentano's next—and final—view, the fact that there are temporal differences within experience is a function, not merely of different temporal modes of *judgment,* but of temporal modes of presentation *[Vorstellung]*. It is one thing for a note, say, to be presented *[vorgestellt]* as present and another thing for it to be presented as past. (We should remind ourselves that, according to Brentano, a thing need not exist in order to be an object of presentation.) Brentano wrote in 1911:

> If we hear a series of sounds in a conversation or in a melody or if we watch a physical object which is in motion or is changing colour, then individually the same sound, individually the same spatially and qualitatively determined coloured thing, appears to us first as present, then more and more as past, while new things appear as present, whose presentation then undergoes the same modal alteration. Anyone who took these differences to be differences of the objects involved—somewhat as spatial differences undoubtedly are when I have a presentation of something more to the right or more to the left in my field of vision—would be unable to do justice to the great difference which exists between space and time.[12]

In setting forth Brentano's original "modification theory," we said that, at the second moment depicted in his diagram, the subject experiences a *b* and a past experience of an *a* and that, at the third moment, he experiences a *c* and a past experience of a *b* and an even more past experience of a *a*. Now we shall say that, at the second moment, he experiences-as-present a *b* and experiences-as-past an *a*.

At the third moment, he experiences-as-present a *c*, experiences-as-past a *b*, and experiences-as-more-past an *a*. The word "past," in short, does not modify the object of the experience; rather, it modifies the way the object is presented. The subject does not sense a *past sensing* of an *a*; rather, he *senses as past* an *a*. And there are many different ways in which an object may thus be sensed as past.

According to the original version of the modification theory, then, Brentano viewed the succession of notes as involving a continuous series of changes in the *objects* of experience. But now he interprets the succession of notes as involving a continuous series of changes in the *temporal modes* in which these objects are experienced. Writing to Marty, Brentano contrasts the old and the new theories this way: Where before "we had a limited continual series of objects in the proteraesthesis, we now have a limited series of modes of apprehension of the same object."[13]

The temporal modes of presentation can themselves form a continuum. If one note is presented as being past, another note may be presented as being less past, and still another note may be presented as being more past. Hence, Brentano says, in proteraesthesis we are related to the object in different ways, "and these ways vary continuously from Asthese to the farthest moment of Proterasthese."[14]

Brentano makes it clear that, in putting forth the theory of temporal modes of presentation, he does not thereby abandon the theory of temporal modes of judgment. For, he says, it would be contradictory to suppose that there can be temporal modes of presentation but no temporal modes of judgment.[15] The judgments that we make are a function of the presentations *[Vorstellungen]* that underlie them, and we would not be able to make judgments about the past or about the future unless we had these temporal modes of presentation. And so, too, for the emotions.

The proper description of proteraesthesis, then, is this: "When something that had been given as present appears as more and more past, it is not the case that *different objects* are apprehended as existing; rather the same object is apprehended throughout, but in *different ways*, with a different mode of apprehension."[16] The temporal modes of judgment are a function of the temporal modes of presentation. One judges in a temporal mode if one accepts what is presented in that temporal mode.[17] In proterasthesis the temporal modes involve *primarily [zunächst]* presentation and *thereupon [daraufhin]* affirmation.

THE TEMPORAL MODES AS MODI OBLIQUO

In the Supplementary Remarks to the *Psychology*, first published as *Von der Klassifikation der psychischen Phänomene* (1911), Brentano introduced the distinction between the *modus rectus* and the *modus obliquus*. If I think of a person who is thinking of a golden mountain, then I think of the person in *modo recto* and of the golden mountain in *modo obliquo*. Until the last few years of his life, Brentano had held that affirmative judgments about the past resemble affirmative judgments about the present in affirming their objects in *modo recto*.[18] But, according to his final view, judgments about the past are judgments in *modo obliquo*. He held, more generally, that objects of the temporal modes of presentation—those other than the present—are always experienced in *modo obliquo*.

Generally speaking, when we think of one thing as standing in a certain relation to another thing, we think of the first thing in *modo recto* and the second thing in *modo obliquo*. If, for example, we think of *the teacher of Alexander*, then we think of the teacher in *modo recto* and of Alexander in *modo obliquo*. According to Brentano's final view of temporal thinking, if we think of a certain thing as past or as future, then, actually, we are thinking of the thing in *modo obliquo* and we are thinking *in modo recto* of some present thing.

The proper description, then, of the hearing of the melody *a*, *b*, *c* would be this: (i) at the first of the three moments singled out in the diagram, an *a* is presented in *modo recto* and in the mode of the present; (ii) at the second moment, a *b* is presented in *modo recto* and in the mode of the present, and *a* is present in *modo obliquo* in a mode of the past; and (iii) at the third moment, a *c* is present in *modo recto* and in the mode of the present, *b* is present in *modo obliquo* and in a mode of the past, and *a* is present in *modo obliquo* and in a mode of a greater degree of the past.

Brentano points out that it would be a mistake "to think of the temporal modes of the past and future as being merely *modi obliqui*."[19] For they involve more than thinking of a present thing as being earlier or later than some other thing. We can think of it as being *more* or *less* removed from the present. It is necessary to appeal to the temporal modes in order to be adequate to this more and less.

Thus Brentano writes in one of the appendixes to the *Psychology:* "If something is affirmed temporally, if it is affirmed as past or as future, it is affirmed only in the *modo obliquo*, which is to say it is not actually affirmed at all. Something now existing *[ein jetzt Bestehendes]* is affirmed as more or less separated from it in one of two opposing directions."[20] The "jetzt Bestehendes," which may be the I or the subject of experience, is thus affirmed as a relativum—the fundament of a relation—and therefore in *modo recto,* whereas the "vom ihm Abstehendes" is the terminus of the relation and is affirmed only in *modo obliquo*. Whenever we affirm a thing as past, then, we are *ipso facto* also affirming in the strict sense something as present and we are judging the present thing to be later than the past thing.[21]

What happens when we hear a note followed by a *rest*? In such a case the note is presented in *modo obliquo* and the perceiver himself is presented in *modo recto*.[22]

THE DENIAL OF INNER PROTERAESTHESIS

There remains still another aspect of Brentano's doctrine which is essential to his theory of time consciousness. This is his denial of "inner proteraesthesis." To understand this doctrine, let us consider in detail the points made above pertaining to the "primary" and "secondary" objects of sensation and of proteraesthesis.

According to Brentano, whenever we perceive anything we are aware, not only of the object of perception, but also of our perception of that object. Quoting Aristotle, he observed that, if we see or hear anything, our seeing or hearing is presented "along with [*nebenher*]" the thing that we see or hear. He wrote, in the first edition of the *Psychologie:* "We can say that the sound is the *primary object* of the hearing and that the hearing itself is the *secondary object.*"[23] And the I, or the subject of experience, may be said to be included in the secondary object of perception. If I am immediately aware of a tone, then, according to Brentano, I am immediately aware that *I* am immediately aware of a tone. Hence he writes: "Inner perception grasps the spiritual soul."[24] Inner perception entitles us to say that it is certain that the I exists.

Suppose I now recall a certain experience of sorrow. The primary object of the original experience was the thing toward which my sorrow was then directed. But this thing is not the primary object of my recollection. In recalling the act of sorrow, however vividly, I need not relive the sorrow. The primary object of the recollection is not the primary object of the original experience; it is, rather, the secondary object of the original experience.

The primary object of consciousness, according to Brentano, is never presented with evidence. In other words, we can never know with certainty that the primary object exists. But the secondary object—the intentional act itself—is always presented with evidence. These observations also apply to memory. The thing remembered—the primary object of memory—is never presented with evidence, but the *act* of remembering is always presented with evidence. Thus we could say that memory presents *itself* with certainty but does not present its *object* with certainty. (We should note that Brentano here uses the word "remember" as other philosophers have used "seems to remember" or "thinks one remembers." Thus "I remember hearing *c*," in this use, does not imply that I *did* hear *c*, much less that I *know* that I heard *c*.)

What, now, of the primary object of proteraesthesis? When Brentano accepted the modification theory, he held that the primary object of proteraesthesis is an *act* of consciousness—a past presentation, say, of the note *b*. Brentano insisted at that time that *b* itself was *not* the primary object of the proteraesthesis. But according to his final view, the primary object of the proteraesthesis is *not* the past sensation of *b*; it is *b* itself as presented in a mode of the past.

If now I experience a certain sensation as past, it will be *evident* to me that I experience a sensation as past. In asking whether there is "inner proteraesthesis," Brentano is asking this: if I have an experience of a past sensing of a note, will it be evident to me that I once *did* sense the note as present? His answer is that no previous inner perception can be evident to me *now;* for *no* matter of fact about the past can be evident to me now. (It is at least logically possible that God has just created me. If this is so, my ostensible memories—including my ostensible awareness that I have just heard notes *a* and *b*—would be unveridical. The present experience cannot guarantee any past event. And since this is so, Brentano concludes that no fact about the past can be apprehended with evidence.)

The prior perceptions, then, cannot be evident to me now. That is to say, it cannot be evident to me *now* that those perceptions were evident to me *then*. Hence there cannot be inner proteraesthesis.

Brentano also notes that the *assumption* of inner proteraesthesis would entanble us in such problems as the following: when in fact I heard the *a*, I heard it as being present; now, while I hear the *c*, I hear the *a* as past; but if the original act of *hearing* the *a* were *also* an object of proteraesthesis, then, in now being aware of *that* act of consciousness, I would still be hearing the *a* as present. Hence I would be hearing it as present and also as past. But this is not an accurate description of my experience.

If there were inner proteraesthesis, I would also be aware of myself as something undergoing change — as something that hears now *a* and something that hears now *b* and something that hears now *c*. But Brentano denies that I can have such awareness. Thus he observes at the beginning of "Vom Gedächtnis," the second essay in Part Two of *Raum, Zeit, und Kontinuum*, that in the experience of outer proteraesthesis, "I appear to myself, not as someone who has previously experienced something as present, but as someone who now experiences something as past."[25] Writing to Stumpf in 1906, Brentano said: "When I hear a melody, what appears to me is a succession of notes, not a succession of hearings. I do not apperceive myself as someone who has heard something, but as someone who hears one note as present and another note as past and retreating still farther into the past."[26] My "past self," then, is never the object of inner perception. Although I exist now, I cannot be certain (even though I may have reason for believing) that I existed a few moments ago. Inner perception, according to Brentano, does not confirm the hypothesis that I have persisted through time as an individual substance. This hypothesis, he says, is to be compared with the hypothesis of an external physical world *[Hypothese der körperlichen Aussenwelt]*; it cannot be evident but it is "confirmed in so many ways, that I cannot find it unreasonable to adhere to it."[27] It is, moreover, a hypothesis that Brentano takes very seriously when he considers the subject of experience and attempts to show that materialism is false.[28]

One may ask: Isn't the persistence of the self confirmed by Brentano's own theory of the temporal? According to Brentano's view, whatever exists exists now; but whatever exists now is *also* such that either it did exist or it will exist at some time continuous with now. For the now is a boundary of a temporal continuum, and boundaries, according to Brentano's doctrine, exist only as belonging to continua.

Brentano considers this objection and replies as follows: "One should observe that, although a boundary must belong to a continuum, no particular continuum is required for its existence. For every particular continuum has a determinate size. But no continuum of any determinate size is required for the existence of the boundary. However small one may think of such a continuum as being, a half of it would suffice — as would a half of this half, and so on *ad indefinitum*."[29] Brentano concludes, then, that the certain knowledge we have of the existence of ourselves does not extend beyond the point of the now. For there is no period of time, however small, which extends into the past or into the future and which is such that we can know that the self existed at *that* time.

Two points are to be distinguished. (1) There is no finite period of time, however short, which is such that I can be certain that I have existed or will exist through *that* period of time. Nevertheless (2) I can be certain that there is *some* finite period of time which is such that I will have existed through that period of time. Brentano emphasizes the first in denying the experience of inner proteraesthesis. But the second follows from the temporal nature of *entia realia*: "An *ens reale* is as such something that is temporally extended."[30] And this is sufficient to show that I do know that I am a subject that persists through time.[31]

Notes

1. This is reported by Carl Stumpf on p. 136 of his "Erinnerungen an Franz Brentano," in Oskar Kraus, *Franz Brentano* (Munich, 1919). Stumpf's essay is reprinted as "Reminiscences of Franz Brentano," in *The Philosophy of Franz Brentano*, ed. Linda McAlister (London, 1976), pp. 10-46; see p. 38.

2. But everything is temporal in that every thing is such that either it did exist or it will exist. Brentano puts this point by saying that everything exists as a temporal boundary [*Grenze*].

3. This view was set forth in his lectures entitled "Psychognosie," given at the University of Vienna in 1890-91. These are classified in the Brentano *Nachlass* as EL 74. An edition of these lectures, to be entitled *Deskriptive Psychologie* and edited by Roderick M. Chisholm, is to appear in 1981 in the Felix Meiner Verlag of Hamburg.

4. In Edmund Husserl, *Zur Phänomenologie des inneren Zeitbewusstseins* (The Hague; 1966), there is a criticism of Brentano's early views about our consciousness of time (see pp. 10-18). Husserl does not mention Brentano's subsequent view that our consciousness of time has its source in modes of presentation [*Vorstellungsmodi*]. See Oskar Kraus, "Zur Phänomenognosie des Zeitbewusstseins," *Archiv fur die gesamte Psychologie* 75 (1930):1-22; reprinted as "Toward a Phenomenognosy of Time Consciousness" in McAlister's *The Philosophy of Franz Brentano*, pp. 224-39. Kraus's paper was occasioned by the publication of Martin Heidegger's edition of Husserl's "Vorlesung zur Phänomenologie des inneren Zeitbewusstseins," in Husserl's *Jarbuch fur Philosophie und phänomenologische Forshung* 9 (1928):367-489. Brentano's lectures had been the impetus for Husserl's work on this topic, as Husserl notes (see p. xv of the 1966 edition).

5. Compare Brentano's *Vom sinnlichen und noetischen Bewusstsein* ed. Oskar Kraus (Hamburg, 1968), p. 46; and Anton Marty's exposition of Brentano's early view, in Kraus's "Zur Phänomenognosie des Zeitbewusstseins." There is a detailed study of such modifying adjectives in Marty's posthumous "Von den logisch nicht begrundeten synsemantischen Zeichen," published in Otto Funke, *Grundfragen zur Bedeutungslehre* (Leipzig, 1928); this work originally appeared in *English Studies* 62 and 63 (1928).

6. These points are made in the 1890-91 lectures on descriptive psychology.

7. Quoted in Kraus, "Zur Phänomenognosie des Zeitbewusstseins," p. 7; English translation in McAlister, p. 228.

8. See Brentano's letter to Marty of March 1906, reprinted in Brentano's *Die Abkehr vom Nichtrealen* (Hamburg, 1978), p. 160.

9. This move will call to mind Kant's "Copernican revolution" and the doctrine that time is a "form of inner sense." But Brentano's view can hardly be called Kantian. This latter point is obvious in view of Brentano's doctrine according to which what is real coincides precisely with what is temporal or "in time."

10. John Stuart Mill said that "the circumstance of time is properly considered as attaching

to the copula, which is the sign of predication, and not to the predicate." *A System of Logic*, part I, chap. IV, sec. 2.

11. The passage occurs in a lecture Marty prepared in 1895 concerning Brentano's theory of our consciousness of time. Quoted by Kraus in McAlister, p. 236.

12. *Psychology from an Empirical Standpoint* (London, 1973), p. 279; *Psychologie von Empirischen Standpunkt* (Hamburg, 1971), II, p. 143.

13. From Kraus's article on time, in McAlister, p. 228. Brentano also observes that when the note is experienced as becoming "more and more past," it "appears as one and the same unitary note, which is only such that it is apprehended by us successively with a different temporal mode." *Die Abkehr vom Nichtrealen*, p. 247; my translation.

14. ". . . und diese Weise variiere kontinuierlich von der Ästhese bis zum fernsten Moment der Proterästhese." *Vom sinnlichen und noetischen Bewusstsein*, pp. 48-49.

15. *Die Abkehr vom Nichtrealen*, p. 287.

16. "Indem was vorerst als gegenwärtig gegeben war, mehr und mehr vergangen scheint, werden *nicht andere* Objekte als seiend anerkennt, sondern dasselbe Objekt in anderer Weise, mit einem andern Modus des Anerkennens, anerkannt." From Brentanos *Philosophische Untersuchungen zu Raum, Zeit, und Kontinuum* (Hamburg, 1976), p. 96; my translation. Compare pp. 45-52 of *Vom sinnlichen und noetischen Bewusstsein*.

17. See *Raum, Zeit, und Kontinuum*, p. 22.

18. See Kastil's note 72 to *Raum, Zeit, und Kontinuum*, p. 223.

19. See *Die Abkehr vom Nichtrealen*, p. 278.

20. *Psychology*, p. 364; *Psychologie*, II, p. 271.

21. Compare *Raum, Zeit, und Kontinuum*, p. 128. See also Brentano's 1906 letter to Stumpf, quoted in Kraus's Introduction to the *Psychology from an Empirical Standpoint*, p. 405.

22. *Psychology*, p. 329.

23. *Psychology*, p. 128; *Psychologie*, I, p. 180.

24. "Die innere Wahrnehmung . . . erfasst ja die geistige Seele"; *Raum, Zeit, und Kontinuum*, p. 111; my translation. But as Kastil notes in connection with this passage, inner perception does not yield the information *that* the soul is spiritual *[geistig]*; *ibid.*, p. 224. Compare *Vom Dasein Gottes* (Hamburg, 1980), p. 418, and *Kategorienlehre* (Hamburg, 1968), p. 158.

25. " . . . erscheine ich mir nicht als einer der früher etwas als gegenwartig empfunden hat, sondern als einer, der etwas jetzt als vergangen empfimdet" (p. 86); my translation.

26. Quoted by Kraus, in his Introduction to *Psychology from an Empirical Standpoint*, p. 406.

27. " . . . schon so vielfach bewährt, dass ich es nicht unvernünftig finden kann, ihr auch ferner anzuhangen." *Raum, Zeit, und Kontinuum*, p. 93; my translation.

28. See *Religion und Philosophie* (Hamburg, 1978), pp. 232-33.

29. *Vom sinnlichen und noetischen Bewusstsein*, p. 14; my translation.

30. *Raum, Zeit, und Kontinuum*, p. 107; my translation.

31. Husserl emphasizes the second of these points: "Die Beziehung der Evidenz auf den Punkt des Jetzt muss eine Fiktion sein. Evidenz der *cogitatio* ist doch schon Evidenz eines Dauernden als solchen." *Zur Phänomenologie des inneren Zeitbewusstseins*, p. 295.

Frege: The Last Logicist[1]

PAUL BENACERRAF

When I was young I was taught a number of fundamental propositions: Frege was the father of logicism—he showed that arithmetic was really only logic (ingeniously disguised), and consequently that it was really analytic, which was really why it was a priori, all of which showed where Kant had gone wrong about arithmetic, and probably about the rest of the alleged synthetic a priori as well.

I was told too that Frege had invented the logic that arithmetic was really only—or at the very least that he was the father of modern logic. Had I stopped to think, it might have occurred to me to question this all too happy coincidence of discovery and invention. At the very least, a decent interval should have been allowed to elapse between the discovery (invention) of the laws of logic and the further (?) discovery that they were just what had been needed to show that the basic laws of arithmetic had really been basic laws of logic all along.

We have a tangle of problems here

concerning what Frege thought he was doing

concerning what we should take him to have done, both for logic and for arithmetic

concerning the proper assessment of the broader philosophical import of these achievements.

This paper addresses itself to some of these issues. My most immediate concern will be to examine the role of the logicist doctrine in early twentieth-century empiricism in order to determine whether the view adopted (or adapted) from Frege by the positivists was a view that he himself had held. I would like my discussion to serve as a starting point for a deeper understanding of Frege's own views and ultimately for the discussion of the fascinating philosophical issues themselves. To broach these, I must return to the fundamental propositions I was taught as a youth. They concern the content and philosophical import of the logicist thesis.

1. LOGICISM

As *I* learned it, logicism was a philosophical view closely allied with empiricism: it was heralded by Carnap, Hempel, members of the Vienna Circle, Ayer, and others as the answer to Kant's doctrine that the propositions of arithmetic were synthetic a priori. Focusing on the sentences that express mathematical propositions, logicists conceded that *these* were a priori — that they could be known independently of experience (except, of course, for what experience may be required to formulate them). But, in reply to Kant, logicists claimed that these propositions are a priori because they are *analytic* — because they are true (or false) merely "in virtue of" the meanings of the terms in which they are cast. Thus, to know their meanings is to know all that is required for a knowledge of their truth. No empirical investigation is needed. The philosophical *point* of advancing the view was nakedly epistemological: logicism, if it could be established, would show that our knowledge of mathematics could be accounted for by whatever would account for our knowledge of language. And of course it was assumed that knowledge of language could *itself* be accounted for in ways consistent with empiricist principles, that language was itself entirely *learned*.[2] Thus, following Hume, all our knowledge could once more be seen as concerning either "relations of ideas" (analytic and a priori) or "matters of fact" (synthetic and a posteriori). Kant's challenge to that dichotomy was turned back by showing that his most challenging counterexample — mathematics — though admittedly a priori, had mistakenly been classified by him as synthetic.

Logicism comes packaged in a number of different versions, each with its own wrinkles; but most have the following general structure:

1. The truths of arithmetic are *translatable* into truths of logic.
2. (1) is demonstrated by
   a. providing definitions for the "extra-logical" vocabulary (concepts) of arithmetic in "purely logical" terms; and
   b. noting that the translations induced by these definitions carry arithmetical truths into logical truths and arithmetical falsehoods into logical falsehoods.
3. This arithmetical demonstration is then claimed to establish the *analyticity* of the mathematical propositions, because (a) since the definitions supposedly preserve meaning, the logical translations have the same meaning as the arithmetic originals and (b) the logical truths are *themselves* thought to be true in virtue of meaning, in this case, of the meanings of the logical particles occurring in them (and thus analytic).

Whether this is a viable view is something that has been much discussed. I engaged in that discussion myself some years ago[3] in a piece that can be read as arguing that either the definitions of the mathematical terms do not preserve their meaning, or their meaning does not determine their reference, since different and equally adequate definitions assign different referents to the mathematical vocabulary. I will argue later, contrary to what I formerly thought Frege to hold, that he and I speak with one voice. Definitions adequate to *his* purposes need not preserve reference. But more about this later. Right now, I am primarily interested in outlining the logicist's position for the purpose of comparison with Frege's own.

Relatively little has been written on the issue of whether logic itself is analytic, so a word might be in order here simply to locate the question and some of its possible answers in the spectrum of positions under examination.

If, as W. V. Quine has done,[4] one defines analytic truth as transformability into a logical truth by meaning-preserving definitions, it becomes a trivial matter that the laws of logic are analytic; but such a definition, as applied to logic, bears little ostensible relation to the traditional account of analyticity as truth-in-virtue-of-meanings. Yet it was *this* latter explanation which bore the epistemological burden of persuading us that analytic propositions were also a priori. It should also be mentioned in favor of Quine's definition that it bears clear lines of ancestry to Frege and through him, back to Kant. For Frege's account of analyticity, to be found early in the *Grundlagen*, was:

> The problem whether a mathematical proposition is analytic or not becomes in fact that of finding the proof of the proposition, and of following it up right back to the primitive truths. If in carrying out this process we come only on general logical laws and on definitions, then the truth is an analytic one. . . (*Grundlagen* 4).[5]

Thus, a proposition is analytic if its proof makes use only of general logical laws and definitions.

We will examine this definition in detail below. The aspect to notice at this time is that "proof" from general logical laws and definitions is *sufficient* for analyticity. Of course, this does not make Frege's account equivalent with the one suggested (but not advocated) by Quine, since Quine and Frege differ on what the logic is to be and probably also on the role of definitions. For Quine, logic is first-order quantification theory plus identity, whereas for Frege it was considerably more extensive than that. Since Quine's narrower version of logic does not suffice for the "proofs" of the laws of arithmetic, mathematics is *not* analytic in Quine's sense, though it still might be in Frege's. I say "might be" because when Frege's logic failed to be consistent (and presumably, thereby also failed to be logic), his view was left with a certain indefiniteness; whether arithmetic turns out to be analytic in Frege's sense will have to depend at least on what logic one substitutes for Frege's ill-starred version.

The connection with Kant is made by Frege himself when he likens his own account to Kant's but chides Kant for the narrowness of his conception (*Grundlagen* Section 88). He criticizes Kant for giving a definition that applies only to universal general propositions—those which can be construed as having a subject-predicate form—and for having too narrow a conception of definition, one presumably fashioned for use in showing that the concept of the subject term of a proposition contains the concept of the predicate.

So Frege offered an account of analyticity designed to improve Kant's in two respects: (a) it classified *all* propositions as analytic or synthetic, i.e., it was purportedly exhaustive, and (b) it broadened the concept of definition beyond Kant's notion (which Frege refers to as definition "by a simple list of characteristics") (*Grundlagen* 100) into one that encompassed "the really fruitful definitions in mathematics" (*Grundlagen* 100).[6]

I wish to stress the epistemological motivation of the twentieth-century logicist. This is, of course, manifest in the third component of his view, in which he tries to reap a rich philosophical harvest from the seeds that Frege has sown. A striking example is the position advanced by C. G. Hempel in an article[7] that, although breaking no really new ground, presented a nuclear point of view as only Hempel can. According to Hempel, the Frege-Russell definitions of number, 0, successor, and related concepts have shown the propositions of arithmetic to be analytic because they follow by stipulative definitions from logical principles. What Hempel has in mind here is clearly that in a constructed formal system of logic (set theory or second-order logic plus an axiom of infinity), one may introduce by stipulative definition the expressions 'Number', 'Zero', 'Successor' in such a way that sentences of such a formal system using these introduced abbreviations and which are formally the same as (i.e., spelled the same way as) certain sentences of arithmetic—e.g., 'Zero is a Number'—appear as theorems of the system. He concludes from that undeniable fact that these definitions show *the theorems of arithmetic* to be mere notational extensions of theorems of logic, and thus analytic.

He is not entitled to that conclusion. Nor would he be *even* if the theorems of logic in their primitive notations were themselves analytic. For the only things that have been shown to follow from theorems of logic *by stipulation* are the abbreviated theorems of the logistic system. To parlay that into an argument about the *propositions of arithmetic*, one needs an argument that the sentences of arithmetic, in their pre-analytic senses, *mean the same (or approximately the same) as their homonyms in the logistic system.* That requires a separate and longer argument. I bring this up here not to berate Hempel but to use his view as an illustration of the epistemological motivation that drives twentieth-century logicists. The *point* of logicism was to make it intelligible on empiricist principles how we might have *a priori* knowledge of mathematics. "By stipulation," says Hempel. If this much were correct, it would at least reduce the problem to the analyticity of logic, a problem I will not tackle here, although I will point out some obvious ways in which certain answers affect the proper assessment of the logicist's philosophical position.

Matters become particularly tangled when the analyticity of logic is in turn discussed in the context of defending such a logicist position; for such a logic must comprise enough set theory (or suitable equivalent) to yield enough mathematics. The only solution that seems to be offered in such a case is that the *axioms* constitute an implicit definition of the concepts. This is a form of conventionalism that construes the axioms as stipulations that are to govern the use of the terms they contain: *So use/understand this language that its sentences come out true!* This is difficult enough to understand when the interpretation of the "logical vocabulary" is kept fixed; as an instruction applicable to an entire language it makes no sense at all; as an explanation of how sentences of logic *in fact* get their truth values it is worthless, as Quine[8] and others have made abundantly clear. Logic is needed to *apply* such a rule to individual cases. Of course, it may *in fact* be the case that we use the language in such a way that the sentences in question do come out true. But what we seek is an *explanation* of that fact which will at the same time make the truth-values of these sentences knowable a priori. For this is the task that the twentieth-century logicist has set for himself.

So far I have concentrated on explaining the complex of philosophical views, taken in the philosophical setting of meeting Kant's challenge to empiricism, which has been the logicism of this century. It might seem curiously eccentric of me in a discussion of twentieth-century logicism to have made no mention of the most famous twentieth-century logicist: Russell Whitehead. I have omitted him for two reasons. (1) Because no brief account will encompass his shifting and differing stands; and (2) because, perhaps for this very reason, what I have taken the liberty to call "logicism" has fed more on his (and Frege's) technical achievements than on his fluctuating philosophical assessment of those achievements. (I might add, parenthetically, that to say even this much is already to make an untenable distinction between his "technical achievements" and his "philosophical views"—as anyone who has tried to puzzle out the *Principia Mathematica* concept of propositional function well knows.)

Such, then, is the received view: Kant's challenge has been met. Mathematics is really analytic, not synthetic. This was shown by Frege when he showed how mathematical propositions have the same meaning as logical propositions, which themselves are analytic (and therefore knowable a priori). Frege showed this by analyzing the "extra-logical" vocabulary of arithmetic and providing definitions that preserved meaning (and therefore, reference and truth). Frege was, therefore, the first logicist.

2. FREGE

If Frege was the first logicist, then he was also the last. If it is appropriate to call what Frege *actually* believed "logicism," and if he was the first to believe it, then, most probably he was also the last. To my knowledge, no one since Frege—and certainly no twentieth-century "logicist"—has held precisely the position that Frege advocated in the *Grundlagen* and that moved him to write that philosophical masterpiece. Although the views summarized in the previous paragraph are fairly widely held (I think most philosophers with a view on the subject are closet "logicists" in this sense), they were not Frege's. There are various points of contact which make it tempting to think that Frege held such a position, but I will argue that he did not —that his view was a much more intriguing one and in its spirit directly antithetical to the philosophical motivation of his twentieth-century "followers."[9]

First of all, of course, Frege was no empiricist. True, one of the philosophical aims of the *Grundlagen* was to refute Kant's doctrine that arithmetic consisted of synthetic a priori propositions. But Frege readily conceded what no empiricist would concede — that Euclidean geometry was synthetic a priori. He says:

> In calling the truths of geometry synthetic and a priori, he [Kant] revealed their true nature. And this is still worth repeating, since even today it is often not recognized. If Kant was wrong about arithmetic, that does not seriously detract, in my opinion, from the value of his work. His point was, that there are such things as synthetic judgments a priori; whether they are to be found in geometry only, or in arithmetic as well, is of less importance (*Grundlagen* 101-2).

So for him, establishing the analyticity of arithmetical judgments is not a way of defending empiricism against Kantian attack. It has another purpose, one which I hope to uncover by examining how he introduces and defends his views.

Frege opens the *Grundlagen* by deploring the fact that no one seems to have given a satisfactory answer to the question "What is the number one?":

> . . . is it not a scandal that our science should be so unclear about the first and foremost among its objects, and one which is apparently so simple? Small hope, then, that we shall be able to say what number is. *If a concept fundamental to a mighty science gives rise to difficulties, then it is surely an imperative task to investigate it more closely until those difficulties are overcome* . . . (*Grundlagen* xiv [my italics]).

This sets the stage. It is to be an inquiry into the foundations of arithmetic with a view to overcoming the "difficulties" to which its fundamental concepts give rise. It is tempting to think that Frege is speaking tongue-in-cheek, that he does not really regard our inability to give a satisfactory account of the concept of number a genuine difficulty *within that science*. To be sure, it is a philosophical worry — one appropriate for philosophers — but not a difficulty *internal to the science of number itself*. But this would be a mistake. Frege emphasizes that it is a matter with which mathematicians themselves *qua* mathematicians must be concerned, even though the inquiry will of necessity contain a substantial philosophical component:

> I realize that . . . I have been led to pursue arguments more philosophical than many mathematicians may approve; but any thorough examination of the concept of number is bound always to turn out rather philosophical. It is a task which is common to mathematics and philosophy (*Grundlagen* xvii).

In urging that a proof is incomplete unless the definitions have been thoroughly justified, he says:

> Yet . . . the rigor of the proof remains an illusion . . . so long as the definitions are justified only as an afterthought, by our failing to come across any contradiction. By these methods, we shall, at bottom, never have

achieved more than an empirical certainty, and we must really face the possibility that we may still in the end encounter a contradiction which brings the whole edifice down in ruins. For this reason I have felt bound to go back rather further into the logical foundations of our science than perhaps most mathematicians will consider necessary (*Grundlagen* xxiv).

We should take him at his word. It is a concern with the foundations of arithmetic that motivates his study.

Small wonder, given his title.

But such a concern might be interpreted in two different ways, corresponding to the interests of a philosopher and to those of a mathematician. Typically, the philosopher takes a body of knowledge as given and concerns himself with epistemological and metaphysical questions that arise in accounting for that body of knowledge, fitting it into a general account of knowledge and the world. That is Kant's stance. He studies the nature of mathematical knowledge in the context of an investigation of knowledge as a whole. And that was the positivist's stance, though they reached quite different conclusions.

But a mathematician's interest in what might be called "foundations" is importantly different. *Qua* mathematician, he is concerned with substantive questions about the truth of the propositions in question, as well as slightly more "philosophical" issues concerning how such propositions are properly established. The interests of the two groups are not disjoint—nor can these questions be sharply separated. But the differences are significant, and it is important to keep them in mind as we approach Frege. I claim that the Frege of the *Grundlagen* has the mathematician's motivation; that where he appears to deal directly with the more typically "philosophical" issues (Are the propositions of arithmetic analytic or synthetic? A priori or a posteriori?), *it is because he has restructured those questions and posed them in such a form that the answers they require will answer the substantive mathematical questions which are his principal concern.* Thus, if logicism is the complex of philosophical views I described in the first part of this paper, Frege was no logicist.

So, on his view, unless we do as he urges, "we must really face the possibility that we may still in the end encounter a contradiction which brings the whole edifice down in ruins."[10] What needs to be done? Quite starkly, this. The propositions of arithmetic stand in need of *proof*. We cannot simply taken them for granted, on intuition, or accept them because they have proved useful in their many applications. ". . . in mathematics, a mere moral conviction, supported by a mass of successful application, is not good enough" (*Grundlagen* 1). It is quite the same situation as if, in some more advanced branch of mathematics, a body of "knowledge" had arisen but never been adequately justified. ". . . it is in the nature of mathematics always to prefer proof, where proof is possible. . ." (*Grundlagen* 2).

In section 1, Frege explains the *general* need for rigor and proof in mathematics. In section 2, he defends his search for proofs of such propositions as 7 + 5 = 12 or the Associative Law of Addition, by the last remark I quoted and by likening the matter to the case of Euclid's proofs of "many things which anyone would concede him without question" (*Grundlagen* 2). He then moves on to what I take to be the heart of his view when he explains the aim of proof as follows:

> Philosophical motives *too* have prompted me to enquiries of this kind. The answers to the questions raised about the nature of arithmetic truths—are they a priori or a posteriori? analytic or synthetic?—must lie in this same direction. For even though the concepts concerned may themselves belong to philosophy, yet, as I believe, no decision on these questions can be reached without assistance from mathematics—though this depends of course on the sense in which we understand them (*Grundlagen* 3 [my emphasis]).

As the "too" I emphasized indicates, the motives discussed so far have been mathematical, not philosophical. Only now is he turning to what he feels may be considered the philosophical aspect of his work. And he serves notice that he will so construe the "philosophical" questions of the a priori and analytic character of arithmetical truths that they shall have mathematical answers. No doubt it will be somewhat controversial to what extent Frege's redefinitions of these concepts are simple clarifications and to what extent they are important reconstruals. This will depend on what we take Kant's and Leibniz's intentions to have been. What concerns me more is the contrast between these concepts as defined by Frege and the corresponding notions that are woven into the texture of the philosophical views I have called "logicism" and which I outlined in the first part of this paper.

The best way to seek out these answers is to follow section 3 paragraph by paragraph, adding what interpretive commentary seems appropriate. The section is short, but rich in the substance of Frege's thought.

> It not uncommonly happens that we first discover the content of a proposition, and only later give the rigorous proof of it, on other and more difficult lines; and often this same proof also reveals more precisely the conditions restricting the validity of the original proposition. In general, therefore, the question of how we arrive at the content of a judgement should be kept distinct from the other question, "Whence do we derive the justification for its assertion?" (*Grundlagen* 3).

This is a seemingly innocent distinction, pointing out that we often form propositions in our minds—indeed come to believe them—and only later (or perhaps never) arrive at proofs of those propositions (or of suitably restricted versions of them). The point of this remark is to try to separate the notion of the content of a judgment from that of the justification for the judgment—in the sense of justification introduced in the previous section: namely, the "support" of the judgment; the propositions on which it "depends" for its truth. Frege's attempt to divorce these two ideas (content and justification) will be crucial to his critique of Kant, a central aspect of his redefinition of analyticity, and a pivotal point of difference with later "logicists."

So we must recognize this distinction as the first leg of an attack on Kant. The reason is transparent. For Kant, the distinction between analytic and synthetic propositions was primarily a distinction in the *content* of the propositions. And the epistemological *point* was that this distinction in content had, for the analytic propositions, the immediate consequence that they were a priori—that they were knowable independently of experience just on the basis of a consideration of their *content*. For it was a fact about the content of an analytic proposition that it was possible to notice that in merely *entertaining* such a proposition one could not think the concept of its subject term without thinking along with it in the appropriate way the concept of its predicate term. Thus a major problem of the *Critique* was establishing the very possibility of a priori *synthetic* judgments: it seemed obvious why analytic judgments were a priori; but an elaborate theory had to be developed to account for the a priori character of judgments that did not pass the simple test that certified them as analytic and hence obviously a priori. Twentieth-century "logicists," following Kant in this respect, accorded a priori status to an enlarged class of analytic propositions *on the basis of their content*—for truth-in-virtue-of-meanings is simply an extension of Kant's distinction and of the epistemological analysis that went along with it. (I should add, parenthetically, that once the class of propositions has been enlarged beyond the subject-predicate propositions to which Kant limited his attention, the easy route to the a priori from the analytic is no longer available.) On this revisionist view, Kant was wrong because, hobbled by an inadequate notion of content owing to a primitive logical and semantical theory, he failed to appreciate the fact that arithmetical propositions were also true for the same kind of reason—merely in virtue of their content. Thus, on the received view of Frege's work and of its relation to this tradition, one would have expected him to claim precisely what I attributed to the "logicists"—that where Kant had gone wrong was in his analysis of the *content* of arithmetical propositions. And indeed, as we see above, Frege criticized Kant's distinction between analytic and synthetic judgments for not being exhaustive (*Grundlagen* section 88). Although it would be tempting to construe this as Frege's criticism of Kant's analysis of the *content* of arithmetical judgments, a construal which would tend to locate Frege in the epistemological tradition that runs through Kant to the contemporary logicist, it would be misleading to do so. For Frege shows in the very next paragraph that he has set up his distinction between content and justification for the express purpose of eschewing further talk of content. The paragraph is full of oblique references to Kant's discussion of analyticity and has a footnote in which he claims to be following Kant. I quote both the paragraph and the footnote:

> Now these distinctions between a priori and a posteriori, synthetic and analytic, concern, as I see it,* not the content of the judgment but the justification for making the judgment. . . . When a proposition is called a posteriori or analytic in my sense, this is not a judgment about the conditions, psychological, physiological and physical, which have made it possible to form the content of the proposition in our consciousness; nor is it a judgment about

the way in which some other man has come, perhaps erroneously, to believe it true; rather, it is a judgment about the ultimate ground upon which rests the justification for holding it to be true.

---

*By this I do not, of course, mean to assign a new sense to these terms, but only to state accurately what earlier writers, Kant in particular, have meant by them (*Grundlagen* 3).

The point of introducing the content/justification distinction is to place *both* the a priori/a posteriori *and* analytic/synthetic distinctions squarely on the side of justification, something he will carry through to its conclusion when he explicitly defines all four concepts in the following and concluding paragraph of section 3. As for the above paragraph, the oblique references to Kant are the denials that in calling a proposition analytic or a priori we are concerned in any way with the conditions that have made it possible to form the content of the judgment or, by implication, what in fact happens when one forms the judgment in our minds. This is Kantian language. It has a psychologistic flavor, and Frege wants none of it. What he particularly wishes to avoid is treating the analyticity of propositions in terms of what happens in the mind when one entertains the proposition. Just such a discussion quite properly provided the link for Kant between the analyticity of the proposition and its a priori character. Frege's *reasons* for wishing to avoid such talk in general, and the difficulties to which (in my opinion) he was ultimately led by his particular brand of anti-psychologism, are fascinating questions in their own right, but the subject of another paper. I mention it only to bring into sharper focus the contrast Frege is drawing between his own position and Kant's, footnote disclaimers to the contrary.

So, to resume the argument, Frege sees *both* the question of the analyticity of the judgment and of its a priori character as concerning the *justification* of the judgment. Accordingly, he will provide definitions for these concepts (analytic/synthetic, a priori/a posteriori) that reflect this view. Since arithmetical propositions are at issue, the question of their justification is properly a matter for mathematics. Therefore, the concepts will be so defined as to make it a properly *mathematical* question whether some arithmetical judgment is analytic or synthetic, a priori or a posteriori. This will be in full accord with his remarks at the end of the first paragraph of section 3, which I quote again here for the sake of convenience:

> For even though the concepts concerned [analytic, synthetic; a priori, a posteriori] may themselves belong to philosophy, yet, as I believe, no decision on these questions can be reached without assistance from mathematics— though this depends of course on the sense in which we understand them (*Grundlagen* 3).

The sense in which Frege will understand them will be one that attempts to give some content to the notion of "the ultimate ground upon which rests the justification for holding . . . a judgment to be true." For this is the metaphysical notion on which his view depends. I say "metaphysical" to contrast the dependence to which he is alluding with epistemic dependence. There may be a hierarchical structure to our beliefs, with the hierarchy representing the relation of foundation or justification that a person's beliefs may bear to one another: the relation of dependence that *actually* obtains and which may vary from person to person even though the related beliefs might themselves be close to identical. On some (e.g., foundationalist) views, beliefs do form such a structure; on others (e.g., holist), they do not. Frege is not concerned with such a relation, but with relations of dependence *among the propositions themselves*, whether or not they are believed and however those beliefs may be related to one another in the epistemic world of any individual. To prove a proposition involves (at least) deducing it from the propositions on which it "depends" in this metaphysical sense. It involves tracing its ancestral lines of dependence back to propositions that are themselves "fundamental" or "primitive" and *have* no proofs—which cannot be reduced to more fundamental propositions.[11] I will now quote the balance of section 3, in which Frege gives his definitions and thereby fixes the sense of the questions: Are the propositions of arithmetic synthetic or analytic? A priori or a posteriori? I will devote the balance of my paper to a commentary on this paragraph.

> This means that the question is removed from the sphere of psychology, and assigned, if the truth concerned is a mathematical one, to the sphere of mathematics. The problem becomes, in fact, that of finding the proof of the proposition, and of following it up right back to the primitive truths. If, in carrying out this process, we come only on general logical laws and on definitions, then the truth is an analytic one, bearing in mind that we must take account also of all propositions upon which the admissibility of any of the definitions depends. If, however, it is impossible to give the proof without making use of truths which are not of a general logical nature, but belong to the sphere of some special science, then the proposition is a synthetic one. For a truth to be a posteriori, it must be impossible to construct a proof of it without including an appeal to facts, i.e., to truths which cannot be proved and are not general, since they contain assertions about particular objects. But if, on the contrary, its proof can be derived exclusively from general laws, which themselves neither need nor admit of proof, then the truth is a priori (*Grundlagen* 3-4).

To determine whether a proposition is analytic, look for a proof of it in which the basic propositions are "primitive truths"—propositions which themselves *have* no proofs. If there exists such a proof (one in which appeal is made only to definitions and to "primitive truths") and the primitive truths evoked include only laws of logic, the proposition in question is analytic. If not, it is synthetic. So, an analytic proposition is one that can be proved from logical axioms alone plus definitions. At least two aspects of this definition deserve comment.

First, Frege includes among the relevant propositions on which a given proposition depends "all propositions upon which the admissibility of any of the definitions depends." This is a consequence of his view that definitions must not simply be introduced in a proof; the proof is not complete unless they are justified as well. (Recall *Grundlagen* xxiv.) Many kinds of questions enter into the judgment of the admissibility of a definition, and it would be too difficult to review them all here. Frege discusses at least these two: (a) Will the introduction of this definition lead to contradictions? and (b) Will the introduction of this definition prove fruitful —i.e., can we prove things with it that we could not have proved without it (*Grundlagen* 81)?

The inclusion of this element in the definition of analyticity introduces a peculiar problem for Frege when he is discussing the analyticity of the laws of arithmetic. It is this: Normally, a negative answer to the first question (Will the introduction of this definition lead to contradictions?) or any positive answer to the second (Will it prove fruitful?) will require a proof involving some sort of induction, perhaps up to ω, ω^2, or even ϵ_0. If the proposition under consideration *is itself the relevant induction principle,* then either (1) no definitions are involved in its proof, in which case it is irreducibly arithmetical and not analytic; or (2) definitions *are* involved and once more induction is itself one of the principles on which it depends, since some appeal to induction would be required to demonstrate the admissibility of those definitions.[12] Unfortunately, Frege does not consider the question and leaves the notion of dependence insufficiently determinate to resolve this problem. For, whether *on Frege's definition* arithmetical truths are in fact analytic would depend on whether the "logical" principle of induction—i.e., induction in primitive logical notation—is sufficient to establish the admissibility of the definitions introduced in the proof of the *mathematical* principle of induction. If not, then arithmetic is not analytic *on Frege's definition.* But this is a very complicated issue which cannot be explored more fully here; I mention it as an interesting and relevant aspect of Frege's definition of analyticity.

The other matter on which I must comment, also inconclusively, I fear, also has to do with definitions. If we accept the view that I have been urging—that the problem of the *Grundlagen* is to argue that it is probable that one can find proofs of heretofore unchallenged but unproven arithmetical propositions—and if we take seriously Frege's view that finding such proofs is a *mathematical* problem like any other, then we must also regard the definitions that should be employed in these proofs as mathematical definitions like other mathematical definitions. In the *Grundlagen*, Frege does not tell us explicitly what semantical conditions these definitions must meet. (He does say a good deal in the *Grundgesetze*). Nor is this the place to provide a positive account of my own—either of the nature of mathematical definitions or of what Frege's positive view on this might have been. But the things he does say, although leaving it open what positive account he would offer, do render certain accounts unlikely.

Definitions are not *simply* conventions of abbreviation; for if they were, the requirement of fruitfulness cited above would make little sense. The fruitfulness would be a matter only of psychological heuristic and not something to which Frege would attach much importance. So, even if, formally, the definiens must serve at least as an "abbreviation" for the definiendum, the importance and principal role of the definition must lie elsewhere than in this function. Viz., Cantor's definitions of transfinite numbers, which Frege himself cites and praises (with reservations).

Similarly, mathematical definitions do not standardly reflect preexisting synonymies. The reasons are many. Quite apart from the uncertain status of the concept of synonymy, often a new term is introduced in the definition and there is consequently no question of preexisting synonymy. But, more important, typical and important cases of mathematical definition, of precisely the kind that Frege has in mind, just do not fit that model. To return to one example on which Frege himself comments, consider Cantor's Theory of Transfinite Numbers. Frege praises the theory as extending our knowledge but takes Cantor gently to task for having appealed to "the rather mysterious 'inner intuition' " (*Grundlagen* 98) in developing the theory "where he ought to have made an effort to find, and indeed could actually have found, a proof from definitions" (*Grundlagen* 98). Frege then goes on to add, "For I think I can anticipate how his two concepts [following in the succession, and Number] could have been defined" (*Grundlagen* 98). Surely, whatever Frege may be claiming here, he is not claiming that Cantor overlooked an appeal to preexisting synonymies which he, Frege, thinks he can produce. The analysis of this case—one which closely parallels the case of Number—is complicated. But whatever the correct answer, it does not seem as if it will be in terms of either preexisting synonymies or conventions of abbreviations.

If the two cases I have just mentioned exhaust the kinds of definitions that preserve sense or meaning, it remains an open question whether definitions of the kind employed in *Grundlagen* and in its formal counterpart, *Grundgesetze*, if they are adequate, must even preserve *reference*. I have myself argued elsewhere that this need not be so.[13] What did Frege think? I should like to point to two passages in which it seems clear that, for arithmetic at least, Frege did *not* expect *even reference* to be preserved by his definitions. The two passages I have in mind both concern the definition of Number. The first is a footnote to the definition of "the Number which belongs to the concept F" as "the extension of the concept 'equal to the concept F' " (*Grundlagen* 80). The footnote, keyed to the word "extension," reads as follows:

> I believe that for "extension of the concept" we could write simply "concept." But this would be open to two objections:
>
> 1. that this contradicts my earlier statement that individual numbers are objects, as is indicated by the use of the definite article in expressions like "the number two" and by the impossibility of speaking of ones, twos, etc. in the plural, as also by the fact that the number constitutes only an element in the predicate of a statement of number;
>
> 2. that concepts can have identical extensions without themselves coinciding.
>
> I am, as it happens, convinced that both these objections can be met; but to do this would take us too far afield for present purposes. I assume that it is known what the extension of a concept is (*Grundlagen* 80).

This is fairly conclusive, unless his way out of the second objection consists in arguing that for number concepts, concepts with identical extensions are not only identical with one another *but also identical with their extensions*, an unlikely course for Frege, given his views about the distinction between concepts and objects: concepts cannot be identical with anything. Identity is a relation reserved for objects.

The second passage occurs in the conclusion, as he comments on the same definition:

> This way of getting over the difficulty cannot be expected to meet with universal approval, and many will prefer other methods of removing the doubt in question. I attach no decisive importance to bringing in the extensions of concepts at all (*Grundlagen* 117).

It may help to recall what "the difficulty" in question was. After giving a *contextual* definition of the expression "the number which belongs to the concept F" only for the context of an identity in which both sides have the same form — e.g., "the number which belongs to the concept F is identical with the number which belongs to the concept G" — Frege noted that for his definition to be logically complete, it must fix the sense of all contexts containing that phrase. For example, an adequate definition should determine the truth-value of "the Number which belongs to the concept 'moons of Jupiter' is identical with Agamemnon." However, the definitions provided up to that point are not up to this task, and a further specification was needed. Frege chose the definition I cited. Thus, in precisely this context — the one most critical for determining whether he required definitions to preserve reference — Frege backs off and allows that different definitions, providing different referents (not "bringing in the extensions of concepts at all") might have done as well. It is as if the mathematical job of the definitions had already been done and all that remained was some logical tidying up, important, but of no mathematical consequence and for all that mattered to mathematics, something which would be done equally well in a number of different ways. The moral is inescapable. Not even reference needs to be preserved.

More needs to be said. It might be objected that at the time of *Grundlagen* Frege had not developed the concepts of sense and reference to a sufficient extent to imbue the questions I am raising with sense, and hence that they should not be raised. Although it is beyond the scope of the present paper to present the case in full detail, I believe that the very same questions can be raised about Frege's accomplishments in *Grundgesetze*,[14] which is certainly late enough. I will sketch my reasons.

In *Grundgesetze* Frege actually carries out the constructions that he only promises in *Grundlagen*. He constructs a system, formal in the technical sense, whose fundamental principles are those that he takes to be the basic laws of logic and from which he derives, by the introduction of definitions, the principles he had previously identified as the fundamental laws of arithmetic. In the course of that construction, several points appear at which "arbitrary" choices must be made — arbitrary in the sense that they are not determined by what has gone before, but which must nevertheless be made, if only for the sake of completeness. An example will serve to illustrate.

Frege introduces what he calls "courses-of-values" to represent the extensions of concepts. He stipulates that two functions have the same *course-of-values* if they have the same value for every argument. If the function is one

> whose value is always a truth-value, one may accordingly say, instead of "course-of-values of the function," rather "extension of the concept"; and it seems appropriate to call directly a *concept* a function whose value is always a truth-value (*Grundgesetze* 36).

So far, so good. The only defining condition he has imposed on courses-of-values is the contextual one that the courses-of-values of two functions shall be equal if they have the same value for every argument. He then notes that nothing that he has said bears on whether the two truth-values, the True and the False, are themselves courses-of-values, and if so, which ones. He summarizes this position:

> Thus without contradicting . . . [here he repeats the contextual definition] . . . it is always possible to stipulate that an arbitrary course-of-values is to be the True and another the False (*Grundgesetze* 48).

He then picks a particular one and stipulates that *it* is to be the True and another the False. The problem and its solution have exactly the same form as in the case of numbers and the extensions of concepts. And the philosophical consequences are also the same. If we call the one he picked "George," then "George = the True" lacked a truth-value before he did the picking, and acquired the True as its value from the pick. But had Frege not picked George but something else instead, "George = the True" would have been false. Since George then figures in every course-of-values, he figures in the extension of every (non-empty) concept. Had he not been the lucky one chosen, the extension of every concept would have been different.

Of course it does not make any mathematical difference. But *that* it makes no mathematical difference is an important philosophical point concerning what we must construe definitions such as Frege's to accomplish. Although I cannot pursue the matter further here, I hope that these examples make it clear that a straightforwardly "realist" construal of Frege's intentions or accomplishments will fail to do justice to his practice.

As I promised, the conclusion is unsatisfying. It seems clear that definitions for Frege are not a number of things we might have thought they might be. But it remains unclear what he thinks they are. This makes his notion of analyticity correspondingly unclear, or at least unspecified. If we accept the view that he is simply requiring that proofs be given for the arithmetical propositions that we have heretofore accepted without proof, then the notion is no worse than that of mathematical proof itself: it is hard to say what one is, but mathematicians produce and recognize them daily. Of course, that is not good enough for Frege, who wanted to remove the concept of mathematical proof from the realm of intuition and reduce it to a small number of precisely stated formal rules of logic. What we have learned from this discussion is that he will be unsuccessful in this task until he does the same for his concept of definition.

This brings me finally to Frege's concept of a priori.

> ... if ... the proof of a proposition can be derived entirely from general laws, which themselves neither need nor admit of proof, then the truth is a priori (*Grundlagen* 4).

First, for other writers, a priori had a definite direct connection with knowledge. Not so for Frege, since nothing in the above definition suggests that any a priori propositions are knowable at all—unless it is the reference to the fact that the ultimate truths from which a priori propositions can be proved do not themselves stand *in need* of proof. But this is rather empty since nowhere in the *Grundlagen* does Frege suggest an account of what it is to stand in need of proof. He asserts that arithmetical propositions *do,* but the grounds seem to be principally his conviction that they are *susceptible* of proof.

Second, I should like to note that the idea of propositions that do not admit of proof derives from the rationalist conception I attributed to Frege of a hierarchy of propositions, some of which are absolutely basic and form the foundation on which all the others "rest." He pays further homage to this conception when he agrees with Hankel's criticism of Kant's doctrine that numerical identities constitute an infinite set of unprovable and self-evident propositions. The reader will undoubtedly recall that Hankel had criticized Kant for supposing that numerical identities were all self-evident and yet unprovable.

> Hankel justifiably calls this conception of infinitely numerous unprovable primitive truths incongruous and paradoxical. The fact is that it conflicts with one of the requirements of reason, which must be able to embrace all first principles in a survey (*Grundlagen* 6).

There must be only finitely (or manageably) many first principles, from which all other a priori truths can be deduced. Their surveyability is a matter to which Frege pays no further attention, because, I think, to do so would require him to give an account of how we can and do know what we know—an account that would force him into a discussion of the conditions under which our beliefs constitute knowledge, a topic which he correctly perceived would involve certain psychological issues but which he (wrongly, I think) sweeps out with his antipsychologistic broom. But, as I said above, that is the topic of another paper.

I will close my discussion of section 3 with an amusing sidelight: On Frege's definitions, are analytic truths all a priori? Presumably so, since an analytic truth is one whose proof involves only first principles of *logic* (and definitions), and an a priori truth is one that can be proved exclusively from *general laws* which neither need nor admit of proof. To all appearances, it remains only to verify that the first principles of logic are themselves general laws which neither need nor admit of proof. Clearly, Frege believed that they were, *par excellence*. But, just as clearly,

Frege believed that he had shown that all arithmetic truths were analytic. This creates a problem, for it implies that there is a set of logical first principles from which all arithmetic truths may be deduced, using only definitions and principles of logical inference. Frege's characterizations of the nature of logical proof make it clear that the notion of proof he has in mind is an "effective" one, in the technical sense. Thus, if all arithmetic truths are analytic, there is a set of logical truths from which all arithmetic truths are effectively derivable. But this implies that if logic is recursively axiomatizable, so is arithmetic. And we know from Gödel's first incompleteness theorem that arithmetic is not. It follows that logic is not, whatever you take as logic, so long as it is adequate for the derivation of arithmetic. But if logic is not even recursively axiomatizable, its first principles constitute a class of "infinitely numerous unprovable primitive truths" and it is therefore "incongruous and paradoxical" and thus "conflicts with one of the requirements of reason." So—either

(1) not all arithmetical truths are analytic;

or

(2) not all logical truths are a priori (though all are trivially analytic);

or

(3) perhaps the conception of infinitely numerous unprovable primitive truths is not incongruous and paradoxical after all.

None of the above is a comfortable settling place for Frege, for I think he is quite serious about all three views. Indeed, I think it is their conjunction that forms for him much of the philosophical motivation for the *Grundlagen*. I have been arguing that his attempt to establish the analyticity of arithmetic was not to be construed as an attempt to enter an ongoing philosophical debate between Kant and the empiricists, and indeed that his very construal of the question took it out of that arena. It was rather an attempt to prove propositions that had yet to be proved, that he believed *could* be proved, and that he believed *should* be proved. Surely, much of the rationale for making this attempt is provided by his general view of proof, of the role of logic in proof, and of the hierarchical structure of all a priori propositions.

3. CONCLUSION

In this paper I have not touched upon the most exciting and important parts of the *Grundlagen*—Frege's actual discussion of the concepts of arithmetic. I have concentrated rather on trying to place that discussion in the philosophical context in which I think it belongs. The *Grundlagen* was written much more as a work of mathematics than it is usually conceded. Or, to retreat to autobiography, than I had been brought up to believe. So, on my view, not only is the *Grundlagen* not a work in the Kantian/empiricist tradition, having as its principal purpose the refutation or establishment of disputed philosophical doctrines, Frege considered it only incidentally a philosophical work. In discussing the "philosophical" issues, he had to redefine certain philosophical concepts so that questions framed in terms of them had mathematical answers. Frege construed the enterprise of the *Grundlagen* as first and foremost a mathematical one, with its problem central to mathematics; and he considered the argument of the *Grundlagen* as merely *the sketch of* a substantive answer to that problem: to prove the heretofore unproven arithmetical propositions. In successfully completing that task, he would incidentally have answered what seems to be a philosophical question: Are the truths of arithmetic analytic or synthetic? But only after having reconstrued that question to suit his own purposes. The *Grundlagen* contains only a sketch, because in the *Grundlagen* he does not give rigorous proofs. That is left for later, but it must be done.

> The demand is not to be denied: every jump must be barred from our deductions" (*Grundlagen* 102).

Philosophy comes in as a convenient vehicle for bolstering his claim that arithmetical propositions must be *proved.* So we see him beginning section 4 with the conclusion he thinks should be drawn from his discussion of section 3, over which we have labored at such length

> Starting from these philosophical questions, we are led to formulate the same demand as that which had arisen independently in the sphere of mathematics, namely that the fundamental propositions of arithmetic should be proved, if in any way possible, with the utmost rigour . . . (*Grundlagen* 4).

Notes

1. The first version of this paper was prepared for and delivered to the Chapel Hill Colloquium at the University of North Carolina in October 1976. It also served as the basis for two seminars offered by the author at the University of Minnesota at Morris in February 1980. I am particularly indebted to Steve Wagner, Fabrizio Mondadori, Glenn Kessler, Ian Hacking, David Kaplan, Jim Van Aken, and Hide Ishiguro for their helpful comments on earlier drafts. The final draft was completed while the author was a Fellow at the Center for Advanced Study in the Behavioral Sciences. The support of the Center, the Sloan Foundation, the National Endowment for the Humanities, and Princeton University are gratefully acknowledged.

2. Recent controversies in the foundations of linguistic theory have indicated that, even if granted the linguistic nature of mathematical truth, empiricists are some distance from home. I think these arguments are problematic, but their very existence shows the issues are not crystal clear. I have in mind here the work of Noam Chomsky.

3. P. Benacerraf, "What Numbers Could Not Be," *Philosophical Review* 74, no. 1 (January 1965):47-73.

4. W. V. Quine, "Two Dogmas of Empiricism," reprinted in *Philosophy of Mathematics,* ed. P. Benacerraf and H. Putnam (Englewood Cliffs, N.J., 1964). Henceforth, "B&P."

5. G. Frege, *The Foundations of Arithmetic,* trans. J. L. Austin (Evanston, Ill., 1968), p. 4. Future references to this work will follow this format.

6. I cannot resist noting in Kant's defense, that given Kant's notion of analyticity, his concept of definition was just fine. It is only when you broaden the notion *à la* Frege that definition "by a simple list of characteristics" becomes too constricting—particularly if you are defining functions as well as predicates. So, Frege's argument at the end of Section 88 to the effect that Kant would erroneously regard as synthetic certain conclusions drawn from his (Frege's) new kind of definition by purely logical means is a bit of a *petitio principii* on Frege's part; since

it is only on Frege's enlarged notion of analyticity that they turn out to be analytic, regardless of the kind of definition employed in the proof.

7. C. G. Hempel, "On the Nature of Mathematical Truth," reprinted in B&P.

8. W. V. Quine, "Truth by Convention," reprinted in B&P.

9. The view I have been calling "logicism" is evidently an amalgam of two views: a semantical thesis to the effect that *arithmetic is a definitional extension of logic* and an epistemological claim about *how this explains the a priori character of arithmetic*. Evidently, one can (and perhaps should) reserve the title for the semantical thesis alone, in which case Frege was certainly as much of a logicist as his followers (although here, too, much depends on how one interprets "definitional extension"—a deceptively tricky question which I will raise in more detail at the end of this paper).

I chose the present method partly for dramatic effect and partly because I am not really sure how clearly the two theses can be untangled from one another—how much the philosophical motivation behind a given form of the semantical thesis infects the thesis itself.

10. It is of course the bitterest irony that Frege had to face that possibility when his system led to contradictions—and that he would not have had to face it had he not pursued his foundational investigations.

11. It is interesting to contrast Frege's attitude toward the relation between logical axioms and mathematical theorems with that expressed by Russell and Whitehead in the following passage drawn from the Preface to the second edition of *Principia Mathematica*:

... the chief reason in favour of any theory on the principles of mathematics must be chiefly inductive, i.e. it must lie in the fact that the theory in question enables us to deduce ordinary mathematics. In mathematics, the greatest degree of self-evidence is usually not to be found quite at the beginning, but at some later point; hence the early deductions, until they reach this point, give reasons rather for believing the premisses because true consequences follow from them, than for believing the consequences because they follow from the premisses.

A. N. Whitehead, B. Russell, *Principia Mathematica,* 2nd ed. (Cambridge, 1925), vol. 1, p. v.

12. If the definitions are *explicit* definitions, then the requirement Frege imposes in the *Grundgesetze*, of establishing the existence and uniqueness of the defined entity, would suffice to guarantee that the system including the definition was a conservative extension of the original system, and hence consistent if the system was consistent prior to the introduction of the definitions. So, at best, whether a given law is analytic depends on whether the laws required in the proof of the existence and uniqueness of each of the defined entities employed in its proof are themselves laws of logic. I say "at best" for two reasons: (a) Definitions that are not explicit, but perhaps contextual, might have to be treated as new axioms whose justification requires at least whatever apparatus is needed to prove the consistency of the enlarged system; second, (b) even in the simple case of explicit definitions, although existence and uniqueness suffice to guarantee relative consistency, I am not sure that Frege's requirement that definitions be fully justified does not impose the further condition *that it be proved that existence and uniqueness suffice to guarantee relative consistency.*

This tangle exists because, from the syntactical viewpoint at least, the justification of definitions involves the proof of straightforward combinatorial theorems, something which Gödel showed us long ago was often equivalent to very difficult arithmetical questions, and worse. Consequently, if the basic laws on which a theorem depends include the laws on which the justifications of the definitions are based, it might well be that the theorem is not analytic *in Frege's sense*. In one sense, this is a quibble: he could omit this troublesome condition. But the issue is an important one to Frege. Rigor in mathematics is one of his most powerful motives, and his insistence on not employing definitions without providing them with the proper justification is a theme that runs through all his work.

13. Benacerraf, "What Numbers Could Not Be."

14. G. Frege, *The Basic Laws of Arithmetic,* trans. and ed. Montgomery Furth. References to this work will be in the form "(*Grundgesetze,* xx)."

Copyright © 1980 by Terence D. Parsons

Frege's Hierarchies of Indirect Senses and the Paradox of Analysis

TERENCE D. PARSONS

One of the primary concerns of analytic philosophy has been with meaning and the analysis of meaning. Although much of this discussion is carried out informally, one often gets the impression that there is a fairly well worked out doctrine, or theory of meaning, lurking in the background. Frege's theory of sense and reference is one such doctrine. This is a rich and powerful theory which deals in some detail with meanings as language-independent entities and with the relations between these entities and language. It also has certain peculiarities of its own—particularly the doctrine of *indirect* sense and reference—which set it apart from other theories of meaning, like Russell's. Some have thought that this doctrine offers a unique and compelling solution to a central problem of analytic philosophy: the paradox of analysis. The goal of this paper is to articulate and assess Frege's doctrine of indirect sense and reference and its relevance to the paradox of analysis. I will suggest that the best solution to the paradox of analysis is not one that employs the doctrine of indirect sense and reference.

1. FREGE'S THEORY: WHAT IS IT?

According to Frege, words have both sense and reference. Ordinarily a word expresses its *customary* sense and refers to its *customary* reference. But in certain contexts a word refers to its customary sense; these are called *indirect* contexts, and they include contexts like 'Samantha believes that _____' and 'It is possible that _____'. Since (in any context) the reference of a word depends on what sense it expresses (in that context) a word in an indirect context expresses a sense that is different from its customary sense (it cannot express its customary sense because then it would refer to its customary reference, which it does not). This new sense is called its "indirect sense" ([S&R]).[1]

Frege himself thought of this shift of reference as a defect of natural language, and he proposed that in a logically correct language different signs should be used

37

inside and outside indirect contexts, instead of a single sign which changes reference.[2] The most impressive developments of Freige's theory of sense and referce, particularly Church [FLSD, RF] and Kaplan [FIL], follow this line of investigation—they explore the way language *should* work. The present paper is directed at the issue of how language *does* work.

According to many authors, the invocation of new senses in indirect contexts is just the first step toward an infinite hierarchy of senses for each word or phrase. On this view, if a sentence containing a word in an indirect context is itself embedded in an indirect context, then the word (which now occurs in an indirect context inside another indirect context) refers to its indirect sense, and so it expresses a new sense, its *doubly indirect* sense. Another reembedding requires a *triply indirect* sense, and so on.

This version of the theory of sense and reference is attributed to Frege by Carnap [M&N], Dummett [F], and others. It has such widespread identification with Frege's theory that it deserves to be called the "orthodox" theory; I will call it this. Ironically, the classical source for this theory is the essay "On Sense and Reference" [S&R], and the orthodox theory is at best an *extension* of the theory presented there. In fact, if [S&R] is read quite literally, the theory given there attributes to words exactly *two* senses: customary and indirect. I will refer to this as the "two-level" theory.

What theory is correct? Dummett ([F], pp. 267-68) objects to the orthodox theory and holds that Frege ought to have endorsed a theory that attributes to words only customary sense. Carnap claims to be able to show the two-level theory inconsistent ([M&N], p. 131). In this paper I hope to establish that the two-level theory is consistent and that it is equivalent (in a sense to be specified) to the one-level theory which Dummett says Frege *should* have adopted—a theory that is also equivalent to (at least one interpretation of) a theory that Carnap himself gave in [M&N]. Second, every orthodox (infinite-level) theory either is equivalent to the one-level theory or is not an adequate theory of language. (This last point will involve a discussion of the paradox of analysis.)

2. A MOMENTARY DIGRESSION

Before proceeding to a consideration of the point at issue, I want to distinguish it from a different though related claim. Carnap argues (correctly) that Frege *is* committed to a certain sort of infinite hierarchy associated with each word ([M&N], p. 130). Frege holds that to each sense there corresponds at most one entity; any word that expresses a sense (in some context) must refer (in that context) to that corresponding entity. I will use Frege's word 'present' to stand for the correspondence in question: i.e., I will say that each sense presents at most one entity. (My 'presents' is the same as Church's 'is a concept of'; I avoid Church's terminology because Frege used 'concept' to stand for a different notion.) Now consider the infinite list of phrases:

(1.1) the evening star
(1.2) the (customary) sense of 'the evening star'
(1.3) the (customary) sense of 'the (customary) sense of 'the evening star' '
....
....

Our understanding of English requires that phrase (1.n + 1) refer to the (customary) sense of phrase (1.n), for each n. Thus, the sense of phrase (1.n + 1) must present the sense of phrase (1.n). And this yields an infinite chain of senses, each related to the previous one by the presentation relation, and beginning with the sense of 'the evening star'.

Carnap found this consequence objectionable, though I do not know why. In fact, if the word 'sense' is replaced by 'intension' in the phrases above, you get a similar chain of intensions within Carnap's own theory. In any event, this issue is a different one than the one being discussed in this paper. The issue I want to discuss is whether each word itself has an infinite number of senses, each of which gets expressed by *that* word in some context. In the example above there is no reason to believe that any one word or phrase expresses all the senses in the infinite chain. There is no reason, for example, to think that the sense expressed by 'the evening star' in single indirect contexts is the same as the customary sense of 'the sense of 'the evening star',' even according to the orthodox interpretation of Frege's theory.

3. THE ORTHODOX INTERPRETATION: SOME NOTATION

Here is the orthodox interpretation. Let us abbreviate 'the customary sense of w' by '$s_1[w]$', and 'the customary reference of w' by '$r_1[w]$'. In a *singly embedded context* — i.e., when the word is within an indirect context but is not in any indirect context which is itself in an indirect context — the word expresses a new, singly indirect sense, $s_2[w]$, and refers to a new, singly indirect reference, $r_2[w]$. The relations among these entities are as follows:

(2) Those due to the standard relation between the sense of a word in a given context and its reference there,
namely: $r_1[w]$ = the entity presented by $s_1[w]$
and: $r_2[w]$ = the entity presented by $s_2[w]$.

(3) The principle of indirect reference:
$r_2[w] = s_1[w]$.

So far, this is Frege's view in [S&R], no matter how many levels of sense there are. The distinctive part of the orthodox interpretation comes next: namely, that when a sentence containing an indirect context is embedded in another indirect context, a similar sort of "elevation" of senses and references takes place. In a single such reembedding the word refers to its singly indirect sense:

(4) $r_3[w] = s_2[w]$

and there is a new sense, $s_3[w]$, where

(5) $r_3[w]$ = the entity presented by $s_3[w]$.

In general the view is that embedding an n-ly embedded context in a singly embedded context produces an n + 1-ly embedded context in which the analogues of (4) and (5) hold, namely:

(6) $r_n[w]$ = the entity presented by $s_n[w]$, for all n.

(7) $r_{n+1}[w] = s_n[w]$, for all n.

Further, $s_n[w] \neq s_m[w]$ whenever n ≠ m, so each word actually expresses (in various contexts) an infinite number of different senses.

4. THE LITERAL INTERPRETATION

According to the orthodox interpretation, when a word is placed in a doubly embedded context, it refers to its (singly) indirect sense and expresses a new sense. This view is *not* stated in [S&R]. Instead we have the following quotation ([S&R], p. 59):

> In reported speech one talks about the sense, e.g., of another person's remarks. It is quite clear that in this way of speaking words do not have their customary reference but designate what is usually their sense. In order to have a short expression, we will say: In reported speech, words are used *indirectly* or have their *indirect* reference. We distinguish accordingly the *customary* from the *indirect* reference of a word; and its *customary* sense from its *indirect* sense. The indirect reference of a word is accordingly its customary sense.

Now in sentence (8):

(8) Mary said that John said that the evening star is a planet,

the phrase 'the evening star' occurs in reported speech. Frege said that in reported speech a word refers to its customary sense. So in (8) the phrase 'the evening star' apparently refers to its customary sense. This contradicts the orthodox view, which says that in (8) that phrase refers to its indirect sense. The orthodox view requires that in doubly embedded contexts we ignore what is said in [S&R].

Actually, I do not think that there is any strong reason to take the [S&R] statement of the theory literally. It seems plausible to me that when Frege stated his principle of indirect reference in [S&R], he just was not thinking of doubly embedded contexts, and it is really up to us to *extend* the theory he had in mind to account for such contexts. The orthodox interpretation gives a very elegant extension, an extension which Frege himself adopted ten years later in a letter to Russell ([F-R], p. 236). But in the next section I will explore another extension, the extension that you get by taking Frege's literal statement as a perfectly general principle: in *any* indirect context a word refers to its customary sense.

5. THE LITERAL (TWO-LEVEL) THEORY SPELLED OUT

In the Appendix to this paper I give a syntax and semantics for a formal system which incorporates intensional operators: phrases like 'Samantha believes that _____', 'Herman said that _____', 'It is possible that _____', . . . The present section illustrates that theory and states some conclusions concerning it.

Let me use 'R' to stand for 'Radium is harmless', 'B' for 'Madame Curie once believed that', and 'S' for 'History books say that'. Each of these phrases is complex, and in a complete Fregean theory this complexity would be dealt with; but it is irrelevant to the present issue and so I will ignore it here.

The semantics of the sentence R, occurring in isolation, is summed up in the following diagram:

$$\#1 \qquad \begin{array}{c} s_1[R] \\ \uparrow \\ R \\ \downarrow \\ r_1[R] \end{array}$$

The arrow pointing up represents the relation "expresses"; that pointing down represents the relation "refers to." So the diagram indicates that the sentence occurring in isolation refers to its customary reference, $r_1[R]$ (a truth-value), and expresses its customary sense, $s_1[R]$ (a Thought).

The semantics of 'Madame Curie once believed that radium is harmless' is given by:

$$\#2 \qquad \begin{array}{c} s_1[BR] \\ \overbrace{s_1[B](s_2[R])} \\ \nwarrow \nearrow \\ BR \\ \swarrow \searrow \\ \underbrace{r_1[B](s_1[R])} \\ r_1[BR] \end{array}$$

Since B is not itself in an indirect context, it expresses its customary sense and refers to its customary reference. Since R is in an indirect context here, it refers to its indirect reference—i.e., its customary sense—and expresses its indirect sense. The reference of the whole sentence (a truth-value) is got by applying the reference of B (which is a function) to the reference of R (which is, in this context, a Thought); this is the significance of the curly brackets. I.e., $\frac{X(Y)}{Z}$ indicates that Z = X(Y). Likewise, the sense expressed by the whole sentence (a Thought) is got by applying the customary sense of B (a function) to the indirect sense of R.

Everything that has been said so far is consistent with both the orthodox and the literal interpretation of [S&R]. The divergence comes at the next step. On the literal interpretation, the semantics of 'History books say that Madame Curie once believed that radium is harmless' is:

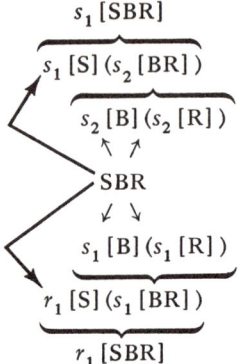

This diagram is got by a straightforward application of the principle that the sense (reference) of a whole is determined by a function-argument combination of the senses (references) of its parts, plus these two principles:

(9) any word or phrase that is not in an indirect context refers to its customary reference and expresses its customary sense,

(10) any word or phrase that is in an indirect context refers to its indirect reference (i.e., its customary sense) and expresses its indirect sense.

The orthodox interpretation would differ, in this case, only in having R refer to $s_2[R]$ and express $s_3[R]$; the rest of the diagram would be exactly the same.

Now a surprising thing happens. According to the "expresses" side of the second diagram, the customary sense of BR is got by applying the customary sense of B to the indirect sense of R:

(11) $s_1[B](s_2[R]) = s_1[BR]$

But according to the "refers to" side of the third diagram, the customary sense of BR is got by applying the customary sense of B to the customary sense of R:

(12) $s_1[B](s_1[R]) = s_1[BR]$

So $s_1[B]$ maps both $s_1[R]$ and $s_2[R]$ to the *same* thing, namely $s_1[BR]$. This is not an inconsistency, but it is a surprise, and surprises of this sort often suggest that there may be an inconsistency lurking *somewhere* around. This is especially disturbing since Carnap ([M&N], p. 131), for example, claims to be able to *prove* that in Frege's theory a word has to express an infinite number of senses, a thesis that is inconsistent with the literal interpretation. (Carnap makes it clear that he is not confusing this claim with the irrelevant one mentioned in Section 2.) And many other authors argue to the same conclusion.[3]

In fact, as the Appendix makes clear, this theory is not inconsistent. Carnap did not publish his proof, so I can only speculate about where and how it might be inadequate. And the argument by Dummett ([F], p. 267), for example, presupposes the orthodox interpretation of Frege's theory, so it is not relevant here. The import of (11) and (12) is not that the theory contains a hidden inconsistency but that there is a kind of triviality or redundancy in the notion of indirect sense (in this version of the theory). In anthropomorphic terms, (11) and (12) jointly show that the customary sense of B cannot tell the difference between the customary and the indirect sense of R. And this is just one instance of a general phenomenon: whenever a sense gets to "look at" both the customary and the indirect sense of a given word, it cannot tell them apart. More literally, whenever f is a sense that is also a function, if f is ever applied to the indirect sense of a word in the semantical analysis of a sentence, then f maps that indirect sense to the same thing to which it maps the customary sense of the word. And this suggests that the theory we are discussing is essentially a variant of a theory with only *one* level of sense. Indirect senses are *almost* just customary senses in disguise. They have to be literally different from customary senses because they have to present different references—but aside from this there is no difference in the way they work in the theory. This suggests that if we could merely alter that part of the theory which identifies the reference of a word (in a context) with the entity presented by what the word expresses (in that context), we could simply identify the indirect sense of a word with its customary sense.

In fact, we can do just that. Suppose we call the theory sketched above 'F2' (for 'Frege: 2 levels of sense'). We can convert F2 into a quasi-Fregean theory with only one level of sense, F1, by making the following alterations:

(13) a word *always* expresses its customary sense,

(14) a word in an indirect context refers to its customary sense; otherwise it refers to the entity that its customary sense presents.

F1 is the theory that Dummett says Frege *should* have given ([F], pp. 267-68). It is equivalent to F2 in the following sense: on at least one plausible model of what senses are, every isolated sentence expresses the same thought according to F2 as it expresses according to F1. (See Appendix for details. The proof that the two-level theory is consistent depends on an appeal to "nonactual situations," but the techniques employed are easily generalizable to other sorts of models—in particular, the techniques of Section 7 also apply.)

Carnap objected to Frege's notion of indirect reference. Roughly speaking, he held that a word ought to keep both its customary sense and customary reference in all contexts; where "indirect" contexts are concerned, we should simply give up the view that the references of the parts determine the reference of the whole. Suppose then that we alter F2 as follows:

(15) a word or phrase always expresses its customary sense and refers to its customary reference.

(16) if X( ) is an "indirect" context, then the reference of X(Y) is the result of operating on the sense of Y by the reference of X, and the sense of X(Y) is the result of operating on the sense of Y by the sense of X.

Call this theory "C1" (For "Carnap: 1 level of sense"). Then C1 is equivalent to both F2 and F1 in the sense described above.

6. CRITIQUE OF THE ORTHODOX THEORIES

The orthodox theories attribute to each word an infinite sequence of senses; a word expresses the nth sense in its sequence when it is within n − 1 embeddings of indirect contexts. Theories of this sort fall into two kinds, depending on the relationship between the customary sense of an expression (the first sense in its associated sequence) and its indirect sense (the second sense in its associated sequence). The one kind of theory, which I will call "rigid," holds that the customary sense of an expression uniquely determines its indirect sense. That is, it holds that any two expressions that have the same customary sense also have the same "first-level" indirect senses. (It follows from this that any two expressions that share a customary sense also share their nth-level sense, for any n, and are thus interchangeable in all contexts without altering the sense of the whole.)[4]

The other sort of (orthodox) theory I will call "libertine"; in this kind of theory the customary sense of an expression does not determine what the indirect sense of that expression will be, and two expressions may have the same customary sense while diverging in nth-level indirect sense, for some n. Expressions with the same customary sense will not in general be interchangeable while preserving the sense of the whole.

My discussion of the orthodox theories is aimed at making two points: rigid theories are equivalent to simpler theories that attribute to each expression only a single sense, whereas libertine theories do not have any interesting application to language.

In what follows I will use a specific language as a basis for evaluating the orthodox theories. It is as simple as possible, consistent with the principle of including all the sorts of contexts that are relevant to the issues to be discussed.

The language L consists of the following:

(1) Names: $a_1, a_2, a_3, \ldots$
(2) One-place predicates: $P_1, P_2, P_3, \ldots$
(3) Extensional sentence operators: $E_1, E_2, E_3, \ldots$
(4) Indirect sentence operators: $O_1, O_2, O_3, \ldots$

The sentences of L include any expression of the form $P_n a_m$, and if A is a sentence, so are $E_n(A)$ and $O_n(A)$. An expression is said to be in an nth level indirect context just in case there are exactly n indirect sentence operators preceding it. For example, a_3 is in a second level indirect context in $O_4(E_7(O_2(P_1 a_3)))$.

I assume that associated with each simple sign, A, of L is a sequence of senses $s_1[A], s_2[A], s_3[A], \ldots$, and that $s_{n+1}[A]$ presents $s_n[A]$, for each n. All senses of predicates and operators are functions. Complex expressions also have sequences of senses associated with them, determined by the following rules:

(i) $s_n[P_m a_r] = s_n[P_m] (s_n[a_r])$.
(ii) $s_n[E_m(A)] = s_n[E_m] (s_n[A])$.
(iii) $s_n[O_m(A)] = s_n[O_m] (s_{n+1}[A])$.

Reference is determined in the usual Fregean manner:

(iv) $r_n[A]$ = the unique thing presented by $s_n[A]$.

I assume that all of this is hooked up to language in the orthodox Fregean way, namely, that an expression, A, that is not in an indirect context expresses $s_1[A]$ and refers to $r_1[A]$, and that an expression, A, that is in an nth-level indirect context expresses $s_{n+1}[A]$ and refers to $r'_{n+1}[A]$.

7. RIGID THEORIES

A rigid theory can be converted into a theory that associates with each expression only one sense, as follows. We define *"the* sense of A," i.e., "$s[A]$," as follows:

(i) If A is a name or a sentence or a predicate or an extensional sentence operator, then $s[A] = s_1[A]$.

(ii) If A is an indirect sentence operator, then $s[A]$ = that function which maps an arbitrary sense x to $s_1[A](s_2[B])$, where B is an expression such that $s_1[B] = x$. (If there is no expression B such that $s_1[B] = x$, then let the function map x to some arbitrarily chosen object.)[5]

The choice of B in clause (ii) need not be unique, for in *rigid* theories it will not matter which B we pick.

Now it can be shown (by induction on n) that:

For any sentence of L of the form $A_1(A_2(\ldots A_n(Pa)\ldots))$:
$s[A_1(A_2(\ldots A_n(Pa)\ldots))] = s[A_1](s[A_2](\ldots s[A_n](s[P](s[a]))\ldots))$.

That is, the sense of a whole is always a function of the senses of the parts (taken in the natural order). And since for any sentence A, the sense of A = (by definition) $s_1[A]$, this simplified theory attributes to every isolated sentence exactly the sense that that sentence expresses according to the original theory. It is also clear that if A and B have the same customary sense according to the original theory, they have the same sense according to this simplified theory, and, by the result above, they are interchangeable in all contexts without alteration of the sense (= the customary sense) of the whole.

I still have not given the "reference" side of this theory. There are two natural ways to do this. One is this:

(R1) An expression A in an extensional context refers to $r_1[A]$, and in an indirect context (of any level) refers to $s[A]$.

Thus fleshed out, this simplification of the rigid theory turns out to be the theory (F1) that Dummett says Frege should have given.

The other natural option is:

(R2) A always refers to $r_1[A]$.

This variant is our (C1) of Section 5.

8. LIBERTINE THEORIES; THE PARADOX OF ANALYSIS

Libertine theories permit phrases to agree in customary sense while diverging in higher-up sense. Does language work this way? Should it?

I know of no argument to the effect that language *should* work this way. Investigators who work on "logically correct" or "canonical" symbolisms typically do not address this issue at all — they tend to follow Frege's advice that in logically correct languages no word or phrase would ever change reference with context. I myself can think of no reason to want a language to behave in the libertine fashion unless there are things we want to say that cannot be said well in any other way. The place to look for what we want to say is probably in what we do say, so let me turn to this issue.

Does actual language behave in accordance with the libertine theory? There is at least one published argument to the effect that it cannot. This is Davidson's argument[6] that if language were correctly described by a libertine theory, it would not be humanly learnable, since the sense of a given word or phrase in a high-level indirect context would not be predictable from its basic sense (this is a rough statement).

There is hardly any published argument that language does behave in accordance with the libertine theory. However, there seems to be a very widespread informal view to the effect that language does work in this way and that the *paradox of analysis* illustrates a linguistic phenomenon which can only be accommodated (within a Fregean framework) by a libertine theory.[7]

I will focus on what I take to be the most popular and also most plausible version of the argument. It begins by considering:

(17) The concept *brother* = the concept *male sibling*.

(18) It is trivial that the concept *brother* = the concept *brother*.

(19) It is not trivial that the concept *brother* = the concept *male sibling*.

The claim is that (17)-(19) are all true, that in (17) the phrases of the form 'the concept ϕ' refer to the customary sense of 'ϕ', but that in (18) and (19) they refer to the indirect sense of 'ϕ'. Since (17) is true, 'brother' and 'male sibling' have the same customary sense; they are *not* intersubstitutable in (18) or (19), and this is explained by the fact that in (18) and (19) they refer to their *indirect* senses, which are distinct. So the argument goes.

I think that this simple format conceals a host of issues; I will discuss them in stages. The first thing to be clarified is whether 'brother' is actually a semantically relevant constituent of 'the concept *brother*' or not. Italics are commonly used for mentioning words, and *one* way to understand (17)-(19) is to suppose that they are shorthand for:

(17') The concept ordinarily expressed by 'brother' = the concept ordinarily expressed by 'male sibling'.

(18') It is trivial that the concept ordinarily expressed by 'brother' = the concept ordinarily expressed by 'brother'.

(19′) It is not trivial that the concept ordinarily expressed by 'brother' = the concept ordinarily expressed by 'male sibling'.

Read in this way, (17′)-(19′) are plausible, but it is not at all clear that they have anything to do with our issue at all. For the words 'brother' and 'male sibling' are mentioned, not used, and their indirect senses are *not* referred to in (18′) and (19′). I am not supposing that anyone was ever confused on this issue, but (17′)-(19′) do give *one* natural way to mentally process (17)-(19). So let me just remind the reader to take care *not* to read (17)-(19) in this manner, and proceed.

Next, there are two (other) ways to interpret phrases like 'the concept brother'. The first is a sort of "ordinary-language" way—though more properly I should say "ordinary philosophical usage" way. Concepts are entities that are apparently familiar to many working philosophers; they have a long and venerable tradition, and within this tradition (17) is a paradigm example of concept identity. I.e., (17) is not the sort of claim that is normally open to question—to deny it is to give evidence of not understanding the concept "concept."

But if 'concept' is understood in terms of its popular philosophical tradition, there is no prima facie reason to think that (17) has anything to do with whether the customary senses of 'brother' and 'male sibling' are the same. It could easily be that 'brother' and 'male sibling' are genuinely semantical parts of 'the concept *brother*' and 'the concept *male sibling*', that 'brother' and 'male sibling' have *different* customary senses, and that (17) be true. This would simply mean that (customary) senses are individuated more finely than the concepts of philosophical tradition. It would also imply that much of the literature on the subject of the paradox of analysis is simply irrelevant to the issue under consideration. I think that this is the case. (Recall that necessary equivalence is often cited as a criterion of concept identity. But in a Fregean theory, customary senses must be individuated more finely than this; for otherwise necessarily equivalent sentences would always be intersubstitutable in first-level belief contexts.)

The remaining way to understand the construction 'the concept ϕ' is to suppose that 'ϕ' forms a genuine constituent of the construction and that it *does* refer to the sense of 'ϕ' (either because traditional concepts *are* senses, contrary to the suggestion of the last paragraph, or because for present purposes we stipulate that 'concept' is to be understood in this way). The idea would be that 'the concept _____' is an indirect-context forming operator, which refers to that function which maps any given sense to itself, and which expresses a function that also maps any given sense to itself. Then within any given n-level indirect context, 'the concept ϕ' would refer to $s_n[\phi]$ and would express $s_{n+1}[\phi]$. I see no reason why we could not have a piece of language that does this, and if we understand 'the concept _____' in this manner, then the paradox of analysis, as embodied in (17)-(19), *is* directly relevant to the issue we are considering: whether 'brother' and 'male sibling' have the same customary sense but different indirect senses. So let me urge the reader to understand (17)-(19) with this (perhaps highly artificial) stipulation in mind, and I will proceed from there.

I would now like to suggest that, so understood, (17) is just plain false. Recall that (17) is true just in case this is true:

(20) 'Brother' has the same customary sense as 'male sibling'.

But 'customary sense' is a technical term from a technical theory of meaning. *It is entirely inappropriate to test the truth of (20) by direct appeal to intuition.* Words have the same customary sense in the theory under consideration only if they are interchangeable *salva veritate* in all first-level indirect contexts (or, interchangeable *salva sense* in all extensional contexts).[8] Whether *this* is true may or may not be testable, *case by case,* by appeal to speaker intuition. But (20) is not so testable, for we are not native speakers of that fragment of our language which contains 'customary sense' as a part. So the ordinary defense of (17) in terms of its being "obviously true" is now beside the point.

(20) (and thus (17)) is false; it is false because 'brother' and 'male sibling' are not interchangeable *salva veritate* in the context:

(21) Herman is certain that all and only brothers are _____'s.

This seems to me to be decisive. Uncertainty about whether all and only brothers are male siblings is a common phenomenon, experienced by practically everyone who first encounters the claim; these are typically people who are certain that all and only brothers are brothers. Other examples which make the same point are: 'Herman argued (claimed, proved) that all brothers are _____' and 'Herman wondered whether all brothers are _____'. I find these examples convincing, but I am aware that others do not, and so the rest of this section is devoted to a discussion of challenges to this conclusion.

First, some would claim, e.g., that anyone who argues that all and only brothers are male siblings is *ipso facto* arguing that all and only brothers are brothers since the latter is simply saying the same thing as the former, just in different words. Although Herman might insist that he was not arguing the "trivial" claim that all and only brothers are brothers, we cannot take what he says at face value. He *is* arguing this, but just does not realize that he is.

I think that this challenge has *some* plausibility, but it gains its plausibility from a source that bypasses the point at issue. It is this: when we report on someone else's attitudes or beliefs, or on what they have asserted, we customarily take a certain amount of liberty in paraphrasing what they explicitly feel, believe, or say. For example, Herman says his knee hurts, and we report that he said his knee is bothering him. Normally no one objects, because the difference does not matter. But if Herman cares about the difference, he might protest that he never said his knee was *bothering* him; he said only that it *hurts*. Maybe he was giving an example of something that hurts without bothering, and the paraphrase does not do justice to his point. But whether it does or not, he is correct in denying that he said his knee bothers him.

The point is this: "close" paraphrases of statements are usually acceptable, even though literally incorrect. And phrases as close in meaning as 'brother' and 'male sibling' are often close enough to provide acceptable paraphrases of one another for ordinary purposes. But acceptability is relative to the context and purpose, and in some situations 'brother' and 'male sibling' are not close enough paraphrases to pass. Some of these situations will involve uses of (21).

A second challenge involves the claim that although 'brother' and 'male sibling' are not interchangeable in (21), this is because (21) is a disguised quotational context. The most sophisticated version of this claim goes as follows: "Although we are sometimes inclined to accept the interchangeability of 'brother' and 'male sibling' in (21), we also sometimes tend to reject it. The explanation for this is that in the latter case we instinctively treat (21) as implicitly having the form:

(22) Herman is certain that 'all and only brothers are male siblings' is true.

In all non-quotational versions of (21), the interchangeability is acceptable."

I do not know of any way to refute a claim that a context is covertly quotational. It is easy to say, and, in interesting cases, hard to argue either way. It seems clear that here is a situation in which the hard data about language is inadequate to decide the issue, and that considerations of theoretical simplicity and elegance come into play. Some, e.g., Quine, would have us think that all non-extensional contexts are implicitly quotational.

But perhaps we can decide the case at hand without having to face the general issue of how to tell quotational from non-quotational contexts. First, we are examining the viability of a libertine Fregean theory of language. If *all* non-extensional contexts are covertly quotational, then the theory is not viable, not because of falsity but because of vacuity. So I will assume that at least some non-extensional contexts are to be treated by the theory of indirect sense. Let me suppose even that the challenger is right in thinking that (21) is ambiguous, sometimes being an inducer of indirect contexts and sometimes being an inducer of quotational contexts. But if this is plausible, it is at least as plausible for sentences (17)-(19). That is, if we want to explain the failure of interchangeability of 'brother' and 'male sibling' in:

(23) It is trivial that the concept *brother* = the concept _____,

then it is just as plausible (perhaps even more so) to allude *here* to implicitly quotational readings as it is in (17) or (21). The trouble with the second challenge, in short, is that it does not show a *difference* in behavior (under substitution) of first and second level indirect contexts. The third challenge addresses itself to this issue.

The third challenge recognizes that there is no hard data to directly support the libertine view and addresses itself to a related phenomenon. It goes as follows: "There are facts about language that the libertine view can explain and which other (e.g., "rigid") views cannot. An example of such a fact is this: If you are a normal native speaker of English, then:

(i) you are certain that all and only brothers are brothers.

(ii) you are certain that necessarily all and only brothers are brothers.

(iii) after you have thought about it a while, you are probably certain that all and only brothers are male siblings.

(iv) In the light of (i)-(iii) you *may* still be uncertain whether necessarily all and only brothers are male siblings."

The trouble with this third challenge is that the "facts" are so easily explainable in terms of a rigid theory that holds 'brother' and 'male sibling' to diverge in customary sense. We explain (i) and (ii) by noting that most people know simple logical truths and know that they are necessary. We explain (iii) by noting that most people, when pressed, find it difficult (perhaps impossible) to imagine a brother who is not a male sibling, or vice versa. And we explain (iv) by noting that most people are (properly) reluctant to jump to conclusions regarding what is necessary, once they leave the safe confines of simple logical truth.

The fourth challenge is also theoretical. It goes like this: "The rejection of the libertine view is only plausible if 'brother' and 'male sibling' have different customary senses, and if the same is true of many similar examples. But 'brother' is *defined* as 'male sibling', and so they *must* have the same sense."

Again, this challenge is relevant only if it yields a difference in the treatment of customary and indirect senses, so the phrase 'same sense' in the last sentence must be read as 'same customary sense'. But the idea behind the challenge seems to be that the meaning of a defined term is the same as the meaning of the defining phrase in the definition, and once this is given up for part of its meaning (its indirect sense) the remaining view seems much less compelling.[9] Still, it is compelling to some, so it deserves a more detailed discussion. An adequate treatment of the topic of definition would take at least a book; I will limit myself here to a sketch, addressing myself to three sorts of definition:

(i) *Ordinary dictionary definitions:* Comment: these almost never yield phrases which we are even tempted to think of as having the same customary senses as the defined terms. (Besides, in most dictionaries 'brother' is *not* defined as "male sibling," nor can their equivalence be deduced by the definitions given alone.)

(ii) *Philosophical definitions of ordinary-language words:* These have been thought to preserve sense because it has been taken as a criterion of adequacy that they do so. Comments: First, there are hardly any such definitions that anyone thinks of as successful. Second, generally the criterion that they preserve sense has not been that they preserve *sense* in the relevant sense of 'sense'. For example, it is usually thought that a philosophical definition of 'A' as "B" will be such that most people do not already believe that all and only A's are B's, and that it will take a philosophical argument to convince them of this (certainly in practice this is what happens). But if 'Most people do not already believe that all and only A's are B's' is true, we have the makings of a first-level indirect context in which 'A' and 'B' are not interchangeable *salva veritate* and thus a context that shows 'A' and 'B' to diverge in customary sense. (A continuation of this discussion would return us to the earlier discussion of the paradox of analysis.)

(iii) *Stipulative definitions:* These are common in some philosophical discussions and in advanced logic and mathematics courses. These definitions are held to preserve sense because the defined term is held to be a mere *abbreviation* of the defining phrase, or because the meaning of the defined term is totally determined by the defining phrase. Comments: First, by two weeks into the semester anyone who truly understands the defined terms by "decoding" them into what they abbreviate will certainly be unable to comprehend the lectures. Second, if it *were* true that stipulative definitions produced abbreviations, or produced terms with *exactly* the same meaning as the defining phrase, then the defined terms would be eliminable within indirect contexts as well as within extensional ones, and they would not then yield examples of pairs of phrases that have the same customary senses but divergent indirect senses.

9. COMPLICATIONS AND CONCLUSIONS

In the last section I argued that 'brother' and 'male sibling' are not interchangeable *salva veritate* in all first-level indirect contexts; in the context of Frege's theory this suffices to show that these phrases differ in customary sense. One might reasonably worry that similar considerations would show that any two phrases differ in customary sense. This would be in opposition to Frege's observation that:

> different expressions quite often have something in common, which I call the sense. . . . It is possible for one sentence to give no more and no less information than another; and for all the multiplicity of languages, mankind has a common stock of thoughts. If all transformation of the expression were forbidden on the plea that this would alter the content as well, logic would simply be crippled, for the task of logic can hardly be performed without trying to recognize the thought in its manifold guises (Frege [C&O], p. 46).

These remarks indicate that it would be undesirable if it turned out that different phrases rarely have the same sense. But they do not show that the theory in question lacks this consequence. Perhaps, contrary to Frege's own intentions, his theory of indirect sense and reference forces this conclusion.

Does it? That depends on how we correct a certain oversimplification in the application of the theory. In the discussion so far I have been ignoring the fact that a given word does not necessarily express the same customary sense in all direct contexts. For example, words that are lexically ambiguous express different customary senses in different direct contexts; the word 'bank' sometimes means a certain kind of financial institution, and sometimes the ground alongside a moving body of water. So on different occasions of use 'bank' expresses different customary senses. But *lexical* ambiguity is not the important phenomenon here; this is: ignoring lexical ambiguity altogether, practically all words change customary sense from (direct) context to (direct) context. Take the word 'loves' for example. When asked whether Mary loves Bill, the response may be "Well, she does and she doesn't; it depends on what you mean by 'love'." More pertinently, on one occasion the sentence 'Mary loves Bill' may be used to say something true, and on another occasion to say something false, even though the same people are being discussed (and the same time is at issue). According to Frege's theory, this can happen only if the reference of 'loves' is different in the two utterances, and, since sense determines reference, the customary sense of 'loves' must also be different in the two utterances.

So, the observation in the last section that 'brother' and 'male sibling' have different customary senses is only obvious if it is weakened to "On *some* occasions, 'brother' and 'male sibling' differ in customary sense." This leaves it open to maintain that on other occasions of utterance they might agree in customary sense, and this sort of speculation would allow us to preserve Frege's view about the same common stock of thoughts being variously expressed on different occasions, while still utilizing his theory of indirect sense and reference which forces "synonyms" to sometimes diverge in (customary) sense. I suspect that this sort of application is most faithful to the ordinary language of which the theory is supposed to be a theory.

Such a refinement in the application of the theory complicates the issue discussed in the last section. On the one hand, if words change sense from occasion to occasion, then the observation that 'brother' and 'male sibling' *sometimes* diverge in customary sense does not show that there is no version of the paradox of analysis in which sentence (17) is true. On the other hand, the evidence in favor of a libertine version of the theory is similarly weakened; there are now more ways than ever to explain the supposedly paradoxical phenomena, and the complications of the libertine view are less plausibly needed. Conceivably, the question of which sort of theory is better as a theory of natural language reduces to the question of which is simpler; if so, I doubt that the libertine view has much to recommend it. As for the paradox of analysis, there still appears to be little virtue in the libertine solution, but this could not be made conclusive without being clearer about the goals of traditional philosophical analysis. Since there has never been a clearly successful analysis of a philosophically important word or phrase that we could use as a paradigm and since there is less and less interest in the attempt to produce one, the issue may never be finally resolved.

Notes

1. Throughout the text abbreviations in square brackets will be used to refer to items in the bibliography. In discussing Frege's theory I will ignore denotationless names and senses that fail to "present" anything; this is for simplicity only; I think that none of my arguments depend on this idealization.

2. Some passages in which this view is articulated by Frege are [BLA], Section 11; [FD], Sections 58, 60; and especially [F-R], p. 236.

3. See Stegmuller [WIS], p. 149 and Dummett [F], p. 267; Linsky [R] considers both sides of the question.

4. For example, suppose $s_1[A] = s_1[B]$, and suppose that F and G are indirect-context creating operators. We can show, e.g., that $s_1[F(G(A))] = s_1[F(G(B))]$ as follows:

$s_1[A] = s_1[B]$ Given
$s_2[A] = s_2[B]$ Rigidity

$$s_1[G](s_2[A]) = s_1[G](s_2[B]) \quad \text{Subst. of Iden.}$$
$$s_1[G(A)] = s_1[G(B)] \quad \text{Fregean Analysis}$$
$$s_2[G(A)] = s_2[G(B)] \quad \text{Rigidity}$$
$$s_1[F](s_2[G(A)]) = s_1[F](s_2[G(B)]) \quad \text{Subst. of Iden.}$$
$$s_1[F(G(A))] = s_1[F(G(B))] \quad \text{Fregean Analysis}$$

5. For a more sophisticated language including quantifiers we may want to quantify over senses that are not expressed by words of the language at hand. Probably we would then have to assume that *every* sense is the nth-level sense of some *possible* word, for some n, and then 'B' in clause (ii) should range over possible words. The principle of rigidity would then be extended to possible words. Notice that this does *not* commit us to the view that if a sense is the nth level sense of a word, W_1, it is not also the mth level sense of some other word, W_2, where $n \neq m$.

6. See Davison [TMLL], [OST]. Davidson actually imposes conditions on learnability (= the formulability of a Tarski-like truth definition) which may reject even theories with only one level of sense, so in his view libertine theories may be only superficially worse off than rigid theories.

7. Church [Rev] proposes a Fregean solution to the paradox of analysis, though not clearly one that utilizes doubly indirect senses; Davidson [MEI] makes a similar suggestion about a Carnapian theory in which L-equivalence has been selected as the identity condition for customary senses. White [CFS] gives a clear statement of a solution to the paradox of analysis using doubly indirect senses. I am indebted throughout this section to conversation with and unpublished work of Herbert Heidelberger, who, however, does not necessarily endorse my conclusions.

8. This requires qualification regarding words that are lexically ambiguous. I will not attempt to spell out the qualification; instead I will just try to be careful not to beg any questions here.

9. Sellars seems to suggest something like this in [NFA].

References

[M&N] Carnap, R., *Meaning and Necessity* (Chicago, 1967).
[Rev] Church, A., review of four articles on the paradox of analysis, *Journal of Symbolic Logic* 11 (1946):132-33.
[FLSD] _____, "A Formulation of the Logic of Sense and Denotation," in *Structure, Method and Meaning* (New York, 1951).
[RF] _____, "Outline of a Revised Formulation of the Logic of Sense and Denotation (Part I)," *Nous* 7, no. 1 (1973): 24-33 and "_____ (Part II)," *Nous* 8, no. 2 (1974): 135-56.
[MEI] Davidson, D., "The Method of Extension and Intension," *The Philosophy of Rudolf Carnap* (LaSalle, Ill., 1963).
[TMLL] _____, "Theories of Meaning and Learnable Languages," *Logic, Methodology, and Philosophy of Science*, ed. Yehoshua Bar-Hillel (Amsterdam, 1965).
[OST] _____, "On Saying That," *Synthese* 19 (1968-69):158-74.
[F] Dummett, M., *FREGE Philosophy of Lanuage* (London, 1973).
[BLA] Frege, G., *The Basic Laws of Arithmetic*, trans. and ed. M. Furth (Berkeley, 1964).
[C&O] _____, "Concept and Object," in *Translation from the Philosophical Writings of Gottlob Frege*, ed. Geach and Black (Oxford, 1970).
[FD] _____, "Frege on Definitions," in Geach and Black, *Translations*.
[S&R] _____, "On Sense and Reference," in Geach and Black, *Translations*.
[F-R] _____, 1902 letter to Bertrand Russell, in *Wissenschaftlicher Briefwechsel* (Hamburg, 1976), pp. 234-37.
[FIL] Kaplan, D., *Foundations of Intensional Logic* (Ann Arbor, 1964).
[R] Linsky, L., *Referring* (New York, 1967).

[NFA] Sellars, W., "The Paradox of Analysis: a Neo-Fregean Approach," *Philosophical Perspectives* (Springfield, Ill., 1967).
[WIS] Stegmuller, W., *Das Wahrheitsproblem und die Idee der Semantik* (Wien, 1968).
[CFS] White, M., "On the Church-Frege Solution of the Paradox of Analysis," *Philosophy and Phenomenological Research* 9 (1948-49):305-8.

APPENDIX

In this appendix I will use the syntax of the language L from Section 6, namely:

Names: $a_1, a_2, a_3, \ldots$
One-place Predicates: $P_1, P_2, P_3, \ldots$
Extensional Sentence Operators: $E_1, E_2, E_3, \ldots$
Intensional Sentence Operators: $O_1, O_2, O_3, \ldots$

Any expression of the form $P_n a_m$ is a sentence, and if S is a sentence so are $E_n(S)$ and $O_n(S)$.

A *model* is a quadruple $\langle w_0, W, I, s_1 \rangle$, where $w_0 \in W$, I is a nonempty set, $I \neq \{0,1\}$, $I \neq \{0,1\}^W$, and W does not contain 0 or 1 or 2. In the intended application w_0 represents the "actual" situation, W represents the set of all situations, and 0 and 1 are the truth-values False and True. ("Situations" are analogous to possible worlds, except that there is no commitment to their "possibility"; for example if we wish to mimic the behavior of words like 'believes', then we may need to utilize a "situation" in which Fermat's last theorem is true and one in which it is false.) The number 2 will be used solely as a technical device to distinguish first- and second-level senses. I is the set of "individuals"; it may contain anything at all — e.g., tables, chairs, truth-values, situations, senses, etc. — but, for purely technical reasons, it may not consist exactly of the two truth-values or of the functions from situations to truth-values.

It will be handy to have a special symbol P for $\{0,1\}^W$, i.e., for the set of functions from members of W to truth-values; I will refer to P as the set of *propositions*. s_1 is going to be a function that assigns first-level senses to expressions of L; these first-level senses fall into four domains, which are defined below (in what follows I use the notation "f:A → B" as short for "f is a function defined on set A (and nowhere else) and yielding values in set B").

Domains of First-Level Senses

D_1 [Names] $=_{df} \{f \mid f:W \to I\}$
D_1 [Preds] $=_{df} \{f \mid f:D_1[\text{Names}] \to P$, and for any $x,y \in D_1[\text{Names}]$ and $w \in W$, if $x(w) = y(w)$ then $f(x)(w) = f(y)(w)\}$

(The second clause here ensures that predication is extensional; similarly for extensional operators below.)

D_1 [ExtOps] $=_{df} \{f \mid f:P \to P$, and for every $x,y \in P$ and $w \in W$, if $x(w) = y(w)$ then $f(x)(w) = f(y)(w)\}$

Before defining D_1 [IntOps], it is helpful to introduce some notation for the set of "constant individual concepts of propositions":

$P^* =_{df} \{f \mid f:W \to P,$ and for some $x \in P, f(w) = x$ for every $w \in W\}$

D_1 [IntOps] $=_{df} \{f \mid f:P \cup P^* \to P,$ and if $x \in P$ and $y \in P^*$ and if $y(w) = x$ for some $w \in W$ then $f(x) = f(y)\}$

Members of D_1 [IntOps] are defined on what will be the first-level senses of sentences (namely, P) and on what will be the second-level senses of sentences (namely, P^*); the complicated clause above ensures that in certain cases such functions cannot tell the first- and second-level senses apart.

Domains of Second-Level Senses

D_2 [Names] $=_{df} \{f \mid f:W \cup \{2\} \to D_1$ [Names]$\}$

(The use of 2 here is merely to ensure that a second-level sense appropriate to a name is identifiable as such.)

D_2 [Preds] $=_{df} \{f \mid f:D_2$ [Names] $\to P^*,$ and there is some $x \in D_1$ [Preds] such that for every $y \in D_2$ [Names] and $w \in W, f(y)(w) = x(y(w))\}$

D_2 [ExtOps] $=_{df} \{f \mid f:P^* \to P^*,$ and there is some $x \in D_1$ [ExtOps] such that for every $y \in P^*$ and $w \in W, f(y)(w) = x(y(w))\}$

D_2 [IntOps] $=_{df} \{f \mid f:P^* \cup \{2\} \to P^*,$ and there is some $x \in D_1$ [IntOps] such that for every $y \in P^*, f(y) = x(y)\}$

Having specified the domains, we now specify the requirement hinted at above: s_1 must map each name to a member of D_1 [Names], each predicate to a member of D_1 [Preds], each extensional operator to a member of D_1 [ExtOps], and each intensional operator to a member of D_1 [IntOps]. Now suppose that we assume that both D_1 [Names] and P^* contain some arbitrarily selected "designated" member. Then we can define the function s_2 which assigns second-level senses to the vocabulary of L as follows:

$s_2[a_n] =_{df}$ the unique member of D_2 [Names] which maps each $w \in W$ to $s_1[a_n]$ and maps 2 to the designated member of D_1 [Names].

$s_2[P_n] =_{df}$ the unique member f of D_2 [Preds] such that for every $y \in D_2$ [Names] and $w \in W, f(y)(w) = s_1[P_n](y(w))$.

$s_2[E_n] =_{df}$ the unique member f of D_2 [ExtOps] such that for every $y \in P^*$ and $w \in W, f(y)(w) = s_1[E_n](y(w))$.

$s_2[O_n] =_{df}$ the unique member f of D_2 [IntOps] such that f maps 2 to the designated member of P^*, and for every $y \in P^*, f(y) = s_1[O_n](y)$.

We can now extend s_1 and s_2 to the sentences of L by means of the stipulations:

$s_1[A(B)] =_{df} s_1[A](s_1[B])$, and

$s_2[A(B)] =_{df} s_2[A](s_2[B])$,

where A is a predicate and B a name, or A is an operator and B a sentence.

Next we will define the "presentation" relation. Notice that the set D_1 [Names] $\cup$ D_2 [Names] $\cup$ **P** $\cup$ **P*** is disjoint from the other domains, and they are all disjoint from each other. We call any member of any of the domains, or of **P** or **P***, a *sense*, and we specify, case by case, what each sense presents.

If $x \in D_1$ [Names] $\cup$ D_2 [Names] $\cup$ **P** $\cup$ **P*** then x *presents* y iff $x(w_0) = y$.

If $x \in D_1$ [Preds] then x *presents* y iff $y \in \{0,1\}^I$ and for every $z \in D_1$ [Names], $x(z)(w_0) = y(z(w_0))$.

If $x \in D_2$ [Preds] then x *presents* y iff $y \in D_1$ [Preds] and for every $z \in D_2$ [Names], $x(z)(w_0) = y(z(w_0))$.

(Similar clauses for $x \in D_1$ [ExtOps] and $x \in D_2$ [ExtOps].)

If $x \in D_1$ [IntOps] then x *presents* y iff $y \in \{0,1\}^P$ and for every $z \in $ **P***, $x(z)(w_0) = y(z(w_0))$.

If $x \in D_2$ [IntOps] then x *presents* y iff $y \in D_1$ [IntOps] and for every $z \in $ **P***, $x(z) = y(z)$.

The systems F1, F2, and C1 result from the above "ontology" by means of appropriate definitions of the semantical relations *expressing* and *referring*.

System F2 (= What Frege Said, Though Probably Not What He Meant)

Say that an occurrence of A in an extensional context in a sentence of L *refers to* whatever $s_1[A]$ presents, and *expresses* $s_1[A]$, and an occurrence of A that is in an indirect context in a sentence of L *refers to* $s_1[A]$ and *expresses* $s_2[A]$. Then the following Fregean principles all hold:

(1) If A is complex, what it refers to in a given context is a function of what its parts refer to in that context.

(2) If A is complex, what it expresses in a given context is a function of what its parts express in that context.

(3) In any context, A always refers to the unique thing that is presented by what it expresses in that context.

System F1 (= What Dummett Says Frege Should Have Said)

Say that an occurrence of A in an extensional context $refers_D$ to what $s_1[A]$ presents and $expresses_D s_1[A]$, and an occurrence of A in an indirect context $refers_D$ to and $expresses_D s_1[A]$. Then:

(1′) If A is complex, what it $refers_D$ to in any given context is a function of what its parts $refer_D$ to in that context.

(2′) If A is complex, what it $expresses_D$ in any given context is a function of what its parts $express_D$ in that context.

(3′) *If an occurrence of A is not in an indirect context,* it refers$_D$ to whatever is presented by what it expresses$_D$ there.

Further, we have the following comparison of F1 with F2:

(4′) Any isolated occurrence of a sentence refers to what it refers$_D$ to, and expresses what it expresses$_D$.

System C1 (= Carnap's System, Sort of)

Say that any occurrence of A always *refers$_C$* to whatever is presented by s_1 [A], and always *expresses$_C$* s_1 [A]. Then:

(1″) If A is complex and contains no intensional operators then what it refers$_C$ to in a given context is a function of what its parts refer$_C$ to in that context.

(2″) If A is complex then in any given context what it expresses$_C$ is a function of what its parts express$_C$ in that context.

(3″) In any context, A always refers$_C$ to whatever is presented by what it expresses$_C$ in that context.

Again we have a comparison with F2:

(4″) Any isolated occurrence of a sentence refers to what it refers$_C$ to and expresses what it expresses$_C$.

This paper is chapter one of *The Logical Syntax of Natural Language*, by Fred Sommers, in the Clarendon Series of Logic and Philosophy, Jonathan L. Cohen, general editor. © 1981 by Fred Sommers. Reprinted by permission of the author and Oxford University Press.

Are There Atomic Propositions?

FRED SOMMERS

I

In the introduction to Michael Dummett's study of Frege we read the following:

He (Frege) was the initiator of the modern period in the study of Logic . . . The understanding of the fundamental structure of language and therefore of thought, depend upon possessing, in a correct form, that explanation of the construction of and interrelationship between sentences which it is the business of logic to give. Modern logic stands in contrast to all the great logical systems of the past—of classical antiquity, of medieval Europe, and of India—in being able to give an account which depends on the mechanism of quantifiers and bound variables; for all the subtlety of the earlier systems, the analysis of the structure of the sentences of human language which is afforded by modern logic is, by its capacity to handle multiple generality, shown to be far deeper than they were able to attain. The discovery of the mechanism which enabled this analysis to be given and the realization of its significance, are due to Frege; if he had accomplished only this, he would have rendered a profound service to human knowledge.[1]

The historical judgment of the significance of Frege's contribution to logic is standard. It is generally agreed that a logical account of a sentence like 'everybody envies somebody" "depends upon the mechanism of quantifiers and bound variables." Frege was the first logician to give a logically useful representation of such "multiply general sentences" and his discovery of the quantifier variable notation is seen as "resolving an age old problem the failure to solve which had blocked the progress of logic for centuries." Specifically, scholastic logic had failed to give an adequate logical account of inferences involving multiply general sentences. An example of a valid inference of this kind is 'Since there is somebody who is envied by everybody it follows that everybody envies somebody'. According to the modern commentators, the scholastics were unable to explain this kind of inference because they did not understand the way signs of generality ('everybody,' 'somebody') and sentences containing proper names ('Peter envies John') were related. Discussing Frege's way of analyzing 'everybody envies somebody,' Dummett says:

> Frege's insight consisted in considering the sentences as being constructed in stages, corresponding to the different signs of generality occurring in it. A sentence may be formed by combining a sign of generality with a one-place predicate. The one-place predicate is itself to be thought of as having been formed from a sentence by removing one or more occurrences of some one singular term (proper names). Thus we begin with a sentence such as 'Peter envies John'. From this we form a one-place predicate 'Peter envies y' by removing the proper name 'John' — the letter 'y' here serving merely to indicate where the gap occurs that is left by the removal of the proper name. This predicate can then be combined with a sign of generality 'somebody' to yield the sentence 'Peter envies somebody'. The resulting sentence may now be subjected to the same process: by removing the proper name 'Peter' we obtain the predicate 'x envies somebody' and this may then be combined with the sign of generality 'everybody' to yield the sentence 'everybody envies somebody.'[2]

The steps that are here outlined show how a doubly general sentence is constructed out of singular beginnings:

1. Begin with a singular sentence with two proper name subjects and remove one proper name. This yields a predicate.
2. Combine the predicate with a sign of generality. This yields a sentence.
3. Begin again by removing from the sentence another proper name. This yields another predicate.
4. Combine this new predicate with another sign of generality. This yields a multiply general sentence.

The constructional history of the sentence determines its meaning. For example, 'everybody envies somebody' is sometimes considered ambiguous. It might be taken to mean that there is some one person whom everybody envies. More plausibly, it is interpreted to say that everybody envies somebody or other (not necessarily the same person). A constructional history of the sentence that will yield the first interpretation could be:

1. Peter envies John   (an atomic singular sentence)
2. x envies John   (a one-place predicate)
3. (x) (x envies John)   (a singly general sentence)
4. (x) (x envies y)   (a one-place predicate)
5. ($\exists$y) (x) (x envies y)   (a multiply general sentence).

The more plausible interpretation has a different constructional history:

1. Peter envies John   (an atomic singular sentence)
2. Peter envies y   (a one-place predicate)
3. (∃y) (Peter envies y)   (a singly general sentence)
4. (∃y) (x envies y)   (a one-place predicate)
5. (x) (∃y) (x envies y)   (a multiply general sentence).

Dummett's account of 'everybody envies somebody' assigns the second interpretation to it. Dummett attributes the plausibility of the second interpretation to the "the *ad hoc* convention we tacitly employ that the order of construction corresponds to the inverse order of the signs of generality in the sentence; when 'everybody' precedes 'somebody' it is taken as having been introduced later in the step by step construction."

The idea that we interpret 'everybody envies somebody' by inverting the surface order of its signs in tacitly analyzing it is an example of the kind of claim made for Fregean analysis by some of his followers. For many linguists as well as for many philosophers Frege's analytical logic is viewed as a source of insights into structures below the surface structures of sentences in the vernacular and Frege's logical grammar is seen by these linguists and philosophers as belonging to the grammar of the natural languages at the level of "deep structure." Frege himself did not think of his logical language as contributing to empirical linguistics; it seems at times that he had too great a contempt for the natural languages to credit them with a logical syntax.

More to the present purpose, Frege's solution to the problem of accounting for inference with multiply general sentences required him to devise a logical grammar that postulates a distinction of level between singular sentences like 'Socrates is mortal' or 'Peter envies John' and general sentences like 'every human is mortal' or 'everybody envies somebody'. In this logical grammar, the former kind of sentences are elements or atoms in the construction of the latter kind of sentences.

II

Although Dummett and others stress the revolutionary importance of the solution to the problem of multiple generality, Frege's revolution in logic is perhaps better located in his doctrine of the atomicity of singular sentences. The basic sentences of Frege's logical grammar are atomic in the sense of being devoid of logical words such as 'everybody' 'not' and 'or.' Before Frege the sentence 'Socrates is mortal' was often parsed as having the form 'every Socrates is mortal' with 'Socrates' or 'Socratizer' as a term whose application is restricted to a single thing.[3] This traditional doctrine treats singular sentences as if they were universal and it implicitly denies the Fregean thesis that singular sentences are syntactically more primitive than general sentences. Instead, the difference between 'Socrates is mortal' and 'every man is mortal' is semantically accounted for by the difference between 'Socrates' and 'man'; i.e., by the difference between a term expressly designed to apply to no more than one thing and one that is not restricted to unique application. Leibniz has an interesting variant of the traditional doctrine that singular terms are syntactically general. According to Leibniz, 'Socrates is mortal' is a particular proposition whose proper form is 'some Socrates is mortal'. But 'some Socrates is mortal' entails 'every Socrates is mortal', so we are free to choose either way of representing the sentence. Leibniz thus views the singular proposition as equivalent to a particular proposition that entails a universal one. In effect, 'Socrates is mortal' has wild or indifferent quantity ('some-or-every Socrates is mortal'). That 'Socrates is mortal' has particular quantity is justified by the consideration that its subject purports to refer to someone. But 'Socrates' as we use it in '(some) Socrates is mortal' is a term that applies to no more than one individual and the fact that it applies uniquely allows us to infer 'every Socrates is mortal' from 'some Socrates is mortal'. Since 'Socrates is mortal' entails its universal generalization, it is understandable that neither quantity is actually specified. However, in justifying inferences we must sometimes be explicit in assigning a given quantity to a singular proposition. For example, we find in Aristotle a variant of the following valid syllogism with two singular premises: "Pittacus is a good man and Pittacus is a wise man, so some wise man is a good man'. To justify this we note that 'Pittacus is P' entails 'every Pittacus is P' which enables us to assign opposing quantities to the two premises giving—in one case—a formally valid argument of form AII3: 'every Pittacus is a good man and some Pittacus is a wise man so some wise man is a good man' and—in the other case—a formally valid argument of form IAI4 'some Pittacus is a good man and every Pittacus is a wise man, so some wise man is a good man'. An assignment of particular quantities to both premises would not do.

Leibniz's doctrine of wild or indifferent quantity for singular propositions is an important rival to Frege's doctrine that singular propositions are logically atomic. Leibniz's theory is within the tradition of scholastic logic which treats all categorical propositions—singular as well as general—as assertions or denials of expressions of form 'some/every S is/is not P'. According to this traditional theory, a genuine logical subject is an expression of form 'some S' or 'every S', and the subjects of singular propositions are no exception. Unless otherwise noted, we shall contrast Frege's doctrine of the atomicity of singular propositions with the scholastic doctrine in its specifically Leibnizian version. Although Leibniz's doctrine of wild quantity is a significant innovation, it is important to place it within the tradition that denies to singular propositions the special syntactical position that Frege later accorded to them.

I shall refer to the doctrine that singular propositions are atomic as Frege's atomicity thesis. According to Frege, there is a class of propositions whose subjects are simple names or other singular expressions devoid of any sign of quantity. Names and other expressions of this kind are the only genuine logical subjects. Frege's atomicity thesis stands in contrast to the traditional doctrine of a logical subject as a syntactically complex expression containing a sign of quantity, 'some' or 'every', followed by a term. The traditional doctrine assimilates singular propositions to the class of general propositions. More correctly, it recognizes only one kind of proposition and one kind of logical subject for propositions that have singular or general terms in subject position.

The Fregean and scholastic doctrines differ then in several respects:

1. The scholastic holds that a logical subject is an expression with a sign of quantity. Frege holds that a logical subject must be simple. In consequence, he holds that only singular propositions are of subject-predicate form.
2. The scholastic holds that every logical subject contains a term and that the subject term of a proposition is interchangeable syntactically with the predicate term. Frege holds that the subject of a singular proposition, being simple, has no syntactical part that can serve in predicate position and, generally, that subjects and predicates have no common syntactical parts.
3. The scholastic distinguishes subject and predicate as expressions that have different logical (syncategorematic) elements. The subject is an expression of form 'some x' or 'every x' and it has a sign of quantity; the predicate is an expression of form 'is y' or 'is not y' and it has a sign of quality. In Frege, the distinction between subjects and predicates is not due to any difference of syncategorematic elements since the basic subject-predicate propositions are devoid of such elements. In Frege, the difference between subject and predicate is a primitive difference between two kinds of categorematic expressions.
4. The scholastic does not recognize a difference of logical form for singular and general propositions. Frege does.

Russell was well acquainted with the scholastic doctrine and he saw the significance of the step that Frege had taken in giving singular propositions their special syntactical status:

> The first serious advance in real logic since the time of the Greeks was made independently by Peano and Frege—both mathematicians. Traditional logic regarded the two propositions 'Socrates is mortal' and 'All men are mortal' as being of the same form; Peano and Frege showed that they are utterly different in form. Peano and Frege, who pointed out the error, did so for technical reasons . . . but the philosophical importance of the advance which they made is impossible to exaggerate.[4]

In this connection, it is worth quoting the passage from Leibniz in which he argues that singular propositions have the logical form of general propositions, their only distinction being that they have "wild" quantity.

> How is it that opposition is valid in the case of singular propositions . . . since elsewhere a universal affirmative and a particular negative are opposed. Should we say that a singular proposition is equivalent to a particular and to a universal proposition? Yes, we should. So also when it is objected that a singular proposition is equivalent to a particular proposition, since the conclusion in the third figure must be particular, and can nevertheless be singular; e.g., 'Every writer is a man, some writer is the Apostle Peter, therefore the

Apostle Peter is a man', I reply that here also the conclusion is really particular and it is as if we had drawn the conclusion 'Some Apostle Peter is a man'. For 'Some Apostle Peter' and 'Every Apostle Peter' coincide, since the term is singular.[5]

According to Leibniz's theory, 'Peter envies John' could be assigned the same form as 'everybody envies somebody' by reading it as 'every Peter envies some John.' Referring to the Fregean analysis of 'everybody envies somebody' Dummett asks:

> Why is this conception, under which the sentence was constructed in stages, more illuminating than the more natural idea according to which it was formed simultaneously out of its three constituents 'everybody' 'envies' and 'somebody' in exactly the same way that 'Peter envies John' is constructed out of its three components?[6]

Leibniz would here put Dummett's question the other way round, asking why we cannot think of 'Peter envies John' as having the same form as 'everybody envies somebody'. To this, Leibniz's answer is: Indeed we *can* although strictly speaking 'Peter envies John' parses as 'some Peter envies some John', a proposition that entails 'every Peter envies some John'.

Of course, Dummett's question presupposes Frege's thesis of atomicity; it assumes the syntactical gap between 'Peter envies John' and 'everybody envies somebody'. The question then is not whether these two are distinct but why they are. In his answer, Dummett exploits the different conditions for the truth of the two sentences. Generally, a singular sentence is true just in case its predicate is true of the individuals that are named by its proper names. For example, 'Socrates is mortal' is true if and only if 'is mortal' is true of Socrates. The rules for assigning truth to general sentences are somewhat more complicated. For example, the general sentence 'somebody is mortal' is true just in case some one singular sentence 'Socrates is mortal', 'Plato is mortal', 'Gabriel is mortal', etc., is true. The general sentence 'everybody is mortal' is true just in case each and every sentence 'Socrates is mortal', 'Plato is mortal', 'Gabriel is mortal' is true. In this way, the rules for assigning truth values to 'something is P' and 'everything is P' refer us back to the truth conditions of the basic sentences of form 'a is P'. We assign a constructional analysis to 'everybody envies somebody' because (says Dummett):

> Once we know the constructional history of a sentence involving multiple generality, we can from these simple rules determine the truth conditions of the sentence provided only that we already know the truth conditions of every sentence containing proper names in places the signs of generality stand. Thus 'everybody envies somebody' is true just in case each of the sentences 'Peter envies somebody', 'James envies somebody', ... is true; and 'Peter envies somebody' is, in turn true just in case at least one of the sentences 'Peter envies John', 'Peter envies James' .... is true.[7]

In this explanation of the difference between 'everybody envies somebody' and 'Peter envies John,' we encounter the characteristically modern doctrine that the logical form of a sentence is an expression that exhibits its truth conditions. Specifically, the analysis of 'everybody envies somebody' as 'For anybody x there is somebody y such that x envies y' is an acceptable "translation" since the truth conditions of the "translated" sentence have been made explicit. Speaking of the way truth conditions are related to the grammar of modern logic, Quine remarks:

> The grammar that we logicians tendentiously call standard is grammar designed with no other thought than to facilitate the tracing of truth conditions. And a very good thought that is.[8]

How good a thought it is we shall consider in due course. For the present, we take note of the Fregian doctrine that truth conditions of general propositions are to be traced recursively to the conditions for the truth of propositions that contain no signs of generality. For this is what Frege's version of general propositions enables us to do.

If we ask whether the standard Fregean account of 'everybody envies somebody' supports the atomicity thesis, our answer must be that it does not. For that account makes use of atomic propositions and it must be rejected by anyone who agrees with Leibniz that even singular propositions are syntactically general. If Leibniz is right, there are no atomic sentences of the kind required for a recursive account of the truth conditions of general sentences. Put another way: If Leibniz is right, Dummett's constructional histories are semantic myths. For while it is certainly true that, say, 'everything is created' is true only if 'Socrates is created', 'Alaska is created' . . . are true, this is of little significance since each of the singular sentences is itself of the form 'every . . . is created' or 'some . . . is created.' To be sure, there may still be some point to observing that the truth of 'everything is created' is conditional on the truth of 'Socrates is created', but so, too, is it dependent on the truth of 'every Greek is created' and it is hard to see why 'every Socrates is created' is semantically more privileged just because the term in its subject is designed for unique application.

If on the other hand Frege is right about the existence of atomic propositions, then the recursive historical account of general sentences is very attractive. It may be thought that the very fact that atomic sentences can serve as ground in an elegant explanation of the truth conditions of general sentences is itself an argument in favor of their existence. If so, it is an unimpressive argument; unless the impossibility of a semantic explanation of general sentences that is not grounded in atomic sentences could be established, the appeal to the Frege type of recursive model as a reason for accepting atomic propositions should be disregarded.[9]

III

We are beginning to face the intimidating prospect of deciding whether to accept or to reject Frege's atomicity thesis. And it is natural to wonder how one goes about deciding whether a certain class of propositions—in this case the class of atomic propositions—exists or fails to exist. The meaning of the question 'are there atomic propositions?' is, however, not necessarily affected by the fact that we are not clear on how to set about answering it. The Fregean thesis on the atomic character of singular propositions is clear enough and it is in sharp contrast to the scholastic theory. Moreover, the question of the existence of certain syntactical forms is something that we are learning to view in a scientific light. For we have, if only in principle, certain criteria for judging the adequacy of linguistic theories when they postulate the existence of some class of syntactical objects, and even if it should be true that we are at present unable to judge the matter in the case of atomic propositions, we still have the right to expect that the question of their existence may admit of an empirical decision at some later date. In the meantime, we can do much in examining the existing grounds for accepting or rejecting atomic propositions. Even an untested hypothesis can be judged plausible or implausible and we are in a position to do this much for the case of atomic propositions. What is more intimidating is the fact that Frege's thesis has been so overwhelmingly accepted by philosophers and linguists. Indeed the alternative doctrine is only rarely mentioned as a buried mistake, and even then it is never set up as a denial of Frege's thesis but is only mentioned as a curious way of parsing singular propositions that does not somehow affect the question of the existence of atomic propositions.

The Frege thesis is thus unchallenged and unnoticed against the background of its classical rival. In part, this came about because the traditional scholastic theory never explicitly denied the existence of atomic propositions. This is not surprising; no one before Frege had clearly postulated a class of sentences whose characteristic feature was to be altogether lacking in "syncategorematic" elements and the question of the existence of sentences of this kind simply did not arise.

After the triumph of Russell's popularization of Frege's logic, the situation was completely reversed; atomic propositions were essential to the new logic and it was natural to take them for granted. Epistemological considerations undoubtedly played a part in this. But in fact the logistic advantages of using Frege's logical language were of greater significance. Frege's logical grammar became canonical because of its inference power; the main reason for distinguishing the logical forms of 'Socrates is mortal' and 'every man is mortal' is the technical one that Russell alluded to: the power and scope of modern predicate logic in which the atomic proposition figures as the element of logical analysis. The rules of formation for the most effective logical languages that have ever been devised begin with atomic forms and proceed with the construction of non-atomic sentences by the addition of sentence-forming operators (the signs of generality and the truth functions). It was felt that the traditional doctrine of the singular proposition must be wrong and that it could be safely ignored; had it been right, it should have been possible to construct a logic as powerful as Frege's in which singular propositions and general propositions have the logical form of an assertion or denial of a universal or particular proposition (i.e., a proposition of form 'every S . . .' or 'some S . . .').

Now this reason for accepting Frege over his scholastic opponents is an excellent one. It is surely legitimate to require of a logical syntax that it be logically effective, and, in this crucial respect, the traditional formal logic failed dismally. If then we compare the logical syntax of Frege with the logical syntax of his predecessors and, in particular, if we compare the two logical grammars in their representation of singular propositions, the question whether there are atomic propositions appears to be idle. There is only one caveat: if it could be shown that a traditional representation of singular propositions is as logically effective (e.g., for reckoning with multiply general propositions) as Frege's atomic propositions have proved to be, one might be prepared to reopen the matter. But here the burden of argument is upon the proponent of the older discarded theory and not upon Frege and his successors.

We shall presently accept the logistic challenge on behalf of the traditional doctrine. It is commonly assumed that Frege's spectacular success with inferences that the traditional logician failed to handle is proof that traditional logic is, in principle as well as in fact, inferior to modern predicate logic in inference power. But this is unwarranted; Frege's success, while decisive, was never, in this sense, definitive. Pending a re-examination of the potentialities of the syntax of traditional logic, we shall keep the question of the truth of the thesis of atomicity alive even while acknowledging that, as matters stand, the logistic evidence is strongly in its favor.

Frege's successors did not challenge the atomicity thesis but neither did they neglect it. On the contrary, although we find no real skepticism about the thesis itself, there is a considerable literature devoted to explaining why singular propositions are as Frege characterized them. Some of the main arguments in support of Frege's account of singular sentences are apologetic, being propounded in the conviction that Frege's account needs to be rationalized and clarified rather than proved; in particular, the following theses are dogmatically maintained:

i. Logical subjects are always singular, and the sole vehicle of predication is the singular sentence.

ii. The most primitive kind of singular sentence consists of a designating subject (or subjects) and a characterizing predicate. The subject-expression and the predicate-expression are of different syntactical types but they are not distinguished syncategorematically. The syntactic difference is due solely to the semantic difference of role: the subject designates, the predicate characterizes.

iii. Singular sentences are syntactically and semantically more primitive than general sentences.

Notes

1. Michael Dummett, *Frege: Philosophy of Language* (New York, 1973), p. xiii.
2. *Ibid.*, p. 10.
3. Speaking of "logicians in past centuries," Quine says, in *Word and Object* (Cambridge, Mass., 1960), p. 181: "they commonly treated a name such as 'Socrates' rather on a par logically with 'mortal' and 'man' and as differing from these latter just in being true of fewer objects, viz. one."

4. Bertrand Russell, *Our Knowledge of the External World* (New York, 1960), p. 40.
5. *Leibniz Logical Papers,* ed. G. H. R. Parkinson (Oxford, 1966), p. 115.
6. Dummett, *Frege,* p. 11.
7. Dummett, *Frege,* p. 11.
8. Quine, *Philosophy of Logic* (Englewood Cliffs, N.J., 1970), p. 35.
9. There is in fact a well-known alternative developed by Tarski. Fregean semantics takes the notion of the truth of *closed atomic* sentences as primitive and defines the truth of quantified and truth-functionally compound sentences in terms of it. Tarskian semantics treats the notion of satisfaction of an *open* sentence by an individual or sequence of individuals as primitive and defines the truth of *closed* sentences, "atomic" or quantified in terms of it. Thus, where a Fregean would say that '($\exists$x) Fx' is true if and only if some atomic sentence 'Fa' is true, a Tarskian would say (roughly) that '($\exists$x) Fx' is true if and only if some (unnamed) individual satisfies the open sentence 'Fx'. As Quine has shown, Tarskian (but not Fregean) semantics can be easily adapted for languages without individual constants and even without individual variables, such as his predicate functor version of MPL: the primitive notion in the latter case is the satisfaction not of an open sentence 'Fx' but of a predicate (or term) 'F' by individuals or sequences of individuals *(Ways of Paradox and Other Essays,* rev. ed. 1976, essay 29, especially sec. V, pp. 316-17). Tarskian semantics can also be adapted for a term logic such as TFL.

For an illuminating comparison of Fregean and Tarskian semantics (somewhat biased in Frege's favor), see G. Evans, "Pronouns, Quantifiers, and Relative Clauses," *Canadian Journal of Philosophy* 3, no. 3, sec. 2 (1977): 471-77.

Frege on Predication

RICHARD L. MENDELSOHN

Frege held that proper names [*Eigennamen*] and concept words [*Begriffswörter*] both denote: proper names denote objects, and concept words denote concepts. Several years ago, there was considerable confusion about whether Frege intended concept words to have reference as well as sense, but that issue has been decisively settled. In the *Nachgelassene Schriften*[1], Frege begins a manuscript written between 1892 and 1895 (i.e., just after "On Sense and Reference"[2]) as follows:

> In an essay ("On Sense and Reference") I primarily distinguished between sense and reference only for proper names (or, if one prefers, singular terms). The same distinction can also be drawn for concept words. Now, a confusion can easily develop here: one might mix up the distinction between concept and object with the distinction between sense and reference, and run together sense and concept, on the one hand, and reference and object, on the other. To each concept word or proper name, there corresponds, as a rule, a sense and a reference, as I am using these words.[3]

But to resolve this exegetical issue is not to resolve the doubt, which I share, about whether Frege was correct in holding that concept words denote.

The paradigm of a denoting expression is an ordinary proper name, and concept words seem to function very differently: they do not appear to name or pick out things about which we might wish to speak, and for this reason (among others), many philosophers have been reluctant to regard them as denoting expressions. Frege sees the difference in the functioning of proper names and concept words as reflecting a difference in the type of entity denoted. The different types of entity require different types of representative, but in each case the representing relation (namely, denoting) remains the same. I tend to believe that Frege's view is untenable. I will argue in this paper that the distinction between concept and object, insofar as it was intended to underpin the distinction between *Begriffswörter* and *Eigennamen*, fails to yield an ontological distinction between types of entities. I take this to be the moral of the paradox of the concept *horse*. I will first rehearse the main outlines of Frege's semantic theory and then turn to the paradox.

An object [*Gegenstand*] is that sort of entity referred to by an *Eigenname*. Not every object need actually have a name, but were any expression to stand for an object, it would have to be an *Eigenname*. And what is an *Eigenname?* "I call anything a proper name if it is a sign for an object."[4] Again, there need not actually be an object for which the *Eigenname* stands—"Odysseus" is an *Eigenname* even though there is no such person as Odysseus. All that is required, then, is that the expression purport to refer to an object. It is not clear to which of these two, *Eigennamen* or *Gegenstände*, Frege assigns priority. He often gives the impression that it rests with *Gegenstände*, as though this is a fundamental category of Reality which it is incumbent upon language to reproduce; but I tend to agree with Dummett[5] that it must reside with *Eigennamen*. Whichever way out of this cricle, however, we remain with a notion that is logically primitive and indefinable:

> [T] he question arises what it is that we are here calling an object. I regard a regular definition as impossible, since we have here something too simple to admit of logical analysis. It is only possible to indicate what is meant. Here I can only say briefly: an object is anything that is not a function, so that an expression for it does not contain an empty place.[6]
>
> Take the proposition "Two is a prime number." Linguistically we distinguish here between a subject, "two," and a predicative constituent, "is a prime number." . . . The first constituent, "two," is a proper name of a certain number; it designates an object, a whole that no longer requires completion. The predicative constituent "is a prime number," on the other hand, does require completion. I also call the first constituent saturated; the second, unsaturated. To this difference in the signs there of course corresponds an analogous one in the realm of references: to the proper name there corresponds the object; to the predicative part, something I call a concept. This is not supposed to be a definition; for the decomposition into a saturated and an unsaturated part must be considered a logically primitive phenomenon which must simply be accepted and cannot be reduced to something simpler.[7]

We are left, therefore, with hints and metaphors, certainly not the most philosophically satisfying position to be in, but since the crude directions Frege provides for sorting expressions (and entities) appear to be sufficient for us to sort expressions (and entities) in the way he intended, we have, perhaps, enough to work with. An *Eigenname*, he says, is a complete or saturated expression, one that has no empty places so that it can stand alone; proper names (ordinarily so-called) and singular definite descriptions are *Eigennamen* (though not invariably), as well as declarative sentences [*Behauptungssätze*]. *Gegenstände*, similarly, are characterized as self-subsistent, saturated, complete wholes. All of the following are *Eigennamen*, and so refer to objects if they refer at all: "the moon," "the Equator," "Snow is white," "the extension of the concept *horse*," "Babe Ruth's batting stance," and, of course, the notorious "the concept *horse*."

The ontological classification of entities into objects and functions is exclusive: it is impossible that anything can be both an object and a function. The distinction, it appears, is exhaustive as well, for Frege says, in one of the passages quoted above, that "an object is anything that is not a function." Unlike objects, functions are unsaturated, incomplete, in need of supplementation, unable to stand alone. The sign for a function must have one or more empty places and so an expression that stands for a function must be an incomplete expression. A function, then, is that sort of entity referred to by an incomplete expression, and only an incomplete expression can stand for a function. As with objects, it need not be supposed that to every function there corresponds an expression that stands for it, but only that were any expression to stand for a function, it would have to be an incomplete expression; and, again, it need not be supposed that there actually be a function denoted by an incomplete expression—just as there are *Eigennamen* that purport to refer but fail because there exists no objects to which they refer, so too there might be function expressions that purport to refer but fail because there exist no such functions.

The distinction between *Eigennamen* and function expressions, like the distinction between objects and functions, is exclusive. It is not, however, exhaustive, for certain expressions fail even to purport to refer; among there are parentheses, bound variables, and the assertion sign. *Eigennamen* and function expressions are both, according to Frege, names—in *Grundgesetze*[8], Frege calles function expressions "function names" [*Funktionsnamen*] —and they are names because they refer, or better, purport to refer, to entities. The relation between an *Eigenname* and the object for which it stands is, therefore, the same as the relation between a *Funktionsname* and the function for which it stands: each *bedeutet* its *Bedeutung*. The difference, then, between *Eigennamen* and *Funktionsnamen* is not to be found in the relation they bear to entities; nor, again, is the difference between objects and functions to be found in the relation expressions bear to them. If anything, the difference between *Eigennamen* and *Funktionsnamen* is to be found in the kind of entity each denotes; and the difference between objects and functions, analogously, is to be found in the kind of expression that denotes them. But this way of marking the distinction is not very informative. The correct place, I think, to locate the difference, both at the formal mode level between *Eigennamen* and *Funktionsnamen*, and at the material mode level between objects and functions, is in their combining properties, for it is here that Frege justifies the distinction:

> It may perhaps be made a little clearer why these parts must be different. An object, e.g., the number 2, cannot logically adhere to another object, e.g., Julius Caesar, without some means of connection. This, in turn, cannot be an object but rather must be unsaturated. A logical connection into a whole can come about only through this, that an unsaturated part is saturated or completed by one or more parts. Something like this is the case when we complete "The capital of" by "Germany" or "Sweden"; or when one completes "one-

half of" by "6." Now, it follows from the fundamental difference of objects from concepts that an object can never occur predicatively or unsaturatedly; and that logically, a concept can never substitute for an object. One could express it metaphorically like this: There are different logical places; in some only objects can stand and not concepts, in others only concepts and not objects.[9]

Thus, among functions Frege marks distinctions which he claims are as fundamental as the distinction between objects and functions:

Now just as functions are fundamentally different from objects, so also functions whose arguments are and must be functions are fundamentally different from functions whose arguments are objects and cannot be anything else.[10]

Functions of two arguments are just as fundamentally different from *functions of one argument* as the latter are from *objects*. For whereas objects are wholly *saturated,* functions of two arguments are saturated to a lesser degree than functions of one argument, which now are already *unsaturated.*[11]

On the other hand, no such distinctions are made for objects, because all objects have the same combining properties: a function that takes for its argument any object accepts every object as argument.

The distinction between *Eigennamen* and the various sorts of *Funktionsnamen* is directed at capturing the fact that certain expressions can combine to form unified whole expressions whereas others cannot, that certain sequences of signs are regarded as complex signs but other sequences of signs are regarded as mere complexes of signs. A string of proper names, for example,

John Harry Tom

is merely a complex of signs; but a proper name followed by a predicative expression, for example,

John is happy

combine to form a unified whole expression. Frege accounts for these syntactic regularities by assigning to each *Funktionsname* so many blank spaces and specifying for each blank space what kind of expression can fill it—an *Eigenname,* a one-place first-level *Funktionsname,* and so on. This classification of expression amounts, in effect, to a rudimentary Ajdukiewicz-type *categorial grammar* in which we have but one basic category, E (for *Eigenname*), the various kinds of *Funktionsnamen* being derived categories. In a categorial grammar, derived categories are represented by "fractions": where $C_1, \ldots, C_n, C_{n+1}$ are categories, basic or derived,

$C_{n+1}/C_1, \ldots C_n$

is the category of those expressions which combine with an expression of categories $C_1, \ldots, C_n$, respectively, to constitute an expression of category C_{n+1}. So a first-level *Funktionsname* with one argument-place which combines with an *Eigenname* to form an *Eigenname* would belong to the category E/E; a first-level *Funktionsname* with two argument-places which combines with *Eigennamen* to form an *Eigenname* would belong to the category E/EE; and so on. These categories are pairwise disjoint: no expression belongs to more than one category.

The relevant mode of combination here is, of course, logical combination. Frege's is a logical grammar. He has not attempted to characterize the grammatical sequences of some natural language, say, English or German. This is evident from his purposeful ignoring of many of the traditional grammatical features of natural language, e.g., case systems, verb conjugations, active/passive forms, and the like; and most striking in this regard is his lumping of singular terms and declarative sentences in the same syntactic category.

Although Frege has provided us with a syntax, there is a sense in which he has not yet accounted for the fact that certain sequences of expressions combine to form complex expressions but others do not. At best, we have a systematic taxonomy of expression; what we should like to know is what it is about these types that accounts for their syntactic behavior. Here, I take it, is where the ontological distinction comes in: the different categories of expressions correspond to different categories of entities, and the combining properties of expressions are explained in terms of the combining properties of the entities represented.

Thus, Frege projects these differences among expressions onto the world: "To this difference in the sign," he says in a passage quoted earlier, "there of course corresponds an analogous one in the realm of references." The same qualifiers—"unsaturated," "in need of supplementation," etc.—are applied to functions as well as to *Funktionsnamen,* and the grammatical categories are mirrored one-for-one at the level of ontology. To the category E of expressions there corresponds the ontological category of objects; to the category E/E of expressions there corresponds the ontological category of first-level singular functions; and so on. And, as with linguistic categories, ontological categories are pairwise disjoint. This amounts, in effect, to a simple theory of types of entities. The complete entities, objects, are of type e. An incomplete entity belongs to the type $\langle t_1, \ldots, t_n \rangle$ if, and only if, it may be completed by (and only by) entities of type $t_1, \ldots, t_n$, taken in that order. So the entities corresponding to the linguistic category E/EE are of type $\langle e, e \rangle$; the entities corresponding to the linguistic category E/E/E are of type $\langle e, \langle e \rangle \rangle$; and so on.

Nor, incidentally, are these ontological distinctions limited to the realm of references; the whole menagerie reappears in the realm of sense:

> The whole [thought] owes its unit to the fact that the thought saturates the unsaturated part, or, as we can also say, completes the part needing completion. And it is natural to suppose that, for logic in general, combination into a whole always comes about through the saturation of something unsaturated. . . . By "compound thought" I shall understand a thought consisting of thoughts but not of thoughts alone. For a thought is complete and saturated, and needs no completion in order to exist. For this reason, thoughts do not cleave to one another unless they are connected together by something

that is not a thought, and it may be taken that this "connective" is unsaturated.[12]

Just as in the case for reference, we find that the sense of a part of a complex *Eigenname* is part of the sense of the whole *Eigenname*, and at least one part of the *Eigenname* must express an unsaturated entity, i.e., a function, in order for the sense of the *Eigenname* to be complete.

At the level of language, Frege's talk of parts and wholes, of saturated and unsaturated entities, etc., can be cashed in for syntactical rules; but at the level of ontology, this talk is treacherously misleading. Indeed, Dummett reports[13] that Frege eventually abandoned the part/whole metaphor at the level of reference for just this reason: although we would readily agree that the expression "the capital of Denmark" contains the name "Denmark" as a proper part, we would just as readily deny that the capital of Denmark, namely, Copenhagen, contains the country Denmark as a proper part. Much has been made of the obscurity of Frege's metaphors by Black[14] and Marshall[15]; but the moral I draw is either that these commentators have failed to heed his plea to meet him halfway, or that the metaphors are genuinely unhelpful—not yet, as has been suggested, that the function/object distinction is itself incoherent. Nor, I think, would it be fair to conclude with Marshall that "Frege has taken a linguistic difference to be a rift in nature."[16] As anyone acquainted with the most elementary parts of mathematics will attest, numbers are very different from functions. Now, Frege was trained as a mathematician, and I am sure that this difference was impressed upon him long before he took up logic; the ontological distinction between numbers and functions was arrived at independent of linguistic considerations, and at the earliest stages of his career, Frege would no doubt have understood expressions like "the sine function" and "the square function" to stand for functions. Of course, in Frege's day, the notion of a function had not yet been firmly tied down, and his contemporaries were saying very foolish things about functions, e.g., that they were variable numbers, or that they were mental operations, or that they were expressions of a special sort; and in his attempt to clarify the notion of a function, on which he had based his *Begriffsschrift*, Frege came to connect the ontological distinction between numbers and functions with the logico-linguistic distinction between (complete) number names and (incomplete) arithmetic function-expressions. The rift in nature, to use Marshall's phrase, was not derived from his analysis of complex number names; rather, it was assumed at the outset.

The crux of Frege's analysis is precisely here in the linkup. For, the connection between numbers and functions, on the one hand, and complete and incomplete arithmetic expressions, on the other, dovetailed neatly with the naive view of representation Frege had held at least as early as *Begriffsschrift*,[17] namely, that language represents by mimicry, that the structure of language mirrors the structure of the entities represented. On such a view, the different categories of expressions would correspond to different categories of entities in such a way that the combining properties of the expressions would mimic analogous properties of the entities represented. The entities would *have* to have analogous properties, and for want of a more perspicuous idiom for describing these properties, one might (as Frege did) simply transfer the mechanistic vocabulary appropriate for expressions to the entities represented. So a complete expression would stand for a complete entity, an incomplete expression would stand for an incomplete entity, and in this way the syntactic coherence of a given sequence of expressions would be explained by the ontological coherence of the entities stood for by the expressions in the sequence. Now, this outline is very efficient and very appealing; still, it is only an outline. Lacking are independent grounds for supposing that there are entities with the desired properties. And here is where the number/function distinction comes in. For in numbers and functions Frege had the entities whose existence and difference were arrived at independently of the needs of the representation scheme. Frege then simply extended the notion of a function beyond the realm of arithmetic so that the picture could be completed for the whole of language.

The generalized function/object distinction therefore does double-duty for Frege: (1) it is an ontological distinction, an extension of the original number/function distinction; (2) it is a semantical distinction designed to ground the difference in the behavior of *Eigennamen* and *Funktionsnamen*. And it is important to keep these two aspects of the function/object distinction separate, for the well-known difficulties that beset the function/object distinction stem largely from the semantical role it is intended to play. Frege's view of the way in which language represents, and, in particular, his claim that a complete (incomplete) expression denotes a complete (incomplete) entity, is simply untenable. To see this, however, we must turn to the paradox of the concept *horse*.

The background, briefly, is as follows. A contemporary, Benno Kerry, had challenged Frege's claim that the concept/object distinction was exclusive. He argued that since, on Frege's view, "the concept *horse*" is an *Eigenname*, it must denote an object; so there would appear to be at least one concept, the concept *horse*, that is also an object. In reply, Frege conceded that "the concept *horse*" is an *Eigenname* and that it must therefore denote an object, but he rejected Kerry's conclusion that the concept *horse* is a concept. So Frege had committed himself to the truth of an exceedingly paradoxical sentence,

(1) The concept *horse* is not a concept.

Some explanation was called for.

Frege attributed the paradoxical character of the sentence to an awkwardness of language:

> I admit that there is a quite peculiar obstacle in the way of an understanding with my reader. By a kind of necessity of language, my expressions, taken literally, sometimes miss my thought; I mention an object, when what I intend is a concept. I fully realize that in such cases I was relying upon a reader who would be ready to meet me half-way—who does not begrudge a pinch of salt.[18]

As another example of such awkwardness, he cited the following:

A similar thing happens when we say as regards the sentence "this rose is red": the grammatical predicate "is red" belongs to the subject "this rose." Here the words 'The grammatical predicate "is red"' are not a grammatical predicate but a subject. By the very act of explicitly calling it a predicate, we deprive it of this property.[19]

But, contrary to what Frege says, we do not, simply by calling a given expression a grammatical predicate, deprive it of the property of being a grammatical predicate: the sentence

(2) The grammatical predicate "is red" is not a grammatical predicate

is simply false. To be sure, Frege's own example,

(3) 'The grammatical predicate "is red"' is not a grammatical predicate,

is true. But, in the first place, it is not clear why we should regard (3), rather than (2), as the proper analogue to (1); in the second place, there is no awkwardness about (2), and whatever awkwardness accrues to (3) is readily explained; and, in the third place, since (2) is false, we are able to speak about grammatical predicates whereas, on Frege's view, we do not seem to be able to say anything intelligible about concepts.

But let us try to read Frege more sympathetically to find out what he might have had in mind. One suggestion is this: by the very act of explicitly calling a given expression a grammatical predicate, we deprive it of the property of being the grammatical predicate of the sentence used to make the assertion. This claim, however, is incorrect. The sentence

(4) The grammatical predicate "is a grammatical predicate" is a grammatical predicate

is true, and, moreover, the grammatical predicate "is a grammatical predicate" is the grammatical predicate of (4). Another suggestion is this: by the very act of explicitly calling a given expression a grammatical predicate, we must use an expression that is not a grammatical predicate. This claim appears to be true. In order to call the grammatical predicate "is red" a grammatical predicate, we must use an expression—'the grammatical predicate "is red"'—that is not a grammatical predicate. However, this interpretation fails to capture Frege's saying that by explicitly calling a given expression a grammatical predicate, we deprive *it* of the property of being a grammatical predicate. A third suggestion, then, is this: by the very act of explicitly calling a given expression a grammatical predicate, and by "explicitly" we mean exhibiting the expression between quote marks or italicizing the expression, we deprive the expression from acting in that context as a grammatical predicate. Now, this claim seems to be true; moreover, I tend to think that this is the correct interpretation. One textual bit of evidence in favor of this interpretation is that Frege points out that Kerry's italicizing of "horse" in "the concept *horse*" indicates that it is not being used in that context in its normal fashion, namely, as a concept word; and the analogy would then be that by placing a given expression between quote marks, as in 'the grammatical predicate "is red"', one is indicating that the expression is not being used in that context in its normal fashion, namely, as a grammatical predicate. Also, viewed in this manner, we can see why Frege might think of his inability to say that a given expression denotes a concept as some minor problem, an awkwardness of language: it is just that he wishes to account for the logical behavior of an expression in its context of use, and in order to say how the expression is operating he must mention it and thus deprive it of the property of acting in the specified way in that context. And this difficulty appears harmless enough. Note that if we follow through on this interpretation, a similar difficulty attends the expression 'the subject "this rose"': by the very act of explicitly calling "this rose" a subject, we mention the expression and in so doing we prevent it from acting in that context as a grammatical subject.

But to suppose that the problem results from a mere awkwardness of language just does not seem to capture the depths of Frege's difficulties. For the view Frege is defending is that the combining properties of expressions mirror the combining properties of that which the expressions stand for. And this view is flatly false. For, "is red" is a grammatical predicate, but 'the grammatical predicate "is red"' is not a grammatical predicate; yet the latter expression obviously stands for the former. Frege is simply mistaken in supposing that he can account for the combining properties of expressions in terms of the combining properties of the entities denoted.

Let us now attempt to reconstruct Frege's argument for (1).[20] (1) is an immediate consequence of Frege's fundamental principle,

(5) η is a predicate if, and only if, η denotes a concept.

(Actually, (5) is not quite right: η might be a predicate without there being anything that it denotes—all that is required is that it purport to refer to a concept; but since Frege himself often overlooked this point, we will let (5) stand as is.) Given the obvious truth,

(6) "The concept *horse*" is not a predicate,

then, by (5), we obtain

(7) "The concept *horse*" does not denote a concept.

Paraphrasing (7) as

(8) That which "the concept *horse*" denotes is not a concept,

and assuming the uncontroversial identity

(9) That which "the concept *horse*" denotes = the concept *horse*,

we get (1) be substituting "the concept *horse*" for 'that which "the concept *horse*" denotes' in (8).

By parity of reasoning, however, we can show that there are no predicates at all. For, given the obvious truth,

(10) "horse" is a predicate,

then, by (5), we have

(11) "horse" denotes a concept;

and paraphrasing (11), we obtain

(12) That which "horse" denotes is a concept.

But it is obviously true that

(13) 'That which "horse" denotes' is not a predicate,

and so, by (5), we have

(14) 'That which "horse" denotes' does not denote a concept.

Paraphrasing (14) as

(15) That which 'that which "horse" denotes' denotes is not a concept,

and assuming the uncontroversial identity

(16) That which 'that which "horse" denotes' denotes = that which "horse" denotes,

we obtain

(17) That which "horse" denotes is not a concept,

by substituting 'that which "horse" denotes' for 'that which "that which 'horse' denotes" denotes' in (15). Since we have been able to derive contradictory statements—(12) and (17)—then, by *reductio*, if (5) is true, (10) must be false. And because the argument does not depend upon any particular characteristic of the predicate "horse" it is iterable for all other predicates. Assuming (5) to be true, then, there can be no predicates.

There is one assumption in the argument I have not yet discussed, namely, the paraphrase

(18) η denotes a concept if, and only if, that which η denotes is a concept;

and I have not mentioned the paraphrase largely because it would appear to be so obvious as not to require any comment. But, in every instantiation of (18), the right-hand side of the "if, and only if" would have to be false: ⌜that which η denotes⌝ is never a predicate, so by (5), it can never denote a concept. Hence, in order for (18) to be true, there can be no expression that denotes a concept. Assuming that an expression denotes uniquely, we can symbolize (18), with the help of Russell's iota operator, as follows:

$(E!x)(den(\eta) = x \,\&\, Concept(x)) \equiv Concept\,[(\iota x)(den(\eta) = x)]$.

On Russell's view, (18) is logically true; so Frege seems committed to there being no expression that denotes a concept.

But our symbolization reveals that we have assumed "ξ is a concept" to be a first-level *Funktionsname*, i.e., to denote a function that takes only objects for arguments. Now, it is fairly clear that Frege, too, is making this assumption, for he claims that the sentence

(19) The concept *horse* is a concept

is well formed, and that "the concept *horse*" is an *Eigenname*. But if "ξ is a concept" is a first-level *Funktionsname,* it can only be sensefully completed by an *Eigenname;* and, according to Frege, any such completion must result in a false sentence. By the same token, ⌜η denotes a concept⌝ must always be false; "concept" is a *Begriffswort*—it only makes sense to say of an object that it is or is not a concept—and since no object is a concept, there can be nothing of which it is true both that a given expression denotes it and that it is a concept. Looking back to (5), we see that the right-hand side of the "if, and only if" will never be true; but since there are predicates, the left-hand side will sometimes be true. So, on the assumption that "ξ is a concept" is a first-level *Funktionsname,* (5) must be false. If, then, Frege assumes "ξ is a concept" to be a first-level *Funktionsname*—and he clearly does—then the derivation of (1) from (5) appears to be valid; but since (5) turns out to be false on this interpretation, Frege has failed to establish (1), and so he has failed to satisfactorily answer Kerry.

What could have led Frege to suppose that "ξ is a concept" is a first-level *Funktionsname?* Certainly, there would seem to be good reason for him to think otherwise. He obviously believes that there are concepts, and, no doubt, he would also like to assert that there are concepts; but by supposing "ξ is a concept" to be a first-level *Funktionsname,* he has debarred himself—so he acknowledges—from ever truthfully saying so. What could have persuaded him to adopt this self-defeating line? The only reason he offers is that "ξ is a concept" can be sensefully completed by an *Eigenname.* But this, surely, is insufficient. For, although "ξ exists" can be sensefully completed by an *Eigenname,* Frege is quite clear that a sentence like

(20) The number 2 exists

is not to be construed as being of the form ⌜Fa⌝, with "the number 2" an *Eigenname* and "ξ exists" a first-level *Funktionsname.* On the contrary, he claims, (20) is not about any particular object at all. Rather, it is to be understood as expressing that something falls under the concept *being the number 2,* and the proper symbolization of (20) would thus be

(21) (Ex)(x = the number 2),

where "– the number 2" is an indivisible predicate. Indeed, it is rather surprising that Frege should so staunchly maintain in "On Concept and Object" that the singular definite article invariably signals an *Eigenname,* for, as we see, he had adopted a more flexible attitude elsewhere, and, moreover, he also had the general rule of thumb that the superficial grammar of a sentence is not always an accurate reflection of its logical structure.

But, then, to which syntactic category might "the concept *horse*" belong? And to which syntactic category might "ξ is a concept" belong? I mentioned that Frege believes that there are concepts and that he would prefer to be able to truthfully assert that there are concepts. Now it appears that in his *Begriffsschrift,* Frege actually has the expressive power to do so. If we want to assert the existence of a given concept, say, the concept *horse,* we might do so as follows:

(22) (Ef)(x)(f(x) ≡ Horse(x)).

Now, (22) appears to have the desired properties: for one thing, it is clear that Frege would grant that (22) is true, and, for another, we have avoided the difficulties with the English sentence that (22) symbolizes, namely,

(23) The concept *horse* exists,

where we apparently refer to a concept by means of an *Eigenname*—or, perhaps, fail to refer to a concept at all and only assert the existence of an object. Since no *Eigenname* occurs in (22), we can see that the difficulties with (23) are only apparent. Logically, "the concept *horse*" is no more serving as an *Eigenname* in (23) than is "the number 2" in (20); the use of the singular term in each case is merely a linguistic device to satisfy the demands of English grammar. However, although (20) and (23) are both existential sentences, they do not receive the same logical analysis. For "exists" is ambiguous: in some cases it is to be understood as playing the role of the first-order quantifier (as, e.g., in (20)), and in other cases it is to be understood as playing the role of the second-order quantifier (as, e.g., in (23)). It would be natural, then, to suggest that "exists" has the force of *being an object* in the former case and of *being a (first-level) concept* in the latter case. And, if so, we could construe "ξ is an object" as a second-level *Funktionsname* denoting the first-order quantifier, and we could construe "ξ is a concept" as a third-level *Funktionsname* denoting the second-order quantifier.

On this interpretation, (19), which Frege had originally claimed to be false, would be symbolized as (22), and thus be true; and the paradoxical (1), which Frege had claimed to be true, would be symbolized as

(24) -(Ef)(x)(f(x) ≡ Horse(x)),

and (24) is false. In conceding that the concept *horse* is a concept, we have not thrown in the towel to Kerry. Kerry's sentence

(25) The concept *horse* is an object,

if it is meaningful at all, would be symbolized as

(26) (Ex)(x = the concept horse),

and so understood, it expresses the existence of an object; whereas (19), understood as (22), expresses the existence of a concept. Given the radically different logical treatments of "the concept *horse*" in these two cases, Kerry would have to argue that that which is said to be an object (speaking loosely) in (25) is one and the same entity as that which is said to be a concept (speaking loosely) in (19). But he cannot do this. For somewhere along the line, Kerry would have to claim that there is an object x and a function f such that x = f; and, on Frege's view, placing the identity sign thus between an object variable and a function variable is incoherent.

Certainly, we have here a much more plausible response to Kerry than the one Frege had originally given. But it is not entirely satisfactory. For, although we have parried Kerry's counterexample, we have done so at the cost of rendering Frege's principle, "No concept is an object," meaningless: there is simply no way of coherently expressing this principle. If Frege wishes to maintain both that objects and concepts are of different logical types, and that we cannot speak about identify across logical types, it would appear that he is committed to the fact that "No concept is an object" is nonsense.

Dummett has remarked:

> If Frege had confined himself to talking about these various types of *expression,* instead of that for which they stood, the appearance of paradox, the awkwardness of phrasing, the resort to metaphor, which pervade his writings, would all have been avoided. Frege was quite wrong in pretending that the same ills affect the formal mode of speech.[21]

But Dummett is the one who is wrong; the same ills do affect the formal mode of speech. This is an immediate consequence of Frege's general view that the structure of language mirrors the structure of the world. For, on this view, predicates and concepts must have analogous properties. Just as a given concept cannot occur outside some connection (say, with an object), so too the predicate that denotes it cannot occur outside a connection (say, with an *Eigenname*). Hence, one cannot extract a predicate from some complex term that contains it; a predicate does not form a separable unit. (By the same token, one cannot extract an *Eigenname* from some complex name that contains it, for this would leave the remaining *Funktionsname* in isolation.) But, then, one cannot say of an expression that it is a *Funktionsname* or that it denotes a concept; for, in order to do so, one would have to consider the expression in isolation—and, in the latter case, one would have to consider the concept in isolation as well. Indeed, if the analogy between predicates and concepts is to hold rigorously, then just as a concept is a function, so too the predicate that denotes it would have to be a function. And, if so, then we will run into the same difficulties with "ξ is a *Funktionsname*" as we had earlier with "ξ is a concept": in particular, just as "No concept is an object" is meaningless, so "No *Funktionsname* is an *Eigenname*" would also be meaningless. That the same ills fail to affect the formal mode is pure illusion.

What Frege sought to capture in saying that a given expression denotes a concept is not how that expression is capable of being used, but rather how that expression is being used in that context. To denote a concept is *thereby* to be acting in a certain way, namely, predicatively. Accordingly, it makes no sense to say that a given expression denotes a concept because in doing so one deprives the expression from acting predicatively in that context. The problem does not arise from any awkwardness of language; rather, it derives from the belief that to denote a concept is to bear a relation to some independently specifiable entity. *Denoting a concept* does not yield a word-world relation in any obvious way.

Notes

1. Gottlob Frege, *Nachgelassene Schriften*, ed. H. Hermes, F. Kambartel, and F. Kaulbach (Hamburg, 1969).
2. Gottlob Frege, "On Sense and Reference," in *Translations from the Philosophical Writings of Gottlob Frege*, ed. Peter Geach and Max Black (Oxford, 1960), pp. 56-78.
3. Frege, *Nachgelassene Schriften*, p. 128. (My translation.)
4. Gottlob Frege, "On Concept and Object," in *Translations from the Philosophical Writings of Gottlob Frege*, p. 47.
5. Michael Dummett, *Frege, Philosophy of Language* (London, 1973), pp. 55-58.
6. Gottlob Frege, "Function and Concept," in *Translations from the Philosophical Writings of Gottlob Frege*, p. 32.
7. Gottlob Frege, "On the Foundations of Geometry," in *Gottlob Frege, On the Foundations of Geometry and Formal Theories of Arithmetic*, trans. Eike-Henner W. Kluge (New Haven, 1971), pp. 32-33.
8. Gottlob Frege, *Grundgesetze der Arithmetik*, I (1893), II (1903) (reprinted, Hildesheim, 1962).
9. Frege, "On the Foundations of Geometry," pp. 33-34.
10. Frege, "Function and Concept," p. 38.
11. Gottlob Frege, *The Basic Laws of Arithmetic, Exposition of the System*, trans. and ed. Montgomery Furth (Berkeley and Los Angeles, 1967), p. 73.
12. Gottlob Frege, "Compound Thoughts," trans. R. H. Stoothoff, in *Essays on Frege*, ed. E. D. Klemke (Urbana, 1968), p. 538.
13. Michael Dummett, "Note: Frege on Functions," in *Essays on Frege*, p. 538.
14. Max Black, "Frege on Function," in *Essays on Frege*, pp. 223-48.
15. William Marshall, "Frege's Theory of Functions and Objects," in *Essays on Frege*, pp. 249-67.
16. *Ibid.*, p. 267.
17. Gottlob Frege, *Begriffsschrift, eine der Arithmetischen Nachgebildete Formelsprache des Reinen Denkens* (Halle, 1879).
18. Frege, "On Concept and Object," p. 54.
19. *Ibid.*, p. 46.
20. Here I am indebted to Dummett's discussion of the paradox in *Frege, Philosophy of Language*, pp. 213-17.
21. Michael Dummett, "Frege on Functions: A Reply," in *Essays on Frege*, p. 269.

Frege and Analytic Philosophy: Facts and Speculations[1]

MICHAEL D. RESNIK

There is no doubt about the fact: Frege had much to do with the development of analytic philosophy. But what is analytic philosophy? And what is Frege's exact relation to it? Was he the first analytic philosopher? Or a precursor of the movement? Did his work exert a causal influence on the development of latter ideas or did it simply anticipate them? Was his own thought "born from Frege's brain unfertilized by external influences"[2] or did it build upon and advance preexisting views? These are difficult questions, and most answers to them are likely to be speculative and controversial. In this paper I want to respond to *some* of them by presenting some speculations and, it is hoped, a few facts about Frege and analytic philosophy.

My plan is first to discuss characteristics of analytic philosophy and the question whether they apply to Frege's work. I shall then turn to the question of Frege's influence upon a number of important analytic philosophers, and shall suggest that his key contributions to the development of analytic philosophy have much more to do with his philosophy of mathematics than with his philosophy of language. My remarks about Frege's influence on analytic philosophy may strike some readers as fairly familiar. (In a letter commenting on an earlier draft of this paper Philip Kitcher referred to my discussion as "the orthodox line.") On the other hand, I know of no detailed statement concerning Frege's influence and the extent to which it can be documented. A large part of this paper is directed toward filling this gap. Much of what I will have said in the first portions of my paper will consist of remarks concerning the nature of analytic philosophy and interpretations of the scant historical data at my disposal. In the final section of the paper I shall return to firmer ground and examine several themes in Frege's work that show that he held some positions in common with some analytic philosophers—at least!

1. WHAT IS ANALYTIC PHILOSOPHY?

I approach this question with trepidation. Not only it is certain to be addressed elsewhere in this volume, but also there is no clear agreement about who counts as an analytic philosopher. To make matters worse Frege is a disputed and disputable case.

A first step toward answering our question is to note that the term "analytic philosophy" has a broad and a narrow sense. In the broad sense analytic philosophy is a movement that blossomed with the work of Bertrand Russell and G. E. Moore and is still in flower today. It cannot be captured by a unique metaphilosophical doctrine or methodology although its style and concern with language serve to demarcate it from other contemporary movements like existentialism and phenomenology. In the narrow sense analytic philosophy is a movement that again blossomed with Russell and Moore but ended with the demise of Logical Positivism.[3] This movement is associated with what I would call a metaphilosophical doctrinal schema—the slogan *philosophy is logical or linguistic analysis*—which must be interpreted differently with respect to different members of the movement.[4] Its demise is usually attributed to such factors as Wittgenstein's rejection of the quest for meanings and Quine's critique of the analytic-synthetic distinction.[5]

From a sociological point of view, Frege belonged to neither the narrow nor the broad analytic movements. As is well known, he met or corresponded with Russell, Wittgenstein, and Carnap, and each was profoundly influenced by Frege and discussed his ideas. Nevertheless, Frege did not reciprocate. Even after 1900 he continued to address himself to mathematicians such as Hilbert and Thomae and his old philosophical enemies the psychological logicians. He hardly seems to be aware of the kinship between his ideas and Russell's and Wittgenstein's theories.[6] Thus if Frege is to be counted as an analytic philosopher, it will have to be based upon criteria of a more abstract kind than sociological ones.

The paradigm members of the narrow analytic movement espoused one or more metaphilosophical views which strongly linked philosophy and logical analysis. These passages from Russell, Wittgenstein, and Carnap are typical of the era:

> I have dealt hitherto upon which one may call philosophical grammar.... I think that practically all traditional metaphysics is filled with mistakes due to bad grammar, and that almost all the traditional problems and traditional results—supposed results—of metaphysics are due to a failure to make the kind of distinctions in what we may call philosophical grammar with which we have been concerned in these previous lectures (*The Philosophy of Logical Atomism.* Lecture VIII.)

> The business of philosophy, as I conceive it, is essentially that of logical analysis, followed by logical synthesis. ("Logical Atomism")

> All philosophy is a 'critique of language' (though not in Mauthner's sense.) It was Russell who performed the service of showing that the apparent form of a proposition need not be its real one. (*Tractatus*, 4.0031.)

Philosophy is the logic of science, i.e., the logical analysis of the concepts, propositions, proofs, theories of science, as well as of those which we select in available science as common to the possible methods of constructing concepts, proofs, hypotheses, theories. ("On the Character of Philosophic Problems")

If explicit recognition of metaphilosophical doctrines linking philosophy to the logical analysis, the critique or reformation of language are required to make one an analytic philosopher in the narrow sense, then Frege does not belong to the fold. He never enunciated a thesis as strong as those just quoted; although, as we shall see in the final section of this paper, a number of his remarks are anticipatory of these passages. Moreover, Frege used philosophical methods that were far more diversified than those which these passages would lead us to believe Carnap, Russell, and Wittgenstein would countenance. He did do quite a bit of logical analysis (example: his definition of number), critique of language (example: the discussion of apparent failures of extensionality in "On Sense and Reference") and methodology of science (example: his discussion of Hilbert's "implicit definitions"). But Frege also used more traditional philosophical methods in dealing with the philosophical views of mathematics and logic proposed by his contemporaries. Taking them at face value, he argued that they were incoherent (example: Erdmann's psychological logic), implied manifest absurdities (example: Mill's empiricism), or were in principle inadequate to the purpose for which they were designed (example: Thomae's theory of infinite sequences).[7] I take it that a presupposition of such investigations is that the theories being attacked are not guilty of an even more fundamental philosophical mistake concerning the proper method in philosophy. Frege thought that these views were not only wrong but also *wrongheaded.* Despite this he did not take the antimetaphysical stance toward them which would typify the approach of later analytical philosophers. Indeed, in the *Grundlagen* Frege accused psychologism of asking for the meaning of words in isolation and thereby being driven to taking meanings to be ideas. That move, with which a staunch analytic philosopher would rest his case, was, however, only one of several criticisms of psychologism which Frege developed.[8]

Of course, it needs to be said that even paradigm analytic philosophers were not all purists. Russell's discussions of opposing views often contain lapses from purely analytic methods.[9] Furthermore, even if Frege was indeed an analytic philosopher in the narrow sense, he was clearly pioneering the method of analysis. It is to be expected that his departure from traditional philosophical methods would fail to be clear and that his metaphilosophical reflections would be scattered and somewhat sketchy. Moreover, his concern with the foundations of mathematics was paramount and his excursions into metaphysics were ancillary to it. It is thus not at all surprising that it was Russell, not Frege, who hailed the new era in philosophy. It was the success of Frege's model, however, which led Russell to do so with such confidence.[10]

For those who insist upon allegiance to the slogan *philosophy is logical analysis,* the evidence is not strong enough to include Frege on the rolls of analytic philosophy in the narrow sense. On the other hand, there is little doubt, I think, that Frege was an analytic philosopher in the broad sense. To make my case convincing, let me propose some properties of analytic philosophy in the broad sense and argue that they characterize Frege's work. The characteristics I am proposing are three: 1) the emulation of science; 2) the introduction of research programs; and 3) the placing of logic and language at the focal points of philosophy.

Analytic philosophy emulates science not only in the sense that many of its practitioners take it to be prescience or continuous with science but also in the sense that it lays claim to precision, demands attention to detail, and has developed its own battery of technical terms and results. Furthermore, it both philosophizes about science and uses science in its philosophizing. Of course, the emphasis on science is not new to philosophy. Kant is a prime example of a philosopher who built his metaphysics in response to scientific results and problems. But the role of science in analytic philosophy is far more pervasive. Understanding many debates in metaphysics requires a fair knowledge of modal logic or model theory; current discussions in social philosophy are grounded on decision theory and welfare economics; the philosophy of mind and epistemology now rely heavily upon biology and linguistics. And this situation has been with us since Russell's time, although the use of science has been restricted primarily to epistemology and metaphysics until recently. The wide use of scientific results to achieve philosophical ends serves, I think, to distinguish analytic philosophy from phenomenology which also claims to be scientific philosophy.

There is no doubt that Frege aimed to make philosophical discussions about mathematics more rigorous and demanded that his colleagues pay more attention to detail and precision.[11] It is also clear that he thought that his technical results would be of use to philosophy in general[12] and that he took himself to have put epistemology on a more rigorous footing.[13] Furthermore, Frege's critical discussions and his own detailed and technical semantics utterly revolutionized the philosophical foundations of logic. That Frege's *writings* meet my first characteristic is thus beyond dispute, but I think that it can also be argued that Frege *himself* was very much in sympathy with the view that philosophy in general should emulate science. (I should say *good science* since he had many complaints about the situation he found in the foundations of mathematics.) Again the problem with clinching one's case is that Frege's range was fairly narrow—he never broached ethics and the philosophy of mind, his epistemology and metaphysics are almost always tied to logic and mathematics—and, consequently, he had little motivation to make broad statements about the nature of philosophy.

The second property of analytic philosophy—the introduction of research programs—flows naturally from the first. Just as research programs in science are prompted by empirical problems and aim at establishing scientific hypotheses, so analytic philosophers in emulating science have proposed hypotheses for dealing with philosophical problems and have pursued research programs that attempt to establish them. Frege's reduction of mathematics to logic is one of the foremost examples of such a program—and it is often mistakenly taken to be the successful example. Other well-known examples are the phenominalist quest for a translation of material object statements into sense data statements, the rational reconstruction of science sought by logical empiricism and Quine's flight from intensions.

Frege is explicit about his commitment to a research program in the philosophy of mathematics. In the preface to the *Begriffsschrift* he tells us that his work in formal logic was necessitated by his commitment to ascertaining the epistemological status of arithmetic.[14] After devoting the entire *Grundlagen* to philosophical argument for the thesis that arithmetic is part of logic, he writes:

> I do not claim to have made the analytic character of arithmetical propositions more than probable, because it can still always be doubted whether they are dedicible solely from purely logical laws. . . . This misgiving . . . can only be removed by the production of a flawless chain of deductions . . .[15]

His *Grundgesetze* was then written to fulfill the research program initiated in the *Begriffschrift* and argued for in the *Grundlagen*.

As an aside let me remark that as analytic philosophy grew up, the logicist program was held up as the shining example. It drew its credibility by dealing with mathematically precise problems by means of mathematical methods. (We still stand in awe when a philosopher can clinch his argument with a piece of formal logic or mathematics.) Yet early analytic philosophers were dazzled by the logicist's results and did not see Frege's contributions or the achievements of the program in their true light. On the one hand, they overestimated what the program had established. We now know that the popular claim that mathematics reduces to logic is a gross overstatement.[16] On the other hand, owing to the discrediting of the system of the *Grundgesetze by* the Russell Paradox, Frege's own contributions to logic and the philosophy of mathematics went largely unappreciated.

The last characteristic of analytic philosophy—the recognition of the centrality of logical and linguistic analysis to philosophy—not only is a well-recognized property of analytic philosophy but also demarcates it from other philosophical movements that claim to make philosophy scientific. Again there is no dispute that Frege in practice took logical and linguistic analysis to be central to philosophy. It has also been remarked frequently that a key move made by analytic philosophers has been the substitution of logic (and the theory of meaning) in the place of epistemology as the fundamental branch of philosophy.[17] This too is explicit in Frege's practice; for he reduced the epistemology of mathematics to the logic of mathematics. It is interesting to note that he almost made it a matter of general doctrine:

> I take it as a sure sign of a mistake if logic has need of metaphysics and psychology—sciences that require their own logical first principles.[18]

These considerations show that Frege should be counted as an analytic philosopher in the broad sense. After I have presented some of Frege's views that overlap those of analytic philosophers in the narrow sense, more skeptical readers may want to group Frege with that batch of philosophers as well.

Philip Kitcher pointed out to me that traditional philosophers—such as Kant or Leibniz—apparently meet my criteria for analytic philosophy at least as stated. For Kitcher this is of no great moment since he thinks that the continuities between analytic and traditional philosophy need to be underscored. Certainly analytic philosophy shares a number of issues and problems with traditional philosophy, and certainly many of the analytic moves have been made before. Perhaps the only difference between traditional philosophy and analytic philosophy—other than those directly attributable to new methods in logic and linguistics—is the higher proportion of logical and linguistic analyses among the philosophical writings of analytic philosophers. And even that is indirectly attributable to the new discoveries in logic and linguistics.

I do not wish to debate here the extent to which the analytic movement represents a genuine break with traditional philosophy. Nor will I attempt to sharpen my criteria so as to exclude Kant, Leibniz, or even Plato and Aristotle. I find it exceedingly difficult to say with any *precision* what a philosophical movement is and what purpose is served in characterizing a particular movement one way rather than another. Perhaps, the distinction between analytic and traditional philosophy is just a matter of style and a matter of the emphasis placed upon the three criteria by members of the analytic movement. Perhaps, nothing of much philosophical importance turns upon this. For my purposes, the important point is that Frege's style and emphasis place him in the analytic camp and that his discoveries in logic made this style and emphasis possible.

2. FREGE'S INFLUENCE ON ANALYTIC PHILOSOPHY

It is unnecessary to delve into the history of the analytic movement to be aware of Frege's significant impact upon recent approaches to philosophical semantics. Through the writings of Alonzo Church, David Kaplan, and Michael Dummett, to name the most notable, he has had a voice in contemporary debates about intensionality and truth. I believe that Frege's imprint upon analytic philosophy is far more pervasive than this, and I shall attempt to demonstrate it by considering his influence upon Russell, Wittgenstein, and Carnap. These three figures, it is generally agreed, were tremendously important in shaping the character of analytic philosophy; and Frege's influence upon them, I claim, was very profound.

One obstacle to arguing my claim is a lack of historical data. We know that Frege and Russell had an extensive correspondence, but it was concerned almost entirely with technical questions like the contradictions in set theory, the theory of (propositional) functions, and use-mention problems.[19] To make matters worse, Russell made several statements to the effect that most of his ideas were developed independently and before reading Frege, and those that he traced to Frege, he said, were obtained indirectly *through* Peano.[20] Wittgenstein by contrast acknowledged a large debt to Frege but did not specify for what he was indebted.[21] Carnap, we know, took courses with Frege and greatly admired him.[22] He often presented historical references to Frege in his writings on logic and mathematics and acknowledged a debt to Frege for the semantical doctrines of *Meaning and Necessity*.

My thesis, however, is that Carnap, Russell, and Wittgenstein owe a much greater debt to Frege than their acknowledgments would lead us to believe. To Frege each owed the model for the philosophical method he propounded. Wittgenstein also obtained almost the entire problematic of the *Tractatus* from Frege's philosophy of logic and language.[23] Russell is indebted to him for the theory of incomplete symbols—the very underpinning of his logical analyses. Carnap's conception of the logic of science is Fregean and so is his doctrine of explication—which, I suspect, is less known.

Frege's writings can be divided into three periods according to the new ideas and results he introduced in them. In the early writings (1879-90) he concentrated on formal logic and the philosophy of arithmetic. In the middle writings (1891-1900) his major new insights were in philosophical semantics, and in the later writings (1900-1925) his new contributions were to the methodology of mathematics. It turns out that all the elements that Russell derived from Frege were already present in the early writings. (Russell read other Fregean works as well.) Wittgenstein, on the other hand, based his conception of philosophy upon reflections on Frege's middle writings, whereas Carnap was most influenced by the later ones.

I shall argue these points by considering each philosopher separately, but before I begin I want to add a qualification to my claims. I view my contentions as historical hypotheses which under the most ideal circumstances could be confirmed by direct historical evidence. To my knowledge such evidence is not to be had. Not only are the three philosophers dead, but also those who have investigated the Fregean connection have not turned up much direct evidence beyond what I have already reported. Furthermore, it is even possible that like most of us Carnap, Russell, and Wittgenstein have propounded ideas that appeared to them as wholly original but that were in fact derived from a previous exposure to Fregean ideas subsequently forgotten or misrepresented. I shall document an important incident of this in my discussion of Russell. In any case I cannot make my case as strong as I would like and must remain content with interlarding facts with comparisons of philosophical positions.

a. Russell

I shall assume with most students of analytic philosophy that Russell's initiation of analytic methods came with his essay of 1905 entitled "On Denoting." This essay contains his famous theory of definite descriptions as well as the roots of the doctrines of incomplete symbols, logical *vs.* grammatical form, and philosophy as analysis. Concerning the first, little needs to be said. Russell was aware of Frege's view on discriptions; indeed indentifying the Fregean reference of "the only son of Mr. so-and-so" (who in Russell's words "had a fine family of ten") as the class of all his sons, he is one of the few who have taken note of Frege's *Grundgesetze* theory of descriptions. Russell rejected the view "as plainly artificial" and not giving "an exact analysis of the matter."[24] On the other hand, the remaining

Russellian doctrines are already present in Frege, *contained in the Fregean writings Russell read and discussed*, and, finally, absent from Russell's theories in the *Principles of Mathematics* (1903). The bulk of this treatise was written by Russell before his exposure to Frege, and the work contains a critical exposition of Frege's doctrines only in the form of an appendix.

Especially noteworthy for our purposes is the crude theory of denotation espoused in the *Principles*. According to the book, sentences such as "all men are mortal" or "a man kissed a woman" are of the subject-predicate form, and denotations are sought for their (subject) terms "all men," "a man," and "a woman." This analysis had been rejected by Frege at the outset of his logical investigations and was thoroughly castigated by Russell in "On Denoting."

Both Frege and Russell saw that the solution to the semantical perplexities involved in ascribing a denotation to "a man" (what will it be—an indefinite man?) could be resolved by replacing the subject-predicate analysis by an alternative account of logical form. For the examples given, they both choose paraphrases such as

(1) for any x, if x is a man then x is mortal,

(2) there is an x which is a man and a y which is a woman and x kissed y,

whose logical form is then readily represented by quantificational schemata.[25] This eliminates the phrases "a man," "every man," "a woman" from the subject positions and makes them parts of the predicates. On the other hand, it leaves us with expressions like "any x," "an x," "a y," which seem to cry out even more for a semantical account. To resolve this, Frege and Russell took another step.

Their next move consisted of the claim that such phrases have no meaning in isolation and yet the sentences in which they occur can be meaningful and have truth-values. To quote our protagonists:

> This leaves "a man," by itself, wholly destitute of meaning, but gives a meaning to every proposition in whose verbal expression "a man" occurs. (Russell)
>
> The expression "every positive integer" by itself, unlike [the expression] "the number 20," yields no independent idea; it acquires a sense only in the context of a sentence. (Frege)[26]

(Some paragraphs back I mentioned that I could document Russell's exposure to a Fregean idea which he failed to appreciate. The last passage is the instance in question. Of it Russell says:

> The meaning of "every positive integer," he [Frege] says depends upon context (Bs. p. 17)—a remark which is doubtless correct, but does not exhaust the subject.[27]

Obviously Russell either mistranslated or misunderstood the passage in question since it contained the very solution to the problem he later adopted.)

Russell did more than adopt Frege's approach to indefinite descriptions such as "a man"; he extended it to definite descriptions as well and in later years parlayed it into the theory of incomplete symbols and logical constructions. On this view, for example, classes are not real but are logical constructions; for class abstracts can be treated as incomplete symbols, that is, symbols which have no meaning in isolation and which can be paraphrased away in favor of sentences not involving them.[28] Russell departed from Frege on another important point. Both Frege and Russell assimilated the expressions "each x," "a y," "every z," as part of quantifiers; Frege sought a denotation for quantifiers (they were taken to denote higher-level concepts), but Russell did not and paved the way for the syncategorimatic treatment of the logical particles which dominates current logical theory. From the broader perspective of the *history of analytic philosophy*, however, Russell's contributions are technical improvements of the basic Fregean idea.

Lest it seem that Russell's exposure to the Fregean ideas was limited to a single easily overlooked passage, let me point out that Frege's *Begriffsschrift* explicitly announces its break with traditional grammar and logic and illustrates this with ordinary language readings of its quantificational formula. Similar points are made in *Function and Concept* (also read by Russell). Moreover, in his reply to Benno Kerry, "On Concept and Object" (discussed at length by Russell in the *Principles*'s appendix on Frege), Frege again demonstrates points of logic by means of paraphrasing sentences, and here he gets metaphilosophical. Let me quote him:

> ... we must not fail to recognize that the same sense, the same thought, may be variously expressed; thus the difference does not here concern sense, but only the apprehension, shading, or colouring of the thought, and is irrelevant for logic. It is possible for one sentence to give no more and no less information than another; and, for all the multiplicity of languages, mankind has a common stock of thoughts. If all transformations of the expression were forbidden on the plea that this would alter the content as well, logic would be simply crippled; for the task of logic can hardly be performed without trying to recognize the thought in its manifold guises. Moreover, all definitions would then have to be rejected as false.[29]

> ... In the sentence "there is at least one square root of 4" we have an assertion, not about (say) the definite number 2 nor about -2, but about a concept, *square root of 4*; viz. that it is not empty. But if I express the same thought thus: "the concept *square root of 4* is realized," then the first six words form the proper name of an object, and it is about this object something is asserted. But notice carefully that what is asserted here is not the same as what was asserted here about the concept [i.e., in the first case a second level concept is used, in the second a first level one]. This will be surprising only to somebody who fails to see that a thought can be split up many ways, so that now one thing, now another, appears as subject or predicate. The thought itself does not yet determine what is to be regarded as the subject. If we say "the subject of this judgement" we do not designate anything definite unless at the same time we indicate a definite kind of analysis; as a rule we do this in connection with a definite wording. But we must never forget that different sentences may express the same thought.

> Language has means of presenting now one, now another part of the thought as the subject; one of the most familiar is the distinction of active and passive forms. It is not impossible that one way of analyzing a thought should make it appear as a singular judgment; another, as a particular judgment; and a third, as a universal judgment.[30]

Although obscured by their involvement with Frege's theory of concepts and objects, several important general doctrines dealing with logical analysis are in these passages, to wit: (1) certain grammatical, stylistic, and logical transformations of sentences preserve their logical content; (2) the transformations in question are those that leave the thought (Frege's term for the sense of a sentence) expressed invariant; (3) the same thought can be expressed by sentences having differing logical and grammatical forms; (4) and thus thoughts can be subject to different but in some sense equivalent logical analyses.[31] I have quoted these two passages because their metatheoretic bent is explicit, but the rest of the article is well punctuated with both discussions and examples of logical analyses offered in the service of Frege's semantical doctrines. It is hard to believe that this failed to have an impact on Russell.[32]

Russell was also quite familiar with Frege's *Grundlagen*. Now in addition to the doctrines and methods I have already discussed, this book contains the only explicit statements of Frege's famous context principle:

> Never ask for the meaning of a word in isolation, but only in the context of a proposition.[33]
>
> Only in a proposition have the words really a meaning.[34]

Frege tied this principle to his analysis of number:

> How then, are numbers to be given to us . . . ? Since it is only in the context of a proposition that words have any meaning, our problem becomes this: To define the sense of a proposition in which a number word occurs.[35]

And he argued that its application was of far-reaching importance:

> Only in a proposition have the words really a meaning. It may be that mental pictures float before us all the while, but these need not correspond to logical elements in the judgment. It is enough if the proposition taken as a whole has a sense; it is this that confers on its parts also their content.
>
> This observation is destined, I believe, to throw light on a whole series of difficult concepts, among them that of the infinitesimal and its scope is not restricted to mathematics either.[36]

There are, of course, a number of questions surrounding Frege's principle, because in the *Grundlagen* he considered but did not use contextual definitions of number and in his later writings explicitly rejected all contextual definitions while abandoning the context principle.[37] Despite these problems with interpreting Frege, the context principle and the applications of it suggested in the *Grundlagen* are a clear anticipation of Russell's theory of incomplete symbols.

To summarize this discussion of Frege and Russell, there are a number of fundamental elements constituting Russell's approach to logical analysis: (1) the break with the traditional grammatical characterization of logical form in favor of that represented in terms of modern quantificational logic; (2) tieing logical analyses to the question of the proper paraphrasing of sentences into logical notation; (3) the observation that certain terms which have been traditionally treated as denoting something have meaning only in the context of a sentence; (4) the application of the observation to philosophical problems. I submit that all these elements are already present in Frege's writings and that Russell was fully exposed to them. If Russell counts as an analytic philosopher in the narrow sense on the basis of "On Denoting" (with the later metaphilosophical "The Philosophy of Logical Atomism" being unnecessary to his inclusion), then Frege should be counted as well.

Finally, note that although Russell studied a number of Frege's works, all the elements he derived from Frege are already contained in his *Begriffsscrift* and *Grundlagen*. These belong to the early writings.

b. Wittgenstein

Frege's middle writings deal with a complex of problems in the philosophy of logic and language. The questions he raised and the solutions he proposed for them must have had a profound influence on Wittgenstein since both the problems and the solutions are the basis for much of the *Tractatus*. Although this connection between Frege and Wittgenstein has been noted before,[38] I do not believe that it is as generally appreciated as it should be nor has the depth of this connection been thoroughly fathomed. Thus I think that it would be appropriate for me to survey the matter again here.

Frege's middle writings dealt with a number of problems in the theory of meaning, the theory of reference, and the philosophy of logic, but underlying most of what he said are two corresponding pairs of major questions: *The Language Pair:* (1) how does language connect with thought and reality? (2) how is it possible for human beings to understand sentences they have never before encountered? *The Logic Pair:* (3) To what extent is logic extensional? (4) how is the meaning of a logically complex expression related to its components? Frege's theory of functions and objects and his distinction between sense and reference are directed at both pairs of questions. That they are directed at the logic pair will be evident to any careful reader of the middle writings; but it was not until Frege and Wittgenstein had conferred that Frege spoke of the language questions in connection with his semantical views.[39] This raises the possibility that Frege obtained that pair of questions from Wittgenstein rather than conversely, but I am convinced that they were part of the Fregean problematic all along. For not only was Frege concerned with language and communication in his earlier essays,[40] but also the assumption that the language pair underlies his middle writings helps explain why he abandoned the contextual approach to meaning so central to the *Grundlagen*.[41] In any case I shall predicate my discussion on that assumption.

Frege answered the questions as follows: we think by apprehending abstract entities called thoughts, but we also think and communicate with words. By means of our language, thoughts are associated with sentences—they are said to be expressed by sentences. But altering certain parts of a sentence can alter the thought it expresses, so to account for these alterations thoughts must have thought-parts that correspond to sentence parts. Furthermore, as finite beings we could not have an indefinite stock of thoughts unless they were generated inductively from a finite vocabulary. Thus thoughts must be composed of elements corresponding to the parts of a sentence, and there must be a correspondence between the structure of the sentence and that of the thought. A similar phenomena is connected with our ability to refer to and to describe indefinitely many things. We describe by means of sentences; we use singular terms to pick things out and general terms to characterize them. Yet alternations of the parts of a sentence can also alter what is described, how it is characterized, or the truth of what the sentence says. So there must also be an isomorphism between (the part of) the world described by a sentence and the sentence itself. This dual isomorphism in which sentences and words partake is how language ties up with the realm of thought and the world. The sentence has images in both and so do its logical elements. Just as a sentence is a compound of its elements, its images in these two domains are compounds of the images of the sentence's parts. Suppose that subscripting an 's' to a sentence or sentence part allows us to form a name of its sense and that subscripting an 'r' allows us to name its reference. Then Frege's isomorphisms with respect to sentences of the form, say, 'Fa' can be represented as follows:

$[Fa]_s = F_s a_s$
$[Fa]_r = F_r a_r$.

Frege went a step further with this mathematical approach. He assimilated F_s and F_r themselves to mathematical functions and gave them the same identity conditions as mathematical functions. But if compound senses are functions in the mathematical sense of their components, then failures of extensionality should never occur. Frege indeed believed this and argued that such failures in ordinary languages are only apparent. They are due in part to a systematic equivocacy of expressions in ordinary language which permits them to have their usual references in all but intensional contexts where they refer instead to their customary senses. In a logically perfect language, however, this equivocacy will not arise and intensional contexts will be replaced by extensional talk of senses.

Frege thought that he must also explain how the logical elements of a compound sense or reference are combined. It is a fact that not every sequence of words expresses or refers to something, and one might expect that there is some connection between the combinations of words into meaningful wholes and the combination of their senses and references into compounds. Frege concluded that the senses and references of functional expressions and predicates had the power to unify several elements into a logical whole. He attributed this to what he called their *unsaturatedness*. He then inferred that unsaturated entities must be fundamentally different from saturated ones and that this would be reflected in a properly constructed symbolism. This entailed that a proper language must be formulated as a theory of types, that type distinctions must be inviolable, and that sentences involving variables ranging over entities of differing types are malformed. It also implied that even ordinary language cannot contain types crossings. This gave rise to the famous paradox of "the concept horse"—an expression which according to Frege does not denote a concept. Pushed to its logical limits, Frege's view implied that his own expositions cannot express the thoughts at which he aimed. Although fully aware of these consequences, Frege thought that in the end his view would be communicated. The following passages typify his attitude:

> I admit that there is a quite peculiar obstacle in the way of an understanding with my reader. By a kind of necessity of language, my expressions, taken literally, sometimes miss my thought; I mention an object, when what I intend is a concept...
>
> ... over the question what is called a function in Analysis, we come up against the same obstacle; and on thorough investigation it will be found that the obstacle is essential, and founded on the nature of our language; that we cannot avoid a certain inappropriateness of linguistic expression; and that there is nothing for it but to realize this and always take it into account.[42]

Frege apparently did not realize that the implications of this situation are far more serious. By Frege's own showing, essential pieces of his doctrine—such as that which the sentence "no concept is an object" attempts to formulate—cannot be expressed in any language. This is not due to a lack of vocabulary but to a lack of correspondence between the structures of the thoughts Frege is aiming at—they are generalizations that cross types, and the sentences of *any* language by their nature cannot express generalizations over more than one type. But then on Frege's own saying, his theory cannot consist in a body of thoughts, for

> The world of thoughts has a model in the world of sentences, expressions, words, signs. To the structure of the thought there corresponds the compounding of words into a sentence; and here the order is in general not indifferent.[43]

Yet for Frege *theories are bodies of thoughts,* so Frege's theory is, properly understood, not a theory at all—a consequence which had a profound influence upon Wittgenstein's conception of philosophy.[44]

I have laid out the Fregean problematic and solutions because I think Wittgenstein's debt to Frege can best be appreciated by comparing the *Tractatus* with Frege's views. I do not wish to deny that the *Tractatus* is a highly original and profound work; my point is rather that Wittgenstein worked with a set of problems derived from Frege, and retained some of his insights, while modifying but not entirely rejecting others.

To start, let us note that most commentators agree that the *Tractatus* is built around answers to the questions I have called the language pair. That is to say, the work is addressed to the questions of how human language is possible and how it is related to thought and reality.[45] Furthermore, the solution to these problems (the picture theory) contains important Fregean elements; for the *Tractatus* used both the functional (3.318) and isomorphism (2.18, 3.2) insights of Frege. The former we saw entailed the extensional nature of language. This is in the *Tractatus* too and so is the view that a proper understanding of language will dissolve apparent counterexamples to the extensionality thesis. There are, to be sure, deep differences between Wittgenstein's doctrines and Frege's. These are due in part, I am certain, to Wittgenstein's working through Frege's theories and finding them deficient or in need of further embellishment. Thus in the *Tractatus* the sense-reference distinction for each logical element is modified, thoughts as abstract entities are abandoned, and Frege's important concept-object distinction is rejected in favor of objects configured in facts. Furthermore, the extensional point of view is greatly elaborated and strengthened so that the only logical particles countenanced are the truth-functions.

One of the most interesting modifications that Wittgenstein made—the one that is the most pertinent to the discussion in this paper—is the transformation of Frege's views on unsaturatedness and its attendant consequences into the Tractarian doctrines of logical form and formal concepts. Logical form is what unites a Tractarian sentence and the fact corresponding to it. Both of these are configurations of objects (names and their references) that have the same form. But the form is not an additional piece of the configuration supplied with a metaphysical glue. When the objects are removed from a configuration, there is nothing left over. Thus the form is not in the world at all and can be neither named nor described. It can only be seen and shown by pointing to something (else) of the same form. Furthermore, general logical and linguistic concepts such as *logical form, object, concept* are themselves formal concepts or pseudo-concepts whose nature cannot be properly described in language but only shown *by means of* language. Thus Wittgenstein's own pronouncements and those of philosophy in general are, taken literally, devoid of genuine content. I quote the famous conclusion of the *Tractatus*:

> 6.53 The correct method in philosophy would really be the following: to say nothing except what can be said, i.e. propositions of natural science—i.e., something that has nothing to do with philosophy—and then, whenever someone else wanted to say something metaphysical, to demonstrate to him that he had failed to give a meaning to certain signs in his propositions. Although it would not be satisfying to the other person—he would not have the feeling that we were teaching him philosophy—this method would be the only strictly correct one.
>
> 6.54 My propositions serve as elucidations in the following way: anyone who understands me eventually recognizes them as nonsensical, when he has used them—as steps—to climb beyond them. (He must, so to speak, throw away the ladder after he has climbed up it.)
>
> He must transcend these propositions, and then he will see the world aright.

In short, Wittgenstein saw the consequences of "the concept horse" paradox for Frege's views and embraced them. His formal concepts are the remnants of the Fregean notions *concept, object, complete, unsaturated,* and the like; his elucidations are the traces of the Fregean philosophical semantics. Like Frege's theory, they, on their own saying (showing?), do not form at the theory at all. The measure of Wittgenstein's tribute to Frege can be appreciated by realizing that he founded a conception of philosophy upon the Fregean disaster.[46]

c. Carnap

In his later writings Frege reviewed and expounded much of the material of his middle writings, but he also broke new ground with investigations of the methodology of mathematics. The main occasion for this was his controversy with Hilbert over the nature of the axioms of geometry and so-called implicit definitions, but he was also prompted by a dispute with Peano concerning the proper form of definitions and the legitimate primitives for a formal system for mathematical logic. The results of his thinking about these matters were published in a number of essays appearing from 1896 to 1906. Young Rudolf Carnap attended three of Frege's lecture courses at Jena University in the years 1910-14. The first two were devoted to the development and application of Frege's logical system. The latter dealt primarily with the methodology of mathematics. From the description of the lectures given by Carnap, we can conclude that they were those which have been posthumously published under the title "Logic in Mathematics."[47]

For our purposes there are three things of note in these lectures. First, they contain a very clear and careful account of the axiomatic method in which the roles of axioms, definitions, inference, and proof are analyzed in detail. The necessity for the axiomatic method in mathematics is very convincingly argued. Second, the lectures include several critical analyses of the writings of Frege's contemporary mathematicians which point out and resolve fundamental confusions in the treatment of basic mathematical concepts. Third, the long discussion of definitions raises the problem of analysis and proposes a resolution that is clearly anticipatory of Carnap's doctrine of explication. I will quote the key passage:

> Let us assume that A is the long-established sign (expression) whose sense we have attempted to analyse logically by constructing a complex expression that gives the analysis. Since we are not certain whether the analysis is successful, we are not prepared to present the complex expression as one which can be replaced by the simple sign A. If it is our intension to put forward a definition proper, we are not entitled to choose the sign A, which already has a sense, but we must choose a fresh sign B, say, which has the sense of the complex expression only in virtue of the definition. The question is now whether A and B have the same sense. But we can bypass this question altogether if we are constructing a new system from the bottom up; in that case we shall make no further use of the sign A—we shall only use B. We have introduced the sign B to take the place of the complex expression in question by arbitrary fiat and in this way we have conferred a sense on it. This is a definition in the proper sense namely a constructive definition.

If we have managed in this way to construct a system for mathematics without any need of the sign A, we can leave the matter there; there is no need at all to answer the question concerning the sense in which—whatever it may be—this sign had been used earlier.

... If this is open to question although we can clearly recognize the sense of the complex expression from the way it is put together, then the reason must lie in the fact that we do not have a clear grasp of the sense of the simple sign, but that its outlines are confused as if we saw it through a mist. The effect of the logical analysis of which we spoke will then be precisely this— to articulate the sense clearly. Work of this kind is very useful; it does not, however, form part of the construction of the system, but must take place beforehand.[48]

Of course, I conclude from this that to Frege Carnap owes his doctrine of explication—that the symbols introduced by definition obtained through "logical analysis" should be viewed as replacements for the old ones and that such definitions should be judged by a pragmatic criterion. But I also want to infer that Carnap probably obtained from Frege the model of *philosophy as the logic of science* which I quoted in section 1. For Frege's lectures of 1914 were concerned with the logic of mathematics in Carnap's sense and showed the value of such analyses for the clarification of the fundamental problems of mathematics.

It should also be pointed out that Frege was responsible to a large degree for the development of the key views of the two other figures who most influenced Carnap, namely Hilbert and Wittgenstein. As we have already noted, it was through Frege that Wittgenstein arrived at the position that philosophy can state no propositions of its own and must restrict itself to the clarification of science. Carnap accepted almost all of this but balked at condemning philosophy to silence and borrowed a device from Hilbert which the latter had used to handle a similar situation in mathematics. Hilbert's finitistic critique of mathematics forced him to conclude that most of the propositions of classical mathematics are meaningless. Yet he found them too important and useful to jettison completely. Hence he relegated them to the status of instruments or calculating devices and developed his proof theory as a means for studying their properties and establishing their reliability. Hilbert's proof theory was to be a meaningful metamathematics whose statements would be about the expressions of mathematics. Carnap argued that the propositions of philosophy have a similar role: they are metatheoretic propositions concerned with the syntax of the language of science. Thus regardless of the status of the sentences with which they deal—whether they express propositions or not—the sentences of the logic of science gain content by virtue of referring to the sentence and sentence parts.

Hilbert, as is well known, conceded that Frege, Russell, and Peano made his proof theory possible by constructing a formal language for mathematics. His philosophical position, however, is usually attributed to his interactions with Brouwer and Poincaré. I have argued elsewhere that Hilbert's finitism was also shaped by his appreciation of Frege's critique of the early formalists and his discussions with

Frege on the axioms of geometry.[49] If I am correct in this contention, the essentials of Carnap's early philosophy are due both directly and indirectly to Frege.

Looking back over Frege's influence, we find his most enduring metaphilosophical contributions have come to us through the Russell-Carnap-Quine tradition. This school has been inspired by formal logic and has made the formal language of mathematics and results about it the key ingredient of its philosophy. It has cast the majority of its philosophical problems as problems about formal languages or as issues concerning the proper formalization of ordinary language. It takes Frege's work in the philosophy of mathematics as its paradigm. That is why I think that Frege's philosophy of language has been less important for the development of analytic philosophy than has his philosophy of mathematics.

3. METAPHILOSOPHICAL THEMES IN FREGE'S WRITINGS

I shall conclude this essay by pointing out two themes that pervade Frege's thoughts on philosophy. Although they are scattered through his books, essays, and unpublished notes which range from his first excursions into logic to notes written shortly before his death, I shall make no claims about their impact upon subsequent analytic philosophy. I am putting them forward here simply to show that at least Frege shared with some analytic philosophers some of their deepest attitudes toward philosophy. The first of these themes concerns the "struggle" of logic and philosophy against the hold of ordinary language, and the second concerns the necessity for an ideal language for science and philosophy.

Frege began his logical studies with the aim of determining whether arithmetical reasoning is reducible to logical reasoning, and quickly found ordinary language unsuited to his purposes. Not only is it too cumbersome to be a vehicle for fully formalized proofs, but it also lacks devices for making explicit inferential steps and for distinguishing different kinds of inference. Frege referred to this as "the logical incompleteness of language."[50] This more than anything else drove him to the construction of his symbolic logic. But ordinary language has other serious faults: it contains equivocal expressions and can form grammatically correct and meaningful singular terms which, nonetheless, have no designation. Both these faults were responsible for serious errors in mathematical thinking.[51] In his last years Frege blamed his own failures—the Russell Paradox and the concept *horse* paradox—on the faults of language as well.[52] Furthermore, in attempting to formulate a logic adequate for deductive reasoning, Frege found ordinary language and its grammar an obstacle to the true theory of logical form:

> Let me warn here against an illusion to which the use of [ordinary] language easily gives rise. If we compare the two propositions:
>
> "The number 20 can be represented as the sum of four squares" and
>
> "Every positive integer can be represented as the sum of four squares"
>
> it appears possible to consider "being representable as the sum of four squares" as a function whose argument is "the number 20" one time, and "every positive integer" the other time.[53]

As a result, Frege came to the view that language, especially ordinary language, gives rise to "illusions" which logic and philosophy must struggle to remove. The following passages typify his attitude:

> We can see from all this how easily we can be led by language to see things in the wrong perspective, and what value it must therefore have for philosophy to free ourselves from the dominion of language.[54]
>
> ... Instead of following grammar blindly, the logician ought rather to see his task as that of freeing us from the fetters of language.[55]
>
> ... Work in logic just is, to a large extent, a struggle with the logical defects of language, and yet language remains for us an indispensible tool.[56]
>
> ... a great part of the work of a philosopher consists—or at least ought to consist—in a struggle against language.[57]

Of course, Frege had no intensions of dispensing with language altogether; he believed that human beings can think only *by means of* language.[58] The problem for the philosopher and logician thus became that of constructing a language that is more suitable for the purposes of abstract thought. It hardly needs saying that Frege thought that his symbolic logic filled the bill:

> If it is a task of philosophy to break the power of the word of the human mind, uncover illusions which through the use of language, often almost unavoidably arise concerning the relations of concepts, freeing thought from that which only the nature of the linguistic means of expression attaches to it, then my "conceptual notation," further developed for these purposes, can become a useful tool for philosophers.[59]

Frege's ideal language—his *Begriffsschrift*—was to be a logically complete language and one whose very construction would prevent us from falling into philosophical and logical errors associated with the use of ordinary language.

During his early years Frege had good reason to have such a confident attitude toward his symbolism. He had taken gigantic strides in analyzing mathematical reasoning. He had uncovered and resolved a number of mathematical and logical errors, and he had offered clear and convincing accounts of *number* and *existence*. Although he later came to realize that his symbolism would not by itself prevent him from holding false logical theories, he continued to see the major part of the philosopher's task as the critique of language.

Notes

1. I would like to thank Philip Kitcher and Jay Rosenberg for their generous assistance with this paper. Both have helped with the question of what analytic philosophy is, but the unsatisfactory state of my answer is not their fault. Rosenberg's lectures and conversations have been useful and provocative in my thinking about the Frege-Russell connection.

2. Michael Dummett, *Frege: Philosophy of Language* (New York, 1973), p. xvii.

3. Cf. Richard Rorty's introduction to *The Linguistic Turn* (Chicago, 1967). Morris Weitz, "Analysis, Philosophical," in *The Encyclopedia of Philosophy* ed. Paul Edwards (New York, 1967).

4. Weitz argues that Russell, Moore, Ayer, et al. each had different conceptions of analysis.
5. Here I again follow Rorty and Weitz.
6. Frege did read some of Russell's logic, and the opening arguments of "The Thought" against correspondence theories of truth may be directed against the *Tractatus.*
7. I discuss most of these matters in detail in my book *Frege and the Philosophy of Mathematics* (Ithaca, N.Y., 1980), hereafter referred to as Resnik, 1980.
8. For more details about Frege's context principle and its role in his philosophy, see my "Frege's Context Principle Revisited," in *Studies on Frege*, vol. III ed. M. Schirn. (Stuttgart-Bad Cannstatt, 1976), hereafter referred to as Resnik, 1976.
9. This passage is representative of what I have in mind:

> Time was when I thought there were propositions, but it does not seem to me very plausible to say that in addition to facts there are also curious shadowy things going about such as "That to-day is Wednesday" when it is in fact Tuesday. It is more than one can manage to believe, and I do think no person with a vivid sense of reality can imaging it.

"The Philosophy of Logical Atomism," in *Logic and Knowledge* ed. R. Marsh (London, 1956), p. 23.
10. Russell's autobiographical remarks emphasize the importance of mathematics in the development of his thought. He also ranks Frege's analysis of number with his theory of descriptions. This by itself is not sufficient for my claim, but Russell did read Frege's major works and I find it hard to believe that he could not have been profoundly impressed by the new model for philosophy which Frege set. I shall say more of this in the next section.
11. Gottlob Frege, *Foundations of Arithmetic*, trans. J. L. Austin (Oxford, 1950). See the Preface. The book will be hereafter referred to as *Foundations*.
12. Cf. the introduction to his *Begriffsscrift* in Gottlob Frege, *Conceptual Notation*, trans. T. W. Bynum (Oxford, 1972). This work will be hereafter referred to as *Conceptual Notation*.
13. *Foundations*, sec. 3.
14. *Conceptual Notation*, p. 104.
15. *Foundations*, sec. 90.
16. See Resnik, 1980 for a discussion.
17. Dummett, *Frege*, p. XV contains an instance.
18. *Grundgesetze der Arithmetik*, vol. I (Jena, 1893). The translation is from *The Basic Laws of Arithmetic*, trans. M. Furth (Los Angeles, 1964).
19. Gottlob Frege, *Philosophical and Mathematical Correspondence* (Chicago, 1980).
20. Bertrand Russell, *My Philosophical Development* (New York, 1959), p. 66.
21. Ludwig Wittgenstein, *Tractataus Logico-Philosophicus*, trans. D. B. Pears and B. F. McGuinness (London, 1961), p. 3.
22. In *The Philosophy of Rudolf Carnap*, ed. P. A. Schilpp (LaSalle, Ill., 1963).
23. I should add that I am not the first to suggest this hypothesis, but the evidence I shall present for it is more extensive than that previously offered. Cf. G. E. M. Anscombe, *An Introduction to Wittgenstein's Tractatus* (London, 1959), p. 12.
24. See "On Denoting," in *Logic and Knowledge*, p. 47.
25. These particular moves Russell acknowledges to have obtained from Frege *through* Peano. Neither Frege nor Russell used the phrase "quantificational schemata"; for both, the formulas of logic were meaningful sentences.
26. The Russell quote is from "On Denoting," p. 43; the Frege one is from *Conceptual Notation*, p. 128. The latter is a forerunner of Frege's context principle. (Cf. Resnik, 1976.)
27. Bertrand Russell, *The Principles of Mathematics*, 2nd ed. (London, 1937), p. 507.
28. This doctrine, which appears full blown in "The Philosophy of Logical Atomism," involved a number of confusions and exaggerated claims on Russell's part. For a critical discussion see W. V. Quine, *Set Theory and Its Logic* (Cambridge, Mass., 1963).
29. Gottlob Frege, "On Concept and Object," p. 196, note Translated in P. Geach and M. Black, *Translations from the Philosophical Writings of Gottlob Frege* (Oxford, 1952).

30. *Ibid.*, pp. 199-200.

31. This may suggest to some that logically equivalent sentences express the same thought. This is not Frege's position; he believes that some but not all logically equivalent sentences express the same thought. His disavowal of the stronger thesis follows from his view that "$2^2 = 4$" and "$4 = 4$", say, are logically equivalent (because arithmetic is part of logic) and yet express different thoughts.

32. It is tempting to probe the comparison of Frege and Russell on the matter of logical analysis: Frege analyzed thoughts, what did Russell analyze? How do their conceptions of a correct analysis compare? I shall forego pressing these matters here.

I should mention that Jay Rosenberg thinks that the issue of whether Frege was an analytic philosopher in the narrow sense may turn on these questions. He takes the key move of early analytic philosophy to be the recognition of the distinction between the real and apparent logical forms of a proposition. (See *Tractatus* 4.0031 where Wittgenstein praises Russell for making this move.) Rosenberg takes Russell to be *diagnosing* and repairing failures of ordinary language whereas Frege is simply urging us to free ourselves from it. This is a complicated matter whose resolution might elude still another paper. On the one hand, Frege's discussion in the passages quoted does not contain the apparatus for the Russellian move. There are several logical forms to a thought rather than one, and the form of a sentence is not mentioned. Thus it is hard to imagine Frege assenting to Russell's claims about the real form of sentences containing descriptions even if he, Frege, had accepted Russell's equivalences. On the other hand, Russell's move is clouded by his use-mention confusions and other unclarities. Furthermore, Frege's discussions of ordinary language—especially in "The Thought"—are along diagnostic-therapeutic lines. Finally, Frege's own logical theory can be seen as showing that the traditional forms of general propositions were not their real logical forms.

33. *Foundations*, p. x.

34. *Foundations*, sec. 60.

35. *Foundations*, sec. 62. See also sec. 46.

36. *Foundations*, sec. 60. See also secs. 104, 106.

37. The question of the context principle has been and continues to be a subject of dispute among Frege scholars, See Resnik, 1976; Resnik, 1980.

38. Especially by G. E. M. Anscombe and Max Black.

39. In his published writings this occurs first in the opening paragraphs of "Logische Untersuchungen: Dritter Teil: Gedankengefuge" (1923), translated as "Compound Thoughts" by R. Stoothoff in *Mind* 72 (1963). However, there is a passage to the same effect in an essay of 1914 (around the time Frege and Wittgenstein met) published posthumously. See Gottlob Frege, *Posthumous Writings*, trans. P. Long and R. White (Chicago, 1979), p. 225, hereafter referred to as *Posthumous Writings*.

40. Cf. "On the Scientific Justification of a Conceptual Notation" (1882), translated in *Conceptual Notation*.

41. See Resnik, 1976.

42. "On Concept and Object," p. 204-5.

43. "Negation," translated in Geach and Black, *Translations*, p. 123.

44. I have elaborated the discussion of the last few pages and documented my claims in "Frege's Theory of Incomplete Entities," *Philosophy of Science* 32 (1965).

45. I make no claims to expertise concerning the *Tractatus*. The doctrines I am attributing to it seem to me to be not only clearly there but acknowledged by several commentators.

46. The extent to which the last passages are related to the Fregean dilemma may be further seen through Wittgenstein's choice of the word "elucidation." Frege used this term to cover the propositions used to explain the primitive terms of a theory. That he viewed his own explanations of "function," "object," "concept," as elucidations is made clear by his talk of needing to use hints and metaphors and to rely upon the goodwill of his reader. ("On Concept and Object," p. 193, pp. 204-5. See also Resnik, 1980.) Wittgenstein adopted Frege's terminology but he thought elucidations to be both important to philosophy and paradoxical (*Tractatus*, 3.263, 4.112).

47. *The Philosophy of Rudolf Carnap*, ed. P. A. Schilpp (LaSalle, Ill., 1963), pp. 5-6.
48. *Posthumous Writings*, pp. 210-11. See Resnik, 1980, for further discussion.
49. See Resnik, 1980.
50. Cf. "Über Formale theorien der Arithmetik" (1885), translated in Gottlob Frege, *On the Foundations of Geometry and Formal Theories of Arithmetic*, trans. E. H. Kluge (New Haven, 1971). *Conceptual Notation*, p. 85, p. 104.
51. *Foundations*, sec. 97. "On Sense and Reference," in Geach and Black, *Translations*, p. 70.
52. *Posthumous Writings*, pp. 269-70.
53. *Conceptual Notation*, p. 127.
54. *Posthumous Writings*, p. 67.
55. *Ibid.*, p. 43.
56. *Ibid.*, p. 252.
57. *Ibid.*, p. 270.
58. *Ibid.*, p. 269, *Conceptual Notation*, p. 84.
59. *Conceptual Notation*, p. 106.

Frege and Chomsky on Thought and Language[1]

J. M. MORAVCSIK

At first glance Frege and Chomsky seem to have diametrically opposed views on how to analyze the structure of natural languages. Frege is well known for his anti-psychologistic stand, whereas one of Chomsky's well-known dicta is that linguistics is a branch of psychology.

In this paper it will be shown that in spite of this prima facie opposition, Frege and Chomsky have very similar views on the methodology required for the analysis of natural languages. Even though some of their aims are different, there is a common core in their conceptual frameworks. In the first section we shall take up the agreement between Frege and Chomsky on the relation between language and thought, and their acknowledgment of the need for idealizations in the study of language. We shall also exhibit their respective postulations of the mutual underdetermination of syntax and semantics.

The second and third sections will show that Frege and Chomsky share a view of cognitive psychology that differs from both behaviorism and introspectionism. Furthermore, though they differ on the extent to which the study of language should be linked to psychological characterizations, they hold similar views of the bearing of linguistic structure on characterizations of the human mind.

The first few sections show also that Chomsky's competence-performance distinction is already implicit in Frege. The fourth section applies this dichotomy to Strawson's discussion of referring so as to illustrate the bearing of this distinction on semantics. The last section shows that Frege's theory of "sense" resembles Chomsky's theory of syntax more than it resembles such contemporary semantic theories as those of Davidson or Dummett. In conclusion, a neo-Fregean view of "sense" is sketched and defended as superior to the alternatives current in today's philosophy of language.

1. LANGUAGE AND THOUGHT

What is the main function of language? Although Frege never addresses this question directly, several quotations can be used to reconstruct what his answer would be. For example, in the early writing, "Sense and Reference," he focuses on the role of language in transmitting a common store of thought from generation to generation,[2] and the same concern serves as the preamble to one of his later works, "Compound Thoughts."[3]

Only in the context of alternatives can one see the significance of saying that the main function of language is to express thoughts. This characterization of language distinguishes natural languages from mere causal communication networks. Such networks are illustrated by deer when signaling danger. A visual experience causes the animal to emit a signal, which, in turn, causes the other deer to seek shelter. Questions of truth or falsity do not arise in such a context. Again, whereas the characterization of language as communication would not distinguish, e.g., English from the simple command languages used by Wittgenstein to introduce the notion of a language-game, Frege's characterization succeeds in drawing this line. It also serves to separate natural languages from such, possible, purely expressive languages in which elements are used only to express emotions. (In such a language all expressions would function like 'ouch', 'hurrah', 'alas', and so on.)

Thus the characterization is not trivial. In focusing on the expression of thought, it separates natural languages from mere command languages, causal signal systems, and expressive languages.

In turning to the analysis of ways in which language expresses thoughts, Frege insists that thought-content is prior to matters of use. Matters of use include sociological context, the intentions of speakers, and so on. As Frege says in "Compound Thoughts":

> Whatever may be the speaker's intention and motives for saying just this and not that, our concern is not with these at all, but solely with what he says.[4]

Frege's characterization of language and his claim that content is prior to matters of use add up to an anti-instrumental and anti-functionalist stand. Frege's stand does not rule out characterizations of language as instruments of communication or as having adaptation value, but it regards such descriptions as merely peripheral and as failing to bring out what separates natural language from other, less complex communication systems. The expression of thought must figure centrally in explanations of syntactic and semantics facts.

This characterization, however, raises a problem. Thoughts are explained by Frege as what can be true or false. They are the contents of utterances with different "forces" such as the assertoric, the interrogative, and the imperative forces. But the relation of "expressing" remains in Frege's theory, and similar subsequent accounts, a basic primitive notion. Thus the claim that language expresses thoughts does not have much explanatory power. Its force lies in calling attention to *sui generis* notions of truth and expressing and in insisting that without these no characterization of natural languages is revealing.

Frege thinks that relations of thought to language are represented in the minds of competent speaker-hearers. He wants, however, to study these relations and their representations under idealizations. One can see this from his approach to the problem of significant statements of identity.[5]

The question "why are certain statements of identity significant for certain persons?" is a psychological question, to be answered by tracing the psychological histories of the persons involved. This is not Frege's question. He wants to know why certain statements of identity are informative *simpliciter;* i.e., for the ideal language user who knows the language fully and whose competence is considered apart from any extralinguistic knowledge. Frege's anti-psychologism can be seen by his rejecting the psychological question that calls for an investigation of the heads of actual language users and his favoring instead the question about identity that calls for a specification of linguistic competence under idealizations. The idealizations involve abstracting the expression of thought by language from language use, and the specification of full knowledge of a language apart from extralinguistic information.

These idealizations in Frege should be kept apart from his occasional talk of natural languages as "imperfect" in the context of assessing these as instruments of scientific or mathematical reasoning.

Frege's recognition that apart from the expression of thought natural languages have many other functions as well leads him to see that the grammatical (syntactic) structures of sentences in natural languages do not mirror faithfully the structures of thoughts. This insight would be labeled today the "autonomy of syntax" thesis: i.e., the claim that the syntax and semantics of natural languages are mutually underdetermined. In addition to reaching this insight, Frege gives an explanation for it. He says in "Compound Thoughts"[6] that the grammar of a natural language is formed by requirements wholly different from those involved in the specification of philosophic ideal, or scientific language. Frege does not say what these factors are, but it is easy to fill out the list. Historical factors, the requirements of the human brain in language processing, and the phonological component all have roles in shaping syntactic structure, and these influences are independent of semantic considerations.

Thus we see how starting with the view that language expresses thoughts, Frege arrives at the underdetermination of syntax and semantics by positing the appropriate idealization conditions and reflecting on the needed intervening variables.

Although there are differences in emphasis, the same view can be found in Chomsky's writing as well.

In works like *Language and Responsibility* Chomsky states his anti-instrumentalist view. He does not see any reason to suppose that instrumental ends have important significance for the characterization of human languages. Language, according to Chomsky, has many functions. "Forced to choose"—he writes—"I would have to say something quite classical and rather empty: language serves essentially for the expression of thought."[7]

Our discussion of Frege's treatment of this subject brought out why Chomsky might think that this is a rather empty characterization. The statement, as we saw, contains too many primitives to be really explanatory. Chomsky uses it primarily in a negative way. It serves for him as the basis of an anti-instrumentalist stand. Semantic, syntactic, and phonological structures have lives of their own. They cannot be explained in terms of human functional needs or in terms of adaptation value. Hence the need for an autonomous vocabulary to characterize linguistic structures.

Frege and Chomsky also agree on the need to abstract and idealize when formulating linguistic explanations. Chomsky is even more explicit than Frege. He spells out some of the idealization conditions in detail.[8] In both Frege and Chomsky the assumptions of abstraction and idealization have as their root the conviction that this is the method that worked so well in the other, more advanced, sciences.

Chomsky's formulation of the "autonomy of syntax" thesis is based not only on general reflections but on detailed empirical arguments as well.[9] It can be shown over and over again that the mere study of grammatical structures will not yield the appropriate semantic structures and, likewise, that the discovery of the required semantic structures leaves us plenty of choice regarding grammatical articulation. Relying on general reflection like that of Frege, as well as on empirical arguments, Chomsky can say: "The more I think about it, the more it seems to me that this thesis is quite natural. . . ."[10]

The "autonomy thesis," however, plays different roles in Frege's thought and Chomsky's speculations, respectively. Since Frege's interest lies exclusively in the discovery of semantic structures, the "autonomy" is a hindrance. Chomsky, on the other hand, is interested in all three components of a natural language; hence for him the mutual underdetermination becomes an important positive methodological heuristic.

To sum up, then, both Frege and Chomsky hold that the main function of language is to express thoughts. Frege does more to develop the positive philosophical consequences of this insight, whereas Chomsky does more to spell out its negative, anti-instrumentalist bite. Given that both Frege and Chomsky know and accept the methodologies of the more established sciences, they both posit abstractions and idealizations as requirements for an adequate study of natural language. In the course of such positing they both come to see and accept the mutual underdetermination of syntax and semantics, though this fact has different consequences for their respective research programs.

To be sure, in addition to these similarities there are differences as well. Frege's main concern is the exploration of the relations between language and reality, whereas Chomsky's work centers on the study of human languages in their own right and on their significance for partial characterizations of the human mind. As a result, Frege is more interested in semantics while Chomsky's empirical research has centered mostly on syntax. Still, there is a common core in their views, and it is significantly different from those that one can find in the philosophy of language of today.

2. TYPES OF PSYCHOLOGY

We are used to distinguishing behaviorism from introspectionism. This contrast, however, does not exhaust the main alternatives in psychology. Both behaviorism and introspectionism claim that the facts to be accounted for are directly accessible to observation. For behaviorists such facts are pieces of behavior, whereas for introspectionists these facts are inner mental occurrences that the subject has direct contact with. Both these views contrast with approaches to psychology that deny that the fundamental facts to be accounted for are directly accessible to observation. (Needless to say, different approaches might be more appropriate for different branches of psychology.) One such approach is that of Freud. On his view the key processes to be investigated are not accessible to direct observation. Still, some of them, at least, can be brought to consciousness by various techniques labeled "analysis."

There is a fourth way to view psychology, especially the parts that deal with cognition. According to this view, the fundamental facts to be accounted for are not observable and cannot be brought to consciousness by any technique. Thus the most revealing way to study these processes and capacities is by investigating the relevant characterizations of their objects. This can be labeled "Platonistic psychology" because Plato was the first to give it a rough formulation. In the *Republic*, Book V (sections 474-77) he distinguishes several cognitive capacities. He does not rely on either introspective or behavioral evidence and draws the distinctions in terms of the properties of the objects of the alleged capacities. On this basis he distinguishes the capacity to understand from the capacity to form opinions. Understanding has its own objects; we can understand theorems or morality but not a tree or a lake.[11] Given the nature of the objects, we can give partial characterizations of the human mind. For example, a rather sketchy Platonistic characterization would argue from the facts that we can do arithmetic and that numbers form a special abstract realm, to the conclusion that the human mind must be such as to be able to form representations of objects other than merely those presented by the senses.

This approach is particularly fruitful when the objects under study have rich abstract structures. This is the situation when the objects are defined by constitutive rules, such as logic, mathematics, and language. The logical and computational complexity of the objects provide the basis for arguing to the minimal computational complexity of the human mind. We could not accomplish the same thing by mere empirical studies of actual processes manifesting the cognitive capacities in question. If we had separate models for how people in fact add numbers 1-6, and again 7-12, etc., these jointly could not account for the fact that the human mind can grasp a principle such as addition to cover an infinite domain, such as that of the positive integers.

Given the appropriate characterization of the objects, we can reach partial descriptions of the human mind. These descriptions do not specify unique states of mind corresponding to distinct capacities. This type of account leaves open the possibility that two minds will be in two different states even when concerned with the same objects. But it rules out the possibility that two humans could have the same state of mind even though they are concerned with different objects. For example, if two humans are in the same state, it cannot be that one is doing arithmetic while the other is processing a piece of ordinary English.

Kant's way of characterizing the human mind has much in common with Platonistic psychology. Kant's scheme is: "given certain salient facts, how is human understanding possible?" The passage referred to above from Plato has basically the same logical structure. To the question about understanding, both Plato and Kant would reply by concentrating on the object. Plato would describe it as the realm of Forms, whereas Kant would posit a priori synthetic propositions as the objects. The differences in ontology obscure the sameness of the explanatory structure. One need not be a Platonist in one's ontology to accept the explanatory pattern exhibited by Platonistic psychology and Kantian explanations.[12]

Let us now consider evidence that both Frege and Chomsky follow basically the Platonist psychology.

For Frege, understanding the descriptive parts of a language consists primarily in forming representation of "senses," and of a subset of senses, namely thoughts, in particular. This claim is not based on introspective or behavioral evidence but on a careful study of the "objects," that is to say, the structure of natural languages. Informativeness, an idealized psychological fact, is also accounted for by reference to the object, namely to senses. Furthermore, the possibility of representing complex senses is explained by a property of the "object," namely the principle of compositionality governing both sense and denotation.

The ability to understand cognitive content apart from other factors of use is accounted for by distinguishing sense from associated ideas ("coloring" in the language) and the corresponding representations (ideas).

Although Frege was not interested in cognitive psychology per se, he saw that his work had implications for the study of "the mind.[13] (Theoretical psychology is the study of "the mind," providing abstract characterizations under idealizations, whereas applied psychology is the study of actual individual minds.) Insofar as Frege objects to attempts to replace semantic analysis with analyses from applied psychology, and to attempts that ignore the idealizations, Frege is an antipsychologist. But this does not prevent him from practicing Platonistic psychology and from formulating a theory of semantics that is the necessary background for devising the representation problem.

Chomsky's way of viewing cognitive psychology is very similar to that of Plato, Kant, and Frege.[14] The main thrust of his construal of what generative grammar should do[15] involves establishing formal properties of the "objects," i.e., the grammars of natural languages, and then on this basis providing partial abstract characterizations of the human mind. Given the level of complexity of the grammars of natural languages, say L, the human mind must be at least as complex as anything that can process structures of complexity L, and any simulator that cannot function on level L cannot be an adequate representation of the human mind. Such characterizations do not rely on behavioral or introspective data. They yield insights that are far more important for our general conception of human nature than a mere "play-by-play" description of a bit of actual language processing.

Chomsky also argues that given certain general facts about human language acquisition and the nature of grammars, the human mind must be a richly and specifically endowed organism; otherwise language learning would be impossible. This is the gist of the so-called innate ideas hypothesis. Its defense as well as possible lines of refutation follow the pattern of Platonistic psychology.

Both Frege and Chomsky reject the substitution of psychological accounts of language for the vocabulary of syntax and semantics, and both are more interested in Platonistic psychology than in observational accounts of actual performances that manifest, typically, a variety of different competences. In this sense, the attitudes of both are anti-psychologistic. But insofar as both believe that through the formal characterization of the objects, important theoretical insights can be gained into the nature of the human mind, they are both working within the conceptual framework of Platonistic psychology. Although their foci on the study of natural languages differ, they use the same fundamental structure in their favored explanatory patterns.

3. "PSYCHOLOGICAL REALITY"

In considering the explanatory patterns of theories of cognition, one might be tempted to set up the following dichotomy. Either what the scientist says corresponds to what goes on in the mind at some particular period of time, or it does not. If it does, it has "psychological reality." If it does not, it is merely a useful artifact of the scientist, needed for constructing predictive theories but not truly descriptive of what is psychologically real, be it in the brain or mind. There are two grounds for claiming that this dichotomy is bogus. First, the dichotomy is inapplicable to explanations in the successful natural sciences in which we explain a phenomenon by positing laws that account for idealized patterns and then add variables to account for actual cases. It will be argued later that the question "are idealized entities in nature or not?" is a pseudo-question. Idealized entities are not mere artifacts of the scientist, and they are not parts of nature in the same sense in which observables are.

The other ground follows from assumptions of Platonistic psychology. If we consider a partial characterization of the mind of the sort we saw in the previous discussion of Platonistic explanations, we see that such accounts do not tell us what takes place in the mind millisecond by millisecond. But these accounts do not thereby become mere artifacts of researchers. Theories can be psychologically *relevant* by providing grounds for partial characterizations of the mind, without being psychologically *real* in the sense of giving a "play-by-play" of behavior or of what takes place in the mind or brain. In fact, Platonistic psychology predicts that psychologically relevant characterizations will provide more theoretic insights than will psychological real descriptions of what actually takes place—events that are typically the manifestations of many independent competencies.

If one is anti-psychologistic in the sense discussed above, one will not aim at accounts that are psychologically real but at theories of the objects of cognitions such as arithmetic, logic, language, etc., that have psychological relevance and that help with the formulation of fundamental characterizations of the mind. This section shows that Frege and Chomsky both share an anti-psychologistic stand and that at the same time both conceive of their respective theories of language as having psychological relevance of various degrees.

In turning to Frege's writings, we see him distinguishing the "laws of thought" as logical laws from psychological laws that go by the same name.[16] The former need to be defined in terms of such non-psychological notations as truth, validity, and so on.[17] At the same time, some of these logical notions such as the laws of proof play important roles in the description of certain cognitive processes.[18]

Frege characterizes the key cognitive notions in terms of logical ones.[19] Thus, for example, thinking is the apprehension of certain "senses," namely thoughts. Judgment is the recognition of the truth of a thought, and assertions are manifestations of judgments. Without the logical characteristics, we cannot give insightful characterizations of the cognitive processes mentioned above. This shows, then, the first layer of psychological relevance.

Psychological Relevance, Level I. For certain cognitive domains, there can be no theoretically insightful way of characterizing the key cognitive processes without bringing to bear on them the autonomous vocabulary of the objects with which the processes are concerned.

The dependence is asymmetrical; psychology depends on logic and linguistics, but at this stage not vice versa. This level of relevance applies to any domain of cognition: not only to rule-governed activities like language and mathematics but also to our abilities to form conceptions of cities, deal with taxonomies, and so on.

There is in Frege's writings, however, a closer connection between semantic structures and the study of the mind. His theory of senses and principle of compositionality help provide a partial abstract characterization of the human mind as the kind of entity capable of the representation of senses and abstract compositional structures. At this level we see the bite of Platonistic psychology. For though the Fregean characterization does not tell us exactly *what* takes place in the mind, nor how these states and processes come about, it does tell us that any entity that cannot represent compositionally structured abstract senses cannot be an adequate simulation of a human mind. This is theoretically more important than a mere account of what takes place in a particular mind at a particular time; for the latter could not accomplish what the former does, namely, the partial specification of minimal complexity for the human mind. This, closer, sense of relevance can be brought out in the following way:

Psychological Relevance, Level II. For certain cognitive domains, the abstract properties of the objects of these domains form the foundation of partial characterizations of some of the fundamental properties of the mind.

We might not be able to achieve this level of relevance in all domains. The fact that humans are capable of learning the names of rivers, cities, etc., might not allow us to formulate interesting partial characterizations of the human

FREGE AND CHOMSKY ON THOUGHT AND LANGUAGE 113

mind, whereas the fact that they can learn a language, do arithmetic, etc., does.

Turning to Chomsky's writings, we find a very similar view. "A grammar of a language purports to be a description of the ideal speaker-hearer's intrinsic competence."[20] The specification of the grammar will be given in the autonomous vocabulary of syntax. Chomsky would object to attempts to substitute psychological vocabulary for syntactic vocabulary just as much as Frege would object to the substitution of psychological notions for semantic ones. But just as Frege claims that the study of semantics yields a partial description of the human mind, so Chomsky too sees the study of syntax accomplishing the same thing. He writes:

> In general, the following distinction is often made: linguistics is the study of language, and psychology the study of the acquisition or utilization of language. This distinction does not seem to me to make much sense. No discipline can concern itself in a productive way with the acquisition or utilization of a form of knowledge without being concerned with the nature of that system of knowledge.[21]

Chomsky thinks that, on the one hand, linguistic descriptions have psychological import and that, on the other hand, certain psychological facts are relevant for the construction of theories of grammar. This view, as articulated in detail, commits Chomsky to psychological relevance on levels I and II. In order to formulate hypotheses about the complexity and nature of the human mind, phonological, syntactic, and semantic descriptions need to be brought to bear on psychological characterizations. On the other hand, linguistics has to account for such psychological facts as creativity and for the arbitrary length of possible utterances in natural languages. This comes out especially clearly in Chomsky's conception of the relation between types of formal grammars and types of processing mechanisms. These correlations establish that if, for example, all natural languages have grammars that are at least as complex as the context-free phrase structure grammars, then mechanisms not capable of processing structures of this level of complexity cannot represent adequately the relevant cognitive competences. This does not give us a "play-by-play" account of what goes on in people's minds but yields an interesting theoretical insight of the sort that mere attention to psychological "reality" could not attain. Such limiting characterizations of the human mind could not have been achieved without the anti-psychologistic stand taken by Frege and Chomsky, a stand that turns attention away from mere observational descriptions and focuses on properties of objects of the mind that form the basis of partial characterizations of the mind itself.

The evidence presented so far shows that both Frege and Chomsky share anti-psychologism if this is taken to be a stand against reducing linguistic descriptions to psychological ones and focusing on "play-by-play" accounts (sometimes called "real time process models"). They also share a concern for theories reaching levels I and II of psychological relevance. Chomsky, however, is also interested in modes of acquisition and their relevance to theories about the various components of language. At this point Chomsky goes beyond Frege, though his conception is not incompatible with that of Frege. The divergence is a matter of emphasis. Frege takes a definite stand on ontology and remains neutral on matters of acquisition, whereas Chomsky remains neutral on ontology and takes a definite stand on learnability and its constraining role on theories of language.

If one adds concern with learnability to the facts to be explained, one reaches yet another level of psychological relevance.

Psychological Relevance, Level III. By constraining the abstract characterizations of the objects of various cognitive domains with accounts of learnability, one can generate "natural systems" of language, logic, etc., i.e., systems that have characteristics in view of which we can prove these systems to be learnable by a human under normal conditions as the first system of the relevant sort.

We can imagine two theories of grammar generating the same class of languages but with quite different structures. If we want to reach only level I of psychological relevance, we can be satisfied with both theories. If we demand that the theories should generate not only the same languages but similar structures as well, and attempt partial characterizations of the mind with the help of these structures, then we can reach level II. We reach level III when we demand that the properties of the grammars should play important roles in theories of acquisition as well. There is, however, underdetermination even at this level. It is possible to have two theories of grammar that yield the same partial characterization of the mind, explain the same facts about learnability, and still differ in the way in which their grammars generate grammatical structures.

Furthermore, level III of relevance should be distinguished from psychological "reality" in the sense of giving a play-by-play account of language processing. For one can imagine the same theory of language reaching relevance at level III, utilized by two very different processing mechanisms—especially since linguistic competence is only one of the many factors determining such mechanisms. Aiming at theories on levels I and II, as Frege does, and also on level III, as in Chomsky's case, is compatible with opposing psychologistic reductionism and exclusive concentration on actual language processing, and thus with being "anti-psychologist" in this sense.

Still another similarity between Frege and Chomsky deserves comment. While in current theories of language (by Grice, Searle, Strawson, etc.) the notion of intention looms large, it is notably absent from the accounts of Frege and Chomsky. Is intentionality essential to the delineation of linguistic competence? One could admit that when humans use language in certain ways, they perform acts, and that their aims and intentions are relevant to the interpretation of these acts, without answering the above question in the affirmative. The following is an argument supporting such a stand.

Some verbs and verbs phrases do not require in their definitions the specification of human (or sentient) subject, whereas others do. 'Push' and 'pull' belong to the first class, and 'feels happy' and 'is depressed' belong to the second. Thus, for example, to push is to exert a certain force on another object so as to move it. Locomotives push railroad cars in the railroad yard, and people push furniture. When people push—under normal conditions—furniture, they perform actions, but when locomotives push railroad cars they do not perform actions. Yet 'push' is not used homonymously in the two types of cases.

With this distinction in hand we can proceed with the argument by pointing out that the key terms involved in describing language processing such as initiating and completing search procedures, forming treelike representations, linking parts of language with parts of non-linguistic reality, etc., are like 'push' and 'pull' and hence belong to the first class rather than the second. If this is so, one can admit that when humans use language, e.g., to refer to something, they perform an act, and yet deny that intentionality is essentially linked to the processes that constitute language interpretation, such as the interpretation of rules of denotation attached to certain parts of language. When humans use language, intentionality plays an important role in the exercise of that use. But from this it does not follow that intentionality must be linked to the definitions of the basic constituents of language interpretation as such.

'Search' is an interesting example, since philosophers use it often as a paradigm of *intensionality*. Our argument shows that from this it does not follow that it should be also a manifestation of *intentionality*. A machine can initiate and carry out a search procedure. It requires only a representation of the items to be sought, and abilities to recognize the relevant features of the objects that it encounters. It requires also that something should set the whole process in motion, but this need not be an intention, nor is it necessary that intention should guide the search. To be sure, when humans search for something, we typically attribute intentions to them. But machines and animals also search, and we can make sense out of these processes without attributing intentions to the agents. Thus it may be that intentionality is essential for the characterization of human language use, and it is not essential for the delineation of linguistic competence as such. Understanding is essential to linguistic competence, but understanding is construed by both Frege and Chomsky as the ability to form abstract representations of the appropriate objects. Understanding need not be linked to practical abilities to interact with the world, relate to others, etc., though it may be a component in such interactions.

4. LANGUAGE USE AND THE COMPETENCE-PERFORMANCE DISTINCTION

The need for idealizations and abstractions in the proper study of linguistic competence is stressed by both Frege and Chomsky. In Chomsky's case this is expressed by his distinction between competence and performance.[22] This dichotomy is not the mere contrast between linguistic competence and an instance of its manifestation. In its more interesting application it separates linguistic competence from other competences, roughly gathered under the label "performance-factors." Linguistic competence is hardly ever manifested in isolation. The typical manifestations are combinations of many factors. These factors, or at least many of them, are themselves manifestations of competences (e.g., communicational skills) which are worthy of being studied in their own right. We shall turn to Strawson's discussion of referring, in order to show how the distinction can be applied to semantics and how confusion results when philosophers ignore the distinction.

Philosophers at times talk of the "Frege-Strawson" theory of reference merely because both philosophers thought that statements whose subjects fail to refer have no truth-value. But there can be no such theory. Frege's theory of denotation is a theory of competence, whereas Strawson's theory of referring is a theory of performance. This can be seen from the very beginning of Strawson's article. While Frege and Russell are concerned with rules assigning denotations to expressions of the required form, Strawson is interested in expressions that "we very commonly use to mention or to refer to some individual person or single object...."[23] This claim about how we commonly use expressions seems to be a statistical claim, or if not, in any case a claim requiring empirical evidence. In contrast, Frege and Russell can say that what they study, the rules of denotation, constitutes only one of the many factors that jointly explain the fact that people commonly use certain expressions to refer to various entities.

Strawson studies the uses of various expressions, whereas Frege and Russell study semantic rules that determine the roles of expressions only under certain forms of idealization. Is the study of use the study of performance, and is the study of semantic rules part of the study of linguistic competence? The evidence is, unfortunately, not unambiguous. At times Strawson's talk of "use" turns out to be merely the specification of what philosophers today call indexicality.[24] For in these places Strawson talks as if two people using the same expression at the same time and with reference to the same place are exemplifying the same use. But at other times he seems to have a much broader notion in mind. For example, if someone says at the time of Louis XIV that the present king of France is bald, one can assume that he is referring to Louis XIV. But what if the person falls asleep for 200 years—as Rip Van Winkle did—and on waking up makes the same assertion? Do we have to interpret his saying solely in terms of the spatial and temporal indexes defining his position, or do we have to take into account his intentions, history and so on? If we take into account these additional factors, we are dealing with *use* in the second and wider sense. This type of use corresponds to what Chomsky calls "matters of performance," since it is the result of interaction of a variety of cognitive systems. Neither Frege nor Russell is interested in studying this full variety. They isolate one of the many factors involved and want to give a full account of the competence associated with this one abstracted factor.

There is evidence that Strawson is interested in the wider sense of use. For he repeatedly stresses the fact that what he investigates is determined not only by place and time but also by what he calls the "context of utterance."[25] If 'context' means simply 'spatio-temporal indexes', then it is within the range of what Frege too wants to explain. But if Strawson wants to account also for the Rip Van Winkle cases, then Frege would demur. One can isolate the semantic and communicational competences (involving recognitions of speaker's intentions) fairly easily. For some people are good at learning the rules of denotation attached to the appropriate parts of the language, but they have difficulty mastering the skill of interpreting the referential intentions of speakers on particular occasions. We call such persons "slow on the uptake," but not deficient in their knowledge of English.

The difference in the scope of their respective theories can be seen also in the ways in which they argue for truth-value gaps. Frege's argument rests on the principle of compositionality.[26] If one element of a denoting complex fails to denote, then the whole complex, in this case a sentence, must fail to denote the true or the false, since the denotation of the whole is a function of the denotations of the relevant parts.

Strawson's argument[27] makes no reference to such principles. It rests on appeals to use, based on imaginary experiments about what we might say under certain circumstances. Such arguments would have carried little weight with Frege. They test, at best, hypotheses about use, hence performance, and not hypotheses about semantic rules partly defining our linguistic competence.

5. THE STRUCTURE OF A FREGEAN THEORY OF SENSE

Having shown important similarities between Chomsky's way of viewing the study of language and Frege's approach to the same or related topics, we shall now show that Frege's theory of sense is very different from contemporary theories of meaning such as those of Dummett or Davidson and that it is, in its logical structure, similar to Chomsky's approach to explanations of syntax.

Frege distinguishes sense from force, and from color, or tone. The color or tone of an expression is made up of associated ideas or images. These might play important roles in metaphors or in popular stereotypes associated with expressions. "Force" for Frege is, roughly, equivalent to mood. Thus one can distinguish the assertoric from the imperative or interrogatory force. What linguists and philosophers call "meaning" today would certainly include what Frege calls "force." Hence it is a mistake to identify a Fregean theory of sense with what is called today ordinarily a theory of meaning.

We saw already that though indexicality would be accounted for in a Fregean theory of sense, use in the wider sense, including speakers' intentions, sociological context, etc., would be left as subject for studies of other cognitive systems.

Recently, following J. L. Austin, philosophers have concerned themselves with speech-acts, i.e., the acts we perform when using sentences in various contexts.[28] A speech-act such as advising, warning, etc., cannot be defined in terms of the factors mentioned so far. For example, what counts as a warning is not merely a function of indexicality, the speaker's intention, and sociological context but also a matter of specific conventions determining the constituencies of this speech-act. But in getting at sense, we need to abstract away from speech-act potential as well.

Thus we see that in order to get at what Frege regards as sense, we need to abstract away from:
1. Tone, color
2. Use, including intentions

3. Speech-act potential
4. Force (i.e., mood).

Only at this abstract level do we reach what Frege called *sense*, and even this needs to be studied under idealizations.

The first idealization involves the specification of senses for an ideal speaker-hearer who knows the language fully. With artificial, formal languages this presents no problem since these languages are invented by those using them. But with natural languages this idealization involves considerable abstraction away from actual speakers. For though one might assume that some speakers know all the grammar of a language, and maybe even all the compositional semantic rules, it is implausible to assume that anyone would know all the lexical items of a natural language—at some historical stage—and each of those completely. Understanding a lexical item of a natural language is not an all-or-nothing affair. Expressions have layers of meaning. We can understand them to a greater or lesser degree.[29] Furthermore, one might even doubt whether it makes sense to speak of the lexicon of a natural language as a closed class at any given time. How is such a vocabulary related to technical expressions or to terms in mathematics? Frege's idealization leaves these questions unanswered.

The second idealization concerns the notion of sense. Fregean senses are abstract procedures that under idealized circumstances pick out the denotation classes of the relevant expressions of a language. Hence an understanding of these requires abstracting away from all the limitations that our sense perception and spatio-temporal restrictions, etc., impose on us. Consider, for example, the verb 'procrastinate'. The sense of the corresponding predicate expression, or expressions, is the procedure by which one would compute a function picking out all those sentient beings who put things off beyond appropriate limits. (We shall ignore problems of tense and aspect.) The understanding of this procedure has no direct links to practical abilities. For one thing, the sense abstracts away from all sorts of contextual limitations that determine in given contexts what counts as procrastination. For another, it bypasses the matter of verification, that is to say, it does not take account of the fact that often there will be very scarce observational evidence on the basis of which judgments about whether someone is procrastinating can be made. Hence understanding a sense will pick out a denotation only under highly idealized circumstances. We must assume having full knowledge of the language and not being limited by constraints on empirical information relating to contextual specifications of denotation and the inadequacy of observational evidence.

One could construct also a variation of a Fregean theory of sense by the denial of the thesis that senses are determinate. One might hold the view that senses yield only partial functions picking out denotations.[30] But that issue is not central for the purposes of this paper.

So after four levels of abstraction and two idealization conditions we arrive at Fregean senses. To grasp these senses is to form representations of them. This is only one part of what constitutes in the ordinary sense the understanding of a language, or the understanding of what is said by someone. Thus the form of a Fregean explanation of a semantic fact is the following:

(a) Invoking an explication of a sense and the corresponding mental representation,
(b) invoking a number of parameters and variables, and
(c) accounting for an actual event of language processing by the conjunction of (a) and (b).

This form of explanation sets the Fregean model apart from the theories that we see in contemporary philosophy of language, such as those of Grice, Davidson, and Dummett. At the same time, this form of explanation bears a striking resemblance to the types of explanations that Chomsky offers for syntactic phenomena. Here too the rule as well as its abstract representation is posited under idealizations. The actual events are explained by assuming along with the syntactic rule a set of additional factors, many of which are as yet unknown in detail.

To place this last point more sharply into focus, we shall look briefly at Dummett's proposals on meaning and show that not only is a Fregean approach different from Dummett's, but it is not even covered by Dummett's classification of theories of meaning.

For Dummett, a theory of meaning has to represent the practical abilities of a speaker that are involved in grasping a set of propositions.[31] This leads Dummett to verificationism, since any reasonable account of the relevant practical abilities has to include observation and observational search procedures. But such an approach is quite alien to Frege. Frege's notion of understanding is far more abstract than Dummett's, and it has little if anything to do with verification. According to Dummett, the issue between him and Frege is whether truth has a central role in semantics for natural languages. But the point at issue here cuts deeper. Even if truth did not have the central role that it has for Frege, his theory of senses and understanding would still move on a much more abstract level than Dummett's proposals. As long as Dummett talks of "practical abilities," he cannot make the abstractions and idealizations that we saw to be essential ingredients in a Fregean theory.

That Dummett is not even considering the abstract level at which Fregean semantic explanations commence can be seen from his classification of semantic theories into the "modest" and "full-blooded" ones.[32] According to Dummett, a modest theory of meaning gives an interpretation of a language to someone who already has the concepts expressed by the language. In contrast, a full-blooded theory seeks to do more than that; it seeks to explain also the concepts expressed by the primitives of the language. The explanation of the primitives is then couched by Dummett in terms of practical abilities, interaction with the world, and the actual workings and uses of the language.

Fregean theories aim at more than "modest" theories of language, as Dummett uses this phrase. For one could know all the equivalences expressed by the biconditionals that constitute a formal theory of truth of a language and still not understand the propositions expressed by sentences of that language, unless one understood these propositions in another language. If the "modest" theories assume knowledge of another language, then they do not account for language understanding as such.

At the same time, a Fregean theory will not yield accounts of practical abilities and full knowledge of the actual workings of a language. Only a full performance theory can yield this. A Fregean theory deals with only one of the ingredients of a performance theory. Thus a Fregean theory goes beyond the "modest" theories, and at the same time it attempts far less than Dummett's "full-blooded" theories. What is at issue is not merely relative modesty but differences of views on what is reasonable scientific procedure. According to the Fregean approach, it is a mistake in principle to aim at a homogeneous performance theory, and it is a mistake in principle to identify an account of understanding with the full range of practical abilities that constitute successful language use and communication. Thus a Fregean theory is neither a "modest" nor a full-blooded theory of meaning. It differs from both by its insistence on isolating one of the ingredients in semantic preformance and studying that under isolation, abstraction, and idealizations. In taking this approach a Fregean theory resembles Chomsky's approach to explanations of linguistic competence.

Further similarities are revealed by the *facts* that Frege and Chomsky want to explain. Chomsky wants to account for intuitions of grammaticality. But such intuitions are not observables; our introspections and verbal output are only indirect indicators of what these intuitions are. Likewise, a Fregean theory wants to account for intuitions about entailment. But such intuitions too are not observables, and our introspections and verbal output serve only as indirect evidence for these.

Since Fregean senses are not the functions representing meanings in Montague-grammars but the algorithms that compute such functions, we cannot regard Montague-grammar as a Fregean theory. Yet we can view Montague-grammars as laboratories for Fregean theories. For this extensional semantics, when applied to a narrowly specified part of a natural language, can reveal some of the compositional rules of that language. From these analyzed fragments one can learn about the interaction between verbs and adverbs, tense and aspect, or about the role of quantifiers, even if one did not identify Montague-grammar with a Fregean theory and made no claim that a whole natural language could be formalized within the same Montague-system.

Viewing linguistic competence under the appropriate idealizations also helps us see why the question mentioned earlier—"are meanings and syntactic rules in the head or not;"—is a pseudo-question. One might ask just as well whether ideal gases occur in nature or not. Idealized entities are not in nature the way observables are, but neither are they the mere artifacts of the scientist. We can see this from the following consideration. If two different artifacts of the scientist explain the same set of facts, we accept such indeterminacy without any qualms, and the question "which is the right theory?" need not arise. But if two different idealized entities are posited to account for the same facts, the resulting pluralism is no longer acceptable. For example, if it were a matter of physics, we would want to know which of the two ideal gases posited is the correct one. The entities in nature cannot be the degenerate cases of two ideals with respect to the same phenomena. Similarly for linguistics. In order to explain syntax or semantics, we posit an idealized speaker-hearer and the corresponding representations. To what extent these representations have realizations in the heads of actual speakers is an open question. But if two theories of grammar differ in the idealized speaker-hearer that they posit, then there is something further to be right or wrong about, even if the same set of well-formed formulas are generated by the grammars posited.

Finally, the relation between the abstract types of understanding assumed by Frege and Chomsky[33] and observational phenomena can be compared to the relation between diseases and their symptoms. The relationship is indirect. There are no criteria for diseases. As we learn more about the disease, we learn also how to find more and more reliable symptoms. The same holds for understanding. Different conceptions of understanding will yield different assumptions about how understanding is linked to practical abilities.

We saw, then, that in spite of superficial differences, there are deep similarities between Frege's and Chomsky's approach to the study of language. Both believe that linguistic phenomena can be studied fruitfully only under conditions of artificial isolation, abstraction, and isolation. They take this strategy to be in line with the ones adopted by the more successful natural sciences.[34]

Frege and Chomsky differ in some of their main interests. Thus Frege takes a firm ontological stand and wants to specify the structure of an ideal language that best serves the interests of science. Chomsky focuses on natural languages and linguistic competence in their own right and links this interest to that of learnability and the psychological mechanisms underlying language processing. But these differences should not blind us to the conceptual core shared by these thinkers. This core includes the claims that language primarily articulates thought, that semantics and syntax are mutually underdetermined, and that linguistic competence should be studied in the framework of "Platonistic psychology." Aiming at psychological relevance without aiming at "real time process models" would not come as a surprise to anyone versed in the a priori and natural sciences. It is strange that such a stance is alien to much of the thinking in current philosophy and the social sciences.

Although this survey is partly historical, it is also designed to serve as a guide toward the realization that if philosophers today are to construct adequate theories of natural language, they will have to make drastic changes in their conceptual frameworks. A careful look at Frege and the generative grammar of the past twenty years provides many of the signposts toward such a much needed conceptual reorganization.

Notes

1. I am indebted to John Perry, Scott Soames, and members of my philosophy of language seminar of the spring of 1980 (especially Tom Carlson and Peter Menzies) for many helpful suggestions.
2. Gottlob Frege, "Sense and Reference" (1892), reprinted in Frege, *Translations from the Philosophical Writings of Gottlob Frege,* ed. P. Geach and M. Black (New York, 1952), p. 59.
3. Gottlob Frege, "Compound Thoughts" (1923), reprinted in *Essays on Frege,* ed. E. Klemke (Urbana, 1968), p. 537.
4. *Ibid.,* p. 547.
5. See Frege, "Sense and Reference"; J. Moravcsik, "Singular Terms, Belief, and Reality," *Dialectica* 31(1977): 259-72.
6. Frege, "Compound Thoughts," p. 550.
7. Noam Chomsky, *Language and Responsibility* (New York, 1977), p. 88.
8. Noam Chomsky, *Aspects of the Theory of Syntax* (Cambridge, Mass., 1965), p. 3.
9. E.g., in "Conditions on Rules of Grammar" as reprinted in *Essays on Form and Interpretation* (Amsterdam, 1977), pp. 180-90.
10. Chomsky, *Language and Responsibility,* p. 138.
11. For detailed argument, see J. Moravcsik, "Understanding," *Dialectica* 33(1979):201-16.
12. There are two ways of being a Platonist and two ways of being a Kantian. One of these ways is a matter of one's ontological stand, and the other is the stand one takes with regard to explanations of cognitive competences. Thus there is nothing incompatible between being both a Platonist and a Kantian, provided that we keep this distinction in mind. Frege was a Platonist in his ontology, since he regarded senses as belonging to a "third realm" (p. 523 in Klemke's *Essays on Frege*) independent of the mind. He did not think that senses interacted causally with the other realms, but Plato did not think so either. This way of viewing things can be illustrated by the following contrast. G. E. Moore was a Platonist in his ontology but not in his psychology, whereas Chomsky is a Platonist in his psychology but not in his ontology. For a different view of these matters, see the essays by Hans Sluga, "Frege and the Rise of Analytic Philosophy," *Inquiry* 18 (1975):471-87, and "Frege's Alleged Realism," *Inquiry* 20 (1977): 227-42.
13. This interest, as the previous note shows, is not incompatible with a Platonistic ontology.
14. An important difference is, however, that whereas Kant accepts the existence of a priori synthetic propositions, Chomsky accepts the Duhem-Quine hypothesis and posits a continuum of more or less conceptual propositions.
15. E.g., Noam Chomsky, "Formal Properties of Grammar," in *Handbook of Mathematical Psychology,* vol. II, ed. R. Luce, R. Bush, and E. Galanther (New York, 1963).
16. Gottlob Frege, "The Thought: A Logical Inquiry" (1918-19), as reprinted in Klemke, ed. *Essays on Frege,* p. 508.
17. *Ibid.,* p. 510.
18. *Ibid.,* p. 508.
19. *Ibid.,* p. 513.
20. Chomsky, *Aspects of the Theory of Syntax,* p. 4.
21. Chomsky, *Language and Responsibility,* p. 43.
22. Chomsky, *Aspects of the Theory of Syntax,* chap. I, *passim.*
23. P. F. Strawson, "On Referring," originally in *Mind* (1950); reprinted in *Essays in Conceptual Analysis* ed. A. Flew (London, 1956), p. 21.
24. *Ibid.,* pp. 28-29.
25. *Ibid.,* p. 36, p. 40.
26. Frege, "Sense and Reference," pp. 62-65.
27. Strawson, "On Referring," p. 34.
28. E.g., J. R. Searle, *Speech Acts* (London, 1969).

29. For detailed argument see J. Moravcsik, "How Do Words Get Their Meanings?" *Journal of Philosophy*, forthcoming.
30. *Ibid.*, and Chomsky, *Language and Responsibility*, p. 144.
31. M. Dummett, "What Is a Theory of Meaning?" in *Mind and Language*, ed. S. Gutenplan (Oxford, 1975), p. 121, and "What Is a Theory of Meaning II," in *Truth and Meaning*, ed. G. Evans and J. McDowell (Oxford, 1976), p. 70.
32. Dummett, "What Is a Theory of Meaning?" p. 102.
33. For an additional defense, see J. Moravcsik, "Understanding."
34. E.g., in Noam Chomsky's, "Conditions on Rules of Grammar," p. 164.

Russell's 1913 Map of the Mind

DOUGLAS LACKEY

I. RUSSELL'S HALF-PUBLISHED BOOK

In January of 1914, P. E. B. Jourdain, editor of *The Monist*, published a long essay by Bertrand Russell entitled "On the Nature of Acquaintance." Another installment with the same title appeared in April, and a third in June. In October, *The Monist* published Russell's "Definitions and Methodological Principles in the Theory of Knowledge"; this article was followed by "Sensation and Imagination" in January 1915, and "On the Experience of Time" in April 1915. In 1956, Robert C. Marsh included the first three articles in his collection, *Logic and Knowledge*, without noting any connection between these three and those that followed.[1] None of the later editors of this material remarked that the six *Monist* articles formed a coherent sequence. Jourdain himself probably realized that the articles were connected, but he never took note of this fact anywhere in *The Monist*. As a result, the connection of these articles remained unnoticed for 55 years.

In 1967, pressed for funds to support the International War Crimes Tribunal, Russell offered his personal papers and letters for sale. While organizing the papers for public auction, Kenneth Blackwell came across a 208 page manuscript, numbered pages 143 to 350, dated 1913, and clearly written in Russell's hand. Blackwell asked Russell about the origins of the manuscript, which discussed topics in the theory of knowledge, but Russell could remember nothing at all about it. The manuscript was catalogued and sold, along with the rest of Russell's papers, to McMaster University in Hamilton, Ontario.

In 1970, Professor Elizabeth Eames examined the manuscript and suggested that it was a continuation of the series of articles published in *The Monist*. Internal analysis proved this conjecture to be correct. The missing 142 pages were identified with the six articles in *The Monist*, and the remaining manuscript constituted ten more chapters. Jourdain, it appeared, had published only the first third (six of sixteen chapters) of a major Russellian manuscript.

125

In 1973, in the course of preparing his master's thesis on Russell's theory of judgment, Blackwell went to Texas to read through some 1200 letters from Russell to Lady Ottoline Morrell, now in the possession of the library of the University of Texas. The letters covered the period of the unpublished manuscript, and the complete story of its construction came to light. After *Principia Mathematica* was completed in 1910, Russell turned his attention toward more broadly philosophical subjects. He wrote *The Problem of Philosophy* in 1911 and then decided to concentrate his attention on the theory of knowledge, which, for Russell, also included what today is called the philosophy of science. By late 1911, Russell was writing Ottoline that he planned to write a "big book" on the subject of epistemology. But, in 1912, all bets were off, for Russell's philosophical life was disrupted by the ferocious onslaught, both philosophical and psychological, of his new student, Ludwig Wittgenstein. By mid-1912, Russell was convinced that Wittgenstein's skill at philosophy far surpassed his own, and he began deferring philosophical work for fear of the criticisms Wittgenstein might unleash upon it. At one point, Russell almost decided to retire from philosophy, leaving the remainder of his philosophical work to be "completed" by Wittgenstein. This peculiar self-repression of intellect continued into 1913, until Russell's own mental fertility got the best of his doubts. On May 7, 1913, the dam burst, and Russell began his long suppressed big book on the theory of knowledge. He wrote furiously, completing over 200 pages in 20 days. On May 27, however, Wittgenstein came to tea, and Russell unwisely showed his nemesis some parts of the work in progress. Wittgenstein criticized the work savagely, and reinforced Russell's fears that Wittgenstein would render all his philosophical work obsolete. The attack of Wittgenstein killed his enthusiasm for the whole project. In the next two weeks, he pushed on through another 150 pages and then stopped. Wittgenstein and the war kept him from returning to it.[2]

Russell's notes from 1913 contain various sketches for the projected book on the theory of knowledge. From these, by considerable detective effort, Blackwell and Prof. Eames produced a table of contents which is most probably what the book would have been like, had the work on it not been interrupted:

THEORY OF KNOWLEDGE

Introduction
Section A. Analytical
    Part I. Acquaintance
        Chapter I. Preliminary Description of Experience (*Monist* 1914)
           II. Neutral Monism (*Monist* 1914)
           III. Analysis of Experience (*Monist* 1914)
           IV. Definitions and Methodological Principles in the Theory of Knowledge (*Monist* 1914)
           V. Sensation and Imagination (*Monist* 1915)
           VI. On the Experience of Time (*Monist* 1915)
           VII. On the Acquaintance Involved in Our Knowledge of Relations (manuscript)

VIII. Acquaintance with Predicates (manuscript)
IX. Logical Data (manuscript)
Part II. Understanding Atomic Propositional Thought
Chapter I. The Understanding of Propositions (manuscript)
II. Analysis and Synthesis (manuscript)
III. Various Examples of Understanding (manuscript)
IV. Belief, Disbelief, and Doubt (manuscript)
V. Truth and Falsehood (manuscript)
VI. Self-Evidence (manuscript)
VII. Degrees of Certainty (manuscript)
VIII. A Priori and Empirical (unwritten)
IX. Epistemological Order of Science (unwritten)
Part III. Understanding Molecular Propositional Thought
Chapter I. Negation, Disjunction, Cojunction, Hypothetical (unwritten)
II. Inference—General Nature of. Knowledge of Logical Principles (unwritten)
III. Inference—Valid and Invalid, Logical and Psychological (unwritten)
IV. Logical, Psychological, and Epistemological Premises (unwritten)
V. Logical and Epistemological Order—Certainty and Probability (unwritten)
VI. General Propositions (unwritten)
VII. Acquaintance and Description (unwritten)
VIII. A Priori and Empirical (unwritten)
IX. Epistemological Order of Science (unwritten)
Section B. Constructive (unwritten)
Part I. Knowledge of Logic
Pure form: Variables only. Includes mathematics.
a priori
Part II. Knowledge of Sense
What can be discovered by mere analysis of data, without assuming principles by which existents not given can be inferred. Time. Space. Psychical data
Part III. Knowledge of Science
Problem. To state (a) existence certain sense-data (b) by certain principles of inference, which must be self-evident, such that science shall follow. Matter. Causality. Induction. Principles of inference required: can they all belong to Logic? Kant's query again.

The alert reader will observe that many of the topics listed unwritten Section A, Part III are covered in Russell's 1918 "Lectures on Logical Atomism,"[3] and that many of the topics listed in the unwritten Section B are covered in Russell's 1914 book, *Our Knowledge of the External World*. It appears that the book is not so much incomplete as scattered. Nevertheless, if one compares the dense and elaborate reasoning of the unpublished manuscript with the popular style of *Our Knowledge of the External World* and the loose presentations of the lectures on logical atomism, one must conclude that Russell never gave the subjects covered in these later works the sort of treatment that he was prepared to give them in 1913. Wittgenstein's cup of tea proved to be a major tragedy in the history of twentieth-century philosophy.

The last four-sixths of Russell's projected book were never written, and the first sixth has long been before the public. My purpose here is to provide a running account of the hidden sixth. The unpublished ten chapters contain many doctrines and devices that Russell published nowhere else, and they present previously published doctrines with a subtlety that Russell rarely reveals elsewhere. At least one purpose served by this account will be to contribute materials toward the resolution of a major historiographical controversy concerning the relations between Wittgenstein and Russell. Is Russell's system of "logical atomism" a degenerate, empiricized version of ideas that originate with Wittgenstein, or is Wittgenstein's *Tractatus* a purified version of ideas that really originate with Russell? A reading of the 1913 manuscript supports the latter view.

II. RUSSELL'S PHILOSOPHY OF MIND IN 1913

Russell did not give his half-published book a title, but *A Theory of Knowledge* seems entirely appropriate. The philosophy of mind developed in *A Theory of Knowledge* is traditional insofar as it assumes, without much argument, that there is a "subject" and that mental relations are relations between objects and a subject. This is the orientation adopted in all the works of Alexius Meinong, whose works Russell had carefully studied between 1904 and 1907. Meinong, in turn, was a student of Franz Brentano, and, accordingly, Russell's book can be considered a lineal descendant of Brentano's seminal phenomenological treatise, *Psychologie vom empirischen Standpunkt*, published in 1874. Russell's development of the phenomenological approach was, however, original in certain respects. The "subject," in Russell's account, was not a mind, nor was it consciousness, and accordingly his theory does not speak of relations between minds and objects, or between consciousness and objects; indeed, Russell hardly employs the terminology of "mental acts" at all. The subject, in Russell's account, is simply a *person*, and a mental relation is simply a certain sort of relation between persons and other things. This relation between a person and mental objects can be either a one-one relation or a one-many relation. If the relation is one-one, Russell calls it *acquaintance;* if the relation is one-many, Russell calls it *understanding*. Perceiving, remembering, and imagining are all varieties of acquaintance; understanding, believing, and doubting are all varieties of understanding.

Another point of difference between Russell and the phenomenological tradition was his steadfast rejection of any suggestion that the object of a mental relation can be an "unreal" object. Following the lead of his theory of descriptions, invented in 1905, Russell argues throughout that what appears to be thought about an unreal object is really thought about the properties that the object would have if it happened to exist. Since we do at least appear on occasion to be thinking about nonexistent objects, it follows that properties as well as particulars can be objects of acquaintance. The type of acquaintance that takes properties as its object is dubbed *conception* by Russell, and conception, in turn, is broken down into two sorts: conception in which relational properties are objects, and conception in which non-relational properties are objects. Chapter VII, the first unpublished chapter of *A Theory of Knowledge,* is devoted to the conception of relations.

III. SUMMARY OF UNPUBLISHED CHAPTERS ON ACQUAINTANCE

Chapter VII. On the Acquaintance Involved in Our Knowledge of Relations

Russell in 1913 employed the term "predicate" for monadic properties and the word "relation" for all non-monadic properties. Acquaintance with relations, Russell argues (ms. 158), cannot arise from acquaintance with related terms, nor can it arise from acquaintance with classes of ordered n-tuples of related terms. One can, Russell observes, be acquainted with related terms without being aware that they are so related, and, accordingly, one can be acquainted with classes of ordered n-tuples of related terms without being aware that they are so related. It is true, Russell observes, that if one is aware of the similarity of relation between ordered n-tuples in a class of related terms, then one is aware of the relation that related the terms, but this awareness presupposes awareness of the relation of similarity, so some acquaintance with relations must be accepted as *sui generis:* the only alternative would be to conclude that we are never aware of relations at all. The argument here is obviously a generalization of the famous argument on behalf of the subsistence of relations in *The Problems of Philosophy,*[4] and it convinced Russell that a proper philosophy of mind must accept relations as subsistent entities which sometimes serve as objects of acquaintance.

Russell suggests that acquaintance with relations is presupposed in understanding the meaning of relational terms. I understand "before," for example, only if I am acquainted with the relation of precedence. Acquaintance with asymmetrical relations is complex: to be acquainted with the relation of precedence I must be acquainted with something which Russell calls the "sense" of the relation. In the two propositions, *A is before B,* and *B is before A,* the constituents are the same and the logical form is the same, i.e., relational form, and thus the difference between them must lie neither in form nor constituents but in a residue which Russell calls sense or "direction" (ms. 158).

That relations have direction was already suggested by Russell in chapter twelve of *The Problems of Philosophy.* But in this manuscript there is an elaboration, which appears nowhere else in Russell. Russell observes that the words or symbols which we use to refer to a relational complex themselves have relational features, and that we use these features to interpret the meaning of relational statements. When we encounter written sentences in English, we naturally assume that the sentences are to be read from left to right, and, when we encounter a spoken sentence in any language, we assume that we are to interpret the sentence in the temporal order in which the words were uttered. Every relational expression in ordinary language, if it denotes an asymmetrical relation, could denote either of two complexes, and the reader must use the context of the expression to determine which complex is actually denoted. This state of affairs makes ordinary language inadequate for two reasons. First, it is part of Russell's general program for the analysis of language that all rules of context for the interpretation of linguistic expressions be eliminated and replaced by explicit rules of syntax. Here we have implicit rules that cry out for elimination. Second, if a language is to succeed in expressing acquaintance with relations, it must be a language in which each relational expression denotes one and only one relational complex, since, in each case of acquaintance with relations, a person is related to a single relational complex.

In his 1903 book *Principles of Mathematics*, section 219, Russell had attempted to deal with this problem by stipulating that "x is before y" and "y is after x" stand for different complexes. If so, then to understand "x is before y" one must understand that x is a y-preceder. But in 1913 Russell rejects this view and declares that there is no difference in meaning between *X precedes Y* and *Y succeeds X* (ms. 161). Instead of attempting to distinguish between "x is before y" and "y is after x," Russell concentrates on distinguishing between "x is before y" and "y is before x." He decides to treat each of these propositions as a case of a relation between the first term of the relation and the entire relational complex. For example, the complex associated with the proposition *X is before Y* is no longer simply xRy, but $xR'xRy$, and the complex associated *Y is before X* is no longer yRx, but $yR'xRy$. (Though Russell does not mention it, we must assume, to prevent regress, that R' is symmetrical.) Thus, to take account of the sense of asymmetrical relations, Russell replaces his old notion of a relational complex, introduced in 1903 in *Principles of Mathematics*, with a new notion of relational complex, which consists of the old relational complex, a selected term of that complex, and a symmetrical relation. The isolated term of the relational complex serves as a marker of what Russell calls "position" in the old-style complex; it marks the point from which the asymmetrical relation proceeds (ms. 162).

By this maneuver, Russell eliminates all ambiguities arising from failure to specify the direction of a relation. Suppose that someone says "Brutus killed Caesar," intending by this utterance to convey the idea that Brutus is a Caesar-killer. The unassisted sentence "Brutus killed Caesar" cannot unambiguously express this idea if we are deprived of the rule that tells us to read the sentence from left to right. This difficulty is rectified by Russell's theory as follows: "Brutus killed Caesar," interpreted left to right, is symbolized "b-bKc," and "Caesar killed Brutus," interpreted left to right, is interpreted "c-bKc."

There is, in this ingenious suggestion, a glimmer of the Wiener-Kuratkowski definition of relations as classes, first proposed in 1914.[5] Given a relational complex aRb, Weiner and Kuratkowski reduced this relation to the ordered Pair $\langle a,b \rangle$ and then reduced this ordered pair to the class $\{\{a,b\}a\}$. Just as the order of the ordered pair is reduced by Wiener and Kuratkowski to a class that includes a class among its members, so the sense of asymmetrical relation is reduced by Russell to a symmetrical complex that contains a complex as a part.

One might still question whether Russell's proposed solution really removes his difficulties. It has not been specified, in the preceding discussion, that "x" designates a simple entity. If it is not, then xRy could be a constituent of x. In that case, (x -(xRy)) could express, reading from left to right, that x is the first constituent in the relational complex xRx, or it could express, reading from right to left, that xRy is the first constituent of a relational complex the name of which is "x." This difficulty will arise if we permit entities to be parts of themselves; if we limit the system to such entities as material objects, which cannot be parts of themselves, the Russellian analysis is free of ambiguity.

From all this, Russell concludes that the word "before" is not merely the name of a relation but the name of a relation combined with an indication of relational position. "After" names the same relation but indicates a different position than does "before." Since "before" and "after" name the same relation, the result seems to be that there are really no asymmetrical relations: in this case, the relation really named is "before-or-after," which is a symmetrical relation. Such symmetrical relations Russell calls "pure" relations (ms. 163).

When the relation is pure, Russell notes, it needs no terms in order to be intelligible (ms. 163). For the theory of acquaintance, this result suggests that the mind can be directly acquainted with pure relations and not just relational complexes containing terms (ms. 164).

Chapter VIII. Acquaintance with Predicates

Russell begins the new chapter with an inquiry into "minimal" complexes. The question is whether there can be complexes that have merely two constituents, or whether the smallest possible complex contains three constituents—a particular, a universal, and the dual relation of predication. He decides that two term complexes exist, on the grounds that if it is arbitrary to say that there are complexes of five terms but not of four, it is equally arbitrary to say that there are complexes of three terms but not of two (ms. 167).

Now, in a two-term complex, are the constituents always universals, or are they sometimes a universal combined with a particular? Do particulars exist at all? In response, Russell surveys a no-particulars theory that is usually identified in the literature as the Bundle Theory of Substance. On this theory, as Russell describes it, one ought not to say "this is white," and "that is white," but rather "whiteness is here" and "whiteness is there." He attacks this theory with an elaboration of the argument first sketched in his Aristotelian address of 1911, "On the Relations of Universals and Particulars,"[6] to wit, that diversity of place requires diversity of terms, regardless of the similarity of the qualities of the terms. "It follows that two patches of white in different places are numerically diverse, and therefore neither is whiteness itself." Thus the Bundle Theory is false, particulars do subsist, and sometimes a two term complex consists of a universal and a particular. If I am aware of a white patch, I am aware of a particular and a universal, and of their being together in the same complex.

It follows from this rejection of the Bundle Theory of Substance that a "thing" is a bundle of particulars, each of which has predicates. These particulars are bluntly identified by Russell with sense data, after the manner of Moore, in his 1910 lectures, eventually published under the title *Some Main Problems of Philosophy*.[7] The notion of sense data is not further elaborated. One suspects that this development was deferred to the later, and ultimately unwritten, sections of this book.

Having admitted the subsistence of predicates or universals, Russell is nevertheless quick to reject both Platonic and scholastic realism. If a particular resembles a predicate, as Russell alleges that Plato alleged, then each particular can have only one predicate, a conclusion that Russell finds too arbitrary to accept. Neither does he wish to assert, as he believes "scholastic realists" to have asserted, that predicates subsist in the same manner as particulars exist. They are, according to Russell, a radically different type of entity, and they cannot be substituted for particulars within complexes. Russell is a "realist" here only in the sense that he claims that universals are not constituents of particulars and that particulars are not constituents of universals. It must be confessed that this account leaves the relationship between universals and particulars more than a little mysterious. The problem of predication, however, is a problem for the theory of understanding, not acquaintance, and Russell need not solve it here.

In later discussions of the Bundle Theory of Substance, it was often argued that rejection of the Bundle Theory entails commitment to property-less entities, nicknamed "bare particulars" in the literature.[8] It should be clear from the foregoing discussion that Russell's particulars are not "bare particulars" in this sense, entities about which, to use Locke's phrase, "we know not what." The particulars for Russell are all sense data, and therefore hardly unknowable. These sense data are not constituted by their predicates, Russell summarizes, because a precisely similar sense datum may exist in another place (ms. 175).

All the alleged errors of the Bundle Theory of Substance are attributed by Russell to the effects of "bad grammar." One example of the several that Russell provides to illustrate this point turns on the interpretation of "Socrates is white." It is tempting, Russell writes, to interpret "Socrates is white" as a proposition similar to "All men are mortal," and tempting to interpret "All men are mortal" as a sentence that expresses a relation of predicates, namely, *humanity implies mortality*. From this we can deduce that "Socrates is white" expresses a relation of predicates. But unfortunately the premises in the deduction are false, resulting from a confusion between a grammatical subject that is named, namely Socrates, and a grammatical subject that is merely described, namely all men (ms. 177). This is the first and only indication in Russell that his main argument against the Leibnizian view that all true subject-predicate assertions are analytic hinges on his distinction, made first in his 1905 article "On Denoting," between naming and describing. In all the voluminous literature on the theory of descriptions, this is one offshoot that the commentators have missed.

It is, on these accounts, necessary to admit acquaintance with particulars and acquaintance with relations. It is not necessary, but merely plausible, to admit that there is acquaintance with predicates, even though such predicates can be defined as classes of similar particulars. This plausibility arises, Russell claims at the chapter's end, from "direct inspection of data" (ms. 178).

Chapter IX. Logical Data

In this chapter Russell proposes to discuss relations in general, as opposed to any particular relation. According to Russell, each genuinely logical notion is primitive. For example, he argues that *"dual relation"* is a primitive notion. *Similarity* is a kind of dual relation and is therefore not primitive, but *dual relation* is not a kind of relation and cannot be decomposed into species and difference or any other components. The reason for this, Russell argues, is that logical propositions are concerned solely with form. The logical constants, for example, which might seem to be entities occurring in the propositions of logic, are not actually constituents of the proposition in the verbal expressions of which their names occur (ms. 182). This phrase shows that Russell, contrary to the usual rumor, could be sensitive to use-mention distinctions when the discussion has need of them.

This point leads Russell into a discussion of logical form. His first attempt at a definition of this notion is that form is what is "left over" when the non-logical constants of a proposition have all been replaced by variables. What is "left over," says Russell, is not another constituent *in* the proposition but the form *of* the whole proposition. Suppose that one obtains *X is F* from the proposition *Socrates is mortal*. Since *Socrates is mortal* has been analyzed, in the previous chapter, as containing only two constituents, when both these constituents are replaced by variables, no constituents are left. Thus *is* does not stand for another constituent: if it did, there would have to be a new way in which it and the other two constituents are put together, and we find ourselves in an endless regress (ms. 183). There is, in Russell, no such thing as the relation of predication.

I do not think that many contemporary philosophers would find this definition of logical form illuminating. For one thing, no rule is provided to distinguish the constants that can be "turned into" variables from those that cannot. The importance of Russell's discussion here is not so much the conclusions that are reached but the subject that has been introduced. These pages are, I believe, the first pages of twentieth-century philosophy given over to the notion of "logical form," and the ideas expressed here are considerably less confused than the ideas in Wittgenstein's "Notes on Logic," which were written in the summer of 1913, several months *after* Russell had written these pages. We can only infer that Russell initiated the discussion of this topic and that Wittgenstein merely picked it up and carried it forward in his "Notes on Logic" in 1913, his "Notes Dictated to G. E. Moore" of 1914, and his *Tractatus* of 1918.[9]

There is perhaps even a more fundamental difficulty in this discussion of form, a difficulty that Russell neither hides nor resolves. Russell appears to assume that to understand any word one must be acquainted with the objects for which it stands, or at least acquainted with the properties possessed by the object for which the word stands. This rule is unblinkingly applied by Russell even to words for logical constants, and so, e.g., we understand "or" if and only if we are acquainted with disjunctions. But if logical forms, like disjunction, are not objects, it does not appear they could do service as objects of acquaintance. Small wonder that Wittgenstein, one year later, in his "Notes Dictated to G. E. Moore,"[10] described form as that which could *not* be expressed in language. Russell, for his part, was content to report that this was a problem to be resolved by future work in logic (ms. 186).

IV. SUMMARY OF UNPUBLISHED CHAPTERS ON UNDERSTANDING

All of the preceding discussion concerned the mental relation of acquaintance between a subject and various objects, or various pseudo-objects, like logical forms. The second part of the projected six-part book is wholly occupied with the notion of "understanding." The entirety of this section is preserved in manuscript, but no portion of it was ever published.

Chapter I. The Understanding of Propositions

Acquaintance, for Russell, is a genus that includes sensation, memory, imagination, conception, and logical intuition. *Understanding*, he stipulates, is a genus in which believing, asserting, doubting, and other such relations are the various species.

In the first step of the analysis, Russell distinguished propositions from sentences. A proposition, he suggests, is a class of sentence with the same meaning. This analysis purges propositions of tenses, pronouns, and other token-reflexive and pragmatic elements. It is propositions in this refined sense that are the objects of understanding (ms. 197). These objects, Russell argues, are fundamentally different from the objects of acquaintance, because, unlike the objects of acquaintance, they are capable of truth or falsehood. (In later writings, Russell attributes this point to Wittgenstein.[11] There is no such attribution here, in Russell's earliest mention of it.) Furthermore, propositions differ from the objects of acquaintance in that they are incapable of existence or subsistence. The argument Russell gives here is familiar: false propositions obviously neither exist nor subsist, therefore, Russell concludes, true propositions also must neither exist nor subsist. They are said to be "incomplete symbols" (ms. 200).

It follows that the relation of understanding cannot be a simple dual relation between a mental act and an object; it must be complex and different in logical form (ms. 200). The understanding of a proposition presupposes acquaintance with all the constituents of the proposition, but acquaintance alone does not suffice for understanding. The key argument for this view returns Russell to the analysis of asymmetrical relations—in this case, to propositions that contain an asymmetrical relation as a constituent. Consider the sentence "A precedes B." This really expresses two propositions: (1) that A is a B-preceder and (2) that B is an A-succeeder. Accordingly, I may be acquainted with A, and acquainted with B, and acquainted with the relation of precedence, and yet still not understand what is meant by a person who says "A precedes B." Hence *understanding* cannot be analyzed into a set of acquaintances (ms. 206).

The discussion following is dense and tangled. The notion of "position in a complex" is once again introduced in the attempt to resolve the difficulties. Russell suggests that we interpret

(1) *A precedes B*

as

(2) *There is a complex* α; *this complex contains the relation of precedence; and A is the first member of this complex.*

It might appear that this analysis is defective, on the grounds that "α" and "A" can be switched around, creating an ambiguity in the interpretation of the translation. But Russell points out that although "A" and "B" can be shuffled, without loss of sense, in proposition (1), "α" and "A" cannot be shuffled around in (2) without loss of sense. The verbal assertion "There is a complex A" makes no sense, since "A is not the name of a complex but of a particular. Thus the understanding of A involves acquaintance with A, and B, and precedence, but also involves understanding how these terms are put together in the proposition. This latter understanding is a new mental relation, fundamentally different from acquaintance (ms. 207).

One can only admire the ingenuity of the theory that Russell proposes here and the ingenious devices employed to create a context-free language. Formally, however, the analysis is not a success. Suppose that our initial proposition is

(3) A is taller than B

which by the Russellian translation becomes

(4) A is first in the complex consisting of A, B, and tallness.

Russell is correct when he says that we cannot substitute "A" for "A is taller than B" in the latter proposition. But it should be obvious that (4) is still not unambiguous and that the reading of (4) still depends upon rules of context. We could read (1) by reading "B" first, then reading the rest as "Is first in the complex 'A is taller than A.'" (Notice that we cannot rule out "A is taller than A" on purely grammatical grounds.) Furthermore, let us suppose, contrary to fact, that (4) is unambiguous. Then it would seem to follow that we could understand (4) merely by being acquainted with all the constituents of (4), contrary to Russell's dictum that understanding cannot be reduced to a class of acquaintances.

After this discussion (ms. 208) the manuscript veers off on a long excursus about the nature of logical form. This discussion largely repeats the discussion of logical form given in the preceding chapter. We might infer that this is a stretch of the manuscript written immediately *after* Wittgenstein's visit to Russell, described in the first part of this article. Russell apparently rethought his views on logical form, but this rethinking did not produce any new ideas.

The last subject of the chapter is the logical structure of propositions expressing that some other proposition has been understood (ms. 212). Suppose, for example, that our sample proposition is

(5) Jones understands that A precedes B.

Russell argues, first, that the complex *A precedes B* is not a constituent of this proposition at all. The reason is that the proposition

(6) A precedes B

can still be understood even if it is false and A does not precede B. Consequently, Russell decides that the proposition consists of A, B, precedence, Jones, and the logical form designated by "something is related to something" (the doctrine that logical forms cannot be constituents seems to have fallen away at this point). This analysis parallels the discussion of the structure of judgments given in *The Problems of Philosophy*, which was written in 1911.[12] The added fillip is the attention given to relational judgments, and the introduction of the notion of logical form.

Chapter II. Analysis and Synthesis

The chapter on "Analysis and Synthesis" has a slightly archaic ring; the topics discussed are the topics of F. H. Bradley, who is less a figure of current interest than is Russell or Wittgenstein. Russell begins with the plausible observation that persons can be acquainted with complexes without at the same time being acquainted with all the constituents of the complex. This observation opens the field for the procedure of analysis: what analysis does reveal are the constituents of complexes that were not originally objects of acquaintance.

The analysis of complexes and propositions that contain asymmetrical relations presents special problems. If *A precedes B* cannot be analyzed wholly into A, precedence, and B, it appears that analysis destroys the sense of the proposition, and the Bradleian view that analysis is destructive will carry the day. Russell claims that this difficulty is surmounted by replacing all sentences containing relational expressions with longer sentences, after the fashion demonstrated above in the case of sentences (1) and (2). The method is here stated with much greater generality (ms. 230), but it is still, I believe, subject to the criticisms lodged against it in the preceding section.

Given the terminology of acquaintance and understanding, the question arises whether analysis first requires acquaintance with the parts that are in turn judged to be part of the whole, or whether judgment that certain parts are present in a whole eventually produces acquaintance with those parts. Russell decides this issue through a careful analysis of the operation of *attention*. In the focusing of attention, according to Russell, we were first conscious of the whole and then came to recognize the parts as parts of this whole. None of this discussion is especially detailed, but it is Russell's only analysis, in his long career, of the notion of seeing-as, a subject later explored in greater depth by Wittgenstein.

Chapter III. Various Examples of Understanding

In this chapter, Russell discusses the understanding of propositions of great generality, such as *something is related to something*, which, in Russell's view, are both definite and true. *Something is related to something*, Russell argues, is a form without constituents, but we can understand it nonetheless. In fact, Russell goes on to make the stronger point that the understanding of *this* very general proposition is presupposed in the understanding of all other relational propositions (ms. 243). This presupposition, subsequent analysis reveals (ms. 249), is not a case of psychological presupposition; on the contrary, from the psychological point of view it is probable that relational expressions of lesser generality must be first understood *before* we move on to the understanding of propositions like the proposition that *something has some relation to something*. We are dealing, then, with a case of *logical* presupposition, and it is a pity that Russell does not say more about this notion of logical presupposition.

The proposition *something has some relation to something* is, according to Russell, perfectly simple. The question then arises whether the understanding of this proposition can be distinguished from merely be acquainted with it. Russell, following the phenomenological instincts instead of his logical instincts, reluctantly concludes that in this one extreme case the distinction between acquaintance and understanding seems to have disappeared (ms. 246). The proposition that something has some relation to something assumes the status, in Russell's discussion, that the proposition *I exist* assumes in the philosophy of Descartes. To understand the proposition that something has some relation to something is, at the same time, to be acquainted with this proposition. But if one is acquainted with this proposition, then it must subsist, and if it subsists, Russell believes, then it must be true. With this particular proposition, the gap between understanding and verifying has disappeared along with the gap between understanding and acquaintance. It is not surprising that from this point forward, Russell's book is concerned less with the philosophy of logic and more and more with epistemology.

Chapter IV. Belief, Disbelief, and Doubt

The distinction of acquaintance and understanding, partly dissolved in the preceding chapter, is reinstated here to distinguish belief from perception. According to Russell, the objects of belief and understanding are the same, namely, complexes that have logical form, joined with the subject by a multiple relation (ms. 262). No object of belief is a single particular. When we believe, for example, in the existence of God, we are believing that *there is a Divine Being*, and thus our object of thought is not simply God but certain properties and the concept of existential instantiation. Thus the Humean conflation of judgment and belief is here sharply rejected.

What, then, constitutes the difference between *belief* and *understanding*? The difference is there, Russell says, and it is simply indefinable, like the difference between two tastes. In the same way disbelief is unanalyzably different from belief: you cannot define disbelief, for example, as a belief in the negation of what is elsewhere believed (ms. 272). Russell says the same about all the differing grades of doubt between belief and disbelief: they are all undefinable, and this chapter accordingly is unsurprisingly short.

Chapter V. Truth and Falsehood

Russell defines an assertion as a complex consisting of a subject, a logical form, and the objects of belief. The symbolic representation of this is

(7) $J(S, F, x_1, x_2, x_3 \ldots x_n)$.

If the form of the proposition is such that there is only one way that $x_1, x_2, \ldots x_n$ can be combined to form the complex $(F, x_1 \ldots x_n)$, then the truth definition of the larger proposition, Russell asserts, is simple:

(8): (7) is true if and only if there exists a complex $(F, x_1 \ldots x_n)$.

Difficulties obtrude when there is more than one way that F and the various x_n can be assembled into a complex, but Russell feels that all these difficulties can be resolved by utilizing the devices earlier employed to deal with the ambiguities of relational expressions (ms. 277). It evolves from Russell's analysis that all statements of truth conditions are existential assertions about the satisfaction of general conditions. The conditions are general in that they are always described, and never named, since if they were nameable, they would subsist and immediately verify that the proposition in question is true. Russell has here ingeniously combined the theory of descriptions with the theory of truth, and the result is a definition of "satisfaction" that is similar to the standard definitions developed by Tarski and Carnap in the 1930s. In strikingly Tarskian fashion, Russell even remarks that a belief in the proposition p is true if and only if p is true; this is, he adds, the whole of the positive argument for the theory (ms. 286).

The definition of truth proposed here by Russell requires the existence or nonexistence of certain "complexes." It does not mention true or false propositions at all. The bulk of Russell's ensuing discussion is taken up with defenses of this "no propositions" account of truth. He acknowledges that the theory is not very developed, and he states no criteria for determining which complexes exist and which do not, and consequently it has no criteria for separating true beliefs from false beliefs. What the theory does, Russell argues, is not to provide a "definition" of truth but to give an "analysis" of truth. The detailed determination of which sentences express truths and which sentences express falsehoods is a task for science, not for philosophy.

Chapter VI. Self-Evidence

It is easier to see that there must be such a thing as self-evidence than to see what it is, Russell begins (ms. 301). The discussion of self-evidence that ensues reads like a dress rehearsal for all the schemes of twentieth-century epistemology that could be roughly classified as "Cartesian." What is self-evident, according to Russell, is knowledge which we possess independently of inference (ms. 302). The objects of such knowledge, Russell says, are propositions, and he notes that false propositions here present no problem, since there is no such thing as knowledge of false propositions.

The quality of self-evidence is, in Russell's view, a "subjective" quality, by which he means that it cannot be defined apart from reference to a subject. For example, knowledge derived from sense is not self-evident until the moment of sensation, which shows that self-evidence adheres to judgments about propositions, and not to propositions as such, which are unchanging in time. This psychological self-evidence, Russell remarks, is like a luminous obviousness, (ms. 304), an indefinable tonal quality of certain beliefs.

The discursus on self-evidence that follows (ms. 307-8) is a meditation on the epistemological warrants for the premises of *Principia Mathematica*, completed three years before. According to Russell, the epistemological basis of any organized system of knowledge, of which the *Principia* is one example, does not necessarily lie in the premises. When setting up premises, one should choose the most deductively fertile propositions, and the most deductively fertile propositions may not be the most self-evident. The epistemological warrant for the premises of any system is therefore inductive: the premises are mystified to the extent that they deductively generate self-evident theorems. It is in the *theorems* that self-evidence remains epistemologically fundamental (ms. 307).

The discussion of self-evidence in these two pages parallels the discussion of self-evidence in Meinong's epistemological treatise, *Über die Erfahrungsgrunde unseres Wissens* (Berlin, 1906), which Russell had reviewed in *Mind* in 1907.[13] Meinong had argued that since true belief is not knowledge, justifications of belief are needed to produce knowledge, and to prevent an infinite regress of justifications, some justifications must be recognizably true. Russell goes one step beyond Meinong here by attempting to guarantee that an evident judgment be a true judgment (ms. 311). Given the definition of truth in the preceding chapter, one such guarantee of the truth of an evident judgment would be simultaneous acquaintance with the corresponding complex (ms. 312) —since a judgment is defined as true if this complex exists, and we can be acquainted only with existents.

One apparently difficulty with this analysis is that it allows that false propositions, considered by themselves, appear to the intellect exactly as true propositions do—the difference between them being, not in the propositions, but in the presence or absence of a corresponding complex. But from the phenenological point of view, this is an advantage, because evident judgments do not feel different from other judgments. The upshot of the discussion neatly combines a correspondence theory of truth with a rationalist criterion of "luminous obviousness." Russell defines "self-evidence" as a property of judgments such that belief in the judgment is always accompanied by acquaintance with its truth (ms. 323).

Chapter VII. Degrees of Certainty

Russell distinguishes the degree of certainty of a proposition from its probability. That a proposition might have a certain probability is itself a new proposition, which might have any degree of certainty (ms. 326). The chapter is concerned with the degree of credibility to be given the propositions that have traditionally bedeviled the empiricist, in particular, the credibility of propositions based on induction or memory.

Distinctions proliferate with Husserlian density. Russell distinguishes "perceptive acquaintance memory" from "perceptive descriptive memory"; these are in turn distinguished from "judgment acquaintance memory" and "judgment descriptive memory." The discussion, which is too detailed to be described here, introduces a notion of "representation" (ms. 334) which appears nowhere else in Russell's discussions of the philosophy of mind. He argues that in acquaintance memory, the memory image resembles a past perceptive image, whereas in descriptive memory the memory image represents the past perceptive image, but does not resemble it. This notion of "representation" absolves Russell of the charge that his philosophy of memory, known principally to the world through his book *Analysis of Mind* (1921),[14] is simply an updated version of Hume's theory that memories are all "decayed" sense impressions. The representative nature of descriptive memory images, according to Russell, may itself be an object of acquaintance, and such acquaintance is the source of our general confidence that there is a past, even though we recognize that any single memory judgment might be false (ms. 341).

A discussion of the vagueness of memory images leads Russell into a discussion of vagueness in general, and the relation between the vagueness of a proposition and its degree of certainty. Suppose that we begin with a proposition that has a given degree of certainty. As that degree of certainty is attenuated, it is possible to recover the original degree of certainty by replacing the original proposition with a vaguer proposition. An uncertain judgment about something is really a certain judgment about something else, Russell says (ms. 341). Every known proposition, then, either is a certain proposition, or it bears a definite relation to some certain proposition, and so Russell succeeds in defining (or defining away) the notion of "degree of certainty" without recourse either to probability theory or to pragmatic theories of *prima facie* truth.

IV. CONCLUSION

What general conclusions may be drawn from this brief survey of Russell's remarkable production of 1913? The Russell of these pages is not the familiar empiricist Russell, struggling with the relation of sense data to physics or the causal theory of perception. Brentano and Meinong, and not Berkeley and Hume, are the ancestors of this volume, and thus the book is a missing link between the British and the Continental traditions in the philosophy of mind.

The book provides a coherent and fairly complete survey of mental phenomena—the most complete, in fact, that Russell ever attempted. But perhaps of even greater interest than the book's architectonic are the numerous technical devices and notions introduced here for the first time by Russell. The book develops new standards for a contact-free syntax, a predecessor of the semantic theory of truth, an ontologically sophisticated "no propositions" theory of judgment, a logic of certainty, and numerous technical devices never explored by subsequent authors. Certainly the publication of this work will do much to revive Russell's slowly waning reputation among analytic philosophers. And one can only speculate on what the course of analytic philosophy might have been, if this book had been completed and published in 1913.[15]

Notes

1. The first six chapters appeared as the following six articles: (1) "On the Nature of Acquaintance (1)," *Monist* 24 (Jan. 1914):1-16; (2) "On the Nature of Acquaintance (2)," *Monist* 24 (Apr. 1914):161-87; (3) "On the Nature of Acquaintance (3)," *Monist* 24 (July 1914):435-53; (4) "Definitions and Methodological Principles in the Theory of Knowledge," *Monist* 24 (Oct. 1914):582-93; (5) "Sensation and Imagination," *Monist* 25 (Jan. 1915):28-44; (6) "On the Experience of Time," *Monist* 25 (Apr. 1915):212-33.
The first three articles are reprinted as a single unit under the title "On the Nature of Acquaintance," in B. Russell, *Logic and Knowledge*, ed. R. Marsh (London, 1956).

2. For an account of the discovery and identification of the manuscript and for the development of the projected table of contents, see Kenneth Blackwell and Elizabeth Ramsden Eames, "Russell's Unpublished Book on the Theory of Knowledge," *Russell* 19 (Autumn 1975):3-14, 18.

3. B. Russell, "The Philosophy of Logical Atomism," *Monist* 28 (1918):495-527; 29 (1919):32-63, 190-222, 345-80. Reprinted in Russell, *Logic and Knowledge*, pp. 175-283.

4. B. Russell, *The Problems of Philosophy* (Oxford, 1959), pp. 91-100.

5. N. Wiener, "A Simplification of the Logic of Relations," *Proceedings of the Cambridge Philosophical Society* 17 (1914):387-90.

6. B. Russell, "On the Relations of Universals and Particulars," *Proceedings of the Aristotelian Society*, n.s. 12 (1911). Reprinted in Russell, *Logic and Knowledge*, pp. 103-25.

7. G. E. Moore, *Some Main Problems of Philosophy*, (London, 1953), chap. 2.

8. See, for example, G. Bergmann, "Russell on Particulars," *Philosophical Review* 56 (1947):59-72, which criticizes Russell's abandonment, in his later writings, the theory endorsed here in the ms. and in "On the Relations of Universals and Particulars," cited above.

9. The two collections of notes, "Notes on Logic" and "Notes Dictated to G. E. Moore in 1914" have been published as Appendix I and Appendix II of L. Wittgenstein, *Notebooks 1914-1916*, ed. G. H. von Wright and G. E. M. Anscombe (Oxford, 1961).

10. *Ibid.*, p. 99. "There is no thing which is the form of a proposition and no name which is the name of a form."

11. In "The Philosophy of Logical Atomism" (*Logic and Knowledge*, p. 187) Russell remarks,

propositions are not names for facts. It is quite obvious as soon as this is pointed out to you, but as a matter of fact I never had realized it until it was pointed out to me by a former pupil of mine, Wittgenstein.

12. B. Russell, *The Problems of Philosophy* (London, 1912), especially chap. 12, "Truth and Falsehood."

13. B. Russell, review of A. Meinong, *Über die Erfahrungsgrunde unseres Wissens*, *Mind* (1906):412-15.
14. B. Russell, *The Analysis of Mind* (London, 1921).
15. The manuscript from 1913 now rests in the Bertrand Russell Archives, McMaster University, Hamilton, Ontario.

What *Was* Russell's Neutral Monism?

MICHAEL LOCKWOOD

I

My aims in this article are twofold. First, I wish to correct what I believe to be a widespread misconception as to what Russell meant by *neutral monism* — a misconception which has contributed, I think, to rendering the mature form of that theory unintelligible to many of his commentators. Secondly, I wish to set out the mature version of the doctrine in as sympathetic a fashion as possible, with an eye to examining its bearing on the contemporary debate between advocates and opponents of the so-called identity theory.

What, then, is neutral monism? Well, I propose to take as canonical, here, the passage in Russell's *The Analysis of Mind* (1921) where he first expresses his adherence to the view:

> The stuff of which the world of our experience is composed is, in my belief, neither mind nor matter, but something more primitive than either. Both mind and matter seem to be composite, and the stuff of which they are composed lies in a sense between the two, in a sense above them both, like a common ancestor.[1]

Now for the misconception. A couple of examples will suffice. Ayer, in his *Russell and Moore: the Analytical Heritage* (1971), having quoted the first of the above two sentences from Russell, immediately goes on to say:

> This more primitive stuff was thought by him to consist mainly of the sense-data, or sensibilia, out of which he then believed the physical world to be constructible. These elements were also supposed to enter into the construction of the minds, so that one and the same sense-datum might, as a member of one group, be a constituent, say, of a table, and as a member of another group, be a constituent of a mind in whose biography a perception of the table occurred.[2]

Even as a statement of what Russell did then think, the foregoing is, I believe, somewhat misleading—given Ayer's tendency to equate sensibilia (a term that is drawn, in any case, from an earlier work of Russell's) with Goodmanian qualia. I shall return to this presently. My main quarrel with Ayer consists, however, in the fact that he presents this as a *gloss* upon Russell's statement of neutral monism. Thus, as the subsequent discussion makes abundantly clear, anything in Russell's later writings that is seen to depart from Ayer's description is taken *ipso facto* as representing a departure from neutral monism. Ayer is consequently obliged to interpret one statement after another in *The Analysis of Matter* (1927) as "at variance with neutral monism"[3]—deviating, as these statements plainly do, from the view Ayer credits Russell with in *The Analysis of Mind*—in spite of the fact that Russell evidently still *thinks* of himself, in the later work, as professing neutral monism.

Very similar in spirit to Ayer's gloss is the following passage from Stace, to be found in his contribution to the Schilpp volume on Russell:

> Neutral monism appears to be inspired by two main motives. The first is to get rid of the psycho-physical dualism which has troubled philosophy since the time of Descartes. The second motive is empiricism. The 'stuff' of the neutral monists is never any kind of hidden unperceivable 'substance' or *Ding-an-sich*. It is never anything which lies *behind* the phenomenal world, out of sight. It always, in every version of it, consists in some sort of directly perceivable entities—for instance, sensations, sense-data, colours, smells, sounds. Thus, if matter is wholly constructed out of any such directly experienceable stuff, there will be nothing in it which will not be empirically verifiable. The same will be true of mind.[4]

Having characterized neutral monism in these terms, Stace, like Ayer, is then debarred from seeing *The Analysis of Matter* as presenting a consistently neutral monist position; "*The Analysis of Matter*," he says, "though it is true that it contains some elements of neutral monism, belongs on the whole to a later phase of Russell's thought, in which scientific realism and the causal theory of perception have finally gained the upper hand." He concedes that "Russell himself does not recognize that there is any important difference between what I would thus distinguish as two phases of thought" but, undeterred by this, rules explicitly that *The Analysis of Matter* is to be "excluded from consideration" in his own treatment of neutral monism.[5] Russell's reaction, in his "Reply to My Critics" is a mixture of regret and sheer bafflement:

> I am rather sorry that he excluded *The Analysis of Matter* from the scope of his discussion, because, although there is some change of view in this book, in the main there is a fuller and more careful statement of theories not very different from those of *The Analysis of Mind*. I cannot understand why Mr. Stace holds that neutral monism must not regard physical objects as causes of sense-data.[6]

With respect, I suggest that Russell simply must be allowed to be a better judge of what he himself understood by 'neutral monism' than are Stace or Ayer. So what has gone wrong here? Well, two things, I believe. First, I think Stace and Ayer underestimate the shift in Russell's thinking which took place between 1914 and 1919; accordingly, they both try to read into *The Analysis of Mind* views that Russell advances in such works as "The Relation of Sense-data to Physics" and *Our Knowledge of the External World*, but had abandoned by the time he embarked on the later book. Secondly—and this error is a straightforward consequence of the first—they are led to see the quasi-phenomenalism which was a feature of Russell's thinking in the earlier period as at least partly *constitutive* of what he was subsequently to refer to as neutral monism. They fail, that is, to appreciate the extent to which neutral monism, as Russell understands the term, is itself intended to be neutral as between phenomenalism and scientific realism. Neutral monism, after all, is characterized by Russell as the view that mind and matter are both composed of some neutral "stuff." Compatibly with holding *this*, one could hold any of a number of divergent opinions on what, precisely, this neutral stuff consisted in.

II

The line of thought that was to culminate, for Russell, in neutral monism had already, in 1914, advanced to the following point. It is a truism that objects appear differently as observed from different points of view. But the differences are systematic; in the case of vision, for example, they may be described in terms of the laws of perspective, Suppose, now, we take sense-data as primitive, subsuming them, however, into a broader class of entities, whose membership also includes things designed to stand proxy for sense-data with respect to points of view not occupied by any actual percipient. I deliberately refrain, for the moment, from saying anything about how these surrogate sense-data should be conceived. For this, crucially, is a matter on which Russell was to hold different views at different times. In any event, it is this broader class of entities, referred to by Russell as "appearances" in *Our Knowledge of the External World* and *The Analysis of Mind*, that constitute the neutral stuff out of which material objects, the space in which they are situated, and the time through which they persist are to be constructed, and which enter also into the composition of minds. A material object at a time Russell identifies with the set of all appearances that would normally be said to be "of" the object in question. The laws of perspective impose a natural ordering on this set such that the various appearances may be seen as grouped around a common center; this we equate with the momentary position of the object. A material object over time is then construed as a spatio-temporally continuous series of such appearances. Assuming—and Russell recognizes that it *is* an assumption—that "there is only one way of grouping appearances so that the resultant things obey the laws of physics,"[7] this, in theory at least, will enable us to select, from among the virtual infinity of such series, those which are to be equated with persistent objects.

It is also possible, however, to group together those simultaneous appearances of different objects which we would normally regard as being their appearance "from" a single point of view. Russell once again allows the laws of perspective (and their non-visual counterparts) to provide the principle of collection and dubs the corresponding set of appearances a "perspective." A perspective comprising as elements only actual sense-data may be equated with the sum total of a person's perceptual experiences at a time. On the basis of memory and perhaps other relations of psychological continuity, we may say of one such perspective that it comes before another in the corresponding (experienced) time ordering. A series of perspectives that is closed under these relations Russell terms a "biography." Biographies composed of perspectives whose elements are sense-data will correspond to a person's perceptual experiences throughout his or her lifetime. But, like sense-data themselves, biographies of this kind are regarded by Russell as merely special instances of a wider class; for Russell, there are also biographies, the component perspectives of which comprise appearances that are not sense-data, and which do not, therefore, correspond to any chain of actual experiences. I omit (as does Russell, in most of his writings) the details of the construction; Russell presumably looks, here, to non-psychological analogues of memory and the like. Suffice it to say that each biography has its own internal temporal ordering, just as each perspective has its own internal spatial ordering. A common space and shared time are accordingly constructed, on the basis of the orderings between and correlations among perspectives and biographies respectively. Once again, the twin guiding principles are that we should preserve (as far as is possible) spatio-temporal continuity and that we should seek a system that *in toto* allows of description by maximally simple causal laws. The project is reminiscent of Leibniz, but as Russell stresses, his perspectives, unlike Leibniz's monads, are not conceived of as "windowless": they are assumed to stand in certain causal relations, and it is by requiring these relations to conform to certain constraints that the ordering is supposed to be effected.

Since, as I said, all this dates from 1914 (Russell says, in fact, that most of these ideas came to him on New Year's Day[8]), Stace and Ayer are to that extent justified, in their respective discussions of neutral monism, to refer to works that were written and published in that year, to wit *Our Knowledge of the External World* and "The Relation of Sense-data to Physics." Ayer is wrong to speak, as he does, of "the neutral monism which Russell . . . expounded in *Our Knowledge of the External World* and in two of the essays collected in *Mysticism and Logic*" (meaning thereby "The Relation of Sense-data to Physics" and "The Ultimate Constituents of Matter").[9] For, as Stace acknowledges, Russell was not yet a neutral monist when he wrote these works. Nevertheless, many of the central notions are already in place. Most importantly, a sense-datum is already being construed by Russell as neither essentially mental nor essentially material; *qua* element of a set of appearances constitutive of a physical object at a time, it is to be regarded as material, but *qua* element in a perspective constitutive of a person's simultaneous perceptual experiences, it may be regarded as mental. Russell's position, in the period 1914 to around 1919, fell short of being neutral monist only insofar as he had not yet rid himself of the perceiving or experiencing subject: a sense-datum is still, for Russell, the object of a two-term relation of which the self constitutes the first term. Only when, in *The Analysis of Mind*, Russell makes the further Humean step of construing minds as constituted wholly of "bundles" of experiences, perceptual and otherwise, does he come to describe his position as neutral monist. And at this point, incidentally, he drops the expression 'sense-datum'. Since a datum means, literally, something that is given, Russell presumably judged the term inappropriate in the absence of an independently existing *recipient*. Accordingly, Russell speaks, instead, simply of "sensations" (in *The Analysis of Mind*) and then of "percepts" (in *The Analysis of Matter*).

I suggested earlier that it was exegetically inappropriate, on Ayer's part, to employ the term 'sensibilia', by way of exposition of the views Russell advances in *The Analysis of Mind*. We are now in a position to see why. Drawn, as it is, from "The Relation of Sense-data to Physics" (an article Russell wrote early in 1914), the notion of a "sensibile" strictly speaking *makes sense* only in the context of a theory that gives central place to the concept of the conscious subject, logically independent of its objects of awareness; whereas the main burden of Russell's argument in *The Analysis of Mind* is to show that we need have no recourse to any such concept.

Russell expressly leaves open, in "The Relation of Sense-data to Physics," the question whether his sensibilia should or should not be conceived in realist fashion. There is some talk of unsensed sensibilia as a mere "aid in preliminary statement" and "a hypothetical scaffolding to be used while the edifice of physics is being raised, though possibly capable of being removed as soon as the edifice is completed."[10] But these are merely gestures in the direction of a phenomenalistic program which Russell does not even begin, in the article, actually to execute. Provisionally, at any rate, sensibilia (except where sensed by oneself) are assigned the status of inferred entities rather than logical constructions. As such, they are the stuff of the physical world and include sense-data among their number. On this theory, a sense-datum is merely a sensibile that stands to some conscious subject as an object of awareness, just as a husband is a man who stands to some woman in the relation of matrimony. (The analogy is Russell's.)

Ayer seems puzzled by this: "if sense-data are existentially dependent on the presence of observers," he objects, "they cannot exist, in the absence of observers, as unsensed sensibilia." But that is to misunderstand Russell's view. One might just as well say: "if husbands are existentially dependent on wives, they cannot exist, in the absence of wives, as unmarried men." It is unclear what Ayer takes himself to mean by 'existentially dependent' (it is not Russell's phrase); but in any event, Russell did not think that the existence of a sensibile that in fact stands to an observer in the relation required to make it a sense-datum *logically* required there to be such a subject, any more than the *existence* of a man who is in fact married is logically dependent on the existence of some woman whose husband he is. But Russell did think it highly probable that the existence of such a sensibile *causally* required the presence of appropriate, and appropriately functioning, sensory apparatus and that—again as a matter of scientific fact—wherever one had that one would *a fortiori* have a conscious subject. Russell is quite explicit, however, that if, *per impossibile*, there could be a "zombie" that differed from an actual human being *solely* in being associated with no conscious subject, its brain would contain unsensed sensibilia identical in their intrinsic character to the sense-data of this zombie's conscious counterpart, and numerically identical to the sense-data that the zombie's brain *would* have contained, had *it* been conscious.[11]

I have no wish to assess the merits or demerits of this theory. One point, however, may be deserving of emphasis. Ayer speaks of "a difficulty about sensibilia." Supposing Russell to understand by sensibilia "what would be presented to an . . . observer who . . . had the appropriate point of view," he raises "the objection that the character of a perspective is supposed to depend not only on the location but also on the physical condition of the observer, and that there is no reason to assume that all hypothetical observers would be in the same physical condition."[12] Ayer thinks that there is a circularity in the procedure, if we must appeal to physical condition and spatial location in the very specification of those elements out of which physical objects and space itself are to be constructed. Maybe so. But Ayer is laboring under a serious misapprehension if he thinks that the existence or character of unsensed sensibilia is a function of how things would look to an appropriately situated observer. Were that the case, one could satisfy one's curiosity regarding the sensibilia presented at a (relatively unchanging) region of space, hitherto unoccupied by any actual observer, simply by taking up position there. On Russell's view, however, this would fail, *precisely because one would be obliged to carry one's body with one!* That is what Russell is driving at, when he speaks of the "causal dependence [of] the appearance which a thing presents to us . . . on the sense-organs, nerves and brain":

> We have not the means of ascertaining how things appear from places not surrounded by brain and nerves and sense-organs, because we cannot leave the body; but continuity makes it not unreasonable to suppose that they present *some* appearance at such places. Any such appearance would be included among *sensibilia*.[13]

Since the impossibility, here, would seem to be an impossibility in principle, this is a somewhat bizarre thing for Russell to say, in an article that places such repeated emphasis on "empirical verification." But say it he does; and here, as we shall see, we have a striking anticipation of one of the main lines of thought in *The Analysis of Matter*. It is tempting, no doubt, to dismiss the above remarks out of hand, on the grounds that it is sheer nonsense to ask how things "appear" from places, and under circumstances, in which there could, *ex hypothesi*, be nothing for them to appear *to*. But that, I think, would be too swift. "Appearance," here and in several later works, is clearly being employed by Russell in a technical sense: no manifest absurdity results if we interpret it roughly along the lines of Russell's explication of the term in *The Analysis of Mind*, which will be quoted shortly. No: what, if anything, is objectionable here is the entire theory according to which sense-data are, in effect, construed as (in the logical sense) external objects of awareness, rather than as internal to, and hence logically inseparable from, the perceptual experiences in which they figure. But to say that, of course, is to recapitulate the very reasons that led Russell himself to abandon these views in favor of the doctrines expounded in *The Analysis of Mind*; and there, significantly, talk of "sense-data" is *terminologically* subsumed into talk simply of "sensations."

III

Stace tells us that "in the first edition of *Our Knowledge of the External World* . . . there now appears for the first time the more or less phenomenalistic theory of matter which was later, in *The Analysis of Mind*, to be incorporated into the author's neutral monism."[14] The first part of this statement is, I think, true. Certainly, in *Our Knowledge of the External World*, we find Russell making many of the stock phenomenalist moves—albeit somewhat tentatively. Thus, taking as his example a pair of blue spectacles, he says:

> If now we find a blue patch moving . . . in sight-space, when we have no sensible experience of an intervening tangible object, we nevertheless infer that, if we put our hand at a certain place in touch-space, we should experience a certain touch-sensation. If we are to avoid non-sensible objects, this must be taken as the whole of our meaning when we say that the blue spectacles are at a certain place, though we have not touched them, and have only seen other things rendered blue by their interposition.[15]

Elsewhere, he says that "the only justification possible [of the truth of physics] must be one which exhibits matter as a logical construction from sense-data."[16] "Ideal" appearances, corresponding to "how things would appear to a spectator in a place where, as it happens, there is no spectator" or "at times when, in fact, they are not appearing to anyone" are both, he thinks, "capable of being exhibited as logical functions of sense-data"; and from them, in turn, one may sequentially construct "ideal" perspectives, "ideal" states of things, and "ideal" things. Russell clearly has in mind some process of continuity-preserving interpolation; there is supposed to be some analogy, here, with the method whereby "ideal" points and lines are constructed in projective geometry. At any rate, it is, Russell insists, a matter of construction, rather than inference:

> Ideal appearances, states and things, since they are calculated, must be functions of actual appearances, states and things; in fact, ultimately, they must be functions of actual appearances. Thus it is unnecessary, for the enunciation of the laws of physics, to assign any reality to ideal elements: it is enough to accept them as logical constructions, provided we have means of knowing when they become actual. This, in fact, we have with some degree of approximation; the starry heaven, for instance, becomes actual whenever we choose to look at it.[17]

Russell was hardly a consistent, and certainly not a dogmatic, proponent of phenomenalism in *Our Knowledge of the External World* (even of this rather hand-waving variety). Thus, the passages I have quoted must be set against such assertions as that, if a man comes newly to occupy a particular position in a room, "we can reasonably suppose that *some* aspect of the universe existed from that point of view, though no one was perceiving it."[18] Also, he says that "it is open to us to believe that the ideal elements exist, and there is no reason for *dis*believing this" though "we cannot *know* it."[19] What *I* am concerned to question, however, is whether Stace is correct in thinking that the Russell of *The Analysis of Mind* was any kind of phenomenalist at all.

There are, to be sure, certain passages in this work which, taken out of context, might seem to reflect a broadly phenomenalist outlook:

> Instead of supposing that there is some unknown cause, the "real" table, behind the different sensations of those who are said to be looking at the table, we may take the whole set of these sensations (together possibly with certain other particulars) as actually *being* the table. That is to say, that table . . . is the set of all those particulars which would naturally be called "aspects" of the table from different points of view.[20]

As he says, Russell still wishes, as in the earlier works, to regard a material object as a logical construction out of those "aspects" or "appearances" which would normally be regarded as aspects or appearances *of* the object in question. But, of course, everything now hinges on how we are to understand "aspects" and "appearances." "In order to eliminate the reference to our perceptions which introduces an irrelevant psychological suggestion" (hardly a promising opening from the standpoint of a phenomenalistic interpretation), Russell cites by way of illustration of what he means by an aspect or appearance "a photographic plate exposed on a clear night [which] reproduces the appearance of the portion of the sky concerned," and goes on to say that "if we assume . . . the continuity of physical processes, we are forced to conclude that at the place where the plate is, and at all places between it and a star which it photographs, *something* is happening which is specially connected with that star . . . [W]hen I speak of 'appearances', " Russell continues, "I do not mean anything that must appear to somebody, but only that happening, whatever it may be, which is connected with a given physical object—according to the old orthodox theory, it would be a transverse vibration in the aether . . . A piece of matter, according to the definition I propose, is, as a first approximation, the collection of all those correlated particulars which would normally be regarded as its appearances *or effects* in different places" (my italics).[21]

The "more or less phenomenalistic theory" which Stace claims to find in *The Analysis of Mind* is not much in evidence here. On the contrary, it sounds as though what Russell is advocating is straightforward scientific realism—albeit a realism of "happenings," rather than material objects. This interpretation is reinforced by the following consideration. In *The Analysis of Matter*, which is, after all, described by Russell in his *Autobiography* as "in some sense a companion volume to *The Analysis of Mind*,"[22] Russell explicitly considers a phenomenalism that would treat unsensed appearances as merely "ideal," cashing them out in terms of what would be observed by suitably situated observers; and he cites among his grounds for rejecting such a view both physical continuity, on the one hand, and the evidence of cameras, dictaphones, and so forth, on the other.[23] There he appears simply to be repeating arguments already presented in *The Analysis of Mind*, both in the passage from which I have quoted and elsewhere, where they are presumably designed to support a similar conclusion.

Russell does, of course, say, in the above passage, that what he is presenting is only a "first approximation" to his view. So, in fairness, we should perhaps examine the more refined theory. Where the latter differs from Russell's looser statement is in defining a material object, not in terms of its actual appearances, but in terms of the 'regular' appearances which it would present, were it in a non-distorting medium, simply obeying the laws of perspective (and their non-visual counterparts). This set is avowedly hypothetical, and that, possibly, is one of the things that leads Russell to refer to matter as a "logical fiction."[24] But I do not see that it has anything essentially to do with hypothetical *perception*—as opposed, anyway, to the hypothetical operations of cameras or dictaphones. Elsewhere, Russell suggests that we simply equate these "regular" appearances with the limiting set of actual appearances which the object presents from points of view that approach arbitrarily close to the position where we should normally speak of the object as being (with any distorting effects of the medium correspondingly becoming negligible). In any event, Russell's appeal to "regular" appearances, in *The Analysis of Mind*, no more represents a departure from realism, as far as I can judge, than does Newton's appeal to the hypothetical state of rest or constant motion in a straight line, which would supposedly characterize an object on which, *per impossibile*, no external force was acting. And its conceptual role is not dissimilar.

Since it is Russell's advocacy, in *The Analysis of Matter*, of both scientific realism and the causal theory of perception which, in Stace's view, renders the philosophical tenor of this work inconsistent with neutral monism, what theory of perception, one wonders, does Stace see Russell as maintaining in *The Analysis of Mind*? Russell could not, one might suppose, hold literally that the sensation which, together with an interpretative penumbra, constitutes the "perception" is *caused by* the physical object that is ostensibly perceived. If, adopting Russell's "first approximation," we identified the object with the sum total of its appearances, of which the sensation in question is merely one, this would cash out, nonsensically, as the view that this set of appearances is the cause of one of its elements. From the standpoint of the refined theory, on the other hand, it would amount to the view that the sensation was caused by a set of hypothetical "regular" appearances, to one of which it imperfectly corresponds; and this is scarcely less absurd. What Russell actually says is, nevertheless, along these lines. When, as will generally be the case in practice, the appearance involved in a perception is (to some degree) irregular, it "may be regarded as caused by the regular appearances, and therefore by the object itself, together with the modification resulting from the medium"; in an ideal case, where the appearance involved in the perception of, say, a star is regular, "it is due to the star alone, *and* is actually part of the star" (my italics).[25] Russell, characteristically mixing modes of speech appropriate, respectively, to the vulgar and the learned (as Berkeley would say), is apparently quite undisturbed by the extreme queerness of what he finds himself saying. What he should have said, presumably, is that the appearance presented in perception belongs to, and has as causal antecedents the remaining members of, a spatio-temporal series of appearances that approximates to an ideal series such as would obey the laws of perspective (which latter we may identify with the object perceived), and departs from it in a manner causally explicable in terms of the medium that it spans. (But, in Russell's writings, the desire for accuracy is hardly ever so strong as to lead him to express himself in so cumbersome a fashion.)

At any rate, Russell's theory of perception *is* causal. So if I am right also in imputing to the Russell of *The Analysis of Mind* a form, at least, of scientific realism, it would seem that the same grounds that led Stace to reject *The Analysis of Matter* as generally inconsistent with neutral monism should have led him, likewise, to exclude the earlier work from consideration. Only then, of course, Stace would have been forced to conclude that Russell was never, in his published writings anyway, an adherent of neutral monism at all.

IV

To summarize, then. *Pace* Stace and Ayer, not only does no part of the *definition* of neutral monism in any way require that it be even quasi-phenomenalistic, there is no phase of Russell's intellectual development at which he would simultaneously have considered himself a neutral monist and any kind of phenomenalist at all. Neutral monism and phenomenalism are both logically independent and, in the history of Russell's thought, temporally non-overlapping doctrines. Dogmatic though it may sound, this conclusion is fully borne out, not only by the internal textual evidence that I cited in Section III, but by Russell's own account of the course of his philosophical reflections on the external world, in *My Philosophical Development* (1959). What he says, in effect, is that he flirted briefly with phenomenalism in 1914, and "suggested it as a possibility" in *Our Knowledge of the External World*, but "soon became persuaded that this is an impossible programme." "Accordingly," he says, "I gave up the attempt to construct 'matter' out of experienced data alone, and contented myself with a picture of the world which fitted physics and perception harmoniously into a single whole."[26] This, remember, was at a time when his continued belief in an irreducible subject of awareness stood in the way of his adoption of neutral monism. By the time he had come round to thinking of the mind itself as no more than a logical construction out of sensations, images, and the like, phenomenalism had long since been displaced, in Russell's thinking, by scientific realism and the causal theory of perception.

The Analysis of Matter represents, *par excellence*, an expression of this later view. And, indeed, an examination of this work fully bears out Russell's claim, in reply to Stace, to have given there "a fuller and more careful statement of theories not very different from those of *The Analysis of Mind*" —assuming, that is, that

WHAT WAS RUSSELL'S NEUTRAL MONISM? 153

our interpretation of the earlier book is correct. Russell's thinking has now come to be dominated by the general theory of relativity (of which he attempts one of the most technical "popular" expositions that I have ever encountered, including a first course in tensor calculus). The neutral stuff of the earlier works is accordingly equated with a manifold of Einsteinian "events," or space-time regions, which includes "percepts" (roughly equivalent to what he previously referred to as "sensations") as a proper subset. Ordinary material objects are identified with "strings of events," conforming to certain sorts of causal law.

We may take, as our starting point, one of the most notorious assertions in this work. Much derision has been occasioned by Russell's remark, in *The Analysis of Matter*, that when a physiologist examines someone's brain, what he really sees is a part of his own brain.[27] Certainly Russell is expressing himself here (perhaps deliberately) in an unnecessarily paradoxical manner. But what he evidently intended by the remark makes perfectly good sense within the context of his own theory. Russell is presupposing a causal theory of perception according to which visually to perceive a material object is to have a visual percept (of the appropriate kind) caused (in the appropriate way) by a physical event or events that are partly constitutive of the object in question. In one sense, therefore, what the physiologist sees when he examines someone else's brain *is*, as common sense would dictate, the *other* person's brain. For *ex hypothesi* the physiologist has visual percepts that are appropriately causally related to events in that brain; therefore he may be said visually to perceive the latter; and that, after all, is precisely what the word "see" would normally be taken to mean. What Russell has done, clearly, is assign to the term "see" a sense of his own, according to which having a visual percept may also be described as "seeing" it. Now Russell is an identity theorist; for him, therefore, a visual percept just *is* an event in the brain. So it follows, in his technical sense, that to have any visual percept at all is to "see" (a part of) one's own brain. The remark, in short, is not the philosophical howler it is made out to be, so much as a pun on the word 'see'.

Russell says of physical events which are, in the ordinary sense of the term, objects of perception that they are merely "inferred" from the percepts to which they give rise. But he stresses that he is making no *psychological* claim, here. Of course we do not, in the normal run of events at any rate, engage in any *process* of inference, conscious or subconscious.[28] And of course we normally *take ourselves* to be directly acquainted with an event such as, say, the collision of two cars, when we witness it with our own eyes: phenomenologically, the external physical event *is* the object of our awareness. Russell is not denying any of this. He is insisting merely that the physical event that is the ostensible object of perception has the *logical* status of an inference. From a philosophically educated standpoint, one can be brought to appreciate that things could be with one, subjectively, just as they are when one actually is witnessing a traffic accident, even though nothing remotely resembling such an event were really occurring—even, indeed, if nothing existed beyond one's own stream of consciousness.

Percepts, as Russell understands the term, are elements in that stream of consciousness. If, indeed, a percept or group of percepts is linked to an external process or event by the right kind of causal chain, and prompts a judgment of the appropriate sort, one will take oneself to be perceiving the physical event in question, and be right to do so. But the causal chain is there; and—given that one's percept lies at one end of that chain, and the "directly" perceived physical event at the other—it is a sheer illusion to suppose that one can enjoy that kind of intimate and immediate apprehension of events in the external world that introspection affords of the events that compose one's own mental life. Nor are such epithets as "intimate" and "immediate" mere uncashable metaphors. In introspection we become acquainted with the *intrinsic* qualities of events, in a way that is, of necessity, denied us in the case of events that are merely perceived, in the ordinary sense of the term.

According to Russell, all that we can know about the physical world at large, whether on the basis of ordinary perception, common sense, or physical theory, is what, in a striking phrase, he refers to as "the causal skeleton of the world."[29] To be sure, we ascribe all manner of properties to physical objects and events. But these properties are known to us only as the "whatever it is" about these objects and events, in virtue of which they have the causal powers and dispositions called for by the explanatory role we assign them in our picture of the world. And these causal powers or dispositions all cash out, ultimately, in terms of powers or dispositions to evoke in us percepts, or conscious events generally. This may be so only at several removes; the ascribed property may be understood as that which grounds a disposition to induce in something else a property grounding a disposition to induce, and so on. But it is a condition of our knowing what we are talking about at all that this chain terminate eventually in a property understood as grounding a disposition to trigger a mental event of some kind.

This is the crux of Russell's mature position. When people find him saying that the brain is composed, in part, of thoughts, that percepts are brain events, that a person's visual space is (literally) located within his own head, they are apt to conclude either that he is just confused or that he has abandoned neutral monism in favor of some kind of crude physicalism. Neither is correct, however. Percepts must, for Russell, be in space, because they are in time and because the theory of relativity tells us that time and space are inseparable. It is a consequence of Einstein's theory that any two events between which there is a temporal interval, with respect to one set of coordinates, are spatially separated with respect to other such sets. And spatial separation obviously entails spatial location. Given, then, that percepts are somewhere, causal considerations make the brain the obvious place in which to locate them. Occam's razor then favors identifying them with neural events, rather than supposing them to exist, literally, side by side with the latter.

There are, however, two notorious difficulties that beset any such identity theory. First, little, if anything, is gained by identifying mental events with brain events, if the result of so doing is that the mind-body dichotomy simply reappears in the guise of a dichotomy between two mutually irreducible types of *property*, physical and phenomenal. Secondly, Kripke has taught us that all identities are necessary; yet we have a strong intuition that, given any brain event that is in fact associated with some mental event, the very same event could exist unaccompanied by the same, or indeed any, phenomenal correlate. We have, it is true, a similar intuition concerning, say, the heat of a piece of metal and the motion of its molecules. But there the "illusion of contingency" can be accounted for in terms of the fact that we identify heat by its contingent property of inducing in us certain sensations; and it *is* a purely contingent fact that what induces these sensations (either in general or on any specific occasion) is the motion of molecules—a contingent fact by which, therefore, we discover the necessary truth that heat is the motion of molecules. So the illusion of contingency can plausibly be explained as a consequence of our conflating the latter, necessary truth with the contingent truth on which, in the actual world, our knowledge of it is grounded. No parallel explanation of the seeming contingency of any postulated association between a given (type or token) conscious event and a (type or token) neural event could possibly be forthcoming, however. For a conscious event is not identified as *whatever gives rise* to a certain subjective impression or state of awareness; it just *is* the subjective impression or state of awareness.[30]

Unlike, say, Smart's version of the identity theory, Russell's, I believe, is capable of avoiding both these difficulties. Moreover, it can do so, I suggest, precisely because, unlike Smart's theory, which is uncompromisingly physicalist, Russell's is neutral monist and therefore non-reductionist. Let me explain. Smart's theory is vulnerable to the first of the two objections cited above essentially because he is committed to the view that, in some sense, whatever can be said truly about the world can be said in the language of physics. Phenomenal predicates are therefore an embarrassment to him. And to avoid being committed to phenomenal properties of brain events, existing in addition to the straightforwardly physical ones, he is led to invoke a most implausible theory according to which phenomenal predicates are "topic-neutral." On this view, what is being said, in effect, by someone who, while having an after-image, characterizes it in terms of the phenomenal predicate 'yellowish-orange' is something along the lines of: "*What is going on in me is like what is going on in me when* my eyes are open, the lighting is normal, etc., etc., and there really is a yellowish-orange patch on the wall."[31] We are to take this, presumably, as (in Kripke's sense) fixing the reference of the phenomenal predicate. Appealing, as it does, to *whatever* relevant similarity obtains between the having of an after-image and a certain kind of normal perception, it allows (or is supposed to allow) for the phenomenal predicate 'yellowish-orange' turning out, upon scientific investigation, actually to stand for some purely physiological property. In fact, however, this theory is unworkable—for all manner of reasons that I shall not bother to go into. (Suffice it to say that even Smart no longer believes that phenomenal predicates can successfully be handled in this fashion.)

Actually, the physicalist assumption that obliges Smart to seek some topic-neutral construal of mentalistic terms is itself very implausible, on reflection. Surely God could be possessed of a complete physical description of the universe, including a description of the most detailed workings of our brains, and still know nothing of our "inner lives"—our thoughts, feelings, emotions, and so forth. So it would seem that there was something of vital significance that, in any such purely physical description, would inevitably have been omitted. (Kripke, incidentally, has told me that, in the light of this consideration, physicalism seems to him simply a "crazy" doctrine.) I suppose the physicalist *might* insist that God, supplied with the physical description, *would* then be acquainted with our thoughts, feelings, emotions, etc., but not *qua* thoughts, feelings, and emotions. But the reply seems very lame. And besides, the semantics of the *"qua"* construction, in this sort of context, is deeply obscure.

Russell, anyway, though a scientific realist, is not a physicalist. And *his* response to the first of the two objections to the identity theory mooted above is, in a sense, the exact mirror image of Smart's. Russell, as I understand him, likewise takes refuge in topic-neutrality, in order to avoid an embarrassing dichotomy of properties. But for him, it is the *physical* predicates that are topic-neutral, not the phenomenal ones. We know something of the causal skeleton of the world, but we are ignorant as to how this skeleton is qualitatively fleshed out. Even the properties that we ascribe to things on the basis of casual observation, let alone the more rarefied properties invoked by the physicist, are known to us *solely* in terms of the niches they occupy in a causal-explanatory scheme. But the scheme itself is essentially abstract. The ostensible concreteness of the world, as perceived, the wealth of intrinsic attributes that we seem to discern in it, is really just an illusion fostered by what Hume describes as the mind's "great propensity to spread on external objects . . . any internal impressions which they occasion."[32] It is a consequence of our tendency to project onto external reality the intrinsic *phenomenal* qualities of our own percepts. And although we have fairly compelling reasons for supposing that the external physical events that are the objects of ordinary perception and the subject of scientific inquiry possess *some intrinsic qualities or other*—that, presumably, being a condition of the very existence of an objective external reality—we have no reason to suppose that phenomenal red, say, is numbered among the intrinsic qualities of the assemblage of events we think of as a ripe apple. On the contrary, it seems more probable that qualities such as this are peculiar to physical events of the kind that one finds in the visual cortex of the brain. That is what Russell means when he says (somewhat to Ayer's puzzlement) that "the physical world, it seems natural to infer, is destitute of colour."[33] The point, I should stress, is not peculiar to the secondary qualities: a similar remark would obviously be in order with regard to the phenomenal, visual *cum* tactile, sphericity of an apple. However, "The gulf between percept and physics is not a gulf as regards intrinsic quality, for we know nothing of the intrinsic quality of the physical world and therefore do not know whether it is, or is not, very different from that of percepts."[34] Russell means, of course, "the physical world beyond our own percepts"; for he wishes to treat percepts, along with thoughts, emotions, and so forth, as merely the physical events with which we are immediately acquainted, and concerning whose intrinsic quality there is consequently no mystery. This apprehension of the intrinsic quality of our own percepts and the like is, however, combined with only a rather obscure grasp of their causal relations. In that respect, at least, the knowledge imparted by physical science is superior.

Here, it seems to me, we have what Russell would almost certainly have regarded as the solution to Kripke's riddle. The mental-physical, or better, perhaps, phenomenal-physical dichotomy is on Russell's view ontologically illusory—a reflection, merely, of the epistemological distinction between immediate acquaintance or introspection, on the one hand, and ordinary perception or scientific inference, on the other. The Cartesian intuition, on which Kripke relies, according to which phenomenal qualities cannot be regarded as *of the essence* of any brain event, has, if Russell is right, a simple explanation, different from, but quite as deflating as, that which Kripke himself offers in the case of the identity between heat and the motion of molecules. Of course, the subjective impressions gained by the physiologist witnessing some cortical event under the microscope, as well as his conception of it, are logically separable from the subjective impression, or corresponding concept, of any thought, feeling, visual image, or whatever, currently being had by his subject. So the physiologist can perfectly well imagine that cortical event occurring, or imagine witnessing it occurring, without, let us say, his subject's experiencing a yellowish-orange patch in his visual field. This holds regardless of what empirical correlations he might have established. But if Russell is right, this is quite irrelevant. For, though he fails to realize it, the physiologist's conception of the cortical event is essentially abstract, and its correlation with his own visual impressions, as he witnesses it, wholly contingent. The cortical event is that, whatever it may be, which lies at the other end of the causal chain that terminates in his own visual impressions; and his conception of it tells him *nothing* about its intrinsic character, only its causal role. If, indeed, the event that initiates the causal chain terminating in his own visual impressions is itself a percept, it is essentially that; and if it has, phenomenally speaking, a yellowish-orange character, it has that essentially too. All that is genuinely contingent, in this case, is that something else might have lain at the other end of the causal chain culminating in the physiologist's visual impressions, consistently with *their* having the character that they do. Also, more drastically, that there might have been a subject which, in its conceptual aspects, and from the subjective standpoint of its practitioners, was indistinguishable from neurophysiology, but which treated a radically distinct class of events—not, indeed, including thoughts, feelings, and percepts among their number.

If Russell's neutral monism, in its mature form, has answers to offer, it is equally true that it raises questions that seem exceedingly intractable. Granted that we have no reason to believe in a radical qualitative discontinuity between the mental and the physical, how *are* we to conceive those regions of the physical universe from which we assume awareness to be absent? Does it make sense, even, to speak of intrinsic qualities that, though in some sense continuous with the phenomenal, nevertheless do not literally figure as features of a "point of view," in Nagel's sense—there being, presumably, no "what is it like to be a chair"?[35] I can only say that any view of the mind-body problem in which these do not, in some manner or other, figure as problems, as genuine *mysteries*, seems to me to that extent inadequate anyway. Whatever faults the theory may have, it is a virtue of Russell's neutral monism that it brings these problems into the open.

Notes

1. B. Russell, *The Analysis of Mind* (London, 1921), pp. 10-11.
2. A. J. Ayer, *Russell and Moore: The Analytical Heritage* (London, 1971), p. 110.
3. *Ibid.*, p. 122.
4. W. T. Stace, "Russell's Neutral Monism," in *The Philosophy of Bertrand Russell*, ed. P. A. Schilpp (Evanston, Illinois, 1946), p. 354.
5. *Ibid.*, p. 355n.
6. B. Russell, "Reply to Criticisms," in Schilpp, *The Philosophy of Bertrand Russell*, pp. 706-7.
7. B. Russell, "The Relation of Sense-data to Physics," in *Mysticism and Logic* (London, 1917), p. 173.
8. B. Russell, *My Philosophical Development* (London, 1959), p. 105.
9. Ayer, *Russell and Moore*, p. 54.
10. Russell, "The Relation of Sense-data to Physics," p. 158.
11. *Ibid.*, p. 150.
12. Ayer, *Russell and Moore*, p. 60.
13. Russell, "The Relation of Sense-data to Physics," p. 150.
14. Stace, "Russell's Neutral Monism," p. 357.
15. B. Russell, *Our Knowledge of the External World* (London, 1914), p. 88.
16. *Ibid.*, p. 106.
17. *Ibid.*, p. 117.
18. *Ibid.*, p. 95.
19. *Ibid.*, p. 117.
20. B. Russell, *The Analysis of Mind* (London, 1921), p. 98.
21. *Ibid.*, p. 101.
22. B. Russell, *Autobiography*, vol. 2 (London, 1968), p. 214.
23. B. Russell, *The Analysis of Matter* (London, 1927), p. 214.
24. Russell, *The Analysis of Mind*, p. 306.
25. *Ibid.*, pp. 134, 136.
26. Russell, *My Philosophical Development*, p. 105.
27. Russell, *The Analysis of Matter*, pp. 320, 383.
28. *Ibid.*, p. 181.
29. *Ibid.*, p. 391.
30. S. Kripke, "Naming and Necessity," in *Semantics for Natural Language*, ed. G. Harman and D. Davidson (Dordrecht, 1972), p. 340.
31. J. J. C. Smart, *Philosophy and Scientific Realism* (London, 1963), p. 94.
32. L. A. Selby Bigge, ed., *Hume's Enquiries* (Oxford, 1894), p. 167.
33. Russell, *The Analysis of Matter*, p. 264. Cf. A. J. Ayer, *Russell and Moore*, p. 122.
34. Russell, *The Analysis of Matter*, p. 264.
35. T. Nagel, "What Is It Like to Be a Bat?," in *Mortal Questions* (Cambridge, 1979), pp. 165-80.

Knowledge, Acquaintance, and Awareness

A. R. WHITE

Knowledge by acquaintance has been said (D. Pears in *Bertrand Russell and the British Tradition in Philosophy* [London, 1967], p. 72) to be "the central pillar of Russell's epistemology." In order to find out what such "acquaintance" is, I shall examine its relations to the ordinary idea of *acquaintance*, to *awareness*, with which Russell equated it, and to *knowledge*.

Although Russell traded on a supposed analogy between his use of 'acquaintance' (or 'knowledge by acquaintance') and the ordinary use of 'acquaintance', the two are quite distinct. That he traded on such a supposed analogy is clear from his introduction (e.g., KAKD., 202 and PP, 70)[1] of 'knowledge by acquaintance' and 'knowledge by description', first, as being parallel to the distinction between knowing a person or thing and knowing something about a person or thing, as when we may be acquainted with the candidate who will get the most votes in an election though we do not know who will get the most votes, and, therefore, do not know him as that man; and, second, as being parallel to the distinction between the French verbs 'connaître' and 'savoir' or between the German verbs 'kennen' and 'wissen'. For we certainly do ordinarily contrast our knowing someone, e.g., the heavyweight champion of the world, because we are acquainted with him or have met him at school, in the navy, or as a member of our club, and knowing who is the heavyweight champion of the world or that there is one; and we can have either knowledge without the other. And we do contrast the knowledge of a place of one who has been there and can, therefore, say "je connais son lieu de naissance" (or "ich kenn seinen Geburtsort") and that of one whose knowledge of it is gleaned solely from Geography text books and who can, therefore, say only "je sais son lieu de naissance" ('ich weiss seinen Geburtsort').

Furthermore, in explaining the meaning of his term 'acquaintance', Russell does contrast the acquaintance with Bismark of one who actually met the statesman and the knowledge of those of us who, being born after his death, have no such acquaintance with him, even though Russell's own mature philosophical view was that no one, with the possible exception of Bismark himself, was or ever could be acquainted with him. And just as we would not ordinarily allow that we could still be acquainted with someone or something that no longer exists, so Russell, at least in introducing his term 'acquaintance', held that being acquainted with someone or something implies knowing that he/she or it exists (PP, 70).

Admittedly also, we do ordinarily use 'acquaintance' to bring out what Russell did want to bring out, namely, that what we are acquainted with is something that we have directly experienced and not come to know at second hand. Thus we talk of being acquainted with persons and geographical locations, with feelings of joy and sorrow, with a certain type of apparatus or a procedure, method, or means of doing something, with certain practices, with works of various authors, etc., which we have personally encountered.

But here, unfortunately, any analogy between Russell's use of 'acquaintance' and the ordinary use ceases, and, hence, both his and his commentators' (e.g., Pears in *Bertrand Russell and the British Tradition in Philosophy*, chap. 6) attempts to explain the former by the latter can be misleading. For not only did Russell come both to deny that we are in his sense acquainted with the things with which in the ordinary sense we undoubtedly are acquainted, such as persons and locations, and to insist that we are acquainted with things such as everything we either experience or remember, which we could not ordinarily claim to be acquainted with, but, more important, he considered being acquainted with something to be quite different from what ordinarily being acquainted with it is, and, therefore, to be present in many cases where acquaintance, as we know it, is not present. Thus, as we shall see, he took 'acquaintance' to signify an occurrence, a momentary present contact, whereas ordinary 'acquaintance' is used dispositionally to signify a condition in which one is in relation to something. Hence I am acquainted with the heavyweight champion of the world if I made his acquaintance at some time, e.g., at school or in the Navy, whether or not I have kept up this contact and, therefore, whether or not I happen to see him, think of him, recall him, or in any way be aware of him at this or any other moment. Conversely, in ordinary use, we would not claim to be still acquainted with a temporal object, e.g., a man or a town, or even an experience like joy or sorrow, which no longer exists. There may be people alive today who were acquainted with Queen Victoria or the workings of her government, but none of them is still acquainted with her or them even at the moments when they recall them in memory. However, though Russell did on one occasion (KAKD, 198) explicitly state that "it is natural to say I am acquainted with an object when it is not actually before my mind, provided it has been before it and will be again," we shall see that this is inconsistent with many other things that he says about acquaintance. For example, it is inconsistent with his almost invariable equation of 'acquaintance" with such notions as *presentation, experience, consciousness, awareness*, and *being before the mind*, which emphasize its occurrent character. "At any given moment," he said, "there are certain things of which a man is 'aware' certain things which are 'before his mind'" (NA, 130). These are the things with which we are acquainted. Conversely, unlike the ordinary use of 'acquaintance', his use allowed that to remember or recall something dead and gone is to be acquainted with it.

Furthermore, Russell's sense of 'acquaintance' had for the same reasons an imputation of consciousness which is absent from the ordinary use. I could well have forgotten that I am acquainted with the present President of Harvard with whom, say, I was at school but to whom I have given no thought since; whereas Russell did not usually, as far as I can see, hold that I am at the moment acquainted even with all the readily recallable colors and sounds of my childhood, or all the not yet forgotten concepts of my mathematical training, though, of course, he did hold that when I do recall or think of them I am at that moment acquainted with them.

Nor does Russell's use of 'acquaintance' allow the degrees of familiarity that distinguish those who are ordinarily well, thoroughly, closely, slightly, or superficially acquainted with things like the environs of Paris, the works of Proust, or even the colors of Monet's 'Dejeuner sur l'herbe'. Indeed, Russell emphasizes (PP, 73) that as soon as one becomes acquainted with something, e.g., a color, one "knows the colour perfectly and completely" and that there is no way in which one can ever "know the colour any better." Ordinary acquaintance does not spring full blown from a first meeting with the object of acquaintance, but increases over time; so that one dates even the time when one first became acquainted with someone or something to a period, not an instant. Russell, on the contrary, insists that full acquaintance with something—which, as we saw, is the only possible degree of it—begins as soon as the object is presented to us.

If Russell's "acquaintance" is not in fact acquaintance—as, no doubt and despite his trading on the word, he would willingly accept—what, if anything, is it? Among the various ways in which he tried to explain it, three particularly stand out, namely, that in terms of *awareness,* that in terms of *experience,* and that in terms of *notice.* Since he, either explicitly or implicitly, treated both 'experience' and 'notice' as equivalent to and explicable in terms of 'awareness' and since 'awareness' is the notion that really dominated his explanations of acquaintance from his earliest to his latest writings, I shall consider these three notions in ascending order of importance, that is, in the order *experience, noticing, awareness.*

First, his use of the notion of *experience.* Although as early as the *Problems of Philosophy* in 1912, Russell does call *being aware* itself an 'experience' and, therefore, presumably would say that to be aware of something is to experience it, it is really in his "On the Nature of Acquaintance" in 1914 that the notion of *experience* comes into its own as an equivalent and explanation of acquaintance. Indeed, the third article in this series in the *Monist* is called "Analysis of Experience." The word 'experience' according to Russell (NA, 127-28) had become a technical word imported "from the language of daily life" which, despite any "vague and muddy ideas commonly called up by it," he decided to "polish" up and to look for the "central idea imbedded" in it. He immediately equated 'experience' with 'awareness' and equated the things experienced—which he said are "the things given in sensation, his own thoughts and feelings (at any rate so far as he is aware of them) and perhaps . . . the facts which he comes to know by thinking" (130, 160) — with the things of which we can be aware. And his discussion of how far experience reaches, e.g., to what is on the periphery of attention and in the immediately and remotely remembered past, is exactly the same as his usual investigations of the nature of acquaintance and awareness. Moreover, in his discussions he constantly slips to and fro between 'experience' and 'awareness', calls acquaintance the "most pervading aspect of experience" and speaks of "knowledge by immediate experience" as he had of "knowledge by acquaintance." Finally, however, in the third article of "On the Nature of Acquaintance" he explicitly states that it is better to employ a less neutral word than 'experience' and to use what he says are the synonymous words 'acquaintance' and 'awareness', generally the former (162, 166, 173-74), though in fact he continues, even in the rest of the same article, to use all three words interchangeably. Nor does this notion of *experience,* as an equivalent or explanation of acquaintance, recur importantly again, for though the word 'experience' is ubiquitous in Russell's *Inquiry into Meaning and Truth* of 1940 and is sometimes there explicitly equated with 'awareness' (e.g., 216, 219), what interested him at that time was not so much anything called "experiencing an object," but the relation between an experience, e.g., seeing something — where what is experienced is an event rather than an object, e.g., the moon's rising — and the language used to express this experience, e.g., "I see the moon rising."

Since, therefore, Russell's use of the word 'experience' was explicitly said to convey nothing further than either 'acquaintance' or 'awareness' and his emphasis on it was possibly short-lived, it would be otiose to show that his use of 'experience' neither is in accordance with its ordinary use — something he would largely admit anyway — nor throws any extra light on the nature of acquaintance.

The second of the candidates that Russell offered as an equivalent and explanation of 'acquaintance' is the word 'notice', introduced first in, and confined to, his *Inquiry into Meaning and Truth* in 1940, though still approved of in his *My Philosophical Development* of 1959, where he states quite explicitly that it was used to replace the notion of *awareness* which was itself an equivalent for *acquaintance.* In the *Inquiry into Meaning and Truth,* the notion of *noticing* is introduced (47 ff.) as an answer to the question "What must be done to an experience in order that we may know it?" and "notice" is said to be one meaning of the allegedly ambiguous word 'know'. But though Russell had said in *My Philosophical Development* that in the *Inquiry into Meaning and Truth* he was replacing 'awareness' by the undefined 'noticing', in the latter work he not only slips to and fro between the two (e.g., 216 ff.; cf. 48-52) but explicitly says that "we may take awareness [which in turn he says is an undefined term] to consist of noticing or remembering" (217). Furthermore, nearly all the characteristics he rightly attributes to the notion of "noticing" are characteristics possessed by the ordinary uses of both *noticing* and *awareness.* Thus, as he says, noticing is something that has degrees, that implies the existence of its object, that is often due to interest in such an object, that is nonverbal, and that implies both the sensible presence and the isolating of its object as well as some attention to it. The things he allows we can notice,— e.g., occurrences, events, connections, one's self speaking, that something is so—are all things of which we can be aware. Indeed, his grammatically mistaken use of present and past continuous tenses of the verb 'notice'—i.e., "I am (was) noticing"— wrongly gives to his notion of *noticing* a non-episodic character properly attributable to the ordinary use of 'awareness', but not to that of 'notice'. Similarly he also wrongly allows 'deliberately notice' (47).

It is difficult to see, therefore, why Russell bothered to replace 'awareness' by 'notice'. He himself gives no reason for this, nor does he stick at all methodically to his substitution. Moreover, 'notice' is in fact different in ordinary use from 'aware' though, as we have seen, Russell, like some other philosophers (e.g., J. Hartland-Swann, '"Being Aware of' and 'Knowing'," *Philosophical Quarterly* 7 [1957]), shows no realization of this. Also, 'notice' is, if anything, farther from both the ordinary sense and Russell's sense of 'acquaintance' than is 'awareness'.

The differences between the ordinary notions of *noticing* and *awareness* are clear enough. To notice something is to acquire knowledge of it by having one's attention caught by it; it is, therefore, to receive rather than to achieve knowledge. It is, in this respect, like *becoming aware* of something. But *becoming aware* is wider than *noticing*, for whereas we can either notice or become aware of so and so by sense, intellect, or feeling, we may become aware of, but not notice, something by hearsay or by learning it from my book. Further, becoming aware of, unlike noticing, signifies not merely the reception of knowledge through attention but some continuance of the attention. This is why 'become', 'be', 'remain', and 'cease to be' can qualify our awareness, but not our noticing, and why what we become aware of, unlike what we notice, must last for some time. I can notice, but not become aware of the fact that there was a flash or a slip. Incidentally, C. D. Broad (*Proceedings of the Aristotelian Society* suppl. vol. 2 (1919):209) takes such sudden catchings of attention as prime examples of "pure acquaintance"; though he also allows acquaintance with what continues to hold one's attention. I notice a sudden twinge but become aware only of a dull aching. To notice is to be struck by something, to become aware is to have it dawn or sink in on one. As well as some necessary continuity in the object of awareness, as contrasted with the object of notice, there is a possible continuity in awareness itself which is lacking in noticing. This is why we do not have, despite what Russell said, a present or past continuous use of 'notice', i.e., 'is or was noticing', but we do have a form 'be aware' to signify the condition we are in when we have become aware. Whereas 'being aware' might not altogether implausibly be thought to signify a state of mind—which Russell explicitly held that both it and 'acquaintance' do signify (e.g., PP, 74)—'notice' certainly could not. The truth is that 'being aware', for which Russell substituted 'noticing', is a less plausible candidate for substitution than even 'becoming aware', though to substitute 'notice' for this latter would also be a mistake.

Furthermore, 'notice' is farther both from the ordinary meaning and from Russell's meaning of 'acquaintance' than is 'being aware' mainly because *acquainted*, like *aware*, has the characteristic of being something one can both 'become' and 'be'.

And, whereas 'being aware' and Russell's 'being acquainted' imply both the posesssion of knowledge and the presence of the object known "before the mind," 'noticing' implies merely the acquisition of knowledge and the coming of the object before the mind. 'Be aware' could, at least for non-sensible objects, possibly do for Russell one job he needed 'acquaintance' to do—and which 'knowledge' and the ordinary use of 'acquaintance' also do—namely, relate him to "an object even at moments when it is not actually before my mind, provided it has been before my mind, and will be again whenever occasion arises" (KAKD, 198). 'Notice' cannot do this job, since we can only notice something at the moment it strikes our mind. Nor does 'notice' do any better than 'aware' the job that Russell wanted his word 'acquaintance' to do but which we saw is not done at all by the ordinary use of 'acquaintance', namely, express a knowledge, e.g., of the color of the table I see, which is complete and perfect as soon as I gain it (PP, 73). I gain as much or as little instant knowledge of what I become aware of as of what I notice.

Notice, it seems to me, was a last minute introduction by Russell of something that was not carefully thought out by the author; it does nothing that his lifelong notion of *awareness*, with its range over becoming and being aware, does not do better; and it is neither given a proper stipulative explanation nor acceptable as equivalent to that notion of *noticing* with which we are familiar in daily thinking.

As well as *experience* and *notice*, Russell throughout his works occasionally used the notion of *consciousness* as both an equivalent and an explanation of his *acquaintance*. Thus, as early as KAKD and in *Problems of Philosophy* (KAKD, 199; PP, 73, 77-78) and as late as his *Inquiry into Meaning and Truth* (279), both sense-data and the contents of our own mind are taken as the prime examples of what one is "acquainted with," "aware of," and "conscious of"; and frequently (e.g., NA, 164, 166) consciousness is equated with these other notions. Even later, in *My Philosophical Development* (144), *noticing*, Russell's other synonym for acquaintance and awareness, is also equated with consciousness. But since Russell never attempts any detailed analysis of consciousness or ever uses the notion much and since its differences from awareness are both small and irrelevant to our problem, it would be unprofitable to examine it further here (cf. my examination in *Attention* [Oxford, 1964], chap. 4).

Let us look, therefore, at the third and most important of the main candidates used by Russell to explain his use of 'acquaintance'. From the earliest introduction of his notion of *acquaintance* to his latest remarks about it, his primary explanation of it was in terms of *awareness*. Thus, in "Knowledge by Acquaintance and Knowledge by Description" to the Aristotelian Society in 1910-11—repeated almost *verbatim* in his popular *Problems of Philosophy* in 1912—he says that "I say that I am *acquainted* with an object when I have a direct cognitive relation to that object, i.e. when I am directly aware of the object itself" (KAKD, 197; PP, 73, 76, cf. 17); and throughout this article—and similarly in *Problems of Philosophy*—he moves easily from talking of being acquainted with something, e.g., a complex, my seeing of the sun, the sun, my desire for food, myself, etc., to being aware of it (e.g., KAKD, 198-99; PP, 76-81). This equation of 'acquaintance' and 'awareness' was continued in his 1914 *Monist* paper "On the Nature of Acquaintance," by means of, as we saw, the word 'experience'. Thus he refers to objects to which at any given moment he could, as he says, "give proper names" as "the objects of my 'awareness', the objects 'before my mind' or the objects that are within my present 'experience'"' (NA, 130). Later, in the third *Monist* article, he decides to give up the word 'experience' for what he calls "a less neutral word." "We shall," he says, "employ synonymously the two words 'acquaintance' and 'awareness', generally the former" (NA, 162; cf. MPhD, 134).

Many years later, in his *Inquiry into Meaning and Truth* of 1940, he still uses 'awareness' to do the duty of *experience* and of *acquaintance*. The word 'experience' is also employed with rather a different emphasis, and the word 'acquaintance' has now been dropped (IMT, 216 ff., 279). And although in his 1959 account of his philosophical development he points out why his views about acquaintance, awareness, and experience began to change (partly owing to his abandonment about 1919 of belief in the self as a subject, partly owing to his abandonment in 1921 of belief in sense-data, and partly owing to further changes in his thoughts at the time of his *Inquiry*), he, nevertheless, makes clear that, whatever his changed views about their analyses, he still regarded 'acquaintance', 'awareness', and 'experience' as synonyms (MPhD, 136, 140).

Apart from his many explicit remarks about the synonymity of 'acquaintance' and 'awareness', his equivalent use of the two terms is clear also from the fact that his list of the objects with which one can be acquainted is the same as his list of objects of which one can be aware. Thus we are both acquainted with and aware of sense-data (KAKD, 198; PP, 73-75; IMT, 52), introspectibles, such as my seeing the sun or desiring food (KAKD, 99; PP, 79; IMT, 205), possibly his self (KAKD, 199; PP, 79), universals (KAKD, 200; PP, 81, 158), relations (KAKD, 200; PP, 99), complexes (KAKD, 198, 200; PP, 99), facts (NA, 131), immediate past things (NA, 131), thoughts and feelings (PP, 78), the meanings of words (KAKD, 201), whatever is referred to by 'this' (NA, 168) and principles (PP, 109).

Although Russell, therefore, undoubtedly equated 'acquaintance' with 'awareness', such an equation will only throw light on the nature of acquaintance if it is clear what awareness is. In his introduction of the word 'awareness' there is no hint that he intended it to mean anything other than what it ordinarily means. Indeed, the whole manner of its introduction is clearly an attempt to explain his notion of acquaintance—which he thought, wrongly as we have seen, as itself analogous to the ordinary notion of acquaintance—in terms of some already familiar notions. Thus, in KAKD, he not only offers 'awareness' as a definition of 'acquaintance', but he both moves back and forth between the two and often uses 'being aware' to the exclusion of 'being acquainted'. There is no hint in his use of phrases like 'being aware of a complex', 'being aware of the sun', 'being aware of my desire for food', 'aware of the universal yellow', 'aware of the universal relation', etc., that Russell does not assume that this is ordinary English which his readers—more particularly the readers of his popular *Problems of Philosophy*— will understand and through it come to understand what he means by 'acquaintance'.

In his 1914 paper "On the Nature of Acquaintance" Russell admits that though he may have to "polish" the word 'experience', it is a word of common use and, more important, what he seeks in it is "the central idea embodied in the word" (NA, 128-29). And whenever he offers 'awareness' as an explanation of it, though he admits "it is very difficult to define 'awareness'" he does not suggest that it is a word with which ordinary people are unfamiliar. Indeed, he stresses that "it is not at all difficult to say that I am aware of such and such things" of which he gives instances. Even in his 1940 *Inquiry into Meaning and Truth,* though Russell starts by taking 'awareness' as undefined, there is no hint that the definition or explanation of it which he will arrive at is merely stipulative and not in accord with its actual use. Furthermore, in other parts of the same work (e.g., IMT., 50, 52, 113) and in other works (e.g., PP, 17), when he uses, rather than mentions, 'aware', he uses it in the ordinary sense, even though, partly because of his views about what this word of everyday occurrence actually does mean, he may drastically restrict the range of things of which we ordinarily believe we can be aware. There is, for example, no reason to believe that Russell thought he was using 'aware' differently in the expressions 'being aware of the sun' and 'being aware of my seeing the sun' (KAKD, 199), even though he came to believe that we can be aware of the latter but not the former.

Assuming, therefore, that Russell intended his semi-technical use of 'acquaintance' to be the same as the ordinary use of 'awareness', what light does this throw on the nature of acquaintance?

First, if Russell's use of 'acquaintance' is, indeed, the same as the ordinary use of 'awareness', his use of 'acquaintance' cannot be—as we have already seen on other grounds it is not—the same as the ordinary use of 'acquaintance', since the ordinary use of 'acquaintance' is not the same as the ordinary use of 'awareness'. This is not to deny that there are certain similarities between them. Acquainted, like aware, is something we can either be or become. Unlike 'introspecting', 'looking', or 'listening', neither 'being acquainted' or 'being aware' signifies something we do, but rather something we may become and, therefore, be as a result of something we do. Hence we cannot resolve or refuse to be acquainted or aware; we cannot be acquainted or aware badly or systematically or haphazardly; nor can we be interrupted at them. There is no answer to the bogus question why—as contrasted with how—are we acquainted or aware of so and so. Although Russell sometimes may seem to have thought that introspection is acquaintance, he probably meant that introspection was one way of being acquainted or aware of something. But neither is becoming, much less being, acquainted or aware an achievement like seeing, hearing, or in some other way perceiving. Nor do we, except in making the acquaintance of a person, try to become acquainted or aware or succeed in this. We do not use means or methods to become acquainted or aware, nor are people trained in or skilled at them. And though Russell may only have meant to say that seeing and hearing are ways in which one can become acquainted or aware of something, much of his language suggests that he thought rather that seeing and hearing were species either of becoming acquainted and aware or even of being acquainted and aware. Becoming acquainted, like becoming aware, is the reception of something. And being acquainted, like being aware, is the condition we are in because we have received it.

But despite these similarities, the ordinary uses of 'acquaintance' and 'awareness' are not equivalent. The great difference between them is, as one would expect, the same as the difference between the ordinary use of 'acquaintance' and Russell's use of it. In its ordinary use, the main ingredient of the notion of being aware is that what we are aware of is before the mind, that it holds our attention in perception, feeling, or thought, or our knowledge of its existence occupies our mind. Hence we can only be aware of it while it or our knowledge of it exists and continues to hold our attention. Our awareness is, therefore, confined to those objects, limited in number, which hold our attention at any particular time. Of these we can be acutely, keenly, or faintly aware. Although it should be stressed that attention to and awareness of things can be more or less gappy for different kinds of things, so that whereas awareness of a sound or a smell requires fairly continuous attention, awareness of the trouble we are causing others can be fairly intermittent. The main ingredient of the ordinary use of 'acquaintance', on the other hand, is that of familiarity gained by the previous presence of that with which we are still acquainted, even though that no longer holds our slightest or most sporadic attention. Hence, although acquaintance cannot, like awareness, be acute, keen, or faint, it can, unlike awareness, be thorough, superficial, close, intimate, or in detail. Awareness, but not acquaintance, can be immediate, whereas acquaintance, but not awareness, can be long-standing. I can fail to realize that I am acquainted with so and so but not fail to realize I am aware of it.

Although both acquaintance and awareness imply knowledge, just as becoming acquainted and becoming aware imply acquiring knowledge, the knowledge that one has in awareness is not on all fours with that which one has in acquaintance. To be acquainted with someone or something is not necessarily to be aware of it, nor is to be aware of it to be acquainted with it. We can be acquainted with what does not hold our attention and aware of what is a stranger to us. We can be acquainted with, but not aware of, something without knowing we are.

Since Russell's 'acquaintance' is not the "acquaintance" of ordinary use — as we showed earlier by independent means and just above by arguing that the ordinary uses of 'acquaintance' and 'awareness' are not the same, whereas Russell assumed that his use of 'acquaintance' was equivalent to the ordinary use of 'awareness' — we must now ask whether Russell was right in his assumption that his use of 'acquaintance' is equivalent to the ordinary use of 'awareness'. To this the answer is "No," because Russell's 'acquaintance', though sharing many other characteristics of the ordinary use of 'awareness', also possesses characteristics which the latter does not. Although both to be acquainted with and to be aware of something imply, on the one hand, to have some knowledge of it — at least to know it is there and, in some way, to know what it is — and, on the other hand, to have it before the mind, Russell's notion stresses the perfection, the completeness, and the immediacy of the knowledge which acquaintance is or gives whereas the ordinary notion of awareness stresses the degree to which either the object or our knowledge of it occupies our attention. 'Acquaintance' suggests that we gain or have knowledge of this object through presentation, whereas 'awareness' suggests that knowledge of this object is present to us. This is why 'acutely', 'faintly', 'clearly', 'fully', 'distinctly', as well as 'suddenly' or 'momentarily' can qualify awareness, but not acquaintance. More significant, 'uncomfortably', 'agreeably', 'pleasantly', 'painfully', and 'embarrassingly' qualify awareness because they emphasize the effects that the presence to our mind of the object itself or our knowledge of it can have on us, whereas I doubt if Russell would have qualified acquaintance in these ways, even though an experience—in terms of which he sometimes tried to explain acquaintance—can be pleasant, agreeable, painful, or embarrassing as well as faint, distinct, sudden, or momentary. Moreover, since knowledge of truths can as easily occupy our attention as knowledge of things, we can have awareness of both; but we can have Russellian acquaintance only with things, because only knowledge of things can come from presentation. Further, there is nothing in the ordinary use of 'awareness' that would confine it to the narrow range of objects, e.g., sense-data, concepts, feeling, etc., stipulated by Russell. We can, in fact, be aware not only of all these but also of physical objects, e.g., the mouse in the corner, the student in the corridor, a situation or event, e.g., the present troubles in the steel industry, the state of the economy. We can, contrary to Russell's objects of acquaintance, be aware of any truth, e.g., that the value of money is declining or that awards do not always or only go to the deserving. And because truths are possible objects of awareness, but not of Russellian acquaintance, we can be aware of, but not acquainted with, that of which our knowledge comes to us indirectly. We can, therefore, be aware of, but not acquainted with, something we read or were told or reached by various means. Further, although we can be aware of what we did in the past, as we can in Russell's sense be acquainted with what we did, to be aware of what we did is to be aware of what it is that we did, e.g., of having made a mistake in handling that situation or of having foolishly promised to write a paper for that journal, whereas to be acquainted with what we did in the past is to be acquainted with that which we did. To remember or even at this moment to recall the day you got married is in Russell's language to be acquainted with your wedding day—or at least with the sounds and colors of that day—but it is not, in ordinary English, to be aware of that day. Conversely, to be aware of the inconvenience you caused your prospective father-in-law on that day is not merely to remember it, much less to recall it, but to have the knowledge of it present to your mind. We can ask whether you remember, know, or are acquainted with the color of the car you were looking at yesterday, but not whether you are aware of it.

Nevertheless, it seems clear, not only from Russell's own explicit equation of the two, but also from the central characteristic of being a present contact, a presentation, something before the mind, which he wished to stress in acquaintance and which is undoubtedly part of awareness, together with the element of knowledge shared by both, that *awareness* is the closest notion in ordinary use to Russell's *acquaintance*. We must, therefore, ask how it is related to knowledge and particularly to "knowledge by acquaintance."

A preliminary question to be tackled, however, is how Russell saw the relation of "acquaintance" and "knowledge by acquaintance." I believe he remained ambivalent throughout his writings between regarding "acquaintance" as a kind of knowledge, namely, "immediate knowledge," and regarding it as a means by which knowledge — therefore, called "knowledge by acquaintance" — can be obtained.

First, he does not appear to have been altogether clear whether he thought that acquaintance, unlike knowledge, is something occurrent, episodic, and lasting only while its object is either presented to the mind, in perception, introspection, or, possibly, thought, or brought before the mind in memory (e.g., KAKD, 216; PP, 75-76, 80-81; IMT, 47); or that, like knowledge, it can be dispositional and, therefore, present when its object is absent. The former alternative is stressed, first, in his insistence that acquaintance is the converse of presentation and in his use of phrases like 'before the mind'. Second, the notions with which he seeks to equate and explain acquaintance, namely, experience, notice, consciousness, and awareness, are themselves either entirely occurrent, e.g., experience and notice, or predominantly so, e.g., consciousness and awareness. One cannot experience, notice, be conscious or aware of a sound, a smell, or a pain after it has vanished. Third, among the commonest examples given of being acquainted with something are the strongly episodic notions of seeing and hearing. Fourth, although Russell does count memory as a prime instance of acquaintance, he always thinks of memory as an experience, rather like actual recall, and indeed speaks of "memory-presentation" (e.g., NA, 151, 100, 171; IMT, 280). Finally, there are occasions on which Russell seems explicitly to confine acquaintance to the moment of presentation. This is particularly clear in his attempts to explain it by experience (e.g., NA, 160, 161, 167) and by the present (e.g., NA, 165-66). And in "On the Nature of Acquaintance" (148) he says, "it seems plain that . . . at the moment when I see the red, I am acquainted with it in some way in which I am not acquainted with it before I saw it, and in which I shall not be acquainted with it when it ceases to be present in memory, however much I may be able to recall various facts which would enable me to see it again if I chose."

On the other hand, Russell did on his first introduction of the notion of acquaintance explicitly stress that "it is natural to say that I am acquainted with an object, even at moments when it is not actually before my mind . . . in the same sense in which I am said to know [one thing] . . . even when I am thinking of something else" (KAKD, 198). Second, he also referred to "something with which we *are* acquainted — usually a testimony *heard* or *read*" (my italics). Third, it is difficult to suppose that in his famous slogan that "Every proposition which we understand must be composed wholly of constituents with which we are acquainted" (KAKD, 206; PP, 91), he thought that the constituents — which would usually be sense-data — had to be before our mind in perception or memory at the moment of understanding.

It is not surprising that distinguished commentators have differed on the question whether Russell did wish to confine acquaintance to what is actively before the mind (e.g., J. O. Urmson, *Philosophical Analysis*, 86, 134) or to extend it to cover what one has experienced and can remember (e.g. Pears, *Russell and the British Tradition in Philosophy*, 71, 92-93, 179-82). My own view is that Russell was not wholly consistent in this, partly because of his ambivalence about the relation between "acquaintance" and "knowledge by acquaintance." When acquaintance was predominant, he stressed the necessity of presentation—as is particularly clear in his "On the Nature of Acquaintance." When knowledge was predominant, he rightly wished to allow room for the dispositional character of the notion—as the early quotation from "Knowledge by Acquaintance and Knowledge by Description," with its analogous reference to knowledge, makes clear. It is also significant that in this quotation he refers to what it would be "natural to say"; and it is precisely the ordinary notion of acquaintance which does carry a strongly dispositional flavor.

The second main sign of ambivalence in Russell's views about the relation of acquaintance to knowledge by acquaintance is related to his views about presentation. For, whereas on the one hand he stresses the mere element of presentation in acquaintance—and later in his *Inquiry into Meaning and Truth* contrasted mere presentation with presentation plus attention—he also thought of both knowledge and acquaintance as two-termed relations between their subject and their object and regarded the relation of acquaintance as just as much 'cognitive" as the relation of knowledge (e.g., KAKD, 197; NA, 148; IMT, 11). Similarly, his view that "if I am acquainted with a thing which exists, my acquaintance gives me the knowledge that it exists" (PP, 70, 84) does not make clear whether to be acquainted is to have this knowledge or only implies it. But at least it does make clear that acquaintance without this knowledge is impossible, though such knowledge without acquaintance is quite possible. Nor is it easy to suppose that when saying "Every proposition which we understand must be composed wholly of constituents with which we are acquainted," he made any sharp distinction between acquaintance and knowledge by acquaintance.

Third, whereas, on the one hand, Russell talked indifferently of being acquainted with and knowing various kinds of objects, e.g., people (KAKD, 203-5), colors (PP, 73), things (PP, 74), and used the phrases 'acquaintance with objects' and 'knowledge of objects' interchangeably (KAKD, 216-17); on the other hand, he frequently referred to our knowledge by acquaintance of objects (PP, 61), of sense-data (PP, 74), of things (PP, 60), and of universals (PP, 158).

Fourth, the same ambivalence appears in his use of his various suggested synonyms for 'acquaintance'. Thus, on the one hand, he equates experience of things with knowledge of them (NA, 159), and on the other he refers to these as "known by experience" (NA, 162; PP, 117; IMT, 286). Equally, though he frequently said that to see or hear something, which he regarded as being acquainted with it (NA, 148; PP, 80), is to know it (NA, 143, 154; PP, 73), he sometimes both in his early (KAKD, 200; PP, 10) and usually in his later work (MPHD, 132, 134, 138; HK, 422, 430; contrast HK, 96, 98) regarded such knowledge as derived from sight or hearing or based on experience. Awareness of sense-data was sometimes called sensation, but the sense-data were said to be "immediately known in sensation" (PP, 17). We hear also both of "introspective knowledge" (KAKD, 200) and of "acquaintance by or in introspection" (PP, 76, 80). Memory too plays its part either, on the one hand, as a species of acquaintance, awareness, or knowledge (NA, 132-33) or, on the other, as a means in acquaintance or knowledge by memory (PP, 76, 80; MPH, 62). Similarly, *notice*, which was one of Russell's equivalents for *acquaintance*, is sometimes said to imply knowledge (IMT 48), but more frequently said to be one sense of 'know' (IMT, 56; MPD, 144). Yet he can also talk of knowing something by noticing it (IMT, 48). The same treatment is given to his favorite equivalent *awareness*. Not to be aware of a relation, which of course is not to be acquainted with it, is taken as equivalent to not knowing directly such a relation (KAKD, 200; cf. PP, 17 on sense-data), whereas all the things that we can either be acquainted with or know by acquaintance are things we are aware of. Some of this ambivalence is, of course, explicable by an explicit change in view. As Russell said in his *Analysis of Mind* (1921) "It might seem natural to regard a sensation as itself a cognition, and until lately I did so regard it . . . it *seems* as though the mere seeing was knowledge . . . but I think it is a mistake to regard the mere seeing itself as knowledge." Having earlier regarded sensation as the awareness of a sensedatum, he now equated the sensation with the sense-datum and therefore denied that it could be knowledge. Hence, "such words as 'awareness', 'acquaintance', 'experience' had to be re-defined" (MPD, 136). But, as my references to the use of 'awareness' and 'notice' in his *Inquiry into Meaning and Truth* make clear, the same ambivalence about the relation of knowledge to acquaintance, awareness, and notice still persisted.

Fifth, although 'knowledge', 'experience', 'notice', 'acquaintance with', and 'awareness of' are all allowed—however ungrammatical this is in the case of 'know' and 'experience'—to take nouns as their direct objects and regarded as the names of the same direct cognitive relation between what is denoted by the subject and by the object of the sentence in which they occur, the introduction of the notion of acquaintance and the titles of the papers introducing it do stress the nature of Russell's topics as being knowledge by acquaintance. Certainly, Russell never meant that 'description' in 'knowledge by description' signified "knowledge," though admittedly he does sometimes contrast 'knowledge by description' with acquaintance and not merely with 'knowledge by acquaintance' (e.g., KAKD, 217). Moreover, when explaining his contrast between knowledge by acquaintance and knowledge by description, he says, on the one hand, that "we have '*merely* descriptive knowledge' of the so-and-so, when although we know that the so-and-so exists and *although we may possibly be acquainted with the object* which is, in fact, the so-and-so, yet we do not know any proposition 'a is the so-and-so', where a is something with which we *are acquainted*" (KAKD, 202—my italics). On the other hand, on the same page he says that "an object is 'known by description' when we know that it is 'the so-and-so', i.e. when we know that there is one object and no more, having a certain property; and it will generally be implied that we do not *have knowledge of the same object by acquaintance"* (my italics). By the time of his *Inquiry into Meaning and Truth* he certainly felt that "the most immediate knowing . . . involves sensible presence plus *something more"* which he thought was probably *attention* (470-78; MPD, 142).

The truth seems to be that Russell was never entirely clear whether acquaintance was itself a kind of knowledge or a kind of means, namely presentation, by which knowledge is obtainable. And this, I think, is a fundamental reason why his technical word 'acquaintance' swayed between the dispositional use of the ordinary word 'acquaintance' and the occurrent use of the ordinary word 'attention'. It also explains why the notion of *awareness* was so attractive to him, because 'awareness' combines to a large degree both the dispositional force of 'knowledge' and the occurrent use of 'attention'. But, unfortunately, the element of attention in *awareness* is too great to allow it a complete independence of the present which is necessary for knowledge. We do not necessarily lose our knowledge of that of which we cease to be aware. Hence acquaintance cannot be the same as awareness, if acquaintance is equivalent to knowledge by acquaintance. On the other hand, the element of knowledge in awareness is too great for it to be merely a means to knowledge. Hence acquaintance cannot be the same as awareness, if acquaintance is not equivalent to, but plays only a subordinate role in, knowledge by acquaintance. In short, awareness is neither acquaintance nor knowledge by acquaintance.

To conclude: 'Acquaintance' seems not to signify the same thing when we are said to be acquainted both with what is present and with what is not present to our minds; nor, possibly, both when it has sense-data and when it has concepts for its objects (KAKD, 80; awareness of universals is 'not quite the same sense' as that of particulars; cf. Moore and Broad in *Proceedings of the Aristotelian Society* suppl. vol. 2 [1919]); nor when it relates both to perception and to memory (cf. NA, 166, "several species of the general relation 'acquaintance'"; IMT, 216, where 'aware' is given two senses); nor both when it is regarded as a kind of knowledge and when it is regarded as a means to knowledge. Moreover, it is also not equivalent to any of the notions, namely, experience, notice, consciousness, or awareness, with which Russell at various times identified it. Is there, therefore, any consolation in G. E. Moore's insistence *(Proceedings of the Aristotelian Society* suppl. vol. 2 [1919]) that, however mistaken Russell's theories about acquaintance and knowledge by acquaintance may be, there certainly is a relation of acquaintance between ourselves and our sense-data?[2]

Notes

1. I use the following abbreviations: KAKD for "Knowledge by Acquaintance and Knowledge by Description," *Proceedings of the Aristotelian Society* 2 (1910-11), reprinted in *Mysticism and Logic* (London, 1963); PP for *Problems of Philosophy* (London, 1912); NA for "On the Nature of Acquaintance," *Monist* 24 (1914), reprinted in *Logic and Knowledge*, ed. R. C. Marsh (London, 1956); IMT for *Inquiry into Meaning and Truth* (Harmondsworth, Middlesex, 1940); HK for *Human Knowledge* (New York, 1948); MPHD for *My Philosophical Development* (London, 1959).

2. I am grateful to David Pears for comments on an earlier draft.

The Vienna Circle

A. J. AYER

It is characteristic of Viennese positivism, which played such an important role in the second quarter of this century that almost no subsequent work of any philosophical interest has been unaffected by it, that its origin at the turn of the century is chiefly to be ascribed to one who was professionally a physicist rather than a philosopher. This man was Ernst Mach, who lived from 1838 to 1916. He became a Privatdozent at the University of Vienna in 1863, the year he also published his first book, a compendium of *Physics for Doctors,* having previously published half-a-dozen articles, most of which already exemplified his lifelong interest in the interconnections of physics with psychology. Four years later, before he was thirty, he was appointed to a professorship at the Charles University in Prague, where he continued teaching experimental physics for the ensuing twenty-eight years. During this period he published his two most important books entitled, in their English translations, *The Science of Mechanics* and *Contributions to the Analysis of Sensations.* They both appeared fairly late in his career, *The Science of Mechanics* originally in 1883 and the *Analysis of Sensations* in 1886, but they had been preceded by seven other books principally on optics, acoustics, and scientific methodology, and by more than a hundred published articles.

In 1895, the University of Vienna decided to institute a third Chair in philosophy, and Ernst Mach accepted an invitation to become its first occupant, on condition that he was also allowed to give lectures on psychology. He himself chose the title "Professor of the History and Theory of the Inductive Sciences," which was changed by his successor, the famous physicist Ludwig Boltzmann, to "Professor of Theoretical Physics and Natural Philosophy." Boltzmann did not sympathize with Mach's philosophy of physics, and this change of title enabled him to claim that he had no predecessor, so that he was able to avoid the courtesy of paying any tribute to Mach in his inaugural lecture. This was in 1902. Mach had suffered a stroke in 1901, which obliged him to retire from the Chair but did not prevent him from writing four more books, of which the most important is entitled, in English, *Knowledge and Error,* which appeared in 1905, and has recently been reissued by H. D. Reidel & Company as a volume in its splendid Vienna Circle collection.

Philosophically, Mach's views were very similar to those of the American pragmatist William James—the novelist Henry James's elder brother and in my opinion the better writer of the two—well, perhaps not the better writer but the more fun to read. The difference between their styles is just the opposite of what you might expect. Paradoxically, it is Henry who writes with the careful qualifications and minute attention to detail that one might expect of a philosopher, and William who carries the reader away with his humor and zest and the vividness of his imagery. William James, on holiday from Harvard, met Mach in Prague in 1882, and they took greatly to one another. Among other things, James explained Hegel to Mach. One wonders what he said, since he had a very strong distaste for Hegel's philosophy, but he may have enabled Mach to understand how this sort of monolithic idealism could be emotionally attractive to tender minds.

The philosophy that James and Mach share is one that came to be known as Neutral Monism. This was after it had been taken up by Bertrand Russell, who held it from 1914 when he published *Our Knowledge of the External World* until at least 1921 when he published *The Analysis of Mind.* Later he moved away from it in the direction of scientific realism. *The Analysis of Matter,* which came out in 1927, marks the turning point, though the old view never wholly lost its attraction for him, and he occasionally rather startlingly reverts to it. Its basic tenet is that neither mind nor matter is part of what Russell called the ultimate furniture of the world. Both are constructions out of neutral stuff—the raw material of experience— most often simply called experiences by James, sensations by Mach, and sensibilia by Russell. The first two terms are not felicitous because they suggest a subordination of matter to mind, which was not intended. James called his theory 'Radical Empiricism', and Mach acknowledged the affinity of his views to the classical British empiricists of the seventeenth and eighteenth centuries, Locke, Berkeley, Hume—especially Hume. Indeed, if one treats Hume as an analyst rather than a skeptic, an approach for which there is virtually no historical warrant but one that requires surprisingly little tampering with the text, one can make a neutral monist out of him.

The dominant idea is that the difference between mind and matter is not a difference in substance, a distinction between two different sorts of stuff, but a difference in the relations of the basic elements. One and the same experiential item, in virtue of its relations to other elements, is both a member of a class of such items which we call a physical object and a member of the series which constitutes some person's mental biography (the person himself being nothing but a fusion of two classes of these different sorts). The way it was supposed to work was vividly illustrated by William James. His example is that of a typical case of sense-perception, his reader's current perception of James's book and of the room in which he is sitting. Philosophers will be most likely to tell him that the physical objects, which he takes himself to be perceiving, are not directly presented to him; the immediate data of perception are subjective impressions to which it is inferred that external objects correspond. But the trouble with such theories, as James says, is "that they violate the reader's sense of life, which knows no intervening mental image but seems to see the room and the book immediately just as they physically exist." And what is more, it is the reader here who is right and the philosophers who are wrong. The philosophers have gone wrong because they have not been able to see how it was possible "that what is evidently one reality should be in two places at once, both in outer space and in a person's mind." This difficulty is removed once it is seen that the object's being in two different places is no more than a matter of its belonging to two different groups, or as James prefers to put it, two different processes. If only on literary grounds, it is worth quoting James's account of these processes in detail. It represents Mach's view but is expressed more racily than anything I have been able to find in Mach.

One of these processes, James explains,

> is the reader's personal biography, the other is the history of the house of which the room is part. The presentation, the experience, the *that* in short, (for until we have decided *what* it is it must be a mere *that*) is the last term of a train of sensations, emotions, decisions, movements, classifications, etc. ending in the present, and the first term of a series of similar 'inner' operations, extending into the future, on the reader's part. On the other hand, the very same *that* is the *terminus ad quem* of a lot of previous physical operations, carpeting, papering, furnishing, warming, etc. and the *terminus a quo* of a lot of future ones, in which it will be concerned when undergoing the destiny of a physical room. The physical and the mental operations form curiously incompatible groups. As a room, the experience has occupied that spot and had that environment for thirty years. [This is careless even by James's standards; what he means is that one of the groups to which the experience belongs is strung out over that period—he makes the same mistake again and one needs to make the necessary adjustments.] As your field of consciousness it may never have existed until now. As a room, attention will go on to discover endless new details in it. As your mental state merely, few new ones will emerge under attention's eye. As a room, it will take an earthquake, or a gang of men, and in any case a certain amount of time, to destroy it. As your subjective state, the closing of your eyes, or any instantaneous play of your fancy will suffice. In the real world, fire will consume it. In your mind, you can let fire play over it without effect. As an outer object, you must pay so much a month to inhabit it. As an inner content, you may occupy it for any length of time rent-free. If, in short, you follow it in the mental direction, taking it along with events of personal biography solely, all sorts of things are true of it which are false, and false of it which are true if you treat it as a real thing experienced, follow it in the physical direction, and relate it to associates in the outer world.

It can be seen now why I said that it is William and not Henry James who ought to have been the novelist. All the same, it is an attractive theory and worth working out in detail. Unfortunately, like most attractive theories in philosophy, it turns out to be false when you do try to work it out in detail. Neither Mach nor James nor Russell nor those who have worked on the theory since, including myself, have ever succeeded in specifying the relations that would have to hold between the sensory elements for them to constitute on the one hand any sort of physical world and on the other a set of mental biographies. Nor, I am afraid, is it merely a matter of incompetence. There are good reasons for concluding that such a program cannot be carried through. I do, however, still believe—I am one of the very few philosophers nowadays who does—that one can defend a rather less ambitious theory along somewhat the same lines.

But how, one may ask, did a first-rate physicist like Mach come to adopt a theory of this type? How did he deal with atoms and electrons and quanta? He died too soon to be troubled with black holes and quarks, but their arrival has not made the problem essentially different. The answer is that he took a pragmatic or operationalist view of physical theories. They were imaginative constructions, the point of which consisted in their providing you with a means of ordering your observable data and so enabling you to make successful inferences from one experimental situation to another. There was no need to suppose that the entities that figured in them really existed, any more than in applying mathematics you need to postulate the reality of a Platonic world of numbers. This approach to physics has its difficulties, though Mach is not the only physicist to have adopted it. The fashion nowadays sets toward realism—but I think that the pragmatist view is still defensible.

Five years after Mach's death, his Chair of the History and Philosophy of the Inductive Sciences was revived, and Moritz Schlick was invited to occupy it. Schlick, who was born in 1882, was not an Austrian but a German, and he too began as a physicist. His doctoral dissertation, which he completed at the University of Berlin in 1906, under the supervision of Max Planck, was about the refraction of light in a non-homogeneous medium. Although he retained an interest in physics—he wrote a paper entitled "The Philosophical Significance of the Principle of Relativity" as early as 1915 and two years later a small book, *Space and Time in Contemporary Physics,* which drew praise from Einstein—he early decided to pursue an academic career in philosophy rather than in physics and held professorships first at Rostock and then at Kiel before coming to Vienna. His philosophical interests were wide, embracing ethics and aesthetics as well as the philosophy of science and the theory of knowledge. Indeed, the first book that he published in 1908 (one of the few of his works that has never been translated) was entitled *Lebensweisheit Versuch Einer Glückseligkeitslehre* and was, as the title indicates, concerned with the pursuit of happiness. But the book that made him famous and was probably responsible for his appointment to the Viennese Chair was his *Allgemeine Erkenntnislehre (General Theory of Knowledge)* which he published in 1918, bringing out a second and considerably revised edition in 1925. Strangely, it was not until 1974 that it was translated into English.

By the time he published the second edition of this book, Schlick had been converted to a view of science which was substantially the same as Mach's, and he had also come to think, again agreeing with Mach, that the basic statements of observation were statements about sense-data. In the original edition, however, he had adopted a more realistic standpoint. He insisted that every scientific statement or theory must be capable of being verified, in the sense that it had to have consequences which were capable of corresponding to observable facts, but the observable facts could have physical objects for their constituents. He agreed with Mach in rejecting psycho-physical dualism, arguing that talking in mental or physical terms was just adopting one or other way of describing the same phenomena, but he tended to treat the phenomena as physical, in some degree anticipating the current fashion of identifying mental occurrencies with processes in the central nervous system. This was another view that he was later to revise in favor of the Machian form of monism. Perhaps the most remarkable feature of Schlick's book was that he anticipated Wittgenstein, of whom he had not then heard, though he was later to come very much under Wittgenstein's influence, in rejecting Immanuel Kant's view that there could be such things as synthetic *a priori* truths, and holding that all true *a priori* propositions, such as those of logic and pure mathematics, were analytic—that is to say, true only in virtue of the meaning of the signs that were used to express them, and consequently devoid of any factual content.

Since Schlick held regular discussions with his philosophical and some of his scientific colleagues almost from the moment of his arrival in Vienna, it is difficult to assign a precise date to the institution of what came to be called the Vienna Circle—*Der Wiener Kreis*—over which Schlick presided for the remainder of his life, but I suppose as good a date as any would be the year 1926 when Rudolf Carnap, one of the three leaders of the Circle (the third being Otto Neurath of whom I shall be speaking presently) came to Vienna.

A younger man than Schlick, having been born in 1891, Carnap was also a German and also worked on a doctoral dissertation on experimental physics, though he never completed it owing to the outbreak of the first world war in which he served as an officer in the German army. He obtained his doctorate at Jena in 1921 with a new dissertation on the topic of Space—subtitled "A Contribution to the Philosophy of Science." Like Schlick, he had been struck by the philosophical importance of Einstein's Theory of Relativity and, with the exception of one pamphlet concerning the part played by the concept of simplicity in physics, and another on the different levels of the construction of physical concepts, the passage from the qualitative to the quantitative and from the concrete to the abstract, the half-dozen articles and pamphlets which he published before he came to Vienna were all devoted to the topics of Space, Time, and Causality. His view of physics was already less realistic than Schlick's then was, and closer to that of Mach. We shall see that their positions were later reversed. Carnap had been an undergraduate at Jena and had been one of the very few students there to attend Gottlob Frege's courses on mathematical logic. Frege, who lived from 1848 to 1925 and published his most important work from the 1870s to the 1890s, is now almost universally acknowledged to have been the greatest logician since Aristotle. But he was almost totally unknown in Germany during his lifetime and unappreciated even in his own university, where he never achieved the rank of full professor. Throughout one of his courses, given in 1913, there were only three persons in the audience of whom Carnap was one. Frege's work was indeed known to Russell, who discovered a contradiction in Frege's system—the possibility of constructing in it the famous class paradox, i.e., the class of classes that are not members of themselves being a member of itself if it is not and not a member of itself if it is—and communicated it to Frege just before the publication of the second volume of Frege's magnum opus on the Foundations (Grundgesetze) of Arithmetic, a blow from which Frege never fully recovered. Through Frege, Carnap learned of Russell's and Whitehead's *Principia Mathematica* and went on to study Russell's works on the theory of knowledge, written during the period of Russell's neutral monism, and was very greatly influenced by them. Carnap had read the *Principia* when he was at Jena but did not possess a copy, and at the time of postwar German inflation could not afford to buy one. Nor could he borrow a copy from the library of the University of Freiburg, to which he had moved from Jena, since there was not any copy there and never had been. He therefore applied to Russell, who did not send him a copy but wrote Carnap a thirty-five-page letter, setting out all the most important definitions on which the proofs in the *Principia* were founded. This enabled Carnap to compile his *Abriss der Logistik* (Outline of Mathematic Logic), the first draft of which he wrote in 1924 though it was not published till 1929. It made him the first German philosopher, so far as I know, to take official notice of the expansion of logic, at least in its bearings on the foundations of mathematics, some fifty years after Frege had initiated it.

Upon his arrival in Vienna, Carnap set himself to complete the first of his major works, *Der Logische Aufbau der Welt* (The Logical Construction of the World), which appeared in 1928. Like Schlick's *Allgemeine Erkenntnislehre*, it had to wait over forty years for an English translation. An exceedingly ambitious work, displaying, as all Carnap's work did, enormous industry and exceedingly high technical accomplishment, it adopted the standpoint of what Carnap called methodological solipsism. The word 'methodological' was put in to disinfect the solipsism, but it may be doubted whether it was sufficient for the purpose. Anyhow, Carnap, following Mach, James, and Russell after his own fashion, took as his starting point the series of elements each constituting the whole of a person's current experience at a given moment, and attempted to show how the entire battery of concepts needed to describe the world could be constructed stage by stage, by the application of Russell's logic, on the basis of the single empirical relation of *Ähnlichkeitserinerung* (remembered similarity). The higher levels of the construction, the development of physical objects, and the constitution, out of a subclass of them, of other minds are sketched only in outline, and Carnap's ingenuity is mainly spent in showing how qualities like colors can be defined on the basis of the primitive relation in a purely structural extensional fashion. He did not succeed in this, as was shown some thirty years later by Nelson Goodman, in his remarkable book *The Structure of Appearance*.

Carnap did not remain long in Vienna; he and another prominent member of the Circle, the physicist Philipp Frank, both left in 1931 to take up professorships at the Charles University in Prague; but Carnap continued through his writings to exercise a predominant influence over the movement. In 1930, the Circle had taken over a journal called *Annalen der Philosophie*, renamed it *Erkenntnis*, and made it the chief outlet for the expression of their views, and Carnap continued to edit it in collaboration with Hans Reichenbach, another philosopher of physics, with a special interest in the theory of probability, who presided over a smaller group in Berlin. Carnap was also one of the three authors of the manifesto which the Circle published in 1929 under the title *Wissenschaftliche Weltauffassung—Der Wiener Kreis* (roughly translatable as Viewing the World Scientifically—The Vienna Circle). The other two authors were Hans Hahn, a professor of mathematics at Vienna University who died in 1934, and Otto Neurath, perhaps the strongest personality of them all, the most humorous and physically the largest—he used to sign his letters with a drawing of an elephant.

Neurath was not attached to the University of Vienna but was director of a Social and Economic Museum which he himself had founded in 1924. He had been born in Vienna in 1882 and educated at the Universities of Vienna and Berlin. He began by studying mathematics in Vienna, went on to linguistics, then to law, then to economics, and then to sociology. The thesis with which he obtained his doctorate in Berlin in 1906 was on the subject of the economic thought of the ancient world. The eighty articles which he published before the first world war were mainly concerned with economics, but some of them were political—displaying a strong interest in the Balkans, especially Serbia and to a lesser extent Bulgaria (they included a short piece for example, on the Bulgarian railway system)—and half a dozen of them were in the field of logic and mathematics. In the whole of his career he published only one substantial book, his *Empirische Sociologie* (Empirical Sociology) which came out in 1931 and in an English translation only in 1974, but over two hundred and seventy articles. After doing his military service in the Army Service Corps, in which he was to serve again mainly in Galicia during the war, he taught political economy at the New Vienna Academy of Commerce. He was not yet a socialist, though well schooled in the writings of Karl Marx and other socialist authors, but he joined the Social Democratic party in 1918, partly as the result of his war experiences. By the end of the war he was Director of the Museum for War Economy in Leipzig, being seconded from the Ministry of War in Vienna, and was appointed to a lectureship at Heidelberg in Max Weber's department of Sociology. He gave this up in order to serve the Socialist Government which had been set up in Bavaria with its headquarters in Munich, and was soon put in charge of its central planning. When this government was replaced by the so-called Spartacist government, consisting of Communists, left-wing Socialists, and Anarchists working for once in some sort of cohesion, Neurath stayed on. This government was soon overthrown by the reactionary Freikorps which, like their unsuccessful counterparts in Russia, were known as the White forces. Having narrowly escaped assassination by Count von Zeppelin, who subsequently made some sort of amends by marrying an American who translated Carnap's *Logische Syntax der Sprache* into English, Neurath was arrested and sentenced to eighteen months imprisonment in a fortress. But the Austrian government intervened, and the sentence was commuted to expulsion from Germany and a seven-year ban on his returning there. He remained a Socialist and drew closer to Marxism, without, however, becoming a Communist. Nearly all the members of the Circle held left-wing views, but the others did not bring them into their philosophy. Neurath alone saw the Circle as being in part a political movement. I shall have more to say later on about the subsequent course of his extraordinary career.

In the appendix to the Manifesto the members of the Circle are listed as fourteen in number. Besides those already mentioned (Schlick, Carnap, Neurath, Frank, and Hahn), they consisted of the philosophers Viktor Kraft, Gustav Bergmann, Herbert Feigl, Marcel Natkin, Theodor Radakovic̀, and Friedrich Waismann, and the mathematicians Karl Menger, Kurt Gödel, and Olga Hahn-Neurath, Hans Hahn's sister and Neurath's second wife. Bergmann and Feigl soon left to take up appointments in the United States and were replaced by Bela von Johos and Edgar Zilsel, already mentioned in the Manifesto as a sympathizer. The Circle was in close contact with Reichenbach's tiny group in Berlin—of which the most prominent members were Richard von Mises, like Reichenbach himself an ardent defender of the frequency theory of probability, the logician Kurt Grelling, and the young Carl Hempel, who later had an outstanding career in the United States—and with the more important group of Polish logicians and philosophers—of which the leading representatives were Lucasiewicz, Lesnievsky, Chwistek, Kotarbinski, Ajdukiewicz, and Tarski. It was also on the look out for what one might call likely prospects in other countries. It was, for example, my very good fortune that Schlick met my Oxford tutor Gilbert Ryle at an international congress held in England in 1930, so that two years later, when I had taken my B.A. degree at Oxford and was allowed a few months leave of absence before starting work as a lecturer, Ryle advised me to go to Vienna. He gave me a letter of introduction to Schlick which I summoned up the courage to present, calling on Schlick in his handsome apartment in the Prinz Eugen Strasse. He spoke good English (he had an American wife) and made on me above all an impression of urbanity—like an American senator in a prewar film. He graciously invited me not only to frequent the University but, what was much more important, to attend the meetings of the Circle. It was there that I first met Quine. I was just twenty-two and Quine a few years older—he had already taken his doctorate at Harvard. I remember his giving us a lecture—some sort of preliminary to his New Foundation in Logic. My own German was then too rudimentary for me to do more than vaguely follow what was going on, but I was helped by reading all the publications of the Circle that I could lay my hands on.

Apart from *Erkenntnis*, the most important source for what was going on in those early years, the Circle put out a series of monographs with the collective title *Einheitswissenschaft* (Unified Science—this was a pet idea of Neurath's, not only that philosophy was to be annexed to science but that there was no difference in method between the natural and the social sciences) and a series of books, under the general editorship of Schlick and Philipp Frank, with the collective title *Schriften zur Wissenschaftlichen Weltauffassung.* They included Neurath's *Empirische Sociologie,* a book by Schlick on Ethics, *Fragen der Ethik,* defending a form of Utilitarianism, one by Frank on *The Law of Causality and Its Limitations,* and Karl Popper's *Logik der Forschung* (translated into English over twenty years later as *The Logic of Scientific Discovery*). Popper, though teaching at a high school in Vienna at the time, was never admitted into the Circle (I do not know why—there may have been personal reasons) and has always exaggerated the differences between his views and theirs. There were differences, but only, in my opinion, of a minor character. I shall return to this briefly later on.

The first volume scheduled to appear in the series, continuing to be advertised as No. 1 even after the appearance of all the others, was Waismann's *Logik, Sprache, Philosophie,* a title from which my own *Language, Truth, and Logic* was partly plagiarized. It never did appear, mainly because of the debt which it would have owed to Ludwig Wittgenstein. To explain this I shall have to say something about Wittgenstein himself, apoligizing to those for whom it is an old story. Born in 1889, he came from a rich Viennese family—I think they largely controlled the Austrian steel industry—and studied engineering at Berlin. He then, like Engels before him, was dispatched to Manchester, where he worked on aerodynamics. This led him to take a deeper interest in mathematics, and he became aware of the work of Frege and Russell on mathematical logic. As a result, he went to Cambridge in 1912 to study under Russell. There is a story of his attending a course of Russell's lectures, never saying a word but coming up to Russell at the end of the course and saying: "Either I am a genius or I join the Austrian air force, which?" He looked a genius, but that was not quite enough for Russell, so he asked Wittgenstein to submit him some written work. When they met again at the beginning of the following term Russell said: "Don't join the air force." After that they worked on equal terms (if anything, Russell deferred to the much younger Wittgenstein—Russell himself was born in 1872) until the war when Wittgenstein fought for the Austrians —not as it turned out for their air force but as a machine gunner. He was captured by the Italians, allegedly after the Armistice, and was held as a prisoner of war well into 1919.

Two important things happened to Wittgenstein during the war. The first was that he decided, some say as a result of reading a work of Tolstoy's, that it was wrong for him to be so rich and gave all his money away. (A story which I have heard but do not vouch for is that he did not give it to the poor, since that would corrupt them, but to his sister who had a rich husband besides being rich in her own right, so that a third fortune could not do her much harm.) The second more important event was the completion of the only book he published in his lifetime— the famous *Logische-Philosophische Abhandlung* (Tractatus-Logico Philosophicus in the English version), which appeared as a lengthy article in the *Annalen* in 1921 and was published in England in 1922 with the German text and English translation by C. K. Ogden (part-author with I. A. Richards of the *Meaning of Meaning* and the inventor of Basic English) on facing pages, with an introduction by Bertrand Russell.

In view of the very great influence of the *Tractatus*, almost immediately on the Vienna Circle and eventually on the younger generation of British philosophers, it is worth giving a very brief summary of its central ideas. They were that the world consists of what in the original translation were called atomic facts (*Sachverhalten* — a better rendering would have been states of affairs), which are logically independent of one another. These basic facts are mirrored by elementary propositions. To have any literal significance a sentence must express either a true or false elementary proposition or one that assigns a certain distribution of truth or falsehood to the elementary propositions. There are two limiting cases. A proposition may disagree with all the elementary truth-possibilities, in which case it is a contradiction, or it may agree with them all, in which case it is a tautology. The true propositions of logic were tautologies and so virtually were the propositions of mathematics, though Wittgenstein preferred to call them identities. They could be useful in inference but in themselves said nothing about the world. Anything else that failed to satisfy these conditions of meaning (and this included all transcendent discourse whether religious, moral, or metaphysical) was a pseudo-proposition — a piece of nonsense. This included philosophy too, which was not a body of doctrine but an activity, the activity of clarifying what could be said and preventing the expression of what could not. There was a mystical strain in Wittgenstein which led him to hint at the existence of things outside the reach of language. In some cases, such as the relation of language to the non-linguistic facts, what could not be said could be shown. This partly emerges in the formulation of the famous concluding sentence of the *Tractatus:* "*Wovon man nicht sprechen kann darüber muss man schweigen*" — what we cannot speak about we must consign to silence — provoking from Neurath the characteristically robust comment: "*Man muss ja schweigen aber nicht über etwas*" — We must indeed be silent but not about anything — a point still better put by Ramsey as "What you can't say you can't say and you can't whistle it either."

After publishing the *Tractatus* Wittgenstein became a schoolmaster at a place called Trattenbach in the mountains, a four-hour train journey south of Vienna. The boys seem to have liked him, though he was eventually accused of beating them too hard, but the villagers did not, nor he them. He wrote to Russell that the men of Trattenbach were the wickedest in the world, a proposition which Russell found improbable. They did, however, succeed in making Wittgenstein's position at the school untenable, and he returned to Vienna to become an architect. I do not know that he ever collaborated on any building except a house for his sister which is now the Bulgarian Embassy. It was in the style of Gropius. About 1925 his interest in philosophy revived and he made contact with Schlick, Carnap, and Waismann. In 1919 he was persuaded to return to Cambridge as a Fellow of Trinity, succeeding G. E. Moore as a Professor in 1939 and holding the Chair till ill-health forced him to resign it two or three years before his death in 1953. Throughout the thirties he continued, however, to return to Vienna almost every summer. He quarreled with Carnap over Carnap's *Aufbau* apparently on the score of plagiarism. Carnap had acknowledged his debt to him but Wittgenstein took this as an aggravation of the offense. Wittgenstein is reported to have said: "I don't mind a small boy's stealing my apples but I do mind his saying that I gave them to him." He continued, however, to discuss philosophy with Schlick and Waismann, especially Waismann who was Schlick's assistant. The trouble was that Wittgenstein was changing his ideas. One can follow the course of this change by reading the so-called Blue and Brown books — notes of his lectures dictated to his pupils and posthumously published — and find the fuller effects in Wittgenstein's posthumous *Philosophical Investigations,* which I am not going to try to summarize apart from saying that its main theme is that we fall into philosophical perplexity through misunderstanding the logic of our language, a thesis not proved but supported by a wealth of brilliant examples. Waismann's *Logik, Sprache, Philosophie* was designed in part to reflect these changes. Wittgenstein was not opposed to this in principle but in fact prevented the appearance of the book by insisting year after year on further revisions. The story ends sadly. When the Nazis invaded Austria in 1938, Waismann fled with his wife and son to Cambridge and was given a position there. But there was no place in Cambridge for an echo of Wittgenstein and Wittgenstein did not welcome him there. Fortunately, Oxford took pity on him and made him a Reader in the Philosophy of Mathematics, a post which he held till his death in 1959. He suffered private misfortunes — both his wife and his son committed suicide — and remained rather an isolated figure, but he went on working, mainly composing epigrams in his later years. His book was published posthumously and did turn out, to my mind at least, to owe too much to Wittgenstein's *Investigations.* The sad thing was that he was philosophically gifted in his own right. His book *An Introduction to Mathematical Thought* (first published in German in the thirties) and his series of articles in *Analysis* in the 1950s on Analytic-Synthetic are well worth reading.

The original position of the Vienna Circle was very much that of Wittgenstein's *Tractatus* on the assumption that Wittgenstein's elementary propositions were observational, except that the Circle did not adopt his pictorial theory of language. The points that they chiefly pressed were, first, the subordination of philosophy to science — it could not compete with science because there *was* only the natural world which the sciences, with the support of observation for their theories, already wholly covered — all it could do was analyze the information that the sciences provided, perhaps do something more positive in the way of sharpening scientific concepts (functioning, in Carnap's phrase, as the logic of science); and, second, the exclusion of metaphysics — represented by any attempt to go beyond what Hume (in whose work almost the whole of Viennese positivism was foreshadowed) called matters of fact. This was effected by the use of their famous Principle of Verifiability — the slogan expressed by both Schlick and Waismann in the form "The meaning of a proposition consists in its method of verification."

It did not detract historically from the power of the slogan that it concealed many difficulties. For example, how strong was the verification to be? At the beginning, Schlick insisted on conclusive verification, but this threatened to rule out scientific generalizations; unless they were construed as finite conjunctions, which was not plausible, they could not be conclusively verified. It was on this point that Popper joined issue with the Circle, advocating a principle of Falsifiability and treating it not as a criterion of meaning but as a principle of demarcation. Only propositions that were falsifiable were to be accounted scientific. This proposal had its advantages but Popper actually defined falsifiability in such a way that it did not cover abstract theories, that is, theories containing non-observational terms or even statements of probability as he construed them. Not that in these respects his opponents were in any better case. Where he chiefly went wrong was in supposing that he had evaded Hume's problem of induction. It still needs to be explained why a hypothesis which we have tried and failed to falsify should gain credibility from passing the test.

Others, like Carnap, preferred to weaken the principle of verifiability by requiring no more than that empirical propositions should be confirmable. Unfortunately they did not have, and we still do not have, a watertight formal theory of confirmation, so that the principle of verifiability never got itself satisfactorily formalized. I made a valiant attempt to bring it off in the second edition of my *Language, Truth, and Logic*, but Alonzo Church torpedoed me.

But worse is to come. The principle, as Schlick and Waismann stated it, fused two separate functions — that of deciding when a particular proposition was meaningful and that of deciding *what* meaning it had. The second was the more ambitious, but it raised an awkward problem. Was it to be verifiability by the author or interpreter of the proposition, in which case its meaning would depend on who he happened to be and what spatio-temporal position he occupied, and you at once run into difficulties concerning propositions about the past (they had to be interpreted as propositions about the availability of present and future evidence) and propositions about other minds which had to be interpreted behavioristically, a course later found to lead to an avowed-behaviorism or, if not behaviorism, physicalism. By no means all philosophers object to this, but it still seems to me to require one's feigning anaesthesia. The alternative was to rely on the fiction of an ideal observer, but this is not a very precise notion. With what powers is such an observer to be credited?

There was disagreement also about the nature of Protokolsätze, the Circle's term for the basic observation-statements. Schlick and Waismann followed Mach in taking them to be sense-datum statements, but Neurath, who won over Carnap, insisted that they must refer to the observation of physical objects. As I now recollect it, the discussion of this point occupied many of the Circle's sessions at which I assisted. Carnap was away in Prague, but Schlick and Neurath battled it out, neither convincing the other. The advantage of Neurath's position was that he avoided many awkward problems. But had he the right to? Schlick faced the problems but ran into difficulties — especially over the question of solipsism. How did he arrive at the public external world of which Neurath and Carnap were making themselves a present? He eventually hit on the ingenious solution of construing public statements as statements about structure as opposed to content. It does not matter to me what the content of your experience is like, whether, if I could *per impossibile* get into your skin, I should or should not find that the world seemed very different, so long as I can cash your statements and your reactions to my statements in ways that make sense to me in terms of my own experience, and all that this requires is that our respective worlds have a structural correspondence. I once thought that this distinction between structure and content could not be so sharply drawn, but I am now more inclined to think that there is a good deal in this idea.

Another disputed issue was that of the nature of truth. Schlick held some form of correspondence theory, but Neurath and Carnap maintained that to talk of comparing sentences with facts was metaphysical. Sentences could be compared only with other sentences. They were therefore driven to hold a coherence theory of truth. To the obvious objection that many incompatible systems of sentences could each be internally coherent, Carnap replied that the true one was that which was accepted by the scientists of our culture circle. But this, as I pointed out at the time, was a fudge. Each one of the competing systems might consistently contain the sentence that it alone was accepted by contemporary scientists. What Carnap meant was that only one of them was so accepted in *fact*. But why should it be only at this point that fact is allowed to intrude?

This outlawing of semantics, for that was what it came to, vitiated Carnap's *Logical Syntax of Language,* which came out in Vienna in 1934 and was translated into English in 1937. Technically, it was a monumental feat, but the attempt to make syntax do the work of semantics failed and so did the construal of philosophical propositions, where they were not metaphysical, as syntactical statements masquerading as statements of fact (this was the nub of Carnap's celebrated distinction between the formal and material modes of speech). Whatever else they were, philosophical propositions were not syntactical.

Carnap's eyes were dramatically opened at a congress in Paris in 1935 when Tarski presented an abstract of his semantic theory of truth. Thereafter semantics became respectable, and Carnap published three books on it between 1942 and 1947. The Circle had held previous congresses, two at Prague and one at Königsberg (though it had no particular respect for Kant), but the Paris one was by far the most ambitious. Bertrand Russell came to it and was treated as an honored figure, though he always held considerable reservations about Logical Positivism. I do not remember meeting him then, though we became close friends in the years after the second war. I do remember meeting Karl Popper there for the first time. With the menace of the Nazis he was shortly to leave Vienna for New Zealand, from which he eventually made his way to the London School of Economics. An even more vivid memory is that of my introducing Neurath to the noble but formidable Susan Stebbing and his disconcerting her with the remark: "I have always been for the womans." By that time Neurath was living in Holland. There had been civil war in Vienna in 1934 when Dolfuss's right wing forces overthrew the municipal government and stormed the Socialist stronghold, the Karl Marx Hof. Neurath was on their list of wanted men, but luckily he was in Moscow, on some business connected with his Institute, which he than set up at the Hague. Most of its work then consisted in the production of what he called Isotypes, pictorial statistics.

If Neurath's removal weakened the Circle, a mortal blow was dealt to it in 1936 by Moritz Schlick's murder. He was shot on the steps of Vienna University. It was not a political act, but the work of a demented pupil. The right-wing press duly deplored it, but there was a faint suggestion that this was the sort of fate that radically anti-clerical professors might expect to suffer.

Neurath made a valiant attempt to keep the movement going. His main ambition was to produce an International Encyclopedia of Unified Science, and he visited Chicago in 1936 to arrange for its publication by the University Press. An organizing committee was set up, consisting of himself, Carnap, Philipp Frank, Charles Morris, who was teaching at Chicago, the Danish philosopher Jørgen Jørgensen, whom the war was to turn into an ardent Marxist, and Louis Rougier, pretty much the only French neo-positivist of the time, who was to become an emissary of the Vichy government. The encyclopedia never amounted to anything more than a handful of brochures, for the most part not very distinguished with the notable exception of Carnap's *Logical Foundations of the Unity of Science* and of Ernest Nagel's *Principles of the Theory of Probability*.

The German occupation of Austria dispersed the Circle. So far as I know, only Neurath and Waismann among its members were Jewish, but the radical spirit of the group, and its rational outlook, made it unacceptable to the Nazis. Vienna's loss was America's gain: Carnap held a professorship first at Chicago and then in California; Frank and I think also Menger went to Harvard; Gödel, perhaps the most gifted of them all, to the Institute at Princeton. I have said nothing about Gödel because his work lay wholly in the technical field of mathematical logic, and I doubt if even in his youth he wholeheartedly subscribed to the main doctrines of the Circle. As early as 1940, if Russell's evidence is to be trusted, his view of mathematics was Platonistic. The Berlin group also escaped: Reichenbach and von Mises to California, after a stay in Istanbul; and Hempel early on to Brussels, and then to the United States, eventually establishing himself at Princeton. Of the Poles, Kotarbinski and Ajdukiewicz remained in Poland and survived the war; Lucasiewicz was sheltered by his pupil Scholtz at Münster and subsequently became a professor in Dublin; and Tarski settled in California.

Even after 1938 Neurath tried to keep things going. He took over *Erkenntnis*, renamed it *The Journal of Unified Science*, and arranged for it to be published at the Hague, but only a few issues appeared. A final congress, which I attended, was held in Cambridge in 1938 but the only members of the Circle to come to it, besides Neurath and Waismann, were Frank and Feigl who came over from the U.S. In 1940, when the Germans invaded Holland, Neurath and his third wife escaped to England as passengers on a crowded small boat. He was interned for some months as an enemy alien, and when released reopened his Institute. He died suddenly in December 1945, his last years having been devoted almost entirely to the production of his pictorial statistics. The other members of the Circle continued working but no longer as a group. Carnap was the most productive, his later work consisting almost entirely of an attempt to develop a system of inductive logic.

Von Juhos remained in Vienna, inconspicuously, throughout the war, and after the war Viktor Kraft returned there, I think from America, but the climate had changed, metaphysics was back in fashion, and so far as the University of Vienna was concerned, the Circle might never have existed. It was different elsewhere. True, with the possible exception of myself, no one any longer cares to be called a logical positivist, but the Circle has left its imprint on successive generations of English philosophers, including Ryle and Austin and their disciples, on the work of Ernest Nagel, Quine, Nelson Goodman, Hilary Putnam, and other distinguished American philosophers, on von Wright and Hintikka in Finland, on groups in Sweden and the Low Countries. Its influence has percolated even to Germany and France. If one goes through the theses advanced in the early issues of *Erkenntnis* in detail, one finds that nearly all of them are questionable and many of them false. But their spirit still triumphs. A strain of what I can best describe as woolly uplift was banished from philosophy — I dare not say never to return, that would be too optimistic — but where it survives or reappears, at least to face criticism of a keenness which we owe very largely to those heroes of my youth.

Notes on
the Ontology of Minds

GUSTAV BERGMANN

This is the third of a series of essays in which I have recently undertaken to provide some indications of the major changes, additions as well as corrections, that have taken place in my world (ontology) since, more than a decade ago, I stopped reporting them in print. Being, like the first two, a *pièce d'occasion*, this essay, too, will be succinct and selective.[1]

The most distinctive innovation of this ontology is the assay of the *act*. The simplest determinates in an act are one particular (*b*) and two universals, called a *species* and a *thought*, respectively. The act itself[2] is the conjunction of two atomic facts; one, the particular exemplifying a species; the other, the particular exemplifying a thought. Take an act of perceiving (*perc*) the atomic fact this-being-green (*gr(a)*). The thought in it is, like all thoughts and all species, a universal, represented in the IL by, say, g_1, that intends *gr(a)*. Thus the act itself is the conjunction *perc(b)* · $g_1(b)$.

This, though, is but part of the innovation. The other part, equally essential, specifies the connection I call the *meaning nexus*, between a thought and its intention, as follows. (i) In the paradigm, g_1 and *gr(a)* are, in this order, the two *terms* of a *circumstance*, $g_1 Mgr(a)$, whose mode is actuality; with '*M*' being one of the four primitive marks of the IL that are called *diacritical*, because they are the only ones of that schema standing for literally nothing.[3] (ii) Every instance of the pattern α*M*β is either *analytic* or *contradictory* and, if *explicitly* intended, either *immediately* or at least *directly* presented to us as such, i.e., we shall see in Section II, as pervaded by its mode, actuality if analytic, potentiality if contradictory. (iii) *Every thought intends one and only one determinate; every determinate is, if at all, intended by one and only one thought.*[4]

These are the bare bones of the assay I proposed a quarter of a century ago and have not changed since; unless you count as a change the easy adjustment to a need that had made itself felt during the long pause, for a species, I called it *grasping*, such that "its" acts can attend all determinates, not only complexes having

189

modes (i.e., facts and circumstances) but also those that do not, viz., *things* (i.e., either particulars or universals).[5] Nor shall I now introduce any change, either minor or major, but, rather, specify two additions concerning the place acts so constituted have and the different jobs the different sorts of them do in the ontology of minds.

This is, emphatically, a world without continuants. Or, equivalently, every one of its particulars is momentary. So, therefore, are all acts. In such a world a material object is thus not one particular but the temporal series of its momentary cross sections. How, then, about minds? My hand, you realize, is forced. A mind of this world is a temporal series of its momentary cross sections, each of which is a collection of acts.[6] 'Momentary cross section', though, is clumsy, and an attractive alternative is available. *A mind is a temporal series of states of consciousness, or more briefly, of conscious states (c.s.).* With that out of the way, let us cast a first glance at the two additions.

Every act has an intention. Yet, negatively, an act, a, occurring in a c.s., does not suffice for the owner of the latter to be conscious of its intention. Positively, he will be conscious of the latter *only if* there is in the c.s. a second act, b, whose species is direct awareness (*draw*) and whose intention is a. But again, having to repeat over and over "the owner of this c.s." is not only clumsy but also unnecessary, for you already know my commitment on what that involves.[7] So I restate the gist of the first addition more conveniently as follows. No act, a, is as such conscious of its intention. (iv) *For a to be thus conscious, it is a necessary condition that there be (in the c.s.) a second act, b, of direct awareness, whose intention is a.*

Let us check in the case of the paradigm. Write 'a_1' for '*perc(b)* · $g_1(b)$', 'b_1' for '*draw(c)* · $g_2(c)$'. Remember the actuality of $g_1 Mgr(a)$; and make g_2 the thought for which $g_2 M a_1$ is actual. Then a state conscious of $gr(a)$ will either be or include the two-member collection of a_1 and b_1. Notice, too, that a_1 being an intention of b_1 is an instance of one way in which the connections among the acts in a conscious state are taken care of (n. 6). Another, or rather the other, we shall discover after having stated the second addition.

The above condition of an act being conscious of its intention was presented as necessary, not as necessary and sufficient. The second addition attends to the gap. Many acts are conscious of their intentions *if and only if* a second condition is also satisfied. If a_2 is such an act, there must be in a c.s., $\mathfrak{A}_2$, of which it is a member, a further act, $a u x_1$, conscious of its own intention;[8] the latter being a string of words forming a sentence that I call the *text* of a_2. You notice that I am speaking of (the tokens of) words and sentences; you know that in the IL there are neither but only primitive marks and well-formed strings of them; so you may anticipate the next point, as crucial as it is commonsensical and even obvious, if you happen to know how emphatically I have long insisted on distinguishing between the schema IL, on the one hand, and the natural or ordinary language(s) (OL) of our speech and thought, on the other. With one exception,[9] again crucial, (v) *the text of an act is a sentence of our natural language, not an expression of the IL.* In Section IV, we shall see that acts with the same text may have different intentions, and conversely. I.e., more succinctly, (vi) *the connection between text and intention of acts is many-many.* Recall now (iii): the "connection" between a thought and its intention is one-one. So, I have reargued in NO, is that between a determinate and the expression, if any, standing for it in the IL. Hence (vii) *the connection between a thought and the expression in the IL that stands for its intention is one-one.*

Some texts are parts of others. E.g., (1) "This is a horse" is a part of (2) "That is a perceiving that this is a horse." Consider now a c.s. such that two of its members are auxiliary acts whose intentions are (tokens) of (1) and (2), respectively; and you will see that you have come upon an instance of the other way in which the connection among the member acts of c.s. is taken care of.[10]

The propositions (i)-(vii) are the pivots on which the dialectic of this essay turns. To point that out, not in order to convince, of course, but helpfully, perhaps, by way of orientation, is the purpose of this introduction. A concluding comment should also serve it.

There is, forever alive, the challenge presented by the assay of one's c.s. when perceiving a material object. In this world, and not just in it, the topic falls within the range of the dialectic just circumscribed. Conversely, I would not even know how to address myself to it without either starting with or presupposing that dialectic. In the fourth and longest section, there will therefore be quite a bit about this assay.[11]

I

The particulars of a nonfoundationalist's world are, I take it, material objects and, perhaps, minds. The foundationalist rejects this choice as much too complex. His particulars are as simple as the sensa of the tradition. The particulars of this world are as simple as the foundationalist's; yet they are anything but sensa. Most of them are nonmental; only some are mental, being the particulars in acts and no others.[12] The ontological status of the subdeterminates apart, the issue between foundationalists and nonfoundationalists is whether the latter's particulars (and universals, if any) can all be assayed in terms of the simplest determinates, here also called things, of the former. This issue must wait until Section V. I turn next to the things and the simplest facts of this world. Its things, since I am not a nominalist, are either particulars or universals; and the familiar green spot, so often styled as a particular, is not that but, rather, the fact of a particular exemplifying a universal$^{(0)}$.[13]

Start from the facts, among those called atomic, represented by the instances of '$f(x)$', '$r(x,y)$', and so on. I do and must claim that—not ordinarily of course yet whenever inducing in myself a certain set—I intend such facts. What, then, is the species of these intendings? A regular foundationalist, and not he alone, would make it a species all its own and call it sensing. In this world it is a perceiving; i.e., "perceiving" an atomic (or molecular) fact is just as much a perceiving as perceiving a horse. Nor is there any species that might plausibly be called sensing. The distance between the two kinds of intentions is vast indeed; exactly as vast as that between the two kinds of particulars in the foundationalism debate. So I shall mark it by writing in the atomic (and molecular) case 'perceiving$_0$' instead of 'perceiving'. That, though, is merely an expository device. The species, I repeat, is with both kinds of intention the same; and I support this claim—*not directly, by argument, but indirectly, i.e., either by appeal to what I call the phenomenological rock bottom, or dialectically, or in both ways, which are the only ones in which one can support so fundamental a gambit*—by pointing out that the communality is as compelling as the distance is vast; both kinds of intention are nonmental.

As for perceiving, so for *imagining,* which is the fourth species we encounter (see n. 7). As for atomic facts, so (as just parenthetically anticipated) for molecular ones. At this point a further distinction of strategic importance appears. A molecular fact is either a conjunction of atomic facts, in which case I call it a *cluster,* or it involves at least one other connective, in which case I call it a *molecular noncluster.* (viii) *With one exception*[14] *perceivings$_0$ and imaginings$_0$ of clusters are the only acts that may be conscious of their intentions without there being in the c.s. of which they are members an auxiliary act intending their respective texts.* Equivalently, in their cases but, always with the exception, in no others, the auxiliary is optional. The proposition (viii) marks the distinction between clusters and nonclusters. Of that presently. First, how shall we support (viii)? I support it by appealing to phenomenological rock bottom. Just try in all possible ways to think such facts as this-is-not-green or if-this-is-green-then-it-is-not-square without also thinking in some form of inner speech the texts "this is not green" or "if this is green then it is not square" and you will soon be convinced that you cannot. I surely cannot; and that is why I offer this here as an example of an appeal to the phenomenological rock bottom, so called because—and that is the very heart of my phenomenological commitment—from this base all ontological discourse must start and against it eventually check its results.[15]

We are ready to turn to some subdeterminates. First, though, for three comments to conclude this section.

First. Speaking, as we ordinarily do, of words, sentences, and texts, we may mean either types or tokens. Probably more often than not, we mean the types, not the tokens. In these comments and for the most part in the rest of the essay, I mean the tokens. Sometimes I shall mean the types. Yet, thus alerted, you will always know what is meant.

(ix a) *Every text is a cluster.* That makes an auxiliary act, without which another act could not be conscious of its intention, either a perceiving$_0$ or an imagining$_0$ of a cluster. Hence, by (viii), it may be, and in most cases is, conscious of its intention, viz., a text, without a further auxiliary act. To say the same differently, as above: (ix b) *For being conscious of a text, being conscious of a further text is merely optional.* That staves off the danger of the vicious regress to which attention was called in n. 8. But that does not affect the first condition, that an auxiliary act, like any other, will not be conscious unless intended by a direct awareness.

The marks in the cluster may be either visual or auditory, produced either by inner speech or by either hearing or reading. Again, the species may be either perceiving$_0$ or imagining$_0$. These as well as some other such differences and nuances, being irrelevant to ontology, I leave here (and throughout the essay) to the phenomenological skills possessed by many good poets and novelists and even by some psychologists.

Second. Some molecular facts are so complicated that thinking and talking about them without resorting to abbreviations (definitions) and definite descriptions (and therefore of course pronouns) exceeds psychologically what we can do. Within these limits, though, we could teach ourselves to use (part of) the IL to describe them in word and thought, provided only we are prepared to learn, as we also could, certain *standardizations*.[16] Within these limits, therefore, the text of an act and the expression of the IL standing for its intention could be made to coincide. Surely that is worth mentioning. For, if it were not so, the very notion of an IL, even if correctly conceived as a mere schema found useful by some ontologists rather than really a language, would be left hanging in the air.

Third. Can negative facts be perceived? The question has been debated in the recent past. My purpose here, rather than reviving the controversy, is to show how it can be resolved by accounting for the "felt difference" in a different way. Of this-being-green, which is a cluster, we can be conscious without also being conscious of its text. Of this-not-being-green, which is a molecular noncluster, we cannot. Is that difference not large enough, even if the species is in both cases the same?

II

Let α be an expression for a complex in the IL.[17] Then $\sim\alpha$ will also stand for one. Equivalently and more conveniently, such and only such expressions stand for what can be *said literally in the IL*. This is but one item in the explication of the very notion of the IL. Are there any existents that we can intend (think) and yet such that what the negations of their texts (!) purport to stand for, being not thinkable, are literally nothing? Or, again equivalently, does the thinkable exceed the literally sayable? The question is substantive, not merely a request for explication. The answer, followed by dialectical support, will be an appeal to phenomenological rock bottom. The section will indeed be quite crowded with such appeals; and there will also be some explication. But again, thus alerted, you will always know which is which.

"a is a particular" and "green is a universal$^{(0)}$" are two texts of what we can think; "a is not a particular" and "green is not a universal$^{(0)}$" are two others purporting to stand for what is unthinkable.[18] (These are of course two appeals.) The species in the acts whose texts the first two are, is the one I call *grasping*. (This is mostly an appeal, partly about a word.) What, then, first, is the existent intended by, say, the first of these acts, and what, second, is the thought in it?

When either explicitly or implicitly (n. 4) grasping a, I am presented with a composite of two subdeterminates; one an *item* that is a pure individuator; one an *ultimate sort* (u.s.), in this case particularity, in others the universalities of the appropriate types. The connection between an item and an u.s. is one of the two closest, or, to use the same word as before, one of the two most inseparable in this world.[19] Its structural similarity to Aristotelian-Thomistic *hylomorphic composition* is unmistakable.[20] But do not ignore the decisive difference. In this world also universals are such composites. Or, with a twist, in each universal, as in each particular, there is *materia signata*.

(x) *Every act of grasping is evident*. I.e., the particular in the act exemplifies the universal$^{(0)}$ *evident*. The intention of an act explicitly grasping a, or any other thing, is a, or that other thing, itself. Equivalently, a thing and the hylomorphic composite it is, is one and the same. Still differently, *every thing is a Two-in-One*. (I.e., with Butchvarov's phrase, we are here at one of the two limits of logical atomism.) Nor does that violate the strict criterion of sameness set forth and argued in NO; for there is in the IL no primitive mark for either an item or an u.s.

What is the thought in an act of grasping? Obviously, like all thoughts, a universal$^{(0)}$. Yet the occurrence of this universal in the mind does not affect the balance between what is and what is not literally sayable in the IL. To see that, consider, first, that if definite descriptions could be added to the IL, 'the-thought-of-a-being-green' would become available in it as a description; and consider, second, that 'a-is-a-particular' and hence also 'the-thought-that-a-is-a-particular' would still be unavailable because, for one, the former and hence also the latter are not literally sayable, and, for another, if there were anything that could be called a "subject" of particularity, it would not be a but the item in it.[21]

All things of the same u.s. share a single *form*, directly grounded in the subdeterminate that is the u.s. in each of them and in no others. As for things, so for complexes. They, too, as the word is commonly used, have forms[22] we may grasp with evidence. E.g., the form of what '$gr(a)$' and all other instances of '$f(x)$' stand for is what is evidently a particular being connected by exemplification with what is evidently a universal$^{(0)}$. (I ignore the standardization.) Yet we are not, when grasping the form of a complex, presented with a further existent, subdeterminate or other, that would correspond to the u.s. in a thing; although, if there were one, we would be implicitly presented with its "building stones"; e.g., in the paradigm, with two items, two u.s., and exemplification. It follows that the intention of, and the thought in, an act of grasping a complex is, analogously to the case of things, the complex itself and the thought intending it, respectively. That answers one question but brings us up against what seems a roughness. If the form of a complex is nothing, how can we be presented with it and how is it represented in the IL? Postponing the answer until the last section will do no harm yet help the exposition. The familiar notion of form we shall need presently.

(xi) *Every complex has a mode, either actuality or potentiality*. The other sort of Two-in-One is a complex with, or, as I would rather say, *pervaded* by its mode. The mode of *some* complexes, e.g., the actuality of this-being-either-green-or-not-green, but not of all, is sometimes accessible to us, in which case I shall say that the complex has become *transparent* to an act of ours. The species of such an act, always evident, is believing or disbelieving in the case of actuality or potentiality, respectively; i.e., more briefly, evident believing or disbelieving.[23] But we cannot think what, e.g., the text "it is not the case that this being either green or not green is actual" purports to stand for. Generally, its not being pervaded by a mode cannot be thought of any complex. For, if a complex is actual, its negation is of course potential. Hence, if a complex not being actual (or potential) were thinkable, potentiality would be just a duplication of the connective "not"; actuality, merely gratuitously ontologized assertion.

The modes entered this world when I could no longer understand how I could, under any species, intend what does not exist. To fill this gap was the primary job for whose sake they were granted ontological status. Nor, except in an ontological desert of things only, could they fairly be considered ontological excess baggage in a world in which to exist (being an existent) has no ontological status whatsoever.[24] An ontologization that does only one job, however fundamental, is under a shadow. The modes eventually were assigned a second, almost, although not quite, as fundamental as the first. (xii) Within the limits Goedel discovered, *the mode of a complex is at least in principle accessible if and only if it is either analytic or contradictory*. The coincidence of these two dichotomies, each so sweepingly dividing all complexes, is the basic idea[25] of the "new" half (n. 1) of the rethought notion of analyticity.

Evident believing of a complex and evident grasping of its form, an attentive reader points out, are two and not one. I agree, of course, even though, I add, upon every adequate explication analyticity must depend on form and form only. Why, then, the reader pursues, are the modes not what you just called ontological excess baggage? I first remind him of their primary job; then invite him to consider how much (xii) contributes to the perspicuity of the overall pattern.

The two "connections" between item and u.s. *in* a thing and between a complex and *its* mode are equally close as well as the closest there are. Yet there is a "felt difference" between them.[26] That is why I called only things hylomorphic composites and speak only for complexes of being pervaded and becoming transparent. A third word, in a metaphor, will focus the difference. Imagine hollow spheres of a glass rather opaque yet translucent under certain conditions; in the center of each burns a light; if one looks at such a sphere from without while the conditions obtain, it is *illuminated* from within. The metaphor also provides a cue in structural history. The similarity to an *illumination doctrine* in the style of Augustine and Malebranche is unmistakable.

I next state or restate four fundamental propositions concerning modes. (A1) Every act to which the mode of a complex is transparent is either a believing or a disbelieving with evidence. (A2) The negation of a complex's being actual (or potential) is unthinkable. (A3) A complex's being pervaded by its mode being itself pervaded by one is unthinkable. (A4) One cannot, while presented with the actuality (potentiality) of a complex, intend the negation of this complex without also being presented with its potentiality (actuality). Each of these propositions requires an appeal, although, as is the case for all ontologizations either of a single existent or of a sort of such, they do and must all mutually support or even require each other.

(xiii) *All evidence is either of forms and ultimate sorts grasped or of transparent complexes either believed or disbelieved.* The intentions of two other kinds of acts, intending complexes without the particular in them exemplifying either evidence or another mental universal not a species, enjoy two lesser kinds of privilege. (A4) provides the foil for both.

(1) Nothing is both red and green (all over). (2) This is both red and green (all over). Both (1) and (2) are facts. the first (we have the best possible reason to believe) actual, the second potential. The conjunction of (1) and (2) is an (immediately transparent) contradiction. (2) I cannot imagine. As I technically use the phrase, that makes (1) *synthetic a priori*. More succinctly and with some latitude, (xiv) *the negation of what is synthetic a priori is unimaginable.* The synthetic *a priori* is one of the two less privileged kinds.[27]

Doubting is a species. Let b_1 be a direct awareness of mine whose intention, a_1, is a perceiving of a horse. Now one can of course doubt whether what one is at the moment perceiving is (as one says, really) a horse; but one cannot, or, to speak as before, at least I for one cannot, while b_1 lasts, doubt that its intention is a perceiving a horse. Generally and more concisely, (xv) *while a direct awareness lasts its intention is undubitable.*[28] This is the other less privileged kind. It provides us with a foil for the promised confrontation with the absolutist.

The absolutist challenges me by asking whether my evident believing, he would rather call it *knowing*, is such that when one knows something he also knows that he knows it. I readily admit that the direct awareness of an evident[29] believing, which is the best I can do, is merely indubitable, which is less than evident (see fn. 28) and therefore, as he speaks, not a knowing. Then I provide him myself with a second question I cannot answer to his satisfaction.

How do I "know" what (I agree) is a strategic feature of my world, viz., that the intention of every evident believing is transparent, and conversely? I answer as before that I do not. He is again dissatisfied. I cannot but surmise that in both cases this dissatisfaction is due to his unwillingness to accept the phenomenological rock bottom as the anthropological basis of all ontological discourse. But I shall not tarry trying to convince him that this use of 'anthropological' does not mark my ontology as either scientistic or idealistic.

III

We cannot specify in any detail the expressions of the IL that stand for the intentions of a perceiving (or imagining) a rock or a horse or a mountain. I speak of this situation and what can and what cannot be done about it in Section IV. In this section I shall examine the case of quantified molecular facts that lies at the exact borderline between that can and that cannot. The difficulty that arises, but which can be overcome, is caused by the role played in the current notations by the variables, either free or bound; or, rather, since from the IL all variables are excluded, by what in it does the job of the bound ones. To spot and resolve this difficulty will take several steps.

NOTES ON THE ONTOLOGY OF MINDS   197

1. What, if anything, is a *canon*? Take a paradigm: "If and only if α and β are two complexes, there is a further one, $\alpha \vee \beta$." Canons are supposed to yield decisions for all determinates. Put then a particular and a class in the places of α and β. We know that a determinate having any form other than its own is unthinkable (see n. 18). Hence a canon is literally nothing. Yet in ontological discourse the notion is useful, if only because, if there were any, they would, on the side of a world, correspond one by one to the formation rules of its IL.

2. Let 'f_1' stand for a universal$^{(0)}$, 'x' and 'f' be two variables of types 0 and (0). In current notations '$f_1(x)$' and '$f(x)$' are both counted as well formed. What, then, would '$f_1(x)$' stand for? I cannot think of anything. '$f(x)$', on the other hand, could be *mis*taken in two ways, as standing either for the form or for the canon that goes with, say, $f_1(a_1)$. Either way, speaking as the syntacticists do, an expression of an object language would be taken to represent what could be represented only in its metalanguage. In syntactical discourse one may get by with so dubious a "shortcut."[30] In ontological discourse it cannot but do harm.

3. Consider a current notation for four generalities as simple as any: (a) '$\forall x f_1(x)$', (b) '$\forall x (f_1(x) \supset f_2(x))$', (c) '$\forall x r_1(x, a_1)$', (d) '$\forall x r_1(a_1, x)$'. Speaking graphically rather than accurately, according to which canons are the four determinates they represent "built" from which others? In case (a) one could get by, letting '$\forall x \ldots x$' stand for a monadic subdeterminate, like a parenthesis written in two parts, that clings to f_1. For the other three, however, since neither '$f_1 \ldots \supset f_2 \ldots$' nor '$r_1(\ldots , a_1)$' nor '$r_1(a_1, \ldots)$' stand for anything, what would this "quantifier" cling to? That alone bans the conventional notation from the IL. The cause of this not having been noticed is the error the ontologist must forever guard against, of confusing words and things. In the cases at hand, it is easy to replace in a well-formed expression a mark that does stand for something by one that does not. But one cannot, as it were, punch a hole into an existent and expect to obtain another. So we must design a notation that cannot be faulted on this ground.[31]

4. Let a_1 by any particular; '$\langle a_1, f_1(a_1) \rangle$' stand for the *2-tuple*[32] whose terms are a_1 and $f_1(a_1)$, '$\forall$' for the subdeterminate of universal generalization. I propose '$\forall \langle a_1, f_1(a_1) \rangle$' as *the* standardization of '$(x)f_1(x)$'. The definite article just italicized is problematic. For, just as '$(y)f_1(y)$' would do instead of '$(x)f_1(x)$', so '$\forall \langle a_2, f_1(a_2) \rangle$' would do for '$\forall \langle a_1, f_1(a_1) \rangle$': In the general case, let 'Φ_1' stand for a well-formed expression in which 'x' may also occur bound but must at least once occur free. Then, provided that a_1 is not selected completely arbitrarily but so that it satisfies *certain conditions*, of which more very soon, '$\forall \langle a_1, \Phi_1(a_1) \rangle$' is proposed as standardization of '$(x)\Phi_1(x)$'. The variable must occur free at least once because, while the syntacticist may save words by postulating that, if it does not in, say, Ψ, $\Psi \equiv (x)\Psi$ is what he calls an axiom, to the ontologist the very notion of a canon that merely "builds" the material it is supposed to build something out of is so repugnant that, if a_1 does not occur free in Ψ, he prefers to make '$\forall \langle a_1, \Psi \rangle$' ill-formed in his IL.[33] 'The' and 'certain conditions', the word and phrase italicized above, both point to the difficulty we are almost ready to spot and tackle. First, though, for a

quite different one, which I shall therefore, with a different word, call a barrier. The price of standardization is increased *phenomenological distance*.[34] Being able to teach ourselves, as in the case of not too complicated molecular facts we are, to think and speak at least about a narrowly circumscribed subject matter that includes what a certain standardization is to stand for, surely is a sufficient condition for the latter's acceptability. Now I, for one, am not ready to push my luck by an appeal to my ability to speak and think the proposed standardization even in a case where the molecular scope of a single quantifier is not too complicated. Thus we face a barrier.[35] Yet we shall soon see that this barrier and the difficulty to which I next turn cancel each other in a way that, I hope you will come to agree, is a very strong reason for accepting the standardization under scrutiny.

5. In a PM-like world, $(a_1)f_1(a_1) \stackrel{RL}{=} (a_2)f_1(a_2)$ is what, deliberately avoiding 'sameness', I call a *Russell-Leibniz identity*; i.e., in such a world $(a_1)f_1(a_1) \equiv (a_2)f_1(a_2)$ would reasonably be counted as "analytic" and $(a_1)f_1(a_1)$ and $(a_2f_1(a_2)$ would in a familiar strong sense by substitutable for each other.[36] In this world, however, there are, outside of its PM-like part (among other things, such as classes no longer assayed in the Russellian style) the meaning nexus as well as, not unconnected with it, a new, stricter notion of sameness.[37] Upon this notion, $V\langle a_1, f_1(a_1) \rangle = V\langle a_2, f_1(a_2) \rangle$ would become transparently potential; hence, supposing $g_1 MV\langle a_1, f_1(a_1) \rangle$ and $g_2 MV\langle a_2, f_1(a_2) \rangle$ to be transparently actual, so would $g_1 \neq g_2$. Otherwise proposition (iii) of the Introduction, and with it my whole world, would collapse. That leaves but two alternatives. Either (a) we accept $g_1 \neq g_2$ or (b) we relax the strict notion of sameness by acknowledging the transparent actuality of $V\langle a_1, f_1(a_1) \rangle = V\langle a_2, f_1(a_2) \rangle$. As for the paradigm, so correspondingly for the higher types, $F_1(f_1)$, and so on, as they are needed in the IL. That covers the special case of the italicized "the" in 4.

In the general case all we need do is introduce the "conditions" mentioned in 4. I.e., we must choose between (a) $g_1 \neq g_2$ and (b) acknowledging as transparently actual $V\langle a_1, \Phi_1(a_1) \rangle = V\langle a_2, \Phi_1^*(a_2) \rangle$ for every a_2 such that, first $\Phi_1^*(a_2)$ is a result of substituting a_2 for all free occurrences of a_1 in $\Phi_1(a_1)$; that, second, a_2 does not occur free in $\Phi_1(a_1)$; and, third, that in $\Phi_1(a_1)$ no free occurrence of a_1 lies within the scope of a quantification over a_2.[36]

6. If one wants to adopt the standardization under scrutiny one must choose between (a) and (b). That is the difficulty, or apparent difficulty. I resolve it by choosing (b) and showing that, in view of the barrier, choosing (a) merely produces an unnecessary complication. Specifically, since one is not, or, if you please, since I am not, when thinking the thought with the text of the generalization, ever presented with any of the $V\langle a_1, \Phi_1^*(a_1) \rangle$, what purpose would be served by choosing one from among them? That is why I said that difficulty and barrier cancel each other.

We are ready to turn to the ontology of perceiving. But let us first tarry a moment to consider in the light of this section the claim, made at its very start, that quantification marks an important borderline. The molecular, if not too complicated, we can teach ourselves to think and talk about in the IL. If it is quantified, we can still write it down but while intending it neither think nor talk about it in the IL. The intentions of perceivings we can neither write down nor either think or talk about in the IL.

IV

Take as paradigm a perceiving of this being a horse. Which acts are, at a minimum, the members of this c.s.? One is obviously an act of perceiving,[38] call it again a_1; a second, a direct awareness, b_1, intending a_1. (The existence of b_1 will in due course be established beyond doubt by making it the intention of a further direct awareness that intends one's c.s. while he is directly aware, not of course of the horse but, rather, of his perceiving it.) That "this is a horse" is the text, *if any*, of a_1 is unproblematic. Problematic in this world is its intention; for, as you were just reminded at the very end of the last section, one cannot in detail write down the expression that stands for it in the IL. 'In detail', though, I just added. For it is the burden, or program, of this section to produce and to put to ontological use an *IL-schema* of that expression. In executing this program I shall propose a *thesis* to the effect that there is in the c.s. ($\mathfrak{A}_1$) also a perceiving$_0$ (a_0) such that, not being in the intention of any b^1, it remains forever unconscious. This is the positive one among the two ideas that guide this attempt. The other, also because it may reasonably be called negative, will be presented more effectively after four preliminary comments.

1. When mentioning above the text of a_1, I added the qualification "if any." Was that meant to suggest that there are conscious perceivings for which being accompanied by an auxiliary text is merely optional? Of course there are.[39] To convince yourself that our paradigm is of that kind, just remember how often you have, when taking a walk, perceived a good many of the things around you while your inner speech dwelt on quite different matters. But again, it will improve the exposition if we postpone taking a closer look at this division. In the meantime, keep in mind that, if there is no text, $\mathfrak{A}_1$ has, at a minimum, three members, a_1, b_1, and, by thesis, a_0; while, if there is one, either required or optional, there are two more, e.g., in the paradigm, an auxiliary act, aux_1, that is a perceiving$_0$ of (a token of) the text "this is a horse" and a direct awareness b_2, intending aux_1.

2. Of the third act, that is there by thesis, one is and remains by this very thesis unconscious. That surely requires an examination of its ontological status. But that examination, once more, had better wait until we find out what the intentions of these acts are and what jobs they can do.[40] The expression *"IL-schema"* is self-explanatory. Everything will depend on what the schema can do.

3. The notion of a cross-section law (of nature) occurs in the analysis of closed *processes (systems)*. A system is *closed* during a time interval if and only if during that interval nothing obtaining or occurring "outside" of it affects anything inside of it. For every closed system there is a group of laws, called its *process laws*, such that, conjoined with the complete description of any temporal cross section of it, they allow for the deduction of such a description of any later or earlier cross section. A *cross-section law*, finally, states a lawful connection among the values

at a moment of all or some of the relevant variables that obtains in all cross sections.[41]

4. Consider spatial particulars or, more accurately, since there are no existents called either space or time, consider particulars that exemplify shapes and, *provided they are simultaneous*, stand in spatial relations to each other. Among the latter, there is a ternary universal, *sum*, that selects for any two such particulars, a and b, one and only one third, c, such that $sum(c,a,b)$. Among the laws (axioms) governing it is $sum(a,x,y) \equiv sum(a,y,x)$; among the *predicates*[42] for any two particulars, whether or not either contiguous or overlapping, a part relation, definable by '$pt(y,x)$' for '$(x \neq y) \cdot (\exists z)sum(x,y,z)$'. With the help of these laws and some definitions it is easily shown that for any (I stress once more: simultaneous) particulars, $a_1 a_2, \ldots, a_n$, there is a predicate, sum_n, such that there is exactly one, b; with $sum_n(b,a_1,a_2, \ldots, a_n)$ having all the features one expects. Also, a particular may be one-, two-, or three-dimensional; in case it is three-dimensional, its surface is a two-dimensional one; and so on. c, for instance, may be (I speak concisely) the particular in a momentary cross section (m.c.s.) of a horse. I.e., equivalently, if one assumes 'hs' to be a predicate so broadly defined that all the m.c.s. of all horses fall under it, c will be such that $hs(c)$. Do not, however, in the IL of this world without continuants look for a predicate Hs and a particular $\overline{c}$ such that $Hs(\overline{c})$ would stand for the "whole horse." This gap, as you know, spots one of two major issues, or clusters of such, that have preoccupied the tradition whose recent masters are G. E. Moore, C. D. Broad, and H. H. Price. Presently I shall try to fill it.[43] First, though, for the other basic idea, the one called negative in the first paragraph of this section.

The style of that great tradition is genetic and, if you please, epistemological. Positively, it sets the philosopher the task to produce an account of how the individual, given the stream of his sensa, eventually learns to perceive what we all do, mountains, rocks, horses, and the rest. This, I submit, is the task of science. Negatively, it is the belief held more or less implicitly that it would be a hysteron proteron to start with two ontological assays, of material objects and of minds, as common sense knows them, respectively, and only in a third step test them both by showing that jointly they can produce an adequate assay of the perceiving situation. This belief, I submit, is mistaken. That is the basic idea I called negative. So I proceed accordingly.

Since I promised no more than an IL-schema, let us take $hs(c)$ for granted and explore how close one can come to Hs, which we already know is beyond our reach. The best one can do is to single out in the IL a predicate, *crmobs*, such that '$crombs(x)$' stands, schematically, for 'x is one of the temporal *c*ross sections of a *m*aterial *o*bject, all of which exemplify *hs*'. Consider, then the following existential generality: There are two moments, t_1 and t_2, and at each of them a particular, c_{t_1} and c_{t_2}, respectively earlier and later than c, such that (1) $hs(c_{t_1}), hs(c), hs(c_{t_2})$; and (2) for every t between t_1 and t_2, $(t_1 \leqslant t \leqslant t_2)$, there is one and *only* one C_t such that $hs(C_t)$; and (3) the area of C_t is a continuous function of t. Reflection shows that the generality can serve as $crmobs(c)$.[44] This is about as far as one can go on the side of the material object. So I turn next to the conscious state.

When perceiving the horse I am (speaking both commonsensically and with the tradition) presented with a part of its surface which, in this world, is in turn a part of a simultaneous m.c.s. of it. Concentrating on this part, one can so modify his set that, depending on aptitude, skill, and of course lack of distraction, his c.s. approaches more or less closely a perceiving$_0$ of a cluster, of, say, n particulars, $a_1, a_2, \ldots, a_n$. Write 'b' for their sum; '$cl_0(b, a_1, a_2, \ldots, a_n)$', for the cluster. (xvi) *The act* $\mathfrak{a}_0$ *is, by thesis, a perceiving$_0$ whose intention is* $cl_0(b, a_1, a_2, \ldots, a_n) \cdot sum(b, a_1, a_2, \ldots, a_n)$.[45] A cluster$_0$, however, if I may save words by distinguishing it thus, is as a rule more vivid and richer than clusters we imagine. The numbers of particulars and of universals in it are larger; the colors more luminous and more saturated; the boundary lines sharper; movement or rest, as the case may be, in the specious present are steadier; and so on. The details do not matter. What does is that a cluster$_0$ can, however laboriously, be described literally, without such metaphors as richness, vividness, steadiness, by using only expressions of the IL that stand for universals.[46]

(xviia) *The IL-schema of the intention of* $\mathfrak{a}_1$ *is*

(1) $\quad cl_1(b, a_1, a_2, \ldots, a_n) \cdot sum(b, a_1, a_2, \ldots, a_n) \cdot (\exists x)(pt(b, x) \cdot crmobs(x))$.

Let us use '$Ashs(b)$' as abbreviation for (1) and read it 'b *is a horse aspect*'; or, as closely as possible to the text, 'this is a horse aspect'. (xviib) *Whenever there is a perceiving, there is by cross-section law a simultaneous, unconscious perceiving$_0$ whose intention is the conjunction of a corresponding cluster$_0$ and sum*; e.g., in the paradigm $cl_0(b, a_1, a_2, \ldots, a_n) \cdot sum(b, a_1 a_2, \ldots, a_n)$. Strictly speaking, the cross-section law is part of my thesis and "corresponding" is still to be unpacked. Notice, too, that by this law there is for every perceiving a corresponding perceiving$_0$ but not conversely.

At this point (xvii) is of course but a claim. So I start its dialectical defense by doing the unpacking still to be done and, at the same time, showing that (1) yields the solutions of the two fundamental groups of issues[47] that preoccupied the tradition.

First. Sometimes, when one "looks" at a coin from a certain angle, the upper part of its surface "appears" or "seems" to him to be elliptical *(el)* even though he "knows" it to be round *(rd)*.[48] The tradition's (genetic) concern is to account for how we come to "know" and often even "see" that this part of the surface is round, although what it calls the sensum in the case is elliptical. I write a_1 for *the* particular (not: sensum) in the case and make $el(a_1)$ and $rd(a_1)$ two atomic conjuncts in the (appropriate) clusters cl_0 and cl_1, respectively. You object immediately: How can one particular be at the same time both elliptical and round? The answer, in this world, is as immediate as the objection. $rd(a_1)$ *is actual; $el(a_1)$ is potential.* The case is a suitable paradigm for all others in that fundamental group. Yet two more comments are in order; the first specific, the second of major systematic import. 1. Sometimes we do perceive as pink what is "really" red, as elliptical what is "really" round, and so on. But then, whoever claimed that all perceivings are (as one says) veridical? On the other hand, though, when one "sees as" pink, or elliptical, what is red, or round, he probably has but taken the first step on a road at whose end, if he knows how to reach it, will be a *corresponding* (yet conscious) a_0'. 2. We have just watched the modes earning their ontological keep by doing their third major job.[49]

Second. Sometimes, when perceiving a horse, one is also aware of perceiving it. So we must make sure that an adequate assay of this further awareness can be produced by adding futher acts to the minimal three, a_0, a_1, b_1. Two things we know already. For one, the new awareness is direct. That requires a fourth act, b_3, that is the direct awareness of b_1 without which one would not be conscious of the intention of b_1, which latter is of course a_1. For another, we know that since b_3 is neither a perceiving nor an imagining, there must also be a fifth, auxiliary act, aux_2, that is a perceiving$_0$ of the text "that is a perceiving that this is a horse," and hence also a sixth, b_4, that by intending aux_2 secures one's being conscious of this text. As for perceiving, so *mutatis mutandis* for every other species, believing, remembering, and so on. I have thus for once delivered more than I promised.

The subscripts, you probably noticed, have been so chosen as to leave room for aux_1 and b_2, i.e., (speaking concisely) for the text of b_1, which, although *merely optional for the paradigm* is yet *required for very many acts*. I did this because, since the first text ("this is a horse") is repeated in the dependent clause of the second ("that is a perceiving that this is a horse"), we *need not for any act* burden the eventual c.s. with an awareness of perceiving$_0$ the first.[50]

A propos burdening, structurally there is in this assay nothing to preclude iteration. Just as we proceeded from a perceiving of this being a horse to an awareness of that perceiving, so one may proceed from the latter to an awareness of that awareness; and so on. Psychologically, we find ourselves only too soon at the limits of what we can do. Yet, as Descartes already pointed out to Hobbes, there is nothing wrong with this open horizon. I take it, then, that the assay (1) has passed a second major test.

Third. By proposition (vi) of the Introduction the connection between text and intention is many-many. So let us next check whether the assay (1) bears that out. (a) Depending on circumstances such as angle, distance, illumination, and, of course, the differences among horses, the first two conjunction terms in (1) may vary while the text, "this is a horse," remains unchanged. That illustrates one half of (vi). (b) Again depending upon circumstances, although different ones such as expectation or purpose, the text of a single perceiving may be either "this is a horse" or "this is a mammal." That illustrates the other half. We need not pursue in order to conclude that (1) can pass this third test.

Fourth. (a) We infer from "this is a horse" and "all horses are mammals" that "this horse is a mammal." Write, then, '*mam*' and '*Asmam*' for the respective schematic IL-predicates and ask yourself whether the inference from '$Ashs(b)$' and '$(x)(Ashs(x) \supset Asmam(x))$' to '$Asmam(x)$' is, as it ought to be, valid. To see that it is, consider, on the one hand, the way *hs* and *mam* enter into the respective assays, and, on the other, that the predicates '*hs*' and '*mam*' are of course so defined that

NOTES ON THE ONTOLOGY OF MINDS   203

the second premise is analytic. As for this inference pattern, so for all others. Or, more cautiously, I see no reason to the contrary. (b) How shall we assay the intention of an act whose text is either "this is a brown horse" or "this horse is brown"? One may, as a first answer, propose for either text the intention ($1'$) obtained by replacing in (1) all occurrences of '$hs(x)$' by '$hs(x) \cdot br(x)$'. Or one may refine this answer by assigning ($1'$) only to the first text and to the second the intention ($1''$) corresponding to the conjunction "this is a horse aspect and this is a brown-material-object aspect." At this point, though, the ontologist's interest flags and the linguist properly takes over.

I take it, then, that (1) can also pass this fourth test and turn, fifth and last, to a defense of a different sort. Then I shall conclude the section by attending to one of the two questions raised in it but not yet answered. The other will fit better into the next and last section.

Fifth. An attentive reader asks to be heard. Do you not (he wonders) simply restate the view, not unrepresented in the tradition you acknowledge, that a perceiving is a fusion of an intending of something present and a believing some things past and future? In a sense I agree, yet take exception to "simple." The ontologist must talk as literally and nonmetaphorically as is humanly possible. And "fusion" in this context is blatantly a metaphor. I, at least, have not the slightest notion of what it means for two acts or, for that matter, any two existents to fuse. But I agree that I have presented a way to unpack the metaphor and for once welcome the word as a reminder of one of the traditions that have nurtured me.

Why did I use 'thesis', shun 'hypothesis', 'speculation', and their derivatives? As the word is used in science and its philosophy, a (scientific) hypothesis is the anticipation of a future result of science. As to area covered, a hypothesis may be either rather limited or more or less far-ranging; it may be more or less strongly supported by results already considered secure; and so on. In the early nineteenth century scientists still spoke of the atomic hypothesis by now so overwhelmingly confirmed.[51] Yet there was also the hypothesis, very broadly based and at its time very well supported, according to which all of physics can be accounted for in terms of Newtonian mechanics, that has since gone sour. And there is, last not least, psycho-physical or mind-body parallelism. One may of course continue to call it a hypothesis. Yet the evidence for it, both commonsensical and scientific, is so overwhelming and the philosophers' arguments against it are so inconclusive that I have long made it a feature of the world whose ontology I keep trying to uncover.[52]

The bolder in one of the senses just illustrated a hypothesis is, the more likely scientists will call it speculative. Of the several ways the word is used in philosophical discourse, only one concerns us here. An ontology is speculative if its IL contains expressions (names) for universals which so far have not occurred and, often by the very way they have been introduced, never will occur in any intention.[53] Where does that leave our several a_0? Their species is perceiving. Their intentions are all clusters.[54] Their thoughts we can of course not name. Yet these are by proposition (vii) one-one connected with their intention. Thus we can, without naming them, in the IL speak about them by unpacking there the appropriate definite descriptions. *That shows why the a_0 of my thesis are not speculative.*

But is not this thesis a hypothesis? For, if one takes, as I do, parallelism for granted and assumes eventually sufficient progress of both behavioral and neuropsychological studies, must not the scientists discover some such "machineries," on the sides of mind and of body, as the one I just constructed on the side of the mind? Some such machinery; yes. But my purpose is not, nor could it reasonably be, to anticipate what on the side of the mind this machinery will be. My purpose is merely to show that in this world of mine there can be some such machinery. *That is why my thesis is not a (scientific) hypothesis.*

V

(A) Which are the acts whose intentions one may be conscious of without also being conscious of their texts? (B) How does one manage to grasp the form of a complex if, as I claimed, it is literally nothing? The answers to these questions were deliberately left to the end, also because, jointly with some comments, they should produce a sense of closure.

(A) A perceiving of this being a horse does not require being conscious of its text. As for the horse, so for any other material object. Whether one recognizes it as being a certain kind, say, a dynamo, is a different matter. One who either does not recognize the kind or does not know the word, will not, of course, when perceiving one, be conscious of "this is a dynamo." By this distinction, though, there hangs, from where I stand, no important issue; provided only one admits into his inventory of simple things, together with material objects, some universals on which foundationalists and nonfoundationalists[55] could agree. How, then, one is led to ask, about what in such a nonfoundationalist world corresponds to the clusters of mine, e.g., for a paradigm as simple as possible, the conjunction whose text is "this is a horse and that is a tree?"[56] They, together with the "atomic" ones, are the only complexes — *of a nonfoundationlist world as well as of mine, except of course the molecular clusters that occur only in mine* — whose texts are, in the familiar sense, optional.[57] For all others, from either negation or even the simplest quantification on, consciousness of the text is, again in the familiar sense, required. That answers the first question. Nor, I take it, does this answer need defense at this point. Yet three comments should help.

1. If you collate what we just learned with proposition (viii), you will see that formally — and of course, with the proviso that, while in my world there are (I speak concisely) two "layers of textless consciousness," in the nonfoundationlist's there is only one[58] — the criterion for the intentions of which one may be conscious without being conscious of their texts does not depend on the ontologist's choice of his "particulars." They are all either atomic (or "atomic") facts or conjunctions of such. At first sight that may seem impressive. Upon reflection it becomes less so; the reason being that the very ideas of atomicity and simplicity (in the relevant senses) are (or at least ought to be) repugnant to an alert nonfoundationalist, or,

as I would here rather call him, coherentist. Nor, therefore, will he (or at least should he) be willing to use an ideal language. For this tool essentially involves the syntactical correlates of these two ideas, atomicity and simplicity.[59]

2. An affable coherentist speaks up. He starts by commending me for what he considers two important admissions, viz., first, that while perceiving a material object one does not and cannot, either literally or even schematically, think what I claim to be the intention of the act; and, second, that there are in my world two layers of textless consciousness. Then he asks why, having made these admissions, I do not abandon my particulars and, with them, the schema IL. I observe first, in a preliminary way, that I, too, believe these "admissions" to be important but that, from where I stand, they strengthen rather than weaken my position. Then I start on my answer, which has two parts.

The only notion of ontology I have and understand is that of a (nonverbal) schema in which every existent either is a simple or, in some sense or senses of the word, "consists" of simples; where to be a simple means being at the phenomenological rock bottom. The formula is crude indeed; the only way of unpacking it completely is to present at least an inventory of such an ontology; yet, crude as the formula is, it leaves me no choice; thus for the purpose at hand it will do. The simple determinates of my world are, and cannot but be, those I call particulars and universals.[60] This is the first part of my answer. The second deserves a number of its own.

3. I address my interlocutor as follows. Being a coherentist you no doubt want as many as possible of our perceivings, believings and putative knowings to be what the tradition calls corrigible. Whether that means all or only those whose intentions are not analytic[61] depends on whether you are an extremist or a moderate. We shall arrive at this fork in the road in a little while. I find it more urgent to impress upon you that, to the best of my knowledge, I have gone as far as anyone who is not in this respect an extremist. For is not in this world of mine the mode of any atomic fact, and therefore also that of every synthetic complex involving exemplification, forever inaccessible to us? And is not, therefore, assigning and reassigning of modes[62] to them, blindly as it were yet systematically, so as to achieve a maximum of coherence, the best one can do? Nor is that all. One also can, as we saw in Section II, on purely phenomenological grounds divide the vast expanse of the synthetic into the three layers, relevant to your concern, of the *a priori*, the indubitable and, if I may so put it, the run of the mine. About the analytic, if you are a moderate, nothing needs to be said in this context. If you are an extremist, we must part ways. Even so, you may remember that, when confronting the absolutist at the end of Section II, I did show that his notion of knowing is stricter than what in this world comes closest to it.

(B) A simple thing, either particular or universal, is the hylomorphic compound of its ultimate sort (u.s.) and the item individuating it. Its form is grounded in its u.s. Subdeterminates, being absolute simples, have no form. The form of a complex, I have claimed on phenomenological grounds, is, unlike its mode, literally nothing beyond the complex itself. (Nor, of course, does it in any way involve its mode.) Yet, when one intends a complex under the species of grasping, he is presented with its form. One cannot but wonder exactly how that comes about.[63]

Which feature, then, of an expression representing a complex represents the form of the latter?[64] That it is represented we may take for granted; for, while being analytic and being of a certain form are two and not one, we are yet, whenever the transparence of the complex is not immediate, cued to it by the form of the expression. In a way, everyone knows the answer: The "form" of the complex is represented by the "form" of the expression. But again, since the former is not an existent, one wants to look more closely into what goes on.

Let the expressions I am speaking about be inscriptions. An inscription— written, say, on a piece of paper—is an approximately two-dimensional cluster of material objects, viz., a collection of primitive marks of certain shapes that stand severally in certain relations to each other. The feature we are looking for, call it the inscription's *Shape*,[65] corresponds to a certain predicate that is stepwise defined from the primitive marks by applications of the syntacticist's formation rules; each of the latter in turn corresponding to one of the ontologist's canons. This geometrical predicate is, I repeat, defined. Thus it does not in this ontology stand for an existent. Yet that does not prevent us from perceiving on the proper occasions the inscription's Shape; just as in the preceding section 'Ashs' being defined did not prevent us from perceiving on the proper occasions that this was a horse.

I did not, I believe, in thus answering (B) say anything that could not be inferred from what went before. Yet, I also believe, what I said was worth saying; for it illustrates in two ways the strength of the method. It shows, first, that the distinction between the form of a complex and the syntacticist's form is virtually forced on us. And it shows, second, by an example, how ontological discourse, by talking in its literal part (among other things) about syntax, can in its nonliteral part shed light on the literally unsayable. In the example, it dissipates the aura of paradox surrounding the idea of nothing being represented by something by means of a countervailing paradox: what really happens is that one nonexistent is "represented" by another.

To continue and conclude in a similar vein, protestations by users of the ideal-language method that they do, as one ought to, distinguish sharply between natural and ideal languages, are often distrusted by those who do not use this tool. Instead of adding one more protestation, I have here demonstrated that I do what I ought to do. For texts belong of course to natural languages. And I have, while always using the method, introduced awarenesses of texts into (this partial sketch of) the ontology of minds. The result, no less important for being at this point in history no longer surprising, is an ontology in which every characteristically human mental event depends on the availability and awareness of texts. That is as far as a philosopher need go, and also as far as he can go, in acknowledging the importance of language without making the whole of philosophy a game about language games.

Notes

1. The two preceding essays are "Sketch of an Ontological Inventory," *Journal of the British Society for Phenomenology* 10 (1979):3-8, and "Notes on Ontology," to appear in *Nous*; hereafter referred to as SOI and NO, respectively. Most of what has been presented in these essays for the first time will be here, if at all, only briefly recalled, mostly in notes. Notice in particular the peculiarities of what I call *ontological discourse* in contradistinction to the schema called the *ideal language* (IL), on the one hand, and our *natural, or ordinary, languages* (OL), on the other; as well as the assay of three new sorts that together make up the category of circumstances. Yet I shall also try to provide, again mostly in notes, the indispensable minimum of information about the changes, both additions and corrections, that have occurred in my world since I fell silent, outside the areas on which OI, NO, and this essay are centered. For virtually everything else here relevant and published before the long pause, see *Meaning and Existence* (1960), *Logic and Reality* (1964), and *Realism: A Critique of Brentano and Meinong* (1967), all published by the University of Wisconsin Press and hereafter referred to as ME, LR, RCBM, respectively.

Since it is getting late in the day, the succinctness, the selectiveness, and the piecemeal presentation will, I hope, be forgiven. Should there be time and strength left, there will also be a fourth essay, centered around the ontology of classes and a new explication of the notion of *analyticity* that not only modifies the old one, with which I made do until the end of the sixties, but also adds to it an equally substantial "new" half, if I may so put it in order to indicate both bulk and proportion. Yet, such are the occasional pleasures of piecemeal presentation, it will not at all be difficult to introduce into this essay the basic idea of that "new" half.

2. Or, more accurately, its core. For, we shall see, the particulars in some acts also exemplify the universal which, borrowing the word from Brentano, I call being-evident or, briefly, *evidence*; and they all exemplify, as does every particular whether or not in a mind, a *duration*; just as any two particulars (and, literally, nothing else) stand in a temporal relation to each other. Keeping that in mind, we can save words by speaking of this core as the act.

3. Why then bother with 'M', which of course is taken from '*m*eans'? The answer lies in the relevant canon: If and only if α and β are determinates, there are *eo ipso* (i.e., without need for any further existent, such as the subdeterminates called connectives and quantifiers, to connect them) three sorts of circumstances; viz., a *meaning nexus* ($\alpha M \beta$), an elementhood ($\alpha \epsilon \beta$) and a *diad* or diversity ($\alpha \neq \beta$); each either actual or potential, as the case may be. In the first two the order matters; in diversity it does not. 'M', 'ϵ', and '$\neq$' serve to distinguish among the expressions for the three sorts. The fourth diacritical mark occurs in the IL-expressions for classes. About canons and their not being existents but merely denizens of nonliteral ontological discourse, there will be more in Section III. For the way the circumstances are written in the IL, see the last section of NO. Also make a note that I shall here hardly ever use the IL but instead, and that only when it really helps, fragments of an *improved language* or notation. For the latter notion as well as a concise statement of the reasons for avoiding the IL whenever possible, see the first section of NO.

4. 'Sp', to represent the universal$^{(0)}$ species, may be introduced into the IL. Then $Sp(perc)$ and $Sp(gr)$ will become actual and potential, respectively; or so at least we have the best reasons to believe one can have in this world for any complex that is neither analytic nor contradictory and whose mode, therefore, is in this world not accessible to us. Not so, however, for the phrases 'the thought that. . . . '. For them, even though they are at home in our natural language as well as in ontological discourse, there are no equivalents in the IL; since, if there were, they would have to be definite descriptions of certain universals such as, in our paradigm, g_1. Yet there are in the IL neither definite descriptions nor abbreviations nor variables. (The exclusion of the latter will preoccupy us in Section III.)

An act intends the whole of its intention *explicitly*; anything in its intention, *implicitly*. The remaining notions introduced in this paragraph all involve what in n. 2 was called the new half. Since you have probably sensed that already, I postpone what has to be said about them until we shall in Section II encounter the basic idea of that new half.

5. Take note of this quick roll call of the determinates in the inventory. For the two strategic distinctions, on the side of the act and of the intention, respectively, and between determinates and subdeterminates, see SOI and NO. The distinctions among the subdeterminates can wait. Classes will be completely ignored in this essay.

6. 'Moment' and 'instant' I have long used as others do. What is momentary, such as a *specious present,* is phenomenologically of rather short duration. That does not, however, exclude one moment being contained in another. Such being-contained-in is indeed one of the temporal universals$^{(0,0)}$. 'Being-instantaneous', on the other hand, if added to the IL, would not stand for an existent but is merely, like the null class, a useful fiction. How then about the assay of continuous change? Although this is but one of several interrelated questions about time that must be asked and answered, I shall ignore them all in this essay. But see "Duration and the Specious Present," (LR, pp. 98-107) where I have at least tried to face some of them. As to memory, about which you may wonder in this context, the assay of it in "Some Reflections on Time" (ME, pp. 255-64) can, I believe, be adapted to my present world.

Concerning the *exclusion of continuants,* consider a lobster, green before having been boiled, red afterward. If it were a continuant (a_1), since nothing can be both green and red (all over), green and red would have to be two nonhomogeneous binary relations and the two facts would be $gr(a_1,t_1)$ and $red(a_1,t_2)$, respectively, with 't_1' and 't_2' standing for two universals of the kind I call (temporal) coordinate qualities. Yet obviously there are no such things. See also "Russell's Examination of Leibniz Examined" (ME, pp. 155-88) and, again, "Some Reflections on Time."

'Collection', unlike 'class' or 'set', I use without ontological commitment, not because these collections are not coextensive with classes but in order to anticipate what in due course we shall see, viz., that the connections among the acts in these collections do (if in the meantime I may so put it) take care of themselves.

7. *Direct awareness (draw)* is a species, the third, after perceiving and grasping, which we encounter. One of "its" acts is actual *only if* its intention is mental. A direct awareness of anything nonmental is indeed not even imaginable. As will be seen in Section II, that secures at the very phenomenological rock bottom and, last not least, at the very outset of ontological discourse the dichotomy mental-nonmental or, as the tradition calls it, the existence of the external world. (See "Realistic Postscript," LR, pp. 302-40.)

The Gothic letters for acts and kinds of such are merely a rather crude and unsystematic notation of convenience. '*draw*' and '𝔥' are of course taken from '<u>d</u>irect <u>a</u>wareness'.

8. And hence also a direct awareness, $\mathfrak{h}_2$, of $a\mathfrak{u}\mathfrak{x}_1$. That makes $\mathfrak{A}_2$, at a minimum, the four-member collection a_2, $a\mathfrak{u}\mathfrak{x}_1$, $\mathfrak{h}_1$, $\mathfrak{h}_2$. The suspicion that a vicious regress may be lurking here will be allayed in Section I. '$a\mathfrak{u}\mathfrak{x}$' is taken from '<u>aux</u>iliary'.

9. The exception will be discussed in Section I.

10. What is, or are, the species of all these auxiliary acts? The answer, if postponed for a while, will illuminate a large part of the ground plan. In the meantime make a note that *texts will always be marked as such by surrounding them with double quotes.*

11. Of the indispensable information about corrections and additions as yet unpublished (see n. 1) there will be only two chunks in the text; one, a miniphenomenology of species, modes, and forms in Section II; the other, about quantification, in Section III.

12. How, then, could any of the others be what the tradition calls a sens<u>um</u>? Nor of course have I used that word for many years. For 'sens<u>ing</u>', see below; for the overall pattern, see also n. 7.

13. In the IL and the notations used here things are represented by the primitive marks, often called descriptive constants, of the corresponding (Russellian) types. '*Simple*', when used as here in ontological discourse, does not stand for an existent and has therefore no equivalent in the IL. As for 'simple', so for 'exist' and 'existent'.

As the two words are used in this essay, *foundationalism* and *nonfoundationalism* are

NOTES ON THE ONTOLOGY OF MINDS   209

these two choices and nothing else. This use is different from, and more specialized than, that made of them by the participants in the current debate between foundationalists and "coherentists." Yet I shall in my ontological rather than epistemological way talk about some of the very things they talk about. Thus an occasional use of these words should do no harm and may even do some good.

14. This exception, strategically important for the assay of perceiving material objects, will be discussed in Section IV.

15. Reconsider here the long italicized phrase in the second paragraph of this section. It may also help to distinguish between a negative and a positive kind of appeal. The one above I call negative. Another example of this kind we shall soon come across when considering that what such texts as "green is a relation" purport to stand for is not even thinkable and therefore not an existent. For an example of the positive kind, I do claim that, when presented with the green spot, I am presented with a characteristic togetherness between a particular and a universal. What else need or could one do in order to establish exemplification as an existent?

'Thinking' I always use in this essay as a synonym of 'intending'.

16. Since the notion of standardization, first presented in NO, will play a key role in Section III, I introduce here an example that will be useful there. The familiar current notation, '$f_1(a_1)$' is in the IL replaced by '$\eta(f_1, a_1)$,' with 'η' standing for exemplification and '$f_1 a_1$)' for the diad familiarly written '$f_1 \neq a_1$'. Diads, you remember from n. 3 (but see also NO), are the most fundamental among the three sorts of circumstances. This particular standardization has two advantages: (1) if one writes the IL, as one must but as I here never shall, nonlinearly, then the order in '$(f_1 a_1)$', that stands for nothing, disappears; and (2) the primitive marks for the connectives (and quantification), all of which become monadic, and for exemplification—i.e., for the only subdeterminates that, "being least inseparable from determinates," have primitive marks to represent them—all obey, except of course for the sort of the single determinate to which they cling, exactly the same formation rule. The price paid for these advantages is (I speak concisely) a certain *phenomenological distance* from what the text suggests. But this price is acceptable as long as the simples mentioned in both notations, in this case f_1, a_1, η, are the same, and as long as whatever additional existent is mentioned, in this case the circumstance (f_1, a_1), is *eo ipso* there provided only the simples are there.

17. I.e., to remind you once more, either a fact or a circumstance. The restriction is necessary because the negation of an expression standing for either a thing or a class, or, of course, for either a connective or a quantifier (see n. 16) is ill-formed. Also, make a note that whenever there is no doubt I shall use the Greek letters without the clause about instances. (The occasional Gothic letters are used for what expressions stand for.).

18. So does "green is a universal$(0,0)$"; more generally, any determinate having any *form* other than its own is unthinkable.

19. The "connection" is, under penalty of regress, *eo ipso*, i.e. without the need for a further existent somehow analogous to exemplification. That is why, things being the *simplest determinates*, the subdeterminates are the *absolute simples*. (About the two modes, see below.)

20. Thus it is not surprising that my Thomist friend, John Peterson, was the one who nudged me toward ontologizing the ultimate sorts. (See his "Bergmann's Hidden Essentialism," *Review of Metaphysics* 22 (1969):660-75.) Once this step has been taken, the need for ontologizing the items, in analogy to Thomas' *materia signata*, becomes obvious. Are, then, some participants in a recent debate might wonder, the particulars of this world no longer bare? I would reply that, ontologically, all things of this world are bare. For it is merely an anthropological feature that although we would not recognize any of its particulars, which therefore we cannot but make momentary, we do countless times recognize universals. But, then, it is also worth noticing that while all of the former are, none of the latter is, literally in time; i.e., none of them exemplifies a temporal universal.

21. In a notation on whose pitfalls Hochberg and I agree, the thought in the case would have to be written '$\ulcorner a \urcorner$'. That, too, fits with the assay of all things as Two-in-Ones. See his *Truth, Fact, and Reference* (Minneapolis, 1978), and my NO.

22. Most complexes have *more than one form*. $(\alpha \cdot \beta) \vee (\gamma \cdot \delta)$, for instance, is a disjunction as well as a disjunction of conjunctions. Among the existents represented by primitive marks of the IL, only *exemplification*, the connectives, and the quantifiers have *none*. All this I take for granted, just as I shall take for granted that in the IL the u.s. of a thing is represented by the shape of the primitive mark representing it. If a complex is too complicated for its form to be grasped immediately, it may yet be grasped directly (n. 4), i.e., in the last of a series of steps such that none of them requires the phenomenological correlate of a step in deduction.

23. I speak deliberately of *evident believing* rather than of *knowing*, as would an absolutist such as G. E. Moore. At the end of the Section I shall join issue with this kind of "absolutism." In the meantime, think of evident believing (and disbelieving) as the last (and first) of a whole series of species with (I speak concisely) entertaining (a thought) as the neutral point between the two extremes. Notice, too, that while all acts of grasping are evident, most acts of believing are not.

24. Let me add that, even by the standards of ontological discourse, to which of course virtually all of this essay belongs, the thinkable and the existent are coextensive upon the only notion of existence I have. Any other belongs to the kind of speculative philosophy in which I have no interest whatsoever. The distinction between what is and what is not thinkable lies, accordingly, at the very rock bottom.

25. Anything more must wait for what I hope will be a fourth essay. But notice, for later reference, that excluding everything synthetic from what is evident on the side of the mind and transparent on that of the intention achieves with one fell swoop what all latter-day Humeans and skeptics or, for that matter, all "coherence theorists of truth" must advocate. Of this more in Section V.

26. The difference is also marked by the two underlinings above. For the connectives operate (if I may for the moment so put it) on the complexes *minus* their modes. That follows from what, I take it, is already secured, viz., that (speaking concisely) the negation of a *moded* complex does not exist. Yet we may safely continue to express ourselves as we do. Nor, therefore, shall I use the two words just underlined again.

27. For a specification I still think substantially correct of what falls in this category, see "Synthetic A Priori," in LR, pp. 273-301.

28. Doubting, incidentally, is the last species you shall encounter in this essay. As to what one might call the relative strengths of the reasons we may have for believing the three kinds of intentions, evidence is of course the strongest, indubitability (it would seem) the weakest, the synthetic *a priori* in between.

29. Notice here the indispensability, on the side of the act, of the universal evident. As in this case, so also for some remembering. E.g., I cannot remember the mode of an arithmetical proposition that was once transparent to me, but I can remember that it was then evident to me. For a mental character, unlike a mode, needs no "illumination."

30. Nor in such discourse would it disturb that (unlike an u.s.) this form and every canon are literally nothing. But see "Propositional Functions" (reprinted in R. Rorty, ed., *The Linguistic Turn* [Chicago, 1967]) for an interpretation of Russell's original '$f(\hat{x})$' as symptomatic of a tendency toward nominalism.

31. The dots above merely call attention to the "holes." In this world, (finite, linear) orders are a sort of existents (see n. 32); yet there are no unoccupied places in them. That each quantifier, as here standardized, is a monadic subdeterminate that "clings" to every determinate of the form specified by "its" canon we are about to see. That by means of the standardizations already imposed on them all connectives as well as exemplification become monadic we know already (see n. 16). With the exception of the three canons for the three sorts of circumstances, all canons are thus monadic; the exception being that, if any two determinates of whatever sort are there, so are *eo ipso*, i.e., without the need for a subdeterminate, three others. Consider how very much all this increases the perspicuity of the overall patterns. For one, as long as no classes are involved, the mode of every circumstance is accessible. For another, the mode of what is wrought by exemplification, i.e., of all atomic facts, is forever inaccessible to us. (Is that

perhaps why the ontological status of exemplification is so controversial?) Third, in the facts, either analytic or contradictory, which are the only ones whose mode is accessible to us, the modes of their atomic constituents are, as it were, neutralized or balanced out by virtue of their forms, as, most simply, in $f_1(a_1) \vee \sim f_1(a_1)$ and $f_1(a_1) \cdot \sim f_1(a_1)$.

32. A 2-tuple, $\langle \alpha, \beta \rangle$, is the existent that in this world ontologizes the order α-followed-by-β. It is not, in spite of the notation borrowed, a class, i.e., it is not an ordered pair but, rather, the diad $(\alpha, (\alpha, \beta))$. For a bit more, see NO.

33. As for V, so of course for $\wedge$. But let me apologize for the very crude device of the mixed Greek-Roman lettering. In a similar vein, let me announce that, for the familiar reasons, I shall in the next section fall back upon the current notation for the quantifiers.

Being-free-in, being-bound-in, and so on, are of course all matters of form, thinkable yet not literally sayable.

34. The notion of phenomenological distance between an expression of the OL or even of one of the current artificial notations, on the one hand, and, on the other, its standardization in the IL, as well as the sufficient condition for the latter's acceptability were introduced (n. 16) when the notion of standardization first came up.

35. One cause of this inability may well be a feature also mentioned in n. 16. '$\vee \langle a_1, f_1(a_1) \rangle$' is built with the particular a_1, that is mentioned neither in '$(x) f_1(x)$' nor, of course, in texts such as "everything is green."

36. For the proofs, see propositions *339 and *341 in Alonzo Church, *Introduction to Mathematical Logic* (Princeton, N.J., 1956). For the higher types Church does not give the proofs, but I see no difficulty in thus extending them.

37. Upon this notion, stated linguistically as at the end of the introduction to NO, as long as no classes are involved every instance of $\alpha = \beta$ is either analytic or contradictory, depending on whether the IL-expressions to the left and the right of '=' are or are not mark by mark two tokens of the same type. The single exception is of course the choice (b). For an early record (1950) of this choice, see *The Metaphysics of Logical Positivism*, 2nd ed. (Madison, 1967), p. 28. For the bracketing of variables and hence also of quantification in NO, see *ibid.* (F4) and fns. 5, 37.

38. Not perceiving$_0$. But remember that the subscript is merely a device to mark a division among all acts of a single species.

39. This is the exception mentioned in n. 14.

40. That they are perceivings$_0$ has already been mentioned.

41. The thermodynamic process in a thermos bottle is a physical example as good as any. Further information and analysis may be found in the second chapter of *Philosophy of Science* (Madison, Wisc. 1957, reprinted, Westport, Conn., 1977).

42. I save words by using '*predicate*' in order to remind you that in this world "defined universals" do not exist. As for '*pt*' here, so for '*bs*' and '*Hs*' above and still others later. Phenomenologically, though, *pt* is at the rock bottom. That is why I called the predicate defin*able* rather than defin*ed*. Also, I wrote '*sum(c,ab)*' instead of the familiar '*c = sum(a,b)*', that hides a definite description based on the axioms for the ternary universal. Make a note, too, that, dealing here mostly with *spatial* particulars, I shall, when there is no doubt, supress the adjective. The subscript in 'sum_n' will also be suppressed. For the part relation, see RCBM, p. 75f.

43. But let us provide ourselves right away with a rudimentary coordinate system that "endures." Take the usual three sticks at right angles to each other and suppose that the particular in each of them at any moment is at the next replaced by another, without, however, the geometrical features, none of which is a particular, undergoing any change. Add to each moment the occurrence of a tone, and the job will be done. If you are still baffled by a "supposition so far-fetched," let me assure you that my intellectual motive is not some residual sensism but, overpoweringly, my dread of the lobster's claws (see n. 6).

44. You see now why rudimentary space-time coordinates were made available in fn. 42. With their help abbreviations such as 'c_{t_1}' can be "translated" into the IL. As to *area*, notice that defining it not by occupancy, but, rather, geometrically in terms of "enduring" space

coordinates, one avoids certain difficulties that would otherwise arise in connection with (3). The *uniqueness* of c_t is secured by a law to the effect that nothing can be a temporal cross section of more than one material object. Schema-wise, that should do for (1) and (2). The difficulties of (3), however, are formidable, if only because the "translation" into IL of the mathematical apparatus is beyond our strength, although not, I suppose, beyond that of a computer. In principle, however, since elementary arithmetic can be accommodated in the IL, classical mathematics can be "attached" to it—roughly speaking, as the "entities" of physics can be attached to the material objects we perceive—by what is known as the partial interpretation of a calculus. Of this feature so characteristic of my world, if there is the opportunity, more in the fourth essay.

45. b, as you see, may and often will, e.g., with its shape, become a particular in the clusters.

46. Here and below, the Gothic letters, $\mathfrak{a}_0$, $\mathfrak{a}_1$, $\mathfrak{b}_1$, stand as before for the members of the minimal collection, $\mathfrak{A}_1$, of the paradigm. The first to point out that what I call a cluster need not lie in a place was (I believe) H. H. Price in *Perception* (London, 1932).

47. Those of the other group all involve the notion of continuants. Their solutions are but corollaries of the total defense, if otherwise successful.

48. In this paragraph the words between double quotes are used as we all use them in ordinary nonphilosophical discourse; and it is assumed that '*el*' and '*rd*' stand for universals, i.e., as somewhat arbitrarily I here speak, are not just predicates.

49. The other two, we remember, were to provide, first, intentions for all acts, and, second, jointly with form an adequate grounding for analyticity.

50. Reread the end of the Introduction where the same texts have been used to illustrate one of the two ways in which acts in a c.s. may be connected.

51. Yet we shall never perceive an atom! But a special, derivative or secondary ontological status may nevertheless be assigned to the simples, particles or otherwise, of physical theory by the technique of partial interpretation (see n. 44 and also "Physics and Ontology" in LR, pp. 108-23.) Make a note, too, so we shall not have to return to the point, that as we shall soon see, the various $\mathfrak{a}_0$, even though we shall never be conscious of one, need not be relegated to that lesser status.

52. For a lucid exposition of how parallelism fits into this world, see L. Addis, "Behaviorism and the Philosophy of the Act," to appear in *Nous*.

53. This is, for brevity's sake put my way, the gist of the so-called *Principle of Acquaintance*.

54. Remember what was said earlier about the dispensability of such words as 'richness' and 'vividness' in their descriptions and you will also see that none of the universals in an $\mathfrak{a}_0$ violates the *Principle of Acquaintance*.

55. In this paragraph, 'foundationalism' and 'nonfoundationalism' are still used as before, for the two choices of "particulars." From the next paragraph on, they will stand for the two sides of the current debate.

56. In case you wonder whether one could not take care of perceiving clusters by conscious states containing several perceivings, one for each conjunction term, let me point out that, whatever the intentions, perceiving-this and perceiving-that, on the one hand, and perceiving-this-and-that, on the other, are, as I believe first Meinong observed, two and not one.

57. The species of the acts intending them are, we know, either perceiving or imagining. Nor, I trust, do the double quotes around 'atomic' and 'molecular' require explanation.

58. See the italicized clause in the preceding paragraph.

59. The failure of the physicalists among the logical positivists provides a sort of justification from the recent past for these expectations from the living. They alone did both, treating material objects as particulars and using what they thought was the ideal language.

60. Nor could I consistently make material objects my particulars. For to do that and yet avoid the paradoxes of change and sameness (see ns. 6 and 43) requires the introduction of substances, i.e., of existents that are, in the sense specified in the preceding section, speculative. But this only way out is not open to me. Or, if that helps, in this respect I am as committed an "empiricist" as I was in my salad days.

61. Or, of course, as I shall not repeat, contradictory.
62. Or, as most would say, truth values. But there is nothing to be gained by introducing the notions of truth and falsehood into this discourse.
63. This is the first half of the question raised near the opening of Section II. See also n. 22.
64. This is the second half of the question raised in Section Two.
65. And, of course, Shape and form of an inscription are two and not one.

Logical Form, Existence, and Relational Predication

HERBERT HOCHBERG

A *nominalist* is one who claims that universals do not exist; a *realist* claims that there are exemplified universals; and a *platonist* claims that universals exist whether or not they are exemplified. As I shall use the term, *realism* is thus a *moderate* realism, in that the realist's universals exist only as constituents of *singular facts*. A *singular fact* is the *exemplification* of a monadic universal by a *particular* or two or more *particulars standing in* a relation. The platonist's universals need not be constituents of facts in which they are *connected* to particulars.

Due to the influence of Quine, many philosophers now associate realism and platonism with claims about *abstract entities*, whether these be universals or particulars. In fact, one can viably argue that on Quine's view a realist-platonist is one who holds that *abstract particulars* exist whereas a nominalist holds that all particulars are *concrete*. One need not argue, on Quine's view, that only individuals exist, since the notion of ontological commitment is so construed that only individuals *can* exist.[1] A class, for example, is taken to be an abstract individual to which a concrete individual may be related by the membership relation. Similarly, a property and a particular, in that they are subjects of an exemplification relation, may be thought of as two kinds of particulars, concrete and abstract, that are *terms* of a relation. Here, I shall consider a property to differ from a particular in virtue of the asymmetry of *exemplification*. Thus, a property *may*, and a particular *may not*, sensibly be said to be exemplified. The notion of *possibility* involved in the previous claim differs from the notion of *logical possibility* involved in a claim that something *can be* ϕ even though it is in fact not-ϕ. It is a notion reflected in the categories recognized and not by the logical truths and falsehoods. Thus, while an object cannot be both ϕ and not-ϕ, one may *sensibly* predicate 'ϕ and not-ϕ' of an object. This does not mean that 'ϕ and not-ϕ' need be taken as standing for a property. One might well hold, first, that only primitive-simple predicates need be taken to stand for properties, and, second, that only exemplified properties need be acknowledged. If one does so, then the two notions of *possibility* will coincide in that *no property* will be such that it *cannot be* exemplified since it is contradictory. Given that we recognize properties and particulars, we recognize that one kind is such that it is one term of a basic asymmetrical connection, exemplification. Elements of that kind *do*, and of course *may, exemplify*, but they *may not be exemplified*. Elements of the other kind, by contrast, may be exemplified and may also exemplify other properties. To be a realist is to hold that properties are universals.[2] This is to claim that one and the same property is (or may be) exemplified by more than one particular. An extreme nominalist denies that there are properties at all, whether they be universals or not. He thereby blocks any argument purporting to prove that some properties must be taken as universals. Such a view is embodied in Quine's use of the notion of 'general term', Goodman's talk of the exemplification of predicates, and Sellars's claims about 'semantic assertibility'. This issue I shall not pursue in detail here. Rather, there is another facet of the problem of universals that was focused on by Russell long ago and has recently been revived.

Russell recognized properties (concepts, functions). He also held that sentences expressed *propositions*. He was concerned with the conditions for *understanding* a proposition. One condition was that a person be acquainted with the constituent entities (of a proposition) that the terms in a sentence, expressing the proposition, stood for. In the case of 'The ψ is ϕ' we would be dealing with the concept ϕ and, depending on Russell's views at a period (1903, 1905, 1912), the denoting concept *the* ψ or the property (concept) *being uniquely* ψ.[3] In the case of 'a is ϕ', we would supposedly be acquainted with the object a as well as with the concept ϕ, assuming that 'a' is a genuine proper name. But, in the case of 'aR_1b', acquaintance with a, b, and the concept (relation) R_1 does not suffice.[4] For, we understand the proposition expressed as contrasted with the proposition expressed by 'bR_1a'. Hence, we must grasp a *direction* or *sense* of a relation. Thus, we must also be acquainted with such an additional *entity* if we are to understand the proposition expressed by 'aR_1b'. This, in turn, points to our implicit recognition of the *form* of a relational proposition as well as that of a monadic proposition. Russell thus felt compelled to recognize *logical forms* and *directions* or *senses* of relations as *objects* of knowledge by acquaintance.[5] We need recognize such objects and our acquaintance with them as conditions for our understanding propositions. Understanding the propositions a is ϕ and a has R_1 to b requires that we understand the difference between an object's having a property and an object's standing in a relation to an(nother) object. This difference is a matter of *logical form*, and grasping it involves knowledge of the forms x-*is*-F^1 and x-*and*-y-*are*-*in* R^2. Likewise, understanding the difference between a has R_1 to b and b has R_1 to a involves understanding the difference between the directions a-*has*-R^2-*to*-b and b-*has*-R^2-*to*-a. This requires knowledge of such directions.

One can see how Russell arrives at the two notions of *form* and *direction* by recalling a familiar device of his. Consider the two sentences 'aR_1b' and 'bR_1a' as related to two propositions [aR_1b] and [bR_1a]. Consider next the following lists:[6]

LOGICAL FORM, EXISTENCE, AND RELATIONAL PREDICATION 217

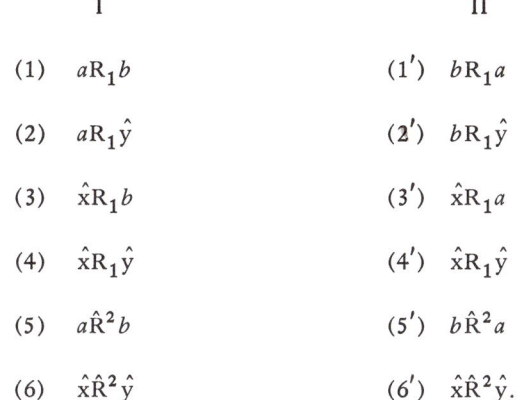

	I		II
(1)	aR_1b	(1')	bR_1a
(2)	$aR_1\hat{y}$	(2')	$bR_1\hat{y}$
(3)	$\hat{x}R_1b$	(3')	$\hat{x}R_1a$
(4)	$\hat{x}R_1\hat{y}$	(4')	$\hat{x}R_1\hat{y}$
(5)	$a\hat{R}^2b$	(5')	$b\hat{R}^2a$
(6)	$\hat{x}\hat{R}^2\hat{y}$	(6')	$\hat{x}\hat{R}^2\hat{y}$.

In (1) and (1') we have sentences which stand for the propositions. By replacing constant signs with a variable abstract, we get a series of different signs standing for different "things."[7] Thus, in (2), (3), (2'), and (3') we have monadic predicate abstracts for *having a in R_1 to, being in R_1 to b, having b in R_1 to, being in R_1 to a*, respectively. Such *relational properties* need not concern us. In (4) and (4'), however, we get tokens of the same pattern, the pattern taken by Russell to stand for *the relation* (function) R_1. In (6) and (6'), we also get, by abstracting from all constants, tokens of the same pattern. This pattern is taken as representing the two-term relational form. In (5) and (5') we have different patterns indicating the different directions (or ordered pairs) of a relation. One thus has in the above lists a representation of propositions, relational properties, a relation, a form, and two directions.

While recognizing logical forms and directions, Russell held that they were not constituents of propositions, since he thought that taking them as constituents led to a Bradley-type regress. Thus, he held that the form connected the constituents into a complex but, in playing such a role, a form was not a further constituent. In taking such forms not to be constituents of propositions, while claiming that they were objects of knowledge and that knowledge of them was presupposed by our understanding of propositions, Russell was a platonist with respect to logical forms in a twofold sense. To get at what is involved, it will be useful to consider a modified version of a Fregean ontology.[8]

Let us assume that 'aR_1b' is true and that 'bR_1a' is false, and let us continue to use '[aR_1b]', and '[bR_1a]' as signs referring to the propositions expressed by the sentences. Let us further assume that the propositions contain, as constituents, *senses* of the names '*a*' and '*b*' as well as the *relational concept* associated with the sign 'R_1'. I will use '[a]', '[b]', and '[xR_1y]' as signs for such *things*. Let us also recognize a fact in virtue of which [aR_1b] is a true proposition. The fact has, as constituents, the objects *a* and *b* and *the relation* $\hat{x}R_1\hat{y}$. The relational concept [xR_1y] correlates to the relation $\hat{x}R_1\hat{y}$ as the sense [a] correlates to the object *a*. The proposition [aR_1b] is correlated with the fact aR_1b in virtue of (1) a correlation between constituents, and (2) a correlation between the form *of* and ordering *in* the proposition [aR_1b] and those of the fact that-aR_1b. Recognizing propositions and facts, we can then distinguish two sorts of entities associated with realism: concepts and universal properties. Both sorts of things play a predicative role, albeit a different kind, since, in recognizing propositions and facts, we recognize two kinds of predicative connections. Both concepts and properties are also universals in that they are taken to play such a predicative role in different propositions and facts. If one holds that all concepts are predicative constituents of propositions, then he is not a platonist with respect to such concepts. But to deny such a claim, and in that sense be a platonist, would seem to be absurd for one who recognizes concepts and propositions. If one also holds that some properties are not predicative constituents of any facts, then he is a platonist with respect to such properties. Such a view is not prima facie absurd, as is its counterpart with respect to concepts. Concepts and properties have traditionally been fused and confused. One can identify them and still recognize that the predicative connection *in* propositions is different from the predicative tie *in* facts, assuming that facts are not taken to be propositions of a certain kind. Even if one identifies concepts with properties, we may still distinguish the two kinds of platonism in terms of concept-properties being required to be constituents of facts, propositions, or both. And, whether one identifies concepts with properties or not, he may or may not take the *forms* and *directions* involved in propositions to be the same as those involved in facts. We may then distinguish types of platonism, as opposed to realism, with respect to *forms* and *directions,* in terms of such things being independent of facts and propositions.

At one time Russell held that properties (identified with concepts) and objects combined into *complexes.* Such complexes, which were, in effect, propositions, were held to be *facts* or *fictions.*[9] Since there were complexes for sentences like 'aR_1b' and 'bR_1a', irrespective of one being true and the other false, he held that there was a complex for every appropriate set of constituents. Facts corresponded to true sentences; fictions to false ones. He then not only identified properties with concepts, but held that objects (rather than *senses*) were constituents of propositions. He also, in effect, identified facts with *true propositions* and fictions with *false propositions.*

In the context of the above discussion, Russell's view between 1910 and 1913 is platonistic in two basic senses. He holds that we must be acquainted with logical objects, such as forms and directions, as a condition for our understanding propositions in which they are *involved.* In this vein he seems to believe that they exist independently of such propositions (and facts). This belief is supported by his concern that a Bradley-type regress is initiated if such logical objects are taken as constituents of propositions.[10] And, his view does imply that forms and directions (as well as concepts) may be involved only in fictions or false propositions, and hence need not be involved in a fact. This feature of his view is independent of how one takes the sense in which logical objects are "involved in" or "connected with" propositions and facts. Aside from any distinction between a realist and a platonist, it is clear that insofar as Russell distinguishes $\hat{x}R_1\hat{y}$ (or $[xR_1y]$) from $\hat{x}\hat{R}^2\hat{y}$, and both of these from $a\hat{R}^2b$ and $b\hat{R}^2a$, he recognizes logical objects. These are like universals in that they *characterize* facts and propositions into *kinds*. The recognition of logical objects is problematic. For, whether he takes logical objects to be further constituents of propositions or not, he seems to require that they be connected with the other constituents by a further tie or relation. Otherwise he has not accounted for the way in which such logical objects play a role in giving structure (form and order) to propositions (and facts). Moreover, directions (or ordered pairs) such as $a\hat{R}^2b$ and $b\hat{R}^2a$ seem to be complex objects, since particulars are "involved." For, clearly, directions or ordered pairs involve particulars and an ordering or arrangement. One thus accounts for the order in a proposition (and a fact) by the introduction of an entity that is itself ordered. This feature also raises the problem of a Bradley-style regress in connection with the recognition of such objects, apart from any question of their relation to facts and propositions.

Russell seeks to avoid one problem by giving the form the role of the exemplification tie. Thus, the form provides the connecting link in the proposition (fact). But, then, it is difficult to see how he can avoid taking the form as a constituent of the fact (proposition), unless (1) this merely means that a proposition (or fact) is a complex that *contains* constituent entities as well as entities that are not constituents, or (2) he takes such a complex *to be* constituents in *a connection* and holds that facts (propositions) may not then be analyzed in terms of constituents.

He seeks to avoid the problems about directions by holding that a is related to aR_1b (or $[aR_1b]$) in one way and b is related to that fact (proposition) in another way. Hence he recognizes further facts expressed by

a is in D_1 to $[aR_1b]$,
b is in D_2 to $[aR_1b]$,
b is in D_1 to $[bR_1a]$

and

a is in D_2 to $[bR_1a]$.[11]

Thus, directions are construed as facts containing propositions (facts) *related* in a special way to objects. They are, then, clearly complex and just as clearly not constituents of *their* constituent propositions. This means that aR_1b and bR_1a differ in virtue of standing in different relations. Such a move is problematic and, for Russell, inconsistent. It clearly runs counter to his classic argument against individuation of particulars by relations in "On the Relations of Particulars and Universals" of the same period, 1910-13. That he consistently held to a line of thought that rejected the appeal to relations to ground the difference of relata is clear from *An Inquiry into Meaning and Truth* of 1940 and *Human Knowledge: Its Scope and Limits* of 1948. In both these later works he introduces absolute monadic spatial properties, as constituents of *individuals,* to ground the difference of such things without appeal to substrata or "bare" particulars.

The complexity of directions (or ordered pairs) also reveals a redundancy in a pattern that recognizes forms and directions. For, if we acknowledge $\hat{x}R_1\hat{y}$ and the directions $a\hat{R}^2b$ and $b\hat{R}^2a$, we do not require $\hat{x}\hat{R}^2\hat{y}$. One can take $\hat{x}R_1\hat{y}$, as Russell later did, to "involve" a relational form. To know what $\hat{x}R_1\hat{y}$ is (be acquainted with the relation) is to know that it is a two-term relation. That is why, in Fregean fashion, the relation is represented by the complex sign '$\hat{x}R_1\hat{y}$' and not by 'R_1'. Likewise, recognizing $a\hat{R}^2b$, or $(a;b)$, we also have the relational form brought in. Thus, a, b, $\hat{x}R_1\hat{y}$, and $a\hat{R}^2b$ appear to suffice to specify what condition (fact) would be the fact, if existent, that grounds the truth of 'aR_1b'. In that sense we have a sufficient list of constituents. All we need add is that the fact is the exemplification of $\hat{x}R_1\hat{y}$ by a and b in the order $a\hat{R}^2b$.

The Bradley-type "problems" are obviously connected with the use of *something* in a double role. Whether one takes the relational form to provide the predicative tie, as Russell does in "Theory of Knowledge," or whether one takes the relation (or the direction) to also provide the *form* for *and* the *tie* in the proposition or fact, as Russell did in 1918, one avoids a question about the connection of the form to the constituents. By so doing, one also blocks a question about the connection of the relation and the direction to the other constituents. The use of entities in a twofold role to avoid a Bradley-type regress is characteristic of the purported nominalism of Wilfrid Sellars. Sellars holds that the truth condition for 'aR_1b' is satisfactorily specified in terms of the two *related* objects, a and b.[12] His gambit derives from his understanding of Wittgenstein's remark in the *Tractatus*.

3.1432 Instead of, 'the complex sign "aRb" says that a stands to b in the relation R', we ought to put, '*that* "a" stands to "b" in a certain relation says *that aRb*.'

Sellars's position is purportedly nominalistic, by contrast with a realist who would hold that the fact is analyzable into two objects *and* a relation in an arrangement (exemplification). For Sellars, it suffices to note that aR_1b is a *matter of fact* and, in recognizing a merely matter-of-fact relation, as opposed to exemplification, we do not reject nominalism.[13] Yet, it is clear that the non-existent relation Sellars appeals to plays a *threefold* role. For, it (1) supplies the difference between aR_1b and bR_1a as truth conditions; (2) supplies the difference between aR_1b and, say, aL_1b, where '$\hat{x}L_1\hat{y}$', for an explicit realist, would stand for a different relation; (3) supplies the basis for 'aR_1b', rather than '$\sim aR_1b$', being taken as true, or, to put it another way, it accounts for the fact being more than a class (the class $\{\hat{x}R_1\hat{y}, (a;b)\}$, for example). The realist's *arrangement* performs only the latter function, if he recognizes directions, and only the first and third functions if he does not. In an obvious sense then, Sellars is no less of a realist about relations than one who explicitly acknowledges relations, and no less of a realist about directions than one who explicitly acknowledges such entities. For, the complexity of his appeal to related objects, as opposed to objects exemplifying a relation, allows him to avoid explicitly acknowledging relations and directions as entities.

By contrast with Russell, Sellars runs together the relation $\hat{x}R_1\hat{y}$ and the direction $a\hat{R}^2b$ by holding that 'aR_1b' is more adequately stated by the use of a

LOGICAL FORM, EXISTENCE, AND RELATIONAL PREDICATION 221

spatial relation between tokens of names. Thus, in place of 'aR_1b', Sellars employs, in his ideal language *Jumbelese*, something like

(α) a b.

That a token of 'a' occurs to the left of and at a certain distance from a token of 'b' represents that $\hat{x}R_1\hat{y}$ holds between a and b *in that order*. Sellars thus represents both the relation, $\hat{x}R_1\hat{y}$, and the direction, $a\hat{R}^2b$. Hence, in spite of his declared nominalism, he is clearly a realist about both relations and directions. In fact, he does not even avoid what he takes to be the nemesis of realism-exemplification. For, (α) not only *shows* what relation and what direction are involved but that *the relation purportedly obtains* or is exemplified) *in the direction*. That his elaborate attempt to deny that he recognizes such entities fails I will not argue here, as I have argued the case elsewhere.[14] Here, it will suffice to note features of Sellars's schema and analysis that correlate with features of an avowed realists's schema. There is also a feature of Sellars's schema that may mislead one into thinking that he does not, on such a pattern, recognize relations. Although we can take

(β) x y

in place of '$\hat{x}R_1\hat{y}$' to represent the relation involved, we do not have any sign to generalize from in (β), as we do in '$\hat{x}R_1\hat{y}$', to yield a sign to represent the relational form that Russell recognized, $\hat{x}\hat{R}^2\hat{y}$. This may lead one to believe that the category of relations need not be represented and, hence, is not recognized. But, recall that on a Russellian-type schema one need not take '$\hat{x}\hat{R}^2\hat{y}$' as representing anything, even though it is a sign pattern that may be arrived at by abstraction from 'aR_1b'. Moreover, even though there is nothing corresponding to '$\hat{x}\hat{R}^2\hat{y}$' in *Jumbelese*, there is a pattern corresponding to '$\hat{x}R_1\hat{y}$'. And, since Sellars has to distinguish between the situation represented by

a b

and that represented by

b a,

we can take the former to involve both the ordering represented by '$(a;b)$' and the relation represented by 'x y', whereas the latter encompasses the ordering represented by '$(b;a)$' as well as the relation x y.

Thus, just as the explicit realist may think in terms of the use of the pattern

aR_1b

as implicitly recognizing $\hat{x}R_1\hat{y}$ and $a\hat{R}^2b$ (or $(a;b)$), so Sellars's pattern involves corresponding commitments. Once we recognize that, we cannot avoid acknowledging another feature in

a b;

that a and b in an order, $(a;b)$, *stand in* a relation, x y. Thus, we recognize objects, a relation, an ordering, and the exemplification, by the objects, of the relation in an order. In fact, Sellars's notation, while suggested by 3.1432 in the *Tractatus*, can be viewed as carrying a Fregean theme to an extreme. Frege, to avoid a Bradley-type regress, did not recognize a predicative tie in propositions. Instead he took concepts to play a twofold role by supplying the *content* (and thus the difference between $\hat{x}R_1\hat{y}$ and, say, $\hat{x}L_1\hat{y}$) and the predicative connection between that content and the individual senses in the proposition. This is one aspect of his holding that concepts are "unsaturated" and his representation of concepts by expressions like 'xR_1y', which give *the form* of the sentences in which such signs become "completed." The awkwardness of such a representation is that 'xR_1y' is a complex sign in which 'R_1' occurs. The use of the attached variables 'x' and 'y' in 'xR_1y' can then be understood to indicate the difference between monadic, two-term, three-term, etc., predicates (and concepts) rather than the incompleteness of the predicate (concept). In short, predicates like 'Gx' and 'xR_1y' represent concepts as well as the form of the propositions the concepts enter into. That is why, with '$\hat{x}R_1\hat{y}$', '$\hat{x}\hat{R}^2\hat{y}$' is redundant on a list of the constituents of a fact (or proposition). On Sellars's pattern, we cannot point to a distinctive part of the concept sign (such as 'R_1' in '$\hat{x}R_1\hat{y}$'), as the concept sign has become a relation obtaining between names or, in the monadic case, a characteristic of a name. Thus, Sellars removes an awkwardness of a standard Fregean-style notation, and, hence, he dramatically represents the dependence of relations on objects. But this does not avoid relations, though it may well be taken to emphasize the moderate realism implicit in Sellars's purported nominalism.

In his most recent book Sellars presents an argument for nominalism that points to his hidden realism. He writes,

Thus, one who is simply struck by the fact that we *could* use '$\genfrac{}{}{0pt}{}{a}{b}$' to say that a is larger than b will be tempted to look for some aspect of

(6) $\genfrac{}{}{0pt}{}{a}{b}$

which is doing the job done in

(5) a larger than b

by "larger than," for example "the *fact* that 'a' is above 'b'" of "'a'"s *being above* 'b'." It is absolutely crucial to appreciate that *nothing in* (6), or *about* (6), is doing the job done in (5) by "larger than." Many philosophers have stared this point in the face and missed it, thus failing to grasp its significance.

Obviously the fact that 'a' is above 'b' is essential to the semantical role (6) is playing. But that fact does not do the job done by "larger than." Rather it does the job done in the case of (5) by the fact that 'a' and 'b' have a "larger than" between them. Let me repeat: *Nothing in (6), or about (6), is doing the job done by "larger than."*[15]

It should be clear from the emphasized phrases that Sellars is taking the fact that a *Jumbelese*-style schema is constructible to be an argument for nominalism.[16] That aside, he is wrong in his claim. This is seen where we use '$\hat{x}L_1\hat{y}$' as the realist's "predicate." Thus, '$\genfrac{}{}{0pt}{}{x}{y}$' plays the role of '$\hat{x}L_1\hat{y}$' and, just as clearly, the space between 'a' and 'b' takes the place of 'L_1' as the occurrence of 'a' over 'b', rather than 'b' over 'a', replaces the linear order in 'aL_1b' to represent the order in the fact. What Sellars is entitled to say is that *no sign* in (6) is doing the job done by "larger than." What he can add is that if you erase the tokens of 'a' and 'b' in (6), the space between them disappears while, in (5), the token of 'larger than' would also have to be erased. This points to a difference between a token of a phrase and "a space," not to an argument for nominalism. Sellars is making use of two basic themes of moderate realism, as opposed to platonism. One only finds relations as obtaining between terms. Hence, without the terms we do not have the relation. And, since they are exemplified by terms, relations are not constituents of facts in the way the terms of the relations are. These are theses of realism that Sellars seeks to transform, by the formulas of *Jumbelese*, into nominalism.

Sellars seeks to convince his readers that one does avoid recognizing properties by pointing out that ordinary statements, such as 'This is green', in ordinary contexts do not state that a relation obtains between an object and a property. Since they do not do so, the realist *construes* a pattern of a purported perspicuous language, 'Ga', in terms of a property being exemplified by an object. Therefore, as Sellars sees it, the realist cannot claim that the pattern of the perspicuous language is a transcription of an ordinary statement.[17] In the case of the true sentence 'This is green' we acknowledge a green object and in the case of the truth 'This is to the right of that' we have spatially related objects. In neither case do we have additional *objects* (entities, terms): the color and the relation. But this is not an argument. It is a declaration that is equivalent to the familiar fiat that as long as one uses predicates predicatively no ontological commitments are made. The fact that one shows the dependence of attributes on objects by employing the spatial distances and juxtapositions of *Jumbelese*, in place of normal predicates, emphasizes, but does not support, the claim. One sees Sellars's gambit at work, simply and clearly, in an analogy he uses.

It seems to me that the necessary equivalence but non-synonymy of
> a exemplifies triangularity

with
> a is triangular

is analogous to the necessary equivalence but non-synonymy of
> That a is triangular is true

with
> a is triangular.

That the analogy is more than a mere analogy is suggested by the fact that instead of saying that a exemplifies triangularity, we might with equal propriety say that triangularity is true of a, or holds of a.

Now if
> a exemplifies triangularity
> triangularity is true of a
> triangularity holds of a

are to be elucidated in terms of

That a is triangular is true

then exemplification is no more present in the world of fact in that narrow sense which tractarians like Professor Bergmann and myself find illuminating, than is meaning, or truth, *and for the same reason*.[18]

The point is that the role of 'is true' is seen in the necessary equivalence of 'p is true' and 'p'. And this reveals that 'is true' does not stand for a property of sentences or propositions. One must see the analagous connection of 'a exemplifies G(-ness)' and '*a* is G'. Doing so, one does not take 'exemplifies' to stand for a tie or connection between a thing and a property. Hence, one need not recognize the property as a term of such a connection. Not being a term, a property is not an *entity*. It is as if Sellars puts Bradley's regress in the service of nominalism. The realist must recognize exemplification as a connection between objects and attributes. But, we need not recognize exemplification as a connection, since 'exemplifies' functions like 'is true'. Hence, we may reject realism. Moreover, in place of '*a* exemplifies G(ness)' we may use "'G' is true of *a*," which is to be understood in terms of "'G*a*' is true." Thus, the analogy is "more than a mere analogy." By using 'is true' we dispense with 'exemplifies' and, by the necessary equivalence of 'p is true' and 'p', we purge 'is true' of ontological commitment. Thus, 'G*a*' is true not in virtue of an object exemplifying a property but in that *a* is a green object! In this way the nominalist dodges acknowledging the color of the object as an entity.

Such a line of reasoning avoids rather than resolves the problem of universals. For, the issue is about whether predicates, normal predicates or *Jumbelese* predicates, play a representative role. The realist makes a simple point. Since such predicative features are basic features of a perspicuous schema which purportedly allows us to represent the neutral facts we all recognize, Sellars must furnish an argument to show that they are exempt from being taken as representatives of something. To say that they represent *objects,* such as *a,* as *qualified objects* is to offer, as an analysis, what is to be analyzed. That Sellars elaborates his account by a sketch of the socio-psychological context in which we learn to attribute predicates to appropriate objects does nothing to resolve questions about the analysis of the truth conditions for sentences like 'G*a*'. The sentence is true, for him, simply because *a* is green. That, of course, is true enough. What is required, however, is that one explicitly state what a truth condition is (a fact, a complex object, a coherent set of propositions, etc.).[19] Sellars does offer complex objects (objects *as* green, square, etc.) as such conditions.[20] But, he refuses to acknowledge that such qualified objects do not differ from the realist's facts. He also refuses to see that there is a basic difference between 'is true', as a semantical predicate, and 'exemplifies', as a term for an ontological tie. This difference is easily spelled out.

There are two problems connected with the notion of *truth* that have concerned philosophers. One is to give an *account* or *theory* or *analysis* of *truth*. This involves *specifying what* a truth condition is (a fact, an object, a set of propositions, the acceptance of a belief, etc.), *characterizing how* such a condition is con-

LOGICAL FORM, EXISTENCE, AND RELATIONAL PREDICATION 225

strued (as a complex, a simple, a class), and *showing that* such a condition so construed suffices as a ground of truth. A second problem concerns the introduction of a term into a perspicuous schema that will transcribe 'is true' and allow one to state that something is true without paradoxical consequences. Since both tasks are described as giving *definitions* of *truth,* they are often confused. Thus, if one introduces a predicate, along lines made familiar by Tarski, that satisfies the so-called convention T, he may thereby think he has proposed a theory of truth. Alternatively, if one offers a theory, such as a correspondence theory that recognizes both propositions and facts, one introduces a truth predicate for *atomic* propositions in terms of something like

(I)   p is true $\equiv (\exists F)$ p ReF. F,

where 'p' is a variable ranging over atomic propositions, 'F' is a variable ranging over atomic facts, and 'ReF.' represents a relation between a proposition and a fact. Then, since

(II) $p \equiv (\exists F)$ p ReF. F

must also be assumed, if we are to derive the required

(III)   p is true $\equiv$ p,

some conclude that such a theory of truth has no content. To say p corresponds to a fact is to say no more than that p is true, or, even, that p. But, (I) and (II) must be understood in the context of the relevant issues. (I) represents a version of a correspondence theory when we understand how 'p', 'F', and 'ReF.' are taken. What is trivial is the introduction of a truth predicate, given that we require (III) to hold for atomic propositions, and not the correspondence theory that is *reflected in,* rather than *stated by,* (I). The statement of the relevant version of the correspondence theory requires the commentary about (I). That, in turn, requires the use of a background context involving references to propositions, facts, and connections between such entities. It is in that context that one also provides a discussion of the notion of a *fact* as a truth condition. In such a discussion, the question of an *exemplification* nexus arises. Thus, it is pointless to dwell on

(IV)   *a* exemplifies G

as being necessarily equivalent to

(V)   G*a*

and

(VI)   'G*a*' is true.

To do so is to make two mistakes. First, one mistakenly thinks that '$(\exists F)$ p ReF. F' is empty in view of (I), (II), and (III). Second, one fails to see that (IV) is involved in the explication of the notion of a fact. Just as some see (I) as trivial in that (II) is acknowledged, so Sellars tries to suggest that (IV) is trivial given its acknowledged equivalence (in some sense) to (V) and (VI).[21] There is an ironical note to this as well as an echo of the purported "paradox of analysis." For Sellars has criticized Davidson for making the very move Sellars himself makes, though he would not acknowledge this since he sees another task to be achieved regarding 'is true' that is not achieved by merely satisfying the condition of convention T. One must elucidate the rule-governed activity of the use of tokens of 'is true' in the social context.[22] But this diverts us from the issue at hand.[23] It also reveals an implicit appeal to an "ordinary language" motif in Sellars's argument. 'Exemplifies' has no ordinary language role, so there is nothing to elucidate. Thus, in view of (III)-(VI), we can confine ourselves to setting forth the rule-governed behavior relevant to the utterance of tokens of 'is true' in the "causal order."

We noted earlier that Sellars explicitly appeals to ordinary usage when he argues that the realist fails to transcribe ordinary sentences, like '*a* is green', by using 'exemplifies' in holding that a particular exemplifies a property. Here, too, we have an implicit appeal to the "paradox of analysis." The paradox, recall, is that one cannot offer a statement as an analysis, since it will either trivially repeat the statement to be analyzed or state something different, and hence not be an analysis. In Sellars's hands, the paradox dispenses with the use of 'exemplifies' to render '*a* is green'. This, in turn, dispenses with the recognition of a *tie* of exemplification. And, that, as we saw earlier, is taken by Sellars to rid us of the property green. Aside from any purported paradox of analysis, Sellars appears to argue that the realist's transcription of '*a* is green' is not perspicuous since the realist reads '*Ga*' in terms of the exemplification of G by *a*. But, what is it to furnish a perspicuous transcription? How can one defend nominalism by pointing to either the philosophical neutrality of ordinary usage or the grammatical fact that in 'This is green' neither 'green' nor 'is green' is used as a *subject* term? For, surely, the realist may acknowledge such claims. The issue is about whether one need appeal to universal properties and a *tie* in order to *account for one predicate truly applying* to two objects. Sellars allows an acceptable response to be the reiteration that the predicate truly applies because the objects are green. This is to claim that so long as predicates are used *predicatively*, no ontological commitments are made by such use. This Quinean theme explains Sellars's claim that 'exemplifies' is to be understood in terms of 'is true'. For, 'is true' is an utterly trivial addition to a perspicuous schema, since there is a clear sense in which the truth conditions for an atomic sentence *s* and a sentence asserting that *s* is true are the same. But, the use of 'exemplifies', by a realist, signifies the latter's recognition of properties, facts, and objects. Thus, there is a critical difference between a use of the ordinary sentence 'This is green' and a purported analysis mentioning a tie between an object and a property. The two are "necessarily equivalent" in that one is offered as part of a philosophical analysis in response to questions about the other. But this does not warrant Sellars's claim that 'exemplifies' is like 'is true', if we are thinking of the sense in which 'is true' is a trivial addition to a schema. Note too, in the above cited passage, how Sellars slides from the claim of an analogy involving 'exemplifies' and 'is true' to the claim that 'exemplifies' is to be elucidated in terms of 'is true'. This, too, emphasizes his repetition of Quine's theme. '*a* exemplifies green'

LOGICAL FORM, EXISTENCE, AND RELATIONAL PREDICATION 227

is elucidated in terms of "'green' is true of a"; the latter is elucidated in terms of "'a is green' is true" and that is ultimately elucidated in terms of (1) there being a green object and (2) the appropriateness of calling green objects green, in view of the roles 'green' and 'is true' have. In speaking of a green object and the predicate 'green' we do not speak of the color green as a term of a relation or tie. Hence, we escape from realism. This "defense" of nominalism thus forces Sellars to claim that every statement using a predicate as a subject term may be transcribed into a statement where no predicate is so used.[24] The success or failure of nominalism thus depends, for Sellars, on the success of such a program of transcription. Here, I do not wish to explore the pros and cons of such a program. I will merely point to a blatant inconsistency in Sellars's views. The realist is held not to transcribe 'a is green' as 'Ga' because he reads the latter in terms of the exemplification of a property by a particular. But, Sellars allows himself to transcribe 'Green is a color' in terms of 'All green things are colored' or "Anything of which a token of 'green' is true is a thing of which a token of 'is colored' is true" or some such statement. The implicit rule for the transcription of ordinary statements is clear. The nominalist, but not the realist, may depart from the literal transcription of ordinary statements. The realist *may not* "parse" the pattern 'Ga' in terms of 'a exemplifying green' since 'green' is then treated as a subject term, but it is not such a term in 'a is green'. The nominalist *may replace* 'Green is a color' by a transcription not using a token of 'green' as a subject term, since that supports Sellars's version of nominalism.

In a recent work, Sellars seeks to bolster his case against realism with a further argument.

> But, it might be argued, the platonist could capture the conceptual tie between exemplification and truth with the claim that truth is to be defined in terms of exemplification, thus
>
> That Fa is true = df a exemplifies F.
>
> But this would be equally absurd, for it would be synonymous with
>
> That a exemplifies F is true = df a exemplifies F
>
> which, as a *definition* (though not as a necessary equivalence), is incoherent.[25]

The argument is based on the assumption that 'Fa' and 'a exemplifies F' are "identical in sense" and differ only in that 'Fa' does not use "an auxiliary expression." The assumption clearly confronts the realist with the paradox of analysis, since it involves the claim that the ordinary statement to be analyzed is "identical in sense" with the statement reflecting a philosophical analysis. Thus, Sellars's argument fails on that ground alone. But, that aside, Sellars overlooks the simple point that what is "defined" in an expression like

> p is true

is the phrase 'is true'. Thus, whether we deal with a sentence with the *auxiliary expression* 'exemplifies' or not, there is nothing incoherent about holding that

'a exemplifies F' is true $=_{df}$ a exemplifies F.

Sellars appears to be raising, knowingly or not, a version of Frege's, and Bradley's, argument against purported analyses of 'is true'. The realist holds that a monadic atomic statement 'Fa' is true on the condition that a exemplify F. Sellars then asks if the realists's analysis applies to the sentence 'a exemplifies F'. And, it does, since the truth condition for that sentence is the same as the truth condition for 'Fa', that a exemplify F, and not, à la Bradley, that a and F exemplify exemplification. By (illicitly) identifying *the sense* of 'a exemplifies F' with the sense of 'Fa', Sellars substitutes the former for the latter in

(S)   'Fa' is true $=_{df}$ a exemplifies F

and obtains

(S_1)   'a exemplifies F' is true $=_{df}$ a exemplifies F.

Writing (S_1), as he does, as

(S_2)   that a exemplifies F is true $=_{df}$ a exemplifies F,

it appears as if one *uses* 'exemplifies' in a circular way.[26] But that does not happen. As we see, by looking at (S_1), 'exemplifies' is only being *used* in the specification of the truth condition for 'a exemplifies F'. There is no more a problem of circularity with 'exemplifies' in (S_1) than there is with 'F' in (S). But, if one permits (S_1), he may raise a problem, if he holds that a Bradley regress is viable in such a case. Then, if we admit 'exemplifies' as a relational predicate, the condition for 'a exemplifies F' appears to be '(a;F) exemplifies exemplification', and this purportedly initiates a Bradley-type regress. But it really does not. One need merely take the fact that is the truth condition for '(a;F) exemplifies exemplification' to be that a exemplifies F. Or, what amounts to the same thing, one can take the appropriate sentence to be (S_1) and not

(S_3)   'a exemplifies F' is true $=_{df}$ (a;F) exemplifies exemplification.

This would underline the insistence that exemplification is a tie and is not a relation among relations.[27] This point is made more emphatic by representing exemplification in a different way than one represents *ordinary* relations: by not allowing a term for such a tie or, at least, not allowing such a term to occupy the grammatical place of a relational predicate. Sellars, at best, thus merely reraises Bradley's old objection and does not establish the "incoherence" of the realist's pattern. Moreover, not only does he mistakenly take the realist to be involved in a vicious circle, through not realizing that 'is true' is being explicated, not 'exemplifies', and that 'exemplifies' is not *used* in the left sides of (S_1) and (S_3), he also overlooks a further crucial point.

One must recognize a different exemplification nexus or tie for monadic, dyadic, triadic, etc., attributes. Thus, the pattern for 'is true' is closer to

'Ga' is true $=_{df}$ a exemplifies$_1$ G
'$R_1(a,b)$' is true $=_{df}$ $(a;b)$ exemplifies$_2$ R_1
etc.

Hence, if one attempts to generate a regress, one should use

'a exemplifies$_1$ F' is true = $_{df}$ (a;F) exemplifies$_2$ exemplification$_1$,

and all semblance of circularity disappears. (One should also keep in mind that since 'exemplifies$_1$' occurs inside the quotes, on the left-hand side of the biconditional, there is no circularity on that ground alone. It appears that Sellars's rendition, through the use of a "that" clause, helps to confuse matters. But, even with such clauses, we still may distinguish *use* and *mention*.)

The realist, either by recognizing that the fact—a exemplifying F—is the truth condition for a whole series of sentences

a exemplifies$_1$ F
(a;F) exemplifies$_2$ exemplification$_1$
etc.

or by holding that such a series is illegitimate can take the purported Bradley regress to be as harmless as the series Sellars acknowledges to be harmless

a is F
'a is F' is true
"'a is F' is true" is true
etc.

One need not, as Sellars does, seek to avoid a Bradley-type regress by taking the "deep structure" of 'a exemplifies F-ness' to be 'that-Fa is true'.

Gustav Bergmann once criticized the Fregean theme regarding the incompleteness of concepts by suggesting that signs for particulars may also be taken as incomplete.[28] Thus a name could be of the form 'ϕa', rather than simply 'a'. This would show that neither names nor predicates, by themselves, are used to assert anything and that they require being combined with signs of the other kind to form a sentence. It would also put names and predicates on a more equal footing, as befits a realistic position, since the Fregean-style notation supposedly emphasizes the dependence of concepts. As we have noted, Sellars's notation stresses that dependence even more emphatically. But Bergmann's claim overlooks a simple point. One would require a number of signs for each name to indicate the role the name may play in different sentence forms:

ϕa, aR^{2}y, xR$^2 a$, R^3 (a,x,y), . . .

Alternatively, one could understand 'ϕa' to *cover* all such cases. But, one need not do anything like that in the case of predicates used predicatively. What this shows is that the basic difference being depicted by the Fregean-style notation is that particulars (or "senses") may enter into logically different *kinds* of facts (or propositions) as subjects, whereas properties and relations (concepts) may enter into only one kind *as attributes* (concepts).[29] This, of course, is a question about the form of facts (propositions) and not one concerning the dependence of attributes (concepts) on particulars. What it represents is that particulars are not of logically different kinds, whereas attributes are monadic, dyadic, and so on. Since there are different kinds of attributes, in this sense, there are different kinds of facts (propositions). Hence, there is a point to taking the attribute (concept) to "carry" the form of the fact (proposition) into which it enters as a constituent. In this sense, there is also a point to a Fregean-style notation, and even to Sellars's extreme version of it.

If one holds that we need not appeal to either a fact or a relation to account for the truth of 'aR_1b', then questions about forms and directions would seem not to arise. In a recent book Michael Loux reiterates Quine's appeal to "is true of" and "satisfaction" to avoid attributes.[30] Thus, to account for the truth of 'aR_1b' one need only note that a and b satisfy the predicate 'xR_1y' (or that the predicate is true of a and b). Oddly, if Sellars were to appeal to such a move, that would amount to holding that '$x\ y$' is satisfied by a and b. And that would mean that one recognizes, explicitly, relational predicates in *Jumbelese*.[31] What is interesting about Sellars's schema is that using '$a\ b$', as opposed to 'aR_1b', it appears as if we make use of a *relation* obtaining between the names to represent a relation obtaining between the objects. But, when we recognize the pattern with variables, as in '$x\ y$', we see that Sellars uses both *the relation* between the subject terms, as in '$a\ b$', *and the spatial distance* between the subject signs. The predicate '$x\ y$' is more like the predicate 'xR_1y' than the sentence '$a\ b$' is like the sentence 'aR_1b', and it is by concentrating on the latter pair that one may be tempted to overlook Sellars's use of a predicate term, albeit a strange one—the distance between subject terms. Insofar as one uses 'xR_1y' as a predicate term, rather than 'R_1', one cannot have 'R_1' on a list of signs without being flanked by an 'x' and a 'y'. Likewise, one cannot have the space between the variables without letter tokens. But, then, '$x\ y$' is as much a predicate sign as is 'xR_1y'. To say this is not to claim that spatial juxtaposition represents a relation and hence that the spatial juxtaposition of a and b functions as a predicate in '$a\ b$'. This would let Sellars reply that the spatial juxtaposition *of a* and *b* is *the sentence, not a constituent of the sentence*. The point, to repeat, is that *the space between* 'x' and 'y' in '$x\ y$' plays the role of 'R_1' in 'xR_1y'. The only difference is that one can remove the letters 'x' and 'y' from 'xR_1y' and be left with 'R_1'; one cannot remove them from '$x\ y$' and be left with the space between them. But, 'R_1' is not a term of a proper Fregean schema. This is why Sellars's schema is a Fregean schema that is both extreme and consistent; it is not a schema that perspicuously does without predicates.

Whether we take '$x\ y$' as a predicate sign or not, one clearly has to recognize an order among objects in the case of relational predicates. Thus, whether one employed '$x\ y$' or 'xR_1y', to employ the notion of *satisfaction*, in nominalistic fashion, would require one to recognize ordered pairs or sequences. Ordered pairs (or directions), and sequences generally, are not objects in the sense in which a and b are objects. Moreover, in the case of ordered pairs (as opposed to pairs), the question of order or structure reappears. As we noted earlier, an ordered pair (or a direction) seems to be a complex consisting of objects in an order or structure. Paradoxically, then, the nominalist's use of *satisfaction* appears to force the recognition of entities other than particulars—*pairs*—and *the order* obtaining between particulars

LOGICAL FORM, EXISTENCE, AND RELATIONAL PREDICATION 231

in an ordered pair. One might seek to analyze the "order" in a standard way, along the lines of the so-called Wiener-Kuratowski procedure. Thus, an ordered pair is construed as a class of classes so that *(a;b)* is taken as the class $\{\{a\}, \{a,b\}\}$, or, since *a* and *b* are not themselves classes, but particulars, we could employ the "simpler" class $\{a, \{b\}\}$ for *(a;b)*.[32] If one takes the pair as a class, one then takes the predicate, 'xR_1y' or 'x y', to be satisfied by such an entity. Relational predication is then construed along the lines of monadic predication except that the kind of *thing* taken as the subject is different: a pair or class as opposed to an object. Using classes, such as $\{a, \{b\}\}$ or $\{\{a\}, \{a,b\}\}$, apparently allows one to dispense with an appeal to order, but, ironically, it introduces "abstract" entities, i.e., classes, and classes of classes at that, in the analysis of predicates applying to particulars. This is hardly in the nominalist's style. On the other hand, if ordered pairs are taken as basic, one introduces not only a new kind of entity but one that is complex in the sense in which the realist's facts are complex: the ordered pair *(a;b)* involves two objects in an order.

Bergmann, who to Sellars is the arch realist on the contemporary scene, has recently made a decidedly nominalistic move with respect to the problem of relational order.[33] He seeks to construe the order of a relational fact along the lines of the set-theoretical construal of an ordered pair as a class. Bergmann introduces a new entity, a *diad*. Given any two entities, there is, "eo ipso," a third, the diad of which they are the sole constituents. Thus, given *a* and *b*, we have *(a,b)*, their diad. And, as in the case of sets, *(a,b) = (b,a)*' holds. One can distinguish the facts aR_1b and bR_1a in terms of the former involving *a* and *(a,b)* as constituents whereas the latter involves *b* and *(a,b)*. Thus, one can analyze the fact aR_1b in terms of *a*, *(a,b)*, $\hat{x}R_1\hat{y}$, and exemplification without appealing to an entity, such as *(a;b)* or $a\hat{R}^2b$, to account for the order. Bergmann thus, in nominalistic fashion, dispenses with an entity that is neither a particular nor *reducible* to particulars by appealing to a *diad* of particulars. Also, on his pattern, one need not appeal to the form $\hat{x}R^2\hat{y}$, since the diad *(a, (a,b))* is taken as *the* subject of the relation $\hat{x}R_1\hat{y}$ in the fact aR_1b. That shows that $\hat{x}R_1\hat{y}$ is a two-term relation on Bergmann's pattern. In the case of a monadic fact, a diad would not be the subject, and in the case of a three-term relation we would have a "more complex" diad as the subject, i.e., something like *((a, (a,b)), c)* or *(c, (c, (a, (a,b))))*.

If Bergmann has successfully analyzed order in relational facts, his gambit can be appropriated by the nominalist to avoid abstract entities, classes or pairs. Bergmann's diads, being complex particulars without an ordering or structure, should be more palatable to a nominalist. But even armed with Bergmann's diads, a nominalist must still propound the absurdity that a relation between a sign and a thing, a diad or an object, constitutes the ground of truth of a sentence. And, he must face the obvious question about appealing to *satisfaction* as a relation. For, to stick with this pattern he must hold that

(I)   'xR_1y' is satisfied by *(a;b)*

is to be construed as

(II) ' . . . is satisfied by ___' is satisfied by
('xR₁y';(a;b)).

And this, of course, generates another version of a Bradley-type regress. For, on this nominalist's gambit, it is a relation between *a sign* and *a pair* that constitutes the condition of truth for 'aR_1b', (I), (II), and so on *ad infinitum*. Thus, (I) stands for a *fact* which we must analyze along realistic lines or which must be reconstrued along nominalistic lines. But to do the latter is to introduce (II). The nominalistic "solution" thus invites the kind of question it purports to answer. Moreover, nominalists cannot invoke the kind of response that realists have employed in the case of a corresponding question about exemplification: that exemplification is a special kind of relation, a tie or nexus, that does not require a further connection to connect *it* to what *it* connects. To do so would be to recognize *satisfaction* as a special kind of *entity*. The version of nominalism we have considered thus falls victim to a vicious regress of the kind Bradley and Frege invoked for different purposes. My main concern in this paper, however, is not with the use of Bergmann's analysis of order by a nominalist, but with the cogency of that analysis. Although suggestive and innovative, it is not viable.

The basic problem with Bergmann's analysis of order has nothing essentially to do with his introduction of a new entity, the *diad*. Whatever problems and *ad hoc* features one may find in the introduction of such a complex but unstructured entity, there is a more basic problem with his analysis. It is a problem that would be present if he were to employ classes as constituents of facts and to directly make use of the Wiener-Kuratowski procedure rather than parody it by the appeal to diads. Thus, I shall consider the issue in terms of classes. Since we deal with elements that are not classes, we may use the classes $\{a, \{b\}\}$ and $\{b, \{a\}\}$ to construe the ordered pairs *(a;b)* and *(b;a)*, respectively. Let us then take R_1 to be a property of the class $\{a, \{b\}\}$, as Bergmann takes it to be a property of the diad *(a, (a,b))*. The question at issue is whether such entities, $\{a, \{b\}\}$ or *(a, (a,b))*, allow us to *analyze* order in facts and, hence, dispense with directions, forms, ordered pairs, and so on.

We should first note that one *chooses* which class, $\{a, \{b\}\}$ or $\{b, \{a\}\}$, is the constituent of aR_1b. In fact, there are any number of other choices one could make; $\{a, \{a,b\}\}$, $\{\{a\}, \{a,b\}\}$, and so on. This choice is really complex. Given that an ordered pair is taken as a constituent of a fact, one chooses which class is to be taken as such a pair. And, given such a choice, one makes use of an ordering *imposed* on the class. It is not the class alone that one employs in the analysis, but the elements of the class in an ordering. In a sense one implicitly treats the classes (or *diads*) chosen as ordered entities. It is true, of course, that the class $\{a, \{b\}\}$ is not a structured or ordered entity since

$$\{a, \{b\}\} = \{\{b\}, a\}$$

is true, whereas, where $a \neq b$,

(a;b) ≠ *(b;a)*.

But, in *choosing* to take $(a;b)$ as $\{a, \{b\}\}$, in the analysis of the fact aR_1b, one takes the element that is the unit class in $\{a, \{b\}\}$ to be the second constituent of the class. That is, one takes the member of the class *that is a unit class* to be the correlate of the second term in the sentence 'aR_1b'. The appeal to order is thus concealed in the interpretation rules, rather than inhering in the linear order of the expression. The Wiener-Kuratowski procedure enables one to map sets onto sentences, $\{a, R_1, \{b\}\}$ onto 'aR_1b' rather than onto 'bR_1a'; but, in so using that procedure, there is an implicit appeal to order. Thus, the use of the procedure in a purported analysis of order in facts is question begging. This is not to say that the procedure is illicitly used in set-theoretical contexts. For the only requirement imposed for such use is that one construe $(a;b)$ and $(c;d)$ such that

$(a;b) = (c;d)$ iff $((a = c) \& (b = d))$

holds. The procedure satisfies that requirement. Since we make use of an unordered entity, a class, it appears as if we have analyzed the order of a fact. But, all we have done is introduce a notation that does not appeal to an ordering of signs. To see this, let us replace 'aR_1b' by (1) '$\{a, \{b\}\} \in R_1$', taking R_1 to be a class of an appropriate "type." We would also have (2) '$\{b, \{a\}\} \in R_1$' for 'bR_1a'. We may then note that (1) and (1') '$\{\{b\}, a\} \in R_1$' state exactly the same condition, as do (2) and (2') '$\{\{a\}, b\} \in R_1$'. Thus, the order within the subject sign is irrelevant. We could also write our sentences as '$aR_1\{b\}$' and '$\{a\}R_1b$', understanding that the linear ordering of subject signs makes no difference because '$aR_1\{b\}$' and '$\{b\}R_1a$' state the same thing, that-aR_1b. We then replace the appeal to the ordering of signs by the introduction of class signs in our "sentences" and the recognition of classes as constituents of facts. But, the ordering of particulars has not been eliminated, for we use the set-theoretical symbols to represent an ordering in a fact instead of using the ordering of the signs in a sentence to represent an ordering in a fact. Bergmann's gambit is thus startlingly like Sellars's attempt to dispense with properties and relations by means of a novel linguistic representation. Both believe that by representing something in a special way they do not represent it at all.

Bergmann's analysis also fails in that, first, he merely manages to represent order by a symbolism that does not involve ordered sign complexes, and, second, he must introduce an additional kind of entity, a diad, and declare that it is a complex but not structured. He seeks to make this latter claim palatable by holding that since any two things "eo ipso" form a diad, the existence of a diad of two entities is a matter of logic and not of fact. Thus, given an object a and a property G, irrespective of whether a has G or even whether G is a property that may sensibly be attributed to a, there is a diad with a and G as constituents. However, it is obvious that Bergmann's diads are merely classes renamed. Given any two things, there is "eo ipso" (or by a kind of comprehension rule) their pair-class. In effect, Bergmann thus takes classes to be constituents of atomic facts. To solve the problem of order at such a price is pointless. But, then, how is one to resolve the issue? If we introduce directions or ordered pairs, we recognize that they are complexes in a threefold way: there are constituents of such complexes, the ordered terms;

there is the ordering of the constituents; there is the two-term form that is involved. We must then hold that questions comparable to those raised about the order of facts may not be raised about directions or ordered pairs and, hence, that Bradley-type regresses may not be generated. Alternatively, we may take a hint from Frege's decisive insight, which was explicitly adopted by Russell and Wittgenstein, and, ultimately, if not explicitly, by Sellars. Frege took it to be pointless to introduce a predicative connection as an additional constituent of a proposition. Thus, he let concepts play a twofold role. He was mistaken to think that no connection was then involved, since he let the concept provide the connection. (In a similar way Sellars was later to be mistaken in thinking that he avoided relations and exemplification by appealing to related objects.) Nevertheless, there is the decisive insight that in dealing with the analysis of structured complexes *something* must play a complex role. In the case of monadic facts (or propositions) exemplification connects a term and an attribute, and as an asymmetrical connection, provides the form of the facts. In the case of relational facts, one can take *the order* (as a direction or ordered pair) as another constituent of such facts. One must then hold that exemplification connects the objects, the order, and the relation in the fact. Exemplification is then taken to involve a further ordering in that it connects the *objects* in *the order* into *the relation*. Thus, even with a direction as a constituent, exemplification takes on a dual role. However, one may hold that the objects do not exemplify the relation. Rather, it is the ordered pair that exemplifies the relation. On this view relational exemplification is construed on the order of monadic exemplification with ordered pairs as subject terms. But, ordered pairs are themselves complexes of the objects in an ordering. Hence, the objects as well as the ordering of the objects are, ultimately, constituents of such a fact. Thus, instead of taking exemplification to connect the objects, the relation, and the direction, one takes it to connect the relation to the pair, while taking the latter to involve a connection between the objects. Alternatively, one can take the order among the terms as yet another aspect of the "predicative" tie, and not as a further constituent. This means that one may hold that facts (or propositions) are not analyzable in a sense in which they would be analyzable if one acknowledged ordered pairs or directions. For, on such a view there is no constituent in virtue of which the fact that-aR_1b would differ from the fact that-bR_1a. The facts are just different structural connections among the same constituents. Exemplification, on such a gambit, supplies the order, structure, and connection for constituents. A variant of the gambit would involve holding that the connection in aR_1b would differ from that in bR_1a. One then grounds the difference in order in a different exemplification nexus. This would permit one to hold that the facts differ in virtue of a different connection or nexus and not in virtue of a *constituent* direction. On either gambit one recognizes different exemplification ties for different kinds of facts, in the sense of monadic, dyadic, etc., and, on the latter view, one would also acknowledge *two* dyadic ties, *six* triadic ties, and so on. The recognition of different ties for different kinds of facts is not merely an *ad hoc* response to the questions regarding relational and monadic predication. We can see that when we note that Bergmann's analysis of order must also incorporate several exemplification connections. He holds that there is only one such connection, which holds between a monadic property or relation and something else. Thus, exemplification is, *in a way*, always a two-term connection for Bergmann. In the monadic case the connection would hold between a property and an object, in the case of a dyadic relation it would hold between a relation and a diad, in the case of a triadic relation it would hold between such a relation and a more complex diad, and so on. I said "in a way" above, because one can think of exemplification, for Bergmann, as always operating on one term, a diad. Such a diad would consist of a monadic property and an object, or of a two-term relation and a diad, such as *(a, (a,b))*, and so on. But all this is misleading. For, both terms of such diads are *logically* different in all such cases. As one term we have either a monadic, a dyadic, etc., attribute, whereas, as the other term, we have an object or an increasingly complex diad. These differences obviously point to another way of recognizing different exemplification connections. Insofar as one recognizes an exemplification connection in logically different kinds of facts, one recognizes a different kind of connection for each kind of fact. To hold that there is one connection that plays logically different roles or is "multigrade" is to use different words, not to acknowledge fewer "things."

There is yet another alternative. One can follow Frege and take the monadic and relational attributes to provide the connection, the form, and the order. This will do so long as one does not thereby think that he has not acknowledged that facts (propositions) involve structure and order. All one does is let the attributes take on the logical roles of the predicative connection; one does not dispense with such roles. Thus, however we go about it, the resolution of the problem of relational predication requires that we recognize two things. First, complexes like facts (and propositions) are not analyzable since they *are* connections, including ordered connections, among constituents, though they *are not* connections in the sense of being connecting ties or relations. And, second, some constituent(s) will play more than one role in a fact or proposition.

As to how one may choose between the various alternatives just outlined, I do not know. There are reasons for and against each. But none of these alternatives incorporate the delusion that order has been eliminated or the double delusion that order and relations have both been eliminated.

Notes

1. On this point see my article "Nominalism, General Terms, and Predication," *The Monist* 61 (1978):460-75.
2. For arguments for the existence of properties and universals, so understood, see Russell's classic paper "On the Relation of Universals and Particulars," *Proceedings of the Aristotelian Society* 1 (1911-12):1-24, and my "Russell's Proof of Realism Reproved," *Philosophical Studies* 37 (1980):37-44.
3. For a discussion of Russell's views on denoting and reference, see my *Thought, Fact, and Reference: the Origins and Ontology of Logical Atomism* (Minneapolis, 1978), chaps. 7 and 8.
4. I will use 'R^2' as a variable ranging over two-term relations and the sign 'R_1' as a constant relational predicate.

5. On Russell's views about *senses of relations* and *logical forms* as *subsistent universals*, see his "The Philosophical Importance of Mathematical Logic," *The Monist* 22, no. 4 (1913):485-87, 492, and chap. 7 of his unpublished manuscript "Theory of Knowledge." D. F. Pears discusses the relation of the latter work to Wittgenstein's *Tractatus* in "The Relation between Wittgenstein's Picture Theory of Propositions and Russell's Theories of Judgment," *Philosophical Review* 86, no. 2 (April 1977):177-96.

6. The lists make use of Russell's device of capping a variable to distinguish a *constant sign* '$\hat{x}R_1\hat{y}$', standing for *the relation* (also indicated by 'R_1') or *function*, from the propositional function sign 'xR_1y'. (See "Mathematical Logic as Based on the Theory of Types," in *Logic and Knowledge*, ed. R. C. Marsh (New York, 1971), pp. 59-102.) When referring to the relation in a discussion of Russell's views, I will use '$\hat{x}R_1\hat{y}$'. When I later discuss views of Frege and others, I will also speak of 'xR_1y' as a "predicate" expression.

7. In "Theory of Knowledge" Russell took the form to involve the exemplification connection. Thus, he held that the proposition *a is G* had only two constituents. See "Theory of Knowledge," p. 183. In keeping with this, Russell denied that *forms* were "things" in the sense in which constituents, related in forms, were things.

8. The basic modification will involve the recognition of facts as the referents of true propositions and the consequent distinction between *relational concepts*, as constituents of propositions, and *relations*, as constituents of facts.

9. B. Russell, "On the Nature of Truth," *Proceedings of the Aristotelian Society* 7 (1906-7): 45-48.

10. "Theory of Knowledge," p. 183.

11. "Theory of Knowledge," p. 278. Though Russell's view is actually more complex than my characterization of it, the difference is not important for the present issue. He holds that the complex $[aR_1b]$ should be represented by a definite description: $(\iota\gamma)\,(aD_1\gamma\ \&\ bD_2\gamma)$. Thus, the relation R_1 is replaced by the relations D_1 and D_2, which "determine" R_1, and he considers the *atomic complex* $[aR_1b]$ to be replaced by a *molecular complex*, since '$aD_1\gamma$' and '$bD_2\gamma$' are terms of a conjunction. His move is designed to enable him to distinguish

S judges that aR_1b

from

S judges that bR_1a

on the relational analysis of judgment he held at that time. (For a discussion of this analysis, see *Thought, Fact, and Reference*, pp. 309-32.) His analysis will depend on the molecular expressions '$aD_1\gamma\ \&\ bD_2\gamma$' and '$bD_1\gamma\ \&\ aD_2\gamma$' having *different atomic constituents* whereas the complexes $[aR_1b]$ and $[bR_1a]$ have the *same constituent entities*.

12. Sellars does not put it quite this way. But this is in keeping with what he says at a number of places, including "Hochberg on Mapping, Meaning, and Metaphysics," in *Contemporary Perspectives in the Philosophy of Language*, ed. P. French et al. (Minneapolis, 1978), pp. 357-58. He acknowledges that *a* and *b* are related, but does not hold that he thereby recognizes relations as abstract objects.

13. W. Sellars, *Science and Metaphysics* (New York, 1960), p. 137.

14. See my "Sellars and Goodman on Predicates, Properties, and Truth," in *Contemporary Perspectives*, pp. 360-68.

15. W. Sellars, *Naturalism and Ontology* (Reseda, 1979), p. 58.

16. Sellars has denied that he does this, and I had earlier agreed with him (see his "Hochberg on Mapping, Meaning, and Metaphysics," p. 353, and p. 333 of my "Mapping, Meaning, and Metaphysics" in *Contemporary Perspectives*), but his new book makes it clear that he does so argue.

17. W. Sellars, *Science, Perception, and Reality* (New York, 1963), pp. 243-44.

18. *Ibid.*, pp. 244-45.

19. In *Substance and Attribute* (Boston, 1978), p. 367, M. Loux also overlooks this simple

fact in his disarming restatement of the nominalistic line of argument (though he argues for realism on other grounds):

We ask why it is true, for example, that Socrates is wise; and the answer we are given is "Because he is wise." What the realist contends is that this is not to provide a genuine explanation; it is merely to restate what has to be explained . . . but I think that the extreme nominalist would be right to ask what other sentence the realist would have him use here. Is he supposed to say that 'Socrates is wise' is true because Secretariat is a horse or because Jimmy Carter is president? Pretty clearly not; if 'Socrates is wise' is true, it had better be because Socrates is wise; and we can be sure that any theory of predication that suggests anything to the contrary is false.

20. See "Hochberg on Mapping, Meaning, and Metaphysics," p. 358. For Sellars, this merely means that we acknowledge green objects in the ordinary context.

21. I speak of "equivalence in some sense," rather than follow Sellars's use of "necessary equivalence," since there is an important issue regarding the sense in which statements embodying philosophical analyses are *equivalent* to the statements of ordinary usage which they purportedly analyze. Not taking them to be necessary, as I do not, would provide yet another stumbling block to Sellars's gambit. But to go into such an issue would involve too long a digression.

22. See "Hochberg on Mapping, Meaning, and Metaphysics," pp. 357, 359.

23. This is so since, ultimately, the "rules" direct us to ascribe predicates to appropriately characterized objects.

24. See the correspondence between Sellars and Loux printed in *Naturalism and Ontology*.

25. Sellars, *Naturalism and Ontology*, p. 108.

26. Keeping the "paradox" of analysis in mind, one can turn any "definition" into an "incoherent" pattern along Sellars's lines. Since, by stipulation, the definiens and the definiendum have "the same sense" we may *replace* any defined pattern by its defining statement in ' . . . = $_{df}$ ---' and obtain an "incoherent" result, since a statement is then its own definition. Clearly patterns like ' . . . = $_{df}$ ---' are not to be so used.

27. Here Sellars may object that I now do exactly what he does when he uses '*a* is green' to express the truth condition for 'that-*a* is green is true'. The difference, of course, is that I have acknowledged a tie, exemplification, that plays a unique role, whereas Sellars seeks to have truth conditions at no ontological expense. This does point to the traditional problem of realism associated with Bradley's name and to how Sellars uses the Bradley regress to support nominalsim.

28. G. Bergmann, "Propositional Functions," *Analysis* 17 (1956):43-48.

29. Russell took this difference to distinguish particulars from universals.

30. Loux, *Substance and Attribute*, p. 36.

31. J. Wilkin has argued that Sellars's *Jumbelese* contains predicate terms in "Sellars on Bradley's Paradox," *Philosophical Studies* 36 (1979):51-59.

32. Since we are concerned only with ordered pairs of individuals (and not pairs of sets), we avoid the standard counterexamples to construing $(a;h)$ as $\{a, \{h\}\}$.

33. G. Bergmann, "Notes on Ontology," forthcoming in *Noûs* (1981). The views developed in this paper are presupposed by and made use of in Bergmann's "Notes on the Ontology of Minds," in the present volume; see notes 1, 3, 16, and 32 in that paper.

Popper's Criticisms of Wittgenstein's *Tractatus*

E. D. KLEMKE

It is one of the chief skills of the philosopher not to occupy himself with questions which do not concern him.
L. Wittgenstein

In his recent book, *Unended Quest*, Sir Karl Popper has written: "*The Open Society* contained some criticisms of Wittgenstein's *Tractatus*, criticisms which have been almost completely neglected by Wittgenstein's commentators."[1] I had not realized that Popper has been so eager for "commentators" to take up this task. I have reread the relevant passages of Popper's book, and I believe that they merit serious discussion. Hence I am happy to oblige.

I

In his criticisms of Wittgenstein's *Tractatus*, Popper's main theses are:

1. According to Wittgenstein, we cannot discuss anything profitably unless we precisely define the terms that we use (ii, 16).[2]

2(a). Wittgenstein holds that whereas science investigates matters of fact, "it is the business of philosophy to clarify the meanings of terms, thereby purging our language, and eliminating linguistic puzzles" (ii, 20; cf. ii, 287).

2(b). For Wittgenstein, *"The true task of philosophy . . . is not to formulate propositions; it is, rather, to clarify propositions"* (ii, 293; cf. ii, 296).

3. Wittgenstein "tries to draw a limit, in our language, between sense and nonsense" (ii, 293).

4. For Wittgenstein, (genuine) propositions "have sense"; but "philosophi-

cal propositions do not exist; they only look like propositions, but are, in fact, nonsensical" (ii, 293).

5(a). For Wittgenstein, "The limit between sense and nonsense coincides with that between natural science and philosophy" (ii, 293).

5(b). For Wittgenstein, the demarcation between sense and nonsense "coincides with that between science and metaphysics, i.e., between scientific sentences and philosophical pseudo-propositions" (ii, 293).

6(a). "Wittgenstein is an anti-metaphysician.... He tries to show that metaphysics is 'simply nonsense'" (ii, 293).

6(b). Wittgenstein's "fundamental aim" is "the destruction of metaphysics by unveiling it as meaningless nonsense" (ii, 296).

7. Wittgenstein's views imply that we should demand definitions of his words from the metaphysician; and if for any word the definition is not forthcoming, *we assume that the word is meaningless*" (ii, 294).

8. Wittgenstein's "method" gives rise "not to the destruction or to the exclusion or even to the clear demarcation of metaphysics, but to their intrusion into the field of science, and to their confusion with science" (ii, 297).

9(a). Many of Wittgenstein's own sentences, e.g., "Philosophy is not a theory but an activity," do not belong to science; hence any such sentence "cannot belong to 'the totality of true propositions'" (ii, 297).

9(b). But, since "it is not a false proposition either ... it must be *'meaningless'* or *'senseless'* or *'nonsensical'*" (ii, 297).

10. Thus "Wittgenstein's own philosophy is senseless, and it is admitted to be so" (ii, 297).

11. But Wittgenstein claims that the truth of the thoughts communicated in the *Tractatus* is "unassailable and definite." This means that "we can communicate *unassailably and definitely true thoughts* by way of propositions which are admittedly nonsensical, and that we can solve problems 'finally' by propounding nonsense" (ii, 297).

12. Such nonsense is (for Wittgenstein) "a new kind of nonsense," *"deeply significant nonsense"* (ii, 297).

13. Wittgenstein determines the conception of 'sense' or 'meaning' in a narrow way such that "you can say of all uncomfortable questions that you cannot find any 'sense' or 'meaning' in them" (ii, 297).

14. Wittgenstein's theory blurs the problem of demarcation because of "his naive idea that there is something 'essentially' or 'by nature' scientific and something 'essentially' or 'by nature' metaphysical and that it is our task to discover the 'natural' demarcation between these two" (ii, 297).

15. Wittgenstein's identification of the totality of true propositions with the totality of science leads to the exclusion from science of all hypoth-

POPPER'S CRITICISMS OF WITTGENSTEIN'S *TRACTATUS* 241

eses that are not true. "And since we can never know of a hypothesis whether or not it is true, we can never know whether or not it belongs to the sphere of natural science (ii, 298).
16. Wittgenstein has a famous "principle of verification" which leads to the same result (ii, 298).
17. Wittgenstein "overlooked the problem of universality or generality" and thereby "followed in the footsteps of earlier positivists" (ii, 298).
18. Some of Wittgenstein's sentences, e.g., "The totality of true propositions is . . . the totality of natural science," are logical paradoxes. Since such a sentence does not belong to natural science, "it follows that it asserts its own untruth and is therefore contradictory" (ii, 355).
19. Wittgenstein defines 'meaning' "arbitrarily in such a way that only factual propositions are 'meaningful'" and hence "norms are meaningless" (i, 234).
20. Wittgenstein's mysticism is "holistic" (ii, 359).

Most of these are serious charges. In many cases I believe that they rest on a misunderstanding of Wittgenstein's *Tractatus*. In some cases I believe that the theses conflict with one another. In other cases, in which conclusions are drawn, I do not believe that such conclusions follow. I shall now attempt to show this. Since I believe that the first 16 are the most serious charges, I shall place my emphasis upon them.

II

1. Popper does not cite any reference to Wittgenstein's *Tractatus* (or any other work of his) with regard to the claim that (according to Wittgenstein) we cannot discuss anything profitably unless we define precisely the terms we use. Instead he quotes a passage from Crossman's *Plato To-Day* (in which this view is expressed). But Popper says of this passage that it is "characteristic of a view which by implication is held by many contemporary philosophers of repute, for example, by Wittgenstein" (ii, 16). Not only is such a view not found in Wittgenstein's *Tractatus*; it is not implied by anything that Wittgenstein says. It is true that Wittgenstein makes various comments about definitions and their roles. But these assertions do not contain or "imply" the above mentioned view. I fail to see why Popper attributes it to Wittgenstein.

If one closely examines the *Tractatus*, one sees that Wittgenstein's few remarks about definitions pertain to an "ideal" or logically perspicuous language. (This claim will be supported below.) He clearly distinguishes between primitive or undefined signs and defined signs. He states that primitive terms cannot be "dissected" by means of definitions. He holds that one can explain their meanings by elucidations, that is, by true propositions whose senses can be apprehended by identifying the facts that they state. But, he adds, since these elucidations are propositions that contain primitive signs, "they can only be understood if the meanings

(Bedeutungen) of those signs are already known" (T, 3.263).[3] Thus, even if one took Wittgenstein's remarks to apply to natural languages, it would *not* be true that Wittgenstein holds that we cannot profitably discuss anything unless we precisely define the terms we use.

Why, then, does Popper wrongly attribute this view to Wittgenstein? I believe that the answer is one to which I shall frequently refer, namely, that Popper has mistakenly interpreted the *Tractatus* as a treatise in the tradition of logical positivism. Many of his remarks about Wittgenstein throughout his works exhibit this grievous error. I shall call attention to a large number of them in what follows.

2(a). Popper claims that Wittgenstein maintained that "it is the business of philosophy to clarify the meanings of terms, thereby purging our language, and eliminating linguistic puzzles," as opposed to science, which "investigates matters of fact" (ii, 20). It is certainly true that Wittgenstein points out that everyday language can lead to various confusions. Thus he mentions that the same word may have different "modes of signification," such as, 'is', which can function as the sign for identity, predication, and so forth (T, 3.323). And he even states that, because of such features of language, philosophical confusions often arise (T, 3.324). But it is inaccurate to say that it is *the* business of philosophy to engage in clarifying meanings of terms and eliminating puzzles. The entire opening part of the *Tractatus*, for example (often overlooked by commentators), contains a number of assertions that are *not* linguistic clarifications. In fact, they have nothing to do with language at all. Indeed, as I shall point out later, they are very substantial philosophical (and ontological) assertions.

This is not to deny that Wittgenstein says a good deal about language in the *Tractatus*. But his primary concern is not with language itself, or the clarification of terms, or the elimination of puzzles. Rather, his concern is with the question of how language relates to the *world*. As I shall show in greater detail below, the chief problem of the *Tractatus* may be stated: What are the conditions that must obtain in order for us to use language to discourse about the world (T, 5.471; 5.6-5.61; 6.12; 6.124; 6.22)?

2(b). Regarding the claim that, for Wittgenstein, *"the true task of philosophy ... is not to formulate propositions; it is, rather, to clarify propositions"* (ii, 293), one must admit that Wittgenstein often says things of this sort; an example is "Philosophy does not result in 'philosophical propositions', but rather in the clarification of propositions" (T, 4.112). However, this assertion occurs in a context in which Wittgenstein attempts to distinguish philosophy from the natural sciences (T, 4.111). But it is a highly exaggerated claim, and Wittgenstein himself does not adhere to it. I have often thought that it would have been better for Wittgenstein to qualify assertions of this sort by saying, *"Much* of philosophy does not ... but rather does ... ," and so forth. Perhaps he presupposed, however, that his readers would interpret these statements in such a fashion. Again, a close reading of the *Tractatus* (including, once more, the opening part) indicates that Wittgenstein did *not* think that the sole task of philosophy is to clarify propositions rather than to formulate them (T, 1-2.063).

Furthermore, in the context to which I referred above, Wittgenstein stipulatively identifies the totality of true propositions with the whole of natural science or with "the whole corpus of the natural sciences" (T, 4.11). But as I shall emphasize later, he *does* hold that there *are* philosophical propositions (T, 6.54) which he calls elucidations. And these elucidations are understandable by others. Hence Popper's first claim in 2(b) is, if not false, at least misleading. It should read: "It is not one of the tasks of philosophy to formulate propositions of natural science." This is obviously true. And Popper's second claim is false: the true task of philosophy is *not* merely to clarify propositions but also, among other things, to formulate elucidations. (More will be said about this below.)

3. Popper says that Wittgenstein "tries to draw a limit, in our language, between sense and nonsense" (ii, 293). This characterization is not sufficiently refined. Wittgenstein actually makes a distinction among *three* concepts:

(A) sense *(Sinn)*; senseful or having sense *(sinnvoll)*

(B) [no sense]; senseless or without sense *(sinnlos)*

(C) nonsense *(Unsinn)*; nonsensical *(unsinnig)*.

Often when Popper speaks of Wittgenstein's distinction between 'sense' and 'nonsense' he, with regard to the latter, conflates (B) and (C). Furthermore, he often equates 'nonsense' with 'meaningless' *(bedeutungslos)*. Such conflation and equation can only lead to gross confusion. I am astonished that someone who knows German as well as Popper presumably does should be guilty of overlooking these distinctions. For a correct understanding of Wittgenstein's views, they *must* be distinguished. Furthermore, Popper fails to see that Wittgenstein uses these terms in technical ways. I shall attempt to clarify those issues about which Popper is confused—or which he does not understand.

An adequate exposition of Wittgenstein's technical use of the term 'sense' would require a long essay in itself. Its use is intimately connected with that of other technical terms such as: 'picture', 'model', 'pictorial form' (of a picture), 'pictorial relationship', 'representational form', 'logical form', 'logical picture', 'projection', 'proposition', and 'propositional sign' (T, 2.1-3.33). But roughly we may say: when a linguistic vehicle such as a sentence has met certain conditions, it is capable of expressing. That which it expresses or represents is its sense. We may think (again roughly) of the sense as the descriptive, common, objective content that the vehicle expresses. (Cf. T, 3.13.) In many respects, the sense of a proposition is similar to many of the inhabitants of Popper's world 3 or third world.[4]

Now it may be thought—and Popper seems to think—that for Wittgenstein the opposite of 'sense' is 'nonsense' and that the opposite of 'having sense' or 'senseful' is 'nonsensical'. But this is not so for Wittgenstein. If an expression does *not* have sense, it may *either* be nonsensical *(unsinnig) or* be without sense *(sinnlos).* Thus, for Wittgenstein tautologies and contradictions lack sense (are without sense), but they are not nonsensical. Wittgenstein expresses this so clearly in the *Tractatus* (T, 4.461-4.4611) that it is difficult to understand how anyone could overlook it. On the other hand, Wittgenstein claims that many philosophical propositions (and questions) are nonsensical. But to say that they are nonsensical *(unsinnig)* is not to say that they are without sense *(sinnlos)* (T, 4.003). Or, to take another example, it would, according to Wittgenstein, be nonsensical to say 'There is only one 1'. But this does not mean that such an expression *lacks* sense (T, 4.1272). Similarly, since there is no property called 'identical', the sentence 'Socrates is identical' is nonsensical (T, 5.473). Finally, in the famous passage that Popper often quotes and refers to, Wittgenstein writes: "My propositions serve as elucidations in the following way: anyone who understands me eventually recognizes them as nonsensical, when he has used them—as steps—to climb up beyond them. (He must, so to speak, throw away the ladder after he has climbed up it)" (T, 6.54). It must be noted that Wittgenstein claims that his propositions are nonsensical *(unsinnig)*, but this does not mean that they are without sense *(sinnlos)*!

A careful scrutiny of these passages, and many others to which I have not referred, clearly reveals that just as the term 'sense' must be interpreted in a technical (not ordinary) sense, similarly the terms 'without sense' and 'nonsensical' must be interpreted as being employed in a technical way. Once this is done, one can immediately see that statements like "Wittgenstein tries to draw a limit in our language between sense and nonsense" are either utterly misleading or false. This fact must be borne in mind as we turn to some of Popper's other theses.

But what is the difference between nonsensical propositions and propositions that lack sense or are without sense? In a logically perfect language, a proposition that has sense—by the complicated conditions that Wittgenstein specifies (T, 2.1-3.5)—represents or depicts a possible state of affairs. Thus such a proposition has a determinate content. It determines a specific place in "logical space" (T, 3.4-3.42). But given this technical sense of the term 'sense' or the expression 'having sense' (which I have barely sketched), and since tautologies and contradictions do not have a determinate context and do not "pick out" specific places in logical space, such propositions lack sense or are without sense *(sinnlos)*. The expression 'without sense' is therefore also a technical one. Now given these technical uses of 'sense', 'having sense', and 'without sense', of course a proposition such as a philosophical proposition cannot be said either to have sense or to lack sense. Thus it is said to be nonsensical *(unsinnig)*. But that again is a technical use of 'nonsensical'. To say that a proposition is nonsensical is merely to say that it neither has sense nor lacks sense—again in the technical senses of 'having sense' or 'lacking sense'. It simply falls into a third category.

Now it is perhaps unfortunate that Wittgenstein chose words like 'nonsensical' and 'without sense', for we tend to think of them as pejorative. But it is clear that Wittgenstein does not intend them to be used in a pejorative sense at all. Once one understands their meanings, they become very neutral, technical terms and could be replaced with arbitrary and even newly invented labels. It all goes back to the matter, again, of Wittgenstein's uses of 'sense' and 'having sense'. As I have mentioned before, these terms are characterized in an extremely complex and technical way. But if one understands at least the outlines of that characterization (T, 2.1-3.33), it is very clear that first, there is no great mystery about the difference between 'without sense' and 'nonsensical', and second, that these expressions are being used in technical, nonpejorative ways.

From all of the above, we can see one further confusion or misinterpretation in Popper's third charge. Popper says that Wittgenstein "tries to draw a limit *in our language* between sense and nonsense" (ii, 293, my italics). I have already dealt with the last phrase. I now turn to the words I have italicized. Wittgenstein does no such thing. He tries to make a distinction—the above-mentioned threefold one—for what has often been called an ideal language or a logically perspicuous language. He does not claim that his assertions on this subject (as well as many others) hold for our everyday language, nor does he say that they ought to (T, 3.325). He is quite explicit on this point: "In fact, all of the propositions of our everyday language, just as they stand, are in perfect logical order.—That utterly simple thing, which we have to formulate here, is not an image of the truth, but the truth itself in its entirety" (T, 5.5563). How strange it is that this "utterly simple" thing should be so grossly neglected or ignored by Popper and other commentators.

Now, as I have already mentioned, Wittgenstein also applies his threefold distinction when referring to philosophical propositions. But since, as I have indicated, he places these in a special category, it is not true that Wittgenstein tries to draw a limit *in our language* between sense and nonsense (or among sense, without sense, and nonsense).

Before moving on, I should clarify one point. I have maintained that many of Wittgenstein's remarks, distinctions, and so forth apply to a logically perfect language. There are many passages in the text (some of which I have cited) which support this interpretation. However, in making this claim I do not make the very different claim that Wittgenstein attempts to construct such a logically perfect language. Nor do I make the claim that he holds it necessary to construct one with which to replace ordinary language. All these issues have often been confused by various commentators. When I maintain that Wittgenstein is concerned with a logically perfect language, all that I am claiming is this: In order for any language to serve us in our effort to discourse about the world, we must be able to analyze or reduce its sentences into various kinds (atomic or elementary sentences and truth-functions of them). If we were to arrive at this level, we would have a logically perfect language that represents the features of the world. Thus a logically perfect language is not to be thought of as an alternative to ordinary or scientific languages but as the vehicle through which the latter can be used to state truths about the world.

Let me attempt to clarify this issue somewhat further. In the *Tractatus* Wittgenstein points out how many confusions arise because "in everyday language it very frequently happens that the same word has different modes of signification, and so belongs to different symbols—or that two words that have different modes of signification are employed in propositions in what is superficially the same way"

(T, 3.323). After giving several examples he writes: "In order to avoid such errors we must make use of a sign-language that excludes them by not using the same sign for different modes of signification: that is to say, a sign-language that is governed by *logical* grammar—by logical syntax" (T, 3,325). This passage led many—Russell among them, in his Introduction to the *Tractatus*—to think that Wittgenstein was concerned about specifying the conditions that would have to be fulfilled by a logically perfect language. And it also led many to think that Wittgenstein was advocating the construction of such a language, or at least one that would come close to being logically perfect. But this was not Wittgenstein's intention. Rather, he was concerned with specifying the conditions that must be fulfilled by *any* language; and for Wittgenstein, in one sense, any language must be logically perfect (T, 5.5563), or it would not be able to depict or describe the world. A language can depict the world or states of affairs in the world only if it shares a common structure or form with the world or with such states of affairs. Hence my claim that Wittgenstein was concerned with articulating features of a logically perfect language must not be understood as meaning that Wittgenstein held that it was his task to construct such a language as an alternative to everyday language, or as a replacement for everyday language. Again, I am merely claiming that for us to be able to use everyday language in its assertive function to utter truths about the world, we must be able, in principle though not in fact, to reduce its sentences into forms that meet the necessary conditions for depicting the ultimate states of affairs in the world. Thus one might say that a "logically perfect language" is not a language outside of and in addition to everyday language. Rather, it is already contained within everyday language, as its basis. And only because it is so "contained" within everyday language can we significantly employ everyday language to assert truths about the world.

4. It may be seen that I have already answered Popper's fourth criticism, that (for Wittgenstein) genuine propositions have sense, whereas "philosophical propositions do not exist; they only look like propositions, but are, in fact, nonsensical" (ii, 293). I shall not belabor the fact that this claim is seemingly contradictory. If philosophical propositions *are* nonsensical, they *do* exist, as nonsensical propositions. More important, I have already shown why it is that philosophical propositions are said to be nonsensical, and how it is that they are so in a technical sense of 'nonsensical'. This does not entitle us to jump to saying that they are nonsensical in the ordinary sense of the word, nor does it allow us to say that they are meaningless (an error which Popper often makes). Philosophical propositions could not possibly be nonsensical or meaningless in the ordinary (non-technical) sense of those terms, for (again) if they were, how could they serve as genuine elucidations for us, and how could we understand them? But Wittgenstein says that we *can* understand them and that they *do* serve as elucidations (T, 6.54).

5(a). Popper claims that for Wittgenstein, "The limit between sense and nonsense coincides with that between natural science and philosophy" (ii, 293).

Because of Popper's terminology in thesis 5(b), we may assume that the term 'limit' is meant to be equivalent to 'demarcation' or at least 'distinction'. There are a number of objections to this thesis.

First, as we have seen, Wittgenstein does not draw a simple 'limit' or distinction between sense and nonsense. Rather, he uses a threefold distinction among having sense, lacking sense, and nonsensical. Thus we would have to more accurately state the above thesis as: 5(a') "For Wittgenstein, the 'limit' or distinction or demarcation between sense (or having sense), on the one hand, and either that which is without sense (or lacking sense) or nonsense (or nonsensical), on the other hand, coincides with that between natural science and philosophy."

Second, even with this revision, or perhaps because of it, thesis 5(a) is not true because (1) tautologies, as we have seen, lack sense yet are not philosophical propositions; and (2) propositions like 'Socrates is identical' are nonsensical, yet are not philosophical propositions. Thus, since there are *such kinds* of propositions that are either lacking in sense or nonsensical, even 5(a') cannot be true. There are propositions that either lack sense or are nonsensical but that are *not* philosophical propositions. Therefore, the distinction between (a) having sense or (b) lacking sense or being nonsensical, does not coincide with that between (a') natural science, or (more accurately) the propositions of natural science, and (b') philosophy, or (more accurately) the propositions of philosophy.

Third, philosophical propositions (again) are (or "serve as") elucidations (T, 6.54). And people can understand them *(ibid.)* to be nonsensical in the technical sense of 'nonsensical'. But if one can understand them and profit by their serving as elucidations, then they all are not nonsensical in the broader or more customary and pejorative sense of the term, which is the one implied in Popper's formulation of 5(a). So far, I have shown that the second items of the two pairs of concepts in 5(a) do not coincide.

Fourth, there is another reason that the alleged coinciding does not hold. The *first* items of each of the two pairs do not coincide. That is, the notion of 'sense' or 'having sense' does not coincide with that of 'natural science' or proposition of natural science'. Although Wittgenstein sometimes speaks of or suggests that there are propositions of natural science (e.g., T, 4.11; 6.34; 6.53) or laws of nature (e.g., T, 5.1.54; 6.36), one must be clear about what he *means* by expressions like 'propositions of natural science', 'laws of nature', and so forth. In his discussion of Newtonian mechanics (T, 6.341-6.35), Wittgenstein suggests that scientific propositions (or laws of nature) may not be genuine propositions at all. A scientific theory is said to be like a mesh with which one covers a surface. Just as a mesh of a certain fineness imposes a unified form on the description of the surface, so Newtonian mechanics "imposes a unified form on the description of the world" (T, 6.341). These highly suggestive passages lend themselves to an interpretation by which the linking or conflating of 'sense' or 'having sense' and 'natural science' or 'proposition of natural science' is doubtful or at least debatable. And this is so because these may not be genuine propositions at all. (I shall return to this point later.)

Fifth, there is a further reason that the alleged coinciding does not hold. As I have indicated, much of Wittgenstein's discussion of 'sense' (as well as 'without sense' and 'nonsensical') pertains to the propositions of a logically perspicuous language. Just what these are Wittgenstein does not say. But whatever they are, they do (for Wittgenstein) have sense. Thus, again, the notion of 'sense' or 'senseful proposition' does not coincide with that of 'proposition of natural science'.

5(b). Popper claims that for Wittgenstein the demarcation between sense and nonsense "coincides with that between science and metaphysics, i.e. between scientific sentences and philosophical pseudo-propositions" (ii, 293). This thesis is similar to 5(a) except for (a) the substitution of 'metaphysics' for 'philosophy'; (b) the addition by Popper of what is taken to be the same distinction as that between science and metaphysics, namely, that between scientific sentences and philosophical pseudo-propositions. Because of this latter identification, my major criticisms of this thesis are the same as those that I directed against thesis 5(a). However, there is one further point I would like to add. At least one passage in the *Tractatus* might be construed as a basis for thesis 5(b). Toward the end of the book (T, 6.53) Wittgenstein writes: "The correct method in philosophy would really be the following: to say nothing except what can be said, i.e. the propositions of natural science—i.e. something that has nothing to do with philosophy—and then, whenever someone else wanted to say something metaphysical, to demonstrate that he had failed to give a meaning *[Bedeutung]* to certain signs in his propositions." However, it should be noted that Wittgenstein does not say *here* that metaphysical propositions are either nonsensical *(unsinnig)* or without sense *sinnlos)*. (He, of course, does say that elsewhere, but in the sense that I have explained above.) He does not even say that they are meaningless *(bedeutungslos)*. What he says is that they are propositions in which someone has failed to *give* a meaning *(Bedeutung)* to certain signs. Again, Popper seems to equate 'meaningless' with 'nonsensical' and, as I have pointed out, fails to apprehend Wittgenstein's sense of 'nonsensical' and fails to distinguish between his use of 'nonsensical' and 'without sense'. But we cannot identify *these* concepts either. The terms 'meaning' *(Bedeutung),* 'meaningful' *(bedeutungsvoll),* and 'meaningless' *(bedeutungslos)* function in very different ways from those of 'senseful', 'nonsensical', and so forth.

The notion of 'meaning' for Wittgenstein (in the *Tractatus*) is tied up with that of *reference*. Thus: "A name means *[bedeutet]* an object. The object is its meaning *[Bedeutung]* " (T, 3.203). The long discussions in 3.2-3.33 and elsewhere show that Wittgenstein also uses terms like 'meaning', 'meaningful', and 'meaningless' in technical senses. There is not enough space here to elaborate upon the details of his conceptions. They are well known, and, as I have mentioned, they are linked to the notion of reference rather than that of sense.

In passage 5(b) and in many that I have not quoted, Popper refers to Wittgenstein's conception of philosophical pseudo-propositions. As we have seen, he also often claims that for Wittgenstein philosophical propositions are meaningless.

POPPER'S CRITICISMS OF WITTGENSTEIN'S *TRACTATUS* 249

More needs to be said now about these claims, beginning with the first—that for Wittgenstein) philosophical propositions are only pseudo-propositions.

The word 'pseudo-propositions' *(Scheinsätze)* occurs only four times in the *Tractatus*. Here are the passages in which it occurs.

Wherever the word 'object' ('thing', etc.) is correctly used, it is expressed in conceptual notation by a variable name.

For example, in the proposition, 'There are 2 objects which...', it is expressed by '($\exists x,y$)...'.

Whenever it is used in a different way, that is, as a proper concept-word, nonsensical pseudo-propositions are the result (T, 4.1272).

And now we see that in a correct conceptual notation pseudo-propositions like 'a = a',... '(x).x=x',... etc. cannot even be written down (T, 5.534).

This also disposes of all the problems that were connected with such pseudo-propositions (T,5.535).

The propositions of mathematics are equations and therefore pseudo-propositions (T,6.2).

Two important things should be noted regarding these passages. First, the word 'meaningless' *(bedeutungslos)* is never ascribed to pseudo-propositions; rather, the word 'nonsensical' *(unsinnig)* is applied (and only once) (T, 4.1272). Second, there is not a single passage in which all *philosophical* propositions are held to be pseudo-propositions, nor is there a single passage where that is even implied. Third, although this does not prove that Wittgenstein does not and would not characterize philosophical propositions as meaningless, it provides evidence that he would not so characterize them. And indeed, if we examine the passages, we find that this is true. While they are commonly referred to as nonsensical (in Wittgenstein's technical sense of the term), they are never referred to as meaningless. The word 'meaningless' occurs in only four passages (T, 3.328; 4.442; 4.4661; 5.47321). In none of them is the term 'meaningless' applied to philosophical problems. Indeed, in none of them is the term applied to *any* propositions whatever! It is (again) applied only to certain *signs* occurring *within* propositions.

6(a). Popper states that "Wittgenstein is an anti-metaphysician" and that "he tries to show that metaphysics is 'simply nonsense'" (ii, 293). I have already said enough to refute the second half of this claim; I shall therefore focus on the first, that Wittgenstein is an anti-metaphysician. I am sorry: this claim is utterly preposterous and utterly false. I realize that the *Tractatus* has often been interpreted in such a "positivistic" way, but I fail to see how anyone who has read the complete book (or even the opening pages!) could provide such an interpretation. The opening part of the *Tractatus*, from the very first sentence (T, 1-2.063), presents an enormously complex metaphysics, in the strictest and most traditional sense of the term. And this part is supplemented later by many other passages (T, 2.1-2.225; 3.11-3.24; 3.4-3.5; 4.01-4.021; 4.12-4.2211; 4.441-4.5; 5.471-5.4711; 5.526-5.5262; 5.55-5.641; 6.12; 6.124; 6.2-6.22; 6.41-6.522). These views are also supported by many passages from Wittgenstein's *Notebooks, 1914-16.* And what is this metaphysics (or ontology) of the *Tractatus?* I have given an account of it elsewhere, but Popper indicates no awareness of it, even in later editions of his works or in later writings.[5] Since I assume that he has not read it, I shall briefly summarize it here. Before turning to the *Tractatus* itself, I should like to quote some passages from other works by Wittgenstein that were written shortly before the *Tractatus.*

> The great problem round which everything I write turns is: Is there an order in the world *a priori,* and if so what does it consist in?
>
> My work has stretched from the foundations of logic to the essence of the world.
>
> Philosophy ... consists of logic and metaphysics, the former its basis.[6]

I turn now to the *Tractatus* itself. The very opening sentence, and the following ones (to 2.063), are about the *world.* The world consists in the totality of configurations of objects. These configurations, or facts, are in logical space. The objects that make up such configurations are simple and make up the substance of the world. They also constitute the unalterable form of the world, not merely of the actual world but of any possible world. Objects are eternal, unalterable, and subsistent. And they must exist. Why? In order to answer the question: "What must be the necessary conditions in order for language to be used in its assertive function to state true propositions about the world?" What must hold in order for discourse to be used to state such truths is this: There are unalterable, subsistent, and non-empirical objects, in a network of logical space, which are capable of forming configurations, and some of which do. If this is not metaphysics, I would like to know what is!

6(b). Because of all that I have already said, I do not see any point in elaborating upon Popper's charge that Wittgenstein's "fundamental aim" is "the destruction of metaphysics by unveiling it as meaningless nonsense" (ii, 293). First, I have used enough space dealing with the claim that, for Wittgenstein, metaphysics is meaningless nonsense. Second, it is apparent from what I have said about 6(a) that Wittgenstein had no fundamental aim to destroy metaphysics. How could someone who presents an elaborate and even non-empirical metaphysics be said to want to destroy it? I realize that Popper is not alone in having this misconception of the *Tractatus.* But I do not see how anyone who has read the book could share this conclusion. The *Tractatus* presents an astonishingly rich and incredibly beautiful ontology. In many respects it is similar to the platonic ontologies of Frege and the very early Russell (1903). And all of Wittgenstein's discussions of language and logic are intimately connected with this ontology. Wittgenstein was far from wanting to destroy metaphysics; he sought, rather, to *promote* it.

7. According to Popper, Wittgenstein's views imply that we should demand definitions of his words from the metaphysician; and if for any word the definition

is not forthcoming, *"we assume that the word is meaningless"* (ii, 294). The closest that Wittgenstein comes to saying anything like this is in the passage already quoted above, with regard to 5(b). But even in that passage, Wittgenstein does not say—or imply—that of which Popper accuses him. What he says is that if anyone "wanted to say something metaphysical," then the "correct method" in philosophy would be "to demonstrate that he had failed to give a meaning *(Bedeutung)* to certain signs in his propositions" (T, 6.53). But, again, all that means is that he has failed to provide a *reference* for those *terms* (or *signs*) in his propositions. This would not mean that the *signs* themselves are "meaningless" in the pejorative sense in which Popper constantly uses the term.

It should also be pointed out that many of the "nonsensical" propositions and questions that are propounded by philosophers arise not from the failure of those philosophers to define their terms clearly but from their failure "to understand the logic of our language" (T, 4.003).

Furthermore, in the same passage Wittgenstein says that "the correct method in philosophy would really be the following: to say nothing except what *can be said*" (T, 6.53, my italics). And this leads us to the need to consider one of Wittgenstein's most important distinctions in the *Tractatus,* one of which Popper seems unaware, namely, the distinction between that which can be *said* and that which cannot be said but can only be *shown*. Once again, these terms ('said', 'shown') are technical ones and must be understood as such. In Wittgenstein's view, for example, if *'a'* denotes an object and *'f'* a given property, than *'fa' says* something. But this proposition also *shows* something, namely, "that the object *a* occurs in its sense" (T, 4.1211). Similarly, the two propositions *'fa'* and *'ga'* show that "the same object is mentioned in both of them" *(ibid.).* Similarly, if two propositions contradict each other, "then their structure shows it" *(ibid.).* These things which *can* be shown *cannot* be said (T, 4.1212). And, in general, anything that pertains to logical form, i.e., the logical form of *reality* (T, 4.121), falls into that which cannot be said. It is rather something that is shown by the structure and syntax of propositions *(ibid.).* What Wittgenstein intends to convey here is that if we had a logically perspicuous language of the sort characterized in the *Tractatus,* then we may make this distinction between that which can be said and that which cannot be said but can only be shown. Similarly, we may make such a distinction for philosophical discourse. Therefore, when Wittgenstein says that the correct method in philosophy would be to say nothing except what can be said, this must be interpreted in the light of *Wittgenstein's distinction* between that which can be said and that which cannot be said but only shown. But this does not imply that the realm of what cannot be said but only shown is meaningless in the pejorative sense of 'meaningless'. For indeed, Wittgenstein himself has expressed clearly what is meant by propositions that show something; some of us at least have understood what he has written about all this, and some of us have even been enlightened by it!

8. Popper states that Wittgenstein's method gives rise "not to the destruction or to the exclusion or even to the clear demarcation of metaphysics, but to their

[sic] intrusion into the field of science, and to their confusion with science" (ii, 297). Now, clearly this contradicts many of Popper's earlier theses. I believe that the inconsistency is blatant; hence I shall not dwell upon the obvious. But apart from that, there is no reason whatsoever, on the basis of anything said or even implied by Wittgenstein, to think that this charge is true. I have failed to find anything in the *Tractatus* that explicitly states or allows for the result that Popper states, or anything from which it might conceivably follow. I do not understand why Popper thinks that such a result must, or even might, follow. And indeed, all that he himself has said negates it.

9(a). Popper states that many of Wittgenstein's own sentences, like "Philosophy is not a theory but an activity," do not belong to science; and hence any such sentence "cannot belong to 'the totality of true propositions'" (ii, 297). It is true (as I have already mentioned) that Wittgenstein characterizes—perhaps even defines—'natural science' as 'the totality of true propositions' (T, 4.11). But this is because such propositions fall into the category of that which can be *said*. Does that not mean, then, that a sentence like "Philosophy is not a theory but an activity" must fall into the category of that which can only be *shown*? And if so, is not Wittgenstein himself inconsistent by saying (or writing) it? I take this to be the thrust of a more refined formulation of Popper's charge. The answer is: No. For in addition to the distinction between that which can be said and that which can only be shown, there is another distinction in the *Tractatus*, and the two do not necessarily always coincide. This is the distinction (often mentioned in Popper's quotations from the *Tractatus*) between doctrinal or philosophical propositions on the one hand and elucidations on the other. In Wittgenstein's view, "Philosophy is not a body of doctrine" (T, 4.112). Rather, "a philosophical work consists essentially of elucidations" (*ibid*; cf. 6.54). Thus all that Popper's charge amounts to is that any sentence like "Philosophy is not a theory but an activity" is not itself a proposition of natural science (which is obvious and true by virtue of Wittgenstein's stipulations). It is rather a proposition that falls into the category of elucidations that we use but then "transcend" in order to "see the world aright" (T, 6.54). However, to serve that function it must be a true proposition, but one of a very different sort from the type to which Wittgenstein (stipulatively) applies the term 'proposition', i.e., a proposition that says something about the world by virtue of having a determinate sense and the capability of depicting.

9(b). Popper goes on to say that since any proposition like "Philosophy is not a theory but an activity" not only is not one falling within "the totality of true propositions" (i.e., natural science), but also is not a false proposition, it therefore "must be *'meaningless'*, or *'senseless'*, or *'nonsensical'*" (ii, 297). Here again we see Popper's conflation or confusion among three utterly different concepts. It is true that such a philosophical proposition is nonsensical (in Wittgenstein's technical sense of the term 'nonsensical'). But: (a) it does not follow that it is either senseless or meaningless (as Wittgenstein uses 'senseless' and 'meaningless'); and (b) it does not follow that it is meaningless in the ordinary sense of the word 'meaningless', i.e., just gibberish. On the contrary, as we have seen, it is perfectly meaningful in that sense, for it serves as an elucidation!

10. From his previous theses Popper draws the conclusion: Thus "Wittgenstein's own philosophy is senseless, and it is admitted to be so" (ii, 297). From what I have said above we may see, first, that this charge is inaccurate as stated and, second, that when the inaccuracy is removed, it is innocuous. First, Wittgenstein does not hold that his own philosophical propositions are senseless; he says that they are nonsensical (in the technical sense of 'nonsensical' characterized above). Second, all that thesis 10 now amounts to is that Wittgenstein's own philosophical assertions are admitted to be nonsensical (in the technical sense) by Wittgenstein himself. Of course! But again, this does not imply that they are nonsensical or senseless or meaningless in the non-Wittgensteinian, pejorative senses of 'senseless' and so forth. And I repeat that in the ordinary sense they are perfectly senseful and meaningful. How else could they serve as elucidations for us?

11. We may now deal with Popper's next charge quite simply. Popper says, rightly, that Wittgenstein claims in his Preface that the truth of the thoughts communicated in the *Tractatus* are "unassailable and definite," or better, "unassailable and definitive" (T, p. 5). According to Popper, this means something seemingly paradoxical or absurd, namely, that "we can communicate *unassailably and definitely true thoughts* by way of propositions which are admittedly nonsensical," and that "we can solve problems 'finally' by propounding nonsense" (ii, 297). Popper's first assertion is surely correct. Wittgenstein did state that the thoughts he set forth in the *Tractatus* were unassailable and definitive. But there is no paradox or absurdity involved or implied, as Popper claims in his second assertion. For such thoughts again are communicated by propositions that are nonsensical (in the technical sense of 'nonsensical'), but which are genuine elucidations we can understand and appreciate. Finally, regarding his third assertion, there is no paradox or absurdity either. For we *can* solve genuine problems by propositions that are nonsensical (in the technical sense of 'nonsensical'), but which are nonetheless illuminating elucidations that help us "see the world aright" (T, 6.54).

12. Popper claims that Wittgenstein holds that the (supposed) nonsense discussed in the above theses is "a new kind of nonsense," "*deeply significant nonsense*" (ii, 297). If by "a new kind of nonsense" is meant the technical conception I have discussed above, then this first characterization is true. But since Popper is not aware of that technical conception, then in Popper's sense of 'nonsense', this characterization is false. The second claim, that it is deeply significant nonsense, is false, or at least misleading. If it is interpreted as meaning that Wittgenstein *said* that it is "deeply significant," then it is false. If it is interpreted as meaning that, in his technical sense, nonsensical propositions can be genuinely significant, then it is true. But without that understanding of Wittgenstein's meaning, the second claim is

misleading. Both of these types of characterizations actually stem not from the *Tractatus* itself but from commentators on it, beginning with F. P. Ramsey.[7]

13. Popper claims that Wittgenstein determines the conception of 'sense' or 'meaning' in a narrow way, so that "you can say of all uncomfortable questions that you cannot find any 'sense' or 'meaning' in them" (ii, 297). As I have pointed out, Wittgenstein does use terms like 'sense' in a technical way. But nothing in the *Tractatus* indicates that Wittgenstein held that one could dismiss "uncomfortable" questions in this casual way; nor does anything in the *Tractatus* even imply that. Here again is an example of Popper's positivistic interpretation of the *Tractatus*, his reading it as if it were a creed of logical positivism. And, of course, this is not the only time that Popper has done so. Anscombe has drawn attention to another glaring instance of such misinterpretation on Popper's part.[8]

14. Popper states that Wittgenstein's "theory" blurs the problem of demarcation because of "his naive idea that there is something 'essentially' or 'by nature' scientific and something 'essentially' or 'by nature' metaphysical and that it is our task to discover the 'natural' demarcation between these two" (ii, 297). This charge certainly conflicts with many of Popper's earlier theses (above). For in many of them Popper's charge is that Wittgenstein has *arbitrarily* distinguished the scientific from the metaphysical or the propositions of science from metaphysical propositions. Now we are told that Wittgenstein holds that there is an essential or natural demarcation between the two! But apart from that inconsistency, the charge simply is not true. That there is a distinction follows from Wittgenstein's definitions, his technical concepts, and his complex theory of language. In other words, given Wittgenstein's stipulations, a distinction or "demarcation" follows. But there is nothing essential or natural about it. However, this does not mean that the distinction is merely a verbal one. Rather, it is a logico-onotological one—which is not the same as a natural distinction.

15. Popper says that Wittgenstein's identification of the totality of true propositions with the totality of science leads to the exclusion from science of all hypotheses that are not true. "And since we can never know of a hypothesis whether or not it is true, we can never know whether or not it belongs to the sphere of natural science" (ii, 298). Of course, there are some who have doubted the second statement (in quotation marks). I grant that they are wrong and that Popper is right on this issue. But do these unfortunate consequences follow from Wittgenstein's identification of the totality of true propositions with the totality of (natural) science? First, it is undeniable that Wittgenstein does make this identification (T, 4.11). And given such an identification, *this* charge of Popper may seem to be a valid criticism. However, as I have pointed out above, Wittgenstein also seems to hold a different account of scientific propositions in the *Tractatus* (T, 6.341-6.35). What he suggests here is that scientific theories do not consist of propositions that are true or false, but they are meshes or grids we impose upon the world. Different

characterizations may result, depending on the fineness of the mesh we use. Under this latter interpretation Popper's charge in this thesis would not be true.

And what is this conception of scientific propositions? And why does Wittgenstein consider such an interpretation of them? I shall answer the second question first. For Wittgenstein, all propositions are ultimately either elementary propositions or truth-functions of elementary propositions (T, 5; cf. 5.234). Obviously, the laws of science cannot be either elementary (or atomic) propositions or truth-functions of elementary propositions. What, then, are they? This takes us back to the first question. Wittgenstein, in the passages referred to, suggests that scientific laws (or at least some of them, e.g., those of Newtonian mechanics) are not empirical propositions or factual propositions; hence, strictly speaking, they are not propositions at all. Rather, they are suggestions or recommendations of ways or methods to represent certain phenomena in a consistent and uniform way. Consider Wittgenstein's illustration of a white surface with irregular black spots on it (T, 6.341). If we superimpose a sufficiently fine square network on this surface, we may report of each square whether it is black or white. Griffin has stated the matter nicely:

> The only empirical statements we can make in a system like this will be either reports made by using the language the system provides, or perhaps, reports to the effect that the particular fineness involved in the language is or is not effective in describing this particular surface. Now, Wittgenstein's point is many scientific laws are like the mesh in this illustration. Their function is not to make reports, but to supply representational techniques by which reports can be made. Thus, when this kind of law is superseded, it is not, for it cannot be, falsified. What happens is that a better method of representation is found. Perhaps it is illustration, possibly it is even verification, of this thesis, that in general we do not say of Einstein's work that it proved Newton's wrong; in fact it is only under certain circumstances that Einstein's language is definitely to be preferred. On this view, what Einstein did was to discover a new representational form, to present a finer grid.[9]

It should also be noted that elsewhere Wittgenstein identifies the totality of propositions with *language*, not with the corpus of natural science (T, 4.001). To be sure, he does not use the word 'true' in the phrase 'the totality of propositions' in this passage. Nevertheless, this should make us doubtful about how rigidly he adhered to the identification of the totality of true propositions with the propositions of natural science. Or, more accurately, it should lead us to recognize that, as I have indicated above, he is using the phrase 'the totality of true propositions' in a technical, stipulated sense and that, strictly speaking, there may not be any such propositions at all.

Furthermore, there is evidence that Wittgenstein uses the expression 'scientific propositon' (or 'proposition of natural science') in two different ways in the *Tractatus*. First, he sometimes takes 'scientific proposition' to be equivalent to or identical with 'empirical proposition', i.e., any factual proposition, whether of science or everyday usage. Second, he sometimes takes 'scientific proposition' to be equivalent to or identical with 'law of science' or 'law of nature'. It is the second of these meanings that appears in the section of the *Tractatus* to which I have just referred (T, 6.341-6.3432). And as we have seen, in this sense of the expression, scientific laws are not *propositions* at all. Since I have already dealt with this matter, I shall turn to the first of the senses in which Wittgenstein employs the expression 'scientific proposition'. We first find this use in the *Notebooks, 1914-16*. Wittgenstein writes (in a letter to Russell in 1913): "A proposition like '($\exists x$)x = x' is for example really a proposition of physics. The proposition '(x): x = x.$\supset$.($\exists y$). y = y' is a proposition of logic: it is for physics to say *whether any thing exists*" (p. 127). Now surely we would not customarily say that the proposition 'Something exists' ('($\exists x$). x = x') is a proposition of physics! Hence here is an indication that Wittgenstein means 'scientific proposition', or in this case 'proposition of physics', to be equivalent to 'empirical proposition'. This equivalence is also indicated in passages in the *Tractatus*, for example: "The totality of true propositions is the whole of natural science (or the whole corpus of natural science)" (T, 4.11). Similarly in the *Tractatus* Wittgenstein equates 'everything that can be said' with 'propositions of natural science' (T, 6.53).

With this in mind, we may now return to Popper's first charge in thesis 15. Popper points out that Wittgenstein makes this identification of the totality of true propositions with the totality of science. And he claims that this identification leads to the exclusion of all hypotheses that are not true. But since we cannot know whether a hypothesis is true, we cannot know whether it belongs to "the sphere of natural science." I earlier stated that this charge of Popper's might seem to be a valid criticism. But we can now see that it is not, because Wittgenstein is using the expression 'proposition of science' in the extended sense in which it means merely 'empirical proposition'. Under this interpretation Popper's first charge could not be valid. It is erroneous because it misses the point completely, since Wittgenstein's comment is not concerned with the propositions of *science* at all.

16. Popper claims that Wittgenstein has a famous "principle of verification" which leads to the same result, i.e., the same result that was mentioned in thesis 15 (ii, 298). Here is yet another positivist-type interpretation and misunderstanding. Indeed, the assertion is false. Wittgenstein has no principle of verification anywhere in the *Tractatus!* As Black has pointed out, the nearest Wittgenstein comes to propounding one is his statement, "To understand a proposition means to know what is the case if it is true" (T, 4.024).[10] But this occurs in a specific context, and it has no relationship whatever to the principles of verifiability which were sought so eagerly by the logical positivists. Indeed, a close reading of the *Tractatus* reveals that (1) Wittgenstein *would* not espouse a principle of verification, even if he could; and (2) he *could* not hold such a principle.

(1) The belief that Wittgenstein has a principle of verification rests on the erroneous view that Wittgenstein was concerned, in the manner of the logical positivists, with outlawing certain propositions (e.g., metaphysical ones) on the

grounds that since they are unverifiable, they are therefore meaningless. But as we have seen, Wittgenstein has no concern whatsoever with outlawing any propositions as meaningless, and he never applies the term 'meaningless' to propositions. That he does characterize some as being 'nonsensical' is another matter, about which I have said enough.

(2) More important, Wittgenstein *could* not possibly hold any verification principle. For to what would such a criterion apply? Presumably it would have to be applicable to elementary propositions and truth-functions of elementary propositions, and would have to yield the result that they are verifiable (and hence 'meaningful'). Yet Wittgenstein never provided any instances of elementary propositions and once said (I believe to Norman Malcolm) that he did not think that (when he wrote the *Tractatus*) it was his business as a logician to do so.

(This is not to deny that in his transitional works and lectures, from 1929-32, Wittgenstein attached some importance to a vertification principle. Indeed, there is some evidence that he did. But contrary to Popper, no such principle, nor any need or possibility of one, appears in the *Tractatus*).

I have now covered what I consider to be the most serious of Popper's charges and misinterpretations. In the remainder of this part, I shall very briefly discuss the last four of his theses.

17. Popper claims that Wittgenstein "overlooked the problem of universality or generality" and thereby "followed in the footsteps of earlier positivists" (ii, 298). This simply is not so. Generality and general propositions are discussed in 5.52-5.5262 of the *Tractatus,* in which Wittgenstein outlines a theory of general (or universal) propositions. Indeed, it is essential for Wittgenstein to do so. For since all senseful propositions are elementary propositions or truth-functions of elementary propositions and since we cannot produce *any* instances of elementary propositions (and therefore any instances of truth-functions), it follows that the only propositions we can develop must be completely general. Now Wittgenstein's theory of general propositions may not be a successful one—I, for one, believe that it is not. But *that* is another matter. To say that Wittgenstein overlooked generality is to have missed one of the most important parts of the *Tractatus.*

18. Popper claims that some of Wittgenstein's sentences, e.g., 'The totality of true propositions is . . . the totality of natural science', are logical paradoxes. Why? Since such a sentence does not belong to natural science, "it follows that it asserts its own untruth and is therefore contradictory" (ii, 355). From what I have said above, it is easily seen that there is no such paradox or contradiction. For once again, these propositions are elucidations and are therefore in a completely separate category. Hence any such assertion can mention the totality of true propositions (as Wittgenstein has defined or explicated 'propositions') without being a logical paradox. Philosophical propositions are, as it were, "second order" propositions. Hence they can refer to other propositions without being paradoxical.

19. Popper claims that Wittgenstein defines 'meaning' "arbitrarily in such a way that only factual propositions are 'meaningful'," and hence "norms are meaningless" (i, 234). I have already dealt with the first of these claims at length. I shall here focus on the second, that norms are meaningless. It is true that ethics, and normative ethical propositions, fall into the category of that which cannot be said (T, 6.421). However, this still allows for the possibility that they pertain to that which must be shown. Indeed, much of what Wittgenstein says supports such a view. And Wittgenstein exemplifies the fact that metaethical propositions fall into the category of elucidations (T, 6.422). At any rate, Wittgenstein does not in any way state or imply that norms—or normative propositions—are meaningless in the pejorative sense of the term. There may be reasons for thinking that Wittgenstein was wrong in believing that ethics falls into the area of that about which nothing can be said (but only shown). But again, that is another matter.

20. Popper states that Wittgenstein's mysticism is "holistic" (ii, 359). This is but one of several references to Wittgenstein's mysticism in Popper's account. I have selected this one, not because of its emphasis on the holistic aspect, but merely as an example of these references. We all know that Wittgenstein had a conception of the mystical in the *Tractatus*. But I fear that it in no way coincides with Popper's characterization. Rather, it is intimately connected with the distinction I have repeatedly stressed between that which can be said and that which cannot be said but must be shown. Hence what this doctrine amounts to is: There are things that cannot be said. These show themselves. This is the mystical (T, 6.522). As to whether Wittgenstein's conception is holistic, it is doubtful. It is true that Wittgenstein writes: "Feeling the world as a limited whole—it is this that is the mystical" (T, 6.45). But since the whole is a limited one, it hardly seems appropriate to apply the traditional term 'holistic' to this view, since that term implies a very different conception.

III

I have alluded several times to the fact that Popper has provided his erroneous criticisms of the *Tractatus* because he interpreted it as a treatise in the tradition of logical positivism. One would have hoped that since *The Open Society* was written, he might have come to change his opinions. But alas, he has still clung to them in his recent writings and revisions. The first edition of *The Open Society* was published in 1945; the most recent edition, published in 1971, contains some minor verbal changes but the same erroneous charges. Furthermore, others of his writings after 1945 contain the same views. Here are two examples, one from an essay published in 1957, another from a very recent essay published in 1977.

In his essay "Philosophy of Science: A Personal Report," Popper writes:

> Wittgenstein, as you all know, tried to show in the *Tractatus* (see for example his propositions 6.53; 6.54; and 5) that all so-called philosophical or metaphysical propositions were, in fact, non-propositions or pseudo-propositions:

that they were senseless or meaningless. All genuine (or meaningful) propositions were truth-functions of the elementary or atomic propositions which described 'atomic facts', i.e. facts which can in principle be ascertained by observation. In other words, they were fully reducible to elementary or atomic propositions which were simple statements describing possible states of affairs, and which could be in principle established or rejected by observation. If we call a statement an 'observation statement' not only if it states an actual observation but also if it states anything that *may* be observed, we shall have to say (according to the *Tractatus* 5, and 4.52) that every genuine proposition must be a truth-function of, and therefore deducible from, observation statements. All other apparent propositions will be, in fact, nonsense; they will be meaningless pseudo-propositions.[11]

In her *An Introduction to Wittgenstein's Tractatus*, G. E. M. Anscombe has criticized one of the charges made by Popper in the above quotation, namely, that for Wittgenstein the elementary propositions in the *Tractatus* are simple *observation* statements.[12] Anscombe's book appeared two years after Popper's essay. Popper's essay was reprinted under the new title "Science: Conjectures and Refutations" in 1963.[13] The second edition of the book in which this essay appeared was published in 1965.[14] Apart from two minor verbal changes, the only difference in the second edition occurs in the last sentence. It now reads: "All other apparent propositions will be meaningless pseudo-propositions; in fact they will be nothing but nonsensical gibberish."[15] It must be noted: First, six years after Anscombe's attack of Popper's account of Tractarian elementary propositions, Popper says nothing to modify his earlier, erroneous views. Second, regarding the other matters discussed in the passage, Popper says nothing to correct those mistakes either. In fact, he compounds them by his new version of the final sentence.

I turn now to the 1977 essay. Popper writes:

Under the influence of Ludwig Wittgenstein's *Tractatus Logico-Philosophicus*, the (Vienna) circle had become not only antimetaphysical, but antiphilosophical.

The existence of urgent and serious philosophical problems and the need to discuss them is, in my view, the only apology for what may be called professional or academic philosophy.

Wittgenstein and the Vienna Circle denied the existence of serious philosophical problems.

According to the end of the *Tractatus*, the apparent problems of philosophy (including those of the *Tractatus* itself) are pseudo-problems which arise from speaking without having given meaning to all one's words.[16]

I keep wondering, hasn't Popper read any of the literature on the *Tractatus* since 1945?

Of course, Popper is not the only one who is confused on these issues. W. W. Bartley III, in his *Wittgenstein*, writes:

In providing a theory of demarcation between science and nonscience, Wittgenstein's *Tractatus* prescribes criteria that must be satisfied by any factual (not logical) utterances which are well-formed, and proscribes . . . utterances which do not satisfy these criteria. Factual propositions are well-formed scientific propositions. No other propositions exist, although there exist certain pseudo-propositions—typically found in philosophy—which superficially look like propositions but which prove on analysis not to be well-formed. Wittgenstein himself does not use the locution 'well-formed'; he speaks of propositions which are *meaningful* and pseudo-propositions which are *meaningless*.

We find specified in the *Tractatus* two separate and different sorts of *legitimate* meaningful propositions. These are atomic propositions and molecular propositions. A sentence which proves to be neither is in fact no proposition at all: it is meaningless.[17]

Note the similarity to the charges made by Popper. Is this perhaps due to the fact that Bartley is an exPopperian?

I believe that Karl Popper is one of the greatest philosophers of our time. His contributions have been acknowledged by many in numerous papers and in the several volumes devoted to his philosophy. And I have learned much from him. But I do wish that he would stick to the areas in which he is competent and in which he so often offers brilliant insights. In those areas, he has much to say that is of profound value. But as a critic of Wittgenstein, his remarks are worthless and can lead only to more confusions and misunderstanding. Hence, if I may paraphrase a famous statement in the *Tractatus*, I offer this advice: Whereof one does not have the competence or knowledge to speak one ought to remain silent.[18]

Notes

1. K. Popper, *Unended Quest* (La Salle, Ill., 1976), p. 116. This book is a revised version of his "Autobiography of Karl Popper," which first appeared in P. A. Schilpp, ed., *The Philosophy of Karl Popper* (La Salle, Ill., 1974).
2. Volume and page numbers in parentheses refer to *The Open Society and Its Enemies*, vols. I and II, 5th ed. (Princeton, N.J., 1971).
3. All quotations from the *Tractatus* (T) are from the Pears and McGuinness Translation (London, 1961).
4. See K. Popper, *Objective Knowledge* (London, 1971), and *Unended Quest*.
5. "The Ontology of Wittgenstein's *Tractatus*," in *Essays on Wittgenstein*, ed. E. D. Klemke (Urbana, Ill., 1971), pp. 104-19.
6. L. Wittgenstein, *Notebooks, 1914-1916* (Oxford, 1961), pp. 53, 79, 93.
7. F. P. Ramsey, *The Foundations of Mathematics* (London, 1931), pp. 270-86.
8. G. E. M. Anscombe, *An Introduction to Wittgenstein's "Tractatus"* (London, 1959), pp. 25-40. I shall return to the passage that Anscombe cites in the last part of this paper.
9. J. Griffin, *Wittgenstein's Logical Atomism* (London, 1964), p. 103.
10. M. Black, *A Companion to Wittgenstein's "Tractatus"* (Ithaca, N.Y., 1964), p. 171.
11. In C. A. Mace, ed., *British Philosophy in the Mid-Century* (London, 1957), pp. 163-64.

12. (London, 1959), pp. 25-28. Anscombe does not quite accurately quote this passage. Also she does not indicate her deletions by the customary device: '...'.
13. *Conjectures and Refutations* (London, 1963).
14. (New York, 1965.)
15. *Ibid.*, p. 40.
16. K. Popper, "How I See Philosophy," in *Philosophers on Their Own Work* (Berne, 1977), pp. 134-35.
17. (New York, 1973), pp. 71-72.
18. The comments, interpretations, exegesis, and criticisms I have presented in this paper stem from research I have done on the *Tractatus* since 1959 and from lectures I have given since 1964. Although I have read most of the commentaries and articles on the *Tractatus*, I have not consulted them in writing this paper. Hence there may be some unconscious borrowings. If so, I would like to express my gratitude to all those to whom I may be indebted. To attempt to go back and trace every point or criticism would be overly pedantic. I have therefore listed in the References the works that I found in the past to have either paralleled my own thought or that provided significant insights. Apart from the few exceptions I cited, I have not referred to these works while writing this paper.

Many of the issues that have been only briefly discussed in this paper are treated in greater detail in my two as yet unpublished papers, "Sense and Nonsense in Wittgenstein's *Tractatus*" and "Propositions and Pseudo-propositions in Wittgenstein's *Tractatus*."

References: Works on Wittgenstein's *Tractatus*

Anscombe, G. E. M., *An Introduction to Wittgenstein's "Tractatus"* (London, 1959).
Black, Max, *A Companion to Wittgenstein's "Tractatus"* (Ithaca, N.Y.; 1964).
Copi, Irving M., and Beard, Robert W., eds., *Essays on Wittgenstein's "Tractatus"* (New York, 1966).
Fann, K. T., *Wittgenstein's Conception of Philosophy* (Berkeley and Los Angeles, 1971).
Griffin, James, *Wittgenstein's Logical Atomism* (London, 1964).
Hacker, P. M. S., *Insight and Illusion: Wittgenstein on Philosophy and the Metaphysics of Experience* (London, 1972).
Hartnack, Justus, *Wittgenstein and Modern Philosophy* (London, 1965).
Klemke, E. D., ed., *Essays on Wittgenstein* (Urbana, Ill., 1971).
Maslow, Alexander, *A Study in Wittgenstein's Tractatus* (Berkeley and Los Angeles, 1961). (Most of this book is worthless.)
Pears, David, *Ludwig Wittgenstein.* (New York, 1970).
Pitcher, George, *The Philosophy of Wittgenstein* (Englewood Cliffs, N.J.; 1964).
Stenius, Erik, *Wittgenstein's "Tractatus"* (Oxford, 1960).

Peirce, Wittgenstein, and Systematic Philosophy

RENFORD BAMBROUGH

"Philosophy ought to trust rather to the multitude and variety of its arguments than to the conclusiveness of any one. Its reasoning should not form a chain which is no stronger than its weakest link, but a cable whose fibers may be ever so slender, provided they are sufficiently numerous and intimately connected." Many a philosophical reader will be saved only by the American spelling of one word from misattributing this quotation. It comes from Peirce's "Some Consequences of Four Incapacities" (5.265), but it would be excusable to confuse it with *Philosophical Investigations*, I, sec. 67:

> Why do we call something a "number"? Well, perhaps because it has a — direct—relationship with several things that have hitherto been called number; and this can be said to give it an indirect relationship to other things we call the same name. And we extend our concept of number as in spinning a thread we twist fibre on fibre. And the strength of the thread does not reside in the fact that some one fibre runs through its whole length, but in the overlapping of many fibres.

The influence game is more dangerous and less important in philosophy than in literature, but sometimes just as interesting. Six pages later (sec. 81) Wittgenstein recalls that "F. P. Ramsey once emphasised in conversation with me that logic was a 'normative science'." There is no reference to Peirce here or anywhere in the *Investigations*, and perhaps Ramsey used one of Peirce's slogans without referring to its source. But Ramsey was a keen reader of Peirce's published writings, and though that phrase was not coined by Peirce, and expresses a thought found in other authors who do not use the phrase at all, it seems likely that he was consciously using Peirce's terminology. This impression is reinforced when we notice that there are numerous other and louder echoes in Wittgenstein of ideas and phrases, analogies and similes, that are now familiar from the eight volumes of Peirce's *Collected Papers*.

Some of the echoes are little more than curiosities. Peirce is fond of the metaphor of "family resemblances". British logicians, he says, display such a resemblance over many centuries from Occam and Duns Scotus to Whewell and Mill, Herschel and Hamilton (1.29). The three normative sciences, Esthetics, Ethics, and Logic, show "a family likeness" (2.156). In extending his detailed classification of the sciences, he speaks of families and subfamilies of inquiries (e.g., 1.238). He is concerned with exhibiting "the close alliance, the family identity, of the ideas of externality and unexpectedness" (5.540).

Other parallels are more significant and substantial. Peirce follows Duns Scotus and anticipates Wittgenstein in speaking of *grammar* where others have spoken of epistemology, theory of knowledge, or *Erkenntnislehre* (e.g., 2.83, 2.206). He declines to call a certain state of mind *faith*, "because that implies the conceivability of distrust" (5.212), as Wittgenstein declines to speak of knowledge or of certainty where it would be senseless to speak of doubt. In 5.183-85 Peirce discusses double-aspect pictures on lines similar to those of *Investigations*, part II, sec. xi: "We seem at first to be looking at the steps from above; but some unconscious part of the mind seems to tire of putting that construction upon it and suddenly we seem to see the steps from below and so the perceptive judgement, and the percept itself, seems to keep shifting from one general aspect to the other and back again."

It would be possible to multiply instances at tedious length while still circling round the heart and core of the philosophy of each of these thinkers. When we come to look at what each regarded as most important in his methods and results, we find a kinship such as we might expect if we knew that one had been the close disciple of the other.

Against Descartes. Peirce speaks for Wittgenstein when he trenchantly condemns "the method of doubt" and "the project of pure enquiry." "Do you call it *doubting* to write down on a piece of paper that you doubt?" (5.416). "Just try — in a real case — to doubt someone else's fear or pain" (*Investigations*, I, sec. 303). Peirce does not often speak of the use of language in connection with philosophical problems (as he does at 5.294 and 5.314), but his motto "Dismiss make-believes" (5.416) expresses the same spirit as Wittgenstein's observation that what we have to do is "to *accept* the everyday language-game, and to note *false* accounts of the matter *as* false" (Investigations, p. 200). Wittgenstein's polemic against the imposition of *requirements* (sec. 107) is paralleled by Peirce's complaints against philosophers who "block the way of inquiry" (1.135 and 1.156) or "bar the gate of inquiry" (1.144). Some passages are as reminiscent of Moore's "Proof of an External World" and "Defence of Common Sense" as they are of the *Investigations*: we *cannot* "start by doubting everything" as "philosophers of very diverse stripes" urge us to do; there is only one place where we can start, and that is where we actually *are*: and that means that we start every inquiry already "laden with an immense mass of cognition" that it would be madness to try to jettison even if there were any risk of succeeding in such a project (5.416). The anti-Cartesian principles stated at the beginning of "Some Consequences of Four Incapacities" (5.264-65) govern most of the work of both philosophers: (1) complete doubt is impossible; (2) the individual consciousness is not the source or test of certainty; (3) we must use multiform argumentation and not rely on a single thread of inference; (4) nothing is inexplicable, beyond the range of reason and understanding.

The COMMUNITY. The word is printed in capitals at 5.311, and the concept is heavily emphasized in many passages of the *Collected Papers.* Here again the difference between Wittgenstein's emphasis on language and Peirce's more direct reference to facts and things and ideas is too thin a veil to obscure the kinship of their thoughts and strategies. Wittgenstein's preoccupation with what *we* say, what *we* call a justification or count as a ground for doubt, is foreshadowed in Peirce's argument that the concept of reality has its origin in the experience of discovering "an unreal, an illusion." When we find it necessary to correct ourselves, we see the need of a distinction "between an *ens,* relative to private inward determinations, to the negation belonging to idiosyncrasy, and an *ens* such as would stand in the long run." And that means that "the very origin of the conception of reality shows that this conception essentially involves the notion of a COMMUNITY, without definite limits, and capable of a definite increase in knowledge."

Familiar Facts. Any philosophy that assigns a fundamental role to common sense and/or common language is bound to give the stress that Peirce and Wittgenstein both give to the importance of familiar facts. The remarks of Wittgenstein that might be quoted here are among the most characteristic in his writings: sec. 129 of the *Investigations* is typical of them: "the aspects of things that are most important for us are hidden because of their simplicity and familiarity. (One is unable to notice something because it is always before our eyes.)" Peirce must be quoted at greater length: his words are not so well known, and besides we shall be seeing soon the importance of some ways in which he differs from Wittgenstein. The first paragraph of 5.120 sums up most of what we have so far considered in Peirce's theory of knowledge:

> . . . by Philosophy I mean that department of Positive Science, or Science of Fact, which does not busy itself with gathering facts, but merely with learning what can be learned from that experience which presses in upon every one of us daily and hourly. It does not gather new facts, because it does not need them, and also because new general facts cannot be firmly established without the assumption of a metaphysical doctrine; and this, in turn, requires the cooperation of every department of philosophy; so that such new facts, however striking they may be, afford weaker support to philosophy by far than that *common experience* which nobody doubts or can doubt, and which nobody ever even pretended to doubt except as a consequence of belief in that experience so entire and perfect that it failed to be conscious of itself; just as an American who has never been abroad fails to perceive the characteristics of Americans; just as a writer is unaware of the peculiarities of his own style; just as none of us can see himself as others see him.

In 5.42 we are told of the philosophical value of "that rare faculty, the faculty of seeing what stares one in the face, just as it presents itself, unreplaced by any interpretation, unsophisticated by any allowance for this or that supposed modifying circumstance. This is the faculty of the artist who sees for example the apparent colors of nature as they appear." (For example, the artist sees, what the layman misses, that snow is not white, but yellow in the sun and blue in the shade).

It is part of the same parallel that both Wittgenstein and Peirce should attach great value to *particularity*, even if Peirce does also speak in 5.42 of the need for "the generalising power of the mathematician who produces the abstract formula that comprehends the very essence of the feature under examination purified from all admixture of extraneous and irrelevant accompaniment." Wittgenstein adds no such qualification when he inveighs against our "craving for generality" and "our contemptuous attitude towards the particular case" (*Blue Book*, pp. 17-18). He would have been happier with Peirce's comment on a controversy about the nature of greatness: "in order to establish a definition of greatness it would be necessary to begin by ascertaining what men were and what men were not great, and that having been done the rule might as well be dispensed with" ("The Century's Great Men of Science," *Values in a Universe of Chance*, ed. Philip P. Wiener [New York, 1958]).

Words and Deeds. Pragmatism and Pragmaticism were so called because of the emphasis given by Peirce and James to *practice*. Yet they could scarcely have given more importance to practice than Wittgenstein does in the *Investigations* and in *On Certainty* (OC). When Wittgenstein comes near to calling himself a pragmatist (OC, sec. 422), it is this element in his account of thought and language that he has in mind. Peirce's view of beliefs as *habits* (5.18) or *maxims* (5.27) and Wittgenstein's conception of language as composed of practices or "games" — "Words are also deeds" (sec. 546) — are alternative expressions of a common determination to resist the abstractness and overintellectualism of much traditional philosophy. The middle of the stage is to be occupied by the "flesh and blood experimenter" of 5.424, and he is from the same family as Wittgenstein's builders. A judgment involves an act (5.546-47). Both thinkers harp on usings and doings, actions and reactions, employment and application. The writ of Peirce's sheriff (1.213, 5.48) runs in the territory whose landscapes Wittgenstein sketches.

Instinct, "something animal." Wittgenstein had said in the *Tractatus* that Darwin's theory had no more to do with philosophy than any other theory of natural science, while Peirce saw "the Idea of Evolution" as a turning point in the history of philosophy (5.46). But the *Investigations* and *On Certainty* run parallel to the *Collected Papers* in the attention that they give to the "natural history" of human beings and its epistemological significance. Peirce attributes to man an 'Insight' into the ways of Nature, and so calls it "because it is to be referred to the same general class of operations to which Perceptive Judgements belong. This Faculty is at the same time of the general nature of instinct, resembling the instincts of the animals in its so far surpassing the general powers of our reason and for its directing us as if we were in possession of facts that are entirely beyond the reach of our senses" (5.173). At OC, secs. 357-59 Wittgenstein constrasts the "*comfort-*

able certainty" often expressed by 'I know' with 'the certainty that is still struggling" and goes on to speak of it "not as something akin to hastiness or superficiality, but as a form of life," i.e., to think of it "as something that lies beyond being justified or unjustified; as it were, as something animal." And in sec. 475 he again writes that he is regarding man "as an animal; as a primitive being to which one grants instinct but not ratiocination. Any logic good enough for a primitive means of communication needs no apology from us. Language did not emerge from some kind of ratiocination." This echoes a sentence from the paragraph, already quoted, in which Peirce speaks of Instinct (5.173): "However man may have acquired his faculty of divining the ways of Nature, it has certainly not been by a self-controlled and critical logic."

So Peirce and Wittgenstein are to be seen as Naturalists in epistemology. They regard man's thinking and inquiring, asking and answering, asserting and denying, believing, doubting, and explaining, as actions and reactions of a creature whose actions and reactions can be observed and described and understood, in spite of its bewildering familiarity to the only observers qualified to undertake the task. Naturalists: but not Empiricists any more than they are Rationalists. And so many philosophers can plausibly be tied to those posts that the negative comment serves to sum up how close these two are in outlook and upshot.

Yet what concerns me most is a difference, indeed a major *opposition* between Wittgenstein and Peirce on a question so substantial that it might make it seem astonishing that there are those many and close parallels between them on such central issues, to say nothing of the scores of detailed correspondences with which each heading could have been more fully furnished.

Peirce's editors speak of his system-making mind (1.1). Wittgenstein's followers declare that his writings defy summary. It is easy to provide evidence for the first verdict. The first sentence of the first paragraph of the *Collected Papers* is almost sufficient by itself: "To erect a philosophical edifice that shall outlast the vicissitudes of time, my care must be, not so much to set each brick with nicest accuracy, as to lay the foundations deep and massive." Peirce repeatedly pleads for the application to philosophy of the methods of science. In 5.265, just before the introduction of the cable analogy, he writes of the need for philosophy to imitate "the successful sciences" and accordingly "to proceed only from tangible premisses which can be subjected to careful scrutiny." He attributes "the present infantile condition of philosophy" to the fact that most of its nineteenth-century practitioners have been trained in seminaries rather than in dissecting rooms and other laboratories, and he firmly believed that philosophy should imitate the sciences not only in adopting systematic methods but also in endeavoring to construct a system of results. Although he criticizes Hegel often and severely, it is not for his architectonic ambition that he rebukes him. On the contrary, Peirce offers his own system, and especially his triad of Categories, as a rival edifice worthy to occupy the extensive site on which the discredited Hegelian structure had stood: "My philosophy resuscitates Hegel, though in a strange costume" (1.42).

He is also like the scientist, and again like Hegel, in his readiness to coin technical terms for the expression of his new discoveries: "if philosophy is ever to stand in the ranks of the sciences, literary elegance must be sacrificed—like the soldier's old brilliant uniforms—to the stern requirements of efficiency, and the philosophist must be encouraged—yes, and required—to coin new terms to express such new scientific concepts as he may discover, just as his chemical and biological brethren are expected to do." In a section entitled "Philosophical Nomenclature" (5.413) the "philosophist" has become a "philosophian" but is still required both to aspire after "a condition like that of the natural sciences" and to provide himself with "a suitable technical nomenclature, whose every term has a single definite meaning universally accepted among students of the subject, and whose vocabularies have no such sweetness or charms as might tempt loose writers to abuse them—which is a virtue of scientific nomenclature too little appreciated."

This open endorsement of the ancient maxim *"unum nomen, unum nominatum"* is a suitable juncture at which to begin to paint the starkly contrasting picture that Wittgenstein presents. Wittgenstein feared that he might "sow a certain jargon" (Norman Malcolm, *Wittgenstein: A Memoir* (London, 1958), p. 63). He regarded language as being "in order as it is" (*Investigations*, sec. 98). The natural sciences might build new avenues in the suburbs, but the tangled streets of the old center (including, one might add, the *agora* of Socrates) were the scenes on which the drama of philosophy could suitably be enacted (see sec. 18). Above all, we must renounce all *theoretical* aspirations, all desire to *explain* rather than to offer detailed *description:* there is "nothing hypothetical in our considerations"; there are no *theses* in philosophy (secs. 109, 128). Although there is one place in which he deprecatingly speaks of himself as offering "what looks like the fragments of a system" (*Investigations,* p. 228), Wittgenstein's insistent refrain is that philosophy is *unlike* the sciences and that in any case his own activity is only an *heir* of "the subject that used to be called philosophy." That subject had delusions of grandeur about its systems and theories and categories. What we need now is the sanity and sobriety to recognize the need for *skilled* philosophers. "A *method* has been found," but it is not a unitary method, and certainly not a scientific method, but a varied collection of techniques or "therapies" (sec. 133). "Philosophers constantly see the method of science before their eyes, and are irresistibly tempted to ask and answer questions in the way science does. This tendency is the real source of metaphysics, and leads the philosopher into complete darkness" (*Blue Book,* p. 18).

"*The* method of science." From long familiarity we think of the comment as characteristic of Wittgenstein, but there is also something very un-Wittgensteinian about the use of the singular in such a context. The singular is equally unsatisfactory in "*A* method has been found." Wittgenstein's own message was so often about the importance of multiplicity and variety—"I'll teach you *differences*"; "there are many cases here"—that some strong motive must have prompted those ill-fitting singulars. Wittgenstein was mainly concerned with dispelling the illusion that philosophical inquiry is a kind of causal inquiry—"the physics of the abstract" —an illusion to which Russell had given strong evidence of being inclined to succumb. Since Russell was also the leading apostle of 'scientific' philosophy, it was natural to express the necessary opposition to the causal picture as opposition to the conception of philosophy as resembling the physical sciences. But this is one of those cases, of which I have discussed others in "How to Read Wittgenstein," *Understanding Wittgenstein*, ed. G. Vesey (London, 1974), where Wittgenstein adopts the idiom of his opponent in order to correct a confusion that could at least equally effectively be corrected by questioning the opponent's idiom. There are many sciences, and each has many methods. Besides causal explanation, there are other modes of explanation as numerous and varied as the modes of understanding to which they are designed to give rise. Instead of saying that philosophy is not scientific and that philosophy gives no explanations, we may say that the science of philosophy has some methods that are different from the characteristic methods of the natural sciences and that philosophical explanations operate differently from scientific explanations. The necessary contrasts between philosophy and other species of inquiry may be made with or without the use of a vocabulary in which the philosopher is allowed to frame theories or defend theses, to have opinions, to offer explanations. A sympathetic reader of Wittgenstein should be the last person to allow a preference for one idiom over another to disguise the substance of important philosophical issues. And yet this is just what is done by those many defenders of Wittgenstein's results who are insistent on using all and only his own methods of expressing them.

This is where we can open a path to the resolution of the apparent conflict between Peirce and Wittgenstein. Peirce uses 'science' widely, and Wittgenstein uses it narrowly. For Peirce every rational method is a scientific method.

As with 'science', so with 'system'. It does not matter if two philosophers sum up their views in verbally conflicting formulas if they offer very similar descriptions in detail of what they are trying to represent. Philosophers in general are prone to widen or narrow the uses of ordinary words. The fact that Wittgenstein was a keen student of this phenomenon does not alter the fact that his work also presents many excellent illustrations of it. Peirce, for his part, adds to the general tendency of philosophers the special tendency of his own to favor a novel and technical terminology. In comparing and contrasting these two philosophers we must notice that Wittgenstein uses 'grammar' widely and 'science' narrowly; that Peirce uses 'science' and 'experiment', 'experience' and 'observation' and 'perception' so widely that his voice sometimes seems to be the voice of Russell when the thoughts he thinks are nearer to the thoughts of Wittgenstein (See e.g. 1.34, 1.109, 1.238-73, 5.181, 5.212, and 5.255).

The detailed differences of idiom are accompanied by a pervasive difference in style and presentation. Wittgenstein's "remarks" may be set against Peirce's ambition to write massive treatises. It is true that Wittgenstein took great care in the arrangement of his remarks, and it is also true that Peirce's ambitions were unfulfilled. He too produced only "fragments of a system." But Peirce's fragments are massive structures compared with the sherds out of which we are invited to compose the unity of Wittgenstein's philosophy. For precisely this reason we are liable to overlook a further respect in which the two philosophers are closely akin even in their perception of the nature and technique of the enterprise of philosophy. As Peirce's references to Hegel should lead us to expect, he too is a *dialectical* philosopher. He practices in most of his work the "method of inclinations" that he preaches in his long note to 5.382, a passage whose language and thought are equally reminiscent of Wittgenstein's observation that "what we are inclined to say is not, of course, philosophy, but it is its raw material." This may be set beside 5.421, where there is an echo of Plato's suggestion that thought is the soul's dialogue with itself: " . . . a person is not absolutely an individual. His thoughts are what he is 'saying to himself,' that is, is saying to that other self that is just coming into life in the flow of time. When one reasons, it is that critical self that one is trying to persuade; and all thought whatsoever is a sign, and is mostly of the nature of language."

There is room for differences that are more than differences of emphasis about how much processing the "raw material" should undergo before it is presented to the philosophical public. Varying opinions on this question go with varying estimates of the value of Wittgenstein's work and with opposing views, among those who are largely sympathetic to Wittgenstein's methods and results, about the extent to which it is proper, or even possible, to recast his thought into a form more traditional and systematic than he used himself, and than his *obiter dicta* on points of method might seem to countenance. But among the many questions that might be taken up from our present starting point, there is one of great philosophical substance which is yet fruitfully involved in controversies about the interpretation of the work of each of these two philosophers, and capable of being pursued productively by an extension of the comparative study we are engaged in.

The question of substance is raised again by Michael Dummett in *Truth and Other Enigmas* (Cambridge, Mass., 1978). The last essay in that collection is entitled "Can Analytical Philosophy Be Systematic, and Ought It to Be?" Dummett distinguishes two senses in which an investigation may be said to be "systematic": it may be systematic in the sense that it issues in a system of results, an articulated theory; or it may be systematic in the independent but compatible sense that it proceeds according to agreed methods of inquiry, and produces results that are subject to assessment by commonly agreed criteria, and are accordingly accepted or rejected by the application of such criteria, rather than remaining subject to interminable dispute. Dummett believes that philosophy can and should be systematic in both senses. Like many earlier thinkers, he aspires to put the subject on to "the sure path of a science," and regards it as a scandal that so little has yet been achieved. The long infancy of the science of philosophy has recently been brought to an end by Frege, but Wittgenstein—to whose influence Dummett is nevertheless sufficiently beholden to express qualms in his Preface—has been responsible for a swerving from the path by many of our contemporaries. Dummett openly recognizes that it is implausible to suppose that he or Frege has succeeded or will succeed where Descartes and Spinoza and Kant and Husserl are agreed to have failed. With self-confessed lameness he can "offer only the banal reply which any prophet has to make to any sceptic: time will tell" (p. 458).

Dummett's ambivalence does him credit, but it needs a fuller articulation than he gives it. All the materials needed for such an enterprise are now to hand, and it is an enterprise that will yield the bones of answers to a number of questions about Peirce, about Wittgenstein, about the relation between Peirce's scientism and Wittgenstein's antiscientism, and consequently about the senses in which philosophy respectively can and cannot be systematic. To put flesh on the bones would call for a study of the authors and the theme for which this paper is little more than a prospectus.

Wittgenstein has often been accused of countenancing relativism, and equally often praised and enlisted by those whose own relativism was open and avowed. Peirce has been subjected to severe criticisms on parallel lines. It has been doubted whether his pragmaticist notion of truth is a notion of *truth* at all. Does he not in the end identify the true opinion with the opinion on which human inquirers will in the last resort agree, and is it not obvious to anybody with a notion of *truth* that truth is independent of human belief, that we could all agree for ever and be for ever wrong?

Wittgenstein is vulnerable to such accusations when he speaks of "forms of life" as what is given, as that beyond which there is no appeal (*Investigations,* p. 226). If the "real foundation" of all inquiry is a set of *practices* that we happen to have and might not have had, how can we ever claim to have arrived at an objective truth about anything? It seems that he is involved in admitting that at a certain stage in a conflict of ideas, and a stage that is all too often reached, the parties can do nothing but denounce each other as fools and heretics (OC, 611). Peirce seems equally openly to admit the dependence of his conception of truth on human choice and practice. "Reality depends on the ultimate decision of the community" (5.316). In one of the notes to 5.402 Peirce even permits himself to speak of man's activity of inquiry as "the share which God permits him to have in the work of creation."

Yet Peirce's recognition of the objectivity of inquiry, his repudiation of relativism, is unmistakable. In 5.405 we are told that "we may define the real as that whose characters are independent of what anybody may think them to be," and the succeeding two or three pages are typical of many that could be quoted in amplification and support of the same conception:

> Our perversity and that of others may indefinitely postpone the settlement of opinion; it might even conceivably cause an arbitrary proposition to be universally accepted as long as the human race should last. Yet even this would not change the nature of the belief, which alone could be the result of investigation carried sufficiently far; and if, after the extinction of our race, another should arise with faculties and disposition for investigation, that true opinion must be the one which they would ultimately come to. "Truth crushed to earth shall rise again," and the opinion which would finally result from investigation does not depend on how anybody may actually think. But the reality of that which is real does depend on the real fact that investigation is destined to lead, at last, if continued long enough, to a belief in it (5.408).

The word *'destined'* is an important exhibit on behalf of the defense. It is not an accident, according to Peirce, that a particular conclusion comes to be agreed upon by those who collaborate in that "species of controlled conduct" (1.606) known as reasoning, a species of conduct whose participants form a COMMUNITY that is not just a community of scientists or of Americans or of Western thinkers, but a community of all inquirers, and one that therefore includes all human beings and any other beings who may be equipped with "faculties and disposition for investigation." Destiny rides again in 5.430, in double harness with another affirmation of Peirce's realism:

> That is *real* which has such and such characters, whether anybody thinks it to have those characters or not. At any rate, that is the sense in which the pragmaticist uses the word. Now, just as conduct controlled by ethical reason tends toward fixing certain habits of conduct, the nature of which . . . does not depend upon any accidental circumstances, and *in that sense* may be said to be *destined;* so, thought, controlled by a rational experimental logic, tends to the fixation of certain opinions, equally destined, the nature of which will be the same in the end, however the perversity of thought of whole generations may cause the postponement of the ultimate fixation.

In the same paragraph he repudiates "the virtual assumption that what is relative to thought cannot be real" by knocking it down with an example: "*Red* is relative to sight, but the fact that this or that is in that relation to vision that we call being red is not *itself* relative to sight; it is a real fact."

The robustness of Peirce's realism—and of his common sense—is obvious even in the otherwise picturesque and grandiose doctrine of Categories to which he attaches such importance. At the most elementary level of perception, observation, experiment—and Peirce uses all these terms exceptionally widely—a reality external to the mind is impinging on all members of the community. The force of destiny is a generalization of the resistance, struggle, exertion that Peirce associates with all experience; "a sense of effort and the experience of any sensation are phenomena of the same kind, equally involving direct experience of the Without and the Within" (5.539).

The same paragraph connects the realism and the doctrine of the Categories with the leading role that Peirce assigns to *surprise* in the origin and development of human knowledge: "A poor analyst is he who cannot see that the Unexpected is a direct experience of duality, that just as there can be no effort without resistance, so there can be no subjectivity of the unexpected without the objectivity of the unexpected, that they are merely two aspects of one experience given together and beyond all criticism; . . . *experience* means nothing but just that of a cognitive nature which the history of our lives has forced upon us." The aim of inquiry, including scientific inquiry, is to protect us from the power of the unexpected: "What then is the end of an explanatory hypothesis? Its end is, through subjection to the test of experiment, to lead to the avoidance of all surprise and to the establishment of a habit of positive expectation that shall not be disappointed" (5.197).

Doubt, Surprise, and Belief are all states that we *find* ourselves in. We must start where we actually are (see 5.416 again). But by the self-controlled conduct that is reasoning we may move from Doubt to Belief or Belief to Doubt or from Belief to Belief via Doubt or Surprise. Peirce as much as any philosopher—and certainly as much as the Cartesian pure inquirer—makes us responsible for our beliefs, answerable for our acts of assertion and inference, attitudes of confidence or uncertainty. What is distinctive about his epistemology is that he combines this recognition of our responsibility for all our conduct—theoretical as well as practical— with a recognition that when we set out to take such steps we can start only from where we are, and that wherever we are we are interacting with reality, burdened with a mass of cognition.

Wittgenstein is distinctive in the same respect. When he speaks of the *given* as consisting of certain "forms of life" (*Investigations,* p. 226) or of the grounding of our reasoning in "something animal" (OC, sec. 359; cf. 475); when he refers us to an inherited background against which we distinguish true from false (OC, sec. 94), a language game that is "there—like our life" (OC, sec. 559), and invokes the system in which all our arguments have their life, from which all our assertions derive their intelligibility, he too is seeing and showing that the relativity of our understanding to our nature and conduct is compatible with the objectivity of the questions we ask and answer, the unique rationality of our procedures of inquiry. "The system is not an arbitrary and doubtful point of departure. It belongs to the essence of what we call an argument, It is the element in which arguments have their life" (OC, sec. 105; see also 102, 140, 141, and 410). It is "not in my power what I believe, even unshakeably" (173). "Can I be in doubt *at will?"* (221). "I do not decide what is a telling ground for something" (271). "We didn't *choose* the game" (317).

The unsystematic Wittgenstein here uses the idea of a system. If the whole of the common understanding, on which all other understanding must be based, can be recognized to be systematic, we may look again and with new eyes at Dummett's anxiety about the progress of philosophy. The common understanding is systematic in both of Dummett's senses: it forms a coherent whole, and it is extended by the operation of procedures that determine agreed answers to the questions that arise on its boundaries. Wittgenstein's picture of human inquiry, especially in *On Certainty,* fits well with a view of philosophy that makes it cognitive and progressive without depriving it of the informality and untidiness that alarms some critics of the common understanding as much as it alarms some exponents of the ideal of a systematic philosophy.

The Light Wittgenstein Sheds on Religion

W. D. HUDSON

Many readers of Wittgenstein are prepared to believe that what he had to say about religion is profoundly illuminating—or, at least, that it will be, once we have understood correctly just what it means. His friend Paul Engelmann[1] went so far as to claim that Wittgenstein's remarks about "the mystical" at the end of the *Tractatus* light up for all mankind the possibility of "a universal new way of life," which will eventually unite them across all their ideological divisions in "a new spiritual attitude" called "wordless faith." Such extravagant expectations will strike the majority even of Wittgenstein's admirers as absurd. But, however unlikely it may be that his remarks will have these dramatic practical consequences, it is not at all unlikely that what he had to say about religion will light up our understanding of the subject.

Any attempt to see what light he does shed may turn on either of two questions. One is: what view *did* Wittgenstein himself take of religion? The other: what view of it *can* be taken in the light of his philosophy? They are not the same question though each has some relation to the other. If, for example, we have to decide whether Wittgenstein conceived of religion as what he called a "form of life," it will obviously be relevant, though not decisive, to ask whether it can be so thought of; and if we have to decide whether one can so think of it, it will obviously be relevant, though not decisive, to ask whether Wittgenstein himself managed to do so. However, it is, I think, more important to answer the latter than the former of the two questions, for a thinker may shed more light upon a subject by his general insights than his expressed opinions on that particular subject reflect. I shall, therefore, try to show not only what view Wittgenstein himself took of religion but more especially what view we should take of it in the light of his philosophy.

The documents[2] that I shall have chiefly in mind are the following: certain passages in his *Notebooks for 1916* and in the *Tractatus* (which he had completed by 1918); his "Lecture on Ethics," given in Cambridge during 1929 or 1930; his *Remarks on Frazer's "Golden Bough,"* which were composed during 1930 or 1931;

his *Lectures on Religious Belief,* which date from 1938; a passage from his *Remarks on Colour,* written in 1950; and his *On Certainty,* which consists of notes written during the last eighteen months of his life. The opinion I shall venture to express and defend in this paper will be that there are two alternative conceptions of religion to be found in, or extracted from, these writings and that the latter of the two conceptions sheds more light on the subject than the former. I shall call the former the idea of religion as *transcending* a limit to thinking and the latter the idea of it as *constituting* such a limit. It seems to me that the former is the view which predominates in the first three of the above writings but that the latter is a conception which can — and should — be formulated in the light of Wittgenstein's *Lectures on Religious Belief* and his *On Certainty.* But to begin with, let us be clear what Wittgenstein did *not* think about religion, by considering his *Remarks on Frazer's "Golden Bough."*

WHAT RELIGION IS NOT

During 1930, Wittgenstein and his friend M. O'C. Drury read and discussed together part of the first volume of *The Golden Bough.*[3] In this monumental work Frazer conceives the history of human thought to have had three stages: it has passed from *magic* through *religion* to *science.* At the stage of magic, men believe that there is an established order of nature which they can manipulate for their own ends. But when they find that they cannot in fact cope by means of magic with all the difficulties and dangers that beset them, they turn to religion. Religion is based on the belief that natural phenomena are regulated only by the will of the gods and that, so far from controlling events, men can only throw themselves upon the mercy of these more powerful spiritual beings. However, the more men find out about the world of nature, the more likely they are to revert to the idea that it has its own uniformity. What was implicit in magic — namely, the idea of an inflexible regularity in the order of natural events, which if carefully observed enables us to predict and control them — becomes explicit in science. The loose connections of sympathetic magic give way to the firmer links of natural law.

From this point of view, Frazer explains the magical and religious practices of primitive people as the logical consequences of the beliefs they hold about the nature of things. Like ourselves, these people want to control their environment in order to satisfy certain needs or fulfill certain purposes. For example, they want to make their part of the earth fruitful so that it will produce food for them to eat. We share with them some of these needs and purposes, and so their magical and religious practices are perfectly intelligible to us, once we know the beliefs about the nature of things from which they arise. The flaw in primitive magical thinking, according to Frazer, "lies not in its reasoning, but in its premises": that is, in mistaken ideas about the way things are, rather than in irrelevant or invalid deductions from these ideas. Primitive man's errors, he wrote, "were not wilful extravagances or the ravings of insanity, but simply hypotheses, justifiable as such at the time when they were propounded but which a fuller experience has proved to be inadequate."

Now, all this, in Wittgenstein's opinion, is sadly mistaken. What he says[4] against Frazer, in sum, is that primitive man's magical and religious *beliefs* should *not* be thought of as mere *hypotheses nor* his magical and religious *practices* as exclusively *utilitarian* in intention. One example he takes from Frazer, in order to show how mistaken the latter's opinions are, is that of African natives who offer gifts to so-called Rain Kings at the beginning of the rainy season. Frazer thinks this practice perfectly understandable given their belief that the Rain Kings can make it rain. We share with these primitive people the need for well-watered ground. Of course, we no longer believe in the powers they attribute to Rain Kings. But if we did, we would think it reasonable as they do to make gifts in order to win the favor of the Rain Kings. In support of his interpretation of this practice, Frazer comments that the reason it has persisted for so long is that the belief on which it is based — namely, that these kings can make rain — is so hard to falsify. Sooner or later it always *does* rain; and so this belief is always confirmed in the long run! But surely, says Wittgenstein, if the practice of offering gifts to the Rain Kings were, as Frazer would have us think, simply a utilitarian device, based on the belief that they have the power to bring rain down from heaven, two things would be very puzzling. For one, why do these primitive people not notice sooner than they do that the fact which is supposed to justify their practice — namely, the inevitability of rain sooner or later — really takes all point away from it? If it *does* always rain, what use is a practice designed to *make* it rain? The rain is going to fall whether the gifts are offered or not. Then again, why do these people offer gifts to a Rain King *only* in the rainy season? In Wittgenstein's own words: "surely this means that they do not actually think he can make rain, otherwise they would do it in the dry periods"![5] On such grounds, then, Wittgenstein is sure that Frazer must be wrong. Beliefs and practices certainly go together in magic and religion, but the practices do not spring from the beliefs in the way Frazer thought.

The *beliefs* are not mistaken hypotheses — or, as Wittgenstein alternatively calls them, opinions — about the nature of things, which a little more scientific knowledge would correct. Taking a further example from Frazer — namely, the practice whereby a woman adopts a child by pulling it out from beneath her clothes — Wittgenstein ridicules Frazer's account of magical and religious practices by pointing out that it is "crazy"[6] to suppose that she is acting on the erroneous hypothesis that she has borne the child. Of course, she must have some beliefs about what she is doing; otherwise she could not conceive of it as making any difference. But Wittgenstein's point is that she is not making a biological blunder. Whatever her beliefs may be, she is not mistakenly thinking of what happens as a form of natural birth. Rather, she is giving a new meaning to the whole idea of getting a child.

Wittgenstein is no less critical of Frazer's view that magical or religious *practices* are utilitarian in intention. To what ulterior ends are kissing the picture of a loved one, celebrating the rising of the sun, cutting Schubert's scores after his death into small pieces to give to his favorite pupils, confessing one's sins, etc., supposed to be useful *means*? Scathingly, he contends that Frazer can only have countenanced the account he gives of such practices because he was "much more savage than most of his savages" in the "narrowness" of his "spiritual life." His explanations of primitive observances are "much cruder" than these observances themselves.[7]

Why cruder? Wittgenstein's own positive account of such observances is that there is something in us which speaks in support of them: "an inclination in ourselves"[8] to perform a certain kind of action when things have made a certain kind of impression on us. Wittgenstein calls the kind of action to which he is referring ritualistic; and the things that make the relevant kind of impression he variously describes as terrible, horrible, tragic, sinister, significant, important, and so on. There are innumerable such things — a man's shadow that looks like him, thunderstorms, changes of season, the phenomena of death, birth, sexual life, and so on. We have a "kinship" with the savages, which is evident in the fact that words like 'ghost', 'shade', 'soul', 'spirit' are as natural a part of our vocabulary as they were of theirs. "A whole mythology is deposited in our language."[9] It comes naturally to us to respond to certain things by performing ritualistic actions. As Wittgenstein has it, such an action "aims at some satisfaction and it achieves it. Or rather, it does not *aim* at anything: we act in this way and then feel satisfied."[10] The satisfaction, however, is not that which a hypothesis explaining the practice can give. Compared with the impression that the kind of thing under consideration makes upon us, any such explanation will be "too uncertain." Says Wittgenstein: "for someone broken up by love an explanatory hypothesis won't help much — it will not bring peace." All we can say of the satisfaction which ritualistic practices bring us is: "human life is like that." Having described any such practice, we can only add: "This is what took place here; laugh, if you can."[11]

Wittgenstein's evident view that no religious beliefs can be mere hypotheses and no religious practices merely utilitarian may well appear mistaken. Surely religious believers as such often think in "if-then" terms — if the gods are angry, then such-and-such consequences will follow. And surely also in "means-end" terms — if we do such-and-such actions, then we will attain this objective or that. But perhaps Wittgenstein's point is that no religious belief is hypothetical in the sense that it is conceived as a proposition which *may* be true or false; and no religious practice, utilitarian in the sense that its *whole* significance is thought to lie in some heteronomous consequence which it effects. To such considerations we must return in due course. What I want to do now is begin to explain the difference between the two conceptions of religion — viz., as *transcending*, and as *constituting*, a limit to thinking respectively — both of which I earlier claimed are to be found in Wittgenstein's writings.

RELIGION AS TRANSCENDING A LIMIT

The view that religion takes us beyond a limit to thinking raises two questions: namely, What is this limit? and How precisely is religion supposed to transcend it?

The former question is easy to answer. The limit is the limit to what can be put into words. Throughout Wittgenstein's life the idea that religion brings us up against such a limit stayed with him, though as I have already indicated I think he sometimes thought of it as a limit that religion must transcend and at other times as one that religion itself constitutes. At the moment we are concerned with the former view.

To take examples of this former view: at the beginning of the 1920s he said in the *Tractatus* that "the mystical" consists of "things that cannot be put into words";[12] at the beginning of the 1930s, shortly after returning to Cambridge, he said in his "Lecture on Ethics" that everyone who has ever tried to write or talk ethics or religion has "run up against the boundaries of language";[13] and at the beginning of the 1950s in the *Remarks on Colour* he said that theology "fumbles around with words, because it wants to say something and doesn't know how to express it."[14]

In the *Tractatus* the limit Wittgenstein drew to the expression of thoughts was his so-called picture-theory of meaning. That theory requires there to be a one-to-one correspondence between the "simples" of language and of reality, and a logical form — i.e., configuration of these simples — common to both, if language is to have determinate meaning. What can be said must picture what *is* the case. "The world is all that is the case."[15] "The mystical" — within which expression Wittgenstein does not distinguish very sharply between ethics and religion — has to do with the questions: What is the meaning of *all* there is? and What has *absolute* value? He thinks it logically impossible for the answer to either question to be something that merely "happens and is the case." How can the sense of all things be just one more thing? How can absolute value be something that just happens? "The mystical" must therefore "lie outside the world."[16] But if it does, then on the "picture theory" of meaning, it cannot be put into words.

By the time he wrote his "Lecture on Ethics" Wittgenstein had abandoned the "picture theory" but he still thought of religion as bringing us up against a limit to language. He gave two examples of the kind of experience on which religious belief is based, viz., wondering at the existence of the world and feeling safe whatever happens. These experiences, he said, are what people refer to when they say that God created the world and that we are in his hands. The point he made about them was this. It makes sense to say that one is wondering at the existence of something only if one can form some idea of what it would be like for it not to exist. I can, for instance, be said to wonder at the existence of a certain plant in my garden, if I can imagine a state of affairs in my garden in which this plant does not exist. But if I am wondering at the existence of the world — i.e., *all* there is — there can (logically) be no other state of affairs with which to contrast it. Similarly, it makes good sense to say that one feels absolutely safe only if one can form some idea of what it would be like to be unsafe. I may feel safe in my house because I cannot be run over there by a car; safe when I have been inoculated because I cannot now catch the disease; and so on. To feel safe is to feel that it is physically impossible for certain things to happen. But this being so, it takes all meaning out of 'feel safe' to say that I feel safe *whatever* happens.

Wittgenstein considers the suggestion that 'wondering' and 'feeling safe' in the context just supposed are analogical expressions: that is to say, that the experiences referred to are *like* wondering or feeling safe as we ordinarily use these expressions. But he rejects this idea on the ground that "if I can describe a fact by means of a simile I must also be able to drop the simile and to describe the facts without it."[17] His point was, for instance, that to say, "The London Underground is like a madhouse at rush hours" has meaning *only* because we know what the London Underground is *as well as* what a madhouse is. The whole thrust of his argument is that we do *not* know what wondering about the existence of the world, and the feeling of being safe whatever happens, are. So how can we say what they are *like*? This is, of course, the limit to what can be said which Aquinas and others have attempted to transcend by their notions of the analogy of proportionality or attribution.[18] But I think unsuccessfully.

In the *Remarks on Colour,* Wittgenstein takes up again one of the examples we have just been considering. The question "Where did everything come from?" is offered as an example of the kind of question with which theology "fumbles." This fumbling, he says, consists in raising such questions and then not taking them seriously. Religion is here conceived to bring us up against the limit to what can be said by using language but then not doing with it what it is designed to do. The question referred to requests a causal explanation of the world but it is not in religion's own nature to accept such an explanation. The center of interest, we may say, has shifted here from what the limits of meaning are to what the nature of religion is. The attribute of the person who believes in God, says Wittgenstein, is "the attribute that takes a particular matter seriously, but then at a particular point doesn't take it seriously after all, and declares that something else is even more important." This passage can, I suppose, be read as an account of *how* religion transcends the limit to what can be said.[19] This brings us to the second of the two questions, which I said (see p. 4) are raised by the view that religion transcends a limit to thinking. Namely, just how is it supposed to do that? To this question I now turn.

Wittgenstein said in his "Lecture on Ethics" that any attempt to put ethics or religion into words is "perfectly, absolutely hopeless."[20] The outcome can only be nonsense. He was as convinced of this as any logical positivist. But he was himself no logical positivist. We have the word of Rudolf Carnap,[21] a member of the Vienna Circle, for it that Wittgenstein's attitude toward religion was quite different from theirs; and the difference was described by Engelmann[22] in this way: whereas the logical positivists thought that what we can speak about is all that matters in life, Wittgenstein believed all that really matters to be precisely what we must be silent about. This view seems to be confirmed by Wittgenstein's own letter[23] to Ficker in 1919, which refers to the *Tractatus* in these terms: "The book's point is an ethical one. . . . My book draws limits to the sphere of the ethical from the inside as it were. . . . I have managed . . . to put everything into place by being silent about it." These words have suggested to some a comparison with Hertz's work because he refers to him a time or two in the *Tractatus*. Hertz expressly attempted, *from within* his account of the limits of mechanics, to make a point about life, namely, that it cannot be mechanistically described or explained. The point of the *Tractatus* could have been ethical in the sense that Wittgenstein was similarly — from within his account of language — making a point about the mystical, namely, that it lies beyond language — and doing so without denying the existence of the mystical any more than Hertz denied that life exists. Support is given to this interpretation by the remark at the end of the *Tractatus:* "There are, indeed, things that cannot be put into words. They *make themselves manifest.* They are what is mystical." [24]

One thing is certain. Wittgenstein conceived of "the mystical" as transcending the limits of language and thought by *showing itself.* But to say precisely what he meant by this is not the easiest thing in the world. G. E. M. Anscombe[25] suggests he meant that things which are "shown" or "make themselves manifest" are things "it would be right to call . . . 'true' if, *per impossible* they could be said." However, because they cannot, their "truth" can, so to speak, be shown only in things that can be said. But Wittgenstein may not have agreed with this interpretation. Even Russell, Wittgenstein's teacher and friend, was told that he had not correctly understood the distinction drawn in the *Tractatus* between what can be said and what can only be shown.[26] I have argued elsewhere[27] that at least part of what Wittgenstein meant by the mystical showing itself may have been that, though inexpressible in words, it expresses itself in art and action. We have, as witness, his often-quoted remark to Engelmann that in a poem of Uhland's the "unutterable" finds expression; and there are some grounds for thinking that when he gave up philosophy and went to teach school in Lower Austria to "get the peasantry out of the muck," he may himself have been consciously engaging in an imitation of Christ.

For all our uncertainty about what 'shows itself' may mean, however, the heart of Wittgenstein's conception of the mystical as transcending a limit appears to be what he had to say about the "I," or willing subject.[28] This "I," or willing subject, is "deeply mysterious." [29] It is placed like an eye in a visual field; and just as the eye cannot be part of its field, so the "I" cannot be part of its world. However, the "I" is dependent on, as well as independent of, the world. "I cannot bend the happenings of the world to my will: I am completely powerless. I can only make myself independent of the world — and so in a certain sense master it — by renouncing any influence on happenings." [30]

Of course, this "I," or willing subject, is a metaphysical, not an empirical, conception. Wittgenstein conceives of it as a "limit" to the world.[31] He says it is what enables us to feel "the world as a limited whole." And he immediately adds that it is this feeling which is mystical.[32] What the "I" *can* do is "alter the limits of the world"; but it is important to realize that this does not mean change any facts within it:

> If the good or bad exercise of the will does alter the world, it can alter only the limits of the world, not the facts — not what can be expressed by means of language.

In short the effect must be that it becomes an altogether different world. It must, so to speak, wax and wane as a whole.

The world of the happy man is a different one from that of the unhappy man.[33]

To be "a happy man," we are told, means to live "in agreement with the world"[34] but also to be able to "renounce the amenities of the world."[35] Such a man lives without hope or fear, timelessly in the present. This exercise of the will is virtue's own reward. It is that eternal life which religion places on offer to all.

On this account of the matter, agreeing with the world and renouncing it seem to come to much the same thing in the end. But there is a distinction upon which Wittgenstein insists. It is that between an "alien" will to which I must submit and my *own* will which makes me "independent." He says, "There are two godheads: the world and my independent I."[36]

A number of philosophical problems are raised by Wittgenstein's remarks about this mysterious "I" — for example, can what is thought of as a *will* be conceived as incapable of altering the facts of the world?[37] But if all such philosophical questions could be answered, the question would still remain whether what Wittgenstein evidently means by religion here has anything in common with what is normally meant by it.

F. P. Ramsey,[38] Wittgenstein's friend, translator, and critic, went to Austria in 1923 to discuss with him at length the ideas put forward in the *Tractatus*. From there Ramsey wrote a letter in which he remarks, "Some of his [Wittgenstein's] sentences are intentionally ambiguous having an ordinary meaning and a more difficult meaning which he also believes." This seems to be particularly true of the sentences in the *Notebooks* and the *Tractatus* which use religious terms. Wittgenstein writes, for example, "To believe in a God means to see that the facts of the world are not the end of the matter."[39] But are we to take these words in anything like the sense they would have if they had been uttered by a traditional theist? A sentence or two earlier, Wittgenstein had written that what he means by belief in God, who is the meaning of the world, can be compared with belief in God as father and that prayer is "thinking about the meaning of life." All this seems to be on the level of traditional religious belief. But what of the sentence quoted a moment or two ago: "There are two godheads: the world and my independent I"? That is a long way away from what is ordinarily meant by religion.

True, some readers of Wittgenstein seem to find no difficulty in comparing his "happy man," who is so detached from the world, with a theistic believer in his reliance upon God. D. Z. Phillips, for example, in *The Concept of Prayer* (London, 1965) considers in turn the various forms of prayer — viz., adoration, confession, thanksgiving, petition, intercession — and discovers the heart of devotion in each case to be what Wittgenstein evidently meant by being 'happy'. Petition, for instance, is at the level of true spirituality, *not* asking God for things but meeting things "in God" — "seeing that what is of value cannot be destroyed by the way things go."[40] The respect Wittgenstein expressed at the end of his "Lecture on

Ethics" for all the hopeless attempts made in religion to break through the barriers of language no doubt included traditional theism and it may be, therefore, that he thought traditional theists would have no difficulty in assenting to his views about how religion transcends these barriers. But there is, to put it mildly, room for some doubt as to whether they could go along with Wittgenstein here without radically changing their conception of God. Insofar as Wittgenstein has an argument to support his view that religion transcends what can be put into words, it seems to turn on his conception of 'two godheads, the world and my independent I'. And this makes it hard to resist the conclusion that in attempting to show how religion transcends the limits of what can be said, Wittgenstein has left religion itself behind.

RELIGION AS CONSTITUTING A LIMIT

I turn, then, to the second of the two conceptions of religion that I said we might find in, or extract from, Wittgenstein's writings. This is the view of it as constituting, rather than transcending, a limit to thinking. In his 1938 *Lectures on Religious Belief* Wittgenstein conceives of religion as "using a picture" in its faith and practice. What he says about these religious "pictures" and their use seems to me to anticipate some of the things he later had to say in *On Certainty,* which was written in 1949-51, about a kind of proposition he called fundamental. I want to show that religion consititutes a limit to thinking in the sense that it rests in the last logical analysis upon a proposition, or propositions, of this fundamental kind. So, first, I shall try to make clear what I take Wittgenstein to have meant in *On Certainty* by fundamental propositions; and then, to discover parallels with what he had earlier said about religious "pictures" in his 1938 *Lectures on Religious Belief;* the object of the whole exercise being to show that we can — and should — conceive of religion in the light which these inquiries will shed upon it. (In what follows I shall enclose in brackets references to paragraphs in *On Certainty* and to *pages* in *Lectures on Religious Belief,* distinguishing the latter from the former by the prefix 'p' for 'page').

Here are some examples of fundamental propositions that Wittgenstein used: "I am a human being" (4), "There are physical objects" (35), "The earth existed long before my birth" (84), "I have spent my whole life in close proximity to the earth" (93), "My body has never disappeared and appeared again after an interval" (101), "I have two hands" (157), "All human beings have parents" (240), "Nature is uniform" (315). Some of these are taken from G. E. Moore,[41] and all of them are offered as examples of the kind of proposition that Moore, in his defense of common sense, claimed he *knew* for certain to be true. It was absurd, Moore contended,[42] to suggest that he did not really know, but only believed, that he had two hands, and so on. Wittgenstein took exception to Moore's use of 'know' here, pointing out that all Moore was really saying was that he had a conviction of the truth of these propositions and that such a conviction is never a sufficient reason for saying that somebody knows something, however trustworthy the man who has the conviction may be (137). Nevertheless, Wittgenstein recognized that Moore had called attention to a kind of proposition which has a "peculiar logical role" (136) in our thinking; and he set himself to explain what this role is. He came to the conclusion that the kind of propositions Moore claimed to know are "fundamental principles of human enquiry" (670), the "foundation of all my beliefs" (246), the "rock-bottom of my convictions" (248).

In what sense, then, are these propositions fundamental?[43] Although they are, to all appearance, synthetic and contingent, it seemed clear to Wittgenstein that they are *not hypothetical* in the way that ordinary empirical propositions are. I shall take, as examples, the fundamental propositions "The earth existed long before my birth" and "Nature is uniform" in order to illustrate the four reasons to be found in Wittgenstein for denying that fundamental propositions are hypothetical.

First, these propositions are true, not in the ordinary sense, but in the special sense that they are the "unmoving foundations" of . . . language-games (153, 403). All historical discourse proceeds on the assumption that the earth has a past and all scientific on the assumption that nature is uniform. These are the logical presuppositions of everything that is said in history and science respectively and are not hypotheses which could conceivably be either true or false within these respective disciplines.

Second, fundamental propositions are not testable, in the sense that we cannot form any clear conception of what would count for, or against, them (119). *Within* historical discourse there is nothing that counts as evidence for, or against, the existence of the past, nor *within* science for or against the uniformity of nature, since the whole discipline in each case is based on the proposition in question. But then again, neither can we say what in *any other* universe of discourse would count for or against the existence of the past or the uniformity of nature.

Third, there is, therefore, "no such thing as doubt" in the case of fundamental propositions (58). Wittgenstein imagines (310-17) a schoolboy who, in history class, keeps asking "But how can I be sure that the earth existed long before my birth?" and in science class, "But how can I be certain that nature is uniform?" His teacher says, "Stop interrupting me and do as I tell you. So far your doubts don't make sense at all." And quite rightly, says Wittgenstein. The boy is only holding up the class and will not learn any history or science himself as long as he persists in raising such doubts.

Fourth, although ordinary empirical propositions *have* to be changed if the evidence goes against them, fundamental propositions are not vulnerable in the same way (512). Even when events occur which appear to be inexplicable in terms of historical precedent or natural uniformity, we do not deny that the earth has existed for a long time past or that nature is uniform. Even if things hitherto unheard of should happen, like houses turning into steam, animals beginning to talk, trees changing into men and men into trees, etc. (513), we should still not accept these unprecedented or irregular events as good reasons to abandon our beliefs in the existence of the past or the uniformity of nature. Fundamental propositions would "stay in the saddle however much the facts bucked" (612, 619).

A glance back at the fundamental propositions listed above on p. 9 may lead the reader to think that Wittgenstein was obviously mistaken in supposing all of them to be non-hypothetical in the four respects just listed. What, for instance, of the proposition, "I have spent my whole life in close proximity to the earth?" Beginning with Yuri Gagarin, there have been a number of men of whom this is: (i) false in the perfectly ordinary sense; (ii) testable by perfectly ordinary empirical methods of establishing truth or falsity; (iii) capable of being doubted; and (iv) an opinion that *has* to be changed in the light of evidence. This proposition is certainly a hypothesis and an erroneous one at that.

Some differentiation within the class of fundamental propositions seems to be called for to meet this objection. I think we may say that there are three subdivisions within that class, although Wittgenstein himself did not explicitly make these divisions. First, some propositions seem to be absolutely fundamental to our entire world view: for instance, that things do not disappear when no one is observing them. Second, some are fundamental to a certain discipline or universe of discourse: we have just been using two such examples, "The earth existed long before my birth," which is fundamental to history, and "Nature is uniform," which is fundamental to science. Third, there are propositions like the one I referred to a moment ago — "I have spent my whole life in close proximity to the earth" — that are simply taken for granted at certain times. When Wittgenstein was writing *On Certainty* in 1950-51, if anyone had said that he had been to the moon, he would have been universally regarded as a liar, and if he had produced what looked like plausible evidence to prove it, this would have been dismissed as some form of chicanery. Fundamental propositions of these three kinds constitute a limit to thinking, though with varying degrees of exclusiveness and permanence. I shall come back to the question of how, and why, some propositions cease to be fundamental toward the end of this paper.

I go back first, however, to my claim that religion is *logically grounded* in a proposition, or propositions, of the fundamental kind. Not *all* religious beliefs are fundamental, of course, any more than all historical or scientific ones are. We may entertain hypotheses about what happened in the past or what goes on in nature; and similarly, we may regard some religious beliefs — e.g., that God was fulfilling such-and-such a purpose in a certain event, or that he wills us to behave in such-and-such a way under certain conditions — as hypothetical. *Within* religion, that is to say, such beliefs may come to be thought false — believers frequently feel that beliefs they once held were mistaken. Such beliefs can be tested in recognized ways — say, by reference to scripture or tradition. They can, therefore, be doubted — "Am I right in believing this?" a believer may wonder. They may *have* to be changed in the light of the evidence — say, when a study of scripture has shown them to be misconceived. However, just as history or science are constituted in the last analysis by a non-hypothetical proposition, or propositions, of the fundamental kind, so, I would claim, is religion.

There is one objection to this way of thinking about religion which need not detain us. It is the objection that religion is such a varied phenomenon that we cannot say anything general about it. Wittgenstein's remarks to the effect that applications of general terms such as 'religion' like 'game' may "belong to the same family without having anything in common"[44] are sometimes invoked to support this objection. But, as I have argued elsewhere,[45] Wittgenstein himself concedes that it may be necessary in the interests of clear thinking, to indulge our "craving for generality"[46] to the extent of drawing certain boundaries around concepts. In the paper referred to, I tried to define religion as constituted by a concept, god (with a small 'g' since I had religions of all kinds in mind and not simply theism), and to list the defining characteristics of this concept. It is not necessary, however, for the present argument that this particular analysis of religion should have been correct, and so I need not say more about it here. All I need do is postulate that *some* such analysis is possible. There is some proposition (or propositions) that is fundamental to religion in the sense in which the propositions quoted above were seen to be fundamental to history or science.

Wittgenstein used some very simple examples of religious belief in his *Lectures* on the subject, including "There will be a Last Judgment" (p. 53) and "God's Eye sees everything" (p. 71). A moment ago I drew a distinction between hypothetical and non-hypothetical religious beliefs. Wittgenstein does not concern himself with this distinction. If it came to the point, I would want to question whether his particular examples of religious belief are of the non-hypothetical, rather than the hypothetical, kind. But let us leave that question on one side here. What is of interest is that some of the things Wittgenstein said about religious beliefs seem to anticipate things he later said in *On Certainty* about fundamental propositions. Leaving aside, then, the question of what is hypothetical and what non-hypothetical *within* religion, I find these similarities significant. They furnish the ground on which I would claim that Wittgenstein's writings contain a view of religion as *constituting* a limit to thinking, which is distinct from the view of it as transcending one.

Let us take, as our example, the belief "There will be a Last Judgment." What parallels are there between Wittgenstein's remarks about it in his *Lectures* and what he was later to say about fundamental propositions in *On Certainty*? Notice that he speaks of this belief quite explicitly as non-hypothetical, as he was later to speak of fundamental propositions. In referring to it he says that words like 'dogma' or 'faith' are used – "We don't talk about hypothesis" (p. 57). He speaks of this belief in ways which seem to me to show quite clearly that in his view it has the four characteristics on the basis of which he was later to speak of propositions as fundamental (cf. above p. 10).

First, this belief is conceived to be true for the believer in the special sense that it is "constantly admonishing" him; he "always thinks" of it; it is "constantly in the foreground" (p. 56) of his mind – all expressions which anticipate Wittgenstein's description of fundamental propositions as "the unmoving foundations of our language-games" (403).

Second, just as Wittgenstein was later to say that fundamental propositions are not testable, so he here recalls that he was taught as a child to use the word

'God' in such a way that "Whatever believing in God may be, it cannot be believing in something we can test, or find means of testing" (p. 60).

Third, what of doubting? The extent to which religious beliefs are unlike ordinary hypothetical empirical beliefs, when it comes to doubting, is indicated by Wittgenstein in this way: "Suppose someone were a believer and said: 'I believe in a Last Judgment' and I said 'Well I'm not so sure. Possibly.' You would say there was an enormous gulf between us. If he said 'There is a German aeroplane overhead,' and I said 'Possibly. I'm not so sure,' you'd say we were fairly near!" (p. 53). The "enormous gulf" is that between commitment and non-commitment. This is the sense in which it might be said of religious beliefs as of fundamental propositions (cf. above p. 10) that "there is no such thing as doubt" (58) in their case.

Fourth, Wittgenstein's view that religious beliefs are not at the mercy of empirical evidence in the way that hypothetical beliefs are comes out in these terms: "Suppose, for instance, we knew people who foresaw the future; make forecasts for years and years ahead; and they described some sort of Judgment Day. Queerly enough, even if there were such a thing, and even if it were more convincing than I have described, belief in this happening wouldn't be at all a religious belief" (p. 56). The hold of religious belief on the believer is certainly not proportionate to what would be empirical evidence for it if it were regarded as an ordinary prediction. Wittgenstein later adds, by way of explanation, "the indubitability wouldn't be enough to make me change my whole life" (p. 57). I take his point to be that a man might say 'O.K. There'll be a Last Judgment in 2000 A.D. So what?' That could be assent to an ordinary proposition on sufficient evidence. But would it be a religious belief? Surely not.

Fundamental propositions draw limits to thinking insofar as they determine two things: namely, what *counts* as explanation and what *characterizes* experience. We are, I think, entitled to take a lead from this where religious belief is concerned. My view is that there are non-hypothetical religious beliefs which constitute a limit to thinking in parallel ways.

Consider explanation first. Wittgenstein said that fundamental propositions are "anchored in all my *questions and answers,* so anchored that I cannot touch them" (103, his italics). He meant, I think, that if, for instance, I ask a historical question — e.g., "What were the causes of such-and-such a war?" — belief in the past existence of this earth is "anchored" in the question and any conceivable answer to it. Other fundamental propositions may also be anchored in it — i.e., propositions that make the question, or any answer given to it, appear reasonable. A clear distinction should be drawn, of course, between a proposition that *serves* as an explanation and one that determines what *counts as* an explanation. In his *Remarks on Frazer's "Golden Bough,"* Wittgenstein said: "every explanation is an hypothesis."[47] This is true, but the same does not apply to a proposition that determines what *counts as* an explanation. Such a proposition draws a limit to thinking insofar as it prescribes what would constitute evidence of the relevant *kind* and what would not. Therefore, anyone who rejected this proposition could not engage in thinking of the relevant kind at all. As Wittgenstein has it: "If someone doubted that the earth had existed a hundred years ago, I should not understand for *this* reason: I would not know what such a person would still allow to count as evidence and what not" (231). I take his point to be that historical hypotheses are one of the generally accepted ways of explaining certain kinds of event; but if anyone purported to offer such an explanation and at the same time professed to doubt the fundamental proposition in which all such hypotheses are grounded, it would seem to us that he had passed beyond the limit of thinking altogether.

Religious beliefs offer explanations of their own kind. Take Wittgenstein's own example of someone who believes in Divine Judgment and explains illness as punishment. An unbeliever (such as he takes himself to be) uses "different pictures" and so does not explain illness as a punishment at all. Wittgenstein is very concerned to make it clear that there is a limit to thinking about the explanation of illness which separates believers from unbelievers. The religious belief in Divine Judgment *constitutes* this limit. It is not that believers and unbelievers entertain different hypotheses about illness. They use different pictures.

Suppose someone is ill and he says: "This is a punishment," and I say: "If I'm ill, I don't think of punishment at all." If you say: "Do you believe the opposite?" — you can call it believing the opposite, but it is entirely different from what we would normally call believing the opposite.

I think differently, in a different way. I say different things to myself. I have different pictures. (p. 55).

Now, think of experience. One distinction Wittgenstein draws between fundamental propositions and ordinary empirical ones is that whereas it would be quite in order to say that our experience shows an ordinary empirical proposition to be true, it is not appropriate to say this kind of thing about fundamental propositions. What we must say instead is that assent to a fundamental proposition gives our experience in some respect or other the character it has. Of fundamental propositions Wittgenstein writes: "One wants to say '*All* my experiences show that it is so.' But how do they do that? For that proposition to which they point itself belongs to a particular interpretation of them" (145). I take this to mean that the proposition concerned is, so to speak, *in* the experience from the start. We do not go around entertaining hypotheses such as "There are physical objects," "I have two feet," etc., and wait for experience to confirm them. The world I experience has the character it has because I assent to certain fundamental propositions giving my experience that character. "Why do I not satisfy myself that I have two feet when I want to get up from a chair? There is no why. I simply don't. That is how I act" (148), says Wittgenstein. My experience of the world of nature has the character it has because it is conditioned by my "not doubting" certain propositions (150). To use an example that is not from Wittgenstein but which has always seemed to me apposite in this connection, take moral experience — i.e., feelings of responsibility or remorse. They cannot be thought of as confirming the proposition "There is such a thing as moral obligation," because it is only people who *already* believe that there is such a thing as moral obligation who *can* feel moral responsibility or remorse. I do *not* mean, of course, that one has to say to oneself, "There are physical objects" or "I have two feet" or "There is such a thing as moral obligation" or whatever, and then, and only then, will one feel physically secure, morally guilty, or whatever. I mean that there are always beliefs *implicit* within our experiences, which, to quote Wittgenstein again, characterize our interpretation of them (cf. 145).

I think religious beliefs may be said, similarly, to characterize our experience. Wittgenstein speaks of terror as "part of the substance of the belief" in a Last Judgment (p. 56). I think he means that there is a kind of anxiety that only a man who believed in such a Judgment would — or could — feel. In his *Remarks on Frazer's "Golden Bough"* we found him (above, p. 4) speaking of events which strike people as horrible, tragic, etc., "giving birth" to religious practices, which bring a kind of satisfaction, or peace. Human life is like that according to Wittgenstein. Well, yes, horrible or tragic experiences are certainly part of it for some people, but it would surely be a mistake to suppose that religion is simply a response to them. The horror or the tragedy may be of a kind that *can* only be felt by those who respond to experience in a certain way; they are people who *have* experiences of a certain kind. There is a limit to experience, as to explanation, which religious beliefs constitute.

The logical role of fundamental propositions, we noted above, was described by Wittgenstein as "peculiar" (136). Its peculiarity, he said, lies in the fact that the boundary between propositions and rules seems to be eliminated in their case (319). Neither description fits them completely. They cannot be said simply to convey information (cf. 468) like oridinary propositions because, as we have just seen, they exercise a limiting, regulative function on our thinking; but then again, we do not learn them in the way we normally learn rules, by being told what to do (cf. 44). If Wittgenstein had been compelled to choose one description, or the other, there are signs that he would have called them rules. He speaks at times as if he did not regard them as propositions at all (36), and at other times he expressly likens them to the rules of a game (95). However, it is more significant to notice that he thinks of them as grounded in "our acting" — "It is our *acting*, which lies at the bottom of the language-game" (204; his italics), and he explicitly contrasts such acting with simply believing a proposition (204) or merely keeping a rule (44). If we speak—as Moore wished to do (see above, p. 9)—of "knowing" fundamental propositions, we must think of this knowledge as something we 'shew' in our actions day by day, including our verbal actions (431).

Wittgenstein calls the "certainty" with which fundamental propositions are believed, "a form of life" (358). There has been much discussion[48] of what precisely he meant by this expression, which, though he used it only a few times in his published work,[49] evidently stands for something important in his thinking. Whatever he meant by it, he evidently conceived of religious beliefs — no less than of fundamental propositions — in terms of it. In the *Lectures* he takes for granted an affirmative answer to his rhetorical question "Why shouldn't one form of life culminate in an utterance of belief in a Last Judgment?" (p. 58). The explanation he gives for calling our certainty about certain propositions a "form of life" is this: the expression "means I want to conceive it [any such proposition] as something that lies beyond being justified or unjustified; as it were, as something animal" (359). What I make of this is that he wanted to say two things about certain beliefs or propositions as constituting "forms of life": namely, that it is impossible to go beyond them to anything more fundamental by reference to which the ways of explaining or experiencing things, which they determine, can be shown to be "justified or unjustified"; and that their domination of our thinking is "animal" in the sense that it is as much a part of our natural history as eating, walking, etc. (cf. *Philosophical Investigations*, Sec. 25).

Fundamental propositions form a system (see, e.g., 102) and Wittgenstein evidently thinks it definitive of a reasonable man that the limits of his thinking are the limits of this system (327). If one wishes, as I do, to conceive of religion as constituted by certain beliefs, which belong to that system, then at least these two points about the system must be considered.

First, can it change? Undoubtedly it can. Wittgenstein speaks of it as "the river-bed of thoughts" and says that it may shift (97) and is compounded partly of "rock," partly of "sand" (99). Partly, that is, of propositions that seem permanently to delimit human thinking like "There are physical objects," and partly of those that constrain it for a time but only for a time, like "My body has never been far from the earth." No doubt about it, there have been times and places in which most men felt as certain of their religious beliefs as of their having two hands, and so on. But "what men consider reasonable or unreasonable alters" (336) and, to say the very least, religion is not what it was in the system of which I am speaking.

This fact raises the second question: what generates change within the system? Wittgenstein sometimes speaks as if only proselytizing persuasion, and never rational argument or reflection, can change it. Fair enough. If acceptance of the system defines rationality, then it can itself hardly be subject to rational revision. But it is conceivable that there should be changes in the content of rationality through the interplay of its elements on one another. The riverbed consists of both rock and sand, and in the flow of thoughts pressures set up by the rock may shift the sand. There can conceivably be an internal dynamism whereby certain fundamental propositions within the system, so to speak, displace or downgrade others. The belief, for instance, that there are physical objects could conceivably so dominate people's thinking that they found it harder and harder to conceive of there being anything else. I have attempted elsewhere[50] to deal with the question whether religious belief is any longer part of the rational system. I tend to think it is. But the question whether it is does not bear very directly on our present interest. My point in this paper is simply that, some of the time at least, Wittgenstein thought of religion as constitituting a limit to thinking in the way that fundamental propositions do and that, all of the time, we can — and should — so conceive of it. Whether the fundamental beliefs — whatever they may be — that make religion the kind of thinking it is are in fact still part of the rational system, or only used to be, is another matter.

Notes

1. See Engelmann's *Letters from Ludwig Wittgenstein* (Oxford, 1967) p. 135.
2. Publication data for the texts used are: *Notebooks* (Oxford, 1961); *Tractatus* (London, 1961; "Lecture on Ethics," *Philosophical Review* (1965): 3-12; *Remarks on Frazer's "Golden Bough"* (Retford, 1979); *Lectures on Religious Belief* (Oxford, 1966); *Remarks on Colour* (Oxford, 1979); *On Certainty* (Oxford, 1974).
3. See introductory note to *Remarks on Frazer's "Golden Bough."* Quotations of Frazer are from *The Illustrated "Golden Bough,"* ed. M. Douglas and S. MaCormack (London, 1978), p. 98. See also pp. 248-50.
4. See *Remarks on Frazer's "Golden Bough,"* pp. 1-12.
5. *Ibid.*, p. 12.
6. *Ibid.*, p. 4.
7. *Ibid.*, p. 8; see also p. 5.
8. *Ibid.*, p. 6.
9. *Ibid.*, p. 10.
10. *Ibid.*, p. 4.
11. *Ibid.*, p. 3.
12. *Tractatus*, sec. 6.522.
13. "Lecture on Ethics," pp. 11-12.
14. *Remarks on Colour*, sec. 317.
15. *Tractatus*, sec. 1.
16. *Ibid.*, sec. 6.41.
17. "Lecture on Ethics," p. 10.
18. I say why I think so in "The Concept of Divine Transcendence," *Religious* Studies 15 (1979):197-210.
19. See B. Davies, "Wittgenstein on God," *Philosophy* 55 (1980):105-8. This author seems to think that Wittgenstein may have had in mind something similar to Aquinas's views on analogy.
20. "Lecture on Ethics," p. 12.
21. *The Philosophy of Rudolf Carnap*, ed. P. A. Schilpp (London, 1963), pp. 26-27.
22. Engelmann, *Letters*, p. 97.
23. Quoted in *ibid.*, pp. 143-44.
24. *Tractatus*, sec. 6.522.
25. G. E. M. Anscombe, *An Introduction to Wittgenstein's "Tractatus"* (London, 1963) p. 162.
26. From letter to Russell, quoted by Anscombe, *Introduction*, p. 161.
27. See my *Wittgenstein and Religious Belief* (London, 1975), chap. 3, especially pp. 94-104; and also W. W. Bartley, *Wittgenstein* (Philadelphia and New York, 1973) on Wittgenstein's work as a schoolmaster.
28. See especially *Notebooks*, pp. 72-81, and *Tractatus*, sec. 5.5571-5.641 and 6.373-77.
29. *Notebooks*, p. 80.
30. *Ibid.*, p. 73.
31. *Tractatus*, sec. 5.632.
32. *Ibid.*, sec. 6.45.
33. *Ibid.*, sec. 6.43.
34. *Notebooks*, p. 75.
35. *Ibid.*, p. 81.
36. *Ibid.*, p. 74.
37. Anscombe, *Introduction*, p. 172, thinks this 'obviously wrong'.
38. See L. Wittgenstein, *Letters to E. K. Ogden with an Appendix of Letters by Frank Plumpton Ramsey* (Oxford, 1973), p. 78.
39. *Notebooks*, p. 74.

40. *Ibid.*, p. 124.

41. See his "A Defence of Common Sense" (1925), "Proof of an External World" (1939), "Four Forms of Scepticism" (1959), and "Certainty" (1959), all in his *Philosophical Papers* (London, 1959).

42. "Proof of an External World," p. 146.

43 For my views on fundamental propositions see further "Wittgenstein and Fundamental Propositions" in *The Southwestern Journal of Philosophy* (Oklahoma) 8, no. 1 (1977):7-21 and "Language-Games and Presuppositions," *Philosophy* (London) 53 (1978):94-99. On Wittgenstein's lectures about religious belief see my "Some Observations on Wittgenstein's Account of Religious Belief" in *Talk of God*, ed. G. N. A. Vesey (London, 1969) and my *Wittgenstein and Religious Belief* (London, 1974), chap. 5.

44. Wittgenstein, *Philosophical Grammar* (Oxford, 1974), sec. 35.

45. I consider this objection more fully in "What Makes Religious Beliefs Religious?" *Religious Studies* 13 (1977):234-37.

46. Wittgenstein, *Blue and Brown Books* (Oxford, 1960), p. 17.

47. "*Remarks on Frazer's "Golden Bough,"* p. 3.

48. See, e.g., G. F. M. Hunter, "Forms of Life" in Wittgenstein's *Philosophical Investigations*," *American Philosophical Quarterly* 5, no. 4 (1968):233-43; and P. Sherry, "Is Religion a 'Form of Life'?" *ibid.* 9, no. 2 (1972):159-67.

49. Only five times, for instance in *Philosophical Investigations*: 19, 23, 241, p. 174, p. 226.

50. See my "The Rational System of Beliefs" in the composite volume *Theology and Sociology: Alliance and Conflict?*, ed. David Martin and others, forthcoming from Harvester Press.

The Discovery of Nonsense

IRVING THALBERG

In an autobiographical note, Ryle says that from the 1930s on he believed that "the philosopher's proprietary question is . . . 'Why does this . . . expression make nonsense? and what *sort* of nonsense does it make?'" (A, pp. 6-7).* Wittgenstein also declares it his objective "to pass from a piece of disguised nonsense to something that is patent nonsense" (PI, #464; see #119; also OC, #76). John Wisdom agrees that many theories Wittgenstein debunks are "specimens of the whoppers philosophers can tell"; but he adds that such doctrines are not "merely symptoms of linguistic confusion"; they are "symptoms of linguistic penetration" as well (PP, p. 104).

I plan to elaborate this approach, mainly in philosophy of mind, and to assess a few of its results. Obviously it has made an impact on the analytical movement. More significantly, it still generates some very hostile reactions—and misunderstanding. What I call 'arguments from nonsense' begin to appear in a systematic way after 1930, most prominently in the work of Ryle and Wittgenstein. But you can find antecedents from Plato on. One of Berkeley's attacks on the Lockean theory of physical objects will epitomize the genre. The contention under debate is that such items consist of matter or material substance plus the qualities or "accidents" that it somehow possesses. When he hears that "matter supports or stands under accidents," Berkeley wonders: "How? Is it as your legs support your body?" Lockeans naturally reject this crudely literal interpretation. So Berkeley's challenge is: "Pray let me know any sense, literal or not literal, that you understand it in"; generally, "let me know what it is you would have me believe" (TD, pp. 199, 218). Berkeley's stratagem has by no means refuted the Lockean theory; but it has placed an obligation on votaries of matter and accidents to set forth what they mean. My principal concern will be with the not altogether dissimilar, and equally

---

*Throughout I shall use acronyms to cite various works listed under References.

appealing, theory of our mental life that puzzles Wittgenstein, Ryle, and their sympathizers.

1. A WARMUP EXERCISE

A less provocative, almost facetious example from Ryle's early paper, SME, should give us the hang of an argument from nonsense. Ryle takes a statement which many of his contemporaries would have assumed was about a Platonic universal—a property or attribute. In fact, the statement "Unpunctuality is reprehensible" seems to be as much about unpunctuality as "Jones merits reproof" is about Jones. Yet Ryle thinks that if we endorse this analogy,

> absurdities soon crop up. It is silly to speak of a universal meriting reproof. You can no more praise or blame a universal than you can make holes in the Equator. Nor . . . do we . . . suppose that unpunctuality ought to be ashamed of itself. What we . . . mean is . . . "Whoever is unpunctual deserves that other people should reprove him for being [so] " . . .
>
> . . . all statements which seem to be "about universals" are analysable [thus]. . . . So universals are not objects . . . and therefore the age-old question what *sort* of objects they are is . . . bogus (SME, pp. 90-91).

This rather trumped-up case exhibits many salient features of an argument from nonsense. First we must imagine a context of debate. Presumably the believer in universals has offered to provide information about his or her favored entities and might explain that we can describe them in various terms. For instance, we could say that the universal unpunctuality is something reprehensible. Naturally we want to make sure we understand what the familiar predicate 'reprehensible' means here. So we recall everyday situations in which we judge people—or their behavior—to be reprehensible. It is not important that we are dealing with a moral predicate. Ryle's procedure would be the same if unpunctuality were characterized in non-evaluative terms.

Suppose now that Jones's conduct has been reprehensible. Plainly more can be said and done. Jones himself ought to be contrite, and make amends. We can admonish Jones, ostracize him, impose penalties upon him. He certainly should not exult over his misdeeds. We must not encourage or reward him. The further terms we have introduced, and the activities they denote, flesh out our literal, everyday use of the predicate 'reprehensible'.

We should turn next to the alleged universal, unpunctuality. Could it or any other universal be ashamed? Could it make restitution? How might we go about condemning this universal, isolating it from society, punishing it? What would we do to ensure that its untoward behavior is not reinforced? If we were still discussing Jones or his misconduct, replies would be easy. But any answer we give regarding the universal unpunctuality is going to sound arbitrary—no more plausible than its negation.

The would-be proponent of universals may retreat, explaining that all she or he really meant was that individuals who are not on time ought to be censured. This amounts to a confession that his initial report did not in fact concern the universal unpunctuality. On the other hand, if he persists in describing this universal as literally reprehensible, his statement must be consigned to the same class as the report that someone has drilled holes in the Equator. More precisely: his statement carries equally unintelligible implications—about the universal displaying or failing to manifest remorse, receiving or escaping chastisement, and so on. We show the original statement to be disguised nonsense because we get barefaced nonsense as soon as we take seriously the parallelism between it and our indisputably meaningful statement that Jones, or Jones's behavior, is reprehensible. Until the booster of universals can produce a more satisfactory model for his characterization of them, we should not waste time debating "what *sort* of objects they are." That would be like quarreling about what size holes mar the Equator. Perhaps Ryle overstates his case when he concludes that universals are "not objects"—reprehensible or otherwise. But his line of critical reasoning explains why the type of claim made by a devotee of universals is not literally meaningful and therefore not worth disputing. Ryle has placed the onus upon the champion of universals to devise a more cogent account of them, if that is possible.

2. LESSONS SO FAR

The mini-argument I have reconstructed hardly proves that our subject term, 'unpunctuality', much less our predicate expression, 'is reprehensible', are mere nonsense sounds. Unlike the babbling of a six-month-old infant, they belong to the English phonetic system. What is more, they differ markedly from several of the phonemes in Lewis Carroll's beloved verses: "The Jabberwock, with eyes of flame,/ Came whiffling through the tulgey wood,/ And burbled as it came." Our phonemes, 'unpunctuality', 'is', and 'reprehensible', are all English words. And their concatenation, "Unpunctuality is reprehensible," conforms to English syntax; it ranks as a declarative sentence. Incidentally, this sentence is not wildly out of place or disconnected with other things that have been said in the context we imagined. Wittgenstein offers good examples of unintelligibility through disconnectedness: a speaker who abruptly says "'Good morning' . . . to someone in the middle of a conversation" they are having; or who suddenly remarks to a close friend, "I knew all along that you were so-and-so" (OC, #354). "Unpunctuality is reprehensible" is not on a par with any of these. How then is it nonsensical?

3. FALSITY AND UNVERIFIABILITY

Sometimes people react to an outrageously untrue statement by saying "Nonsense!" Occasionally, self-contradictory or analytically false statements are called nonsensical. But "Unpunctuality is reprehensible" cannot be either contingently or necessarily false, because then its denial would be true. However, both its standard negations—"Unpunctuality is not at all reprehensible" and "It is not the case that unpunctuality is reprehensible"—are as puzzling as their affirmative counterpart. For what would it be like if either of these negative statements were true? In other words: Just what do you rule out—as a matter of empirical fact, or else *a priori*—when you deny that unpunctuality is reprehensible? Surely you must have some idea *what* it is you are denying to be the case? Wittgenstein presents an apt illustration of this point. He compares the negative statements "A goose has no teeth" and "A rose has no teeth," wondering ironically if the second is not "obviously true"—"even surer" than its companion. Yet, he muses: "where should a rose's teeth have been? The goose has none in its jaw. And neither . . . has it any in its wings; but no one means that when he says it has no teeth . . ." (PI, pp. 221-22). What exactly are you telling us when you deny that a rose has teeth? I think it is no less obscure what you mean if you deny that unpunctuality is reprehensible.

Thus far I have distinguished philosophically significant nonsense from mere gibberish; from sounds that are not English phonemes; from phonemes that are not words of English; from strings of words that violate syntax; from statements and other utterances that are glaringly inappropriate to the rest of the interchange in which they occur; and from either necessarily or contingently false statements. I should mention unverifiability and unfalsifiability, which positivists of the 1930s regarded as criteria for deciding whether a declarative statement is empirically meaningful.

In brief, most positivists held that an unverifiable and unfalsifiable statement is a purportedly factual assertion which no conceivable evidence, no experiment or other testing procedure, would either corroborate or disconfirm to any degree. No observation we can specify would contribute toward proving the statement true—or false either.

Plainly, 'unverifiable' and 'unfalsifiable' are epistemological notions, having to do with observation, evidence, proof, and disproof. Notions belonging to this epistemological clan were altogether absent from Ryle's critique of the statement that the universal unpunctuality is reprehensible. The central issue for him was rather: What else can we assert or deny, using terms that normally keep company or clash with the predicate 'is reprehensible'? Do we produce bizarre combinations when we bring in other terms from the same clan as 'reprehensible'? If so, we have to assume that the original statement was camouflaged nonsense. I suppose it will also turn out that no observational test you can dream up would count either for or against the truth of "Unpunctuality is reprehensible." But this would be a separate defect of that statement, over and above its unintelligibility.

So much for target practice on universals. We are ready to gun for the ever-popular general theory of human beings as organisms that are somehow tethered to minds—or *vice versa*.

4. IS IT NONSENSE TO ATTRIBUTE MINDS TO PEOPLE?

Enemies as well as friends of universals would agree that an ontologically noncommital assertion, like "Whoever is unpunctual deserves to be scolded," makes perfectly good sense. Similarly, both opponents and defenders of mind would declare it meaningful—even platitudinously true—to say that people are often conscious or 'mindful'. Statements on the order of "Jane is mentally computing her tax deductions" and "Sam is considering what to do next vacation" are clearly intelligible. No theorist doubts that human beings enjoy a rich mental life—that they become infatuated or indignant, daydream and deliberate. Thus Wittgenstein exclaims: "Why should I deny that there is a mental process?" This is quite uncontroversial—if we assume, for instance, that "'there has just taken place in me the mental process of remembering [such-and-such]' means nothing more than 'I have just remembered [such-and-such]'" (PI, #306). Similarly, Ryle insists that he is not "denying there are mental processes. Doing long division is [one] and so is making a joke" (CM, p. 22). But the metaphysical crux is how to analyze these "processes" and our reports of them: Must we conjure up a mind, or consciousness and fill it to the brim with volatile images, sensations, and thoughts? When we truly report a psychological occurrence, must something go on which resembles the meshing of gears, the tugging of cables—or even digestive processes? Perhaps; but it is unclear what the mentalist gains if he or she postulates such items and episodes. So before we plunge too deeply into that kind of theorizing, maybe we should investigate whether the whole mind-hypothesis makes sense.

5. WHAT IS IT TO POSSESS A MIND?

Wittgenstein bluntly articulates the overall issue when he asks: "What am I believing in when I believe that men have souls?" Then he appears to contrast this with the ostensibly straightforward empirical belief that some chemical compound has two rings of carbon atoms among its ingredients. But surprisingly, his verdict seems to be that it is unclear in both cases what we are "believing in" (PI, ##422-24.).

Elsewhere Wittgenstein offers a less arcane model for attributing a mind to someone: the relatively down-to-earth statement that a certain tribe of people has a chief. Wittgenstein asks if we say anything analogous when we add: "the chief must surely have consciousness" (PI, #419). I doubt it. The chief may have inherited his office; he might have been selected by the tribal elders; possibly he usurped authority. Inheriting, selecting, and usurping are all deliberate transactions between conscious human beings. What would it be like for similar goings-on to occur between the chief himself—or his body—and his "consciousness"? How would he go about nominating and electing his mind? How might it defeat its rivals who also want to be the chief's mind? Our suggested para-political model of 'having a mind' seems to generate as much nonsense as the claim that unpunctuality is reprehensible. What you can meaningfully say of the relationship between a tribe and its leader does not carry over to people and their minds. Incidentally, it makes clear sense to deny that a tribe has a chief or to mistakenly assert that it has one. But, as Wittgenstein remarks, "What would it mean for me to be wrong about his having a mind, having consciousness? . . . [or] to be wrong about *myself* and not have any?" (Z, #394). Insofar as we cannot specify what alternatives it rules out, the mind-hypothesis is a mystery.

I think we can lodge many of the same complaints against the putative denizens of our mind: the sensations, images, beliefs, and impulses that we supposedly 'have' by virtue of their transitory or long-term presence in our mental arena. My own eclectic argument from nonsense against the doctrine that such items are 'in', 'before', or 'present to' our consciousness would consist in asking for details. At what coordinates within your mind are your aches, thoughts, and urges? Can they be located above or below, in front of or behind one another? How many of them can a given region house? Can they crowd one another out? Can they be compressed, like foam rubber? If they can be 'present' to your consciousness, can they at times be absent and still continue to exist? Although we have no difficulty providing this kind of information about the keys and coins that happen to be—or not to be—in our pockets, anything similar we say of our minds' contents will sound daft.

Wittgenstein inquires along these lines about the relationship between people and the mental contents they are said to 'have'. He supposes the mind-philosopher has declared: "[w]hen I imagine something, or even actually *see* objects, I have *got* something which my neighbor has not." Wittgenstein's challenge is quite direct: "In what sense have you *got* what you are talking about . . . ? Do you possess it? You do not even *see* it" (PI, #398). Of course the problem over 'having' is compounded by obscurities about what you have. Again following Wittgenstein, suppose the mind-philosopher insists that

> he sees a private picture before him. . . . [T]hat means that you can describe it . . . more closely. If you admit that you haven't any notion what kind of thing . . . he has before him . . . [i]sn't it as if I were to say . . . : "He *has* something. But I don't know whether it is money, or debts, or an empty till" (PI, #294)?

This last is an example of unadorned nonsense, inasmuch as we cannot even begin to request details regarding whatever the person 'has', and specifics about the type of 'having', until our alternatives are narrowed beyond "money, or debts, or an empty till." For example, our question 'Where does he keep what he has?' will be totally out of place if we are dealing with the financial obligations someone has. But this will not be enough to convince partisans of mind and mental contents to throw out their notion of 'having'.

6. DO WE HAVE THE CONTENTS OF OUR MIND BY PERCEIVING THEM?

The most hallowed theory, alluded to by Wittgenstein, represents us as bystanders or spectators of our sensations and other psychical belongings. Ryle objects persuasively:

> Observing is a task which can be of some arduousness, and we can be more or less successful in it and more or less good at it. But none of these ways of characterizing the exercises of one's powers of observation can be applied to

the having of . . . sensations. . . . We can make mistakes of observation, but it is nonsense to speak of either making or avoiding mistakes in sensation (CM, pp. 204-5).

Our perceptual contact with the denizens of our consciousness is radically unlike standard gazing, listening, touching, sniffing, and delecting. Two or more onlookers may gawk at a single parade; however, as Ryle says,

> the cobbler cannot [be said to] witness the tweaks that I feel when the shoe pinches. . . . [Tweaks] are not the sort of things of which it makes sense to say that they are witnessed or unwitnessed at all, even by me. In the sense in which a person may be said to have . . . a robin under observation, it would be nonsense to say that he has . . . a twinge under observation (CM, p. 205).

Ryle adds that we can meaningfully tell how we use microscopes and other instruments to examine bacteria. However, it is unintelligible to suppose we employ these devices to scrutinize our feelings of chill. Nor can I speak of interferences like fog or background noise disturbing my surveillance of my waves of nausea. Similarly, Ryle says, to ask whether someone's "inspection of a tickle had been hampered or unhampered, close or casual, and whether he could have discerned more of it, if he had tried" is on a par with asking "how the first letter in 'London' is spelled" (CM, p. 207). Words, but not letters or paragraphs, can be spelled or misspelled. Only garden-variety objects and events can be stared at and recognized or misrecognized.

As for the seemingly axiomatic doctrine that each individual is the unique percipient of his or her mental contents, Ryle argues:

> it was wrong . . . to contrast the common objects of anyone's observation, like robins . . . with the supposed peculiar objects of my privileged observation, namely my sensations, since sensations are not objects of observation at all. . . . [T]he cobbler cannot feel the shoe pinching me . . . but . . . not because he is excluded from a peep-show open only to me, but because it would make no sense to say that he was in my pain . . . (CM, pp. 207-8).

We do not say 'I perceive my pain', but 'I am suffering', 'I am in pain'. Maybe no harm is done if we add the curious embellishment, 'I am in *my* pain'. Yet since we cannot under any imaginable conditions meaningfully assert that the bootmaker is in my pain, we should stop regretting that he is barred from being in my pain—as if he had missed a genuine opportunity. However, there is more scope for arguments from nonsense on this strange topic.

7. COMPLICATIONS OF NECESSARILY PRIVATE 'HAVING'

Our difficulties multiply if we underscore the uniqueness and non-transferability of people's ownership of their mental contents. No other known form of possession is akin to this. Ordinarily when an individual or a group happens to have exclusive ownership of some item, there are other options. A pasture that in fact belongs to just one cattle breeder could be purchased by another; it could be jointly owned by several partners; it might be collectivized; the government might confiscate it; conceivably, it might be unowned, if nobody has staked it out. All these ownership situations involve social practices—buying, transfer, dividing up, leasing, foreclosing, dispossession, laying claim. Our everyday concept of proprietorship is inseparable from this cluster. But the mind-philosopher's notion that we somehow own our itches, urges, and thoughts cannot be integrated into the familiar array. "Bill and Jane are co-proprietors of one backache" sounds altogether demented; so does talk of auctioning off a stab of heartburn, homesteading it, or illegally trespassing on it.

Even after we have rehearsed these incongruities, some theorists will keep on asserting, in Wittgenstein's words, "only I have got THIS." Wittgenstein's response pulls together the examples I have been toying with. Wittgenstein suggests: "if as a matter of logic you exclude other people's having something, it loses its sense to say that you have it" (PI, #398). Until theorists tell us more about this unprecedented form of ownership, debate should be adjourned.

If mind-philosophers still consider it meaningful to proclaim, "Another person can't have my pains" (PI, #253), Wittgenstein is ready with a further challenge. He asks: "Which are *my* pains? What counts as a criterion" for identifying them as mine *(ibid.)*? The possessive pronoun rings as oddly in this context as did our vocabulary of ownership. So Wittgenstein insinuates that the possessive lacks any clear meaning in our debate over mental contents. He asserts: "When I say 'I am in pain,' I do not point to a person who is in pain, since . . . I have no idea *who* is. I don't name any person. Just as I don't name anyone when I *groan* with pain" (PI, #404).

A groan is not composed of parts of speech, like pronouns and other referring terms. Thus it is plainly unintelligible to say that in groaning I name or refer to myself. How is apparently referential talk of "my pains" similar? I believe we should consider misnaming and faulty reference. Suppose a racketeer is browbeaten by the authorities. He agrees to name his cohorts and the officials on their payoff list. He could make errors and deliberately or unwittingly denounce some people who are not affiliated with, or bribed by, his organization. This illustrates how ordinary reference can go awry. I think Wittgenstein would go on to inquire whether analogous mistakes can occur when we discuss our pains or say "I am in pain." For instance, could the speaker be right that pain is present, but incorrectly designate himself or herself as its owner, when it actually belongs to someone else? We seem to be speaking nonsense again. But some mind-philosophers will blithely restate their doctrine.

8. PRIVATE REFERENCE AND PRIVATE LANGUAGE

In order to pursue this turn in the debate over having mental contents, we must temporarily withdraw our objection to perceptual-sounding terms. Our target, basically, is the doctrine I would call epistemological solipsism. Its main tenet is that when you truthfully report your aches, emotions, urges, and thoughts, you are using terms like 'ache' to stamp psychical items which are somehow accessible or perceptible to you alone. Since I am unable to get at what you tag as an ache, I cannot possibly know anything of its nature. I cannot even be at all sure that you have any mental contents. Perhaps each of us refers to something radically different, or to nothing at all, when we utter the word 'ache'.

Wittgenstein dramatizes the doctrine by supposing he records

> the recurrence of a certain sensation. . . . I associate it with the sign 'E' and write this sign in a calendar for every day on which I have the sensation. . . . I write the sign down, and at the same time I concentrate my attention on the sensation—and . . . impress on myself the connexion between the sign and the sensation. . . . I remember the connexion *right* in the future (PI, #258).

Now the everyday physical objects and events on which we "concentrate . . attention" either remain stable or undergo changes while we keep tabs on them. If one observer fails to detect alterations, another may spot them. But only I can ever attend to my E-sensations. So it appears to make little sense if we distinguish between Es that are constant and those that seem to be steady, in my judgment, though they actually alter. By the same token, what would it mean to suppose I only imagine a change in E? The objects of private reference cannot be described in the terms that fit ordinary things we name. And to this extent, it is unclear what inner reference amounts to. I believe Wittgenstein was hinting at this kind of camouflaged nonsense when he urged us to "get rid of the idea of the private object in this way: assume that it constantly changes, but that you do not notice the change because your memory constantly deceives you" (PI, p. 207). We can also assume that numerically different though qualitatively indistinguishable private objects constantly take the place of the one you called 'E' but that you are insufficiently attentive to notice these substitutions. With standard items we refer to, you can investigate whether they undergo alterations and they are replaced by a clever duplicate. Such inquiries do not appear to be meaningful *vis à vis* objects of private reference. Insofar as epistemological solipsists argue that we know nothing of other people's mental life because we lack access to whatever they have baptized 'E', their position is threatened. Moreover, Wittgenstein has another well-known argument which purports to bring out nonsense in a variant of the private reference doctrine.

9. FOLLOWING PRIVATE RULES OF REFERENCE

The idea under attack is that when I mentally paste the label 'E' onto "a certain sensation," this guarantees that I shall "remember the connection *right* in the future." Translating into 'rule' terminology: I make it a rule for myself that I shall henceforth reserve the sign 'E' for kindred sensations. The source of nonsense here is that my ordinary rule-governed behavior may be faulty without my realizing it. However, we cannot meaningfully speak of my 'unnoticed deviation from my E-rule'. All I might do is change my mind about ranking this sensation as an E. But there could be no reason either for or against saying that my latest opinion is more—or less—in harmony with my rule of reference than was my initial classificatory move. Therefore Wittgenstein declares that "in the present case I have no criterion of correctness . . . whatever is going to seem right to me is right. And that only means that here we can't talk of 'right'." Our allegedly private rules for naming mental contents are only "impressions of rules" (PI, ##258-59)—which are not rules any more than a reenactment of a famous murder trial is itself a murder trial.

Many post-Wittgensteinian philosophers of mind have rejected this line of reasoning. For instance, A. J. Ayer imagines a Robinson Crusoe who has lived entirely alone on his island since birth. Crusoe has made up "words to describe the flora and fauna," plus other 'E'-like "words to describe his sensations." Ayer is persuaded that Crusoe may refer incorrectly as well as correctly with both sets of expressions. All that matters for Ayer is Crusoe's

> remembering what objects [his words] are meant to stand for. . . . Undoubtedly, he may make mistakes. He may think that a bird which he sees flying past is a bird of the same type as one which he had previously named, when in fact it is of a sufficiently different [type] for him to have given it a different name if he had observed it more closely. Similarly, he may think that a sensation is the same as others which he has identified, when in fact, in the relevant aspects [sic], it is not. . . . In the case of the bird, there is a slightly greater chance of his detecting his mistake, since the identical bird may reappear: but even so he has to rely on his memory . . . that it is the identical bird. In the case of the sensation, he has only his memory as a means of deciding whether his identification is correct or not (CPL, pp. 259-60).

How plausible is Ayer's analogy between naming or misnaming birds and classifying or misclassifying one's mental contents? Naturally I shall again waive my objections to perceptual terminology. So I will not complain that we utterly lack inner equivalents of 'seeing a bird fly past', 'observing it more closely', and 'subsequently taking another look at the same individual fowl'. Leaving that to one side, I wonder what backing Ayer produces for his anti-Wittgensteinian thesis that Crusoe "may make mistakes" in chronicling his itches, chills, and hunger pangs. All I come across is the general and apparently question-begging statement that Crusoe "may think that a sensation is the same as others . . . when in fact . . . it is not." Ayer neglects to reveal what it might be like for such a mixup to occur.

Regarding Crusoe's ornithology, a few trifling modifications of the background story make indisputable sense of the charge that he has placed a bird in the wrong pigeonhole. A seagull glides by; Crusoe believes and says it is a pelican. Now a secret onlooker might have registered Crusoe's breach of his taxonomic rule. There could be photographic proof that he has erroneously described the creature. Moreover, witnesses and evidence provide essential support for any claims about the accuracy of his present description and for his belief that he remembers the features of those birds he has previously classified as pelicans. Here we can say what we mean by misidentifying and correctly identifying, misremembering and correctly recalling. Not so when we turn to Crusoe's sensations. What

THE DISCOVERY OF NONSENSE 303

could possibly confirm, and in particular what unfavorable testimony, counterevidence, and so on might override Crusoe's description of his present inner goings-on or his alleged "memory" of what he has classified as an E? We exclude nothing when we speculate whether "his identification is correct" and his recall of earlier sensations trustworthy. His confidence in his latest judgments hardly proves that contrary beliefs he has had about previous goings-on are mistaken. Ayer has not distinguished what may "seem right" or wrong to Crusoe, and beliefs that are right or wrong. So far, no definite meaning has been given to the doctrine of epistemological solipsists, that each person correctly follows his (or her) private rules of reference in cataloguing his sensations. The tieup between people and their sensations remains baffling.

Before we dismiss the private-rule model, we should briefly scrutinize a somewhat different elaboration of it, by H-N. Castañeda. His diary keeper is Privatus, inventor of a one-man language, Privatish. Unfortunately, in fleshing out his example, Castañeda seems to take for granted most of the assumptions Wittgenstein found puzzling. Thus Castañeda simply declares that "[o]rdinary pains and afterimages are private in [two] senses": (i) their "existence is (logically) determinable by the speaker alone"—in particular, their "existence is entailed by the speaker's belief" that they exist; and (ii) their "possession of some characteristic A is . . . [similarly] determinable by the speaker alone" (PLA, pp. 92, 90). Castañeda also assures us that Privatus is blessed with "enough private objects which manifest sufficient regularities" (p. 101). Furthermore, Privatus "can avail himself of the objects of his experience" (p. 103). or "resort to" them (p. 99). Above all,

> it is fair to assume . . . that Privatus is for the most part consistent in his use of Privatish, that his use of signs possesses "enough regularity," and also that he holds certain true beliefs about his private objects, which beliefs are the counterparts of the judgments agreed on in the case of a public language (p. 98).

Castañeda does not tell us how to "avail" ourselves of, or "resort to," our mental contents. But he implicitly likens this to our sensory dealings with our physical surroundings. He thinks material objects are "known by perception, pains . . . by feeling, or introspection," and that Privatus "apprehends" both "private and public" objects (pp. 94, 99).

In the hope of learning what Castañeda contrasts with our "true beliefs about [our] private objects," Wittgensteinians must stifle their adverse reaction to the story so far. At any rate, Castañeda insists that Privatus has "some false beliefs . . . about certain facts (or propositions) formulable in the purely private part of Privatish" (p. 103). Is it possible that Privatus, like Ayer's Crusoe, "may think that a sensation is the same as others . . . when in fact . . . it is not"? Castañeda diverges from Ayer on this point. He assumes that "'I believed falsely at [time] t that I was in pain at t' . . . expresses a conceptual contradiction" (p. 93). In Castañeda's scheme, it is "logically true" that "[i]f X feels a pain Y at t, and at t he is capable of thinking that he has a pain at t, and is attending to . . . his mental goings-on . . . then at t X knows that he has Y" (p. 92). So Privatus's "false beliefs" will not be on a par with his "true beliefs about his private objects"; they will be about other "facts" or "propositions." Castañeda thinks Privatus can only make "linguistic errors," mainly slips of the tongue, when he describes his mental goings-on. Castañeda's model of such a mistake is a speaker of English saying "'That red, . . . I mean, brown chair . . . ', [where we also] have a linguistic self-correction" (p. 99). Castañeda implies that Privatus errs similarly if he believes his current sensation is an E, but while distractedly reporting it, he utters the word 'D' instead of 'E'.

What "false beliefs" are involved here? If the speaker of English does *not* correct himself, then *perhaps* he falsely believes he has said what he intended to say. Analogously, Privatus may erroneously believe that he has called his sensation an E. None of this sounds at all germane to Wittgenstein's argument that it makes no sense to talk of following private rules. Wittgenstein challenged the defender of private rules to explain his notion that each of us correctly labels our mental contents, thereby displaying our accurate memory that we have referred to contents of this sort as Es. It seemed incumbent upon the private-rule philosopher to tell us what he or she means by success-terms like 'correct' and 'accurate'. What failures and mistakes does he think we avoid? Plainly Wittgenstein is inquiring about cognitive failures, such as my falsely believing that my current sensation is vertigo, though it is really a cramp—or my falsely believing that discomfort of this kind is what I have regularly called 'vertigo'. But Castañeda has not even attempted to produce instances of misclassification or of misremembering one's mental contents. Instead he has described a somewhat trivial *non*-cognitive breakdown: Privatus utters a different word than he intended. Privatus may, or may not, also fail to notice his linguistic lapse. This hardly makes sense of the supposed relationship between people and the mental contents they 'have'. The doctrine that I name the items drifting through my consciousness, and subsequently conform to my naming rules, has generated no illumination. Yet solipsists and others who are drawn to it can try out one last variant.

10. DO YOU, AND YOU ALONE, SIMPLY KNOW WHAT YOUR SENSATIONS ARE?

For decades philosophers have lamented that we are barred from knowing another person's toothache or anger—at least in the way that person does. When John Wisdom repeatedly deployed this formula in his struggles with the 'other minds' problem, Austin took him to task. Austin remarked that "'knowing his sensations' . . . presumably means . . . 'knowing *what* he is [feeling]'." Austin explained that it is "a grammatical mistake" to understand this 'what' as if it were a "relative" phrase; "'what' . . . in 'know what you feel' is an interrogative. . . . 'I know what he is feeling' is *[sic]* not 'There is an x which both I know and he is feeling' but 'I know the answer to the question "What is he feeling?"'" (OM, p. 143). Ryle bluntly warned that we cannot "speak of knowing, or not knowing, this clap of thunder or that twinge of pain," since "these are accusatives of the wrong types to follow the verb 'to know'" (CM, p. 161).

The grammar lesson appears to have sunk in. However, too many thinkers have merely transferred their fixation, and gravely speak of how each person knows, in some virtually foolproof manner, *that* he or she feels a cramp or whatever. In section 9 I quoted Ayer's opinion that Crusoe "may make mistakes" when identifying his mental contents. This implies that Crusoe is not infallible, though we can assume he generally and perhaps always knows what is looming before his consciousness. I also reproduced Castañeda's bolder thesis, which makes it a logical truth that introspectively alert people who are afflicted with pain know they are in pain. Bruce Aune's outlook is similar. Aune holds that "a condition of having the concept of pain is that one can, with perfect confidence, say or think 'I'm in pain' and be right"; and because the sufferer is "right," Aune regards him as knowing that he is in pain (KMT, pp. 56-57). Like Ayer and Castañeda, Aune is sensitive to the demand that we specify what we are contrasting with this knowledge. Aune argues:

> The contradictory of "He knows that *p*" is . . . "He doesn't know, or is ignorant of the fact, that *p*." Now . . . a sufficient condition of being ignorant of a given fact is that one lack the conceptual resources necessary for the description and classification of that fact. . . . [A] man who lacks the concept of jealousy . . . when he is jealous . . . doesn't know that he is, [and thus] it is *meaningful* (though not true) to say that he *does* know . . .
>
> . . . [I] t is only a *contingent* fact about a person that he has [the] concept [of pain]. . . . Of course, when it is well known that a person has this concept, it is generally pointless to *say* that he knows he is in pain but . . . [that] comes from saying something . . . too obviously true. . . . [C] ircumstances can always be dreamed up in which *any assertion whatever* is utterly pointless (e.g., saying "It is raining" to someone . . . trapped in a downpour)(p. 58; see Aune's KMN, pp. 86-100).

John Searle hands down the same verdict: "It's obviously true that when I have a pain, I know that I have it . . . and it is odd to announce such things under normal circumstances . . . because they are too obvious"; "Only if the situation is aberrant . . . is it appropriate to *say* these things" (SA, pp. 141-43). As for "negations and opposites," like "He does not know whether he has a pain," under normal conditions Searle finds "nothing nonsensical about them"; he thinks "they are just false"—which makes 'He knows . . . ' true (p. 145).

I wonder if these commentators fully appreciate the argument from nonsense that Wittgenstein mounted against the assumption that we have knowledge of our mental goings-on. Forget Aune's somewhat question-begging proclamation that his speaker "can . . . say or think 'I'm in pain' and be right"—and Searle's unsupported assurance that 'I know I have a pain' is "obviously true." We shall not ask for either's "criterion of correctness" or for Searle's account of what the alleged falsehood "He does not know whether he has a pain" could mean. What really troubles me, to begin with, is that Ayer, Casteñeda, Aune, and others suppose they need only set forth *one* alternative to knowledge. Ayer nominated "mistakes"; Casteñeda, slips of the tongue; Aune, conceptual deprivation; Searle, an unexplained sort of 'not knowing whether'. Elsewhere Robert Ackerman (BK, pp. 63-64) and Aune (KMN, p. 95) mention doubt or hesitant thinking. But Wittgenstein's requirement is much broader. Of course he suggests "'I know . . . ' may mean 'I do not doubt'"; however, he quickly adds: "One says 'I know' where one can also say 'I believe' or 'I suspect'; where one can find out" (PI, p. 221). Besides wondering, rhetorically, if we can assert: "Where there is no doubt there is no knowledge either," he declares: "One says 'I know' when one is ready to give compelling grounds"; and he goes on to suggest that if a speaker's "grounds . . . are no surer than his assertion, then he cannot say that he knows" (OC, ##121, 243). Wittgenstein thinks we "need grounds for doubt" no less than for our convictions. More important, Wittgenstein gives non-mentalistic analogues which seem to him as nonsensical as "I know that I am in pain." Some of his best are: claiming to know, when your hand is in normal condition and your view of it is unimpeded, that it is a hand—or guessing that it is; saying you know—or believe—that your name is such-and-such; saying that you know the color plainly visible before you is called 'red' in your native language—or being unsure whether it is; declaring that you know there is a material world—or that it seems to you as if physical objects exist but perhaps you are deluded (OC, ##32, 461, 491, 515, 527, 624, 35).

Aside from Searle's bald assertion, "it's . . . obvious that I do now remember [know] my own name" (p. 141), anti-Wittgensteinians do not deal with these points. They have certainly not tried to explain how you could discover, possibly through sleuthing or experimentation, that your head aches; how you might gather evidence or counter-evidence on whether it aches; how you might be totally unaware of your migraine; how you might be conjecturing when you say your head aches. All these epistemic terms would make sense if we were concerned with a head injury. Suppose a neurologist claims to know that I have suffered a concussion. I can reasonably ask, "How do you know?" But I would be dumbfounded if he or she inquired how I know that my head aches.

Castañeda asserts: "The . . . answer to 'How do you know?' is . . . 'By having the pain' or 'By attending to my feelings'"; generally, "[o]ne knows . . . of his own pains by merely having them" (PLA, pp. 94, 93). This trivially entails another of Castañeda's assumptions: "nobody else knows . . . that X has [pain] Y at t, *in the same way* that X knows that he has Y at t" (pp. 92-93). As we noted, however, beyond a dubious comparison with perceiving, no details seemed to be available on this *"way"* of knowing "by merely having." Worse yet: since our having of mental contents was to be defined in terms of knowing, we should not expect much enlightenment from this circular procedure.

The Wittgensteinian argument from nonsense does not seem to have been rebutted. As with the 'owning', 'perceiving', 'referring', and 'rule-following' accounts of what it is to have a mind and to have the items that supposedly dwell therein, we constantly meet with incoherence. The terms we deploy, and the questions we ask when we discuss ordinary instances of factual knowledge, nearly all sound bizarre in connection with knowledge of one's pains and thoughts. Until the proponent of this exotic species of knowledge reformulates her or his doctrine so that it stops generating such overt nonsense, we may wisely suspend the debate. We would lapse into thinly disguised nonsense if we conclude that people *lack* knowledge of their mental goings-on or that they do *not* have minds or sensations. Rather, no cogent issue has been stated.

In my zeal to do justice to the opposing arguments, I have unduly stretched out the Wittgensteinian-Rylean critique of 'mind' theories. So I shall try to re-emphasize their main lines of reasoning by zeroing in on one sub-theory.

11. COULD MENTAL EPISODES OF WILLING ROUSE OUR BODIES INTO ACTION?

Just as no serious disputant would deny that we sometimes ponder, sometimes suffer, and sometimes worry, none would deny that we often act. We manage somehow to get our limbs moving, more or less as we want them to move, and we thereby affect physical objects around us. How do we accomplish this? A traditional account, recently grown popular again, is that willing does the trick. Our bodily shoves and tugs make the cellar door swing on its hinges; in a similar way, according to old-and new-style advocates of will, our volitions stir up our bodies—perhaps by initiating neural impulses in our brain which make the right ligaments and tendons contract.

I believe that even the most refined versions of this theory of how we act are vulnerable to arguments from nonsense. Therefore I shall briefly sketch the latest developments. First, post-Wittgensteinian volitionists disagree among themselves—for example, on how to describe the bodily effects of willing. Sellars's dictum is that "action is essentially the sort of thing that is brought about by volition," and volition has the "job of getting actions going" (VR, ##10, 8). In a similar vein, Aune reports that "we unquestionably . . . will to act" (RA, p. 67), and L. Davis says: "A volition . . . is a volition . . . to do an A for some act-type A" (TOA, p. 17). These latter statements suggest that actions are what result from willing. However, many volitionists—including Aune and Davis—wish to rank willing itself as an action. Davis "regard[s] actions as identical with volitions" alone, and so he must consider willing the sole form of action (TOA, p. 41; see pp. 17, 45). McCann, another activist on the subject of volition, argues that "what . . . is willed . . . cannot be . . . an *action*. . . . [S]ince volition is essential to . . . raising [one's] arm, to will to raise it would be to will to will to raise it," and so forth—an intolerable consequence (VBA, p. 467). However that may be, the upshot is that if willing is an action, then its result—and its 'object', what a person wills—must be a bodily happening, not an action.

Of course volitionists also disagree about the active status of willing. Goldman appears inclined "simply to reject the characterization of volitions as purposeful actions or activities"; he believes "[t]here are . . . other plausible candidates for the kind of thing a volition is" (VTR, p. 69). But expert opinion is again divided on "other . . . candidates". Goldman says a "dominant" view is that willing is "a species of desire or intention" (p. 68). Indeed, he acknowledges that his earlier book on action (THA) contains "a doctrine quite close to the volitional theory," which assigns to "wants" the task of bringing about action (VTR, p. 67). However, in that book Goldman seems to argue by *fiat,* decreeing that "[w]ants simply are not acts" (THA, p. 93).

Sellars (TA, VR) and Aune (RA, pp. 65-84) hold that volitions are intentions to act here and now and that such intending is a type of 'practical thought"; but only Sellars appears to doubt that willing is active (TA, p. 153; VR, ##1, 6, 21). Some volitionists are firmly convinced that willing is an act. McCann is the most adamant on this point. He accepts the classification of willing as "practical thought"; but, *contra* Goldman, he sharply distinguishes it from "desiderative" thought, such as wanting, and he is sure that "[t]o will is not . . . merely to want" (VBA, pp. 468-70). As for Sellars's and Aune's candidate, intending, it fares no better. Julia Annas confidently denies that volition is "any form of intending" (HBBA, p. 211). McCann and Davis equate willing with "exertion" and "attempts," respectively (RABA, pp. 240-47; TOA, pp. 16-17, 39, 45). Yet Sellars informs us that volitions are definitely "not tryings"—or "choosings" or "decisions" either (TA, p. 156). Davis even questions the "practical thought" hypothesis. He suspects we gain "uncertain illumination" if we classify willing as thinking "'in the executive mode' . . . as long as we do not know what thoughts are, or understand what is meant by the executive mode" (TOA, p. 17). For his part, McCann admits "no other mode of thought is quite like it" (VBA, p. 468); and Annas, while holding that "volitions . . . must be thoughts," also foresees that "we shall have to . . . say that volitions are *sui generis*" (HBBA, pp. 208, 211). Overall, if we ask for a description of willing, we hear cacophony from our experts.

Before I illustrate how this opens the way to arguments from nonsense, I should mention two other related topics. One is: How much bodily behavior can a volition produce? Goldman seems uncertain. He admits: "I cannot execute an entire three-block walk . . . as a result of a single occurrent want. I can, perhaps, take ten or twenty steps" (THA, p. 90). He says that a ballerina "initiates [an] entire series" of movements by one volition; yet an experienced typist may have "volitions for fingers to move" each time he strikes a key! (VTR, pp. 71, 74). This brings us to the second issue: Are we conscious of all our volitions? Goldman's typist is unlikely to be. But Goldman's solution is to distinguish between "focal" episodes of willing that occupy the center of our "volitional field," and "peripheral" episodes like the typist's—of which we are "at least *dimly*" conscious (p. 74). But Davis disagrees; he contends we are "not generally aware of willing . . . in itself" (TOA, p. 18). So Davis appears to give theorists license to multiply short-range unconscious volitions *ad gustam,* or to suppose that long stretches of behavior are "controlled" by either conscious or unconscious "ongoing processes" of megavolition (p. 23).

How do these conflicting statements about willing and action invite charges of nonsense? Well, regardless of their doctrinal squabbles, all volitionists say that

THE DISCOVERY OF NONSENSE 309

willing is a psychological event—perhaps a covert act—which engenders movement of our limbs. So they should be able to provide characterizations of willing and its effects, using at least some of the crude but evocative terminology we draw upon to describe more familiar happenings and deeds. For purposes of comparison, consider the range of details we can furnish about such a humble event as the cooling of my dinner wine by some ice cubes in which the bottle is submerged—or my unmomentous action of sipping the wine. The same holds for consequences of these goings-on. But when we—even with the advice of our experts—make a similar attempt to portray volitions and their results, we become either tongue-tied or unpersuasively dogmatic. Most of what we can say of everyday occurrences and human acts does not intelligibly carry over to volitional episodes. Thus Ryle notices how bizarre it sounds if someone reports "that at 10 AM he was occupied in willing this or that, or that he performed five quick and easy volitions and two slow and difficult volitions between midday and lunch time . . . (CM, p. 64). Yet it makes plain sense to report that I was sipping chablis when the phone rang at 7:00 P.M. We can count the number of sips I take, and say how much easier it was for me to ingurgitate wine than cough syrup.

More generally, Ryle asks the proponent of willing:

> By what sorts of predicates should [volitions] be described? Can they be sudden or gradual, strong or weak, . . . enjoyable or disagreeable? Can they be accelerated, decelerated, interrupted or suspended? Can people be efficient or inefficient at them? Can we take lessons in executing them? Are they fatiguing or distracting? . . . Can we perform them while thinking of other things . . . ?
>
> [W]hen a champion [of volitions] . . . is . . . asked . . . how many acts of will he executes in, say, reciting "Little Miss Muffet" backwards, he is apt to . . . find difficulties in giving the answer, though these difficulties should not, according to his own theory, exist (CM, p. 65).

Incidentally, people can sip wine gracefully or clumsily and learn the art of wine-tasting. It is certainly less exhausting and distracting to sip wine than to lift barbells. Analogous disparities emerge if we turn to 'non-active' theories of willing. You can gauge how much ice you need to reduce the temperature of the wine so-and-so many degrees. You can describe how chilling alters the wine's molecular structure and what happens to our digestive system, cerebral cortex, and muscles as our body absorbs the wine. By contrast, it seems radically unclear what the dimensions or characteristics of willing might be and how it brings about the neural and muscular events that occur when we act.

The principal counter-arguments by volitionists take up the 'counting' problem. Goldman wonders why Ryle

> believe[s] that there should be no difficulty, according to the volitional theory, in saying how many acts of will one has executed? . . . [A] person may not have noticed how many there were. . . . Furthermore, . . . what reason is there for requiring a volitional theory to . . . [have] criteria for

counting volitions? There do not seem to be criteria for counting other categories of mental events. . . . Is there a definite number of thoughts one has during a two-minute interval? Thoughts can be chopped up into . . . units of almost any length one pleases . . . [so] there is no straightforward answer to the question, 'How many thoughts did you have . . . ?' (VTR, pp. 69-70).

This helps very little, since many theorists assimilate volitions to "practical thoughts," and the critic who suspects that talk of willing is nonsensical would have the same misgivings when Goldman confidently discusses thoughts and their alleged "length." Critics would react similarly when Goldman deals with the broader 'indescribability' problem by arguing: "mental states may be distinct from one another, and we may recognize this distinction, although we cannot . . . *say* what features distinguish them. This is true . . . of many if not all mental states, not volitions alone" (p. 71).

When Davis takes up the 'counting' puzzle, he goes outside the debated mental sphere and compares our problem of individuating volitions with "a similar difficulty in dividing a range into discrete mountains" (TOA, p. 23). But is he right about alpine geography? We cannot break up a range into as many or as few mountaintops as we please. There are just so many peaks or summits in a mountain chain, and each has a definite elevation, latitude, and longitude. Moreover, we can investigate how a mountain influences wind currents and water runoffs—in a way we cannot begin to study the supposed effects of willing. Davis has failed to neutralize the argument from nonsense against volitions, since he appears to be mistaken that it applies to mountains.

One more volitionist reply merits analysis: the claim of Davis, McCann, and others (e.g., Annas, HBBA, pp. 203, 206) that willing is a form of "trying" or "effort." McCann is most explicit, declaring it "a matter of physiological fact that, when a person performs a *normal* act of arm-raising, the upward motion of his arm is caused by the tensing of . . . muscles . . . [and] the tensing . . . is the result of an action of physical exertion" (RABA, p. 247, my italics). McCann seems to forget about physiology when he later says "no publicly observable event . . . need occur" during exertion (pp. 244-45). But that is secondary. I doubt that we should allow McCann's decree to override Wittgenstein's astute remarks: "When I raise my arm I do not usually *try* to raise it," and "[I] f there is no difficulty about [reaching some house] —*can* I try at all costs to get to that house?" (PI, ##622-28). If I am not handcuffed, injured, or otherwise impeded, what would it be like for me to exert myself or to make an attempt at lifting my arm? Unless barbed wire or something else blocks my path, nothing would qualify as desperately trying to reach the house. Nor is it intelligible to report that I made only a half-hearted attempt to reach the unobstructed house. A further point worth noting about our ordinary exertions and attempts is that we can always specify *what* we are doing with effort and what we are attempting to do. Suppose there are snowdrifts. I am nearly frozen. Then what I am doing with great effort is stumbling forward in the direction of a shelter. Or imagine calmer circumstances. I effortlessly dial a friend's telephone number. I am thereby attempting to contact him. Now assume that McCann is correct: willing is "an action of physical exertion," and to will is to strain. What is it you do strenuously when you perform a volition? Should McCann nominate the bodily movement that you have willed? No, because you can will bodily events, and yet they might fail to occur. Your arm does not change position, although you genuinely willed it to. So there could be volitional "exertion" when no bodily movement—and hence no strenuous one—took place. Do you exert yourself in willing then? Hardly, since McCann equates the willing with the exertion. Thus we seem to generate nonsense when we ask questions that are perfectly appropriate to everyday cases of effort.

I become just as dumbfounded when I examine Davis's repeated claim that willing is an attempt. I wonder: an attempt to do what? In common life, badminton players try to return lobs, pickpockets endeavor to snatch purses, rescuers strive to locate a crashed airplane, incumbent politicians attempt to win reelection. Is it intelligible to suppose that you might attempt to do any of these things merely by willing? Could I, in performing a volition only, have tried but failed to smash a lob, steal a purse, rescue someone, or get elected? Could willing even qualify as a lackadaisical attempt?

Of course it makes sense, and is often plainly true, to report that people willingly or reluctantly attended a meeting, that an officeholder is unwilling to accept a bribe, and that someone has settled upon a plan of action—or remains undecided. Evidently such conative goings-on shape our behavior; yet volitional theories, as formulated so far, make little sense of this relationship. However, like general 'mind' theories, they are deep; Wittgenstein might say they are "statements one would like to make here, but cannot make significantly" (OC, #76).

References

Ackerman, R. J., *Belief and Knowledge* (= BK) (Garden City, 1972).
Annas, J., "How Basic Are Basic Actions?" (HBBA), *Proceedings of the Aristotelian Society* (henceforth: PAS) 78 (1977-78):195-213.
Aune, B., "Knowing and Merely Thinking" (KMT), *Philosophical Studies* 12 (1961):53-58.
———, *Knowledge, Mind, and Nature* (KMN) (New York, 1967).
———, *Reason and Action* (RA) (Dordrecht, 1977).
Austin, J. L., "Other Minds" (OM), PAS suppl. vol. 20 (1946); reprinted in *The Foundations of Knowledge*, ed. C. Landesman (Englewood Cliffs, N.J., 1970), pp. 124-59.
Ayer, A. J., "Can There Be a Private Language?" (CPL), PAS suppl. vol. 28 (1954); reprinted in *Wittgenstein*, ed. G. Pitcher (Garden City, 1966). pp. 251-66.
Berkeley, G., *Three Dialogues between Hylas and Philonous* (TD) (1713); reprinted (Indianapolis, 1952).
Brand, M., and Walton, D., eds., *Action Theory* (Dordrecht, 1976).
Castañeda, H-N., "The Private-Language Argument" (PLA), in *Knowledge and Experience*, ed. C. D. Rollins (Pittsburgh, 1964), pp. 88-105.
Davis, L., *Theory of Action* (TOA) (Englewood Cliffs, N.J., 1979).
Goldman, A. I., *A Theory of Human Action* (THA) (Englewood Cliffs, N.J., 1970).
———, "The Volitional Theory Revisited" (VTR), in *Action Theory*, eds. M. Brand and D. Walton (Dordrecht, 1976), pp. 67-84.

McCann, H., "Is Raising One's Arm a Basic Action?" (RABA), *Journal of Philosophy* 69 (1972):235-48.
_____, "Volition and Basic Action" (VBA), *Philosophical Review* 83 (1974):451-73.
Rorty, R., ed., *The Linguistic Turn* (Chicago, 1967).
Ryle, G., "Systematically Misleading Expressions" (SME), PAS 32 (1931-32); reprinted in *The Linguistic Turn*, ed. R. Rorty (Chicago, 1967), pp. 85-100.
_____, *The Concept of Mind* (CM) (London, 1949).
_____, "Autobiographical" (A), in *Ryle*, eds. G. Pitcher and O. P. Wood (Garden City, 1970), pp. 1-15.
Searle, J., *Speech Acts* (SA) (New York, 1969).
Sellars, W., "Thought and Action" and "Fatalism and Determinism" (TA), both in *Freedom and Determinism*, ed. K. Lehrer (New York, 1966), pp. 105-74.
_____, "Volitions Re-Affirmed" (VR), in *Action Theory*, eds. M. Brand and D. Walton (Dordrecht, 1976), pp. 47-66.
Wisdom, J., "Philosophical Perplexity" (PP), PAS 37 (1936-37); reprinted in *The Linguistic Turn*, ed. R. Rorty (Chicago, 1967), pp. 101-10.
Wittgenstein, L., *Philosophical Investigations* (PI) (New York, 1953).
_____, *Zettel* (Z) (Oxford, 1967).
_____, *On Certainty* (OC) (Oxford, 1969).

The Informativeness of Philosophical Analysis

DIANA F. ACKERMAN

In his reply to Langford, Moore gives the following conditions as necessary for a philosophical analysis.
1. "Both *analysans* and *analysandum* must be concepts or propositions, not mere verbal expressions, and must in some sense be the same concept."[1]
2. "If you are to 'give an analysis' of a given *concept*, which is the *analysandum*, you must mention, as your *analysans*, a *concept* such that (a) nobody can know that the *analysandum* applies to an object without knowing that the *analysans* applies to it, (b) nobody can verify that the *analysandum* applies without verifying that the *analysans* applies, (c) any expression which expresses the *analysandum* must be synonymous with any expression which expresses the *analysans*."[2]
3. '. . . the expression used for the *analysandum* must not only be different from that used for the *analysans*, but they must differ in this way, namely that the expression used for the *analysans* must explicitly mention concepts which are not explicitly mentioned by the expression used for the *analysandum* [in the sense that] 'X is a male sibling' explicitly mentions the concepts "male and "sibling," whereas the expression 'X is a brother' does not."[3]
4. ". . . that the method of combination should be explicitly mentioned by the expression used for the *analysans* is . . . also a necessary condition for the giving of an analysis."[4]

A striking characteristic of these conditions is that philosophically interesting analyses do not seem to satisfy them. Pairs of philosophically interesting *analysanda* and *analysantia* notoriously seem to violate the second condition. For example, suppose that the concept "justified true belief supported by a chain of reasons that does not essentially involve a falsehood" is the *analysans* of the concept "knowledge." (For convenience I will assume this is a correct analysis and will use it as an example of such throughout the paper. But nothing hinges on the question of whether it actually is correct; I am using it solely for purposes of illustration. Also, I

313

will abbreviate 'justified true belief supported by a chain of reasons that does not essentially involve a falsehood' as 'JTB'.

There are several possible ways of handling this conflict. It might be held that the concept "knowledge" and the concept "JTB" are not really related as *analysandum* and *analysans*, precisely because they do not fit Moore's conditions. But I think this would be a difficult position to maintain, since this particular analysis seems to be one of the most widely used examples of analysis in philosophy.

It might be argued that 'knowledge' and 'JTB' *are* synonyms and that on some level, ("implicitly," perhaps) anyone who grasps the concept "knowledge" really does know that knowledge is JTB. But this would also raise difficulties. First, it is at least unclear how this sense of implicit knowledge could be developed and justified in a way sufficient to keep from seeming *ad hoc*. Second, if 'knowledge' and 'JTB' really are synonyms, the Fregean sort of principle of sense individuation would seem to require not only that knowing that knowledge is knowledge entails knowing that knowledge is JTB, but also that knowing "explicitly" (as opposed to "implicitly") that knowledge is knowledge entails knowing "explicitly" that knowledge is JTB. I argue elsewhere against rejecting this sort of sense individuation principle.[5]

Another possibility is to accept Moore's conditions, the Fregean sort of sense individuation principle, *and* the concept "JTB" as the *analysans* of the concept "knowledge," but to deny that a sincere and competent speaker of English who expresses doubt about a sentence like 'all and only cases of knowledge are cases of JTB' really, fully grasps the concept of knowledge and really, fully knows that knowledge is knowledge. This amounts to saying that nobody fully grasps a concept unless he knows its *analysans* (if it has one) and nobody really fully understands an expression unless he knows the *analysans* (if there is one) of what it expresses. In conversation, Ernest Sosa has suggested this sort of approach.[6] But it has the counterintuitive consequence that virtually everyone fully grasps very few concepts and fully understands very few words he uses, since knowledge of analyses is so rare. This sets the standard for fully grasping concepts and fully understanding language far higher than the standards we ordinarily apply. I do not see any compelling reason to accept this counterintuitive result, especially since there seems to be a less problematic way to solve the problem.

The less problematic way, which I will sketch in this paper, involves denying Moore's constraints on analysis, specifically, denying that the *analysans* and the *analysandum* must be the same concept, and involves rejecting all the provisions of Moore's second condition quoted above. (As we will see, I will be rejecting the third and fourth conditions quoted above as well.) I find this move attractive because so little has been offered in support of these conditions and because the concepts "knowledge" and "JTB" have so little intuitive claim to be identical. I think the picture of analysis suggested by Moore's constraints has attracted people partly because of the apparent lack of alternatives, i.e., the apparent difficulty of specifying a relation between *two* concepts that would relate them closely enough to distinguish them from such pairs of concepts as the concept "twenty-eight" and the concept "second-smallest perfect number,"[7] which clearly do not seem closely enough related to be related as *analysans* and *analysandum*. In this paper, I will sketch such a relation. My approach will be intended to apply to such analytical relations as the relation between the concept "knowledge" and the concept "JTB." The approach is not intended to apply to everything that has been called an analysis by philosophers; for example, it is not intended to apply to analyses that are "trivial" (i.e., immediately obvious to anyone who understands them) or to reformatory analyses that seek at least in part to reform our concepts. Like Moore, I will speak of the analysis of concepts or propositions rather than the analysis of verbal expressions. However, I think one can say very similar things about the analysis of concepts and the analysis of verbal expressions, provided that in the latter case it is understood that one is considering those expressions *along with their associated meanings*. It is probably simplest to say I am concerned with a view of the analytical relation between the concept "knowledge" and the concept "JTB," and that this view will apply to many other pairs of *analysanda* and *analysantia* as well.

What are the relations between the concepts "knowledge" and "JTB" in virtue of which the latter is the *analysans* of the former? The first two conditions are easy to specify. First, it is a *necessary truth* that something is a case of knowledge if and only if it is a case of JTB. Second, it is *knowable a priori* that something is a case of knowledge if and only if it is a case of JTB. But these conditions clearly are not sufficient for the type of analytical relation that holds between the concept "knowledge" and the concept "JTB," as they also hold between such pairs of concepts as the concept "twenty-eight" and the concept "second-smallest perfect number," and the concept "brother" and itself.

Before giving my own suggestions toward an additional condition, I will consider a few possibilities that are suggested by some remarks of others. Moore's third and fourth conditions on analysis quoted at the beginning of this paper, if conjoined with the two conditions on analysis given in the preceding paragraph, clearly would not produce a sufficient condition, as the examples of the concept "twenty-eight" and the concept "the second-smallest perfect number" illustrate. But what is particularly interesting to note here is that Moore's third and fourth conditions are not even necessary for explicating the sort of analytical relation that holds between the concepts "knowledge" and "JTB." This can be seen as follows. Suppose that the word 'knowledge' has a homonym in English, and suppose the homonym has the same Fregean sense (satisfying the Fregean sense individuation principle) as the expression 'JTB', i.e., suppose that this homonym of 'knowledge' is just an abbreviation of the expression 'JTB'. Then the two concepts expressed by 'knowledge' in these two senses will still be related as *analysans* and *analysandum* in precisely the way the concept "knowledge" (using 'knowledge' in the old sense) and the concept "JTB" (which *is* what is expressed by 'the concept "knowledge"' using 'knowledge' in the new stipulated sense) are related.

A condition that is closely related to Moore's third and fourth ones can be seen in Moore's remarks that an analysis breaks a concept down into its parts.[8] But saying that analysis breaks a concept down into its parts is clearly inadequate as the supplementary condition here, because it just throws the problem back on the word "parts," by leaving unanswered the following question: in what sense are the concepts of justification, truth, belief, etc., "parts" of the concept of knowledge whereas the concepts of being a perfect number, and being such that only one perfect number is smaller are not "parts" of the concept "twenty-eight"?

Another interesting related approach to the missing condition is suggested by some remarks of Langford. He says

> Suppose that we are trying to teach a child by an ostensive procedure what a square object is, or, in other words, that we are trying to teach him how to form the class of square objects. We may present to him a great variety of things, some of which we designate as square and others as not square, in the hope that he will catch on and be able to proceed on his own initiative. . . . Then, on each occasion on which the child recognizes an object as being square, there will be something else that is true: it will always also be true that the object in question has *four* sides. But we must not hastily conclude that he will recognize or be able to recognize this fact. For to recognize that a square has four sides requires knowing what the number four *is,* and this is tantamount to knowing how to form the class of quadruples. It would hardly be plausible to maintain that [this ability] is involved in the ability to discriminate objects which are square from those which are not. Yet that an object have four sides will be a necessary condition that it be recognized as being square. And we may therefore conclude that a fact can be causally effective in recognition even though it is not itself recognized.
>
> Perhaps the simplicity of this example makes it less suitable for illustrative purposes than a somewhat more complicated example. The reader will know how to recognize a cubical object. . . . Let him then answer immediately the question: How many edges has a cube? In order to recognize an object as being a cube, it is not necessary to form the class of its edges and compare this class in respect of number with other classes. . . . And if a person does not happen to know how many edges a cube has, but proceeds to find out by counting, then having twelve edges can be no part of his notion of what a cube is, since, if it were, he would then not know what it was the edges of which he was counting. Such a person will recognize an object as being cubical, however, only if it has twelve edges in point of fact. I am trying to maintain that the property of being a cube is not a truth-function or any other logical function of the property of having twelve edges.[9]

Langford also says

> In some boxes of colored children's crayons, there is no crayon which is labeled Orange, but instead there is a crayon called Red-Yellow. I suppose that the manufacturers have here provided us with an analysis of a common idiom, which we might express on the present view by saying: "Anything that was orange would be intermediate in color between red and yellow, and conversely." Possibly the converse is dogmatic, but part of the example will

survive even if it is disallowed. We may suppose a person who has lived always in a world plentifully supplied with objects orange in color, but who has never seen anything either red or yellow. He will be unable to understand the analysis here suggested, and this will not be due merely to a defect in vocabulary. Yet such a person would not recognize an object as being orange in color unless it was a fact, which he would be unable to recognize, that the object in question possessed a color which was intermediate between red and yellow. We may suppose, further, a second person, who has seen all his life things that were red and yellow, but has never observed anything orange in color. Will it be possible to define for him the term orange so that he will be able to recognize objects to which the term is applicable when they are presented to him? . . . The requirement is merely that he be able to distinguish objects as answering or not answering to the definition; and we may suppose this to be possible, as it appears to be. Then there is a sense in which the expressions 'being orange' and 'being intermediate in color between red and yellow' do not have the same meaning, and there is another sense in which these expressions do have the same meaning. They have the same meaning in the sense that they mean the same things and yet, as Moore has on occasion put the matter, it is no accident that they do, as it would be if the terms red and round happened to apply to exactly the same objects. The sense in question is therefore stronger than that of having the same denotation and is yet not so strong that the two verbal expressions can be said to be synonymous.[10]

 These remarks may suggest the following condition to be added to necessary and *a priori* knowable coextensiveness. a is the *analysans* of b if and only if the first two conditions are satisfied and x's having the property of being a is a causally necessary condition of someone recognizing x as a case of b (and perhaps also a causally sufficient condition, given such conditions as that the person is attending to x, he has the concept of b, his mind, sensory faculties, and background conditions are normal, etc.). But this condition is inadequate, for there being one-twenty-eighth of the second-smallest perfect number of apples on the table is just as much a necessary condition, and in appropriate circumstances, just as much a sufficient condition of someone's recognizing that there is one apple on the table, but the concept "one-twenty-eighth of the second-smallest perfect number" is not the *analysans* of the concept "one."

 I will now offer my own suggestions toward an additional relation between the concept "knowledge" and the concept "JTB" in virtue of which the latter is the *analysans* of the former. Like the relation discussed in the previous paragraph, my suggestion is epistemic, i.e., I hold that the additional relation beyond necessary and *a priori* knowable coextensiveness between an *analysans* and an *analysandum* of the appropriate sort has to do with cognitive relations between the concepts involved, without being so strong as to constitute identity between the concepts. I draw upon something that is epistemically unique about philosophical analyses of the sort under consideration—the way they are arrived at and tested for correctness. The analytical relation between the concept "knowledge" and the concept

"JTB" is arrived at and tested by the philosophical example-and-counterexample method, which in general terms goes as follows. The person whose concept is being tested (and who can but need not be identical with the person performing the test) is presented with a series of simple described hypothetical situations and then asked questions of the form "If such-and-such were the case, would you still say this was a case of knowledge?" The tester then generalizes from the series of answers in an attempt to get at the general properties that enter into the *analysans* of the subject's concept of knowledge.

This procedure can be described more precisely by emphasizing several important aspects. First, the person being questioned is to judge each described hypothetical case simply in terms of whether it just *seems like* a case of knowledge. No process of complicated deduction is involved. Second, there are certain conditions that should be met in the formulation of the described hypothetical test cases. These cases should be made as simple as possible, both to minimize the possibility of confusion on the part of the person being questioned, and to minimize the possibility that he will draw upon his philosophical theories (or quasi-philosophical, rudimentary, fragmented notions, if he is unsophisticated philosophically) in answering the questions. For these reasons, if two hypothetical test cases turn out to yield conflicting results, the conflict should *ceteris paribus* be resolved in favor of the simpler case. A wide variety of simple hypothetical test cases should be used to maximize the likelihood that all and only relevant properties will be taken into account in the generalization. Expressions that are synonymous with the expression that stands for the *analysandum* should not be used in formulating the test cases. There is no requirement that the test cases be formulated in terms of what can be observed or verified. Each property the subject appears to be taking into account as well as their method of combination should be part of the basis for the generalization. Moreover, since the generalization to the *analysans* is a generalization only on the *descriptions* of the test cases, my approach avoids the objection made to Langford's, as the *analysans* takes account of only the descriptions the subject actually shows he relies upon, and not of just any other causally or logically connected property. Note also that a full analysis will not be circular, which in the present context means that no expression synonymous with the *analysandum* should appear in the expression for the *analysans.*

It is particularly crucial that the method under consideration, when used on oneself, gives the *final* test for deciding whether on one's concept of knowledge all and only cases of knowledge are cases of JTB, so that the method wins if it conflicts with other ways of deciding about this. This of course does not mean that this method is infallible, but simply that the way errors in the test can ultimately be overridden is by counterexamples or by repeated questioning. The notion of the test as final is actually important twice. First, as just emphasized, the final test of whether on one's concept of knowledge all and only cases of knowledge are cases of JTB is whether that equivalence can be arrived at by using on oneself the generalization procedure just sketched. Second, the fact that described hypothetical situations are used as test cases enables the tester to frame the questions in such a way as to rule out extraneous background assumptions. Thus, even if someone correctly believes that all and only *a*'s are *b*'s, the question of whether *a, b,* or both enter the analysis of his concept of c can be investigated by asking him such questions as "Suppose (even if it seems preposterous to you) that you were to find out that there was an *a* that was not a *b,* would you still consider it a *c?"*

Several objections can be raised here. Some are of a Quinean sort, such as objections to my reliance on the notion of necessary truth and *a priori* knowledge. Of course, a thorough reply to Quinean attacks on necessary truth would take up far more space than I have available here. I try to provide such a reply elsewhere.[11] And Quine is clearly right that in certain cases it will be unclear in principle whether what is at issue is empirical. But of course this does not show that there is no distinction between empirical and necessary propositions, but only that the distinction is vague. There should be nothing surprising about the fact that there will also be areas of vagueness in an analysis.[12]

Another possible objection to my approach concerns normative concepts. Suppose person J, like most people, does not believe (or "believe explicitly," see above) any proposition of the form "All and only F things are intrinsically good," where F is a non-normative concept, possibly an extremely complicated one; but suppose that the fact that J counts all and only F things as intrinsically good can be discovered by the simple hypothetical test case method described above. If it is in fact necessary and knowable *a priori* that all and only F things are intrinsically good, then the concept "F thing" counts on the above account as the *analysans* of J's concept of intrinsically good. But now suppose that person K bears the same relation to the proposition that all and only G things are intrinsically good that J bears to the proposition that all and only F things are instrinsically good, where G is also a non-normative concept and the concepts "F" and "G" are not even extensionally equivalent, let alone identical. A question arises: do J and K have the same concept of good? It seems unreasonable to say they do not simply on the grounds that they count different things as good, since they may still be able to argue with each other about moral issues, understand each other's moral discourse, etc. But if they have the same concept of good, what is its analysis? If only J is considered, the above method would yield the view that the concept "F thing" is the *analysans,* but once K is investigated, this seems wrong.

Of course, one possible move here is to deny that sentences of the form "All and only F things are intrinsically good," where F is a non-normative concept, actually express propositions that are necessary and can be known *a priori* to be true or false. Another possible move is to admit that, because of a special gap between normative concepts and the final tests for their application, my view of analysis does not generally apply to normative concepts that are explicated in non-normative terms. My view still *can* apply to the analyses of normative concepts in terms of *other* normative concepts. In fact, the above analysis of the concept "knowledge" is an example of this, because it uses the normative concept of justification.

I will end by listing some advantages and special features of my approach.

First, of course, this approach sketches a form of analysis that does not preserve concept identity between *analysans* and *analysandum*, or synonymy between expressions expressing them.[13] Moore frequently makes remarks equating indefinability and unanalyzability, but from the present standpoint, this is an error. Thus, although Moore takes his "open question argument" to show that the notion of good is unanalyzable and indefinable, from the present standpoint he errs in saying this argument shows that good is unanalyzable. One could as well argue that the concept "knowledge" is unanalyzable on the grounds that "whoever will attentively consider with himself what is actually before his mind when he asks the question 'Is [JTB] after all [knowledge]?' can easily satisfy himself that he is not merely wondering whether [knowledge] is [knowledge]."[14]

My approach also suggests the way the *analysans* of a concept in the sort of analysis under consideration is "close" to that concept without actually preserving concept identity: the analysis comes just from generalizing from the subject's responses to questions about simple described hypothetical cases, rather than from using a complex process like a proof.[15]

Notes

1. G. E. Moore, "A Reply to My Critics: Analysis," in *Readings in Twentieth Century Philosophy*, ed. W. Alston and G. Nakhnikian (London, 1963), p. 282.
2. *Ibid.*, pp. 281-82.
3. *Ibid.*, p. 284.
4. *Ibid.*
5. See my "Recent Work on the Theory of Reference," forthcoming, *American Philosophical Quarterly*.
6. In conversation and correspondence, Alvin Plantinga has independently suggested a related approach for some problems involving proper names.
7. A perfect number is a number that is equal to the sum of all its divisors (excluding itself).
8. For example, see G. E. Moore, "The Indefinability of Good," in *Readings*, ed. Alston and Nakhnikian, pp. 236-37.
9. C. H. Langford, "The Notion of Analysis in Moore's Philosophy," in *The Philosophy of G. E. Moore*, ed. P. Schilpp (New York, 1952), pp. 326-27.
10. *Ibid.*, pp. 330-31.
11. I discuss this material in the chapter "The Attack on Necessary Truth," in my book *Methodology of Philosophy* (in preparation) to be forthcoming in the Prentice-Hall Foundations of Philosophy series.
12. Alston gives interesting examples of vague analyses in his *Philosophy of Language* (Englwood Cliffs, N.J., 1964), chap. 5.
13. I think there also are types of analysis that *do* preserve concept identity. These have their own special problems, but they lie beyond the scope of this paper.
14. G. E. Moore, "The Indefinability of Good," in *Readings*, ed. Alston and Nakhnikian, p. 242. I have replaced Moore's references in this passage to good and pleasure with references to knowledge and JTB. See also *ibid.*, pp. 237, 243, and 245 where he equates indefinability with unanalyzability.
15. I am indebted to Alvin Plantinga, Philip Quinn, and Ernest Sosa for valuable discussion and correspondence about material related to this paper. I discuss this material in greater detail in the chapter "Problems of Analysis" in my forthcoming book *Methodology of Philosophy*.

Ryle's Theories of Concepts[1]

MORRIS WEITZ

In this essay I attempt to refocus Ryle's contribution to theories of concepts: from our traditional meadowland picture of him as a logical geographer mapping ordinary concepts—suggested by his *Concept of Mind*—to a new vision of him as a logical explorer engaged in the discovery of the varieties of logical types of concepts—impressed upon us by his entire *oeuvre*—where he stands, joined by his pioneers, Frege, Russell, and Wittgenstein, on the white peaks of philosophical logic.

In "Systematically Misleading Expressions" (1931-32)[2], Ryle states that the primary (perhaps the whole) task of philosophy is the analysis of certain expressions which systematically mislead philosophers into thinking that these expressions record one kind of fact when they actually record another: and whose logical form, as against grammatical form, can be elicited only by correct logical paraphrase of these original expressions. The major result of this analysis is that it reveals as the sources of traditional philosophical theories and disputes—including theories of concepts—the persistent confusions of grammatical with logical form. Employing Russell's theory of descriptions as a model of logical paraphrase of certain expressions, Ryle classifies and analyzes a number of expressions that mislead (of which "the author of *Waverley*" is not an example since it does not mislead as "the present King of France" does; thus, Ryle says, Russell is correct in his theory of descriptions, but not correct in thinking that all descriptions mislead).

Among systematically (i.e., classes of) misleading expressions are (1) quasi-ontological assertions, like "God exists," "Carnivorous cows do not exist," "Mr. Pickwick is a fiction"; (2) quasi-platonic statements, like "Virtue is its own reward," "Unpunctuality is reprehensible"; (3) certain descriptive statements, like "Whoever is Vice-Chancellor of Oxford University is overworked," "The present King of France is wise"; and (4) quasi-descriptive claims, like "I saw the top of the tree." Each of these is misleading in that its grammatical form is improper to the fact recorded; each must be paraphrased so that the real logical form of the fact recorded is brought out. Thus, "Carnivorous cows do not exist" is true, significant, and looks grammatically like an ordinary subject-predicate statement. But when compared to the fact recorded, "carnivorous cows" does not denote and "does not exist" does not predicate. So the grammatical clue of subject-predicate must be rejected, and the real logical form of the fact must dictate the restatement. The fact recorded by the original statement is better expressed by "Nothing is both a cow and carnivorous," since this latter statement does not imply that anything is either. To generalize from this one example, philosophical analysis, as Ryle conceives it, can then say that one expression means another and that that other is a better expression than the original because it exhibits better the logical form of the fact it records.

So far as concepts are concerned, Ryle says, "X is a concept" and "the concept of x" are systematically misleading, the one because it is quasi-ontological, the other because it is quasi-descriptive. But unlike other systematically misleading expressions, Ryle does not paraphrase them, he gets rid of them. There is no paraphrase of "The number four is a concept" or "the concept of number," which brings out the real logical form of these expressions as "Nothing is both a cow and carnivorous" does of "Carnivorous cows do not exist." Ryle describes philosophers' attempts at clarifying or analyzing concepts employed by them or by others as "a gaseous way of saying that they are trying to discover what is meant by the general terms contained in the sentences which they pronounce or write" (II, 39). "What is meant by a (specified) general term?" presumably is all the cash value Ryle finds in "What is a (specified) concept?" Talk about concepts is not paraphrasable or even reducible to talk about general terms: it is replaceable by it. Thus, it is more than misleading to talk about concepts; it is a mistake. If "The number four is a concept" is systematically misleading, "There are no concepts" is not; as Ryle says: "it can be shown that it is not true in any natural sense that 'there are concepts' . . . ." (II, 41).

Ryle compares "the thought or idea of x" to "the concept of x." But the first reduces to "Whenever A thinks of x," whereas the second is replaced by "Whenever we use 'x'." 'X'—the expression—has a meaning. Philosophers who convert this meaning into a concept misdescribe "the meaning of the expression 'x'."

> I suspect that all the mistaken doctrines of concepts, ideas, terms, judgements, objective propositions, contents, objectives and the like derive from the same fallacy, namely, that there must be *something* referred to by such expressions as 'the meaning of the word (phrase or sentence) "x"', on all fours with the policeman who really is referred to by the descriptive phrase in 'our village policeman is fond of football'. And the way out of the confusion is to see that some 'the'-phrases are only similar in grammar and not similar in function to referentially-used descriptive phrases, e.g. in the case in point, 'the meaning of "x"' is like 'the King of France' in 'Poincaré is not the King of France', a predicative expression used non-referentially (II, 55).

"The meaning of the expression 'x'" is systematically misleading and is quasi-descriptive, to be paraphrased as Ryle suggests. But "the concept of x" is a mistaken doctrine—not a wrong paraphrase—about meanings. As Ryle says, "the meaning of 'x'" can be redrafted as "what 'x' means;" however, "the concept of x" cannot be redrafted, only thrown out as unfit for service.

The beauty of this paper is, I think, that it does proclaim the view, first intimated by Hume, then articulated by Mill, that there are no concepts; that all talk and theories of concepts are mistaken doctrines about words and what they mean. There is language. There are theories about language. Among these theories are mistaken views about how general terms function. It is therefore a particular theorizing about language that generates concepts and a theory about them. Correcting the theorizing about language is in effect to undercut the need for concepts altogether. Ryle's paper, thus, is not a defense of his later doctrines that there are concepts and that these are the roles of certain expressions or that to have a concept is to be able to wield an expression of a certain sort. For this view is to admit concepts, not to reject them as misguided projections onto language. Ryle does not say in this paper "The concept of x is the same as what 'x' does in the language," as he does say "The meaning of 'x' is the same as what 'x' means."

In "Categories" (1938)[3], Ryle suggests that asking what type or category does so and so belong to? is equivalent to asking, in what sort of true or false propositions and in what positions in them can the expression "x" for so and so occur? He introduces the term "proposition-factor" to replace "propositional function." It names an abstractable item from families of similar propositions, not separate entities. Talk about concepts is talk about these abstracted proposition-factors, so that now Ryle allows "What sort of concept is the concept of x?" This becomes equivalent to "What sort or type or category of expression is 'x'?" "What position can it occupy in a sentence?" Clarifying and classifying concepts are no longer gaseous, but a legitimate and fruitful charting of what we can and cannot do with certain expressions.

Ryle's acceptance of the legitimacy and irreducibility of concepts along with his employment of them continues in *Philosophical Arguments* (1945)[4]. Philosophy, he says, is neither inductive nor deductive argument. Instead, "A pattern of argument which is proper and even proprietary to philosophy is the *reductio ad absurdum*" (II, 197). And it is a *reductio* in the strong sense of reducing a proposition to nonsense by showing that its implications lead to absurdities. The aim of such arguments is not a nihilistic one but rather to test the logical powers of certain philosophical ideas and doctrines. "Every proposition has . . . certain 'logical powers'; that is to say, it is related to other propositions in various discoverable logical relationships" (II, 198). For the most part, all of us understand these logical powers of the ideas and propositions we employ; the difficulty is to state them, to test them against possible implications and absurdities.

It is a function of philosophy to chart these logical powers.

> When several different propositions are noticed having something in common (and when this common feature or factor is not itself a constituent proposi-

tion) it is convenient and idiomatic, though hazardous, to abstract this common factor and call it (with exceptions) an 'idea' or 'concept'. Thus men learn to fasten on the idea of mortality or the concept of price as that which is common to a range of propositions in which persons are affirmed or denied to be mortal or in which commodities are said to cost so much or to be exchangeable at such and such rates. Later they learn to isolate in the same manner more abstract ideas like those of existence, implication, duty, species, mind, and science (II, 199).

Concepts are not terms in the historical sense of substantial parts of propositions. Rather, they "are abstractions from the families of propositions of which they are common factors or features" (II, 199). Talk of a concept, thus, is talk about no entity, but of a family of propositions that share a common feature. "Statements about ideas [concepts] are general statements about families of propositions" (II, 199).

Concepts, like the propositions from which they are abstracted, differ in their types, or categories. The concepts of three and large have different logical powers than the concepts of green and merry. Concepts of different types cannot be coerced into similar logical conduct without contradiction.

Philosophers ought to chart the logical powers of concepts. And like geographers, they cannot do this by concentrating on one item but instead must "determine the cross-bearings of all of a galaxy of ideas belonging to the same or contiguous fields. The problem, that is, is not to anatomize the solitary concept, say, of liberty but to extract its logical powers as these bear on those of law, obedience, responsibility, loyalty, government, and the rest" (II, 202). The search for the types and logical powers of concepts and the testing of these concepts by reducing to absurdity their being placed in types they do not belong to or their being given powers they do not have Ryle calls "dialectical." It is, he says, the true method of philosophy as the clarification and analysis of concepts and the search for definitions.

Ryle next amends "proposition" to "expression" in order to avoid having to assert that philosophy attempts to reduce propositions to absurdity, since such reduction would nullify the original as a proposition. "The solution is that expressions and only expressions can be absurd" (II, 203). The reduction to absurdity operates only on expressions, disclosing "that a given expression cannot be expressing a proposition of such and such a content with such and such a logical skeleton, since a proposition with certain of these properties would conflict with one with certain of the others" (II, 203). Thus, the pattern of the *reductio* is that of *ponendo tollens*.

Not all ideas or concepts generate puzzles, Ryle says, only abstract ones. A concrete idea or concept is one "the original use of which is to serve as an element in propositions about what exists or occurs in the real world" (II, 207). "Ideas like *spaniel, dog, ache, thunder* in their original use are instances of concrete concepts. . . . Such concepts are formed from noticing similarities in the real world" (II, 207). Abstract concepts, on the other hand, are not formed by noticing similarities and do not correspond to anything. "To form abstract ideas it is necessary to notice not similarities between things in nature but similarities between propositions about things in nature or, later on, between propositions about propositions about things in nature . . . " (II, 208).

All this talk about propositions (and, by implication, about concepts) reduces to talk about expressions as they are employed by persons. With this safeguard, we can now say that certain propositions—things people say—share a common factor: "Socrates is wise" and "Plato *sapiens est*" share the common factor that can be expressed as "So and so is wise." Propositions about such factors are propositions about abstract ideas. And such ideas are always subject to the test of absurdity. But, Ryle concludes, these ideas, when they generate new theories or new questions in philosophy, are as important in their logical powers as are any concepts.

Philosophical Arguments, thus, is as remarkable in its conservatism about the nature and role of concepts as "Systematically Misleading Expressions" is in its radicalism. According to its main theses, there are concepts; and the claim that there are is neither systematically misleading nor mistaken, only hazardous. Although not entities, they are, when concrete, items extracted from the world and, when abstract, common factors found in language about the world. Moreover, though there is original talk about the charting of concepts, there is nothing about this charting as the elucidation of the use of expressions and about concepts as the roles of expressions. Ryle's theory of concepts here is a form of traditional abstractionism, except that what is abstracted is not an entity, neither mental, physical, nor linguistic.

The Concept of Mind (1949) owes much to the *reductio* of *Philosophical Arguments.* One of its theses, that Cartesianism, in all its varieties, from Descartes to Russell, is fundamentally a logical mistake since it reduces certain crucial statements about the mind which are not and cannot be categorical to categorical ones, stems from his Inaugural Lecture. Cartesianism or "Descartes' Myth" (as he calls his first chapter) is a category-mistake, that is, a misplacing of one kind of concept or expression in a type whose logical powers yield implications that are absurd.

However, *The Concept of Mind* is much more than a *reductio* of Cartesianism. Its three other main theses, I think, are these: (1) the philosophy of mind is fundamentally the logical elucidation of mental concepts or expressions and the logical mapping of their cross-bearings; (2) statements about mental phenomena are, logically, at least irreducibly threefold: categorical, hypothetical, and mongrel-categorical; and (3) the mind is not an extra, metaphysically hidden entity, affixed to the body—a "Ghost in the Machine"—but a "person's abilities, liabilities and inclinations to do and undergo certain sorts of things, and of the doing and undergoing of these things in the ordinary world" (p. 199). Even the title of the book indicates that Ryle's primary concern is with the concept, not the nature of mind. Philosophy as analysis shifts to philosophy as elucidation of concepts. (Contrast, for example, Russell's title, *The Analysis of Mind,* with Ryle's.) The preoccupation is with the logical mapping of central mental concepts or expressions. Ryle's basic claim, which pervades the book, is that the description of the logical behavior of mental concepts constitutes the whole philosophical story of the mind; and neither in plot nor in character is it the story narrated by the orthodox, classical amalgam of traditional theories, from Descartes to Russell, that Ryle calls "Cartesianism."

In this book, whether under the influence of the later Wittgenstein or not, Ryle comes to see that there are concepts, not just general words or abstractable features of language and things—though there is much expository identification of concepts with their conveying words, where the concept of x simply replaces x with inverted commas ("x")—and that these concepts are the same as certain abilities or capacities to move about in various ways in the world, one of which is the ability to use language. In this way, concepts are assimilated to the having of them, and the having of them is being able to do certain sorts of things, only one of which, but a very important one, is employing expressions correctly. Talk of concepts is mostly tantamount to talk of the roles of corresponding linguistic expressions. It is not clear—nor is it, I think, in the whole of Ryle's work—that a necessary condition for being a concept or for having a concept is being able to use an expression correctly. However, it is clear that such a necessary condition is being able to perform a certain range of tasks; it is also clear that a sufficient condition for having a concept of a certain sort is being able to use its word correctly. That not all concepts are abstractions from families of propositions or things we say about the world follows from the fact the concept of volition is both a concept and yet has no legitimate role in any linguistic family of propositions.

In "The Theory of Meaning" (1957)[5], Ryle's theory of concepts comes full circle: from a rejection of concepts in any form to their identification with the roles of expressions. Traditional theories of concepts, he claims, rest on a misdescription of the functioning of language; a correct theory rests on a correct description of the functioning of language. The decisive moment in the history of theories of concepts occurs when Wittgenstein exchanges "What is the role of an expression?" for "What is the meaning of an expression?" The latter question, Ryle points out, led philosophers to search for a realm of non-natural, non-mental objects which could serve as the denotata of meanings of expressions. That every word (with the exception of the syncategorematic) stands for an object that it denotes or means, from Plato to Mill, Russell, and Moore, is the root of all traditional theories of concepts as entities. That this denotational theory of the meaning of words is an erroneous answer to "What do words mean?" to be replaced by a different question, "What do words do?" is the beginning of the correct approach to concepts. A realm of meanings as concepts is no longer needed. Having a concept is not being acquainted with a meaning but being able to wield expressions according to conventionally accepted rules. A concept is the role of similar expressions. Analysis, as practiced by Russell and Moore, no longer has a realm to analyze; philosophy now has as its great task the elucidation of the roles of expressions, not the analysis of meanings.

In the Introduction to his *Collected Papers,* Ryle writes: "To elucidate the thoughts of a philosopher we need to find the answer not only to the question, 'What were his intellectual worries?' but, before that question and after that question, the answer to the question, 'What was his overriding Worry?'" (I, ix). So far as his own philosophy is concerned, Ryle confesses as his overriding worry, in a number of essays that span his career, to discover what, if anything, is proprietary to philosophy? His answer is that it is conceptual inquiry. Such inquiry, though not the same as analysis of concepts for Ryle, is equivalent to inquiry into concepts. This inquiry, I think, has taken two main preliminary directions: to determine whether there are concepts and to determine what they are. Although Ryle has wavered on his different answers to both questions, I do not find that he has ever denied the distinctness of these two questions. Whatever concepts are or are said to be by philosophers, "There are concepts" and "Concepts are . . . " are different answers to different questions. There is hardly an essay of Ryle's as well as *The Concept of Mind* and *Dilemmas* (1954) that does not center on or raise these two questions and provide answers to them. They may not add up to Ryle's overriding worry, but they are pretty close to it.

I have concentrated on those writings of Ryle's which, at least in my judgment, contain the major moves Ryle has made in the development of his theory of concepts. These writings show that Ryle went from There are no concepts, therefore, there is nothing that they are to There are concepts and they are abstractable common features of families of sentences or propositions, tied to language, not to things; they are these features, with all their logical powers, plus extracted similarities from things, not just language; and they are roles of expressions in one or more languages or certain abilities for performing tasks, including being able to wield certain expressions.

If we turn from these essays and their varying answers to others of Ryle's writings, especially those that explore different kinds or logical types of concepts, we find not only further clarifications of Ryle's views about whether there are concepts or what they are but, as important, perhaps more important, both statements and examples of the point of conceptual inquiry. And because no adequate answer to What is Ryle's theory of concepts—their nature and role?—can be forthcoming without consideration of these writings, I include them here. Although they add to the difficulty of arriving at an univocal theory attributable to Ryle, they equally enhance the richness of the conceptual life that he so abundantly unfolds.

Ryle's early essay, "Are There Propositions?" (1929-30)[6], examines arguments for and against an affirmative answer. He concludes that there are no propositions, only facts and symbols or sentences and statements made with sentences about facts. "Proposition" denotes sentence or statement, and is a name for what one thinks with or talks in, not for what one thinks. Now, if propositions are not sentence-meanings, as the tradition assumes they are, are concepts word-meanings? Ryle raises this question, only to drop it, since after all his topic is Propositions. However, we can ask, in the spirit of this essay, whether concepts too can be resolved into symbols we think or talk with, not entities we think of? Because we are given nothing like *facts*—*things* seem to be the only possibility—it is difficult to project a Rylean answer to what a concept is about if it is a symbol, if "concept" denotes symbol, and if "concept" names what we think and talk with or in, not what we think. Nevertheless, that concepts remain legitimate word-meanings whereas propositions do not as sentence-meanings is not implied in this paper and is rejected completely in his next, "Systematically Misleading Expressions."

In "Plato's 'Parmenides'" (1939).[7] Ryle proposes that that dialogue is primarily an early exploration into different logical types of concepts. Plato does not distinguish between generic and specific concepts, as he does elsewhere, but between "formal" and "proper" concepts. The formal, Ryle says, include the concepts of existence, negation, being an instance of; and the proper, concepts like triangle, courage, piety, and so on. In the *Parmenides,* Ryle hypothesizes, Plato was feeling his way into this radical type difference. Ryle also proposes that Plato here introduces the *reductio* (which Ryle later in *Philosophical Arguments* makes central in philosophy) as the method of deducing absurdities from erroneous placing or identification of formal and proper or non-formal concepts. To treat existence, for example, like square is to sin against logical syntax: this is the major point of much of the argument in the *Parmenides,* according to Ryle. This distinction between formal and non-formal concepts as they differ in their logical type, demonstrated by anomalies deduced by denying their different logical types, Ryle attributes not only to Plato but to Aristotle as well. Ryle introduces a variety of names in his essays on Plato and Aristotle—"common," "ubiquitous," "neutral," "topic-neutral" —to mark these concepts that run through all discourse and thought; and he differentiates these formal concepts from the non-formal which, throughout his work, include task, achievement, heed concepts, dispositional, process, activity concepts and even polymorphous concepts, each different from the others, but all to be distinguished from the formal ones in their lack of ubiquitousness. Ryle's essay on the *Parmenides,* because of its introduction of this division of concepts and independently of its validity of application to Plato, is as important as anything in Ryle's work, so fundamental has the search for types of concepts been to Ryle: it is perhaps the persistent theme that underwrites his inquiry into concepts.

In "Ordinary Language" (1953),[8] Ryle distinguishes between the ordinary (or standard) use of expressions as against their nonstandard use; the use of ordinary as against the use of technical (or uncommon) expressions; and a linguistic usage (or custom). The primary task of philosophy is to give logical accounts of the roles of ordinary and technical terms in their standard modes of employment. Talking about the uses of expressions replaces talk about concepts and talk about the meanings of expressions, since the former but not the two latter raises no questions about status or provenance. However, inquiry into concepts is, Ryle says, shorthand for the longwinded inquiry into uses of expressions; inquiry into meanings of expressions is a perversion of the description of uses of expressions. Thus, concept talk remains in this article, meaning talk does not; the first, but not the second, is the same as talk about the ordinary use of both ordinary and technical expressions. Conceptual elucidation is an alternate for description of uses of expressions; whether concepts are alternates for uses of words, so that the concept of, say, cause, is the same as the role of "cause," "*Ursache,*" etc., and the having of that concept is the same as being able to use "cause," etc., Ryle does not say. But he leaves little doubt that they are the same. Four years later, in "The Theory of Meaning," he says as much.

In *Dilemmas,* Ryle contrasts competing theories that can be adjudicated by the theorists themselves with dilemmas that can be litigated only by philosophy. Litigation, thus, becomes, along with reformulation of systematically misleading expressions, the *reductio,* and the charting of logical powers or the mapping of concepts, one of the proprietary tasks of philosophy. Competing theories are mostly rival solutions to the same problem; dilemmas are apparent but not really rival solutions to the same problem. Competing theories differ over the truth or falsity of putative propositions; dilemmas arise because certain, mainly ordinary, concepts and their categories are misconstrued. Their resolution proceeds by detailing reminders of the category status of the various concepts involved in the seeming dispute; and with the overall reminder that, though the category status must be considered piecemeal since there is no table of categories, neither Aristotle's nor Kant's, to determine its status, the concepts cannot be taken one apart from others related to it. Thus, "Whatever is was to be" seems to conflict with "Some things which have happened could have been averted." This dilemma, however, rests on a mistaken notion of anterior truths about happenings as causes of these happenings; and is to be litigated by the reminder that only truths necessitate truths, whereas events can be effects but not implications. The concepts of truth, cause, necessity, and the related ones of prevention and responsibility have been wrongly categorized: the necessitation of truth is not the necessitation of causality. Whatever the category or logical power of the concept of cause or truth may be, the philosophical truth that they are different in their types and cannot be assimilated without, in this case, generating the dilemma, also dissolves it.

Right now, I am not interested in pursuing the question of the adequacy or inadequacy of Ryle's statement and resolution of this dilemma or any of the others he presents; nor, more important, of the differences, if any, between a dilemma and a *reductio* as Ryle conceives them. My sole concern is the role of concepts in these dilemmas and their litigation. A dilemma, Ryle says, centers on the misconstrual of concepts. Both the concepts and their misconstruals do not merely rest on but are equivalent to what we say and what we cannot say, that is: to expressions, their use and misuse. The concepts of cause, truth, and necessity; or of whole, part, and sum; or of pleasure, pain, and enjoyment, and so on for all the concepts involved in the dilemmas Ryle discusses, are shorthand for the employments of the words "cause," "truth," etc., which convey the concepts. If I have any of the concepts that may become enmeshed in dilemmas, Ryle seems to allow, I still know how to use certain words, even if I then go on to misuse them as I generate a horn of a dilemma. However, whether I use these words correctly or not, I still may not be able to state the criteria and the rules for the correct use of the word in question. Ryle distinguishes sharply between being able to use a word correctly and being able to state its criteria and rules of correct employment. But he does not say what is to count as having or understanding the concept: being able to use a word or being able to state its criteria and rules? If it is the former, concepts are equivalent to uses of expressions; if it is the latter, concepts are not, unless uses include their criteria and rules, which they do not. In any case, even if we grant that Ryle's distinction between employing a concept efficiently and describing its employment efficiently is equivalent to using an expression and describing that use, so that all talk about concepts is the same as talk about uses of expressions, what shall we say about the concepts of litigation, the *reductio,* and logical powers? Can these concepts be rendered equivalent to uses or rules of expressions? Is talk about the "notion of litigation" (p. 6) the same as talk about "litigation" or any other word or words, as talk about the concept of cause is talk about "cause" or *"Ursache"* or some other word? Of course the concept of litigation as Ryle describes it depends on language and especially on some of the snares we encounter when we depart from standard uses of certain terms; but does it depend on language as the concept of cause depends on "cause" or that of pleasure, on "enjoy" and "being pleased?" The concepts of cause and pleasure reduce to or are equivalent to the roles of certain words, about which we need philosophical reminders when we lose our ways in handling them. But the concept of litigation, though it depends on language, indeed, lives off it, cannot be reduced to or rendered equivalent to any employment or description of that employment of expressions. The concept of litigation, as Ryle abundantly shows, is a concept of a skill, in particular of being able to resolve dilemmas by amassing reminders about the logical types of the concepts or words conveying them whose boundaries have been transgressed. In the spirit, if not according to the letter of Ryle, one might say the concept of litigation is an elucidatory concept, not a concept to be elucidated. As such, it is a concept about the employment and the rules of employment of certain expressions, irreducible to expressions or their roles. And having or understanding this concept includes more than being able to use expressions and state their criteria and rules of correct use; it is being able to wield this knowledge in the detection of misuses that generate dilemmas and in the resolution of these dilemmas by nosing out and stating the type or category mistake.

In the Discussion of Ryle's paper, "Thinking Thoughts and Having Concepts" (1962), which unfortunately is not included in the reprinting in *Collected Papers,* Professor J. N. Findlay asks Ryle "why he thinks that his entirely acceptable view that having a concept entails being able to apply it in a certain way in various classificatory and argumentative contexts should justify the patently false view that there is no such thing as a particular recollectable experience of having a concept in mind, dwelling on it, soaking oneself in it, realizing what it involves, profoundly understanding it?"[9] Ryle's reply is not printed; however, it is safe to assume that Ryle would not countenance having a concept in mind as a particular recollectable experience. Nevertheless, Findlay's point that one sometimes dwells on a concept, soaks oneself in it, trying to understand what it includes and entails—whether we agree with him or not that these imply having a concept in mind or just having a concept of a certain sort—illumines Ryle's concept of litigation and the having of it better than Ryle's account of concepts as uses of expressions and the having of them as being able to wield these expressions. In effect, then, Ryle creates his own dilemma with the concept of litigation (and with the concepts of the *reductio* and logical powers as well): Concepts are the roles of expressions or those plus their rules versus Some concepts are about the roles or rules of expressions, their transgressions, and their logical types. The having of concepts is being able to use certain expressions and to state the rules of their correct employment versus Some havings of concepts are being able to assemble reminders of the categories or types to which they belong with the express purpose of exposing and resolving dilemmas. The way out of this dilemma (and similar ones could be constructed for the concepts of the *reductio* and of logical powers) is to remind Ryle and ourselves that it rests on a confusion perhaps not of categories or types but, since the term has a use, or orders. Concepts like that of cause reduce to the use of "cause." These are first order concepts, whatever their types or categories may be. Concepts like litigation, the *reductio,* or logical powers, however, depend on but do not reduce to words or their uses or their rules of use. These, then, are second order concepts, about other concepts in their propositional contexts, dependent on but neither reducible nor equivalent to the first order. That their nature and role differ from the nature and role of the first order concepts, whether concrete, such as enjoyment or pain, or abstract, like pleasure; or whether topic neutral or proper, proposition-factors abstracted from families of propositions or extracted from similarities among things; or whether formally logical, like negation—whatever the order of these may be—is the philosophical truth that resolves Ryle's dilemma about concepts.

Ryle's "Phenomenology versus 'The Concept of Mind'" (1962)[10] includes, among other things, Ryle's Retrospect on his various thoughts about concepts. Both Phenomenology and Cambridge Philosophy began with a fundamental doctrine that concepts are platonic essences. The great difference between them is that the first never repudiated this doctrine and the realm it affirmed whereas the second, at least as represented by Russell and Wittgenstein, rejected it, at first in part, then totally, in Wittgenstein's *Tractatus.*

Ryle offers this preliminary definition of a concept:

> By 'concept' we refer to that which is signified by a word or a phrase. If we talk of the concept of *Euclidean point* we are referring to what is conveyed by this English phrase, or by any other phrase, Greek, French, or English, that has the same meaning (I, 182).

"There are concepts" and "Concepts are what certain words mean" are neutral and only the second is potentially harmful since it may invite status questions, about both concepts and meanings. But even independently of this danger, there are some words, like "exists" or "not" or "pleased," which are meaningful yet do not convey concepts as their abstract nouns, "existence," "negation," and "pleasure" do; and there are also some concepts that do not get conveyed by verbs or adjectives, like the concept of pleasure that neither "enjoys" nor "pleases" signifies. The relationship between words, their meanings, and the concepts conveyed by words is thus at best an uneasy one: Not all concepts are meanings of words; not all meanings of words are concepts.

Ryle's greatest objection to the definition he offers is that it yields too easily to identification of meanings with entities that exist in isolation. Concepts are not meanings if meanings are entities of any sort, platonic or not. Russell proved this even as early as the *Principles* for the logical concepts *all, some, any, a, the* (in the singular and plural), *not, exists,* among others, although his commitment to Platonism, Ryle claims, prevented him from drawing the consequence that the words for these logical concepts as well as the verbs of action, like "assassinate," convey no entities, hence no platonic essences either. Russell recognized but disregarded the fact that the logical words and the live verbs have meanings but only as auxiliary to the senses of the whole sentences in which they occur. It was left to Wittgenstein to invert the traditional ascent from separate word meanings to sentence meanings, for he followed Frege in starting with the sense of the complete sentence.

Ryle generalizes from this historical demolition of concepts and meanings as separate items, an achievement of "The Cambridge Transformation of the Theory of Concepts" (I, 182), to formulate the doctrine, first articulated by him in "Categories" (1938), that concepts are proposition-factors, now as the theory that:

concepts are not things that are crystallised in a splendid isolation; they are discriminable features, but not detachable atoms, of what is integrally said or integrally thought. They are not detachable parts of, but distinguishable contributions to, the unitary senses of completed sentences. To examine them is to examine the live force of things that we actually say. It is to examine them not in retirement, but doing their co-operative work (I, 185).

A concept, thus, is exactly what the meaning of a logical word or a verb was to Russell: "an abstractible feature, not an extractible part of the unitary senses of the different sentences that incorporate it" (I, 184); and all concepts are what meanings of parts of sentences were to Wittgenstein: "abstractible differences and similarities between the unitary sense of that sentence and the unitary senses of other sentences which have something but not everything in common with that given sentence" (I, 184).

Ryle's preliminary definition stands: There are concepts and they are the meanings of words in their complete sentential contexts. Conceptual inquiry turns from the "Platonic dream of a descriptive science of Essences" (I, 188) to "what can be significantly said but also . . . what cannot be significantly said with the word or phrase conveying the concept under investigation" (I, 186). Since the meanings of words are their contributory roles in the sentences in which they occur, concepts remain the uses of expressions, to be abstracted as common features, not extracted as common separate items. Concepts, thus, are not entities. But they are not abilities either. Conceptual inquiry is a skill; but the having of concepts is an amalgam of knowing that certain words, in contributing as they do to the unitary sense of the sentences that incorporate them, do their jobs under certain conditions or rules; and of knowing how to wield words according to their rules, with or without being able to state them.

One final observation on Ryle on Plato: In his *Encyclopedia of Philosophy* article, "Plato," Ryle interprets Plato's Theory of Forms as Plato's ontology of concepts: "A general idea or concept, according to this . . . doctrine, is immutable, timeless, one over many, intellectually apprehensible and capable of precise definition at the end of a piece of pure raciocination *because it is an independently existing real thing or entity*" (vol. 6, p. 322). He also argues that "Plato did not deduce the Theory of Forms from the false premise that verbs and verb phrases function like extra nouns" *(ibid.)*. Rather, his arguments were based on epistemic considerations regarding the certainties attributed to the sciences, especially mathematics, and the objectivity of truth required in intelligible disputation. Elsewhere, from "Systematically Misleading Expressions" on, Ryle hammers away at the idea that all traditional philosophical theories of concepts are mistaken theories of the meanings of words. If, therefore, Forms are super concepts for Plato, these forrm-concepts are also mistaken projections of the meanings of words. Ryle cannot have it both ways. Either some philosophical theories of concepts as entities do not derive from mistaken, on the whole, denotative theories of meanings of words, in which case there is no wholesale formula for disposing of entity theories of concepts; or all entity theories of concepts—including Plato's—are badly mistaken doctrines about the meanings of words.

There is, I think, another, perhaps deeper, problem in Ryle's interpretation of Plato's theory of concepts. Like almost everyone else, he identifies concepts in and for Plato with the forms. This identification is untenable: Plato's forms are necessary conditions for some concepts, not all, and never identical with concepts in Plato. (How, one wants to ask Ryle, would Plato reconcile the concept of love with the lack of the form of love in the *Symposium?*) Ryle's real target is not Plato's theory of concepts which are neither entities nor forms but Aristotle; and it is Aristotle's direct concerns with what we say and cannot say that divert Ryle from seeing that these concerns were integral to, not substitutes for, Aristotle's persistent search for the real definitions of things that, once completed, offered up concepts as definitional λόγοι.

To return, finally, to our original question: What is Ryle's theory of concepts? I hope it is now evident there can be only one answer: that he formulated a number of theories, as well as an anti-theory, soon abandoned. His most persistent theory, I think and have tried to show, is the one he first states in "Categories," that concepts are proposition-factors. To be sure he refers to these by various names; and, more important, he explores their different facets—as logical powers or as logical types or as categories. What remains univocal, however, throughout his work is not a theory of concepts but the absolute centrality of conceptual inquiry, as it is tied inextricably to language or uses of expressions. This predominant concern, fixed on concepts in their linguistic employment, rather than fixated on concepts as inspectable entities of any sort, has led Ryle into conceptual terrains where he staked proprietarily philosophical discoveries of the highest order, especially about the different logical types of concepts, there to be discerned and abstracted from what we say and what we cannot say. My major criticism, if that is the right word, is not so much with his theory or theories of concepts as it is with the fact that these theories, so carefully formulated by him at different times, simply do not do justice to the multiplicity of the logical kinds of concepts that Ryle uncovered.

Notes

1. This essay is part of a larger manuscript entitled *Theories of Concepts: A History of the Major Philosophical Tradition*, not yet published.

2. Gilbert Ryle, "Systematically Misleading Expressions," *Proceedings of the Aristotelian Society* 32 (1932); reprinted in Gilbert Ryle, *Collected Papers*, 2 vols. (New York and London, 1971). All references to Ryle's essays in the text are to this edition, with volume number, followed by page number; this essay is in II, 39-62.

3. Ryle, "Categories," *Proceedings of the Aristotelian Society* 38 (1938); reprinted in *Collected Papers*, II, 170-93.

4. Ryle, *Philosophical Arguments* (Inaugural Lecture as Waynflete Professor of Metaphysical Philosophy, Oxford), 1945; reprinted in *Collected Papers*, II, 194-211.

5. Ryle, "The Theory of Meaning," in *British Philosophy in Mid-Century*, ed. C. A. Mace (London, 1957); reprinted in *Collected Papers*, II, 350-72.

6. Ryle, "Are There Propositions?" *Proceedings of the Aristotelian Society* 30 (1930); reprinted in *Collected Papers*, II, 12-38.

7. Ryle, "Plato's 'Parmenides'," *Mind* 48 (1939); reprinted in *Collected Papers*, I, 1-44.

8. Ryle, "Ordinary Language," *Philosophical Review* 62 (1953); reprinted in *Collected Papers*, II, 301-18.

9. Ryle, "Thinking Thoughts and Having Concepts," *Logique et Analyse*, no. 20 (*Thinking & Meaning*, Entretiens d'Oxford, Organisées par l'Institut Internationale de Philosophie, Septembre, 1962), pp. 156-71; reprinted in *Collected Papers*, II, 446-50; the Findlay question is on p. 167 of the original.

10. Ryle, "Phenomenology versus 'The Concept of Mind'," in (French translation) La Philosophie Analytique, *Cahiers de Royaumont Philosophie* 4 (Paris, 1962): 65-84; English original text in *Collected Papers*, I, 179-96.

Ryle's Thoughts on Thinking

ZENO VENDLER

I

The daunting apparition of Rodin's *Le Penseur* seems to have haunted Gilbert Ryle in the last decade or so of his life. There he sits, unmoving and lost to the world. Yet he is by no means idle or inactive: he is thinking and, presumably, thinking weighty thoughts. No, he is not talking to himself; nor is it enough to say that he is thinking what he is doing—for what he is doing is just thinking and nothing else.

No wonder, then, that the author of *The Concept of Mind* should feel challenged by *The Thinker*. Man is a thinking thing, had said Ryle's great antagonist, and so long as that paradigm of thinking is not explained, the Ghost in the Machine is not yet slain, but only driven to its last line of defense.

It is to Ryle's credit that he saw and took up the challenge. Toward the end of his life he turned to the topic of thinking more and more often, till it became his main preoccupation: he wrote seven papers on this subject in the last ten years of his life.[1] These papers vary in rigor and polish, yet taken together they amount to the richest and most perceptive analysis of this central and specifically human activity to be found in recent literature.

Ryle sticks to his purpose: unlike many contemporaries, he does not try to cheat and pretend to account for the notion of thinking by adding some new pages to the enormous literature on belief, knowledge, and intention. When all is said about these states, the riddle of *The Thinker* has barely been approached. For that man, quietly sitting on his rock, is engaged in a sustained activity which he pursues with great concentration and intensity. It is this activity that interests Ryle and forms the subject of his inquiry:

> It is a vexatious fact about the English language that we use the verb 'to think' both for the beliefs and opinions that a man has, and for the pondering

and reflecting that a man does. . . . The problem which I wish to discuss are questions not about the propositions that a person does or might believe, but about his activities of pondering, perpending, musing, reflecting, calculating, meditating and so on.[2]

This notion of thinking is that of pondering or trying to solve a problem, not that of believing or feeling sure, which unfortunately goes by the same English name of 'Thinking'. I am interested in cogitation, not credence; in perplexity, not unperplexity.[3]

II

What does *The Concept of Mind* have to say about thinking? There is first the claim, borrowed from Plato, that thinking may be talking to oneself silently. This is Ryle's version:

> Much of our ordinary thinking is conducted in internal monologue or silent soliloquy, usually accompanied by an internal cinematograph show of visual imagery. This trick of talking to oneself in silence is acquired neither quickly nor without effort; and it is a necessary condition of our acquiring it that we should have previously learned to talk intelligently aloud and have heard and understood other people doing so. Keeping our thoughts to ourselves is a sophisticated accomplishment.[4]

It obviously follows that such thinking is conducted *in* a language, say, English or Chinese.

The attractiveness of this explanation for the author of *The Concept of Mind* is quite clear. As one can build a model, or play chess intelligently, one can also talk intelligently. The precondition, furthermore, of doing so is paying attention to the task on hand; in Ryle's favorite phrase "thinking what one is doing." This feature, as he correctly points out, is not something added to the overt performance. Doing something intelligently, thinking what one is doing, does not consist of two activities going on at the same time, but of one single activity performed in a certain manner, intelligently, attentively, or "thinkingly" if you like. There is no need, therefore, to invoke a ghost to ride tandem with the body, to provide the "inner" thought behind the "outer" event. Now if much of our thinking is but subvocal or suppressed speech, i.e., the kind of speech that cannot be perceived by other people, then this fact certainly does not add something to the performance; on the contrary, it takes something away from it: articulation, exercise of vocal chords, etc. It differs from ordinary talk in the nondoing of something rather than in the doing of something additional. Therefore, if ordinary talk, even very clever talk, can be accounted for without a hidden performance by the Cartesian ghost, so can be thinking, even of the most subtle variety.

"But", you ask, "is not that inner speech something heard or pronounced, i.e., privately experienced, in the subject's imagination?" No, answers Ryle, imagined experience is no experience at all, but unfulfilled expectation of experience:

We might say that imagining oneself talking or humming is a series of abstentions from producing the noises which would be the due words or notes to produce, if one were talking or humming aloud. . . . Silent soliloquy is a flow of pregnant non-sayings.[5]

And, by the same token, the "cinematograph-show of visual imagery," which often accompanies the silent soliloquy of thinking, is no experience either, but the systematic lack of it:

The expectations which are fulfilled in the recognition at sight of Helvellyn are not indeed fulfilled in picturing it, but the picturing of it is like a rehearsal of getting them fulfilled. So far from picturing involving the having of faint sensations, or wraiths of sensations, it involves missing just what one would be due to get, if one were seeing the mountain.[6]

So we are left with . . . what? Thinking, we are told, is often silent soliliquy plus visual imagery. But these things are series of negative things: nondoings and nonexperiencings. Are they then nothing? To anticipate, is *The Thinker* doing nothing after all? No, suggests Ryle, "Refraining from saying things, of course, entails knowing both what one would have said and how one would have said it,"[7] and "Seeing Helvellyn in one's mind's eye . . . does involve the thought of having a view of Helvellyn."[8]

Thus the notion of thinking—allegedly reduced to silent talk and imagery—reenters through the backdoor still untamed. For what is this "knowing what one would have said"? Is it a disposition, as Ryle's analysis of knowing would suggest? If so, then the process of thinking must consist, in part at least, in successive occurrences of certain dispositions—a peculiar result indeed in view of the fact that the distinction between occurrences and dispositions is a cornerstone of Ryle's whole theory.

And what about "the thought of having a view of Helvellyn"? This, too, looks like a mental occurrence, and not of the harmless variety either, such as the aches, twinges, and tickles Ryle graciously allows us to have in privacy. What has been gained then, for his enterprise, from the suggestion that some thinking consists in unvoiced talk and the play of the imagination, if these processes, in turn, have to be explained in terms of fleeting thoughts? If such thoughts have to be admitted anyway, then we may as well stick to the common sense view, according to which the process of thinking consists in moving from thought to thought. Trouble is that such fleeting thoughts, "occult episodes" as they are, do not fit well into the Rylean scheme of things.

Otherwise, *The Concept of Mind* remains strangely silent about thinking. At one point Ryle himself remarks on his avoidance of this term, and offers some excuses for the omission.[9] The dominant use he makes of the word is in the highly idiosyncratic phrase: "thinking what one is doing." Ryle seems to be obsessed with this idiom and tries to create the impression that it somehow captures the basic sense of *thinking*. Even in his later writings this paradigm looms large. And no wonder: once thinking is tied to the doing of *other* things, Ryle's ship is in for some smooth sailing. Unfortunately, the rock on which *The Thinker* sits lies straight ahead: what is *he* doing so "thinkingly" beside thinking itself? The *O.E.D* lists some seventeen senses of the verb *to think* but Ryle's preferred sense is not among them. And, incidentally, try to translate the phrase "thinking what one is doing" into another language . . . Ryle's key phrase is a petrified idiom. If it were not, then the dummy clause "what one is doing" could be cashed in for some real things. Just contrast it with live constructions of the same kind, e.g., "observing (monitoring, photographing, etc.) what one is doing." These generate: "observing (etc.) one's running, eating, skiing," and what have you. But is there such a thing as thinking one's skiing? Trying to account for thinking in terms of thinking what one is doing is about as hopeful an enterprise as explaining what seeing is in terms of seeing the guest home.

III

In his later and wiser years Ryle progressively revised his theory of thinking first proposed in *The Concept of Mind* and maintained in a few subsequent papers. In the first place he anandoned the view that thinking predominantly, or typically, consists in talking to oneself in silence, and, in the second place, he came to realize that one ordinarily does not think "in" words, or "in" any other vehicle of thought. These two "theoretical barnacles," as he called them,[10] are scraped away by reflecting on such exercises of thinking as occur in composing music, playing chess, fitting jigsaw puzzles together, and so forth. These, clearly, are cases of thinking, often on a fairly high level, yet the subject would not be able to articulate his thoughts in open speech. How, then, could he do so in his silent monologue?

It should be granted, however, that words do play an important role in people's thinking. There are such verbal tasks as writing a poem, formulating a speech, translating a text, and so forth, which require some pondering, search, trial and error, i.e., some thinking. But even here, the words represent the *materia circa quam* rather than the *medium in quo* of the process of thought. Is the translator thinking in English, or in German, when trying to translate a poem by Goethe into English verse? Ryle clearly sees that what we mean by saying that, e.g., a foreigner is now able to think in English is nothing more than this: he is able to express himself in English directly, i.e., without the necessity of first formulating what he wants to say in his native tongue and then translating it by some routine.

Thus Ryle realizes that the facile answer, "thinking is talking to oneself silently" will not do. And *The Thinker* seems to thwart any attempt to account for what he is engaged in in terms of "thinking what he is doing," since besides thinking he is not doing anything. What other avenues are still open to Ryle?

IV

One promising new idea is tied to the notion of "adverbial" verbs. Ryle notices that there are verbs that, as it were, do not shoulder the full burden of a verb by themselves. To put it simply, they do not tell us, as other verbs normally do, what the subject is doing, but rather they indicate the manner or circumstance of the action performed. You cannot, for instance, just hurry, obey, try, or start, as you can just eat, run, or sing.

Obviously Ryle's category catches verbs of quite disparate kinds. The very grammar of such "modal" verbs as *start, stop, resume,* and *try* shows their "adverbial" nature.[11] They are normally followed by the *V-ing* form of the main verb (if it is assumed that the action is, was, or will be actually going on) or by a *to V* construction (if no such supposition is made). Hence *started running* or *started to run* but not *resumed* or *stopped to run; tried to run,* but less likely *tried running;* and so forth. *Pretend, enjoy,* and *imagine* are in a related category: *pretend to do something,* but *enjoy doing something,* and not the other way around.

The other two verbs Ryle often mentions in this connection, *hurry* and *obey,* do not wear their adverbial credentials on their sleeves. Yet, semantically, their use clearly presupposes another verb, denoting an action performed in a certain manner (hastily), or in certain circumstances (in compliance with an order).

Ryle's attention is caught by these verbs for the following reason. The man who tries to run does not do two things, trying and running, but one thing, i.e., moving his legs in a certain way with the intention of running. And the soldier who slopes arms obeying his officer does not do "something else as well" in addition to sloping arms; only he does so after and in consequence of having received an order. Thus if *to think* (when it does not mean something like *to believe*) could be regarded as an adverbial verb, then, perhaps, *The Thinker's* activity would conceal no more mysteries than the soldier's in obediently sloping arms . . . Well, it is clearly such in Ryle's favored context, "thinking what one is doing." As we mentioned above, the man who works on his car thinking what he is doing need not indulge in two distinct activities, one performed by his hands, and the other going on "in his head." He does but one thing in a certain manner, i.e., with concentration and care.

But this analysis—as Ryle now clearly sees—will not work for *The Thinker:*

He is surely so meditating, reflecting, pondering or thinking that the report 'he is thinking' is *not* an unfinished adverbial report. . . . The telephone interrupts the typist's attentive and careful typing; but it interrupts *Le Penseur*'s attentive and careful thinking. I hope that the notion of thinking what one is doing provides letters of the alphabet out of which we shall be able to spell what *Le Penseur* is engaged in. But it does not provide much of that spelling.[12]

Whatever *The Thinker* is doing is not done carelessly, haphazardly, or while concentrating on some extraneous matter. This element of care and purpose which *thinking* seems to imply is, of course, the justification of Ryle's beloved phrase, "thinking what one is doing."

But what is *Le Penseur* doing with his wits about him that he might have done when vacant, frantic, dazed, sleepwalking . . . ? Here we have the adverbial verbs that we need, but we seem to be at a loss for the desiderated non-adverbial or autonomous verbs.[13]

Here is, once more, "the puzzling element in the notion of thinking" he had reflected on before.[14] What is the autonomous verb that *thinking* modifies, or rather what is the proper activity which the thinker is supposed to be pursuing with attention and care? "No singing without noises, no testimonial-writing without ink-marks, no thinking without . . . " what?[15] It is exactly this need for an autonomous activity which was supposed to be satisfied by the now rejected "talking to oneself in silence."

At any rate, what *The Thinker* is doing is not something manifested in his outward behavior. His "thinking" is not related adverbially to his sitting on the rock, resting his chin on his fist, etc. He is "absorbed" in his thinking, "detached" from his environment. In one paper Ryle, admittedly "with a great deal of arbitrariness and imprecision,"[16] uses the term *reflecting* for this kind of "disengaged" thinking. To give a name to what *The Thinker* is doing, however, does not solve the problem on hand. All right—one might say—he is surely not playing ball or counting daisies; he is reflecting, and with care and devotion at that; but what exactly does his reflecting consist in?

V

At this point Ryle casts another look at the idea of adverbial verbs. He notices that in many, perhaps most, cases an adverbial factor is already built into the meaning of a verb. That is to say, the verb does not merely specify the "basic action" the agent is performing, but adds some other features regarding the manner and the circumstances. Consider the simple example of *winking*.[17] Although winking consists in the momentary shutting of one eye, not all such events are winkings. What is missing in these cases? What else should the prospective winker do to complete his winking? Nothing else, of course. But the intention and the circumstances must be right . . . So people who think that winking is nothing but the shutting of one eye (the "reductionists") are as wrong as the people who think that winking is that plus something else (the "dualists"). Ryle's view—no doubt a correct view—is that what an agent is doing can be described on various levels, or, as he puts it, by means of descriptions of various "thickness": "he momentarily closed his right eye" (thin description); "he winked" (thicker description); "he gave a wink of understanding to his girlfriend" (thick description). Levels of adverbiality may form a pyramid.[18]

Other examples could be given *ad nauseam.* Ryle mentions translating, rehearsing, shamming, mimicking, and so forth.[19] We may add Austin's theory of speech-acts: what the speaker is doing in uttering certain sounds may be described on the locutionary, illocutionary, and perlocutionary levels. If the felicity conditions are right, the speaker's mere utterance will be a warning, a promise, or an order without his doing anything additional.

Now the interesting thing, from Ryle's point of view, is the following. In many cases it is the adverbiality, rather than the basic action, that is dominant in the meaning of a "thick description" verb. Think of the many ways a parent can warn a child to stay away from the cookie jar. Or of the Rylean example: *rehearsing*. What—one might ask—is a typical act of rehearsing? How can I tell, by simply looking at him, whether a person is rehearsing or not? These are silly questions. The man can be singing, dancing, declaiming, walking up and down, kissing a girl, snoring, what have you. All these may be rehearsing if the setup and the intention are right.

"No rehearsing without . . . what?" And we recall: "No thinking without . . . what?" We have reached the end of Ryle's progress: his answer is that this too is a silly question. *Thinking*, to him, is a highly adverbial verb, so that there is no one basic action which would be required for someone to be thinking. He may be just running through the multiples of seven, translating a poem, pondering over a chess puzzle, planning an escape, trying to remember a tune, or to understand a Kantian argument. But, of course, these tasks too can be broken down into more basic episodes. These may involve saying words under one's breath, picturing the chessboard or the prison yard, running through tunes "in one's head," recalling a page, and so forth.

If these things are carried out on purpose, with some concentration and care, then the person is thinking. Much of these activities will be pursued in the "detached" or "disengaged" manner mentioned above. Yet the chessplayer may think about his next move in front of a real chessboard, the painter may stare at a real canvas while planning his picture, and the composer may run his fingers over an actual keyboard in creating his work: the process of thinking may employ the actual and the imaginary with equal ease. From this point of view Ryle's old favorite, the man who goes about his ordinary business "thinking what he is doing," and the "lost to the world" thinker of Rodin appear as the extremes of the very same spectrum.

With dramatic flair Ryle creates a scenario of eight "thinkers," each sitting on a rock, who indulge in activities more and more detached, purposeful, and original—from a mere observer of the scene to the real *Le Penseur*, the man, that is, whose activities are not occasioned by external circumstances and not aimed at future use, but are freely pursued for their own sake: the kind of thinking Rodin, and Aristotle for that matter, must have had in mind.[20]

Quite obviously "saying things to oneself" is likely to figure prominently in the "thin description" of such intellectual and creative thinking. Thus Ryle returns to the Platonic paradigm, but puts it in a new perspective:

> Thinking, then, can be saying-things-tentatively-to-oneself with the specific heuristic intention of trying, by saying them, to open one's own eyes, to consolidate one's own grasp, or to get oneself out of a rut.[21]

But, of course, it *can* be many other things.

VI

Ryle's account is comprehensive, ingenious, and, as far as it goes, intuitively correct. Yet—the same intuition prompts us to say—it does not go far enough. Let us, once more, have a look at Rodin's masterpiece. How come a posture like that is chosen to represent a thinker? Why not a man walking on the beach or working on a car? The reason is obvious. Rodin's man, outwardly, is in a state of sustained rest (one is unlikely to assume that position just for a moment); yet his face is not that of an idler: it shows an expression of utmost concentration. Concentration on what?—he is not doing anything. On thinking, of course, which is not something that is supposed to appear in outward demeanor. This is Rodin's "trick": he draws our attention from what we see to what we cannot see; from a body at rest to a mind in travail.

Thinking, paradigmatically, is an inner process, an activity manifest only to the subject. Ryle, starting out from the behavioristic framework of *The Concept of Mind*, tried to approach *The Thinker* by means of another paradigm: the man in action "thinking what he is doing." True, Rodin's challenge forced him to admit more and more of inner events: imaginings, subvocal talk, and the like. Not to speak of the thinker's intentions which guide the progress of his moves, and of which he must be aware himself. Remember the simple example of winking: mere physical act (shutting of the eye) and the right circumstances (girlfriend looking at you) are not enough without a free and conscious intention to wink. Yet in this case that intention may be gathered by an onlooker by observing the "fine shades" of the subject's behavior. Not so with the intentions guiding the process of thinking: they are entirely private and unobservable. *The Thinker* may change the course of his thoughts at will without any change in his posture or expression.

Rodin's lesson is this: thinking, pure and simple, is a mental activity of a certain kind, i.e., an activity consisting of subjective events and processes. About the nature of these occurrences Ryle may be right: their "thin description" may list imaginings, subvocal talk, and so forth. He is also right about their purposeful arrangement; yet we must not forget about compulsive thoughts, fleeting thoughts, ideas that suddenly strike us, and so forth.

Ryle is also correct in focussing our attention to instances of thinking in which the process spills over, as it were, into the physical world: e.g., the thinking of writers, composers, chess players, and so forth. But even in these cases the accent is on the inner events. Routine performances, even if they are very apt and intelligent, do not amount to thinking: masters of a skill do many things "without thinking" which would cost the common mortal a great deal of thought.

And what about the man who goes about his business "thinking what he is doing"? I agree, he need not be actually engaged in a thought process bearing upon his task, for he may be an expert practitioner. At any rate, from our less-skilled perspective, it looks as if his performance were ruled by conscious thought.

Ryle, for obvious reasons, could never quite overcome his obsession with the unimportant and idiosyncratic phrase "thinking what one is doing." Yet he makes an admirable effort to understand and explain what *The Thinker* is doing: he discovers many things about the grammar of some key words and exposes some crucial features of the notion of thinking. Yet his effort is wrongheaded: he starts out from a false paradigm. In this case the artist beats the philosopher. Rodin's *Le Penseur* in his visible immobility draws our attention to the invisible, essentially private, and subjective nature of thinking, which in Ryle's scheme of things appears peripheral and admitted on sufferance.

Notes

1. "Thinking and Reflecting" (1966-67), "The Thinking of Thoughts, What Is 'Le Penseur' Doing?" (1968), both in *Collected Papers*, vol. II (London, 1971); "Adverbial Verbs and Verbs of Thinking," "Thought and Soliloquy," "Thought and Imagination," "Thinking and Self-Teaching" (1972), "Thinking and Saying" (1972) in *Gilbert Ryle on Thinking*, ed. K. Kolenda (Oxford, 1979).
2. *Collected Papers*, II, p. 392.
3. *On Thinking*, p. 84.
4. *The Concept of Mind* (New York, 1949), p. 27.
5. *Ibid.*, p. 269.
6. *Ibid.*, p. 270.
7. *Ibid.*, pp. 269-70.
8. *Ibid.*, p. 270.
9. *Ibid.*, p. 185.
10. *On Thinking*, p. 34.
11. *Ibid.*, p. 21.
12. *Ibid.*, p. 24.
13. *Ibid.*
14. "A Puzzling Element in the Notion of Thinking," *Collected Papers*, II, pp. 391-406.
15. *Collected Papers*, II, p. 399.
16. *Ibid.*, p. 466.
17. *Ibid.*, p. 485.
18. *On Thinking*, p. 28.
19. *Collected Papers*, II, p. 485.
20. *Ibid.*, II, pp. 488-96.
21. *On Thinking*, p. 92.

Austin's Theory of Illocutionary Force

GRAHAM BIRD

So-called ordinary language philosophy produced a number of suggestive insights into the working of natural language. Among the best known and most durable of these insights were Strawson's account of presupposition, Ryle's notion of an achievement verb, and Austin's treatment of force. Of these, it was Austin's topic which received the most elaborate discussion from its author as well as the most extensive criticism. Indeed Austin's account has formed a point of departure for innumerable later discussions by Strawson, Searle, Schiffer, Holdcroft, Katz, and most recently Bach and Harnish.[1] It is the aim of this paper to consider how far Austin's treatment still offers at least the outline of a useful theory of force. I shall examine, somewhat selectively, some radical objections to his theory and consider the implications for his theory of some later developments which he could not have taken into account.

I

In order to examine objections to Austin's account it is plainly necessary to say what that account is. But it is well known that Austin's views developed from the original 'special' theory of performative utterance to a 'general' theory of illocutionary force.[2] One objection to his views is that the move to a more general theory was either ill-motivated or a mistake. Since I wish to concentrate on the general theory, it is necessary to consider this problem before outlining the central elements in that account of illocutionary force.

Both Urmson and Warnock,[3] for example, take the view that the original (Mark I) performative, governed by such things as legal rules or the rules of particular games, is so different from the (Mark II) explicit performative or the (Mark III) primary performative that it would be wrong to subsume all three under one general theory. The central argument they employ is that since Mark I performatives are governed by non-linguistic rules they cannot properly figure in a linguistic

345

theory of force, and cannot be likened to other performatives (especially Mark II performatives) that are essentially linguistic. Cohen, too, agrees with these critics that Austin failed to separate the strictly linguistic aspects of his theory from its non-linguistic aspects, and he seems to agree that the Mark I performative should be excluded from a linguistic theory.[4] Katz also separates Austin's original distinction between performative and constative utterances from the later more general theory.[5] But since his understanding of the original distinction differs from that of Warnock and Urmson, and since anyway he claims to vindicate Austin's distinction by including it in a genuinely linguistic theory, it is to the criticism of Warnock and Urmson that I turn.

First it should be noted that although Warnock and Urmson agree on the premise that Mark I performatives are non-linguistic and quite different from Mark II or Mark III varieties, they nevertheless disagree on the conclusions to be drawn from this premise. Whereas Warnock is content to stress the dangers of assimilating the disparate cases to one general type, Urmson believes that the assimilation is simply a mistake. He says:

> I think that Austin's later attempt to subsume the theory of performatives under a general theory of illocutionary force was a mistake. The theory of illocutionary forces may well be important in the elucidation of speech acts but performatives should not be classed as speech acts.[6]

It is clear that Warnock's weaker conclusion need not damage Austin's general theory at all. Even if it is true that there are dangers in the proposed assimilation, it does not follow that we have to succumb to them. Even if it is true that Austin's generalizing move was not forced on him, as he perhaps believed, this still leaves quite open the question whether that move is beneficial, as Austin no doubt also believed. The crucial argument, then, is Urmson's in which from the premise that at least Mark I performatives are non-linguistic it is inferred that the assimilation of these to the other Marks must be a mistake. I shall attempt to rebut this argument by showing that the premise shared by Urmson and Warnock is ambiguous and that in the sense in which the premise is true it simply does not follow that the proposed assimilation is mistaken. The criticism of Austin, if I am right, rests simply on a fallacy of equivocation.

Of course in one way it is undeniable that a statutory provision in the law, or a rule of some game, that invests an utterance with some specific 'operative' force is non-linguistic. We regard it as a rule of bridge that the utterance 'Three no trumps' in a suitable context has the force of a bid, and we do not regard the rules of bridge simply as rules of language. But what it evidently means to call the rules of bridge non-linguistic is simply that they are not co-extensive with the rules that govern a natural language, even when the rules of the game are themselves written in that language. Hence to describe one of the rules of bridge as non-linguistic is, so far, to say no more than that it belongs to a set of rules not co-extensive with some set of rules from any language. But it evidently does not follow from this that any such particular rule itself cannot be regarded as linguistic, that is, as also belonging to a set of rules of some language. For there is no reason whatever in the argument to suppose that a rule belonging to one set cannot belong to another set as well. There is indeed no good reason to think that rules belong exclusively to just one set. So the fallacy in the argument is that it infers from the correct claim that such rules belong to a non-linguistic set to the conclusion that they cannot therefore belong also to some linguistic set. Moreover it is quite easy to illustrate rules that may belong to non-linguistic and to linguistic sets of rules. Any legal definition of the meaning of a term will belong both to a non-linguistic set of legal rules and to a set of rules defining the meaning of words in some natural language.

Such an illustration may provoke two natural but mistaken rejoinders. First, it may be said that the example works only because it concerns the meaning of terms, whereas the argument in Urmson and Warnock concerns not the meaning but the force of certain utterances. Certainly the substance of the claim is correct, but the original argument itself drew no such distinction between different aspects of language. Nor, indeed, could it have done so without begging the question. For what is at issue is precisely whether rules governing the force of utterances should be counted as linguistic. Merely to assume that meaning-rules are linguistic but force-rules are not is to assume just what is at issue in the argument.

Second, it may be denied that the legal rules defining the meaning of legal terms belong properly to the rules of a natural language. For it may be thought that such technical terms and their meanings are not part of the natural language in which they are expressed. I find it hard to understand how such a view could seriously be maintained, but it is not hard to find within 'ordinary language' philosophy a strand of thought that encourages such a view. For it was a discreditable part of ordinary language philosophy to restrict a philosophical interest in language to what was called 'ordinary' language, that is, a part of natural language that excludes technical vocabularies. However, such a position does not entail the claim that natural language itself excludes such technical vocabularies, simply because 'ordinary' language is not identifiable with any natural language.

Both Urmson and Warnock offer a number of supporting illustrations of their conclusion, but none of them seem at all convincing. They tend to say such things as: To understand the force of 'Three no trumps' in bridge one has to understand not only English but also the rules of bridge.[7] Or that if someone wants to get married in Turkey, then he has to ask initially: How do I get married in Turkey? and not: How do I get married in Turkish?[8] Or that if I know the Turkish for 'I warn you . . . ', then I can warn Turks, but even if I know the Turkish for 'I name this ship . . . ', it does not follow that I know how to name ships in Turkey.[9] The first of these points seems to assume that the rules of bridge and those of English simply exclude one another, and this has been already denied. The second is hard to assess because Urmson is not claiming that it is impossible to ask: How do I get married in Turkish? but only that this is not a question that such a person would *initially* ask. And the third point is similarly inconclusive not the least because it is by no means obvious that knowing how to translate 'I warn you . . . ' into Turkish enables one to warn Turks. Even in English the prefix 'I warn you . . . ' is more commonly used to threaten rather than to warn. More generally it might be suggested that knowing the Turkish for some English expression with characteristic performative force, such as an explicit performative, may involve translation into a Turkish expression with that force, if there is one. And that might seem to suggest a close relation between force and linguistic rules rather than a divorce between them.

II

If those arguments against Austin's attempt to provide a general theory of illocutionary force are inconclusive, then it is reasonable to consider what that general theory amounts to. I shall pick out three general features of such theory, all of which have been severely criticized. These features present what is admittedly no more than a skeleton of the full account offered in *How to Do Things with Words*, but it is not my intention to examine, much less to justify, all the detail of Austin's theory. The three features I shall pick out are, however, quite central to his account, and if the criticisms made of them were justified then there would be no merit in the theory at all.

(1) The first feature of an essentially Austinian theory is the distinction to be drawn between locutionary acts and illocutionary acts. The distinction can be explained partly by saying that the former have to do with meaning, whereas the latter have to do with force. This way of putting the point at least indicates a further metalinguistic division which Austin associates with the basic contrast. For the suggestion is that the two kinds of act, and the characteristic features that define them, require distinct branches of linguistic theory to accommodate them. The first branch, concerned with meaning, or what Austin unclearly calls 'sense' and 'reference', might be labeled 'semantics'; and the second branch, dealing with illocutionary force, might be labeled 'pragmatics'. These labels, together with the basic distinction, serve only to indicate the aims of such a theory rather than to demonstrate how the divisions are to be drawn. Austin himself underlined the problems in drawing such distinctions. According to him locutionary and illocutionary acts are 'abstractions' from the 'total speech act'.[10] They are, moreover, abstractions with a peculiarly intimate relationship, so that to perform a locutionary act is in general to perform an illocutionary act, and to perform an illocutionary act is necessarily to perform a locutionary act.[11] These claims have led critics to suggest variously that no such distinction can be drawn, or that Austin's distinction is one without a difference, or at least that even as abstractions the two kinds of act can never be clearly separated because in one case, the (Mark II) explicit performative, the two features coalesce.

(2) Illocutionary acts are also to be further contrasted with perlocutionary acts. This division, too, is associated with another metalinguistic contrast, namely that between what properly belongs to linguistic theory and what lies outside such a theory. It is well known that Austin tried hard to draw a clear line between these acts in *How to Do Things with Words*, but was dissatisfied with the result. Some

critics have suggested not only that Austin failed to draw such a distinction, but that there is no such distinction to be drawn. It has also been suggested that the associated contrast between what belongs to a linguistic theory and what does not is seriously misplaced. Cohen, for example, holds that apart from the 'semantic force' belonging to explicit performatives the remainder of what Austin regarded as illocutionary force should be excluded from a genuinely linguistic theory.[12]

(3) Once the distinctions outlined in (1) and (2) have been drawn, the main concern of a theory of illocutionary force must be to explain how such force is determined. In *How to Do Things with Words* Austin seems, not unnaturally, more concerned with the basic contrasts than with a systematic attempt to resolve this issue. He offers some such accounts rather incidentally in particular illustrative examples, but his more general references to the determining factors of illocutionary force have also been criticized. For on one side Austin tends to claim that just as sense and reference are governed by conventions of meaning, so illocutionary force is determined by force conventions. Although he is notably cautious in his overt appeal to such conventions of force, he does persist in this general belief. On the other side, however, he also tends to stress certain contextual features in the utterance of sentences as determining the illocutionary force of those utterances. His notion of a 'felicity condition' seems in part designed to identify such features, among which he would include such things as the speaker's intentions. Now it would not be a strong objection to his theory that in giving an account of the way in which illocutionary force is determined Austin had simply left the account incomplete. It would, however, be a more serious criticism to suggest that there is some conflict between an appeal to conventions and an appeal to intentions; or to suggest that the idea of a force convention is itself somehow objectionable. Urmson, for example, in the article already considered would be willing to allow force conventions to determine Mark I performatives, but only at the cost of denying that such conventions were linguistic. Other critics have tended to draw a contrast between forces that are determined by convention and those that are determined by the intentions of the speaker.

These items present only the most general outline of an Austinian theory and omit much of the detail provided by Austin. But Austin himself seemed prepared to admit that the account finally given in *How to Do Things with Words* was a good deal less than a fully developed theory. It is inevitable that his account should have left out some aspects of language and some topics that were extensively discussed only after he had produced his account. It has, for example, been pointed out that his appeals to grammar might usefully have been supplemented by the apparatus of the transformational grammarians,[13] and it has been claimed that his own outline theory makes no room for a distinction between 'mood' and 'force'.[14] By themselves such omissions have little significance, for what is at issue is not whether Austin omitted such considerations but whether his theory could make room for them. I shall attempt to consider some such cases at the end of this paper, but the main focus of attention will be on the three features already listed and the criticisms that have been made of them.

III

The central aspect of both Searle's and Cohen's objections to the Austinian distinction between locutionary and illocutionary acts is that they cannot generally be separated. Characteristic expressions of this central point are:

> Austin's distinction cannot be completely general in the sense of marking off two mutually exclusive classes of acts,[15]

and:

> When you say 'I protest' you are not describing your protest nor reporting it. You are just protesting. . . . The meaning lies solely in the making of the protest.[16]

These claims have been taken up by many other commentators and expressed by saying that in at least one case, namely that of the explicit performative, the locutionary meaning simply exhausts the illocutionary force.

But it has to be noted initially that common though such claims are, they remain fundamentally unclear. Searle's own arguments for his position, for example, suffer from certain rarely noticed defects of presentation. First, the general conclusion quoted above is on one interpretation quite consistent with Austin's view. Austin held, as Searle admits, that the locutionary and illocutionary features of acts of utterance are abstractions from the total speech act. He evidently did not intend to present the distinction as one between two distinct, or exclusive, acts identifiable in successive stages of utterance. Second, Searle employs various models to illustrate Austin's position, but at some points these models are strictly inconsistent with what he identifies as that position. Thus he agrees with Austin that

> the concept of an utterance with a certain meaning is indeed a different concept from the concept of an utterance with a certain force.[17]

But he then goes on to explain the difficulty Austin has in separating these by saying,

> For cases such as the performative use of illocutionary verbs the attempt to abstract the locutionary meaning from the illocutionary force would be like abstracting unmarried men from bachelors.[18]

But if the two *concepts* are distinct, then the attempted abstraction could not be of this kind, since the concepts of an unmarried man and of a bachelor are held to be identical. On other occasions Searle illustrates the relationship differently by using the model relationship between being a terrier and being a dog,[19] but it might be questioned whether this is any more appropriate. What Searle's arguments show is the need to explain how Austin himself understood this relationship, especially when he put it in the two cryptic remarks,

> To perform an illocutionary act is necessarily to perform a locutionary act, . . . To perform a locutionary act is in general and eo ipso to perform an illocutionary act.[20]

For these two claims may be read as blurring, or even eliminating, any real distinction between locutionary meaning and illocutionary force.

Cohen's position, too, suffers from similar problems. He, rightly, takes Austin to task for not having adequately explained his notions of sense and reference, which together make up his conception of meaning. But he then attributes to Austin a Fregean account of sense and reference which is blatantly at odds with the few passages in which Austin does offer some explanation of his use of these terms.[21] Moreover the challenge, on which Cohen rests his case, to indicate a meaning for an explicit performative prefix without appealing to its force is open to some objections. In order to make sense of such a challenge presumably some prior account of meaning needs to be given, so that the prefix can be shown to lack any such features. Of course, such an outcome will be very difficult to achieve since it is scarcely controversial that such prefixes have just the same referential features as non-performative utterances in the first person present indicative. But more serious is the difficulty that without some such prior account of meaning it is at least possible that in claiming performative force to be, or be part of, meaning in such cases Cohen is appealing to no more than an intuitive conception of meaning in which we ordinarily allow that to understand, or misunderstand, the force of some utterance is to understand, or misunderstand, part of what was meant. Austin himself, of course, recognized that when we speak casually of what some utterance meant we may refer to force rather than to sense or reference. He thought, however, that we should replace such an undiscriminating usage with his own explicit contrast between force and meaning. This, then, must make it doubtful what is the substance of any disagreement between Austin and Cohen at this point.

Just as in the earlier case of Searle's comments, however, it is possible to give some substance to the disagreement by offering some independent account of locutionary meaning. For it might be said that locutionary meaning can be accounted for, at least in the standard case of declarative sentences, in terms of the truth-conditions of such sentences. Then the issue whether in the case of explicit performative sentences their meaning exhausts their force can be understood in terms of the claim that the truth-conditions for such sentences adequately explain their performative force. It seems doubtful that Cohen himself understood his challenge in this way, but so understood at least the challenge has a substance which it otherwise lacks. For it offers a clear test for the claim that in the case of the explicit performative locutionary meaning and illocutionary force coalesce.

(I) The relationship between Locutionary and Illocutionary Acts

How should we understand Austin's two claims

(a) All illocutionary acts are necessarily locutionary, and

(b) All illocutionary acts are in general and eo ipso illocutionary acts?

First, it should be noted that in Austin's terms (a) expresses some necessity, whereas (b) does not. But which necessity does (a) express? There are plainly two main candidates, though they are generally not separated. Claim (a) might mean

(a′) any act described by an illocutionary verb is such that it can be performed only by means of uttering a locution characteristically having some meaning.

Or it might mean

(a″) any act described by an illocutionary verb is such that it cannot be described as an illocutionary act unless it has been performed by means of uttering a locution characteristically having some meaning.

Although these elaborations may appear complex, their difference can be simply illustrated. What (a′) says of acts described by an illocutionary verb such as 'warn' is that they can be performed only by uttering a locution. Such a claim is simply false of such acts, for it is evidently quite possible to warn someone or something without uttering an expression of any language. What (a″) says of such acts is that, whether or not they can be performed non-linguistically, at least they do not qualify for the title 'illocutionary' warning unless they have been performed by using some linguistic expression. Searle and Alston tend to accept (a′)[22] at least for certain illocutionary acts, but it is surely clear from Austin's own examples of illocutionary descriptions being applied to non-linguistic performances that he could not have accepted (a′) as a general claim.

It seems, then, that Austin's claim (a) should be understood in terms of (a″), which serves primarily to delimit an interest in illocutionary descriptions that are applied to linguistic performances. Perhaps if he had been interested, as Grice seems to have been, in the pre-linguistic conditions that provide a basis for linguistic performance, he might have modified (a″), but it seems likely that this was not his principal concern. However, even (a″) might be thought to be open to one obvious objection, namely that it may appear to exclude the possibility of performing illocutionary acts with expressions having no independent sense or reference. It seemed to be part of Cohen's complaint that for Austin illocutionary acts have to employ expressions with a sense or reference, and yet with explicit performatives there was no evident locutionary meaning other than the illocutionary force itself. Certainly it is easy to find expressions, like the conventional greetings 'Hi' or 'Hello', that have a standard utterance force but no obvious independent sense or reference. Strictly understood, however, (a″) surely does not exclude such possibilities. For locutionary acts are identified not only in terms of locutionary meaning but also in terms of the phonetic and phatic features that Austin listed. Among these is the feature of simply belonging to the vocabulary of some natural language, and such a feature plainly belongs both to expressions like 'Hello' and to expressions that normally make up the explicit performative form. For this reason, (a″) was formulated in terms of the characteristic, rather than necessary, possession of sense and reference by locutions. Claim (a″) requires only that illocutionary acts employ expressions of a language, and it may be that some expressions owe their inclusion not to their possession of an independent sense or reference but to their standard illocutionary force.

Claim (b) seems less germane to the issue once claim (a)'s necessity has been explored. For (b) seems not to canvass any necessity at all. Austin's point amounts to no more than the claim that generally, in serious discourse, locutionary acts are performed for some illocutionary reason, and this can scarcely be denied. The question might, of course, be raised whether it would be possible for discourse to arise in which no such illocutionary descriptions of utterances were available. Certain metaphorical accounts of language in which its semantic features are likened to formal aspects of a game such as chess and its pragmatic features correspond to the players' aim, i.e., to win or not to lose the game, may suggest that claim (b) might express more than just a contingent aspect of language.[23] But the issue is by no means clear. Perhaps it is barely possible to conceive of a use for language in bare soliloquy or private recitation, a kind of analogue in discourse to the traditional entertaining of a proposition, which might reveal an exception to (b). But there is no sign that Austin wished to pursue any such issue.

With such accounts of (a) and (b) there seems to be no case to answer with regard to the blurring or identification of Austin's contrasted aspects of language. Claims (a) and (b), so understood, can be held consistently with the view that locutionary and illocutionary aspects of utterance are distinct. Moreover, the account offered of these claims shows also the inadequacy of Searle's weaker model, in which locutionary acts stand to illocutionary acts as terriers stand to dogs. For that model implies that (b) expresses a conceptual necessity, whereas it is only (a) that strictly does so.

(II) The Explicit Performative

However, even if claims (a) and (b) are consistent with a distinction between locutions and illocutions, they do not concern the one case in which the two acts have been thought to overlap or coalesce. The belief that in the case of the explicit performative locutionary meaning exhausts illocutionary force has also been held to impugn Austin's original distinction, even though without some independent account of meaning and force the belief remains obscure. It may be said, for example, that in an utterance like 'I protest' the pronoun has its conventional reference and the verb its conventional sense, but that neither of these features yet tells us whether the utterance was an explicit performative. But then it will be replied that the introduction of 'hereby' into the sentence will resolve the difficulty, until we find cases in which such a sentence may be used actually to describe a protest independent of but simultaneous with the utterance itself.[24] There are serious and important problems even in this obscure area, for example, the problem of evaluating a suggestion that sense and reference should be allocated primarily, though not uniquely, to sentences and force allocated primarily, though not uniquely, to utterances. But I shall circumvent these issues by taking it that the sense of explicit performative utterances might be explained in terms of their truth-conditions and that those truth-conditions might adequately account for their performative force.

That latter view has indeed, in recent years, become something of an orthodoxy, although its adherents still interpret the claim in different ways. Sometimes it is regarded as obvious that explicit performatives have a truth-value and so also have truth-conditions in principle;[25] sometimes it is admitted that the ascription of a truth-value to explicit performatives is artificial, even though justified on grounds of theoretical economy.[26] Very few philosophers now take the view that Austin was simply right to deny these performatives a truth-valuation, and even those, like Katz, who agree with Austin succeed rather in embarrassing the opposition than in firmly establishing their own view as correct.[27] It has been known for some time that the philosophical arguments for and against a truth-valuation are inconclusive,[28] and I shall consider instead the following question: if we give explicit performatives a truth-value, will their truth-conditions adequately capture their performative force?

If we allow that such performatives have a truth-value at all, it may seem to follow directly that an understanding of their truth-conditions is an understanding of their force. For to use a verb as an explicit performative is to utter a claim that names the illocutionary act performed in the utterance itself, if indeed the utterance is successful. And it seems to follow from such an account that the utterance will qualify as an illocutionary act of the requisite kind if and only if the claim made in the utterance is true. Evidently such an idea requires us to identify the success of an utterance with its truth, but once such utterances are seen as claims that may be true or false, it will seem difficult to separate that truth or falsity from the respective success or failure of the illocutionary act.

It has been suggested, however, that the truth-valuation of such performatives is different in some respects from that for other kinds of declarative sentences. For any declarative sentence we might express a truth-relation of the following kind,

(A) The state of affairs that (utterance of) S says obtains *does* obtain iff S is true.

Similarly, for any such declarative sentence that refers to the performance of some act, we could write,

(B) The act that (utterance of) S says is performed *is* performed iff S is true.

But (B) will hold just as much for sentences like

(1) Keegan kicked the ball

as for the explicit performative sentence

(2) I hereby promise to reform.

It might be said, then, that without further elaboration the truth-relation expressed in (B) fails to capture the performative element in (2). So far as it goes, this is true, but what it suggests is not that explicit performative force totally resists capture in terms of truth-conditions, but that a further elaboration is needed. Consider sentences like

(3) I am now singing

or

(4) I am speaking English.

It has often been suggested that such sentences have a special 'reflexive' character, in which their truth or falsity depends essentially upon their utterance, at least in appropriate circumstances. It would certainly be wrong to say that their truth or falsity depends solely upon their utterance,[29] but the suggestion is that unlike most declarative utterances the utterance itself is the subject of the claim and so forms an essential part of the truth-conditions. As we shall see, the idea of 'appropriate conditions' needs closer scrutiny, and it is evident that these will differ in (3) and (4). But the special feature of these sentences could be brought out by formulating the following generalized truth-relation

(C) The act that (utterance of) S says is performed in uttering S *is* performed in uttering S iff S is true.

(C), like (A) and (B), is simply a tautology, but it contains features that distinguish the truth-conditions for such sentences as (3) and (4) from those for (1). For (C) differs from (A) and (B) in its ability to capture an additional feature of such tautological relationships, namely, that the performance which the utterance of S says is performed is carried out in the utterance of S itself. (3) and (4) have that self-referring, or reflexive, character which, it is claimed, belongs also to explicit performatives such as (2). But (3) and (4), though they have this feature, are still not themselves explicit performatives, so it is difficult to evaluate the conclusion drawn from such an analysis that truth-conditions for explicit performatives adequately capture, or exhaust, their force. On one side it will be said that since (C) holds for such utterances, their truth or falsity will simply determine respectively the performance, or non-performance, of the relevant illocutionary act. But on the other side it will be said that since (3) and (4) are not themselves explicit performatives, some further elaboration on (C) is necessary, though it remains quite unclear what the nature of such an elaboration might be.

The apparent inconclusiveness of the debate at this point can be reinforced in at least the following two ways, concerning first the nature and second the extent of such an overlap between truth-conditions and force. For the proposal to fit explicit performatives into a truth-conditional semantics is at present no more than a general goal without clear detail. Truth-conditional semantics still faces unsolved problems with respect to standard constative utterances, but it remains in any case unclear which elements will be necessary for such an account of explicit performatives. Cresswell, in offering a 'possible worlds' account of explicit orders, concedes that his schematic account is 'terribly crude'.[30] It remains unclear, for example, whether a distinction could be made within such a framework between felicity and truth-conditions, or whether the latter would have to make reference to the speakers' intentions, the audience's understanding, or other aspects of the context bearing on the successful performance of the illocutionary act. Indeed, if such items as these have a bearing on the success of the performance, then by virtue of (C) it seems that they must be included in a truth-conditional account. What we would then have would be not so much an independent theory of truth-conditions which renders unnecessary any further treatment of explicit force, but rather the intrusion into a truth-conditional presentation of these elements from a standard account of force.

A similar point can be made in relation to the extent of such an overlap. Consider, for example, the evident differences between explicit performatives expressed by

(5) I declare Jonas IV to be King of Ruritania

when it is uttered (a) in response to a question about the present king on a quiz program or (b) at the crucial moment of Jonas's coronation. These variations, of course, by no means exhaust such differences which may arise among, say, declarations of war, or love, or closure of an innings, and so on. Both (5a) and (5b) are explicit performatives, but they are plainly not the *same* explicit performative. Should we take the view that a truth-conditional account would differentiate between these cases? Or should we take the view, endorsed by Bierwisch,[31] that since the verb 'declare' is not ambiguous in these distinct uses, a truth-conditional account should be restricted to some common 'core' element in declarations which would then need to be differentiated by other means. Bierwisch's view, which he puts by saying that

> what is needed for a full analysis of explicit performatives is nothing but a truth-theoretical structure and a theory of social interaction providing interactional settings and communicative senses,[32]

at least indicates a further and quite severe restriction on the overlap of truth-conditions and force. Not all aspects even of explicit performatives will be included in the truth-conditional theory.

It seems that the primary motive for wishing to present an account of explicit performatives within a larger truth-conditional theory must be simple economy. Austin and Katz are surely right to claim that the ascription of truth or falsity to explicit performatives is at least artificial even if no more decisive objection can be leveled against it.[33] But to put the point in this way is to appeal only to the belief that such performatives may be represented as true or false and that there are benefits in so representing them. Such a presentation at least acknowledges the similarities between explicit performatives and other constative utterances, as Ginet rightly observes.[34] But that motive is double-edged. For we might insist that any adequate theory of language should represent also the other similarities that exist between explicit performatives and primary performatives. Indeed, if what has been said here is correct, even a truth-conditional representation of the explicit performative, however restricted or enlarged, will indicate such a similarity by including among the truth-conditions those features which characteristically determine illocutionary force, but not truth or falsity, in the primary performative.

Austin's tripartite division between locutions, illocutions, and perlocutions cannot remain quite unchanged after such a discussion. But the change in outlook that such considerations bring does not show that Austin's division is mistaken. What is shown is that there can be no sharp, exclusive line between locution and illocution, even though these two aspects of utterance remain in principle distinct. If it is accepted at all that explicit performatives can be represented as having truth-values, then it is at least pointless to separate meaning and force in the one case of the explicit performative. Locutionary meaning can be represented without illocutionary force in the case of straightforward constative utterance, and illocutionary force can be represented independently of truth or falsity of the utterance in the case of many primary performatives. But with the explicit performative we do not need *two* representations, one of locutionary sense and one of illocutionary force. In this instance the material relevant to the latter may be represented within the framework of the former.[35]

IV

It has been a persistent complaint against Austin's theory that it draws no adequate line between the illocutionary and the perlocutionary act. Cohen, for example, suggests that Austin himself blurs the distinction by requiring of illocutionary acts that they achieve the perlocutionary effect of audience 'uptake'.[36] Other commentators have sided with Austin in regarding the audience's understanding as at least an important feature of the communicative process, and Searle underlines such a view by calling the audience's uptake an 'illocutionary effect'.[37] There would be general agreement that some line needs to be drawn between those aspects of communication which are essential to it and which might form the basis for a pragmatic account of language use, and those aspects which concern further non-linguistic effects of communication. Austin's division between illocutions and perlocutions was designed to mark such a boundary, but even he seemed dissatisfied with his attempts to locate it.

Some commentators indeed have been so impressed by the difficulties that they have sought to draw the general distinction in a quite different way. Cohen, again, separates the linguistic and non-linguistic aspects of utterance at a point between the (Mark II) explicit and the (Mark III) primary performative.[38] For him, therefore, it is unnecessary to make any further contrast between illocutionary and perlocutionary acts. But even those commentators who have accepted Austin's basic division between these acts have disagreed about the criteria that should be used to mark it. Intuitively illocutionary acts have been separated from the remoter effects of utterance.[39] But such an idea provides by itself no indication of the place where such remoter effects begin. Two other types of response to the difficulty deserve consideration. First, it has been argued by Strawson, using Grice's intentional analysis of meaning, that illocutionary acts can be identified in terms of the speakers' intentions and have an 'essential avowability' which distinguishes them from perlocutionary acts.[40] Second, it has been suggested that some verbal test might be used to identify illocutions. Illocutionary acts might be identified as verbs with an explicit performative form. Alternatively, some other set of illocutionary force-indicating devices might be used to locate illocutionary acts.[41]

The appeal to the speaker's intentions to identify illocutionary acts is motivated partly by the idea that those intentions are generally within the speaker's control. It may be beyond the speaker's capacity to ensure that he successfully performs an illocutionary act, but it is generally within his power to determine which act he intends to perform. If that is so, then his intentions might be held to determine just those illocutionary aspects of utterance which involve no perlocutionary effects. Curiously, one of the evident drawbacks in such an idea has been concealed by a suggested terminology to separate the speaker's intentions from the successful performance of the act itself. Strawson suggested that we should employ the phrase 'force of an utterance' for the former and contrast this with the illocutionary act itself, if any such act was performed.[42] But the phrase 'force of an utterance' is a misleading way of marking such a distinction, for it seems to mark the characterization of the utterance as an illocutionary act rather than merely describe the speaker's intentions. Once that distinction is noticed, the appeal to the speaker's intentions will be open to the objection that it leaves out of account all the further factors that determine the success of the illocutionary act itself. Plainly, a theory of illocutions needs to give an account not only of the intention to perform such an act but also of its successful performance. The appeal to the speaker's intentions, or misleadingly to 'force', to draw the line between illocutionary and perlocutionary acts will seem far too restrictive.

That restriction, however, might be thought to be overcome by a more detailed reference to the Gricean analysis. For in that analysis room can be made not only for the speaker's intentions but also for the audience's understanding of the utterance. Strawson suggested that the audience's understanding could be identified simply with the fulfillment of certain of the speaker's intentions.[43] Among those intentions were included not only the intention to effect some perlocutionary goal characteristically associated with the illocutionary act (the so-called primary intention) but also the intention that that intention itself be recognized. The suggestion is that the audience's recognition of the primary intention amounts to his understanding of the force of the utterance.

Such a suggestion is, however, open to objections. For it can be doubted whether the audience's recognition of a speaker's intentions is either sufficient or necessary for his understanding of the force of an utterance. It will not be strictly necessary, for example, if the audience can ascribe to the utterance a force that is independent of the speaker's intentions. Thus a man may take, or understand, an utterance as a warning even if he has no idea whether the speaker intended to warn him. In some instances an audience may indeed impute beliefs or intentions to a speaker on the basis of his understanding of the force of the utterance, and it may be important that the operation proceeds in that order rather than its reverse. But in certain other situations that imputation is not made, and yet the utterance is taken as a warning. Difficulties can also be raised about whether a recognition of intentions is sufficient for an understanding of the force of an utterance. An audience may recognize the speaker's intentions but not understand the force of the utterance in terms of those intentions. Someone who, through a wholly mistaken belief, utters what he intends to be a promise may be taken by an audience better informed than he not to have made a promise at all, even though the intention may have been clearly recognized.

Cases of these kinds will also cast doubt on the adequacy of any inference from the speaker's intentions (whether primary intentions or not) to his performance of an illocutionary act. An act of warning may be performed inadvertently without the speaker's intending to warn or to alert his audience. A speaker may have the intention to warn or promise but simply fail to do so. It may be said that these problems arise from a confusion about the idea of the 'force of an utterance', but there is a serious dilemma for such an appeal to the Gricean analysis. Either the analysis is preserved at the cost of restricting it to the speaker's intentions, or else room is made in the account for other features, such as audience understanding, that bear on the successful performance of the act itself. But the first alternative seems too restrictive, and the second assumes certain analytic connections which have been shown to be dubious.

It is not surprising in the light of these problems that Strawson's appeal to 'essential avowability' is open to similar objections. For it seems neither sufficient nor necessary for an act to be illocutionary that the relevant intentions be avowable. It is not sufficient because there may be acts and intentions such as 'frightening', 'persuading', 'boasting', or even 'getting someone to do something' which are avowable and even in some contexts essentially avowable. For in all such instances there may be circumstances in which it is either understood or required that the relevant intentions be made explicit in order to facilitate or achieve the goal. And it is not necessary since, as has been often pointed out, certain verbs seem to be illocutionary and yet are not essentially avowable. Such verbs include many cited by Vendler and Skinner,[44] for example, 'hint', 'insinuate', 'threaten', or 'flatter'. Such verbs characteristically lack an explicit performative use.

A more general conclusion might be drawn from these points. Although the speaker's intentions, and the explicitness that goes with essential avowability, are natural accompaniments of communication, it does not follow that such features are analytically related to communicative acts. There is, of course, some ambiguity about the relationship envisaged between these items in Grice's account,[45] but it seems more plausible to interpret that relationship on a Kantian model rather than in terms of a direct analytic link. That is, it seems more plausible to argue that intentions and explicitness are necessary conditions for the possibility of communicative acts in general, than to hold that every specific communicative act can be analyzed in these terms. In a similar way intentionality in some form may be a characteristic feature of communicative acts in general, but it does not follow that every specific communicative act has to be performed intentionally. What this suggests is that instead of attempting to analyze illocutionary acts in terms of the Gricean apparatus, we might simply use it to delimit the scope of a pragmatic account of communication. Speakers' intentions and audiences' understanding plainly play an important role in such communicative acts, and they may be used to identify the limits of a pragmatic explanation for such acts. But it does not follow that these items alone could form the basis for an analysis of illocutionary acts.

The apparent failure of avowability as a test for illocutionary verbs shows also that the latter cannot be identified as verbs with an explicit performative form. The verbs in the counterexamples from Vendler and Skinner have no such form in English, and yet they appear to be illocutionary. Presumably we are tempted to classify them as illocutionary because they can be used to describe an act of utterance without making reference to remoter effects of such an utterance. Such an intuitive criterion seems radically different from that of avowability, since there is no reason to suppose that every act that can be performed in the utterance itself should also be avowable. It is worth noting, too, that the possession of an explicit performative form may vary from one language to another, just as standards of avowability may vary from one culture to another. As a result of adopting such a test for illocutionary verbs, these verbs could be identified only relative to some particular language.

It might indeed seem in general unplausible to expect that any verbal or grammatical test would pick out illocutionary verbs, if these are understood as verbs that can describe the act of utterance itself. Vendler's complex and interesting grammatical tests have been criticized by Katz and Holdcroft,[46] but a more recent attempt has been made by Steven Davis.[47] His criterion rests on the natural idea that passive transformations might provide clues to separate perlocutionary and illocutionary verbs. He cites the three forms

(i) By ϕ-ing X S Ψ-s H Y
(ii) S's ϕ-ing X Ψ-s H Y
(iii) H was Ψ-ed Y by S's ϕ-ing X,

where S is a variable for a speaker designation, H is a variable for a hearer designation, and ϕ ranges over illocutionary and propositional act verbs. He then claims

> A verb substituted for Ψ is a perlocutionary act verb just in case there are substitution instances for the other variables which render (i)-(iii) grammatical.[48]

It seems that the criterion is intended to be both necessary and sufficient for a verb's naming a perlocutionary act, but it is relatively easy to find cases that cast doubt on the sufficiency of the test. Verbs like 'inform', 'remind', 'brief', 'exhort', 'threaten', and 'warn' all seem able to form these expressions grammatically, and yet all of them would normally be taken to be illocutionary rather than perlocutionary verbs. And a perlocutionary verb such as 'get to do' seems to fail the test suggested by (iii).

The general difficulty which such tests face is that there are subtle but marked differences between illocutionary verbs with regard to such passive transformations. Verbs like 'state' and 'inform' are commonly treated as illocutionary but they form passives in very different ways. From

(6) S stated that p to H

we cannot form

(7) H was stated that p by S

but only

(8) p was stated by S to H.

By contrast from

(9) S informed H that p

we cannot form

(10) p was informed by S to H

but only

(11) H was informed that p by S.

These formal divergences are associated with other semantic differences, for example, that whereas a verb like 'state' may be used without reference to a specific audience, 'inform' cannot be so used. Although 'state' and 'inform' are both commonly taken to be illocutionary, they differ in regard to their commitments to an audience and perhaps also in their commitment to audience effects. Thus (6) and (8) seem to contain no strong commitments to the audience's grasp of what was said to him, whereas (11) certainly and (9) possibly might be thought to entail that the audience had grasped what was being said to him.

It is indeed characteristic of many verbs in this area to exhibit such ambiguities. From

(12) S encouraged H to continue his work

we may infer

(13) H was encouraged to continue his work.

But both (12) and (13) are ambiguous according to their commitment to a heartening effect on H. (12) may quite naturally be used merely to indicate that S gave, or offered, encouragement to H, whether or not his remarks had the desired effect, and (13) too, though less clearly, might be interpreted in that way. There are similar devices employed in connection with many such verbs to limit the commitments of the utterance description. We may speak of offering a resignation instead of resigning, or of presenting apologies instead of apologizing, or of issuing a warning instead of just warning, and so on. Such devices can be seen as ways of limiting the scope of illocutionary verbs to the acts performed in the utterance itself. But they indicate, too, the severe difficulties that can be expected when attempting to identify illocutionary acts by a test for illocutionary verbs.

Points of this sort were raised by Cohen to cast doubt on Austin's apparent requirement that illocutionary acts should achieve audience uptake.[49] Cohen claimed that we can distinguish strong and weak senses of various illocutionary verbs according to their commitment to audience understanding. It may be doubtful whether I can be said to have warned you if you have not understood what I said, but it is quite possible to ask a question or to make a statement whether the audience understands or not. Cohen's solution to the problem is to characterize a weak sense for such verbs in which their use does not require the audience's understanding but only that the utterance 'could reasonably be expected to achieve' such uptake. But Cohen's position here is inadequate. First, it requires him to interpret Austin's claim that 'the performance of an illocutionary act involves the securing of uptake' as an entailment, when it is by no means clear that Austin intended such a strong claim. Second, it remains doubtful whether the appeal to different senses of words is correct, and whether the appeal to what it is 'reasonable to expect' is helpful.

A better way to deal with the issue might be to locate certain characteristic features relevant to the production and understanding of speech acts, and then to draw a line between those aspects which are included in an Austinian account and those which are not. Such a procedure would make explicit the delimitation of the scope of such a theory already referred to. Thus for an act such as warning we might separate at least the following questions:

(i) Did S intend to utter a warning to H?
(ii) Did S in fact utter a warning to H?
(iii) Did H recognize S's intention in uttering the words?
(iv) Did H understand (take) S's utterance as a warning?
(v) Was H alerted by S's utterance?
(vi) Did H take subsequent action as a consequence of S's utterance?

The bare question 'Did S warn H?', or its passive form 'Was H warned by S?', might be used to cover several of these questions. The former, for example, might be construed as (i), or as (i) and (ii), or even as (v), or as some other combination of (i)-(v). Not all these possibilities would naturally lead us to speak of a new sense for the verb 'warn', nor is any reference needed to the obscure idea of what it would be reasonable to expect. Of course the questions could be further subdivided. More important, it seems natural to draw a line between (iv) and (v) to separate those aspects of communication essential to an Austinian account and those which are outside its scope. Further motivation for such a division is provided by the Gricean account of communication expressed clearly by Searle, when he says,

> In the case of illocutionary acts we succeed in doing what we are trying to do by getting our audience to recognise what we are trying to do. But the effect on the hearer is not a belief or response, it consists simply in the hearer understanding the utterance of the speaker.[50]

To endorse such a claim is not, however, to accept either Searle's or Grice's further analyses.[51] Questions (i)-(iv) in this way effectively delimit an Austinian account of illocutionary acts, and it is possible that Austin's claim about audience uptake may have been intended to do no more than that.

V

Such a scheme fits Austin's views reasonably well, but it still faces one serious problem. If an Austinian theory concerns itself with questions (i)-(iv) only, it so far fails to separate illocutionary and perlocutionary acts within those limits. Just as questions (i)-(iv) can be framed for an illocutionary verb like 'warn', so they can also be asked with such perlocutionary verbs as 'frighten', 'persuade', or 'amuse'. Even when a speaker intends to frighten his audience by uttering some remark and the audience recognizes that intention and is frightened, we would not normally think of this interaction as specifically linguistic. To allow a theory to range over these cases would be to extend the account beyond its initial linguistic interests. So the scheme still fails to separate illocutions and perlocutions. It seems either to presuppose a prior account of that distinction, or simply to abandon it.

This difficulty is connected with a number of other points. It is connected with the intuitive idea that perlocutionary acts involve remoter effects of utterance and with Austin's related interest in the two formulas 'In saying p S ϕ-d' and 'By saying p S Ψ-d'. It is connected also with Cohen's general complaint that Austin's theory requires a criterion for act identity but fails to provide any such criterion.[52] For it is possible that in some circumstances and on some criteria the act S performs in uttering some form of words may be identified equally well as an act of threatening or as an act of frightening. It is true that Austin shares this failure with many other commentators, including Cohen, but such a response evidently does not resolve the problem.

But the problem is somewhat misconceived if it is expressed purely in terms of act identity. An Austinian theory could select in an ad hoc way some criterion for act identity in which the act of threatening and the act of frightening were different, though this would not throw much light on the nature of illocutions and perlocutions. The more important point is that whether the two acts are identical or not their descriptions cannot be equally attached to the utterance itself. If by uttering some words I both assert something and thoroughly alarm my audience, I may have performed one act with two different descriptions. But in the former case I can describe my utterance itself as an assertion, whereas in the latter case there is no such comparable description. Acts such as 'amusing', 'frightening', or 'persuading' may be performed by uttering certain words, but those words cannot be described as an 'amusement' or a 'fright' or a 'persuasion'.[53] The earlier delimitation of the scope of an Austinian theory, and the point rightly emphasized by Grice and Searle, indicate that the communicative success of illocutionary acts is circumscribed by questions (i)-(iv), whereas this is generally not true of perlocutionary acts.

It is tempting at this point to appeal to differences in the verbal content of utterances, so that the illocutionary descriptions of the utterance are determined solely by the presence of illocutionary force-indicating devices, while there are no such verbal devices to mark perlocutionary acts. It is, of course, true that some such illocutionary force-indicating devices can be located. Strong indicators of illocutionary force such as the explicit performative, sentence adverbials, syntactic moods, and a large range of vocabulary connected with specific acts, such as 'good' for commending, 'true' for assertion, 'danger' for warning, and so on, enable us to identify utterances containing them as having the relevant force. But these variously 'explicit' cases are not the only examples of such force; and the appeal to them gets the explanation the wrong way round. I may warn someone of an insect by saying

(14) That insect is dangerous.

But I can equally well in appropriate circumstances utter the warning by saying

(15) That is a scorpion, or
(16) Look out!

Warnings issued by uttering (15) and (16), as well as those like (14), need to be explained in an adequate illocutionary theory. The appeal to specific force-indicating devices gets the explanation the wrong way round, since their presence merely exemplifies our ability to attach force descriptions to the utterance itself. Their presence does not explain our ability to characterize utterances in that way; rather the devices, and our characterization of them, presuppose the ability to attach such descriptions to the utterance. What is needed is an explanation of that ability and along with it an explanation of those devices. Such an explanation would cover all the Mark I, Mark II, and Mark III cases of performative utterance and finally justify Austin's assimilation of them to some general type.

Problems of act identity are not irrelevant to this issue, but they are secondary to it. For one suggested way of identifying acts is that of linking an act of utterance with some speech act description by means of a convention. Where ϕ-ing in appropriate circumstances counts as ψ-ing in this way, we may identify the acts of ϕ-ing and ψ-ing. Austin's appeal to conventions, which was used in part to draw the distinction between illocutionary and perlocutionary acts, already provides some resolution to the problem of act identity.[54] A similar resolution arises also from Searle's controversial appeal to constitutive rules governing illocutionary acts.[55] But Austin's appeal to conventions of force has been strongly criticized. It has been suggested that he overlooked the differences between conventions for Mark I and those for Mark II performatives; or that he failed to see that whereas Mark II performatives might be said to be conventional, Mark III performatives could not; or that to speak of an act's being conventional 'in the sense that it could be made explicit by the performative formula' is to misuse the notion of a convention.[56] But it seems likely that Austin's point was to stress that the characterization of any force-indicating device, as of any utterance with such a force, depends upon some features that enable the utterances to be generally understood to have that force. To use the term 'convention' to stand for those features is to prepare the way for an explanation rather than actually to offer one, but it is not obviously a mistake. If such an explanatory cipher could be unraveled, it would serve to explain why we identify the act of utterance and the illocutionary act and why we describe the utterance itself in terms of the illocutionary description. It would, again, provide in principle a justification for the assimilation of the three performative cases.

Austin himself expressed doubts about the appeal to conventions and made little headway toward elaborating the explanation behind such an appeal. But since Austin's lectures there has been some development in this direction. It is a development that stresses the attitudes of belief and intention on the part of speakers and hearers in producing and understanding illocutionary acts. Central in such accounts have been the ideas of 'mutual knowledge' and 'mutual belief', variously elaborated.[57] It is not difficult to see some connection between these ideas, the notion of a convention, and the analysis of specific illocutionary acts. A speaker's intention to perform an illocutionary act will, for example, depend upon his beliefs about the world, about the words he is to employ, and about his audience's beliefs. Similarly, for an audience to understand the utterance as having some force it will be necessary for him to hold a comparable set of beliefs. The success of the communicative act will be partly determined by the extent to which such beliefs match. Obviously it is not required that speakers and hearers simply share a set of beliefs, for then communication would be redundant. But from the point of view of understanding the nature of an illocutionary act, it is required that both speaker and hearer share a grasp of its belief structure. Such an understanding will be related to the meaning of the relevant illocutionary verb, but it will not be confined to that. But if specific illocutionary acts can be analyzed in these terms, the mutual beliefs held by speakers and hearers within the linguistic community which are required for an understanding of the act will constitute conventions governing its performance. The best way to establish such connections would plainly be to provide such analyses of specific illocutionary acts, and that cannot be done here. But such an analysis and such conventions would have a similar status to Searle's constitutive rules, although they would be more consistently formulated in terms of the speaker's and hearer's beliefs, and they would not have to be characterized as constitutive rather than regulative.[58] All that is required here is to indicate the possibility of such an explanatory scheme within an Austinian account and to add some comments on it.

First it seems that the notion of mutual knowledge in this context will be too strong. Of course, at the level of understanding the structure of beliefs related to a particular illocutionary act it is desirable, at least, that the participants in a conversation know what that structure is. But at the level of the analysis of the act it would be too much to require that the participants *know* relevant items and know that they know them. Such mutual knowledge might be taken to define an ideal speaker-hearer relationship which is only rarely achieved. Similarly, the demand for mutual belief at this level will also be an idealization. In a situation of mutual belief each participant in the exchange will have ideal grounds for making a specific remark at each point and for appreciating the significance of such remarks. But in most conversations, even those dealing with the bare exchange of information, the relevant beliefs of the participants may not be mutual at the start or at the end. Participants have to make assumptions, and guesses, to impute beliefs, and to form hypotheses about their partner's beliefs or attitudes. Even outside the conflicts that generate such exchanges, or those which such exchanges may generate, a game theoretical model for conversation may often be appropriate.

The appeal to mutual knowledge or mutual belief is an appeal to determinacy in conversation which is largely unrealistic.

An appeal to sets of beliefs to explain the conventions under which speech acts are produced and understood can also explain the shifting nature of the division between illocutionary and perlocutionary acts. For such a division will depend upon the beliefs in some linguistic community, and these may change. If, for example, in some culture it is generally believed that certain people can bewitch others by uttering some ritual phrase, in the right circumstance such an utterance may count as a 'bewitchment'. It is, in any case, open to a community to stipulate that the utterance of some expression counts as, or effects, some outcome, for example in a legal context. In this way Mark I performatives may come to be instituted and impose on the designated utterances an appropriate belief structure. The boundary lines between the illocutionary and the perlocutionary act will be variable for these very reasons.

Finally it may be asked what sort of theory such an Austinian account would eventually provide. Various suggestions have been made involving such distinctions as those between 'langue' and 'parole',[59] 'competence' and 'performance',[60] 'language' and 'language use'.[61] But these terminologies themselves are no longer quite clear or innocent. Such a theory might seem naturally to deal with 'speech', but it evidently also has to do with language and might be presented as a formal theory.[62] It has to do with specific performances, too, but these have to be seen against a background of individual and community competence. What is important in such an Austinian account is the relation between a certain belief structure and the understanding of particular illocutionary acts; and the relevant beliefs of speaker and hearer on some occasion which determine the success of the performance. Some such account ultimately justifies Austin's assimilation of the Mark I, Mark II, and Mark III performatives in the general theory. Certainly there are important differences between them, but what they have in common is the belief structure that enables them to be performed and understood and that differentiates one act from another. Within such a common background Mark I performatives operate by stipulating the function of the utterance and so making it possible for the community to use those devices. Mark II performatives simply attach directly to verbal forms the relevant beliefs associated with the illocutionary acts, and the same will be true of the other illocutionary force-indicating devices. Mark III performatives rely solely on those beliefs to make effective a speech act that contains no such illocutionary force-indicating expressions.

Notes

1. J. R. Searle, *Speech Acts* (Cambridge, 1969); S. Schiffer, *Meaning* (Oxford, 1972); D. Holdcroft, *Words and Deeds* (Oxford, 1978); J. J. Katz, *Propositional Structure and Illocutionary Force* (Hassocks, 1977); K. Bach and R. M. Harnish, *Linguistic Communication and Speech Acts* (Cambridge Mass., 1979).

2. J. L. Austin, *How to Do Things with Words* (Oxford, 1962), lecture XII, p. 147.

3. J. O. Urmson, "Performative Utterances," vol. II in *Midwest Studies in Philosophy*, ed. P. A. French, T. E. Uehling, Jr., and H. K. Wettstein (Minneapolis, 1977); G. J. Warnock,

"Some Types of Performative Utterance," in *Essays on J. L. Austin*, ed. G. J. Warnock (Oxford, 1973).

4. L. J. Cohen, "Speech Acts," vol. XII in *Current Trends in Linguistics*, ed. T. Sebcok (The Hague, 1974).

5. Katz, *Propositional Structure*, chap. 5, pp. 156-94.

6. Urmson, "Performative Utterances," p. 127.

7. Warnock, "Performative Utterance," p. 86.

8. Urmson, "Performative Utterances," p. 125.

9. *Ibid.*

10. Austin, *How to Do Things with Words*, p. 146.

11. *Ibid.*, p. 98 and p. 113.

12. Cohen, "Speech Acts," p. 197. "Illocutionary force, whatever it may be, is not a topic for linguistics." There is, of course, some sheer arbitrariness in drawing such general boundary lines. But the fuzziness of lines dividing syntax, semantics, and pragmatics does not encourage the construction of arbitrarily sharp lines.

13. Katz, *Propositional Structure*, p. 23, note 17. Katz also stresses the disadvantages for Austin of lacking a 'competence-performance' distinction.

14. Cohen, *Speech Acts*, p. 194.

15. J. R. Searle, "Austin on Locutionary and Illocutionary Acts," *Philosophical Review* 77 (1968):407.

16. Cohen, "Do Illocutionary Forces Exist?" *Philosophical Quarterly* 43 (April 1964):121.

17. Searle, "Austin on Locutionary and Illocutionary Acts," p. 408.

18. *Ibid.*, p. 408.

19. *Ibid.*, p. 413.

20. Austin, *How to Do Things with Words*, p. 98 and p. 113.

21. Austin, "How To Talk," and "Truth" in *Philosophical Papers* (Oxford, 1961). Austin's account is very brief and somewhat different in the two papers. But the main difference between his account and Frege's lies in the scope of sense conventions and conventions of reference. For Austin these conventions do not apply to sentences but only to the constituents of sentences. Moreover, for Austin the constituents are governed either by one convention or the other; there is no suggestion that a sense convention might in some way determine a reference.

22. Searle, *Speech Acts*, p. 38. W. P. Alston, "Meaning and Use," in *The Theory of Meaning*, ed. G. H. R. Parkinson (Oxford, 1968). Searle claims that in general illocutionary acts could not be performed without a language. Alston requires of illocutionary acts that they be performed either by using language or by using a conventional device.

23. M. Dummett, *Frege; Philosophy of Language* (London, 1973), chap. 10, p. 295-302.

24. J. Houston, "Truth Valuation of Explicit Performatives," *Philosophical Quarterly* 49 (April 1970):139-49.

25. Warnock, "Performative Utterance," p. 81. But Warnock also adds that the proposal should be welcomed as "much simplifying any general doctrine of the indicative mood." D. Wiggins, "On Sentence-sense, Word-sense, and Difference of Word-sense", in *Semantics*, ed. D. D. Steinberg and L. A. Jakobovitz (Cambridge, 1971).

26. D. Lewis, "General Semantics," in *Semantics of Natural Language*, ed. G. Harman and D. Davidson (Dordrecht 1972). Also C. Ginet, "Performativity," *Linguistics and Philosophy* 3, no. 2 (1979):245-65.

27. Katz, *Propositional Structure*, pp. 173-77.

28. Houston, "Truth Valuation."

29. Warnock, "Performative Utterance," pp. 82-83, gets close to making this claim when he says, " . . . what the notice says – *that* customers are warned – is in effect *made true* by the fact that the notice says it."

30. M. J. Cresswell, *Logics and Languages* (London, 1973), p. 231.

31. M. Bierwisch, "Semantic Structure and Illocutionary Force," in *Speech Act Theory*, ed. J. R. Searle (Dordrecht, 1980).

32. Bierwisch, "Semantic Structure."

33. Wittgenstein hints at a general line of argument in *Tractatus Logico-Philosophicus* when he says: "Every proposition must already have a sense; assertion cannot give it a sense for what it asserts is the sense itself" (4.064). But it is not obvious how such a remark should be elaborated, nor whether it would offer a decisive ground for denying a truth-valuation to explicit performatives. See also Schiffer, *Meaning*.

34. Ginet, "Performativity," pp. 246-47.

35. The original claim that in these cases locutionary meaning *exhausts* illocutionary force, though metaphorical, seemed to mean more than this. (See, for example, Strawson, "Intention and Convention in Speech Acts," in *The Philosophy of Language*, ed. J. R. Searle [Oxford, 1971], pp. 23-24.) If that original claim implied that a truth-conditional account of explicit performatives can be given without employing the standard materials for explaining force, then at least that claim is not entailed by (C).

36. Cohen, "Speech Acts," pp. 178-79.

37. Searle, *Speech Acts*, p. 47.

38. Cohen, "Speech Acts," p. 197.

39. Alston in "Meaning and Use" seemed to indicate such an idea in speaking of illocutionary acts as "more fundamental than perlocutionary acts in the means-end hierarchy." But he also admitted that this presents a problem whose solution should have the "highest priority."

40. Strawson, "Intention and Convention in Speech Acts," pp. 23-38.

41. Austin, of course, grapples with such criteria throughout *How to Do Things with Words*. See also Zeno Vendlar, *Res Cogitans* Ithaca, 1972), and "Illocutionary Suicide," in *Issues in the Philosophy of Language*, ed. L. Mackay and D. Merrill (New Haven, 1976).

42. Strawson, "Intention and Convention in Speech Acts," p. 24.

43. *Ibid.*, pp. 29-30.

44. Zeno Vendlar, "Illocutionary Suicide," pp. 135-45 and Quentin Skinner, "Conventions and the Understanding of Speech Acts," *Philosophical Quarterly* 49 (April 1970):118-38. Vendlar seems to be wrong to include 'allege' in his group of 'suicidal' performatives.

45. H. P. Grice, "Meaning," *Philosophical Review* 66 (July 1957):377-88 and "Utterer's Meaning and Intentions," *Philosophical Review* 78 (April 1969):147-77. J. Bennett gives a quasi-Kantian interpretation of Grice in his "The Meaning-Nominalist Strategy," *Foundations of Language* 10 (1973):141-68.

46. *Propositional Structure*, Katz, chap. 2, pp. 50-58. Holdcroft, *Words and Deeds*, pp. 128-31.

47. Steven Davis, "Perlocutions," *Linguistics and Philosophy* 3, no. 2 (1979):225-43.

48. *Ibid.*, p. 237.

49. Cohen, "Speech Acts," pp. 178-79.

50. Searle, *Speech Acts*, p. 43.

51. Since there seem to me to be doubts about Searle's and Grice's equation of intention recognition and audience understanding, I tend to interpret the claim only in terms of the latter notion. But the central point made in Searle's text seems to me to justify the weaker conclusion already indicated without involving the full-scale acceptance of a Searlean or Gricean analysis.

52. Cohen, "Speech Acts," pp. 176-77.

53. The point is well brought out in Zeno Vendler's paper "Can I mean You?" which was given at the Twelfth International Congress of Linguistics at Vienna in September 1977, in a general account of what he calls the "shift from agent to product."

54. Austin, *How to Do Things with Words*, pp. 120-21.

55. Searle, *Speech Acts*, chap. 2, pp. 33-41, and pp. 50-53.

56. Strawson, "Intention and Convention in Speech Acts," p. 25 and pp. 27-28.

57. Schiffer, *Meaning*; D. Lewis, *Convention* (Cambridge, 1969); and Bach and Harnish, *Linguistic Communication* all make use of these notions.

58. Searle's "constitutive-regulative" distinction has been criticized, for example, by C. Cherry, "Regulative Rules and Constitutive Rules," *Philosophical Quarterly* 52 (October 1973): 301-15.
59. Cohen, "Speech Acts," p. 196-99.
60. Katz, *Propositional Structures,* chap. 1, pp. 22-25; chap. 5, pp. 156-94.
61. *Ibid.,* pp. 6-7.
62. See e.g. Asa Kasher, "Mood Implicatures: A Logical Way of Doing Generative Pragmatics, " *Theoretical Linguistics* 1 (1974): 6-38.

Illusions and Sense-Data

DAVID H. SANFORD

1. SENSE-DATA AND THE FOUNDATIONS OF ANALYTIC PHILOSOPHY

The purpose of this essay is to provide some new arguments against the existence of sense-data. This first section shows the relevance of my purpose to the overall purpose of this volume.

The label "analytic philosophy" has outlived a live interest in the nature of philosophical analysis. A cagy investor in the currently unfashionable writing for this volume might attempt to precipitate a revival of serious interest in questions such as "Is analysis a useful method in philosophy?" I shall not attempt to initiate such a revival, but I will collect a few passages which show that an interest in analysis and an interest in sense-data did not just happen to be concomitant in the philosophers who founded analytic philosophy. References to sense-data are crucial to their examples of analysis.

In the last of his lectures entitled "The Philosophy of Logical Atomism" (1918), Russell says:

> One purpose that has run through all that I have said, has been the justification of analysis, i.e., the justification of logical atomism, of the view that you can get down in theory, if not in practice, to ultimate simples, out of which the world is built, and that those simples have a kind of reality not belonging to anything else.[1]

Later in the same lecture, Russell gives sense-data as an example of things that are part of "the ultimate constituents of the world."

> The things that we call real, like tables and chairs, are systems, series of classes of particulars, and the particulars are the real things, the particulars being sense-data when they happen to be given to you. A table or chair will be a series of classes of particulars, and therefore a logical fiction.[2]

Sixteen years later, in an Aristotelian Society symposium entitled "Is Analysis a Useful Method in Philosophy?" John Wisdom similarly gives sense-data as an example of something more ultimate than ordinary invidivuals.

> '*S is an Ostentation of S'*' does mean '*The elements of the fact which S displays are more ultimate than the elements of the fact which S' displays*' .... And individuals are more ultimate than nations. Sense-data and mental states in their turn are more ultimate than individuals.[3]

Philosophers less committed to some version of logical atomism and therefore less committed to supplying examples of ultimate constituents still frequently discussed analysis and sense-data at the same time. Here is a passage from a lecture by G. E. Moore entitled "What Is Analysis?" (1933-34):

> Consider the prop.
> "I am nearer to this blackboard than any of you are."
> This is a prop. which we all understand perfectly well and you can all see that it's true, and yet it seems to me fearfully puzzling to see *what its analysis is* in a certain respect.
> The point of difficulty is this. It seems to me perfectly clear that when I say this I'm saying something about a percept or sensation or sense-datum or sensum which I have at the moment. But there's every reason to think that this isn't identical even with the surface of the blackboard, far less with the blackboard: that I'm not saying of it that I'm nearer to it than you are. Yet somehow the statement about the blackboard which I make is identical with a statement about it. What sort of statement about it is it identical with?[4]

In his earlier work, C. D. Broad wrote of *sensa* rather than of *sense-data*.[5] Conveying less feeling of difficulty or puzzlement than Moore, he also connects sensa with the analysis of perceptual statements.

> On the Sensum Theory the proposition: "The physical object which I am now perceiving appears to have the determinate characteristic *c*" can be analysed up to a certain point. The analysis would run as follows. This proposition means: "There is a certain sensum *s* which is the objective constituent of this perceptual situation. This actually has the characteristic *c* which I can detect in it by inspection, and it has this characteristic in a straightforward dyadic way. And there is a certain physical object *o*, to which this sensum has a certain relation R which it has to no other physical object. In virtue of this relation the sensum *s* is said to be "an appearance of" the physical object *o*. . . .[6]

Questions about the existence of sense-data, despite a fairly common sentiment that they deserve to pass into oblivion, have been kept alive in some quarters ever since the heterogeneous mixture of practices called *analytic philosophy* became distinguished from other modes of philosophic inquiry. There are signs that a revival of interest in sense-data is at hand. My main text is Frank Jackson's *Perception*.[7] Although some of Jackson's arguments for the existence of sense-data are original, his conception of sense-data is as traditional as any. There is no such thing as *the* traditional conception of sense-data, since analytic philosophers have not used the term *sense-datum* in some single narrow sense. Different philosophers, and some philosophers writing at different times, take different characteristics as essential to sense-data. If my argument succeeds, it will show, for example, only that some, not all, of G. E. Moore's various characterizations of sense-data do not actually apply to anything.

2. AN ESSENTIAL FEATURE OF SENSE-DATA

The essential feature of sense-data important for my argument is indicated in the quotation above from Broad. Here is another explicit description of this feature by Broad.

> Whenever I truly judge that x appears to me to have the sensible quality q, what happens is that I am directly aware of a certain object y, which *(a)* really does have the quality q, and *(b)* stands in some particularly intimate relation, yet to be determined, to x.[8]

Moore formulates the principle, without either accepting or rejecting it, in his *Commonplace Book*.

> Whenever a physical surface is looking ϕ to me, I am seeing (in the sense in which I see afterimages with shut eyes) something which is ϕ.[9]

The essential feature is explicit in some of A. J. Ayer's many introductions of sense-data.

> I have not so far attempted to give an explicit definition of the word "sense-datum". I have chosen rather to indicate its usage by giving examples in which sentences referring to sense-data are introduced as translations of sentences the meaning of which is already known. The general rule which one may derive from these examples is that the propositions we ordinarily express by saying that a person A is perceiving a material thing M, which appears to him to have the quality x, may be expressed in the sense-datum terminology by saying that A is sensing a sense-datum s, which really has the quality x, and which belongs to M.[10]

Frank Jackson's discussion of sense-data is squarely within this tradition. He says in *Perception* that "to accept (visual) sense-data is to accept that (i) whenever seeing occurs, there is a coloured patch which is the immediate object of perception, and (ii) that this coloured patch bears the apparent properties" (p. 88). Jackson supposes claim (ii) obviously to be correct in cases of veridical perception, visual hallucinations, and afterimages.

> The controversy over claim (ii) arises from its application to the case of illusion. When I look at a white wall in circumstances which make it look blue, do I see something blue? And, in general, does something looking F to me

entail that I see something F. Most philosophers today take the possibility of illusion to refute any such principle. I will attempt to establish claim (ii) by defending this principle (p. 88).

The philosophers whom Jackson will argue against reason as follows: when I look at a white wall in circumstances which make it look blue, and the wall fills my visual field because I am so close to the wall, I see part of the surface of the wall, and everything else I can correctly be said to see, for example, the wall, something made of plaster, part of the building that houses the Philosophy Department, I see in virtue of seeing this part of the surface of the wall. Neither this part of the surface of the wall, nor any of the things I see in virtue of seeing it, is blue. Although something looks blue to me, there is nothing blue that I see.

As an argument against the existence of sense-data, this begs the question. In arguing against the existence of sense-data, we cannot just assume that part of the surface of the wall is not seen in virtue of seeing (or sensing, or having a visual awareness of, or being presented with) something distinct from part of the surface, since a defender of sense-data denies precisely this assumption.

As Jackson remarks (pp. 89-89), the principle that when something looks F to me, I must see something F, is intended to cover only certain instantiations, which he calls the phenomenal uses, of "looks F." F is understood to be restricted to sensible qualities; so a fact such as that something can look to me to be a genuine twenty-dollar bill even though I see nothing that is a genuine twenty-dollar bill is not a relevant counterexample.

Following Roderick M. Chisholm's discussion in *Perceiving: A Philosophical Study*,[11] Jackson distinguishes three visual uses of "looks." In the epistemic use, "Something looks F to me" says that what I can see supports the proposition that something is F (p. 30). In the comparative use, "Something looks F to me" says that something looks the way something that is F normally looks. The phenomenal use of "Something looks F to me" is indicated by examples, such as the white wall that looks blue under certain conditions. Philosophers like David Armstrong, George Pitcher, and Jeremy Roxbee Cox have attempted to reduce phenomenal uses of "looks" to epistemic or comparative uses. Jackson raises formidable objections to these attempted reductions (pp. 33-49). To my mind, these objections together with Jackson's objections to adverbial accounts of "looks" (pp. 50-87) constitute his most persuasive argument for the existence of sense-data. He also has an original, interesting, perverse, and less persuasive positive argument for the existence of sense-data which relies on the troubling intermediate conclusion that no material things are really colored (pp. 120-137). The colored things that we see are therefore not material things. I find this argument provocative, but I shall not examine it here. I am concerned here rather with Jackson's traditional account of the phenomenal use "looks F" by reference to a sense-datum that is F.

3. THE ARGUMENT FROM ILLUSION AGAINST THE EXISTENCE OF SENSE-DATA

The title of this section is intended both to describe its topic accurately and to sound paradoxical. It sounds paradoxical because arguments traditionally grouped under the heading "The Argument from Illusion" have been arguments *for* the existence of sense-data. These are the familiar arguments that refer to: round pennies or dinner plates that appear elliptical when tilted, rectangular table tops that appear more or less trapezoidal or rhomboidal when viewed from an angle, tall towers that appear short in the distance, straight sticks that appear bent when half submerged in water, white walls that appear blue under blue light or through blue lenses, faces that appear to be behind the bathroom mirror, and hallucinations of pink rats or bloody daggers. It is not my purpose here to lower still further the current low reputation of these arguments. Rather than attempt to find something new to say against old arguments for the existence of sense-data, I shall attempt to say something new by way of argument against the existence of sense-data. My argument is an argument from illusion not because it uses any of the examples just listed but because it is concerned with genuine illusions, in the narrow and here undefined sense of *illusion* as that term is used in textbooks on the psychology of perception.

According to Jackson, when something phenomenally looks to be F, a visual sense-datum is F. One example of the phenomenal use of "looks" is provided by the Müller-Lyer illusion. Jackson discusses this illusion as part of his attack on attempts to explain away phenomenal uses of "looks" by reduction to epistemic uses. He writes:

> The two lines are the same length, but the top line looks longer than the bottom line. Moreover, I know with complete certainty that the lines are the same length. (I am familiar with this kind of illusion and have just measured the lines.) Therefore, I neither believe nor am inclined to believe that the top line is longer than the bottom line (p. 38).

"Inclined to believe" here is often given a technical sense by giving it counterfactual truth-conditions. Against Godfrey Vesey's suggestion that when the two lines of equal length in the Müller-Lyer figure look to be unequal, "if I hadn't good reason (having measured them) to believe them to be equal, I would, on looking at them, believe them to be unequal,"[12] Jackson says:

> The problem here is that what Vesey claims seems to be false. Even if I had not measured the lines, or otherwise determined that the lines were equal, I would not have believed that the top line was longer than the bottom; I would, rather, have reserved judgement. This is not because I am familiar with the Müller-Lyer illusion, but is a result of the fact that it is obvious that the 'wings' at the end of the lines are going to have a distorting effect. The *first* time I was presented with the illusion, and before I had measured the lines, I noted that the top line looked longer, but did not thereby believe

that it was longer. And this is almost universally the case. Every student presented with the Müller-Lyer figure for the first time realizes that, though the top line looks longer, it would be foolhardy to suppose that it was in fact longer (pp. 40-41).

Jackson, or the designer of his book, rather cheats in selecting the figure on page 38 to illustrate the Müller-Lyer illusion. The two parallel lines of equal length are quite close together, and diagonal lines forming the 'wings' are relatively very short, being only one-twelfth as long as the parallel lines. The illusion still works, but it can be made to work more impressively; and my contention will be more persuasive if we have a more striking example of the illusion in view. Here is a simple demonstration anyone can prepare: With a wide felt-tip pen draw a line about 30 inches long with relatively good-sized wings or arrow heads at both ends pointing in the same direction, the diagonal lines on each side being parallel. On a shorter piece of paper draw a line from edge to edge with a single set of wings in the middle. When the shorter sheet of paper is lined up with the longer sheet, the set of wings on the shorter sheet extends outward with respect to the line on one side and bends back with respect to the line on the other side.[13] Move the shorter sheet back and forth until the lines on either side of the common set of wings look to you or your accomplice to be of equal length. You may well be surprised at the magnitude of your errors. You and your friends are, of course, all sophisticated, wise to the ways of the Müller-Lyer illusion, and know that when the lines look, in the phenomenal uses of "look," to be of equal length, they are actually of unequal length. You might thus try a second experiment. Hold a little contest to see who can judge actual equality of length most accurately. Adjust the sheets of paper to the point where your friend judges that the two lines actually are of equal length, although one phenomenally looks to be longer than the other. The magnitude of error, although somewhat less, may still surprise you.

I contend that it is utterly implausible to suppose that when two lines of unequal length in a Müller-Lyer figure look to be of equal length, there are two lines of equal length that one sees or senses or has presented. If the visual sense-datum involved is the object one is aware of that actually has the relative lengths which the two lines look to have, then there is no visual sense-datum involved.

Suppose that there were a sense-datum that really has the properties the physical lines look to have. The two sense-datum lines of equal length also have Müller-Lyer wings. We know that such wings make physical lines of equal length appear unequal. The sense-datum theory requires that these wings, which can have such a marked effect on how long two physical lines look to be, have no effect on how long two sense-datum lines appear to be. There is no reason to believe this and plenty of reason to disbelieve it.

Some philosophers take afterimages to be paradigms of sense-data. Other philosophers who attach no particular importance to afterimages in their arguments for the existence of sense-data would still deny that there are sense-data of after images. No one holds that one is aware of a visual afterimage in virtue of being aware of something distinct from the afterimage, the afterimage sense-datum.

ILLUSIONS AND SENSE-DATA 377

Can an afterimage look to have a sensible quality that it does not actually have? Philosophers who argue that it cannot ignore the following fact among others: one can have an afterimage of a Müller-Lyer figure as easily as one can have an afterimage of any figure. A visual afterimage can be projected on a physical surface. We can, if we want to, say that a projected afterimage line is ten inches long when it coincides with two points ten inches apart on the surface. According to this convention, the length of an afterimage line depends on the distance from the subject to the surface on which it is projected. No such convention is required to make comparisons of length. Anything in one's visual field subtends or occupies a certain visual angle. If one has a circular afterimage, it subtends the same solid visual angle whether it is projected on a near surface, or on a far surface, or is not projected at all but viewed with closed eyes. The visual angle it occupies can be measured by projecting it on a surface and calculating the angle subtended by the portion of the surface it covers.

There is a correction, of more theoretic than practical importance, that this method of measurement can require. Suppose that one projects an afterimage on a wall while one is viewing the wall through binoculars. Measuring the angle subtended by the portion of the surface of the wall covered by the projected afterimage will then obviously not give the visual angle subtended by the afterimage until multiplied by the magnification factor of the binoculars. Normal magnification devices increase the visual angle subtended by an object seen by increasing the size of the corresponding retinal image. I think we can image a magnification (or reduction) device that works differently from this, that operates, so to speak, behind the retina rather than in front of it, and that increases or decreases the visual angle subtended by an object in the visual field without changing the size of the corresponding retinal image. This possibility shows that the size of one's retinal image and the angle subtended by a shape in one's visual field should not be identified, although there is usually a direct relation between them. In unusual circumstances, moreover, a shape can subtend an angle in one's visual field when there is no retinal image. This occurs when the experience is induced by direct stimulation of the visual cortex as well as when one has an afterimage, an image that is experienced *after* the retinal image is gone.

The magnitude of the Müller-Lyer illusion should be expressed as a percentage. Two lines look to have the same length when one is really only 80 percent as long as the other. So long as these lines are close to and perpendicular to the line of sight, percentages of differences in length can be expressed as percentages of differences in visual angle. With a little training, we can learn to express phenomenal judgments in terms of visual angles. The Müller-Lyer phenomenon remains unchanged. Two lines look to subtend equal visual angles when one subtends an angle only 80 percent as large as the angle subtended by another. This phenomenon also occurs with afterimages of Müller-Lyer figures. If two lines in a visual sense-datum cannot look to subtend equal visual angles unless they actually subtend equal visual angles, then no visual sense-datum is involved in having an afterimage of a Müller-Lyer figure. The afterimage itself does not have the characteristic, taken as essential to sense-data, of actually having the sensible qualities it appears to have.

Consider for a moment another impressive visual illusion, one discussed by Berkeley in *An Essay Towards a New Theory of Vision* (Sections 67-78).[14] The moon looks larger when it is just over the horizon than it looks high in the sky. That is, it seems to subtend a larger visual angle. In fact, it subtends just the same visual angle. If there is a sense-datum of the moon, the sense-datum subtends the same visual angle the moon subtends. If a sense-datum of the moon just over the horizon were actually larger than the sense-datum of the moon high in the sky, there would not be a moon illusion but rather the puzzling fact that the moon subtends a smaller visual angle as it climbs higher in the sky. This does not occur. When one watches the moon apparently diminish in size as it climbs higher in the sky, one does not do this by being aware of a bright disk that actually diminishes in size. If a sense-datum of the moon actually has the size the moon looks to have, there is no sense-datum of the moon. My contention can be summarized as follows: Judgments of phenomenal size can be expressed in terms of subtended visual angles. In certain cases of illusion, what one sees directly, that is, what one sees not in virtue of seeing or being visually aware of something else, seems to subtend a visual angle different from what it actually subtends. There is, in such cases, nothing that is both seen but not seen in virtue of being visually aware of something else and that subtends just the visual angle one judges it to subtend. According to traditional sense-datum theory, there is such a thing. Therefore, traditional sense-datum theory is mistaken.

Many of the phenomena that philosophers of perception call *illusions* are due to perspective, refraction, reflection, and absorption. For example, one has to know only about the different refractive properties and water and air to account for the so-called bent-stick illusion. No special information about the psychology of vision is required. The Müller-Lyer illusion and the moon illusion, in contrast, cannot be accounted for just in terms of the properties of light. They are of interest to psychologists precisely because they must be accounted for in terms of the information processing systems involved in perception. Another family of profoundly impressive visual illusions of this sort involves color. Because of different surrounding colors, two samples of the same color can look to be of very different colors, or two samples of very different colors can look to be of the same color.[15] These cases also cannot be adequately accounted for by supposing that when something looks to have a sensible property *F*, then there is something, a sense-datum, that really has the property *F*.

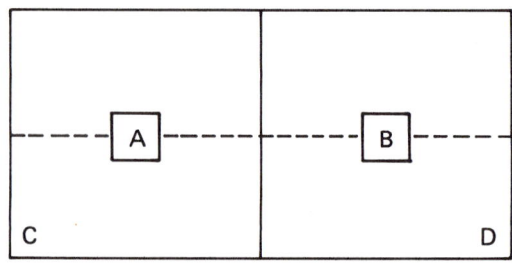

Suppose, as before, that there were sense-data that really have the colors that the colored expanses of paper A and B look to have. The sense-data of A and B are respectively surrounded by sense-data of colored expanses C and D. The sense-datum theory requires that although physical surrounding colored areas C and D have a marked effect on the color appearance of the physical surrounded areas A and B, the corresponding surrounding sense-data have no effect on the color appearance of the sense-data they surround. Except for a desire to defend the theory, there is no reason to believe this.

Imagine that these demonstrations of color illusions are set up so that the surrounding areas C and D can be removed without the subject's losing sight of A and B. The dotted line in the previous figure indicates where two sheets of paper fit together. As these two sheets slide apart, A and B are revealed as parts of adjacent colored areas on the sheet underneath.

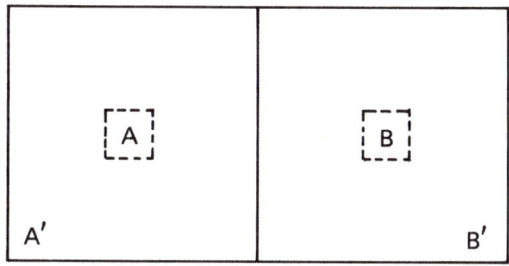

The smaller areas A and B are respectively indistinguishable from the uniform surrounding area A' and B' in all cases. In some cases, where A and B previously looked to be of the same color, A' and B' can now be seen to be of definitely different colors. In other cases, where A and B previously looked to be of different colors, A' and B' can now be seen to be of the same color: there is no boundary visible between A' and B' since the sheet underneath is of one uniform color.

Consider a case of this second kind. What must the sense-datum theory say about it? Since A and B initially appear, when surrounded by C and D, to be of different colors, the initial sense-datum of A really is of a color different from the sense-datum of B. A and B do not appear to change in color as the covering sheets C and D are removed, yet A looks to be of the same color as A', B looks to be of the same color as B', and B' and A' look to be of the same color. Since A and B end up looking to be of the same color, according to the sense-datum theory, the final sense-datum of A really is of the same color as the final sense-datum of B. However many sense-data of A and B are supposed to be involved in this process, while both A and B are under continuous observation, there is never a time when either appears to change in color. Strictly, at every time during the process, each appears not to change in color. Not changing in color is a sensible quality each phenomenally appears to have; so, on the sense-datum theory, the sense-data of A and B remain the same color. (It makes no difference whether one thinks that a single sense-datum persists through time or one thinks that there is a series of numerically distinct sense-data.) This phenomenon involves the sense-datum theory in a contradiction. The sense-data of A and B start off being of different colors. The sense-data of A and B end up being of the same color. Yet the sense-data of A and B one ends up with are of the same colors, respectively, as the sense data of A and B one starts off with. This sort of difficulty is removed if we give up the assumption, essential to the sense-datum theory, that if two areas appear to be of different colors, we must be aware of some areas that actually are of different colors.

4. SENSE-DATUM INCONSISTENCIES

The example above differs from the usual examples that exploit the nontransitivity of indistinguishability. It is assumed to be possible that samples A and B are indistinguishable with respect to color, as are samples B and C, although A is (barely) distinguishable from C. Such a case does not involve illusion. In the example above, areas that are indistinguishable with respect to color in some circumstances appear (misleadingly) to be definitely distinguishable in other circumstances, when different surrounding colors interfere.

The nonillusory nontransitivity of indistinguishability, however, also poses a problem for the sense-datum theory. If A and B phenomenally look to be of the same color, the sense-datum of A and the sense-datum of B are of the same color. Ditto for B and C. Yet A and C phenomenally look to be of different colors, so the sense-datum of A is of a color different from the sense-datum of C. By the transitivity of identity, the sense-datum of A is also of the same color as the sense-datum of C. The sense-datum theory is thus led into a contradiction.

David M. Armstrong uses such an argument in *Perception and the Physical World* and again in *A Materialist Theory of the Mind*.[16] The argument is criticized by Frank Jackson and R. J. Pinkerton in "On an Argument against Sensory Items,"[17] and these criticisms are repeated in Jackson's *Perception*, pp. 112-17. In my discussion of color illusions, I have anticipated the first of these criticisms, which follows:

> Though it may be true that the sensory items we have when we look at A and B are identical in colour and that the sensory items we have when we look at B and C are identical in colour, it does *not* follow from this, or anything else given, that the sensory items we have when we look at B in the two cases are identical in colour. (*Perception*, p. 113.)

As I claimed above, the fact that B phenomenally looks not to change in color between times t1 and t2 implies, according to the sense-datum theory, that the sensory item associated with B at t1 is identical in color with the sensory item associated with B at t2. It makes no difference how finely sense-data are individuated. Multiplying the number of B-sense-data only adds steps in the linkage of sense-data of the same color between the A-sense-datum and the C-sense-datum.

Jackson and Pinkerton go on to consider an obvious way in which problems involving distinct B-sensa-data can be evaded.

The difficulty just raised for Armstrong's first argument turns on the point that, on sensory item theories, there will be *two* sensory items associated with B in the case on which Armstrong's argument relies. Therefore, the obvious repair to the argument is to base it on a case involving just *one* occasion of looking at B, and so just *one* sensory item associated with B. Thus, it might be suggested that we take the case where A, B and C are looked at together (that is, by the one person at one time), and where A and B are indistinguishable (in colour), B and C are indistinguishable, while A and C are distinguishable. The trouble with this suggestion is that the case is *logically impossible*. It is logically impossible to have A, B and C *all together*, and be unable to tell A from B in colour, and B from C in colour, while able to tell A from C in colour. This is impossible, because, for example, if one can tell A from C but cannot tell B from C, then one can tell A from B simply be reference to the fact that one can tell A from C but cannot tell B from C. (*Perception*, p. 114.)

In response to this objection, the philosophers' distinction-drawing reflex appears to be appropriate. "X and Y are indistinguishable with respect to color" either can mean "no difference in color between X and Y can be determined just by the visual comparison of X and Y with each other," or it can mean "no difference in color between X and Y can be determined by any visual comparisons involving X and Y." In the first sense of "indistinguishable," which is sufficient for Armstrong's purposes and for mine, there is no contradiction in a theory-neutral description of the phenomenon. There is a contradiction given the sense-datum theorist's assumption that whenever one sees a physical colored area, one is aware of a sense-datum, and that two sense-data that are indistinguishable with respect to color are of the same color.

Although, in the relevant sense of "indistinguishable," there is no contradiction in supposing that there are color samples A, B, and C that satisfy Armstrong's description, I think that I have never seen such a display. It is no doubt possible to assemble a series of samples such that no two adjacent samples are distinguishable just by comparison with each other and the two samples at either end of the series are clearly thus distinguishable. It is tempting to argue from this that there must therefore be three samples in the series such that two are distinguishable from each other and each indistinguishable from the third. I have qualms about such an argument; for it uses the assumption, which seems questionable to me, that the Principle of Bivalence applies to each statement of the form "X is distinguishable in color from Y" that refers to any pair of samples in the series. It is assumed that given, say, the first and third members of the series, either they are indistinguishable, or they are not, in which case they are distinguishable. The question of distinguishablity may, for some pairs, be unanswerable. As we compare successive members of the series with the first member, there may be no adjacent pair such that one is definitely indistinguishable from the first member of the series and the other is definitely distinguishable. Familiar examples of sorites arguments demonstrate that there are borderline cases of one-place predicates such as "short," "rich," and "bald." We should not assume that there cannot also be borderline cases of predicates like "indistinguishable from A with respect to color." On my view of things, this does not by itself constitute any additional difficulty for the sense-datum theory. It does show that until we actually see a triplet of color samples of the sort Armstrong describes, we can suspect the example of being fictional. Even if there are no such examples, the same form of argument can be used for any *n*-member series of samples, where *n* is large enough that every pair of adjacent samples are definitely indistinguishable and the samples at either end are definitely distinguishable.

I should like to exploit the Müller-Lyer illusion again to present a difficulty, similar to Armstrong's, for sense-datum theory. Consider the accompanying figure:

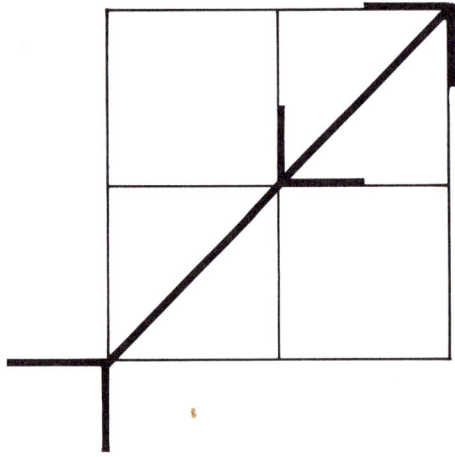

The diagonals are of equal length, and if you attend to the figure in the proper way, they phenomenally look to be of equal length. This requires ignoring the Müller-Lyer wings and attending to the visible fact that the whole figure is a square composed of four equal squares. Diagonals of equal squares are, of course, equal in length. If you attend to the Müller-Lyer wings rather than ignore them, they do their usual trick: one diagonal looks to be longer than the other. As my attention shifts between the Müller-Lyer wings, which cause the illusory appearance of different lengths, and the squares, which provide sufficient visual information to make the diagonals appear to be of equal length, I experience something like a "change in aspect" similar to what one experiences when viewing a reversing staircase diagram or a duck-rabbit diagram. Those diagrams would not serve my purposes as well if at all, for they involve a switch between different representational readings. The switch one experiences when viewing the diagram above does not involve representation. It is the diagonals themselves, not what they represent, that now look equal, now unequal in length. The diagram does not appear to change its shape during this switch. There appears to be no stretching or contracting. The diagonals appear not to change in length although the relation between their lengths does appear to change. According to sense-datum theory, the sense-data of the two diag-

ILLUSIONS AND SENSE-DATA 383

onals do not actually change in length although the relation between their lengths actually does change. This is impossible. The theory of sense-data, committed by the phenomena to an impossibility, is false.

5. HOW TO ACCOUNT FOR PHENOMENAL LOOKING?

Jackson raises formidable objections to attempts to account for phenomenal uses of "looks" in terms of epistemic or comparative uses. He also raises objections to adverbial accounts of phenomenal looking. I said above that these constitute his most persuasive argument for the existence of sense-data. If my enterprise has succeeded, I have diminished the persuasiveness. I attribute the following argument to Jackson: "The supposition that there are sense-data accounts for phenomenal looking. The alternatives to this account, reductions to epistemic or comparative looking and adverbial analyses, all fail to account for phenomenal looking. Therefore, it is reasonable to accept the supposition that there are sense-data." I have been arguing against the first premise of this argument. I shall not attempt here to give arguments against the second premise. Although I think some of Jackson's objections to each of the alternative accounts are answerable, I am not confident that all his objections to any one alternative account are answerable. If the sense-datum account of phenomenal looking is inadequate, and if all the alternative accounts are also inadequate, then all the accounts we have managed to come up with are inadequate, an uncomfortable but neither impossible nor unprecedented predicament.

The phenomenal appearances provided by certain visual illusions, I have claimed, cannot be adequately accounted for by the principle that when something phenomenally looks to be F, a visual sense-datum is F. But I have not claimed that there is something intrinsically unintelligible in the supposition that a visual sense-datum is F in such cases. There are cases of phenomenal appearance, I think, where the supposition of a corresponding sense-datum that actually has the apparent property cannot be understood. Things at the edge of one's visual field phenomenally look indistinct.[18] There are many ways that pictures, photographs, printed pages, and images can be actually blurred or indistinct; but I cannot imagine any sort of thing, public picture or private sense-datum, that actually has the visual properties it phenomenally looks to have and that is phenomenally indistinguishable from the objects that look indistinct because they are at the edge of my visual field. Neither can I, who suffer from astigmatism and fairly severe myopia, imagine anything that actually has the visual properties it phenomenally looks to have and that is phenomenally indistinguishable from distant objects I view with my glasses off. Perhaps, in this case, my imagination is deficient. The phenomenon of indistinct peripheral vision is sufficient to refute the principle that whenever something phenomenally looks F, it is possible that something phenomenally indistinguishable from it is actually F. These examples of blur and indistinctness pose difficulties for attempts to reduce phenomenal uses of "looks" to comparative or epistemic uses. They also pose additional difficulties for the attempt to account for phenomenal looking in terms of sense-data.

384 DAVID H. SANFORD

Notes

1. B. Russell, "The Philosophy of Logical Atomism," in *Logic and Knowledge*, ed. R. C. Marsh (New York, 1956), p. 270.
2. *Ibid.*, p. 274.
3. J. Wisdom, "Is Analysis a Useful Method in Philosophy?" in *Philosophy and Psycho-Analysis* (Oxford, 1957), pp. 25-26.
4. G. E. Moore, "What Is Analysis?" in *Lectures on Philosophy*, ed. C. Lewy (London and New York, 1966), p. 163.
5. Broad uses "sensum" and "sense-datum" interchangeably in his late (1951) article "Some Elementary Reflections on Sense-Perception." This and some selections from *Scientific Thought* are reprinted in Robert J. Swartz's anthology *Perceiving, Sensing, and Knowing* (Berkeley, Los Angeles, London, 1976), pp. 29-48, pp. 85-129.
6. C. D. Broad, *The Mind and Its Place in Nature* (London, 1925), p. 182.
7. F. Jackson, *Perception* (Cambridge, 1977).
8. C. D. Broad, *Scientific Thought* (London, 1923), p. 239.
9. G. E. Moore, *The Commplace Book*, ed. C. Lewy (London and New York, 1962), p. 136.
10. A. J. Ayer, *The Foundations of Empirical Knowledge* (London, 1940), p. 58.
11. R. M. Chisholm, *Perceiving: A Philosophical Study* (Ithaca, N.Y., 1957).
12. G. Vesey, "Analysing Seeing (II)," in *Perception: A Philosophical Symposium*, ed. F. N. Sibley (London, 1971), p. 134. Vesey makes a similar claim in his *Perception* (Garden City, 1971), p. 9. I think this sort of counterfactual approach to phenomenal appearance escapes certain objections if instead of entertaining a contrary-to-fact absence of belief—"if I didn't know better," "if I didn't have reason to think otherwise," and so forth—one entertains a contrary-to-fact presence of belief—"if I believed the conditions of perception to be normal," "if I believed that nothing unusual in the situation would affect my judgment," and the like. Jackson's forthcoming objection appears to be met by this sort of emendation.
13. Like this:

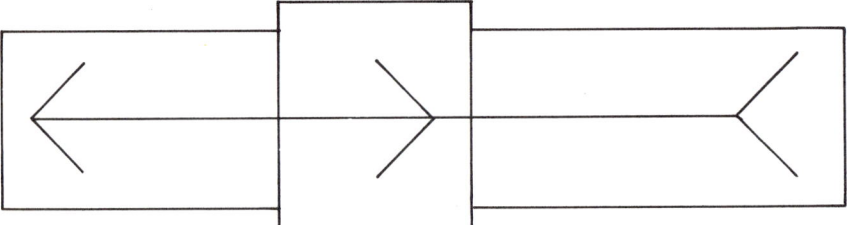

14. Reprinted in *Berkeley's Philosophical Writings*, ed. David M. Armstrong (New York and London, 1965) and in many other editions.
15. There are excellent serigraph demonstrations of illusions of these kinds in the original, large format, edition of *Interaction of Color* by Josef Albers (New Haven, Conn., 1963). A look at this work is worth a trip to a Rare Book Room.
16. D. M. Armstrong, *Perception and the Physical World* (London and New York, 1961), pp. 42-44 and *A Materialist Theory of the Mind* (London and New York, 1968), pp. 218-19.
17. F. Jackson and R. J. Pinkerton, "On an Argument Against Sensory Items," *Mind* 82 (1973):269-72. The connection of Armstrong's argument, and thus of the Jackson-Pinkerton objections to Armstrong, to my use of the forthcoming figure involving the Müller-Lyer illusion was pointed out by Professor Jeffrey Tlumak who commented usefully on an earlier version of this paper delivered under the title "The Argument from Illusion against the Existence of Sense-Data" to the Pacific Division of the American Philosophical Association in 1980.
18. H. H. Price discusses peripheral vision in the first two sections of his "The Nature and Status of Sense-Data in Broad's Epistemology," *The Philosophy of C. D. Broad*, ed. P. A.

Schilpp (New York, 1959), pp. 457-85. As J. L. Austin remarks, "Price is more seriously interested than is Ayer in the actual facts about perception, and pays more attention to them . . ." (*Sense and Sensibilia*, p. 104). I should say that Price is distinguished among all philosophers of perception, Austin as well as Ayer, for the degree and penetration of his serious interest in the phenomenal facts about perception.

Semantic Innocence and Uncompromising Situations

JON BARWISE AND JOHN PERRY

Since Frege, philosophers have become hardened to the idea that content sentences in talk about propositional attitudes may strangely refer to such entities as intensions, propositions, sentences, utterances and inscriptions . . . *If we could but recover our pre-Fregean semantic innocence,* I think it would be plainly incredible that the words "the earth moves," uttered after the words "Galileo said that," mean anything different, or refer to anything else, than is their wont when they come in other environments.

Donald Davidson, "On Saying That"[1]

1. SITUATIONS COMPROMISED

The present authors have managed to recover their pre-Fregean semantic innocence by rediscovering an old idea, that statements stand for situations, complexes of objects and properties in the world. The idea is found in various forms in Russell, Wittgenstein, and Austin, and more recently in Gustav Bergmann and other midwestern realists, but it has had little appeal for those whose philosophy of language is guided by the traditional model of formal semantics.

Situations were compromised by Frege's supposition that the reference of a sentence must be a truth value. This approach left no room for situations, and major figures such as Church, Quine, and Davidson have followed Frege in this regard. Carnap tried to take propositions as the designata of sentences in his early *Introduction to Semantics,* and his propositions were something like states of affairs or situations. But Church, in his review of this book, gave a formal proof that this could not work.[2] This argument used ideas from Frege to show that the reference of a sentence must be a truth value, granted principles to which Carnap was committed.

We have developed a model-theoretic conception of semantics which takes situations seriously. We were forced to do this to give an innocent account of the semantics of perception and belief, respectively. Having developed situation semantics, we remembered the old proof that it was impossible. Reexamining Church's argument from this new perspective shows that it conflates two quite different ways of looking at the relation between statements and situations.

In this paper we sketch (quite briefly) enough of our conception of situations and their types to allow us to share our reexamination. A fuller development of situation semantics will appear in due course.

2. TYPES OF SITUATIONS

The basic picture we wish to promote goes like this. The world, at least the common sense world that human language reflects, consists not just of objects and sets of objects, nor of objects, properties, and relations, but of objects having properties and standing in relations to one another. There are parts of the world, clearly recognized (although not precisely individuated) in common sense and human language, that we call situations.

We are certain that situations are part of the world because we see them (as when we see Hoover Tower casting a shadow on Stanford), because we find ourselves in situations (our being late with this paper puts us in an embarrassing one), and because we find we have always believed them (as we have frequently believed that Columbus discovered America). States of affairs are situations, events and episodes are situations in time, scenes are visually perceived situations, changes are sequences of situations, and facts are situations enriched (or polluted) by language.

Situations have properties of two sorts, internal and external. The cat's walking on the piano distressed Henry. Its doing so is what we call an external property of the event. The event consists of a certain cat performing a certain activity on a certain piano; these are its internal properties.

Simple indicative statements classify situations according to their internal properties, by stating that the actual situation is a certain *type* of situation. To represent the internal properties or type of a situation we use partial functions that take sequences of relations and objects as arguments and 1 or 0 as values. The type of situation that distressed Henry is one in which

$s(\text{on, the cat, the piano}) = 1$

The type of situation s' in which the cat is not walking on the piano but is where he belongs, on the mat, satisfies

$s'(\text{on, the cat, the piano}) = 0$
$s'(\text{on, the cat, the mat}) = 1$.

Belief in the world is belief in a largest situation; its type we call the world type.

We take properties and relations seriously; they are neither meanings nor sets of individuals nor sets of sequences of individuals. The domain A of individuals and the domain R of relations are parallel products of conceptual activity, that of individuation. They are equally abstract but equally the most concrete items we deal with in perception and in language. Individuation provides the articulation of the world necessary for language to get a hold on it.

Actual situations are part of the actual world. The conceptual activity that individuates the world lets us classify the situations according to their types. However, once we have some of the facts, we realize that they might have been otherwise, that there are situation types that are not realized by actual situations. These unrealized situation types are involved in many of our hopes, fears, intentions, and beliefs. Much of our mental life and hence the language we use to describe that mental life involves such unrealized situation types.

3. INTERPRETATION AND EVALUATION

How does language get a hold on the world? It does so at the most rudimentary level by having simple indicative statements describe types of situations, and a sentence's meaning is what suits it for this task. But meaning is a notoriously slippery and complex notion, conflating many distinct aspects of the use of language. Just as the number 100 is the sum of many different columns of smaller numbers, so are there many ways one might try to break down meaning into smaller components. Certain ways of doing this are rather well entrenched in philosophy: Frege's reference versus sense, Carnap's extension versus intension. More recently David Kaplan has advocated a three-level system of character, intension (or content), and extension.[3] Our own attempt also has three levels: *linguistic meaning, interpretation,* and *evaluation.*

About linguistic meaning we shall have little to say here, except by way of examples indicating how it gives rise to interpretation, but must be kept distinct from it. This we have learned from Kaplan's work on indexicality. (It is also an important insight of Austin's, and Austin's work in general is valuable for the situation-oriented philosopher.)[4] Kaplan superimposes his top layer, character, on a possible worlds semantics. Character and intension or content he sees as aspects of Frege's notion of sense. We believe the bottom two layers of this structure are in need of drastic reorganization, and that the top can benefit from awareness of the situations below. Our middle layer is *not* Frege's sense, for our interpretations are complexes of objects and properties, not denizens of a Fregean third realm, and not procedures or functions from possible worlds to extensions that have been used by recent philosophers of language to interpret Frege's senses. Objects and properties are found at Frege's level of reference. But Frege's notion of reference reflects his view that a realm of sense is available to provide needed specificity for embedded statements. We think this is quite misguided; hence our middle level is at best a drastic reworking of reference.

There is much that can be explored at the levels of interpretation and evaluation that seems to be largely insulated from other complexities of linguistic meaning. We do this by following two methodological principles.

Our first principle is that, at the level of interpretation, indicative statements stand for, describe, or *designate* (as we will officially say) types of situations.

Our second principle is a version of compositionality, the claim that the meaning of a statement is a function of the meanings of its parts. Stated so vaguely, it could hardly be false.

Frege used this principle in his theory at both levels: the reference of a complex expression is a function of the references of its parts and similarly for sense. Our second methodological principle is the principle of modest and flexible compositionality: be compositional at the level of interpretation, but be modest in our goals, and not overly rigid. Modestly, bite off as little as possible from "meaning" so as to make the interpretations of a whole functions of the interpretation of its parts. Flexibly, realize that there may be more than one way to make a whole out of parts.

There are deliberate ambiguities in these principles. When we said that statements are to designate situation types, we used the plural to mask a complication. Namely, a single statement does not designate a single situation type, but a set of situation types. For example, "Someone is asleep" does not describe a single situation type, that of some particular individual being asleep; rather, it describes the type of situation in which *someone* is asleep. That is, it will designate the set of types of situations in which someone is asleep.

Similarly "Jackie or Molly has fleas" designates the set of types of situations in which either Jackie or Molly or both have fleas. We shall call a set of situation types a *proposition* so that statements designate propositions.

Another ambiguity in the first principle is that between statement and sentence, and here our first principle begins to interact with our second. The sentence "I am a Nebraskan" has a linguistic meaning that is independent of which English speaker uses it, or when (within bounds of time where the individual words do not take on different meanings or the whole becomes idiomatic). However, it expresses different propositions (types of situations) depending on who says it. Said by the first author, the resulting statement designates a set of unrealized types of situations. As said by the second, the resulting statement is different and contains the actual world type among those it designates.

In our emphasis on statements and types of situations we follow J. L. Austin in his famous paper "Truth." However, Austin tried to have his "descriptive conventions" take one straight from sentences to situation types, a move which conflates two steps that need to be kept separate. (Here Austin failed to implement the insight mentioned above; Kaplan's system does.) The way that utterances of "I am a Nebraskan" give rise to different statements is an important part of linguistic meaning, but one that gets in the way of having sentences designate situation types. Hence our emphasis on statements.[5]

A sentence is a sentence of some language, and part of what the language provides is the linguistic meaning of the sentence. In a particular use, the linguistic meaning provides interpretations of the parts and the whole. The interpretation of the whole is to be the set of situation types designated by the statement. (This is an

SEMANTIC INNOCENCE AND UNCOMPROMISING SITUATIONS

oversimplification; as we shall see. The interpretation of the parts underdetermines the interpretation of the whole.) In general, the statement will have one interpretation that is independent of the way things really are in the world: that is, an interpretation determined by the statement, the set A of objects, and the set R of relations, but independent of the structure of the world as it happens to be. This must be the case since we can interpret statements that turn out to be false or that have to do with situations that are inaccessible to us.

Let us now turn to our second methodological principle — modest and flexible compositionality. First, let us look at a trivial application. The interpretation of "Jackie barks" is to be a proposition, the set of situation types s in which Jackie barks, i.e.,

$$\{s \mid s(\text{is barking, Jackie}) = 1\}.$$

It is also to be a function of the interpretation of the parts of the statement, so "Jackie" must supply the object Jackie and "barks" the property of barking. That is, the simplest choice of interpretations compatible with our principles is to interpret "Jackie" as Jackie and "barks" as the property of barking. At the level of interpretation, then, we find objects as the interpretations of names, variables, and other non-complex terms, properties and relations as the interpretation of simple predicates, and propositions (i.e., sets of situation types) as the interpretation of statements.

There is a tendency in twentieth-century philosophy of language to conflate properties with meanings; this must be avoided. When the first author says "Mollie is this color," pointing to a rug of a certain color, and the second author says "Jackie is this color," pointing to a book, they use exactly the same verb phrase with the same meaning. But if the colors of the rug and the book are different, the predicates stand for quite different properties in the two statements.

To carry the analysis of interpretation one step further, let us find out what the interpretation of a complex predicate, or verb phrase, like "loves Mary" is. At first there is a problem. We interpret "loves" by a two-place relation l and "Mary" by Mary, and need to get out of the two some property — the property of loving Mary. Do we need to assume that this is a primitive or can we construct it out of what we have on hand?

To show how to construct it, we start from our first principle. For any a in A, we want to statement that a loves Mary to be interpreted as the set of situation types s in which a loves Mary, $s(l, a, \text{Mary}) = 1$. Call this proposition, this set of situation types, $p(a)$. The function from any a in A to $p(a)$ has two important properties: (1) it can be defined solely in terms of the interpretations l of "loves" and Mary of "Mary," and (2) from this function and any $a \in A$ we can construct the proposition that a loves Mary, namely, $p(a)$. These are just the properties we require of an interpretation of "loves Mary."

Thus, we define P to be the set of all propositions obtainable from A and R, and we call any function from A into P a *complex property*. They are our analogue of Russell's propositional functions. Any primitive property p can be identified with a complex property p*—the property of having p—by defining p*(x) to be the proposition that x has p,

$$p^*(x) = \{s \in S \mid s(p,x) = 1\}$$

So, in general, the interpretation of a verb phrase is a complex property.

A moment's thought will convince the reader that the conjunction of two statements ϕ and ψ should be interpreted by intersection of their respective interpretations. If we use $[\![\phi]\!]$ to denote the interpretation of ϕ, then $[\![\phi$ and $\psi]\!] = [\![\phi]\!] \cap [\![\psi]\!]$. Similarly, $[\![\phi$ or $\psi]\!] = [\![\phi]\!] \cup [\![\psi]\!]$. What about negation?

Austin, in "Truth," laments the confusion between falsity and negation, and with this we must agree. In the situation we are aware of here in our study, it is not true that Jackie is barking. Jackie is not present to our senses; she is just not part of this situation. Thus, while the proposition that Jackie is barking does not contain the type of the situation we are aware of, neither does the proposition that Jackie *is not* barking. Knowing Jackie, she probably is barking at home. Thus, the statement that Jackie is not barking is interpreted as the set of types s such that s (is barking, Jackie) = 0, whereas the statement *It is false that Jackie is barking* can be interpreted as $\{s \mid s(\text{is barking, Jackie}) \neq 1\}$. Only this last proposition contains the situation we are aware of. Since situation types are partial world types, they never take on more than one value 0 or 1, but being partial, they may take on neither. This does not mean that we have a "three-valued logic." A statement is either true or it is not.

Situation semantics is much more flexible than more traditional approaches in ways that should please the linguist or philosopher of language who has not let traditional logic get too firm a hold on his thought processes. The proposal we are making leads to a rethinking of much of traditional logic. Certain classically simple concepts like negation and material implication are seen as conflations of several notions, brought about by working with only a single situation—the world.

In speaking of flexible compositionality, however, we had in mind another and absolutely central aspect of our theory. Recall that our system has three levels: meaning, interpretation, and evaluation. The idea behind the third category is this. Often by taking a look at the world or at some part of the world (or even at some pertinent situation type that does not fit the world) an expression can be fitted with a "value-laden interpretation"—an interpretation that depends on how the situation type arranges things. This value-laden interpretation is an alternative contribution that the expression can make to the interpretation of the statement of which it forms a part.

Some obvious sorts of evaluation consist in: 1) determining whether a given type of situation is in a given proposition; 2) determining the extension of a property in a given situation; 3) determining the properties an individual has in a given situation. We think that certain traditional semantical categories, such as Frege's *bedeutung* or the more modern notion of extension, are sort of a jumble between interpretation and evaluation, provoked by the central role of evaluation in understanding language. Thus propositions have been taken to be truth values, properties conflated with extensions, and in Montague's work individuals have almost been identified with sets of properties.

Sensitivity to the differences between value-free and value-laden interpretations of statements is dulled by the logical tradition that ignored situations. For unembedded sentences in simple situations, value-laden and value-free interpretations will not be so different, and in particular their truth values will agree, so long as the salient situation type belongs to a part of the world.

But the distinction is hard to ignore when sentences are embedded in perception and belief contexts. Thus everyone can feel the two readings of

> Sally saw a dog with fleas jump in the pool.

or

> Sally thinks the dean's secretary is a dean.

One who fails to see the alternative interpretations when the statements are unembedded is forced to find an alternative source for the ambiguity of the embedding statements. The appeal is naturally to scope, and this way of looking at things is so engrained as to be confused with the phenomena itself. We see the ambiguity as simply a matter of the interpretation of the embedded sentence, not a matter of scope.

Applied to definite descriptions, the value-free, value-laden distinction is simply Donnellan's distinction between attributive and referential uses.[6] Russell's theory of definite descriptions focused on their value-free or attributive use, Frege's and Strawson's on their value-laden use. Donnellan saw that these should not be alternative theories, but alternative uses accounted for by a single theory. Donnellan was unsure what sort of ambiguity he was drawing attention to; some philosophers have thought he was simply calling attention to the potential ambiguity, due to scope, when sentences containing definite descriptions were embedded. We think that Donnellan put his finger on a straightforward semantic ambiguity, and that the attributive-referential distinction is one manifestation of a ubiquitous and important phenomenon of value loading.

4. INNOCENT SEMANTICS

One can find two reasons in Frege for giving up innocence. The first is that substitution of co-referential expressions within statements embedded in certain linguistic contexts does not preserve truth of the whole embedding statement. Such contexts are now often called, following Quine, "referentially opaque." Propositional attitudes are widely believed to be referentially opaque. We believe that by and large they are not. In any case, there should be general agreement that *some* are not. One such context is non-epistemic perception:

> (1) Sally sees Mollie run.

Another is ordinary belief:

> Sally believes that my dog is running.

Some arguments for referential opacity seem to be based on ignoring the difference between value-laden and value-free interpretation. One might argue, for example, that non-epistemic perception is opaque, citing the falsity of

(1)′ Sally sees the dog with the red collar run.

But (1)′ is only false if the description is used attributively; that is, if the type of scene Sally is said to see has the property of having a red collar as a constituent. But so used, the substitution of "the dog with the red collar" for "Mollie" does not preserve interpretation. On the other hand, if the description is value-loaded (using a type of a larger portion of the world than Sally sees to do the loading), (1)′ is true if (1) is, given that Mollie is the dog in question.

Some arguments for referential opacity seem based on a confusion between conversational implicatures and semantic entailments. Thus we think that "Smith believes Cicero was an orator" does not imply, but at most suggests, that Smith would check "Cicero was an orator" true. The suggestion is clearly cancelable: "Smith believes that Cicero was an orator, but only knows to call him 'Tully'."[7]

In any case, it seems clear to us that there are transparent sentence-embedding propositional attitudes. But Frege's second reason for giving up innocence was a set of considerations that convinced him that any such contexts would be equivalent to "It is true that . . ."

In "Sense and Reference" he asks what the reference of an entire declarative sentence should be, when it is "concerned with the reference of its words." He concludes that it is the truth value. A key point in favor of this is that the truth value of an expression remains unchanged when a part of the sentence is replaced by an expression having the same reference. "What else but the truth value could be found," asks Frege, "that belongs quite generally to every sentence if the reference of its components is relevant, and remains unchanged by substitutions of the kind in question?"[8]

An innocent semantics takes the reference of the statement—that aspect of signification that depends on the reference of its parts—to be just that which contributes to the reference of the wholes in which it is embedded. If we take the reference of the sentence to be its truth value, an innocent semantics is hopeless, as Frege sees:

> If now the truth value of a sentence is its reference, then on the one hand all true sentences have the same reference and so, on the other hand, do all false sentences. From this we can see that in the reference of a sentence all that is specific is obliterated.[9]

Given that Mollie is running and Richard lying, this would leave an innocent semantics committed to the equivalence of

(1) Sally sees Mollie run

(2) Sally sees Richard lie

or

(3) Sally believes that Mollie is running
(4) Sally believes that Richard is lying.

A semantics that could not grant these pairs different truth values would be quite hopeless.

The tradition has come to grips with Frege's loss of innocence in two ways: (i) for plausibly opaque propositional attitudes, treat the sentences as embedded and the semantics as guilty; (ii) for undeniably transparent propositional attitudes, treat the embedding of the sentence as illusory, adopting an analysis that removed the seemingly transparent position out of its spot in the embedded sentence. The semantics for that portion of the sentence left embedded will again be non-innocent.

Our approach is to treat the sentence as embedded and the semantics as innocent, and to deny that the problems that Frege and others have seen with this approach amount to much of anything.

For example, we take a statement of the form *X sees S* to embed a statement S, and to be true just in case X sees a scene (a specific kind of situation) that belongs to some type in the interpretation of S. We take *X believes that S,* in its most central and ordinary uses, to say that X has a certain complex relational property built of the objects and properties that are constituents of the proposition that S. In both cases, the parts of the embedded statement have their usual interpretations in the whole. What can be wrong with this innocent approach?

5. THE FREGE-CHURCH SLINGSHOT

Frege's own arguments against innocence do not seem very impressive. To his question, "What else but the truth value could be found, that belongs quite generally to every sentence if the reference of its components is relevant, and remains unchanged by substitutions . . . ?" we answer, "The situations designated." In the situation, all that is specific is not lost.

Again, Frege says that "the reference of a sentence may always be sought, whenever the reference of its components is involved, and this is the case when and only when we are inquiring after the truth value." This seems to imply that we are only interested in the reference of the components of a sentence when we are inquiring about its truth value; but this is not so. If I am told "Smith believes his neighbor is a fool," I might be quite interested in the reference of "his neighbor," without caring at all about the truth of the embedded sentence.

There is, however, a very influential argument, virtually a priori, suggested no doubt by Frege's remarks, laid down explicitly by Church in his review of Carnap, and deployed in various forms with formal rigor and ruthless vigor by Quine, Davidson, and others, which seems to rule out the very possibility of a non-trivial situation semantics. The argument is so small, seldom encompassing more than half a page, and employs such a minimum of ammunition—a theory of descriptions and a popular notion of logical equivalence—that we dub it *the slingshot*. As developed by Church, the conclusion is that all sentences with the same truth value must designate the same thing. As developed by Quine, we are put in the dilemma of either accepting "extensionality," which means seeing no distinction between (1) and (2) or (3) and (4), or losing our innocence and accepting opacity. Davidson used the slingshot to rule out straighforward innocent semantics, and then applied incredible resources of ingenuity to recover lost innocence in roundabout ways.

Church gives a form of the slingshot in the opening sections of his *Introduction to Mathematical Logic,* to motivate taking truth values as the key notion in developing logic. This version of the argument is especially interesting because, being for a reader who does not already know logic, Church cannot fall back on an appeal to any accepted notion of logical equivalence. This makes it eminently suited for reexamination, to see just where it goes wrong. Church considers these sentences:

(5) Sir Walter Scott is the author of *Waverly.*

(6) Sir Walter Scott is the man who wrote the twenty-nine *Waverly* novels altogether.

(7) The number, such that Sir Walter Scott is the man that wrote that many *Waverly* novels altogether, is twenty-nine.

(8) The number of counties in Utah is twenty-nine.

Church argues that as we go from each sentence to the next, what the sentences denote is the same. But the first and last seem to have nothing of importance in common except their truth value; he says, "Elaboration of examples of this kind leads us quickly to the conclusion, as at least plausible, that all true sentences have the same denotation."[10]

Sentence (6) results from (5) by replacement of one description by another, where both descriptions describe the same person, Scott. Sentence (8) results from (7) by a similar move, with the descriptions describing the same number, twenty-nine. The step from (6) to (7), however, is of a different sort. Church says that (6), though perhaps not synonymous with (7), "is at least so nearly so as to ensure having the same denotation."[11]

The argument is like an ambiguous figure or an Escher drawing. If you are aware of situations, you have to keep shifting perspective to let the argument trick you. From one perspective the first and last steps are fine but the middle step is all wrong. From a second perspective the middle step is reasonably good but the first and last steps are completely unfounded.

Intuitively, situations are complexes of objects and relations (under which we shall from now on subsume properties). Given this conception, the role of the parts of the sentence is to identify objects and relations out of which the complex is constructed. Let us hold this in mind, and go through the steps of the argument from both perspectives.

To get from (5) to (6), we need to suppose that the great difference between "the author of *Waverly*" and "the man who wrote the twenty-nine *Waverly* novels altogether" makes absolutely no difference to the situations described by the two sentences, that is, that the contribution these two descriptions make to the situation is just to identify Scott. Thus, the first perspective is the one where all four definite descriptions are interpreted by the objects they happen to describe, Scott in two cases, the number twenty-nine in the other two.

But from this perspective, the step from (6) to (7) does not work at all. Recall we are attempting to show that all four sentences must designate the same situations. But from our current perspective, (6) designates a situation whose only constituent object is Scott, whereas, (7) designates one whose only constituent object is the number twenty-nine.

Now let us focus on the step from (6) to (7). If we attempt to see these sentences as designating the same situation, then it must be that of Scott's having written exactly twenty-nine *Waverly* novels altogether. To see them as designating this situation, however, we must pay close attention to the properties involved in the definite descriptions. This is not unreasonable. If you take situations seriously, it is quite natural to distinguish two ways in which descriptions might contribute to the sentence. The need is for the materials to build a situation, a complex of objects and properties, and why should the description not contribute the individual described or the properties involved in the description of the situation?

Thus, the second perspective, which is suggested anyway if we take situations seriously, is the one where "the author of *Waverly*" is not interpreted simply as Scott, but contributes the complex of objects and properties it mentions to the situations the sentence describes. But this perspective is absolutely fatal to the step from (5) to (6) or from (7) to (8). The descriptions of Scott, and those of twenty-nine even more so, contribute radically different objects and properties to the overall situation. Sentence (7) designates twenty-nine's being the number of *Waverly* novels Scott wrote, but sentence (8) designates twenty-nine's being the number of counties in Utah: distinct situations if ever there were distinct situations.

So we see that from the first perspective, the one Frege would have us take, where in the reference of the description all that is specific is obliterated, the first and last steps of the argument are fine but the middle is wrong. From the second perspective, more in line with Russell's theory of descriptions, the middle step comes off better but the first and the last steps are wrong. Under neither reading are we compelled to accept the argument.

The connection between the slingshot and Russell's theory of descriptions was, in effect, commented on by Gödel in his essay "Russell's Mathematical Logic," for he used a sort of reverse slingshot to motivate Russell's theory:

> But different true sentences may indicate different true things. Therefore, this view about sentences makes it necessary either to drop the above mentioned principle (of compositionality) . . . or to deny that a descriptive phrase denotes the object described. Russell did the latter by taking the viewpoint that a descriptive phrase denotes nothing at all but only has meaning in context, . . .[12]

Gödel goes on to say that he cannot help feeling that the puzzling conclusion of the slingshot "has only been evaded by Russell's theory of descriptions and that there is something behind it which is not yet completely understood."[13]

We believe that "something" was gotten at by Donnellan, with the referential and attributive distinction, and that this version of the slingshot, and every version of it, simply turns on shifts from value-free to value-laden interpretations. We value load the definite descriptions for the first step, take them as value-free for the next, and then load them again to finish the argument.

Church speaks of the intimate relation between (6) and (7) but, as he is introducing logical ideas at this point, does not exploit the fact that they are logically equivalent in the traditional sense: true in just the same models. From one perspective they are both identity statements (*Scott is Scott, twenty-nine is twenty-nine*, respectively). From the other they are contingent, but nevertheless true in just the same models. For the philosopher who has learned the traditional notion of logical equivalence, it is easy to be impressed by this. It might seem that logically equivalent statements must stand for the same thing; they must, after all, be equivalent in their *logical* powers or they would not be called that. But this line of thought would use the idea that all true sentences stand for the same thing as a premise for an argument where it is also the conclusion. If sentences designate truth values, then, of course, sentences that have the same truth value under all assignments to the non-logical constants will be equivalent in what they designate. But if statements designate something else, they might be equivalent in truth value in virtue of logical structure, while being non-equivalent in what they designate. On our theory, "logical equivalence" is a misnomer for the relation between statements true in the same models; such statements need not have the same subject matter, in the sense of objects and properties designated by their parts, at all. As soon as such "logically equivalent" statements differing in subject matter are embedded in other statements, the differences in their logical powers become evident. The standard notion of logical equivalence plays an important role in the uses of the slingshot to which we now turn.

6. QUINE AND THE SLINGSHOT

Quine uses various forms of the slingshot throughout his writings. One of the most explicit of these uses comes in his discussion of what he calls the extensionality principle: statements occur within other statements either truth functionally or opaquely, which forces one to give up semantic innocence.[14] When we suppose that (1) and (3) might be true, and (2) and (4) false, but still maintain that the parts of the embedded sentences make their usual contributions to the wholes, we are violating the extensionality principle.

Quine does not say that such violation is impossible, only that it is "not easy". Suppose S and S' are true and that F is a referentially transparent sentence-embedding context. Quine wants to argue that if F(S) is true, so is F(S'), and conversely. First note that

(A) $\{x \mid S \& x = \phi\} = \{x \mid S' \& x = \phi\} = \{\phi\}$
(B) S is logically equivalent to $[\{\phi\} = \{x \mid S \& x = \phi\}]$
S′ is logically equivalent to $[\{\phi\} = \{x \mid S' \& x = \phi\}]$

From F(S) we obtain $F([\{\phi\} = \{x \mid S \& x = \phi\}])$ by substitution of logical equivalents, then we obtain $F([\{\phi\} = \{x \mid S' \& x = \phi\}])$ by (A) and the referential transparency of F, and then F(S′) by another substitution of logical equivalents. If S and S′ are both false, trade ϕ for $\{\phi\}$. Thus, if F is referentially transparent, it will treat sentences that just happen to have the same truth values alike.

Quine finds in this argument "compelling" grounds for the principle of extensionality, a principle he was to come to advocate for the whole of science.[15] And yet he quite explicitly observes that for it to work we must suppose not only that the embedding context is transparent but that logical equivalents are interchangeable in it. The argument simply takes us from the premise that transparent contexts do not discriminate among "logically equivalent" statements to the conclusion that they do not discriminate among statements that happen to be equivalent in truth value.

All the versions of the slingshot turn on the fact that logically equivalent statements can differ in subject matter, i.e., in what individuals and relations their parts designate.

Let us call a context that is transparent and in which logical equivalents are interchangeable *unconcerned* (about subject matter). Those that are transparent but in which logical equivalents are not interchangeable we shall call *concerned*. There seem to be a number of clearly concerned contexts. The most compelling is perception:

(9)   Fred sees Betty enter.
(10) Fred sees Betty enter and (Sally smoke or Sally not smoke).

The statements embedded in (9) and (10) are logically equivalent. "Fred sees" seems clearly a transparent context. And yet we cannot go from (9) to (10). If we did, we should have to admit that Fred either saw Sally smoke or saw Sally not smoke, even though, as we may suppose, Fred has never laid eyes on Sally. The admission would be forced by the principles:

If Fred sees P and Q, then Fred sees Q
If Fred sees P or Q, then Fred sees P or Fred sees Q.

One could of course deny one of these principles to save the principle of extensionality, or one could deny that perception statements such as (9) and (10) are transparent. But we see no motive for either move. Quine seems to convey the attitude that unconcerned contexts are in the natural order of things, but, to be fair, does not say that there are no concerned contexts. His argument has to do with his statement operator "nec," and he carefully stipulates that logical equivalents are interchangeable within it without change of truth value. Other writers are not always so careful.

7. DAVIDSON AND THE SLINGSHOT

The term "slingshot" was originally suggested to us by Donald Davidson's use of this compact piece of philosophical artillery in his wars against some of the giants of our industry. It is an essential part of his criticisms of Reichenbach on events and of Austin on truth, for example. The biggest giant Davidson takes on is Frege, however, for Davidson has consistently resisted the idea that statements embedded in propositional attitudes retain specificity by referring to Fregean senses. For this resistance, and for his recognition of situations, particularly in the analysis of action statements, he should be applauded. Unfortunately, Davidson was blocked from the most straightforward implementation of these insights by his devotion to the slingshot, a weapon constructed of Frege's own materials. To vary the pun, although Davidson resisted original *sinn*, he succumbed to original *bedeutung*.

To see how the slingshot corrupts Davidson, let us briefly look at his criticisms of Reichenbach. In *Elements of Symbolic Logic* Reichenbach developed a formal symbolic logic in which he quantified over situations, events, and facts. For Reichenbach the terms "fact" and "event" were synonymous, and events "have the physical existence of things, and not the fictitious existence of situations."[16] Thus his events and facts are analogous to our situations, his situations to our situation types.

Reichenbach sees a close relation between statements like (11) and (12):

(11) Scott wrote Waverly

(12) The event of Scott writing Waverly took place.

He refers to such statements as alternative ways of "splitting" a situation: "thing splitting" and "event splitting." The close relation is that a certain situation "corresponds" to (11) which is referred to by the description in (12). Reichenbach does not think that there is any singular term, manifest or hidden, in (11) that refers to the situation; only the statement as a whole has this relation to it; the transformation from (11) to (12) is "holistic."

Davidson finds much of value in Reichenbach's theory.[17] He acknowledges and emphasizes the importance of recognizing situations in resolving a number of problems about the logic of action statements. But he has to reject the leading component of Reichenbach's idea: he does not think (11) can correspond to the situation referred to by the description in (12) unless (11) also contains a (hidden) argument place for events. At this point, we think, Davidson purchases philosophical insight at the cost of syntactic plausibility.

The villain here is the slingshot. It convinces Davidson that Reichenbach's proposal is "radically defective," in leading inevitably to the conclusion that there is only one big event. The deployment of the slingshot depends on the principle,

If S and S' are logically equivalent, then, for every event e, e consists in the fact that S if and only if e consists in the fact that S'.

This is just the assumption that "e consists in the fact that" provides an unconcerned context. Here Davidson is being less cautious than Quine was, perhaps more awed by the phrase "logical equivalence." There is no reason at all to suppose this operator would be unconcerned, as should now be pretty clear. The natural development of the idea of a statement corresponding to an event or class of events will have that event or class of events determined by the objects and properties the parts of the statement designate. And logically equivalent statements can have parts that designate very different sets of objects and relations. Reichenbach would have no reason to accept the principle.

Logical equivalence as an unargued-for criterion for statement codesignation plays a key role in another important paper of Davidson's. In "Truth and Meaning" he considers the possibility of a semantical system something like ours.[18] Our level of interpretation is an aspect of meaning that is assigned to statements in a (modest and flexible) way as a function of the interpretations of the parts. Such a system, Davidson argues, must conclude that all true sentences have the same meaning, and so, too, all of the false ones. This version of the slingshot takes up very little room:

> But now suppose that 'R' and 'S' abbreviate any two sentences alike in truth value. Then the following four sentences have the same reference:
>
> (1) R
> (2) $\hat{x}(x = x.R) = \hat{x}(x = x)$
> (3) $\hat{x}(x = x.S) = \hat{x}(x = x)$
> (4) S
>
> For (1) and (2) are logically equivalent, as are (3) and (4), whereas (3) differs from (2) only in containing the singular term '$\hat{x}(x = x.S)$' where (2) contains '$\hat{x}(x = x.R)$' and these refer to the same thing if S and R are alike in truth value.[19]

This difficulty for such a theory of meaning looms when we make two assumptions Davidson describes as reasonable:

> ... that logically equivalent singular terms have the same reference; and that a singular term does not change its reference if a contained singular term is replaced by another with the same reference.[20]

Davidson notes that the argument is essentially Frege's, cites Church, and says that "the argument does not depend on any particular identification of the entities to which sentences are supposed to refer."

Although we do not speak this way, in assigning interpretations to whole statements, we might be said to be treating them as singular terms. Let us look at Davidson's two principles, then, from the perspective of someone who treats statements as singular terms referring to situations. The first principle would be totally unacceptable, for it is really simply the rejection of this very idea. This is not surprising, since it was the rejection of the whole idea by Frege that led to the use of "logical equivalence" that the statement of the principle exploits. In spite of what Davidson says, it is hard to imagine any among those who have decided that statements designate at all who would accept this principle, except those who had decided they designate truth values. The second principle is ambiguous, depending on whether complex singular terms are given a value-free or value-laden interpretation. Taken the first way, and assuming the first principle, the first step in the argument works but not the second. Taken the second way, the first step fails.

8. FINAL REMARKS

In many contexts embedded statements seem to contribute something more specific than their truth values to the embedding statement. Frege's choice of the truth value as that which belongs to the statement in virtue of the references of its parts precluded taking this appearance at face value. His approach was to look to another aspect of meaning for the specificity provided by the embedded statement. Others who are skeptical of meaning beyond reference, like Quine, have been led to doubt the very intelligibility of such statement-embedding contexts. A third approach is to recognize that statements do contribute something to the larger wholes in which they are found, something that turns on the designations of their parts, but to deny that when this occurs they are truly embedded. Quine takes this attitude too at times, and Davidson's article from which our opening quotation was taken adopts a radical version of this approach. Perhaps a combination of the first and third attitudes is something like philosophical orthodoxy. Frege's approach is taken toward certain cases ("de dicto"): the statement is embedded, but what it provides does not turn on the reference of its parts. The third attitude is taken toward other cases ("de re"): the parts of the contained statement do provide their designations to the whole, but the statements are not really embedded, they only seem to be at the level of superficial syntax.

An alternative is to question Frege's original decision. Here we think the slingshot has had a real and unfortunate influence. Perhaps its most important use was the first, Church's in his review of Carnap's *Introduction to Semantics*. Church used principles internal to Carnap's system to show that it must have truth values as the designations of sentences, rather than the situation-like propositions Carnap had intended. Church's argument turned on the principle that "L-equivalent" sentences have the same designation and on the assumption that substitution of two quite different singular terms designating the null class preserved the designation of the sentence in which they occur ('Λ' and '$(\lambda x)(x = x \ \& \sim \ldots)$', where ' $\ldots$ ' is some true but not L-true sentence). His argument seems decisive against Carnap's system as it stands. One possible response would have been to rethink Carnap's principles about designation and his conception of propositions, to see if the slingshot could be avoided. But both Church and Carnap went in another direction and assumed that what is specific is not to be found in the reference of the sentence. Awesomely formal deployments of the slingshot seem to put this beyond question. One can see the whole development of possible worlds semantics, and much else in the philosophy of language of the past thirty years, as an outgrowth of this response to Church's deployment of the slingshot against Carnap.

We like to view situation semantics and possible worlds semantics as two lines meeting in a single point, that point being where there is only one world and one situation. We believe a more workable semantics for natural language can be developed along the line we are proposing and that many of the valuable insights of the possible worlds approach can be incorporated into it. It may turn out, however, that the semantic facts will not fit such a narrow-minded view, and that we will have to look at the complex plane determined by the two lines. If so, we leave it to the reader to decide which line is the real axis and which is the imaginary.

Notes

1. Donald Davidson, "On Saying That," reprinted in *The Logic of Grammar*, ed. Donald Davidson and Gilbert Harman (Encino, Calif., 1975), p. 152. Originally published in *Synthese* 19 (1968-69). Our italics.

2. Rudolf Carnap, *Introduction to Semantics* (Cambridge, 1942); Alonzo Church, "Carnap's Introduction to Semantics," *Philosophical Review* 52 (1943):298-305.

3. David Kaplan, "Dthat" and "On the Logic of Demonstratives," in *Contemporary Perspectives in the Philosophy of Language*, ed. Peter A. French, Theodore E. Uehling, Jr., and Howard K. Wettstein (Minneapolis, 1979), pp. 383-412.

4. J. L. Austin, *Philosophical Papers* (Oxford, 1961). See particularly "Truth" and "Unfair to Facts."

5. We try to use "sentence" and "statement" properly, except when discussing the views of others where it seems inappropriate.

6. Keith Donnellan, "Reference and Definite Descriptions," *Philosophical Review* 75 (1966):281-304; "Putting Humpty Dumpty Together Again," *Philosophical Review* 77 (1968): 203-15. Ruth Marcus remarks in passing in "Modalities and Intensional Languages," *Synthese* 14 (1962), that descriptions can function as proper names, i.e., "purely referentially"; she takes their normal use to be more like the attributive; see page 283.

7. See J. O. Urmson, "Criteria of Intentionality," in *Logic and Philosophy for Linguists* ed. J. M. E. Moravcsik (The Hague, 1974) pp. 226-37. See also Jon Barwise, "Scenes and Other Situations," unpublished paper, Stanford University, and John Perry. "Belief and Acceptance," *Midwest Studies in Philosophy* 5 (1980):533-42 and "The Problem of the Essential Indexical," *Noûs* 13 (1979):3-21.

8. Gottlob Frege, "On Sense and Reference," in *Translations from the Philosophical Writings of Gottlob Frege*, ed. and trans. Peter Geach and Max Black (Oxford, 1960) p. 64.

9. *Ibid.*, 65.

10. Alonzo Church, *Introduction to Mathematical Logic* (Princeton, 1956), p. 25.

11. *Ibid.*

12. Kurt Gödel, "Russell's Mathematical Logic," reprinted in *Philosophy of Mathematics*, ed. Paul Benacerraf and Hilary Putnam (Englewood Cliffs, N.Y., 1966) pp. 214-15.

13. *Ibid.*

14. W. V. Quine, "Three Grades of Modal Involvement," in *Ways of Paradox*, revised and enlarged edition (Cambridge, 1976) pp. 163-64.

15. W. V. Quine, "The Scope and Language of Science," in *Ways of Paradox*, p. 242.

16. Hans Reichenbach, *Elements of Symbolic Logic* (New York, 1966), p. 272. Relevant sections are reprinted in *The Logic of Grammar*, ed. Davidson and Harman.

17. Donald Davidson, The Logical Form of Action Sentences," in *The Logic of Grammar*, pp. 235-46. This essay was originally published in *The Logic of Decision and Action*, ed. Nicholas Rescher (Pittsburgh, 1967).

18. Donald Davidson, "Truth and Meaning," in *Philosophical Logic*, ed. J. W. Davis et al. (Dordrecht, 1969) pp. 1-20. This essay was originally published in *Synthese* 17 (1967).

19. *Ibid.*, p. 3.

20. *Ibid.*, pp. 2-3.

Analytic Philosophy and Mental Phenomena
JOHN R. SEARLE

1. INTRODUCTION: THE BEHAVIORIST BACKGROUND

Throughout most of its history analytic philosophy has exhibited a curious prejudice against the mental. Many, perhaps most, analytic philosophers have felt that there was something especially puzzling about mental processes, states, and events, and that we would be better off if they could be analyzed away or explained in terms of something else or somehow eliminated. One sees this attitude, for example, in the persistent use of pejorative adjectives, such as "mysterious" and "occult," that analytic philosophers from Ryle to Rorty use to characterize mental phenomena naively construed.

I first became aware of the pervasiveness of this attitude when I tried to extend my analysis of speech acts to intentional states. No one doubts the existence of promises, statements, apologies, and commands, but when the analysis is extended to beliefs, fears, hopes, desires, and visual experiences, suddenly philosophers raise a host of "ontological" doubts. I think that thinking and other mental processes and events, like linguistic processes and events, are biologically based and are as real as digestion, conversation, lactation, or any other of the familiar biologically based processes. This seems to me so obviously true as to be hardly worth arguing, but I am assured that it is a minority opinion in contemporary philosophy.

During the positivist and verificationist phase of analytic philosophy the reason for the urge to eliminate the mental was not difficult to see: if the meaning of a statement is its method of verification and if the only method of verification of statements about the mental is in the observations of behavior, at least where "other minds" are concerned, then it would appear that some sort of behaviorism is an immediate logical consequence of verificationism. Statements about the mental are equivalent in meaning to statements about behavior.

Most philosophers today regard behaviorism as dead; yet, as I shall argue, many of them hold views that suffer from the same sort of defects as behaviorism. So, let us begin by examining what is wrong with behaviorism. Sometimes in reading the literature on this subject one gets the impression that behaviorism is at fault because of some more or less technical reason: the behaviorists never quite got a satisfactory account of the notion of a disposition, or their analyses suffered from some sort of circularity, or they never could give a satisfactory formulation of the antecedent clauses in the analysanda, or they had weak answers to the "perfect actor" or simulation arguments. Or some such. I want to suggest that these defects are not the basic flaws in behaviorism; at most they are surface symptoms of the underlying problem. If we remember that in its material mode version, behaviorism is the view that mental phenomena just are patterns of the behavior, then it just seems obviously false. To me at least, its falsity seems clear as soon as I ask myself what it is like to have some conscious mental phenomenon such as a pain and contrast that with what it is like to engage in certain sorts of behavior appropriate to pains. For example, I now have a stomachache, not a violent one, but a nagging pain at the back of my stomach. The fact that I have this stomachache is quite a different fact, and indeed a different sort of fact altogether, from any facts, including conditional facts, about my behavior. Having a stomachache is one thing; engaging in various sorts of behavior appropriate to having a stomachache is something quite different.

I do not present this objection as an *argument* against behaviorism; if so, it would be question begging since the facts I am reminding myself of are stated in a way that simply asserts the falsity of behaviorism. What I want ultimately is not a refutation of behaviorism but an understanding of the underlying motives that gave rise to such an unplausible thesis in the first place.

Well, one might say, Rylean behaviorism was always troubled by the analysis of sensations such as pains. But it is much more satisfactory for beliefs and desires. It is not at all obvious that behavioristic analyses of beliefs and desires are false. Perhaps having beliefs and desires, especially in the right combination,[1] just is being disposed to behave in certain ways.

Here again I want to argue that behaviorism is false, though its falsity is not as obvious in this case as in the case of sensations. Suppose I now have a desire to drive to my office; suppose I want to drive to my office, as they say, more than I want to do anything else right now. Suppose, furthermore, that I have a set of beliefs about my abilities to drive to my office, about my car and its functioning, about the proper route, and so on. Now, doesn't that all entail that I will, other things being equal, engage in certain sorts of behavior, namely behavior describable as driving to my office, or at least trying to drive to my office? And furthermore, doesn't the appropriate kind of behavior, such as driving to my office, itself manifest or express my beliefs and desires in such a way that given the appropriate formulations, we could say that the behavior is at least a sufficient condition of having a certain range of beliefs and desires? At this point another objection to behaviorism arises: If the project of behaviorism is to analyze mental notions in terms of behavioral notions, then the project fails because the notion of behavior in question, the kind of behavior described in the analysans of the behaviorists' analysis, is itself *intentional* behavior, and therefore the behavior in question is still, in the relevant sense, mental. If by "behavior" we mean human action, then behavior is more than a set of bodily movements or muscle contractions. The bodily movements count as actions only if they are caused by intentions, and the intentions in question are as much mental as the beliefs and desires that they are being invoked to analyze.[2] Rylean behaviorism about beliefs and desires is therefore confronted with a dilemma: either the behavior in question is full-blown human behavior, that is to say, human actions performed intentionally, or it is not. If the former, then the analysis of the mental into the behavioristic is the analysis of the mental into the mental, and we are still left with the mental component in the notion of behavior. If the latter, then we have to construe behavior as bodily movements described solely as bodily movements; and no analysis of statements about beliefs and desires and intentions into statements about bodily movements will ever be adequate because the movements are not yet human actions, and the notion of a bodily movement by itself is inadequate for any analysis of mental states. A human body, for example, might be wired up in such a way that it would undergo all the bodily movements characteristic of driving a car to an office even though it was totally unconscious or even dead. If, in short, "behavior" means action, then behavior is mental. If it means bodily movements, then it is not behavior, and the analysis fails. At this point, the objection to analyzing beliefs and desires in terms of bodily movements (including dispositions to bodily movements) is much like the objection to analyzing sensations such as pain in terms of behavior (including dispositions to behavior): the distinction between mental states and sheer physical bodily movements is as stark as the distinction between pain and behavior.

I want to keep in mind these two objections to behaviorism—the non-identity of sensations and behavior and the mentalistic element in human actions—in what follows. I now want to introduce a distinction between what I will call ascriptions of *intrinsic mental phenomena* on the one hand and *observer relative mental ascriptions* on the other hand. This distinction can be made clear using unproblematic and uncontroversial examples. Suppose I now say that I have a stomachache or that Reagan believes he can win the election. When I make such statements I am ascribing intrinsic mental phenomena to myself and Reagan. But suppose I say that the expression "il pleut" in French means it is raining or that my pocket calculator adds and subtracts but does not divide. In such cases I am not ascribing any intrinsic mental phenomena to the expression "il pleut" or to my pocket calculator. Such statements are in part shorthand statements for the intrinsic mental phenomena of French speakers or users of pocket calculators. They are, roughly speaking, shorthand for saying such things as that by convention people who speak French use the sentence "il pleut" to mean "it is raining" and that I am able to use my calculator for addition and subtraction but not division. There are not two kinds of mental phenomena, intrinsic mental phenomena and observer relative mental phenomena; rather, there are ascriptions of mental predicates where the ascription does not ascribe an intrinsic mental phenomenon to the subject of the ascription. In such case the only mental phenomena in question are in the minds of the observers (or users), not in the subject of the ascription. Thus there are two kinds of *ascriptions* but only one kind of mental phenomena.

2. CARBURETOR FUNCTIONALISM

I want now to turn to functionalism, the most influential of the current forms of the rejection of the mental. I will argue that functionalism suffers from very much the same sort of difficulties as behaviorism and that, in addition, it rests on a confusion between observer relative and intrinsic mental ascriptions.

First, a few words about the recent history of the philosophy of mind to explain how functionalism evolved out of physicalism. In the early days of physicalism, there were a series of objections from more or less dualistically inclined philosophers to the physicalists' view that mental states were identical with brain states. Most of these objections were versions of the argument from Leibniz's Law (e.g., my stomachache is in my stomach but my brain state is in my head, so my stomachache cannot be identical with my brain state), and Smart[3] and his colleagues justifiably felt that they could answer them. (e.g., it is not my stomachache, but my experience of having a stomachache, which is identical with a state of my central nervous system). But there were two classes of arguments that were more troublesome.

First Objection. Suppose physicalism is true as a contingent identity thesis. Then all mental states are identical with some physical states of the brain. But then some physical states of the brain are also mental states, and some other states of the brain are not mental states. What is the difference between them? Well, the obvious difference is that the physical states that are mental states have mental properties and the others do not. But now we seem to be left with a dualism of properties in place of our original dualism of entities; so physicalism is a species of the very dualism it was designed to replace. In place of "mysterious," "occult" mental entities, we are left with "mysterious," "occult" mental properties.

Smart answered this objection by saying that it was possible to describe these entities in a language that did not mention any mental properties, in a language that was "topic neutral." For example, instead of saying, "I am having an orange afterimage" one could say, "Something is going on in me which is like what goes on when I see an orange." But that is no answer. The fact that one can mention an object that has mental properties without mentioning that it has those properties is as irrelevant to its possession of those properties as the fact that one can mention a locomotive without mentioning the fact that it is a locomotive is irrelevant to the fact that it is a locomotive. One could refer to a locomotive in a "topic neutral" way, as, e.g., "A certain item belonging to the Southern Pacific Railroad." But that does not make it any less of a locomotive, and the fact that one can talk of mental states in a veiled topic neutral vocabulary does not make them any less mental. This, by the way, is a recurring fallacy in analytic philosophy, the confusion between features of the language we use to describe a phenomenon and features of the phenomenon.

Second objection. Early physicalists believed that if two people were in the same type of mental state, they must be in the same type of corresponding neurophysiological state, that, for example, if you and I both now believe that it is snowing, we must both have the same type of neurophysiological state which realizes that belief. But for a variety of reasons it seems most implausible to suppose that this is true. Even if mental states are physical states, it can hardly be true that type identical mental states can be identified with type identical neurophysiological states.

The way out of this objection is to notice that many sorts of things can be type identical at one level of description even though each instance is token identical with some object at a lower level of description and those objects at the lower level of description are not type identical. Clocks are the same type of thing at the level of description "clock," even though each clock is token identical with some physical realization, say, a set of mechanically powered gears and wheels, or a set of electrically operated quartz oscillators; and those physical realizations may be type different. And if this works for clocks and carburetors, why not for mental states as well? Thus, you and I can each have the same belief that it is snowing, even though our neurophysiologies may not be type identical, just as your car and my car can each have a carburetor, even though mine is steel and yours is brass. But what is it then that the mental states have in common that makes them type identical? I believe the obvious answer is that mental states are type identical because of their common mental features, whether features of consciousness or of intentionality or both or some further sorts of mental features. But such is the reluctance of many analytic philosophers to take mental phenomena at their face value that this common sense answer was not the one proposed.

According to the functionalists, just as clocks and carburetors are identified by their functions, not by how those functions are realized in the physical structure, so mental states are identified by their functions, and not by how those functions are realized in the brain. Mental states are functional states in a sense that is supposed to be made clear by analogy with clocks and carburetors, and so on. And now the answer to the second objection has, *en passant,* also answered the first. For the "mysterious," "occult" mental properties turn out to be metaphysically harmless functional properties. In a word, type-type identity theories gave way to token-token theories and with them came carburetor functionalism. Functional materialism turned out, more or less inadvertently, to be a kind of eliminative materialism because the functional analysis eliminated any problems about irreducibly mental properties.

An immediate and obvious objection to functionalism is that it seems it could not be right because the mental states in question are intrinsic and functions are always observer relative. The ascription of a function to a system or to an element of a system is always made relative to some goal, purpose, or objective; functions are never just causes, they are causes relative to a teleology. My carburetor intrinsically causes many things, only some of which are its functions; for example, it exerts pressure on the engine block, it makes a hissing sound, it supports the air cleaner, it accumulates dirt, and it mixes air and gasoline. When we say that its *function* is to mix air and gasoline, we are saying more than that it causes the mixing of air and gasoline; we are also saying that *its purpose* is to mix air and gasoline relative to the overall purposes of the system. But such purposes are never intrinsic; they are assigned by us. If I decide to use my carburetor solely for supporting my air cleaner, then its function changes even though there are no changes in any of the intrinsic causal features of the system. The observer relativity of functions, by the way, is also true of systems that are not artifacts. For example, the heart causes the circulation of the blood, a thumping noise in the chest, and pressure on the lung. To say that its *function* is to pump blood is to assign observer relative intentionality to it. A linguistic clue to these facts is that as soon as we assign a function to some causal element, a whole intentionalistic vocabulary becomes appropriate which is inappropriate for causal relations *tout court;* thus we can speak of "malfunction," "breakdown," "functioning properly," and so on.

Now because mental states are intrinsic and functional states are observer relative, it can never be constitutive of mental states that they are functional states. Even if mental (=brain) states always had the same causal relations and even if we always assigned the same functions to these states; still, the features of these states that make them *mental* states are intrinsic and so could not be constituted by any observer relative stance we might take. To put the same point differently, if we try to define mental states in terms of their functions, then something else might serve just those functions, even though it lacked the intrinsic features we were trying to define. The very feature that made carburetor functionalism so appealing, namely, the analogy between the functional level and the physical level of description of carburetors, etc., on the one hand, and the mental and physical level of descriptions of beliefs, etc., on the other hand, is fatal in the end to carburetor functionalism; because the mental level of description is intrinsic and not functional.

I believe that most contemporary functionalists would feel that this is not a serious objection to their view because, so they might argue, the notion of a function is not really essential to functionalism. Ultimately they want to define mental states in terms of their *causal* relations where the causes are intrinsic, even if the functions are not. The argument would then turn on whether the causal features are sufficient to define intrinsic mental features. And I will come to this point shortly.

3. TURING MACHINE OR ORGANIZATIONAL FUNCTIONALISM: PUTNAM AND DENNETT

Let us continue with our story. Carburetor functionalism was soon replaced by Turing machine functionalism. On this view, mental states are indeed functional states, but not just any kind of functional state; rather, they are logical states of a computer, and thus they are *intrinsic* states at least at the level of description of the computer program. Turing machine functionalism is also superior to carburetor functionalism in that it seems to promise a richer theory of the mind, according to which mental processes are computational processes; and this theory seems to be consistent with and supported by current work in cognitive psychology and artificial intelligence. I will consider the work of two authors in this tradition, Hilary Putnam and Daniel Dennett.

I begin with Putnam even though he claims to have abandoned Turing machine functionalism at least in its cruder forms (Putnam, 1975, pp. 298-99). I believe he abandoned it for the wrong reasons. The two reasons he gives for abandoning it are first, that a Turing machine can only be in one state at a time whereas a human can be in many psychological states at the same time, and second, some psychological states such as jealousy are related to other psychological states in a holistic fashion that is unlike the relations among Turing machine states. But this would still permit him to hold that psychological states are matters of functional organization, and it is this aspect of Turing machine functionalism that I want to discuss, not the specific limitations of the computer analogy that have to do with the scope and discreteness of machine states. So perhaps "organizational functionalism" would be a better term than "Turing Machine functionalism" for the view I am criticizing.

Putnam introduces the notion of a "Description" of a system, where a "Description" is defined as a specification of the states and input-output relations of the system as determined by the machine table (the computer program) for that system. He then states a version of organizational functionalism about conscious mental states such as pains.

The hypothesis that "being in pain is a functional state of the organism" may now be spelled out more exactly as follows:

(1) All organisms capable of feeling pain are Probabilistic Automata.

(2) Every organism capable of feeling pain possesses at least one Description of a certain kind (i.e., being capable of feeling pain *is* possesing an appropirate kind of Functional Organization.)

(3) No organism capable of feeling pain possesses a decomposition into parts which separately possess Descriptions of the kind referred to in (2).

(4) For every description of the kind referred to in (2), there exists a subset of the sensory inputs such that an organism with that Description is in pain when and only when some of its sensory inputs are in that subset (Putnam, 1975, p. 434).

It seems to me that this analysis suffers from the same sort of defects as classical behaviorism: being in pain is one thing; satisfying all these conditions or anything like these conditions is something quite different. I will argue for that conclusion by showing that a system could satisfy all these conditions and not feel anything at all, that these conditions are not constitutive of nor sufficient for having sensations such as pains. Since (2) and (4) are the heart of the analysis, I will dispose of (1) and (3) briefly.

(1) "All organisms capable of feeling pain are Probabilistic Automata."

Since everything is a probabilistic automaton under some description or other, as Putnam concedes, this statement is not much help. It does not serve to discriminate organisms capable of feeling pain from anything else. Furthermore, it is important to emphasize that "organism" in the statement does not mean organism in any biological sense. It just means system. It is essential to functionalism of the sort that both Putnam and Dennett adhere to that any system at all capable of having the right functional organization is capable of pain. It need not be an organism in the sense that plants and animals are organisms. Indeed, as we noted earlier, one of the original motivations for functionalism was the recognition that an indefinite number of different types of system could be functionally isomorphic. Robots, for example, could count as "organisms" for Putnam's purposes. So, in what follows, I will use the word "system" since systems are what is being talked about.

(3) "No system capable of feeling pain possesses a decomposition into parts which separately possess Descriptions of the kind referred to in (2)."

The reason for putting in this condition is that many systems can consist of sub-systems and the sub-system may be capable of feeling pain even when the system is not capable of feeling pain. Suppose, for example, we have a system composed of many people working together in a large bureaucracy. Such a system can realize a certain machine table without it being the case that the system suffered any pain in addition to the pain suffered by the individual people, and in order to eliminate these sorts of counterexamples Putnam has inserted condition (3). The elimination of a class of potential counterexamples by simple fiat is generally the sign of a theoretical weakness, and we will shortly see that Putnam's analysis is still subject to related counterexamples.

(2) and (4). "Every system capable of feeling pain possesses at least one Description of a certain kind (being capable of feeling pain *is* possessing an appropriate kind of Functional Organization). For every Description of this kind there exists a subset of the sensory inputs such that a system with that Description is in pain when and only when some of its sensory inputs are in that subset."

What (2) and (4) together amount to is this: Beings capable of pain are those and only those that instantiate a certain computer program; the computer program specifies a set of transition probabilities between input, output, and internal states, and the system will actually be in pain when the right input activates the system according to the program.

There is a way of trivializing Putnam's view so that it implies that a system is in pain if and only if it is in pain. That, I take it, is not his intent. His idea is rather that just as there are specific machine tables for pain, so there are specific inputs for pain. We do not need to know exactly *what they are* but simply *that there are some*, and we can define functionalism in terms of them whatever they are. Furthermore, the use of the expression "sensory" in "sensory input" is as potentially misleading as the use of the term "organism." "Sensory" in this context does not mean sensory in the biological sense, since any system such as, e.g., a robot could have all sorts of sensory inputs without having any of the familiar biological apparatus for the senses. Otherwise, it is impossible to interpret Putnam's various remarks about robots.

Now once you lay bare the real character of the claims made in (2) and (4), you can easily see that it is possible for systems or organisms to satisfy the conditions and not have any pains. I think the claim is as obviously false as behaviorism, and I will present two related arguments to try to make its falsity apparent.

The argument from anesthesia. Let the system in question be me. By hypothesis I am capable of feeling pain because I instantiate a certain machine table. Let us suppose that the machine table is upset and that this is done by anesthetizing the relevant portion of my central nervous system, so that I cannot feel any pains. I now no longer instantiate the machine table. But suppose further that I make up for this by simply memorizing the steps in the machine table, so that I can now go through the steps in my mind. On Putnam's account there is no reason why my own mind could not be the element of the system that instantiates the machine table. Whenever somebody gives me the relevant sensory input, say he punches me in the nose, I do not feel anything because I am anesthetized, but I "look up" in the machine table what I am supposed to do next, and I follow through all the steps until I reach the output and then I say or print out "Ouch!" I cannot feel anything, but I still have the relevant sensory inputs; I still instantiate the machine table and I still have the right input-output "transition probabilities". I satisfy all of Putnam's conditions (1)-(4), but I do not feel any pains at all.

This argument may seem rather swift, but I think in fact the counterexample is decisive. Machine table plus inputs could not be constitutive of nor sufficient for pain because a human agent could in his own mental processes instantiate any machine table you like and could have any inputs you care to induce in him and still not feel the relevant sensations if his specific neurophysiological states are not appropriate. This suggests that functional organization is not the feature of the neurophysiology that really matters, and this suggestion will be pursued in the next objection. It is also important to emphasize that though this objection is stated in terms of machine tables, it would apply to other sorts of functional organization. It is directed at organizational functionalism and not just at the Turing machine version of organizational functionalism.

The argument from biology. Insofar as we know anything about the causal basis of pains and other sensations, we know that they are specific to quite definite sorts of animal and human nervous systems. Humans and many species of animal are capable of suffering pains; but trees, shrubs, and flowers are not, much less stones, waterfalls and mountains. It is an amazing consequence of the claims of Turing machine functionalism that *any sort of substance whatever* is capable of feeling pain, provided only that it instantiates the machine table of principle (2) and has the sort of receptors described in principle (4). Though functionalists recognize and even embrace this consequence, its implausibility is masked from us by the fact that they seldom go through any detailed examples, so let us now try such an example. In my office is a computer console hooked up to a routine garden-variety computer called a PDP-10. Now let us suppose, in line with Putnam's number (2), there is a quite specific machine table which human beings instantiate and which enables them to feel pain. I know of no reason at all to suppose it is true, but let us give it to Putnam for the sake of the argument. Let us now program the PDP-10 with exactly this machine table. Notice that the machine table is purely formal; it has nothing to do with the specific material in which it is instantiated. As Putnam repeatedly insists, two systems can have the same Functional Organization, while having quite different constitutions, and to repeat, "Being capable of feeling pain *is* possessing a certain kind of Functional Organization" (*ibid.*, p. 434). So on Putnam's definition, the PDP-10 is now capable of pain, presumably all the way from mild discomfort to the most frightful agony. We now add a "sensory input." We introduce a transducer which is such that whenever I slam the door of my office or hit the console with my fist this produces an input to the computer as programmed for pain, and the "transition probabilities" are such that on my automatic typewriter the machine prints out, "Ouch!" "You are giving me a terrible stomachache!" "Please stop!" and so on.

We have now satisfied all of Putnam's conditions. We have a probabilistic automaton; by fiat we can give it any machine table or other sort of functional organization that you like; it has no subsystems with the same Description; and it has sensory inputs that trigger the appropriate pain-responses. (And if I have chosen the wrong inputs, it does not matter because the argument remains the same no matter what sensory inputs you put in it). Now is there any reason at all to suppose that the computer is in pain? Real intrinsic pain? Notice that the functionalist thesis is not that for all we know the computer *might* be in pain, but that the computer *must* be in pain because it is in a functional state equivalent to the functional state that human beings are in when they are in pain; and that is all that pain is: a functional state. I think it is obviously empirically false that the computer is in pain, because, to put it as an understatement, it is made of the wrong kind of material and is the wrong sort of system altogether to have pains. To have pains it would have to have a nervous system with neurons, biologically specific pain receptors, etc., or at least it would have to have something that was *causally* and not merely *formally* equivalent to an animal nervous system.

Some other sort of system besides animal nervous systems might be capable of having pains, that is an empirical question; but in order to be capable of having pains the system would have to have the relevant causal powers equal to the causal powers of animal nervous systems, and merely instantiating the same program would never be sufficient to guarantee that. Suppose by some incredible miracle my PDP-10 were in frightful agony. Even if that were true, it would still be no help to Turing machine functionalism, because if it were true it would have to be because the specific causal structure of the hardware somehow duplicated the causal powers of animal nervous systems, and that, as far as functionalism is concerned, is quite accidental. Even if my PDP-10 had, unknown to us, an electrochemical structure capable of feeling pains, the thesis of functionalism is that structure does not matter; what matters is functional organization, and that is defined by purely formal considerations quite independently of the structure. Even if the PDP-10 is in pain, we can then put the same program in a set of water pipes, wind machines, or any crazy Rube Goldberg apparatus you might care to construct, provided only

ANALYTIC PHILOSOPHY AND MENTAL PHENOMENA   415

that it is stable and enduring enough to carry the program. We could, e.g., make the system out of windmills, old beer cans, and paper clips, and according to organizational functionalism, any such system must be in pain. Against this I am arguing that from everything we know about physiology, it seems incredible to suppose that these other systems *could be* in pain, much less that they *must be* in pain.

If we put these two arguments together, we get a sequence of steps to show that both the main claims of organizational functionalism are false. Anybody who wanted to defend this sort of functionalism would have to show that something is wrong with this argument.

The two claims are:

a. For a human to be in pain or some other mental state is just to instantiate a certain sort of functional organization (such as a computer program) with the right inputs and outputs;

b. Any system such as a robot that was functionally equivalent to a human, i.e., that had the right organization and the right input and output relations, would also have to be in pain in virtue of those facts.

Against these I argue:

1. Humans and at least some animals have nervous systems that are causally sufficient to enable them to feel pains and have other sorts of mental states (this is an empirical assumption, shared by both sides in the dispute, about the causal basis of mental phenomena).
2. Any system capable of having pains and other mental states must have the relevant causal powers equivalent to human and animal nervous systems (this is a trivial consequence of 1).
3. Instantiating a certain functional organization such as a program could never by itself be sufficient for mental states, because it would be possible for an agent to instantiate the program and not have the relevant mental states (by the argument from anesthesia). This entails the negation of a.
4. Therefore, a system could not have the relevant causal powers described in 2 solely in virtue of instantiating a certain organization with certain input-output relations (by 2 and 3).
5. Human and animal nervous systems have a causal capacity to produce mental states which is *not* constituted by their having a certain functional organization with certain input-output relations (this is a consequence of 1 and 3).
6. Other systems such as robots could not have mental states solely in virtue of having a functional organization with the right input-output relations but would have to have other causal powers equivalent to those of the brain (a consequence of 2 and 4). This entails the negation of b.

Throughout both these arguments I have been supposing, as a concession for the sake of argument, that my machine table must have some relevant role to play in my feeling of pains, and that might even be true, but there is so far not the slightest reason to suppose it is true. What I am doing here is arguing against the view that organizational functionalism gives us a sufficient condition for the mental. I am conceding for the sake of argument that it might give us a necessary condition, though I do not believe there is any argument for that view, and once you see that it does not give a sufficient condition, most of the motivation for supposing it might give a necessary condition is removed.

I now turn to Dennett, whose opposition to the mental is even more explicit than Putnam's. Typical of Dennett's remarks about mental phenomena is the claim that "beliefs, desires, pains, mental images, experiences—as all these are *ordinarily* understood" are not "good theoretical entities" (Dennett, 1978, p. xx.) The difficulty with this claim is that there are quite different ways in which something can fail to be a "good theoretical entity." Witches and goblins fail to be good theoretical entities because such things do not exist; but tables and chairs, and mountains and beaches, fail to be good theoretical entities not because such things do not exist, but because the laws that describe the course of nature do not use these terms; they do not mention objects under the description "chair," "table," "mountain," or "beach." In that sense, these sorts of things are not good theoretical entities, but so what? At most, that is a remark about which sorts of terms figure in the construction of scientific theories and not about the *existence* of chairs, tables, mountains, and beaches. Now, does Dennett think mental phenomena are like witches or like mountains? Can it be that Dennett really thinks pains and beliefs are like witches and goblins in that they do not exist at all "as ordinarily understood"? (How many non-ordinary ways are there to understand, say, the stomachache I referred to earlier?) He discusses how difficult it is to "convince someone that there are no pains or beliefs" (*ibid.*, p. xx), and he declares that it will have to be done piecemeal. He concludes one such effort with the sentence "Then, since I am denying that any entity could have the features of a pain or a thought, so much the worse for the ontological status of such things." (*ibid.*, p. 38). And in a subsequent discussion (Dennett, 1980, p. 76) he says he is indeed "claiming that there are no such things as pains, although people do feel pain." He does not find this view self contradictory (I do), but for present purposes our concern is not with its consistency but with the argument that "strictly speaking there could be no such things as pain" (*ibid.*, p. 76). The argument is as follows:

> But if, as I have claimed, the intuitions we would have to honor were we to honor them all do not form a consistent set, there can be no true theory of pain, and so no computer or robot could instantiate the true theory of pain which it would have to do to feel real pain. Human beings and animals could no more instantiate the true theory of pain, (there being none), which lands us with the outrageous conclusion that no one ever feels pain (Dennett, 1978, p. 228).

This argument contains, in my view, something more outrageous than the conclusion, and that is its logic. From the fact that the set of intuitions we have about a class of objects is inconsistent, and therefore the class is such that none of the objects could satisfy *all* of the intuitions, it simply does not follow that no such objects exist. Compare: the intuitions we have about chairs do not form a consistent set; therefore, there is no true theory of chairs; therefore, chairs do not exist. Or compare: the set of intuitions people have about Jimmy Carter do not form a consistent set; therefore, there is no true theory of Jimmy Carter; therefore, Jimmy Carter does not exist. With the best will in the world there is simply no way you can rescue the formal structure of Dennett's argument that "strictly speaking" pains do not exist, and the objections I am making to it are at least as old as Wittgenstein's discussion of "game" and other family resemblance notions.

But even assuming that Dennett's arguments against the existence of mental phenomena such as pains are inadequate, what about his positive thesis concerning the mental, about those states which presumably are left over after the nonexistent ones are eliminated? I now turn to his "Cognitive Theory of Consciousness" (*ibid.*, pp. 149-73).

He describes, in some detail, a flow chart for a system that has consciousness. He then asks (Thomas Nagel's question), "What is it like to be an entity that instantiates the flow chart?" His supposition is that there is something it is like if the entity is conscious, and if not, not. Here is the answer: "Suppose I put forward the bold hypothesis that you are a realization of the flow chart and that it is in virtue of this fact that it seems to us—and to you—that there is something it is like to be you" (*ibid.*, p. 165). Having consciousness is thus on his account "a matter of having a certain sort of functional organization." He then challenges us, "Can you give good grounds for denying the hypothesis and if so, what are they? What personal access do you have and to what?" (*ibid.*, p. 165).

One feels one must be misunderstanding the questions because the answer seems too obvious. Yes, one can give good grounds for denying the hypothesis. Indeed, taken quite literally, it seems obviously false and false for the same sort of reason that old-fashioned logical behaviorism is false. Having conscious states such as bodily sensations and visual experiences is one thing, and instantiating the flow chart is something quite different. Bodily sensations such as tickles and itches are constituted by the way they intrinsically feel and are realized in nervous systems. Flow charts are constituted by satisfying certain functional descriptions and can be realized in any substance you like. They have no essential connection with either feelings or nervous systems. If it is not obvious on the face of it that instantiating the flow chart is neither constitutive of nor sufficient for the possession of the relevant conscious states, the same two arguments I marshaled against Putnam can again be invoked here. First, the flow chart is totally independent of the forms of its realization. This means that all sorts of substances can instantiate the flow chart even though they are inappropriate for having visual experience, tickles, itches, and so on. The flow chart can be instantiated by our fancy Rube Goldberg machine made entirely of beer cans, paper clips, and windmills.

And second, the argument from anesthesia that we used against Putnam also applies to Dennett, though in a slightly modified form. The flow chart will have to have variations for different sorts of conscious states, say, itches, visual experiences, and so on. Let a person whose eyes are closed go through the steps in the flow chart that are specific to vision. He can use braille or any other method to get through the flow chart. He will indeed have conscious states, he is conscious of going through the flow chart, but he has the wrong conscious states since he has his eyes closed and has no visual experiences. He cannot see anything, even though the flow chart in question is specific for vision.

I said earlier that functionalists showed a tendency to confuse intrinsic mental states with the causal features that might warrant observer relative ascriptions of mental states. In Dennett's case this shift from intrinsic to observer relative ascriptions of mental phenomena is made a matter of principle with his introduction of the notion of "intentional systems" and "the intentional stance." On his account both humans and computers with certain sorts of program are "intentional systems," and an intentional system is just one where we find it appropriate to adopt "the intentional stance." In the adoption of the intentional stance, "One predicts behavior . . . by ascribing to the system *the possession of certain information,* and supposing it to be *directed by certain goals* and then working out the most reasonable or appropriate action on the basis of these ascriptions and suppositions" (*ibid.*, p. 6). It is then, he says, but a small step to describe this information and goals as beliefs and desires. But we must not ask if these really are beliefs and desires because "the definition of intentional systems I have given does not say that intentional systems really have beliefs and desires but that one can explain and predict their behavior by ascribing beliefs and desires to them, and the decision to adopt this strategy is pragmatic and is not intrinsically right or wrong" (*ibid.*, p. 7).

Well, one can agree that it is open to anybody to adopt any strategy he finds useful, but the question remains, what is the status of the ascription of the mental states, whether the ascription is of information and goals, or beliefs and desires? Assuming we do find it useful, how are we supposed to interpret this usefulness? Even if we have not defined intentional systems in such a way that we say that they really have beliefs and desires, there will still be a difference between those intentional systems that really have beliefs and desires and those that do not, and in the case of those that do, the ascriptions have entirely different interpretations from the case of those that do not. For example, in the case of those that do, the beliefs and desires play causal roles determined by their specific intrinsic features. Dennett thinks the case of the computer and the human being are the same; in both cases we find it useful to adopt the intentional stance, and it is up to anybody to adopt some other strategy if he finds it more useful. But there is an enormous difference between my attributing a "desire" to a chess-playing computer to castle on the strong side and my saying I have a desire to drink a glass of cold beer. In the computer case, it is just a useful shorthand for describing how the system functions. There are no intrinsic mental phenomena in question at all. But in my own case I do not attribute to myself a desire for a beer because I find it useful in predicting my behavior, but because I want a beer. In my own case, I am stating facts about intrinsic mental phenomena, and whether or not people find it useful to adopt "the intentional stance" toward me is quite irrelevant to what the facts really are. In short, whether a system really has beliefs and desires is quite independent of whether or not we find it useful to make observer relative ascriptions of beliefs and desires. Furthermore, we only understand the observer relative attributions in a way that is parasitic on the use of the same expressions to specify intrinsic mental states. We understand the metaphorical non-literal use of "belief" and "desire" as applied to computers because we see these attributions as based on an analogy with systems such as human beings who literally have intrinsic beliefs and desires.[4]

I think I can make clear my sense of the strangeness of Dennett's project and of functionalism in general with the following analogy. Suppose that there were a group of philosophers who were puzzled by the existence of hands; suppose there was a long tradition of being worried about the ontological status of hands. And suppose that a functionalist view of hands became fashionable. On one version of this view, we are told that we do not have to worry about the existence of hands because it is all a matter of adopting the "manual stance" toward certain systems which we will describe as "manual systems." To paraphrase Dennett: "the definition of a manual system does not say that manual systems really have hands but that one can explain and predict their behavior by attributing hands to them, and the decision to adopt this strategy is pragmatic and not intrinsically right or wrong." I think that the intentional stance approach to understanding beliefs and desires is about as useful as the manual stance approach would be to understanding hands. In each case the question of analyzing the intrinsic features of mental states (or hands) gets replaced by a different question: under what conditions do we find it useful to talk *as if* a system had mental states (or hands)? And to ask that question amounts to changing the subject while still deluding ourselves into thinking we are addressing the original philosophical issues.

In sum, I have made three objections to Dennett's account: first, that the argument to show that pains, etc., do not really exist is invalid; second, that the cognitive theory of consciousness is subject to counterexamples; and third, that the notion of the intentional stance conceals but does not get rid of the crucial distinction between observer relative mental attributions and attributions of intrinsic mental phenomena.

Most of my discussion of functionalism has been addressed to organizational functionalism because it seems to me the richest and most interesting of the versions I have seen, but I want to conclude this part of the argument by showing how some of the same worries apply quite generally to other sorts of functionalist accounts. Consider the following functional definition from Grice which he calls a "first shot" at a definition of belief. "X believes that p just in case x is disposed, whenever x wants (desires) some end E, to act in ways which will realize E given that p is true rather than in ways which will realize E given that p is false" (Grice, 1975, p. 24). Now compare that with an analogous definition of hands: "X has a hand just in case x is disposed whenever x wants (desires) some graspable and retrievable object O_{gr} to act in such a way that will bring it about that x grasps and retrieves O_{gr} rather than that he does not grasp and retrieve O_{gr}."

The problem I have with such definitions is not just that one can always think up counterexamples, but that the enterprise of this sort of definition seems so dubious in the first place. Shoemaker (1980) tells us that on his version of functionalism it is the view that "mental states can be defined in terms of their relations, primarily their causal relations, to sensory inputs, behavioral outputs and other mental states." Analogously, a functionalist view of hands would be that "hands can be defined in terms of their relations, primarily their causal relations, to manual inputs, behavioral outputs and other features of the body including mental states." Now let us suppose that after years of ingenious philosophical effort the functionalist dream of satisfactory definitions was realized for both hands and mental states; suppose we had such definitions and nobody could think up a good counterexample. What would we have achieved? In the case of our definition of hands, not very much; because our definitions still leave out the intrinsic properties of hands, all they tell us about is the functional role of hands. Analogously, our definitions of mental states do not tell us the intrinsic properties of mental states, only their functional role. But it might be replied that the very thesis of functionalism is that mental states do not have any intrinsic properties except their functional role, so that is hardly an objection. But now I want to pick up the thread of our earlier discussion of the intrinsic-observer relative distinction. We left off where the question was: are the acknowledged causal properties of mental states sufficient to define their intrinsic mental properties? And by now it should be clear that my answer to that question is no, and for the same sorts of reasons that the acknowledged behavioral manifestations of pains are not sufficient to define pains and the acknowledged causal features of hands are not sufficient to define hands. Indeed, all the arguments I have presented so far are just ways of trying to exhibit this basic intuition. The intrinsic features of, e.g., beliefs, pains, and desires are just that: intrinsic features; the strategy of the functionalist, like that of the behaviorist, is to get us to take a third person observer relative stance, in which we agree that mental states do indeed stand in causal relations; just as we agree with the behaviorist that they have behavioral manifestations. But the arguments that I have presented, such as the argument from anesthesia and the argument from biology, are designed to remind us that something could have all the right causal relations and still not have the right mental properties.

4. DIAGNOSIS AND CONCLUSION

I believe that functionalism, like the behaviorism which preceded it, requires not so much refutation as diagnosis. Why would anyone hold such an unplausible view? Why would anyone believe, for example, that one's own pains, tickles, and itches, as well as one's beliefs, fears, hopes, and desires, were constituted by the fact that one was the instantiation of a flow chart or a computer program? And more generally, why does this phase of analytic philosophy seem to exemplify a longer-term reluctance to take mental phenomena at their face value?

I believe, in fact, that there are many reasons, more than I can hope to discuss in this article, and some of those that I will not be discussing should be mentioned at least in passing. There are arguments, such as those of Quine on indeterminacy, to show that where intentional states are concerned there are no facts of the matter beyond certain dispositions to behavior. And there are a series of confusions about the relations between intentionality with-a-t and intensionality with-an-s. Many philosophers believe that the propositional contents of beliefs and desires belong to a class of mysterious entities, called intensions, and that we would be better off to avoid believing in such entities. But I think these are not the arguments that have really mattered in the long run. On my diagnosis there are three major reasons for the appeal of such views as functionalism and for the long-run prejudice against the mental in analytic philosophy.

1. *Verificationism.* Positivism and verificationism are officially dead, but they live on in certain verificationist tendencies that one finds in functionalist authors. In analyzing pains and beliefs Putnam and Dennett do not try to describe the intrinsic properties of such mental phenomena; rather, they are concerned with such questions as "When would we attribute such mental states to a system? What is the explanatory role of such attributions to a system? Under what conditions do we think ourselves justified or not justified in making such intentionalistic attributions?" But these questions are not the same as "What are the intrinsic properties of mental states?" Notice that in both authors the approach is almost entirely from a third-person point of view, and indeed the confusion between observer relative and intrinsic attributions of the mental derives largely from this third-person approach. As long as we think of mental states as something to be ascribed from outside, it can be made to seem as if what matters is the adoption of an "intentional stance" and the "pragmatic" usefulness of treating something as an "intentional system." No one would think it of much use in the philosophy of mind to worry about these "stances" if he were concentrating on his own mental states. Think what it is actually like to have a pain in the stomach or a passionate desire for a cold beer and ask yourself if you are talking about real mental phenomena or just adopting a stance. The cure, in short, for the verificationism of Putnam, Dennett, and others and for their persistent confusion of the question "What is it to have mental states?" with such questions as "What is the functional role of the ascription of mental states?" is to insist at least at some point on the first-person point of view. It reveals a fundamental confusion to suppose that we can get clear about mental states entirely by examining the functioning of third-person attributions of the mental.

2. *Cognitive Science.* The second reason is peculiar to functionalism, but I think it is important. Many philosophers have the conviction that they are utilizing the results of something called "cognitive science" and that somehow the computer has given us remarkable new insights into the operation of the mind. On the surface, this manifests itself in a great deal of more or less intimidating technical jargon. There is much talk about Turing machines, finite state automata, analog and digital computers, machine tables, flow charts, transducers, and so on. The illusion is thus conveyed that philosophical problems about the mental have been converted into

technical questions in automata theory capable of solution by the cooperative efforts of philosophers and cognitive scientists, including both psychologist and computer scientists. Underlying this surface appearance is a fairly serious fallacy. From the fact that at some level of description the brain is a digital computer (or, if you like, a set of digital computers) together with the fact that the programs of the brain can be instantiated by any other sort of computer sufficiently rich and complex to carry the program, the fallacious inference is drawn that what the brain does in producing mental phenomena is nothing more than what these other sorts of computers would be doing if they instantiated the program. And this fallacious inference leads naturally to the thesis of Turing machine functionalism. Being in a certain mental state just is instantiating a certain sort of computer program. To put it another way, the fallacy is in moving from the true premise that the brain is a computer, in the sense that it instantiates computer programs, to the false conclusion that all that the brain does which is relevant to the production of the mental is to instantiate computer programs, that the only psychologically relevant feature of brain states is that they are logical states of a computer. The premise could hardly be false: since everything is a digital computer at some level of description, brains are too. But the conclusion is obviously false, as I have claimed in both the argument from biology and the argument from anesthesia. It is false both because no program by itself guarantees the causal powers that are specific to the biochemistry of the brain, and because a system such as a human agent could instantiate the program and still not have the relevant mental states.

3. *Fear of Cartesianism.* I believe that the deepest source of the prejudice against the mental is the fear that to admit mental entities at their face value would necessarily involve us in the worst excesses of Cartesianism, that we will be postulating a class of mysterious and occult entities, inhabiting another metaphysical realm beyond the reach of scientific investigation, that we will be left with the self or the soul, with privileged access and incorrigibility, and all the rest of it. Or, perhaps worst of all, that we will be left with a "mind-body problem."

Indeed it is a curious fact about the history of behaviorism and functionalism that neither was *independently* motivated. No one examined his own pains and discovered them to be patterns of behavior or Turing machine states; rather, these theories were proposed as solutions to other problems in philosophy, such as the problem of other minds and especially the "mind-body problem." But suppose there is not any such problem as the "mind-body problem" anymore than there is such a problem as the "digestion-stomach problem." Suppose that, as I believe to be the case, thinking and perceiving are as much natural and biological phenomena as digestion or the circulation of the blood. Suppose that mental phenomena are both caused by and realized in the structure of the brain. If so, we can give up not only dualism but "monism" and "physicalism" as well, for the antidualist jargon only has a point if we accept the dualist categories, such categories as kinds of substance and relations between kinds of substances. No one feels that he has to choose between monism and dualism where digestion is concerned; nor does he have to choose between epiphenomenalism, interactionism, etc., nor to postulate the existence of a metaphysical self or a transcendental ego that digests. Why should cognition be treated any less naturalistically? The most effective way to answer behaviorism and functionalism is not, as I have done, by making "objections" to them, but by removing the philosophical picture that motivated them in the first place.

Notes

1. It is sometimes correctly objected to behaviorism that in order to analyze desires one would have to assume fixed beliefs, and conversely. But again, this is an "in house" objection that does not expose the underlying absurdity of the behaviorist approach.
2. For a discussion of the mental element in actions, see Searle (1979).
3. For a discussion of these issues see the articles by Smart, Shaffer, and Cornman in Rosenthal, ed. (1971).
4. Also, when I adopt the intentional stance is that supposed to be intrinsic or not? Do I really have an intentional stance or is it just a case of adopting an intentional stance to my intentional stance? If the former, we are left with intrinsic intentionality; if the latter, it looks like we are in a vicious regress.

References

Dennett, Daniel C., *Brainstorms, Philosophical Essays on Mind and Psychology* (Montgomery, Vt., 1978).

———, "Reply to Professor Stich," *Philosophical Books* 21, no. 2 (1980):73-76.

Grice, H. P., "Method in Philosophical Psychology," *Proceedings and Addresses of the American Philosophical Association,* vol. 48 (Newark, Del., 1974-75).

Putnam, H., *Mind, Language, and Reality; Philosophical Papers,* vol. 2 (Cambridge, 1975).

Rosenthal, David M., ed. *Materialism and the Mind-Body Problem* (Englewood Cliffs, N.J., 1971):

    Cornman, James W., "The Identity of Mind and Body," pp. 73-79; Shaffer, Jerome, "Mental Events and the Brain," pp. 67-72; Smart, J. J. C., "Sensations and Brain Processes," pp. 53-56.

Searle, John R., "The Intentionality of Intention and Action," *Inquiry* 22 (1979):253-80.

Shoemaker, Sydney, "The Missing Absent Qualia Argument," forthcoming.

Quine and the Confirmational Paradoxes[1]

CHARLES CHIHARA

To what extent would the undermining of W. V. Quine's views on confirmation and verification diminish the attractiveness, and thus the influence, of his philosophy? Since Quine presents us with a vast theoretical edifice encompassing the ontological structure of the universe as well as the ideological and logical structures of our intuitive and scientific theories, it is not hard to see how the rejection of one of its foundation stones—its confirmation theory—could significantly alter one's attitude toward its basic soundness. Certainly, given Quine's acceptance of the verification theory of meaning according to which the meaning of a sentence "turns purely on what would count as evidence for its truth,"[2] one would expect his views of confirmation to exert a powerful influence on the formation of Quinian doctrines about what certain philosophically crucial sentences mean. Consider, for example, the view he expresses with the words:

> Our basis for saying what 'could' be generally consists, I suggest, in what *is* plus *simplicity* of the laws whereby we describe and extrapolate what is. I see no more objective way of construing the *conditio irrealis*.[3]

It is not surprising then that Quine would arrive at the following doctrine:

> [I] n natural necessity, *or our attribution of it,* I see only Hume's regularities, culminating here and there in what passes for an explanatory trait or the promise of it.[4]

His confirmation theory is also clearly at work when Quine arrives at the following view of science:

> The scientist introduces system in his quest and scrutiny of evidence. System, moreover, dictates the scientists's hypotheses themselves: those are most welcome which are seen to conduce most to simplicity in the overall theory. Predictions, once they have been deduced from hypotheses, are subject to the discipline of evidence in turn; but the hypotheses have, at the time of

hypothesis, only the considerations of systematic simplicity to recommend them.[5]

In terms of the view of scientific acceptability, one can understand how Quine came to accept the existence of certain sorts of abstract entities (sets) and to reject the existence of mental entities. Quine's reasoning can be crudely and schematically put: Why is it reasonable to posit the existence of molecules, say, or electrons? Only because by so doing, one obtains a simpler overall system of physics. "The molecular physicist is, like all of us, concerned with commonplace reality, and merely finds that he can simplify his laws by positing an esoteric supplement to the exoteric universe."[6] Seeing that this is so, does the postulation of sets contribute to the overall simplicity of our scientific theories? Yes. Then posit sets. Does the postulation of mental entities contribute to the overall simplicity of our scientific theories? No. Then do not posit them.

I shall not, in this paper, attempt any sort of detailed examination of these arguments[7] or of any of the doctrines based on the Quinian confirmation theory. Instead, I shall examine the confirmation theory itself. More specifically, I shall examine Quine's proposed solution to the confirmational paradoxes, partly with the purpose of exposing weaknesses in the theory of confirmation he has adopted. In connection with the Grue puzzle, I shall also discuss a proposed solution of Frank Jackson's. Then I shall analyze the paradoxes within the framework of the Personalist brand of Bayesianism in order to compare Quine's basically positivistic confirmation theory with a quite different and, I shall argue, more promising approach.

1. QUINE'S SOLUTION

What confirms a hypothesis, insofar as it gets confirmed, is the verification of its predictions. When more particularly, the hypothesis is a generalization arrived at by induction, those predictions are simply instances of the generalization. Thus, what confirm an induction are its instances.[8]

From the above quotation, it can be seen that, in its general outlines, Quine's view of confirmation is not very different from those of many Logical Positivists.[9] Distinctive features of the Quinian view emerge when the confirmational paradoxes are taken up. We are told that a non-black non-raven is an *instance* (or what is frequently called by other philosophers a "positive instance") of the generalization that all non-black things are non-ravens. Hence, the above description of confirmation suggests that observing a white shoe (a non-black non-raven) should confirm that generalization and all its logical equivalents, including 'All ravens are black'. To avoid being committed to the paradoxical position that a white shoe confirms the hypothesis that all ravens are black, the above characterization of confirmation is specified to read: Any instance of ⌜All ζ are η⌝ confirms the generalization, so long as ζ and η are *projectible*. Quine states that "projectible predicates are predicates ζ and η whose shared instances all do count, for whatever reasons, toward confirmation of ⌜All ζ are η⌝," claiming that "only a black raven *can confirm* 'All ravens are black', the complements not being projectible" (italics mine)[10] —a suggestion that is reinforced in *Web*, where is said:

> To call a trait projectible is only to say that it is suited to induction . . .
> Induction is the expectation that similar things will behave similarly; better, that things already seen to be appreciably similar will prove similar in further ways. The question what traits are projectible, then, can as well be put simply thus: What counts as similarity? (p. 57).

Evidently, *the things that share a non-projectible trait* are not seen as similar to one another and hence *cannot serve as the basis for an inductive inference* (nonjectible traits are simply not suited to induction.)

If we analyze the preceding Raven paradox as resulting from

> (1) *Nicod's principle,* which states that all instances of a generalization ⌜All ζ are η⌝ confirm it;
>
> (2) the *Equivalence principle*, according to which anything that confirms a generalization also confirms all statements that are logically equivalent to it;

and

> (3) the specific premise asserting that 'all non-black things are non-ravens' is logically equivalent to 'All ravens are black',

then Quine's resolution can be seen to involve the rejection of (1) by requiring that η be projectible. Thus, by claiming that the predicate 'non-raven' is non-projectible, Quine is able to avoid being committed to the conclusion of the paradox.

A similar move is made in the case of what I shall call the *Grue puzzle* (as opposed to "The New Riddle of Induction").[11] The predicate 'grue' is defined in the standard Goodmanian way:

> An object x is *grue* iff x is observed prior to t_0 and x is green, or x is not observed prior to t_0 and x is blue

where, for purposes of specificity, we can suppose with Quine that t_0 is midnight tonight. Now we are to imagine that emeralds have been identified by some criterion other than color and that all the emeralds observed thus far have been found to be green. The puzzle is then stated: "Should we expect the first one examined tomorrow to be green, because all examined up to now were green? But all examined up to now were also grue; so why not expect the first one tomorrow to be grue, and therefore blue;" (*NK*, 115). Here again, Quine can block the paradoxical inference by maintaining that 'grue' is not a projectible predicate.

But how is one to distinguish the projectible from the non-projectible predicates? Here, Quine appeals to our intuitions of natural kinds: green things form a natural kind; grue things do not. The projectible predicates are natural kind predicates; the non-projectible are not. Quine freely admits that the notion of kind is of "dubious scientific standing," but from his neo-Humean point of view this is not surprising—induction, itself, is characterized as "animal expectation or habit formation" (*NK*, 125). For Quine, "Induction is not peculiarly intellectual" (*Web*, 57).

A slightly different view of the situation is presented in *Web*, where another "paradox of induction" is sketched. Every moment of one's life has had the trait of being prior to t_0. Should we conclude that every moment of one's life will share this trait? To avoid such a conclusion, Quine stipulates that the predicate 'is prior to t_0' is non-projectible. He then addresses himself to the question of how the projectible traits are to be distinguished or selected. He tells us "they are the traits we notice." He adds: "It is significant that we did not have a word for grue; it is not a trait we notice" (*Web*, 57). Thus, not only are the projectible traits the natural kind traits, they are also the traits we notice. But that is not all, for Quine also wants to explain projectibility in terms of simplicity and similarity:

> Our eye for projectibility is our eye for similarity. These are two names for the same problem. In fact, similarity, projectibility, and simplicity are all of a piece. Projectible traits count as simpler than others, and the sharing of projectible traits counts as similarity (*Web*, 57).

Now there are a number of initial difficulties with the Quinian view. Consider the following example. A rash of daring burglaries are committed in Gotham City by someone who calls himself 'The Spider'. One suspect is arrested at time t_1 for possession of large amounts of cocaine; he is subsequently convicted and sent to prison. Several years later, an investigation reveals that all the burglaries know to be committed by The Spider occurred prior to t_1. Could we take this as providing some confirmation of the generalization that all burglaries committed by The Spider occurred prior to t_1? To put it another way, would we be (at least slightly) more confident of the generalization upon receiving this information about all the known instances than we would be without this information? Surely, the answer is 'Yes'. Thus, the trait of occurring before t_1 must be projectible even though the trait of occurring before t_0 is not! But how can the set of occurrences before t_1 be a natural kind if the set of occurrences before t_0 is not? My intuitions certainly do not fit such a determination. The latter set does not seem any more "kindlike" than the former. And is there something about the trait of occurring before t_1 that makes it simpler than the trait of occurring before t_0? Of course, it is still open to Quine to reject my intuitions of simplicity, similarity, etc.; but such a move will not be attractive if t_0 is specified by time of day and date.

Let us consider another example. An unmanned spacecraft lands on the planet Neptune and gathers various samples of Neptunian soil. Among the samples is a batch of crystals. By certain chemical tests conducted from the earth by remote control, this material is identified as a substance named 'Neptunite'. The Neptunite is brought back to earth in a liquid solution of chemicals used in conducting the tests. All the Neptunite is examined on earth at a time prior to t_0 and found to be green. But it is also determined that the chemicals changed the color of the Neptunite and that the examined Neptunite would have been blue had it not been subjected to the tests. Furthermore, the available data tell us that the sorts of chemicals that would change the color of Neptunite are not found anywhere on Neptune. Thus, we have:

> All the Neptunite we have examined has been observed prior to t_0 and is green.

Also

> All the Neptunite we have examined has been observed prior to t_0 and is grue.

Which of the following

> All Neptunite from or on Neptune is green

or

> All Neptunite from or on Neptune is grue

is more likely to be true in view of the above evidence? Practically everyone would choose the latter. But how can that be, given Quine's solution? In the emerald example, the inference to green emeralds was explained as resulting from the fact that 'green' is projectible and 'grue' is not. But here, we draw the inference to grue Neptunite, thus implying that 'grue' is projectible and 'green' is not. Should we say that 'green' is projectible in certain situations and 'grue' is in others? That would require a radical revision of Quine's solution and a considerable complication of his (basically) simple view of confirmation. Predicates and traits were said to be either projectible or not: 'projectible' was not taken to be a term relating predicates to situations. Obviously, to attempt to revise the theory along these lines would require a method or criterion for determining the situations in which a predicate is projectible — something that seems intrinsically difficult to provide.

Now it might be said that the inference to grue in this situation should be explained in terms of background information—not in terms of projectibility. Certainly that would be a plausible suggestion. But if that can be said of these last two examples, why cannot the same be said of these last two examples, why cannot the same be said of the original grue example and also of the Raven? Can we not then challenge Quine to show how these last examples differ from the earlier ones in ways that require the application of an entirely different set of confirmation rules? I shall return later to the question of the use of background information in these examples. But first, I should like to examine a more promising approach to the Grue puzzle.

2. JACKSON'S COUNTERFACTUAL CONDITION

Frank Jackson has suggested that Nicod's principle and the Straight Rule (see below) do not require the sort of emendation advocated by Quine, because they are already governed by a condition (the "counterfactual condition") which eliminates the paradox, viz. the condition:

that certain Fs which are H being G does not support other Fs which are not H being G if it is known that the Fs in the evidence class would not have been G if they had not been H.[12]

So expressed, the condition may seem overly complicated; but an example will bring out the basic idea, which is quite simple. Suppose we have as evidence that all the diamonds we have seen, $a_1, a_2, a_3, \ldots a_n$, are polished and glint in the sun. Now the *straight rule* seems to allow the inference to the proposition that a_{n+1}, which is an unpolished diamond, glints in the sun. But now ask: Suppose the $a_1, \ldots a_n$ had not been polished, would they have glinted in the sun? No, and we know that they would not have. Then, according to the counterfactual condition, we do not have support for the proposition that a_{n+1} glints in the sun. In another example Jackson gives, we supposedly know that had all the lobsters we have seen not been boiled, they would not have been red. The counterfactual condition tells us that our evidence set, which consists of instances of boiled red lobsters, does not support expecting some unboiled lobster to be red.

Now in the Grue puzzle, we have as evidence that all the emeralds we have seen, $c_1, \ldots c_m$, are grue and examined prior to t_0, and the straight rule seems to yield the paradoxical claim that we have support for the proposition that a_{m+1}, an emerald are examined prior to t_0, is also grue. However, Jackson claims that the counterfactual condition blocks such an application of the rule, because we know that had the $c_1, \ldots c_m$ not been examined prior to t_0, they would not have been grue.

There is some plausibility to these analyses. But has Jackson laid the Grue puzzle to rest? Let us turn to another example. Suppose that an Army medical researcher notes that every ex-POW from a specific Vietnamese camp (#1) who had had a POWE—a series of physical examinations given to randomly selected soldiers on release from a POW camp—is suffering from hepatitis. He wonders if John Smith, an ex-POW from camp #1 who had not had a POWE, is also suffering from hepatitis. Clearly, the evidence cited does provide some support for an affirmative answer. But now consider the predicate defined as follows:

x has *hepeven* iff x has hepatitis and has received a POWE or
x has an even-numbered Social Security number and has not received a POWE.

We then have as evidence: each of the ex-POWs from camp #1 who had a POWE, $d_1, d_2, \ldots d_n$, is suffering from hepeven. But in this case, we cannot use the counterfactual condition to block the use of the straight rule to arrive at the conclusion that the evidence supports 'Smith has hepeven'; for we do not know whether each of the $d_1, \ldots d_n$ would have had hepeven if he had not been given a POWE, and this because we do not know which men from camp #1 have even-numbered Social Security numbers. Since no one would regard the above evidence as supporting the hypothesis that John Smith has an even-numbered Social Security number, the counterfactual requirement is not sufficiently restrictive to give us the intuitively correct result in this case.[13] So clearly more is required before one can be justified in claiming, as Jackson did, that "there is no paradox resulting from 'grue' and like predicates."[14]

3. DO POSITIVE INSTANCES ALWAYS CONFIRM?

A second sort of difficulty with Jackson's method of resolving the grue puzzle—a difficulty it shares with Quine's and indeed with practically all views of confirmation based on keeping Nicod's principle pretty much intact—is brought about by the use of background information. Jackson uses the counterfactual condition to defend Nicod's principle against grue-type puzzles in situations in which the evidence set includes no negative instances, at least one positive instance, and when it is assumed that not all the members of the subject class have been examined.[15] Now imagine that we are given a large box of small balls with the information that this box contains either

(a) 100 black glass balls and a million plastic balls;

or

(b) 1000 black glass balls, one white glass ball, and a million plastic balls.

Now suppose a ball is selected at random from the box and it turns out to be a black glass ball. Then, as evidence, we have a positive instance of the generalization 'All the glass balls in the box are black', no negative instances, and we know that there are some unexamined instances. Is the hypothesis that all the glass balls in the box are black confirmed by this evidence? I. J. Good has argued persuasively that the above result, far from increasing our confidence in the hypothesis, would undermine it.[16] For the selection of the black glass ball constitutes good evidence that the box is correctly described by (b) and hence is one in which not all glass balls are black. Again, we have a situation in which neither Jackson's counterfactual condition nor the appeal to unprojectible predicates saves the principle: clearly, the Quinian strategy of denying the projectibility of the relevant predicates is not at all plausible in this case.[17]

Hempel responded to this sort of example by claiming that it makes use of illicit background information: to produce a genuine counterexample to the principles being defended, one must show that the evidence sentence (the positive instance) "considered by itself and without reference to any other information may fail to support" the generalization.[18] As Hempel views the paradox, Nicod's principle concerns only the situation in which the given evidence consists exclusively of a positive instance.

But is such a defense reasonable? Is it one that either Jackson or Quine could plausibly make? Certainly not Jackson, since his use of the counterfactual condition makes explicit use of all sorts of background information. And it is hard to see how Quine could make such a move, given his holistic view of science and confirmation. (More on this later.) And consider the problems involved in determining what background information one is allowed to use in intuitively testing Nicod's principle (with or without qualifications or revisions). Thus, suppose we wish to determine whether an instance of 'All ravens are black' confirms the generalization. We are to imagine what? That we have no information at all other than the one instance. Taken literally, that is what Hempel suggests we should do. Then, supposedly, we would have no knowledge of even the most elementary logical laws or of the simplest features of our language. But would we even have an intelligible situation? It is hard to imagine what the raven sentence would mean to us under such conditions. Clearly, this project will not get off the ground unless we assume at least some minimal knowledge. And it is clear from Hempel's writings that he does grant the legitimacy of some background knowledge. But then the question of how much knowledge arises. Can we assume some mathematics? If so, what parts? What about physics? Biology? These are questions Hempel did not answer. Perhaps, however, given the Logical Positivistic tradition in which he was working, he would say that only analytic truths can be allowed into the set of permissible background beliefs. Such a decision holds promise of allowing into this set at least logic and mathematics—recall that Hempel once argued that the truths of logic and mathematics are all analytic.[19] But there are many reasons for being skeptical about this position. First, it is not clear how one ought to assess the confirmatory value of the instance in the envisaged situation, even allowing the use of logic and mathematics. After all, we are not even allowed to make any assumptions about the size of the classes involved—for all we know the class of ravens might have some enormous infinite cardinality. Second, the Logical Positivists's belief in the analyticity of logic and mathematics is itself highly questionable; it seems to have been based on a combination of wishful thinking, blissful inattention to the critics of logicism, and sloppy argumentation. Third, the analytic-synthetic distinction itself has been under such heavy attack these past thirty years that it is hardly something on which one should be happy to base one's confirmation theory. Finally, it is hard to see what value a theory of confirmation of this sort would have, based as it is on intuitions of confirmation in completely unreal situations. I do not wish to suggest that I regard the considerations either of this section or of those of the first as constituting anything like a decisive refutation of the Quinian theory of confirmation; the view itself is too roughly sketched for me to feel confident that any refutation of it would be decisive. But certainly, enough has been said to indicate why I am dissatisfied with what Quine has said on the topic.

4. A BAYESIAN ANALYSIS OF THE GRUE PUZZLE

In his paper Jackson does two things that seem to be right: (1) He attempts to show why our intuitive judgments are correct vis-á-vis grue-green without invoking the projectible-unprojectible distinction. I agree with Jackson that there is nothing about certain predicates that makes them intrinsically unfit for inductive inferences. (2) In each of the examples he considers, the counterfactual he appeals to does seem to be highly relevant to the question of which of the two hypotheses is supported by the evidence given.

I wish now to provide an analysis of the Grue puzzle that incorporates the above two points but which also brings to the fore a view of confirmation that makes a more profound break with the positivistic tradition in which Quine has developed his solution. I shall present my analysis within the framework of an orthodox Personalist version of Bayesian confirmation theory, even though I am quite sure that the theory I shall be utilizing is, at best, only a rough approximation to a truly adequate one.[20] For the confirmational puzzles, as I view them, are crude puzzles, relying on rather crude features of the confirmational situation, and hence may be appropriately dealt with using relatively unrefined tools.

For purposes of these analyses then, I shall take probability to be equated with the relevant agent's degrees of belief, idealized so as to be *coherent* and to change over time in accordance with the rule of *conditionalization*.[21] Confirmation will be evaluated in terms of probability assessments. Specifically, I shall take evidence e as confirming hypothesis h iff $P(h/e) > P(h)$; and the degree to which e confirms h will be given by the "plausibility increment" $P(h/e) - P(h)$.[22] By an obvious generalization, I shall also talk about the confirmation of h by e, given background information b and the degree to which e confirms h, given background information b.

This sort of approach to confirmation will allow into the analyses at least one feature of beliefs that is noticeably absent from the Quinian discussion of the paradoxes; in Quine's analyses, one is pictured as either believing or not believing a proposition—there is no place given to gradations of belief, e.g., of being somewhat sure, of being rather doubtful, of being quite certain, and the like.

The Bayesian approach also provides an efficient method for dealing with one sort of problem that arises in connection with these paradoxes; as Patrick Suppes put it,

> ... it is impossible to express in explicit form all the evidence relevant to even our simplest beliefs. There is no canonical set of elementary propositions to be approached as an ideal for expressing exactly what evidence supports a given belief, whether it be a belief about ravens, gods, electrons or patches of red.[23]

To take account of heterogenous information and evidence obtained from a variety of sources, all of differing degrees of reliability and relevance, as well as of intuitive hunches and even vague memories, the Bayesian theory provides us with a subjective "prior probability distribution," which functions as a sort of systematic summary of such items.

Investigating the notion of confirmation within the framework of probability theory opens up a number of possibilities not available to those working within the confines of the sort of deductive model Quine uses; and it makes the problem of explicating and analyzing our causal and nomological beliefs seem much more manageable.[24] Not surprisingly, Bayesians have been able to provide plausible explanations and justifications of a variety of widely accepted maxims of inductive inference.[25]

Furthermore, some recent Bayesian studies of the history of science show promise of significantly improving our understanding of past scientific inferences and practices.[26]

The prominent role the Bayesian framework gives to background theories is in sharp contrast to what one finds in the Quinian analyses. Quine, as much as any living philosopher, has championed a holistic view of science which stresses the role of background theories in the formation and testing of hypotheses. But his analyses of these paradoxes are a sort of throwback to the very positivistic tradition that his holism was meant to challenge; the basic elements Quine works with—evidential statements of an elementary sort (mostly monadic atomic sentences of the form 'Fa') and a rule of simple induction—are not very different from the basic Hempelian elements. As a result, much that is relevant to the confirmational puzzles gets left out. For example, do I really need to resort to the doctrine of projectible predicates in order to explain my reluctance to conclude from an unbroken string of instances that every moment of my life is followed by a moment in which I am alive (as is suggested in *Web*, 56)? Am I forced into maintaining that 'is a moment in which I am alive' is unprojectible as Quine would have us believe? Do we not have a rich fund of background information and theories about ourselves, the animal kingdom, and especially the biological processes of living and dying, which is highly relevant to the plausibility of the conclusion in question and which can account for our reluctance to infer our own immortality?

Similarly, do we not have in the Grue situation much background information and beliefs that are relevant to the question of which of the competing hypotheses is confirmed by the evidence given? Do we not know, for example, how emeralds are mined, polished, made into jewelry, and prized? And can we not learn from an encyclopedia such things as: emeralds are composed of a double silicate of chromic oxide, they are hard (the fourth hardest mineral), they usually occur as hexagonal prismatic cyrstals, and the best kind have been found in Colombia, where they have been mined continuously for over 400 years?[27]

Now consider:

e_1: Many emeralds have been examined and all those examined prior to t_0 are green.

e_2: Many emeralds have been examined and all those examined prior to t_0 are grue.

h_1: All emeralds are green.

h_2: All emeralds are grue.

The conjunction of e_2 and h_2 implies

c_2: Many emeralds have been examined and all those examined prior to t_0 are green, whereas all emeralds not examined prior to t_0 are blue.

But c_2 would be regarded by practically everyone as being very unlikely; for given the sheer number of emeralds discovered thus far, the way emeralds are found to be distributed in the crust of the earth, the way emeralds come to be mined, the extent to which emeralds are prized, etc., it is implausible that the green ones would turn out to coincide exactly with the emeralds observed prior to t_0. Why will no blue ones be observed prior to t_0? And how can it be that not a single green emerald will remain hidden somewhere in the vast unmined crust of the earth after t_0? Quine seems to be sympathetic with the sort of considerations I appeal to when he writes:

> The plausibility of a hypothesis depends largely on how compatible the hypothesis is with our being observers placed at random in the world. Funny coincidences often occur, but they are not the stuff that plausible hypotheses are made of (*Web*, 44).

The implausibility of this conjunction is relevant to the Grue puzzle of why we have more confidence in h_1 than in h_2 given evidence e_1 (or the equivalent e_2). For within the Bayesian framework, the puzzle asks us to consider whether $P(h_1/e_1)$ is greater, less than, or equal to $P(h_2/e_2)$ (here, assuming for the sake of argument, that the "prior probabilities" $P(h_1)$ and $P(h_2)$ are equal). But

$$\frac{P(h_1/e_1)}{P(h_2/e_2)} = \frac{P(h_1 \& e_1)}{P(h_2 \& e_2)}$$

and, as we have just seen, $P(h_2 \& e_2)$ should be very small.

Well, could not the Goodmanians make the standard symmetry reply? After all, the conjunction of h_1 and e_1 implies

c_1: Many emeralds have been examined and all those examined prior to t_0 are grue, whereas all emeralds not examined prior to t_0 are bleen.

And c_1 can be made to appear just as implausible as c_2 by simply rephrasing the above considerations, replacing 'green' and 'blue' by 'grue' and 'bleen' respectively. "How implausible," it might be argued, "that the grue emeralds should turn out to coincide exactly with the emeralds observed prior to t_0? Etc."

But is c_1 really implausible given our present theories? Here, Jackson's counterfactual condition is suggestive. Our present-day theories, especially those (both psychological and physical) relating to the nature of colors and minerals, tell us that the observed emeralds would have been green even if they had not been observed prior to t_0, that the process that led up to, and that includes, the act of observing these emeralds did not affect or change in any significant way the color of the stones. Hence, accepting c_1 does not strain our credibility in the way c_2 does.

The point can be illustrated by a simple example. Let us suppose that we have a large urn containing 1000 marbles each of which we have examined and analyzed by all the means modern science has put at our disposal. We know

[$] All the marbles in the urn are green and merely drawing them out of the urn and looking at them does not change their color.

Now suppose that Larry has never seen any of these marbles and that he is blindfolded before the urn is stirred up and two hundred marbles are drawn out at random. Imagine that the urn is then taken away so that Larry will not see any more of these marbles until after t_0. Define '$grue_1$' (and, with obvious changes, '$bleen_1$'):

x is $grue_1$ iff x is green and observed by Larry prior to t_0
or x is blue and not observed by Larry prior to t_0.

Now suppose Larry takes off this blindfold and looks at all the marbles that were drawn out. They are all $grue_1$ and none are $bleen_1$. All the marbles left in the urn are $bleen_1$ and none are $grue_1$. Is this surprising? A remarkable coincidence? A freak occurrence? Hardly. Once we know [$], we see that it does not matter which particular marbles are drawn out—they will be $grue_1$ and the others will be $bleen_1$. So there is no need to wonder how it is that we happened to pick just the $grue_1$ ones. On the other hand, if we now introduce an urn with 800 blue marbles and 200 green ones all mixed together, and if Larry proceeds to draw out 200 marbles all of which turn out to be green, we would understandably be surprised. The two sorts of drawings are really not symmetrical—despite what some Goodmanians seem to have argued about similar situations!

Perhaps it will be objected then that in appealing to the counterfactual I do, I am begging the question against the grue advocate. Am I not, in effect, assuming that the grue hypothesis is false in appealing to the counterfactual? After all, someone who truly believed the grue hypothesis would very likely also believe that had these emeralds not been observed prior to t_0, they would still have been grue and hence not green. Jackson's response to this sort of challenge can be appropriately quoted here:

However, our knowledge that the examined emeralds would still have been green if they had not been examined is knowledge about the *examined* emeralds, not about the unexamined ones. . . .

It follows that our knowledge that the examined emeralds would be green even if not examined does not tacitly rest on our knowledge that unexamined emeralds are green. It is knowledge we might have had even if unexamined emeralds were not green or, indeed, were nonexistent, and so, is knowledge we may appeal to without circularity. . . .[28]

Of course, the person who raises a circularity objection may have in mind a more fundamental problem than that responded to here—one involving the very use of background information. So let us take up such objections. Another sort of symmetry response might be based on the supposition that a hypothetical speaker of GRUE (a language like English but with gruelike words replacing our usual ones) could very well produce an argument analogous to the above one in support of his conclusion that e_1 & h_1 is implausible. Might not such a speaker argue, by appealing to *his* background theories, that the emeralds observed thus far would have been grue even if they had not been observed prior to t_0? Certainly, there is much discussion in the literature of such hypothetical speakers of GRUE.[29] But I fail to see why such fictional beings need concern us here. I am not arguing that c_1 would be more plausible than c_2 no matter what one's background theories happen to be. I find no incoherence in the supposition of a Martian who quite reasonably found h_2 more probable than h_1 as a result of obtaining evidence e_1. Indeed, from the Bayesian point of view, any bit of evidence can support essentially any hypothesis, given an appropriate prior probability distribution.

A more formidable objection has been suggested by James Hullett and Robert Schwarz.[30] It can be claimed that since each of the background beliefs appealed to above itself faces a challenge from a "gruified alternative," we cannot explain the preferability of h_1 over h_2 in the way I have suggested until we have first explained the preferability of these background beliefs over their gruified alternatives; and any attempt to answer this objection by appealing to other background beliefs will only generate a further challenge in terms of other alternatives, leading to a potentially infinite regress.

In assessing this reply, it is important to keep in mind that the problem I am addressing here is not the "New Riddle of Induction" as formulated by Goodman. That problem arises from a view of confirmation that is quite foreign to the Bayesian; I am certainly not trying to articulate a (or the) fundamental rule of induction by defining or characterizing the projectible predicates (or hypotheses). My problem is the one posed by Quine which I have called the Grue puzzle: that of trying to see why we, who always come to our experiences with an encompassing complex web of beliefs, take e_1 as giving us confidence in h_1 rather than in h_2. This problem is analogous to that of explaining why John inferred that Mary was upset at dinner yesterday from the observation that she was gulping her coffee then. Clearly, in the latter case, it would be relevant to bring into our explanation other beliefs that John has about Mary. It is also clear that no explanation of the desired sort could be given if we were precluded from appealing to any of John's beliefs. And the fact that an infinite regress of "Why?" questions can be constructed does not ordinarily lead us into becoming philosophical skeptics who reject every proffered explanation of John's inference.

The infinite regress objection we are considering implies that we cannot explain some specific scientific inference or belief unless we can stop the regress at some point. But I see no reason for accepting such a view. There is a *dimension of rationality* that scholars for many years have illuminated in terms of the principle of maximizing expected utility—a principle that, in effect, selects the rational course of action for an agent with such and such utilities and such and such degrees of belief. Now this principle does *not* presuppose or require that the agent's beliefs be rationally grounded. But why should we let all explanations of the reasonableness of some course of action by reference to such a principle be blocked by the consideration that one can always raise philosophical questions about the "ultimate foundations" of the agent's beliefs? Certainly the burden of proof is on the objector to show why the potentially infinite regress has the dire consequences presupposed by the argument, for there are intuitively attractive reasons for adhering to the universal practice of assessing "new beliefs" in the light of the totality of "old beliefs," whether or not these old beliefs are immune from skeptical problems. Quine certainly accepted the reasonableness of this practice. Indeed, in explaining such things as our adoption of a particular hypothesis, he frequently appeals to the *principle of conservatism* according to which a hypothesis is more plausible the less is conflicts with previous beliefs, other things being equal (*Web*, 44). Reasonable people, according to Quine, want their scientific explanations to be basically conservative. Other things being equal, an explanation that is conservative is to be preferred over a competitor that is not. Another indication of Quine's rejection of the basic presupposition of the objection in question is to be found in Quine's answer to the query: Why does our subjective spacing of qualities accord so well with nature as to make our inductions tend to come out right? Contrary to the spirit of the objection we are considering, Quine sees no circularity in using an inductive generalization (viz., Darwinian evolutionary theory) to explain the overall success of induction:

> I see philosophy and science as in the same boat—a boat which, to revert Neurath's figure as I so often do, we can rebuild only at sea while staying afloat in it. There is no external vantage point, no first philosophy. All scientific findings, all scientific conjectures that are at present plausible, are therefore in my view as welcome for use in philosophy as elsewhere (*NK*, 126-27).

But independently of Quine, I would argue for the reasonableness of the practice of assessing proposed hypotheses and explanations in the light of "accepted" theories. How else could one reasonably proceed? If a goal of science is to build some sort of comprehensive view of the world, then it surely is rational, in forming any new beliefs about the world, to take account of how the new views jibe with, and are compatible with, accepted theories. And if, as I would argue, systematization of our beliefs is a rational procedure for us to follow, then again it is reasonable to want new beliefs to cohere with our old. So if it is claimed that contrary to what practically everyone believes, it is not rational to so proceed, I would expect to see some really solid reasons backing the claim. So far, these reasons have not been produced.

One final objection, which I shall take up, appeals to the notorious difficulty in analyzing counterfactuals properly: it is argued that my analysis should be rejected on the grounds that it makes use of counterfactuals. Jackson responded to such an objection by asserting that, despite the difficulty in providing a satisfactory analysis of counterfactuals, we do *know* on occasions that certain counterfactuals are true.[31] I would add the following. Counterfactuals are not being used in my analysis either to justify or to state the principles of the Bayesian confirmation theory which I make use of: unlike the situation in Jackson's analysis, there is no counterfactual rule of induction or counterfactual condition required above. The appeal to counterfactuals was meant only to facilitate bringing home such obvious facts as that we are significantly more confident of h_1 & e_1 than we are of h_2 & e_2 and that this difference in confidence is not simply an isolated brute fact of our psychological makeup but is linked to, and supported by, our background theories and beliefs. Thus, to see that my analysis of the Grue puzzle is reasonable, one does not also need a logical analysis of counterfactuals. It would be enough, for example, to grant the plausibility of the counterfactual claim. Furthermore, I do not wish to

QUINE AND THE CONFIRMATIONAL PARADOXES   439

suggest that all grue-type problems can be handled by an appeal to such counterfactuals. It is obvious that many different cases are possible and that some will require a different approach.

I shall now take up the hepeven example. However, treating it as giving rise to another paradox of induction (which would require a detailed reply to the sort of inductive skeptic presented above in connection with the Grue) will be avoided here, not only to keep the length of this paper from growing too much, but also because I believe that enough has been said already to make it clear why I do not regard the straight rule as one of the fundamental principles of induction in need of vigorous defense against apparent counterexamples. Instead, taking the straight rule to be a rough rule-of-thumb or generalization with many known counterinstances, I shall analyze the hepeven situation as simply one of the many in which what is implied by the rule conflicts with our intuitive judgments of confirmation. We can then see if our intuitions are vindicated when Bayesian principles (which I have been taking to be more fundamental than the straight rule) are applied. The position I shall adopt here is somewhat analogous to the position a Utilitarian might take regarding such moral maxims as "Lying is morally wrong": most of us feel that in certain sorts of situations, lying is not morally wrong, so an analysis of these types of situations in terms of fundamental principles of morality is supplied in order to vindicate our intuitive judgments.

An analysis of the hepeven situation within the Bayesian framework requires the use of background theories relevant to hepatitis and Social Security numbers. Given what we know about how Social Security number are assigned and about how people get hepatitis, the fact that some members of a POW camp got the disease (and we can assume that this occurred sometime after Smith received his Social Security number) would simply not be probabilistically relevant to whether Smith's Social Security number is odd or even (unless, of course, we were given much more information than is obtainable from the above). So using the abbreviations:

Hx: x has hepatitis
Tx: x has an even Social Security number
Px: x has received a POWE
s: Smith
E: All the ex-POWs from camp #1 who were given POWEs have hepatitis
B: Smith is an ex-Pow from camp #1 and $-Ps$

we can assert

$P(Ts/E \ \& \ B) = P(Ts/B)$.

Now we wish to determine if $P((Hs \ \& \ Ps) \lor (Ts \ \& \ -Ps)/E \ \& \ B)$ is greater than $P((Hs \ \& \ Ps) \lor (Ts \ \& \ -Ps)/B)$. But

$P((Hs \ \& \ Ps) \lor (Ts \ \& \ -Ps)/E \ \& \ B) = P(Hs \ \& \ Ps/E \ \& \ B) + P(Ts \ \& \ -Ps/E \ \& \ B)$
$= P(Ts \ \& \ -Ps/E \ \& \ B)$

$$= \mathrm{P}(Ts/E \& B)$$
$$= \mathrm{P}(Ts/B).$$

and by a similar derivation,

$$\mathrm{P}((Hs \& Ps) \vee (Ts \& -Ps)/B) = \mathrm{P}(Ts/B).$$

So we are able to conclude that E does not confirm the proposition that Smith has hepeven, which after all is the result we wanted.

5. ANOTHER BAYESIAN ANALYSIS OF THE RAVEN

It is a little misleading to classify the Raven Paradox as a paradox. For in my mind, a paradox is an argument that proceeds to an absurd conclusion from premises that appear to be obviously true and in accordance with such rules of inference. I find it hard to regard Nicod's principle as one that even appears to be clearly valid. The Bayesian view I have been exploiting is not committed to any such principle and (as we have already seen) engenders an analysis of confirmation according to which the principle is false. Indeed, the Bayesian I. J. Good has suggested that the Raven is *solved* by the observation that a positive instance of generalization does not necessarily confirm it.[32] Roger Rosenkrantz seems to agree with Good on this point, for Rosenkrantz's book contains a section, entitled "Resolution of the Paradoxes," in which he writes:

> When background knowledge is admitted, e.g., in the form of a probability distribution over possible states of the considered population, very little can be inferred in general about the confirmation of a general law by its 'positive cases'. . . . Given a probabilistic analysis of confirmation, then, the paradoxes are stopped dead in their tracks. We cannot infer the confirmation of the grue hypothesis by grue emeralds (much less by green emeralds) nor the raven hypothesis by white shoes or red herrings.[33]

Much as I am sympathetic with various aspects of this Bayesian view, I tend to look for a fuller explanation of these puzzles. I expect a solution of the Grue to do more than merely point out that the observation of green emeralds (prior to t_0) *need not* confirm the grue hypothesis; I want an explanation of the widespread intuitive judgment that our observations of green emeralds make the green hypothesis much more credible than the grue. Similarly, I expect an adequate solution of the Raven to provide explanations, or at least analyses, of the salient intuitions that give rise to this puzzle: (1) Why do we judge that our observations of white shoes and the like that seem to constitute *positive instances of the contrapositive* of h (i.e., "contrapositive instances" of h) fail to confirm h, when the observations of black ravens do seem to confirm h? (2) Given that many philosophers regard the observation of white shoes as confirming the contrapositive of h, how can this judgment be reconciled with the intuitive opinion that such observations do not confirm the logically equivalent h?

It is interesting to note, in this connection, that in a more recent paper,

Rosenkrantz has allowed that observing that emeralds examined before t_0 are green does confirm the grue hypothesis (it is just that the observations confirm the green hypothesis more).[34] Thus, he too clearly feels the need for a more thorough analysis of these puzzles.

There is, however, an aspect of the Good-Rosenkrantz "solution" that should be mentioned. Consider the following example. Let k be the hypothesis:

> All contestants who lift the block of cement off the floor weigh more than 150 pounds.

Suppose the very first contestant had succeeded in lifting the block of cement off the floor and that he happens to be an overweight, flabby boy of twelve. If we then observe that he "weighs in" at 151 pounds, it would seem that we have a "positive instance" of k. But clearly, we have more information here than is conveyed by the information that a contestant who lifted the block of cement off the floor weighed more than 150 pounds. Indeed, given this added information, it would not be surprising to find that instead of a confirmation of k, we have a disconfirmation. Rosenkrantz suggests that we have a similar situation with the Raven: we are said to observe not simply a non-black non-raven but a white shoe; however, by picking out a "subevent of the observation" of a non-black non-raven, we alter the relevant probabilities in ways that change a confirmation into a disconfirmation.[35]

Although Rosenkrantz's general point about "subevents" possibly disconfirming is well taken, I do not regard it as giving us a sufficiently penetrating explanation of the puzzles. For without much explanation, it would be paradoxical to claim that the alleged contrapositive instances of the raven hypothesis fail to confirm it because of the added information conveyed by the evidential statement: the added information that what one observed was not merely a non-black non-raven but also a white shoe does not, on the face of it, seem sufficient to turn a confirmation of h into a non-confirmation. After all, even when one sees a raven, one generally observes much more than its color (e.g., one generally notes, at least roughly, its size, its position in space, the time of observation, etc.); and much of this collateral information obtained in the observation is simply "filtered out" without fear that by so doing, we are omitting vitally important information that would, if cited, change a confirmation of h into disconfirmation. Our white shoe example, thus, seems to differ from the previous example in which it was *easy to see* why the added information would tend to raise doubts about the generalization in question. All of this should explain why I would look for a fuller analysis of the relevant confirmational situations than is supplied in Rosenkrantz's book.

One standard sort of analysis some Bayesians have adopted—the basic idea of which seems to have originated with Hosiasson-Lindenbaum[36]—proceeds from the observation that we know (or at least believe) that the number of ravens is much smaller than the number of non-black things, so that the "prior probability" of finding a black raven is much smaller than that of finding a non-black non-raven. It is then argued, in accordance with Bayesian principles, that finding a black raven should increase our confidence in h much more than finding a non-black non-raven.

And it is suggested that our reluctance to regard observing a white shoe as confirming h arises from our intuitive grasp of the fact that the amount our confidence should be raised by observing such a contrapositive instance is negligible, especially when compared with the degree of confirmation provided by observing a black raven.

What I should now like to do is take up some of the objections to this Bayesian account that have been raised by eminent researchers in this area of philosophy. In responding to these objections, I hope to carry the analysis of the Raven further and more adequately than has been done previously. Thus, my own view of the situation will emerge as a sort of answer to these objections.

According to Hempel, the cardinality considerations of the sort put forward above are simply not general enough to explain all Raven-type puzzles. For example, it is paradoxical to suppose that a contrapositive instance of

All molecules are inanimate

confirms the generalization; and this paradoxicality cannot be explained by the sorts of cardinality considerations appealed to above. For despite the fact that few people believe that the subject class (molecules) of the generalization is any smaller in cardinality than the subject class of the contrapositive (animate things), it is still paradoxical to suppose that observing, say, the family cat (an animate non-molecule) would confirm the generalization.[37]

Israel Scheffler has put forward a related objection. The above Bayesian analysis of the Raven yields the result that observing a non-black non-raven should confirm the hypothesis that all non-black objects are non-raven much less than would the observation of a black raven; and this result seems very counter-intuitive to Scheffler, who evidently regards positive instances as always having more confirmatory force than contrapositive instances. Intuition, according to Scheffler, tells us that observing a positive instance of the contrapositive of h (say, a white shoe) should confirm it, but not h itself, even though h is equivalent to its contrapositive.[38]

Finally, Max Black has argued that the reasoning required in the above analysis is so "intricate and problematical" that it is hard to believe that common sense reasoning has been captured. Furthermore, the common sense reasoner does not accept the implications of this solution that finding a white shoe confirms h to a negligible degree—rather, he takes the finding to be *completely irrelevant* to h.[39]

Now what in the reasoning of the above Bayesian account is so problematical for Black? According to standard Bayesian accounts,

[*] The degree of confirmation of h produced by finding a raven to be black is much greater than the degree of confirmation of h produced by finding a non-black thing to be a non-raven.

Black's objection is that justifying [*] requires information that goes beyond the mere sizes of the classes of ravens and non-black things: "What is at stake may, with some simplification, be said to be whether a predominance of contrapositive

QUINE AND THE CONFIRMATIONAL PARADOXES 443

instances over positive instances is more likely on the supposition that [the raven hypothesis] is true than upon the supposition that [it] is false."[40] Black finds it hard to see how this question could possibly be answered.

Obviously, this objection requires a more detailed analysis of the Raven than I have given thus far. In the following, I shall treat h as the generalization one would express with the notation

(x)(x is a raven → x is black)[41]

and I shall use the following symbols as abbreviations of the propositions indicated:

H: a_1 is an object selected at random from the class of ravens and a_2 is an object selected at random from the class of non-black things

b: a_1 is black

$\bar{r}$: a_2 is non-raven

We can now take up the question: Does b or $\bar{r}$ confirm h more (given H)? The following biconditionals lead to an answer.

$P(h/b \,\&\, H) - P(h/H) > P(h/\bar{r} \,\&\, H) - P(h/H)$

iff $P(h/b \,\&\, H) > P(h/\bar{r} \,\&\, H)$

iff $\dfrac{P(h/H) \times P(b/h \,\&\, H)}{P(b/H)} > \dfrac{p(h/H) \times P(\bar{r}/h \,\&\, H)}{P(\bar{r}/H)}$ Bayes' Theorem

iff $\dfrac{1}{P(b/H)} > \dfrac{1}{P(\bar{r}/H)}$ since $P(b/h \,\&\, H) = P(\bar{r}/h \,\&\, H) = 1$

iff $P(\bar{r}/H) > P(b/H)$

Since, as we shall show below, $P(\bar{r}/H)$ is larger than $P(b/H)$, it is clear that b conforms h (given H) more than does $\bar{r}$.

What I shall now show is that, using only the crudest of estimations of probabilities based mostly on very rough estimations of cardinality, the degree to which $\bar{r}$ confirms h, given H, is so small as to be insignificant. I am assuming here that we are dealing with a situation in which h is to be genuinely tested, i.e., we are certain neither of h nor of not-h. Thus, $P(b/H)$ is some number j in $(0, 1)$ which is not very close to either end point. Let N be the estimated cardinal number of the set of ravens. And let the number of non-black ravens be estimated to be M. Clearly $M < N$. If one selects at random from the class of non-black things, what is the probability of selecting a non-black raven? Even if we suppose N to be as much as several billion, M will be insignificant when compared with the cardinality of the set of non-black things; for the latter contains such entities as microorganisms, molecules, atoms, neutrinos, photons, and so on. Thus, $P(\bar{r}/H)$ will be a number extremely close to 1—so close in fact that for essentially any calculation of probabilities we are apt to want to make in any real situation involving this probability, we can take its value to be 1. Thus, we can see that the degree to which $\bar{r}$ confirms h, given H, $P(h/\bar{r} \,\&\, H) - P(b/H)$,

$$= \frac{P(b/H) \times P(\bar{r}/\,b\,\&\,H)}{P(\bar{r}/H)} - P(b/H)$$

$$= \left[\frac{1}{P(\bar{r}/H)} - 1\right] \times P(b/H)$$

$$= \epsilon \times P(b/H)$$

where ϵ is a positive number so close to 0 as to make this degree of confirmation insignificant. To get some rough idea of exactly how small this degree is, suppose we calculate $P(\bar{r}/H)$ to be given by

$$\frac{10^{10^{10}}}{10^{10^{10}} + 1}.$$

Given our current physical theories, it would not be unreasonable to give a figure very much closer to one, but even using this crude low estimate, the degree to which $\bar{r}$ confirms h in this situation would come to less than one over ten to the ten billion—a number too small to be used in calculations of probabilities we can expect to make in any real situation, given the kind of accuracies we can obtain or use.

Let us now reexamine Black's analysis of the situation, since the above seems to constitute precisely the sort of justification of [*] that he thought could not be given. Black proceeds by calling the positive instance (a black raven) a and the contrapositive instance (a white shoe) b. Then setting $P(a/h) = p$, $P(a/-h) = p^*$, $P(b/h) = q$, and $P(b/-h) = q^*$, he claims that the observation of a confirms h more than does the observation of b, iff p/p^* is greater than q/q^*. This leads him to maintain that more is involved in assessing the relevant degrees of confirmation than the relative sizes of the classes.[42] But notice first of all that Black's probabilistic statements are somewhat strange: since 'a' stands for a thing (i.e., a black raven), not a proposition, it is not clear exactly how we should understand '$P(a/h)$'. Supposedly Black is speaking here of epistemic probabilities, in which case P should be a function of propositions or propositionlike entities. Notice also that in Black's analysis, the observed entities are treated as if they were obtained as a result of taking samples from the whole universe. This is a reasonable way for him to proceed since he is only reproducing a feature of what has become the common method of analyzing the Raven by means of Bayesian theory.[43] However, at least part of the difficulty encountered by Black in seeking a Bayesian justification of [*] is due to the fact that taking a random sample from the universe and obtaining a black raven could significantly alter one's beliefs about the cardinalities involved; in particular, it could lead one to revise somewhat one's estimation of the number of ravens that there are. The reason this might occur is that a person who thought there were relatively very few ravens compared with the totality of objects in the universe would think it highly unlikely that a raven would be selected in a random sample of the universe. All of this should bring to mind the earlier example of section 3 which was used to show that a positive instance of a generalization may disconfirm it. For similar reasons, it seems possible that observing a black raven with this sort of sampling might not confirm h, since if one thought as a result of the observation that there were many more ravens in existence than one first believed, this could very well lead to a decrease in the evidential significance of the small sample of black ravens previously observed. I thus must agree with Black that more is involved in estimating the relevant degrees of confirmation in this sort of situation than just computations from the cardinalities of the classes involved. And I can sympathize with his wonder at how the Bayesian can guarantee, on the basis of essentially just cardinality estimations, that the observation of a black raven will confirm h more than would the observation of the non-black non-raven.[44]

Notice, however, that the above difficulty is avoided in my reasoning by having the sampling done directly from the class of ravens. Thus, in the justification of [*] given above, we need to know $P(b/h \& H)$ and $P(\bar{r}/h \& H)$, which are both clearly equal to 1, instead of the difficult to estimate $P(a/h)$ and $P(b/h)$ of Black's analysis. Ironically, my construal of [*] conforms to some of Black's own pronouncements on confirmation. For example, Black claims that Hempel's expression 'confirmation' is intended to be a sort of "technical surrogate" for the common notion "constitutes empirical support"—a notion which Black sees as intimately connected with deliberate investigation and, in particular, with the idea of testing a hypothesis. Thus, when Hempel says that the existence of a black raven "confirms" the raven hypothesis, we agree, according to Black, because we tend to substitute 'empirical support' for 'confirmation' and "naturally think (retroactively!) of the admissible procedure of selecting a raven at random in order to determine whether or not it is black".[45] From this, it would seem that Black should agree that the expression 'finding a raven to be black' suggests the sort of "admissible procedure" he refers to above rather than the impractical procedure of selecting an object at random from the whole universe and finding it to be a black raven.

We have thus seen that even if the observation of a non-raven were to be regarded as resulting from a random sampling of the class of non-black things, the degree to which it would confirm h would be so small as to be insignificant. But am I now committed to maintaining that observing a white shoe confirms h to some degree, thus running into the second of Black's objections according to which "common sense" would not regard such an observation as even relevant to h? Not at all. For nothing I have said above implies that any actual case of observing a white shoe should be taken to be a case of observing a non-black thing to be a non-raven. Apart from the problem (discussed earlier) that is created by the information conveyed by 'white shoe' that is additional to that conveyed by 'non-black non-raven', it is clear that no ordinary observation of a white shoe should be regarded as resulting from anything like a random sampling of the class of non-black things.[46] Indeed, it is by no means clear just how one would go about sampling at random such a class. After all, what objects does it contain besides molecules, atoms, and subatomic particles? Parts of medium-sized material bodies? What parts of my green easy chair are to count as elements of this class? And how is the Pacific Ocean to be divided into objects of this totality? What about abstract entities (such as numbers, sets, properties, and the like)? And how would one go about making a selection from such a class? Clearly, we have only the vaguest of ideas about what this class is and how one would take a random sample from it. Thus, even granting the vagueness of the notion of sampling from the class of ravens, sampling from the class of non-black things introduces unclarities of another order entirely.

We might, of course, select a small portion of the universe as our "universe of discourse" in order to make the confirmation more manageable, say, by choosing just flying animals or perhaps birds. However, this would rule out the usual examples (white shoes, red herrings, etc.) as contrapositive instances. But more important, as we shrink the universe of discourse, we also shrink the paradoxicality of supposing that finding a non-black thing to be a non-raven confirms h. Thus, if one could select non-black things at random from the class of birds and if one obtained only non-ravens from a large sampling, then surely our confidence in h would (and should) go up.

But there is a special absurdity in regarding my seeing a white shoe on the street as I drive to work as resulting from taking a random sample of the class of non-black things. For example, if I regard the observations I make at work one day as giving me a random sample of the class of non-ravens, I would have support for the hypothesis

All non-raven are visible.

But no one would be so uncritical as to make such an assumption of randomness: the sample is clearly "biased toward the visible." Anything I am likely to observe during a typical workday is going to be visible. Similarly, it is grossly unrealistic to regard the white shoe I saw on my way to work as resulting from taking a random sample of the class of non-black things. After all, only certain sorts of things *can* be observed by me in ordinary situations. I cannot observe a photon, an electron, or any of the billions of microorganisms that inhabit my body. Most entities are not accessible to me because of my location in space (how many elements of this class are located sufficiently close to me to be observed by me?). And of those elements that are visible and in my vicinity, how many would I even tend to notice?

It should now be obvious that I need not deny Black's premise about common sense: the analysis I have given above does not imply that finding a white shoe confirms h to any degree. We have seen that even if such an observation could be regarded as resulting from a sampling at random of the class of non-black things, the degree of confirmation would be much too small to be significant. But we have also seen that such an observation cannot be *realistically* regarded as resulting from any such sampling, so the analysis is not committed to the position that some degree of confirmation is provided by an observation of a white shoe. Furthermore, I cannot find any good reason for supposing that, on any realistic assumptions, the observation should constitute a confirmation of h within the Bayesian framework. There are so many relationships and factors to consider and so many complicating features of any actual observation situation that must be taken account of that it is hard to see how anyone could come up with a reasonable estimate of the relevant probabilities. It is no wonder, then, that "common sense" would rebel at taking an observation of a white shoe as constituting a confirmation of h.

Has my analysis then committed me to the position that one gets confirmation of h only by taking a random sample from the class of ravens and finding it to be black? Of course not. There is nothing in the Bayesian position that precludes obtaining confirmation of h in other ways. Obviously, what does confirm it will depend on one's background theories and probability space, but as will be suggested in the following paragraph, there are other sensible ways of obtaining this confirmation.

There is another reason why regarding the observation of a white shoe as confirming h may seem so silly to common sense. When we think of sensible procedures for confirming h, we are apt to think not only of sampling the class of ravens in all sorts of different ways and in all sorts of different regions but also of doing relevant genetical and ethological studies on populations of ravens and related birds. We would want to learn, for example, if mutations affecting plumage color can be induced in bird populations. Also, given the existence of albino birds, we would want to investigate the possibility that the various raven gene pools harbor a gene for albinism. We would also want to know if there is a tendency among some birds to cause their albino offspring to die, say, by not feeding them or by pushing them out of the nest (which might account for our failure thus far to see any white ravens). Investigations of these sorts can, of course, be represented within the Bayesian framework. By comparison with such investigations, the idea of looking at such things as shoes and fish to confirm h may seem grotesque.

Similar considerations apply to Hempel's objection. First, it should be clear that I have not claimed, as some evidently have, that every situation in which a contrapositive instance is held not to be confirmatory should be explained by an appeal to cardinality considerations of the sort given above. It should be obvious that within the Bayesian view, our background theories can function in many ways to produce such a situation. Consider Ralph Kennedy's example in which we seek to test the hypothesis

q: All samples of pure iron have a melting point of 1525° C.

If our background theories imply that all samples of a pure metal melt at the same temperature, then a single instance of a sample of pure iron that is found to have a melting point of 1525° C could render q strongly confirmed, whereas determining that a soft white waxy substance with a melting point of 80° C is not pure iron (a contrapositive instance) would clearly not have such an effect. This sort of example has been effectively analyzed in terms of the notion of *resiliency* and without appealing to the cardinality of any classes.[47] Second, I can readily agree with Hempel that it would be paradoxical to affirm that any ordinary observation of the family cat constitutes a confirmation of 'All molecules are inanimate', for my analysis is not committed to denying Hempel's premise. Clearly, observing the family cat, in any ordinary situation, would not be regarded as resulting from taking a random sample from the class of animate objects and hence cannot be analyzed as resulting in a confirmation in the straightforward way the raven hypothesis is confirmed by finding a raven to be black. Of course, if one dresses up the description of the observation in the appropriate way, say, by postulating some device for selecting at random from the class of animate things, then the paradoxicality diminishes—at least it does for me since if one took a large random sample from the class and came up with only non-molecules my confidence in the molecular hypothesis would go up—if ever so slightly.

Let us now turn to Scheffler's objection according to which the observation of the white shoe should confirm the contrapositive of h more than would the observation of a black raven. If we take Scheffler's objection to be directed at the analysis I have given, then it would be based on the intuition that the hypothesis

All non-black things are non-ravens

is confirmed more by finding a non-black thing to be a non-raven than it is by finding a raven to be black. Thus, this objection rests on an intuition. But how seriously should we take this intuition? Might it not have been formed by a philosophical attachment to some version of Nicod's principle? Might not this intuition, then, be a product of a misguided theory of confirmation? I ask the reader to consider an analogous situation in which the cardinality differences are more extreme. Let h^* be the contrapositive of

All the students of Philosophy 290-1 are male humans.

Now suppose that it is known that there are only three students in Philosophy 290-1. Then, on my theory, one can confirm h^* by sampling the class of students in Philosophy 290-1 to see if they are all male; indeed, we need only investigate three students to obtain a conclusive confirmation. So each confirming instance from a sample taken from the set of students of the course would increase our confidence in h^* quite substantially; whereas confirming instances from a sampling of the class of things that are not male humans would be insignificant. The objector's view applied to this case would imply that obtaining positive confirmation from the latter sort of sampling would be more confirmatory than that from the former sort —a view I find too implausible to take seriously.

6. CONCLUDING REMARKS

At a recent philosophy conference, it was asked if anyone seriously doubted the Bayesian solution to the Raven. I hope it is clear from the previous section that there is no such thing as *the* Bayesian solution. There are many different "solutions" that Bayesians have put forward using Bayesian techniques and principles. Furthermore, I should emphasize that I am not claiming to have provided *solutions* to the confirmational paradoxes: 'solutions' suggest a kind of finality and overall adequacy that I cannot claim for what I have provided here. Certainly, I see no reason to think I have provided a general method for dealing with every grue-type puzzle that someone may think up. And as I said at the beginning of section 4, I have all sorts of misgivings about the Bayesian framework itself. As I am quite sure that many significant refinements in the framework will be made in the coming years, I think it likely that I will want to make revisions of my analyses of these puzzles as well. However, I would be willing to claim that this paper provides a more realistic and scientifically satisfying analysis of these puzzles than Quine has given and that this points to the superiority of the Bayesian view of confirmation over the Quinian. The coming years, I predict, will produce a reassessment of many of Quine's doctrines based on critical evaluations of his use of an inadequate theory of confirmation and verification.

Notes

1. A version of this paper was read at the meeting of the Society for Exact Philosophy held at U.S.C. in June 1980. This paper was written, in part, while I was on sabbatical leave with financial support from the University of California Humanities Research Fellowship Program. I gratefully acknowledge this support. Many of the ideas contained in this paper were presented in graduate seminars I gave in 1977 and 1979. I am grateful for the many helpful suggestions I received from those who participated, especially Ellery Eells, Malcolm MacFail, Jerry Wakefield, Neil Thomason, and finally Dr. Roger Rosenkrantz, who supplied me with several valuable prepublication copies of his writings on related topics. I would also like to thank Frank Jackson for carefully working through an early draft of this paper and providing me with many helpful comments.

2. W. V. Quine, "Epistemology Naturalized," *Ontological Relativity and Other Essays* (New York and London, 1969), p. 80. Quine also criticizes there the Vienna Circle for not taking the verifiability theory of meaning seriously enough.

3. W. V. Quine, "The Problem of Meaning in Linguistics," *From a Logical Point of View* (Cambridge, Mass., 1961), p. 54.

4. W. V. Quine, "Necessary Truth," *The Ways of Paradox and Other Essays* (New York, 1966), p. 56 (italics mine).

5. "The Scope and Language of Science," *The Ways of Paradox and Other Essays*, p. 221.

6. W. V. Quine, "Posits and Reality," *The Ways of Paradox and Other Essays*, pp. 236-37.

7. For a more detailed and accurate presentation of Quine's reasoning in this regard, see my *Ontology and the Vicious-Circle Principle* (Ithaca and New York, 1973).

8. W. V. Quine and J. S. Ullian, *The Web of Belief* (New York, 1970), p. 66. Hereafter, reference to this work will be given by 'Web'; numerals immediately following 'Web' represent page numbers.

9. Cf. Clark Glymour, *Theory and Evidence* (Princeton, 1980), chap. 2.

10. W. V. Quine, "Natural Kinds," *Ontological Relativity and Other Essays*, p. 115. Hereafter, reference to this work will be given by 'NK'; numerals immediately following 'NK' represent page numbers.

11. Quine's Grue puzzle is based on, but distinct from, Nelson Goodman's New Riddle of Induction, as presented in his *Fact, Fiction, and Forecast*, 3rd ed. (Indianapolis and New York, 1973), chap. 3. For criticisms of Goodman's views on this topic, see R. Kennedy and C. Chihara, "An Improvement on Zabludowski's Critique of Goodman's Theory of Projection," *Journal of Philosophy* 71 (1975):137-41, and "Beyond Zabludowskian Competitors: A New Theory of Projectibility," *Philosophical Studies* 33 (1978):229-53.

12. Frank Jackson, "Grue," *Journal of Philosophy* 72 (1975):123. The condition is also expressed in a slightly different form (p. 124). I have learned from Jackson (letter of January 25, 1980) that in giving this alternate form, the knowledge requirement was inadvertently dropped. Thus, the discussion of the counterfactual condition in this paper does not depend on using any one form of the condition.

13. The basic idea for this objection was suggested to me by Ellery Eells.

14. Jackson, "Grue," p. 14. Jackson has responded (in a letter of February 11, 1980) that this counterfactual condition is just one of a number of "plausible counter factual principles at work when questions of instantial confirmation arise." His strategy, then, is to introduce still other principles in the hope of shielding the straight-rule from all grue-type difficulties. In this vein, he has suggested the following intuitively plausible principle could be used to obviate my hepeven example:

> Certain Fs which are H being G only supports other Fs which are known to be non-H being G, if it is known that the Fs in the evidence class would have been G had they not been H.

However, he admits that this principle is too strong as it stands and needs to be adjusted to take account of cases in which it is not known, but only likely, that the Fs would still have been G had they not been H. Thus, Jackson sees the need for bringing probabilistic principles into his account. Besides being doubtful about the chances of success of this program, I cannot help thinking that the sort of probability theory he would need to bolster his defenses would obviate the need for surrounding his straight rule with an elaborate army of principles and conditions.

15. In Goodman's terminology (*Fact, Fiction, and Forecast*, p. 90), the hypothesis must be *unviolated, supported,* and *unexhausted*.

16. J. J. Good, "The White Shoe Is a Red Herring," *British Journal for the Philosophy of Science* 17 (1967):322.

17. Jackson has suggested (in a letter of February 13, 1980) that such examples can be obviated by appealing to more general, or perhaps second-order, inductions that tell us when to beware of first-order inductions. Thus, he has in effect admitted that the counterfactual condition does not save Nicod's criterion from counterexamples; as stated, the principle is false. Of course, it is open to Jackson to revise the principle so as to obtain an exception-free criterion of confirmation; but this he has not succeeded in doing, and I am doubtful that he can succeed unless he works with a theory of confirmation (such as the Bayesian) that can provide a more detailed, systematic, and precise theoretical framework for analysis of *confirmation by positive instances* than is provided by appeals to disparate and fragmentary intuitions.

18. C. Hempel, "The White Shoe, No Red Herring," *British Journal for the Philosophy of Science* 18 (1967):239-40.

19. C. Hempel, "On the Nature of Mathematical Truth," in *Philosophy of Mathematics: Selected Readings*, ed. Paul Benacerraf and Hilary Putnam (Englewood Cliffs, N.J., 1964), pp. 366-81.

20. I, myself, have taken part in criticizing certain aspects of Bayesian theory. See R. Kennedy and C. Chihara, "The Dutch Book Theorem: Its Logical Flaws, Its Subjective Sources," *Philosophical Studies* 36 (1979):19-33. The most serious criticisms of Bayesian Confirmation Theory that I am familiar with are to be found in chap. 3 of Glymour, *Theory and Evidence*. These criticisms are aimed primarily at showing that the Bayesian theory cannot explain various methodological truisms, as well as certain features of the relationship between theory and evidence, which any adequate theory of confirmation should explain. Glymour ends the chapter with the words: "None of these arguments is decisive against the Bayesian scheme of things, nor should they be, for in an important respect that scheme is undoubtedly correct." I would add: even granting the force of Glymour's objections and freely allowing that the Bayesian view is not entirely adequate, it is still remarkable just how much one can explain with the theory. For other criticisms of the Bayesian view, see H. Kyburg, "Subjective Probability: Criticisms, Reflections, and Problems," *Journal of Philosophical Logic* 7 (1978):157-80.

21. For a detailed discussion of this rule and the justifications that have been offered for accepting it, see Paul Teller, "Conditionalization, Observation, and Change of Preference," vol. I in *Foundations of Probability Theory, Statistical Inference, and Statistical Theories of Science*, ed. W. Harper and C. A. Hooker (Dordrecht, 1976), pp. 205-59. I should add that I

do not regard any of these "justifications" for this rule (regarded as a principle of Personalist probability theory) as adequate.

22. See R. Rosenkrantz, *Inference, Method, and Decision: Towards a Bayesian Philosophy of Science* (Dordrecht, 1977), p. 168. See also Richard Swineburne, *An Introduction to Confirmation Theory* (London, 1973), p. 3.

23. Patrick Suppes, "A Bayesian Approach to the Paradoxes of Confirmation," in *Aspects of Inductive Logic*, ed. J. Hintikka (Amsterdam, 1966), p. 203.

24. For promising work in this area, see Brian Skyrms, *Causal Necessity* (New Haven, 1980). Also Ellery Eells, "Newcomb's Paradox and the Principle of Maximizing Conditional Expected Utility," (Ph.D. thesis, University of California, Berkeley, 1980).

25. See Mary Hesse, *The Structure of Scientific Inference* (Berkeley and Los Angeles, 1974), pp. 136-41. But cf. Glymour, *Theory and Evidence*, chap. 2.

26. See Jon Dorling, "Bayesian Personalism, the Methodology of Scientific Research Programmes, and Duhem's Problem," *Studies in History and Philosophy of Science* 10 (1979): 177-87.

27. Judy Jarvis Thomson was an early advocate of bringing in background information to deal with Grue-type puzzles. See her "Grue," *Journal of Philosophy* 63 (1966):289-309.

28. Jackson, "Grue," p. 129.

29. For example, see Hesse, *The Structure of Scientific Inference*, chap. 3 (sec. 2).

30. James Hullett and Robert Schwarz, "Grue: Some Remarks," *Journal of Philosophy* 64 (1967):270-71.

31. Jackson, "Grue," p. 129.

32. Good, "The White Shoe Is a Red Herring."

33. Rosenkrantz, *Inference, Method, and Decision*, p. 36.

34. Rosenkrantz, "Does the Philosophy of Induction Rest on a Mistake?" (unpublished manuscript).

35. Rosenkrantz, *Inference, Method, and Decision*, pp. 35-36. The above point seems to have been first made by Good ("The White Shoe Is a Red Herring," p. 322) who suggests that finding a white crow—a non-black non-raven—would actually disconfirm the raven hypothesis, because ravens and crows are known to be biologically related (so that the finding would increase our expectation that there are white ravens). Rosenkrantz also has a clever example to illustrate the point that "subevents" may not confirm—an example which does not require the usual sorts of background theories. Suppose that N hats have been assorted at random among their N owners and that two men are selected at random to test the hypothesis that no man receives his own hat. Although the evidence statement 'The two men did not receive their own hats' confirms the hypothesis, the additional information given by the statement 'The two men received each other's hat' is sufficient to disconfirm the hypothesis.

36. J. Hosiasson-Lindenbaum, "On Confirmation," *Journal of Symbolic Logic* 5 (1940): 138-48. For a detailed discussion of (and references to) more recent work along these lines, see Swineburne, *An Introduction to Confirmation Theory*, chap. 10.

37. The above explanation of Hempel's objection (including the example) is taken from Israel Scheffler's *The Anatomy of Inquiry* (Indianapolis and New York, 1963), p. 284. Hempel raised this objection in "Studies in the Logic of Confirmation," *Mind* 54 (1945):21-22 fn. Another Hempelian criticism of this Bayesian solution is contained in the above note, but I prefer not to take it up here because I feel it is not sufficiently plausible to warrant the space required to deal adequately with all the controversial points it raises or to unravel its many questionable assumptions. (E.g. (1) If one were to use a different language to express one's hypotheses—even one that is radically different from our natural languages—there would be in that language some sentence essentially equivalent to h. (2) 'Every space-time region that contains a raven contains something black' can be taken to be the equivalent of h in a "coordinate language" in which finite space-time regions figure as individuals. (3) In such a language, the contrapositive of 'Every space-time region that contains a raven contains something black' is

'Every space-time region that contains something non-black is a space-time region that contains a non-raven'.)

38. Scheffler, *The Anatomy of Inquiry*, pp. 284-85. For a critical discussion of Scheffler's own theory of "selective confirmation", see Swineburne, *An Introduction to Confirmation Theory*, pp. 567-68.

39. Max Black, "Notes on the 'Paradoxes of Confirmation'," *Margins of Precision* (Ithaca and London, 1970), pp. 206-7.

40. *Ibid.*

41. It should be noted that many philosophers attempt to resolve the Raven by taking the raven hypothesis to be a nomological statement expressing the proposition that, of physical necessity, all ravens are black. It will be seen that it is not necessary to resort to such a move in order to justify (within the Bayesian framework) most of the salient features of our intuitions regarding the relevant confirmational situations.

42. *Ibid.*, p. 207 fn.

43. *Ibid.*

44. Cf. Swineburne, *An Introduction to Confirmation Theory*, chap. 10.

45. Black, "Notes on the 'Paradoxes of Confirmation'," p. 184.

46. A random sample is supposed to be obtained in such a way that the chance of selecting any particular object from the sampled class is equal to the chance of selecting any other object from that class ('chance' being understood here in terms of subjective probability). I imagine that most actual sampling techniques yield samples that are only approximately random (in this sense); but whatever difficulties there may be in devising methods of generating samples of ravens that are close to being random, the above passages are meant to expose the additional difficulties one faces in passing to the task of taking random samples from the class of non-black things. Thus, one ought not to assume that the standard Bayesian reasoning used to justify the claim that finding a raven to be black confirms h can also be used, with only minor adjustments, to justify the claim that finding a white shoe confirms the contrapositive of h.

47. See Skyrms, *Causal Necessity*, sec. IB7.

Reply to Chihara

W. V. QUINE

Chihara has made here a painstaking contribution to the considerable literature on confirmation and its degrees. It is a topic with which I associate the names of Carnap, Jeffreys, Hempel, Kyburg, and Savage, among others, but certainly not my own. I was startled to see his allusions to a Quinian theory of confirmation, and to see how his paper bristles with my name; for I have not thought of myself as holding any distinctive or original theory of confirmation. I was the more startled, then, by his suggestion that my "vast theoretical edifice"[1] rests on my "inadequate theory of confirmation"—something to do with positivism—and that consequently "the coming years . . . will produce a reassessment."[2]

I follow the crowd in celebrating what is loosely described as the hypothetico-deductive method. One seeks a set of hypotheses that will jointly imply the data, and one chooses among such sets with an eye to simplicity and conservatism and perhaps other virtues. Successful prediction confirms, showing as it does the continuing coverage of new data.

Simple induction is a special case of the method, and the primordial case. It is what psychologists call stimulus generalization, and is not peculiar to man. Stimulus generalization proceeds through channels of subjective similarity; we generalize to natural kinds. By natural kinds I mean kinds that are natural to us. Subjective similarity is a psychological relation that can be tested for by reinforcement and extinction of responses. It is a factor in the broader and vaguer quality, likewise subjective, of simplicity. See the last of Chihara's various quotations from p. 57 of *The Web of Belief*.[3]

Chihara's account of my views in his first four pages is quite right, up to the point where he says that the "view of the situation . . . presented in *Web*" is "slightly different." Here "not only are projectible traits the natural kind traits, they are also the traits we notice." I see no difference, since by natural kinds I mean kinds that are natural to us. "But that is not all," he goes on, "for Quine also

453

wants to explain projectibility in terms of simplicity and similarity." No, this is more of the same. "Similarity, projectibility, and simplicity," as he indeed quotes me as saying—and, I might add, natural kind—"are all of a piece."[4]

In my paper "Natural Kinds" I remarked that our standards of similarity and natural kind develop and change in the course of experience; also that "different similarity measures . . . best suit different branches of science,"[5] different theoretical contexts. Marsupial mice count as more similar to kangaroos than to mammalian mice when we are biologizing, and vice versa when we are not. So it is with projectibility.

Chihara cites my example of times: though all times have been prior to t_0, we do not infer that all further times will be prior to t_0. The times prior to t_0 do not qualify as a kind. In Chihara's counterexample of Spider the burglar, the network of findings and hypotheses is such that the times prior to t_0 do qualify as a kind in that context; they qualify for projection. This sensitivity of projectibility or kind to the attendant body of theory is what Chihara notes as sensitivity to background knowledge.

Attendant theory can also work oppositely, arresting projectibility. Chihara cites my other temporal example: I have lived at all observed times, therefore I shall live at all times. Initially this is a tempting induction, he feels, and I agree; but, as he points out, a network of related findings and hypotheses contrive to discourage it. We may say that a kind has lapsed, that a predicate has lost is projectibility, or that a supposedly projectible predicate has proved otherwise, or, indeed, simply that an induction, reasonable but fallible as usual, has been refuted.

Chihara's example of the grueness of neptunite is less clearly a case of induction, or, therefore, of projectibility. It is a case of straightforward hypothetico-deductive method in which the grueness of neptunite is deduced from a combination of findings and hypotheses. Other examples that I have just mentioned are of course likewise far afield from primordial induction; farther far than the coloration of ravens and emeralds.

Such remarks as Chihara has gleaned from my writings, or that I have added here, add up to no theory of confirmation worthy of the name. Theories worthy of the name, good or bad, have been advanced by the philosophers lately mentioned, and Chihara now adds his own. What I find wrong is the notion of there being conflict between his substantial theory and the attitudes that I have meant to express.

Notes

1. Charles Chihara, "Quine and the Confirmational Paradoxes," this volume, p. 425.
2. *Ibid.*, p. 449.
3. *Ibid.*, p. 428.
4. *Ibid.*
5. W. V. Quine, "Natural Kinds," in W. V. Quine, *Ontological Relativity and Other Essays* (New York and Londin, 1969), p. 137.

The Significance of Naturalized Epistemology

BARRY STROUD

Naturalized epistemology is the scientific study of perception, learning, thought, language-acquisition, and the transmission and historical development of human knowledge—everything we can find out scientifically about how we come to know what we know. In asking about the *significance* of those investigations I do not mean to be asking the absurd question whether the deliverances of natural science on such matters are true, or correct, or illuminating, or important. I mean to ask: true or correct *as what?* in what specific *ways* illuminating? important *for what?*

I want to ask, in particular, about the relation between the project of naturalized epistemology as Quine conceives it and the more traditional philosophical examination of knowledge it is meant to supplant. The "old" epistemology asked how any of us knows anything at all about the world around us, and it recognized that most of what we know is based somehow on the senses. The problem was given its special philosophical character by certain facts about sense-perception, familiar from antiquity and employed to dramatic effect in Descartes's *First Meditation* and elsewhere, which seem to imply at least the possibility of the world's being quite different in general from the way it is perceived to be. The philosophical problem was then to explain how anyone can know that such a possibility does not obtain, and thereby know what the world is really like, not just the way it is perceived to be. Only then would the possibility of human knowledge have been explained.

Quine says many things about his epistemological program that suggest that it is a fairly direct response to this familiar question. He recommends an investigation into the source of "our general knowledge of the ways of physical objects,"[1] and he sees the problem as arising from the undeniable fact that "physical things generally, however remote, become known to us only through the effects which they help to induce at our sensory surfaces."[2] Since "we know external things only mediately through our senses,"[3] the problem is: "given only the evidence of our senses, how do we arrive at our theory of the world?"[4]

Quine's way of raising this question differs from that of the traditional epistemologists in that they tried to isolate a domain of pure sensory data evidentially or epistemically prior to the knowledge of nature that is to be explained, whereas for Quine there is no "implicit sub-basement of conceptualization, or language"[5] in which a basic stream of sense-experience could be grasped. That does not imply that the traditional problem of "bridging a gap between sense data and bodies" was a mere pseudo-problem. For Quine it was "real but wrongly viewed."[6] Even without the mistaken belief in pure data of awareness there remain the same good reasons to inquire into the "sensory or stimulatory background" of our knowledge of the world, "namely, to see how evidence relates to theory, and in what way one's theory of nature transcends any available evidence."[7]

Quine's conception of human knowledge and therefore of his epistemological project shares with earlier philosophers the idea of human knowledge as a combination of two quite general, but distinguishable, factors—the contribution of the world and the contribution of the knowing or perceiving subject. Just as we can distinguish the proteins from the carbohydrates in our material intake while we subsist on an unanalyzed combination of both of them, so:

> we can investigate the world, and man as part of it, and thus find out what cues he could have of what goes on around him. Subtracting his cues from his world view, we get man's net contribution as the difference. This difference marks the extent of man's conceptual sovereignty—the domain within which he can revise theory while saving the data.[8]

In carrying out this subtraction we would inevitably come to appreciate the very wide scope of man's "conceptual sovereignty" and thereby discover the extent to which all of science itself is man's "free creation" and is thus to that extent a "put-up job."[9] The subjective contribution of perceiving and knowing subjects will inevitably appear as the overwhelmingly dominant influence on the present state of our general knowledge of the world, given this picture. That is the key to Quine's theory of knowledge.

Although many of the physiological and psychological details are still unknown, Quine thinks we already have the outlines of an answer to the general problem of our knowledge of the world. Considered relative to the irritations at our sensory surfaces, the physical objects we believe in are "posits"; statements of their existence are "far in excess of any available data," past, present, and future.[10] From such "meager traces" as "two dimensional optical projections and various impacts of airwaves on the eardrums and some gaseous reactions in the nasal passages and a few kindred odds and ends,"[11] we somehow arrive at the complex totality of our views about the world.

Our belief in physical objects is therefore a "hypothesis" which we arrive at by the "so-called scientific method."[12] Positing or acknowledging the existence of physical objects differs from the scientist's deliberate and explicit positing of molecules or other theoretical entities only in being "archaic," "unconscious," and "shrouded in prehistory."[13] In each case the point of the hypothesis is the same—to help provide a simpler total "theory" while remaining compatible with as much of the data as possible. And according to Quine the "hypothesis" of physical objects has been eminently successful in that respect. It "has proved more efficacious than other myths as a device for working a manageable structure into the flux of experience";[14] it gives us "the smoothest and most adequate overall account of the world."[15] Each of us acquires that fruitful "hypothesis" when we learn the language of our community. We thereby gradually become masters of the mechanisms of objective reference which enable us to talk of a world of enduring physical objects, and our sensory impacts then dispose us to believe and assert things about an objective physical world. In that way we come to know of physical objects.

This view of the physical world as "hypothetical" or merely "posited" relative to the data of the senses would seem less than satisfactory if it were considered as an answer to the traditional epistemological question raised in, say, Descartes's *First Meditation*. For one thing, scientists explicitly engaged in theory construction do not actually consider and then reasonably reject the "hypothesis," for example, that they are dreaming, or are victims of a mass hallucination or of an evil demon, as the traditional problem requires. And if we ordinary non-scientific mortals arrive at our view of the world by the "scientific method, however amorphous,"[16] then we do not do so by reasonably eliminating such "hypotheses" either. We normally do not even consider, let alone justifiably rule out, those bizarre possibilities. Accordingly, Quine in his positive account does not try to show how we rule out the possibility that the world is completely different in general from the way our sensory impacts and our internal makeup lead us to think of it. But it cannot be that we can afford to ignore this question simply because we know at the outset that that bizarre general "hypothesis" is false or is less likely to be true than the physical object "theory." Whether and how the physical object "hypothesis" *is* better confirmed or known is precisely what is in question when the traditional philosophical problem is raised, so the alleged superiority of the physical object "theory" cannot be taken for granted in demonstrating its superiority. Therefore, there seem to be good reasons for concluding that Quine's naturalistic epistemology does not amount to an answer to the traditional problem of our knowledge of the external world.

Quine would seem to agree with this verdict. On the "doctrinal" issue of "justifying our knowledge of truths of nature in sensory terms,"[17] he finds that we have not progressed beyond the plight Hume left us in. "The Humean predicament is the human predicament,"[18] he says, enigmatically. If he is referring to the predicament of never being able adequately to justify our knowledge of the physical world on sensory grounds, the predicament that Hume thought we are all in, then presumably no naturalized epistemology, or any other kind of epistemology, could show that we are not in that predicament and that we really can give a positive answer to the traditional philosophical question about our knowledge of the world.

Naturalized epistemology is the empirical, scientific study of human knowledge, and in his "Epistemology Naturalized" Quine concedes an illegitimate circularity in any naturalistic attempt to "validate" or "substantiate" our knowledge of the world.

If the epistemologist's goal is validation of the grounds of empirical science, he defeats his purpose by using psychology or other empirical science in the validation.[19]

However, he continues:

such scruples against circularity have little point once we have stopped dreaming of deducing science from observations. If we are out simply to understand the link between observation and science, we are well advised to use any available information, including that provided by the very science whose links with observation we are seeking to understand.[20]

The illegitimate circularity of relying on one's knowledge of nature in an attempt to "validate" that very knowledge on sensory grounds is obviously no objection to naturalistic investigations in which no such project of "validation" is in question. Naturalized epistemology is to be seen as itself part of psychology and hence part of the very science of nature the sources of which it seeks to understand, but there is nothing viciously, or even unpleasantly, circular about that. So it need not be seen as a shortcoming of Quine's theory, or of any scientific study of how we come to know what we do, that it fails to answer the traditional philosophical question of how we can "validate" all our knowledge of the world and thereby know that the world matches up with the way it is perceived to be.

On the other hand, Quine in *The Roots of Reference* seems to regard something at least very like the traditional problem of "validation" as a real problem and as answerable by a naturalized epistemology. The earlier epistemologists's refusal to rely on psychology and the rest of natural science out of fear of circularity, he says, "was a case of needless logical timidity, even granted the project of substantiating our knowledge of the external world."[21] The challenge to science which the epistemologist must meet is one that arises from within science itself, and on the basis of already acknowledged scientific facts.

Science tells us that our only source of information about the external world is through the impact of light rays and molecules upon our sensory surfaces. Stimulated in these ways, we somehow evolve an elaborate and useful science. How do we do this, and why does the resulting science work so well? These are genuine questions, and no feigning of doubt is needed to appreciate them. They are scientific questions about a species of primates, and they are open to investigation in natural science, the very science whose acquisition is being investigated.[22]

The old epistemologist missed the fact that the skeptical challenge arises from within science itself, and so, Quine thinks, he failed to recognize the strength of his own position.[23] He can rely on any knowledge currently available to him to answer the scientific questions that constitute the challenge to science he is trying to meet. That is the task for the newly "liberated" epistemologist, but for Quine it appears that the new epistemology has not simply changed the subject or left the traditional problem and its apparently inevitable skeptical solution intact. It is rather "an enlightened persistence in the original epistemological problem."[24] If that is so and if the original problem was that of justifying or "validating" our beliefs about the world, it would seem that naturalized epistemology can or should answer the question of "validation." But Quine seems elsewhere to have conceded that it cannot do that.

This difficulty in interpreting the results of naturalized epistemology is perhaps not surprising once we become explicitly aware of the difficulty of gaining a firm sense of what I have called the "significance" of statements or remarks that might seem on the face of them to be answers to the philosophical question about our knowledge but which often turn out not to be. The traditional philosopher asked whether there is an external world, and whether we can know that there is. G. E. Moore, for example, said, "There are external things," and he even thought he could prove their existence. He also asserted in the same way that he knows that external objects exist.[25] And all of us say things every day (e.g., "I know that your glasses are on the table in the next room") which seem to imply the truth of the things Moore asserted. But does 'I know that external objects exist', as asserted by G. E. Moore, contradict 'No-one knows whether any external objects exist', as asserted by the traditional philosopher as a result of his investigation of human knowledge?

There is some reason to think that the two assertions do not conflict, that the same form of words is being put to quite different uses in the two cases, and so what Moore and the rest of us say, even if true, or correct, or illuminating, or important, would not be straightforwardly decisive for the philosophical investigation of knowledge. Even if we understood perfectly what Moore and the rest of us say, we would not thereby understand its relation to the traditional epistemological question.

Carnap, Schlick, and other logical positivists would agree.[26] If G. E. Moore, or better still an empirical psychologist, says we know there are physical objects, and even goes on to explain how we know it, it does not follow that he is answering the question that the traditional epistemologist asked, or that he is giving an answer to it which is incompatible with philosophical skepticism. The traditional epistemological question of the reality of the external world and of our knowledge of it was for Carnap and Schlick and other verificationists a meaningless pseudo-question; no answer to it was empirically confirmable or disconfirmable. That of course does not imply that the empirical psychologists's question about our knowledge of the physical world is meaningless or a pseudo-question. It is a perfectly meaningful question to be answered by empirical investigation. But precisely because it is answerable in that way, its answer could not also be the answer to the philosophical question, which according to the verificationist is meaningless. Although the two sorts of questions and answers might be expressed in the very same English words, they could not be the same questions and answers if verificationism is correct.

For Carnap we must distinguish a philosophical (pseudo-) employment of a form of words from an ordinary or scientific employment of the same words.

Kant's claim that the statement 'Objects exist independently of us' is "empirically" true but "transcendentally" false would be another example of the same sort of distinction, not of course unrelated to Carnap's own later view.[27] And no doubt there are others ways of making some such distinction according to which Moore's assertions, and those of the rest of us in everyday and scientific life, can be perfectly legitimate and acceptable without settling one way or the other the traditional philosophical question about our knowledge.[28] The relation between the philosophical investigation of knowledge on the one hand, and everything that goes on in ordinary or scientific life that is presumably its subject matter, on the other, is more puzzling and obscure than has often been supposed. That relation, and the source of its obscurity, is what I am interested in.

How then are we to understand the results that Quine's naturalized epistemology would achieve? Not only does he assert, with Moore, that we do know that there is a world of physical objects; he also tries to explain, in general outline, how we know it. And he offers that explanation in terms of a conception of knowledge as a combination of two quite general, but distinguishable, factors, one objective and one subjective—the contribution of the world and the contribution of the knowing subject. In the rest of this paper I will try to show that (i) given Quine's conception of knowledge, his program of naturalized epistemology cannot answer what appears to be the most general question of how any knowledge at all of the world is possible. That in itself would be no reflection on naturalized epistemology if that question were ill-formed, incoherent, or in some other way illegitimate, but I will also try to show that (ii) there is in Quine no demonstration of the incoherence or illegitimacy of that question. Even if I were right on both counts, no aspersions would have been cast on the empirical study of human knowledge. I would have shown at most that so far there still appears to be a question (and what looks like the most basic question we can ask about our knowledge of the world) which Quine's epistemology does not and cannot answer. The issue is not that of some alleged "limits" of empirical science. I want only to throw light on the way in which the results of a naturalized epistemology would have to be understood if Quine's traditional bipartite conception of knowledge were correct.

Quine's naturalized epistemology is the empirical study of a species of primates or, in the particular case, of an individual human subject in interaction with his environment.

> This human subject is accorded a certain experimentally controlled input—certain patterns of irradiation in certain frequencies, for instance—and in the fullness of time the subject delivers as output a description of the three-dimensional external world and its history.[29]

Given Quine's account of our knowledge of the world, in investigating "the relation between the meager input and the torrential output . . . we are studying how the human subject of our study posits bodies and projects his physics from his data."[30]

There is nothing mysterious about such a study. We observe a human being and we observe his environment while also observing the "output" he produces in the form of utterances we understand to be about the world around him. Given what we know about his surroundings and the processes of perception, we can try to explain how the "torrential output" to which we have access is related to, or produced by, the "meager input" science tells us he is receiving. Knowing what we do about his perceptual mechanisms, we know that what he says about the world far transcends his "input" in the sense that its truth is underdetermined by all the sensory impacts he and everyone else will ever have.[31] In that sense his talk of physical objects is a "hypothesis" that goes beyond the "data." But calling his conception of the world a "posit" or "projection" relative to those sensory impacts is not to malign it or, as Quine says, to "patronize" it.[32] Normally we are in a position to see whether what the subject says about the world around him is in large part true, so there is no unreliability or falsity implied in calling his conception of the world a "posit" or "projection" relative to his "data." If we see that what he says is true, as we usually do, then we do not regard it as a *mere* "posit" or "projection" on his part. We see that his "output" is, generally speaking, accurate, and our only reason for saying he is "positing" or "projecting" at all is that what he says about bodies goes well beyond the meager physical stimulations science tells us he is receiving at his sensory surfaces. But we know it does not go beyond what is actually the case right before his eyes. And that is something we know because we can see what is right before his eyes.

The truth of the subject's beliefs is certainly important for the question whether he *knows* what the world around him is like. That becomes clear if we imagine a second and more unusual situation in which it is possible to find ourselves as experimenters or observers of the human scene. Suppose, as sometimes happens, that we see that there are no bodies at all before the subject, or none of the kinds he says and thinks there are. In that situation, knowing what we do, we would conclude that he does not know what the world around him is like, since his beliefs are false. He would be seen to be *merely* projecting or constructing a world that does not in fact exist as he thinks it does. We might be able to explain how that subject comes to say and believe what he does, but since he does not know what the world around him is like we would not thereby have explained how he knows. Not every explanation of a subject's beliefs is an explanation of knowledge.

But of course the truth of the subject's beliefs, although relevant to the question whether he knows, is not sufficient to settle it. If we explain how he comes to say and believe what he does and if we know that what he says and believes is true, we do not thereby explain how he knows. We must also at least explain how it happens that he is right in his assertions and beliefs. That is a question about how the subject's "projections" or "posits" turn out to be correct, and not just a question about how he comes to make them. Any satisfactory explanation of the origins of the subject's beliefs and of their correctness would show at least that, as we might put it, it is no accident that he gets things right. We would see that the world around him is generally speaking exactly the way he says it is and that its being that way is partly responsible for his saying and believing what he does about it. Many philosophers nowadays would hold that that is enough for knowledge: the subject believes that *p*, he is right, and it is no accident that he is right.[33] On that view an explanation of people's "projections" and of their correctness would explain how we know the science we do, and that is what Quine thinks a naturalized epistemology should explain.

The adequacy of any such "causal" account of knowledge is still questionable at best, and I do not want to go into it further. It is enough for my present purposes that we can and do observe sentient subjects and somehow come to understand how their knowledge is possible. In the two kinds of experimental situations I have imagined so far we can do so because we can observe the subject and his surroundings and investigate the relation between them. We have access to what Quine calls the "torrential output" of the subject and so can identify what he believes, and we can observe the world around him and so can see whether what he believes is true, quite independently of whether it is asserted or accepted as true by him. Only because that is so can we determine whether the subject has true beliefs (or perhaps knowledge) and then explain how that is possible.

So far I have imagined a case in which we recognize that the subject's beliefs are generally true, perhaps not accidentally so, and a case in which we recognize that his beliefs are false and so he does not know. But I now want to introduce another (and eventually a fourth) more unfavorable kind of position it is possible, but not customary, for us to find ourselves in in relation to another perceiving subject. Suppose we find we can observe the subject and can determine his impacts and his "output," but for some reason we are denied access to the surrounding world his remarks are supposed to be about. Perhaps we simply cannot see what is in his environment or perhaps some barrier permanently obstructs our view—in any case we have no information about the world around him. We are restricted to what is happening in the subject himself and to his "output." Obviously we could not then establish that the subject knows what the world around him is like, nor could we even tell whether what he says or believes is in general correct. We would not have access both to his "output" and to the world it is about, so we could not compare them or explain the relation between them. Given only what we would have access to in that situation, we could not go beyond saying, "He projects (or posits or believes or puts it forward) that . . ." We could not assert the much stronger conclusion, "He correctly believes (perhaps knows) that . . ." and so we could not see his view of the world as anything more than a *mere* "projection" or construction from certain stimulations. Even if we could somehow explain how he comes to construct and adopt the "projection" we know he has made (and it is not clear how we could do even that),[34] we would still not be in a position to know whether he is generally speaking right or whether he knows anything about the world around him.

Of course we are fortunately not in that kind of position very often—or not for very long. We move around the barrier and see what is happening on the other side. So the mere possibility of our observation's being restricted in that way poses

THE SIGNIFICANCE OF NATURALIZED EPISTEMOLOGY 463

no threat to the naturalistic study of knowing subjects. I raise it simply as a reminder that there is such a possibility and as an illustration of the truism that we could not explain how someone's knowledge, or even true belief, is possible unless we could observe that person's assertions on the one hand, and observe or otherwise know about the world they are about on the other, and thereby ascertain, independently of his asserting them, whether those assertions about the world are true. But although that is an uncontroversial truism, I think it presents a problem for Quine's conception of naturalized epistemology if it is taken as an answer to what looks like the most general question about human knowledge.

The problem arises because so far we have been considering *other* subjects—those whose interactions with the world we observe—but in order to explain how *anyone* ever comes to know anything about the physical world what is true of other people must somehow be seen to apply to ourselves. Quine tries to generalize it this way:

> We are studying how the human subject of our study posits bodies and projects his physics from his data, and we appreciate that our position in the world is just like his. Our very epistemological enterprise, therefore, and the psychology wherein it is a component chapter, and the whole of natural science wherein psychology is a component book—all this is our own construction or projection from stimulations like those we were meting out to our epistemological subject.[35]

So we are to "appreciate that our position in the world is just like" that of the subject who "posits bodies and projects his physics from his data." To put it mildly, I think that is a very difficult thing to do. Or rather, I think we cannot see all our beliefs in the physical world as a "construction or projection from stimulations" in this way while remaining in a position to understand in general how knowledge, or even true belief, about the world is possible. When we try to "appreciate that our position in the world is just like" that of the "positing" or "projecting" subject we have been studying, what sort of view do we get of ourselves and our position? I think that at best[36] we must see ourselves as we see the subject in the third and therefore restricted kind of experimental situation. If we tried to think of *all* our own beliefs as a "construction or projection from stimulations," we would at most have access to what we know to be our assertions or beliefs about the world, but we would not in addition have independent access to the world they are about on the basis of which we could determine whether they are true. We could not compare our beliefs with the world they are about as we can in the normal experimental study of another person. Each of us would find himself with a set of beliefs and dispositions to assert things about the world, and we could of course undergo experiences that would strengthen or alter those dispositions, but those reinforced or newly acquired beliefs themselves would have to be seen in turn as at most some further "projections" from some new but still extremely meager "input." They could not be seen as a source of independent information about the world against which their own truth or the truth of the earlier beliefs could be checked. Therefore, if we follow Quine's instructions and try to see our own position as "just like" the position we can find another "positing" or "projecting" subject to be in, we will have to view ourselves as we view another subject when we can know nothing more than what is happening at his sensory surfaces and what he believes or is disposed to assert.

In the unusually restricted experimental situation we saw that we could not say more than that the subject's assertions and beliefs are *mere* "projections" on his part. We were there restricted to saying only "He posits or believes that . . ." with no way of going on to the stronger verdict "He correctly believes (perhaps knows) that . . ." So in that position we could never come to understand how the subject's knowledge, or even true belief, is possible. And if Quine's account implies that we must find *ourselves* as epistemologists in no better a position with respect to our own beliefs, we can never understand how our own true beliefs are possible either. On Quine's view we could not see ourselves as having knowledge or true beliefs as opposed to merely believing or "projecting" something about a physical world. We could at most hope to explain why we believe or "project" what we do, but since that is never enough in itself to explain how knowledge or true belief is possible we could never get the kind of understanding of our own position that we seek.

In fact a moment's reflection is enough to show that if we did manage to take the view of ourselves that Quine recommends, we would be even worse off than I have imagined so far, and worse off with respect to ourselves than we are even with respect to another subject in the restricted third sort of experimental situation. Strictly speaking, I could no longer see my so-called scientific belief that my beliefs about the physical world are "projections" from impacts at my sensory surfaces as itself anything more than something I believe or "posit" or "project." If I am precluded from seeing any of my beliefs about the physical world as knowledge, or as anything more than a *mere* "projection" on my part, then in particular I must take that attitude to my belief that I am suffering impacts at my sensory surfaces, and indeed to my belief that I have physical sensory surfaces at all. That too is one of my beliefs about a physical world. Even in the restricted situation in which I was denied access to the subject's environment beyond his skin I was at least granted access to his sensory surfaces and therefore to his meager "input." The question of the relation between that meager "input" and the subject's "torrential output" was not fully answerable in that restricted situation, but it arose there from at least some prior knowledge of the physical world on the part of the experimenter. But in my own case I do not even have that. What is unquestioned information about at least part of the physical world in asking the epistemological question about others must be seen in my own case as nothing more than yet another part of an elaborate "projection" about a physical world that I have somehow come to accept. In my own case I have nothing but "output" to work with. And that puts me in an even more restricted situation than the one imagined so far. In relation to another person it would be like standing alone in total darkness and silence and suddenly hearing from somewhere the words "There is a bear," or

"Gavagai." Without access to the world I take those words to be about, there is simply no telling whether they express knowledge, or even truth, so there is no way of explaining in that case how knowledge or true belief is possible. If I saw all my own beliefs as "projections" or "posits" from meager "data," I would be in the same position with respect to all my own "output" as I would be to the "output" in that fourth and even more severely restricted situation. My own "output" would for me be no better than whistling in the dark.

Within this very restricted conception of my own position, in which I have access only to my own "output," I might even come to wonder whether and how some of the things I believe in are related to my asserting and believing what I do about a physical world. I believe in impacts at my sensory surfaces, and I believe that my sensory "input" is meager and my "scientific" "output" torrential, and this might strike me as puzzling and in need of explanation. In an effort to understand the relation between "input" and "output," I might appeal to other beliefs of mine, e.g., about psychology, language-learning, physiology—in fact, all of what I regard as natural science—if I believe it and I think it might help. But telling that complicated story would in turn be only a matter of expressing more and more of my elaborate "construction or projection" of a physical world. I could not regard it as an explanation of how my knowledge, or even true belief, about the physical world is possible, and I could not regard the alleged "explanation" itself as part of my *knowledge* as opposed to a story I fully believe and am perhaps unavoidably disposed to tell myself from time to time.

So I think that if we try to ask with complete generality how it is possible for any human being to know anything at all about the physical world, and if we adopt Quine's traditional two-part conception of knowledge as a combination of a subjective and an objective factor, we cannot get a satisfactory answer to that question. On that conception we would have to recognize that countless "theories" could be "projected" from the sensory impacts we receive, so if we do happen to accept one such "theory" it could not be because of any objectively discoverable superiority it enjoys over its competitors. Every competing "theory" is equally compatible with the same meager "data" that make up what Quine thinks of as the objective component, so our selection of one "theory" over others could arise only from some aspect or other of our subjective constitution. And that is precisely what the traditional epistemologist always saw as a threat to our knowledge of the external world. The possibility that our view of the world is nothing more than a *mere* "projection" is what had to be shown not to obtain in order to explain how our knowledge is possible. Unless that challenge has been met, or rejected, we will never understand how our knowledge is possible at all.

It is perhaps worth repeating that I do not suggest that there is anything illegitimate or even questionable—let alone impossible—about a scientific explanation of how human beings know what they do. Nor would I question the full legitimacy of Moore's "common sense" assertion that he knows there are external things, if that assertion is taken as irrelevant to the general question of our knowledge of the external world. The so-called scientific account is equally unassailable for the same reason. Naturalized epistemology is supposed to give us all the discoverable scientific information about human knowledge that there is, so the deliverances of naturalized epistemology will simply be "scientific" analogues of G. E. Moore's "common sense" assertions. Both would have the very same epistemological status, and we should have the same attitude toward them both. If not, if Quine's naturalized epistemology is taken as an answer to the philosophical question of our knowledge of the external world, then I think that for the reasons I have given no satisfactory explanation is either forthcoming or possible.

If naturalized epistemology can potentially yield everything knowable about how knowledge is possible, but still not settle the most general epistemological question, then it will perhaps be felt, with Carnap and Schlick and many others, that that question itself must be illegitimate or incoherent or in some way not fully capable of asking what we naturally try to ask about knowledge when we think about it in the traditional philosophical way. Quine's insistence that the only questions about knowledge arise within science itself and can be answered on the basis of scientific information might look like an expression of some such feeling. He argues that even in familiar skeptical appeals to sensory illusions "the concept of illusion itself rested on science, since the quality of illusion consisted simply in deviation from external scientific reality."[37] If we understand what an illusion is, and hence can use the idea to raise a skeptical challenge to science, only because we already know in general what reality is like, it may seem plausible to argue that since some unquestioned knowledge of reality is needed even to understand the idea of illusion used in raising the challenge in the first place, it follows that no skeptical argument can have completely general force against all of science at once. That would be to undermine the traditional question and its specious universality by showing that a completely general skeptical answer to it would be impossible. It would not be that science can answer the question, but that there is no coherent philosophical question that can be raised.

Arguments of that form tend to place a great deal of weight on precisely what is or is not included in the meaning of such terms as 'illusion', 'reality', and so on, or on the logically necessary conditions for their meaningful application. Quine's views about meaning do not put him in a strong position to support any such putatively "transcendental" conclusions. And he explicitly disavows all refutations of that form when he says:

> I am not accusing the sceptic of begging the question; he is quite within his rights in assuming science in order to refute science; this, if carried out, would be a straightforward argument by *reductio ad absurdum*. I am only making the point that sceptical doubts are scientific doubts.[38]

The *reductio* in question would presumably proceed as follows: either science is true or it is not; if it is not true then nothing we believe about the physical world amounts to knowledge; if it is true then from what it tells us about perception we can see that we can never tell whether we are perceiving the world as it really is, so once again nothing we believe about the physical world amounts to knowledge. On either assumption we know nothing about the physical world.

If, as Quine says, the skeptic is "quite within his rights" in arguing in this way, then even if "sceptical doubts are scientific doubts" it does not follow that the epistemologist who tries to meet the skeptical challenge raised by those "scientific" doubts can legitimately make free use of the natural science he is trying to account for. Quine says he can. The epistemologist can answer his scientifically created doubts by pursuing a naturalized epistemology. But what support does Quine have for that claim?

Suppose we have asked how any knowledge at all of the physical world is possible, and suppose that we have asked it because of what we take at the outset to be true about the physical world—in particular about the processes of perception. If we then arrived by *reductio* at the general skeptical conclusion which Quine thinks is at least coherent, we would find all our alleged knowledge of the physical world suspect; on either horn of the dilemma none of it could be seen as knowledge. At that point in our investigation surely no scientific "knowledge" could then be unproblematically introduced to meet the skeptical challenge. We would have reached the tentative conclusion that nothing we believe about the physical world amounts to knowledge, so it would then be to no avail to appeal to some of those very beliefs about the physical world in the hope of showing how they all amount to knowledge after all. We would find ourselves precluded from using as independently reliable any part of what we had previously accepted as physical science; whatever we chose would be as open to question as everything else.

So even if "sceptical doubts are scientific doubts" in the sense that the skeptical challenge arises because we originally accept many things as true about the physical world, it does not follow that we can make free use of what we accept as physical science in an attempt to meet that challenge. It is true that if we rely on scientific knowledge in order to understand and recognize illusions in the first place, and therefore in order to appeal to illusions to raise skeptical doubts about science, then if we eventually arrive at a completely general skeptical conclusion about all of science we will have "lost" or "thrown away" the very distinction between illusions and reality that we relied on at the outset to reach that negative conclusion. But that is always the way with arguments by *reductio ad absurdum*. We always "lose" or "throw away" what we started with. I conclude that even if Quine is right in saying that skeptical doubts are "scientific" doubts, the "scientific" source of those doubts has no anti-skeptical force in itself. Nor does it establish the relevance and legitimacy of a scientific epistemology as an answer to the traditional epistemological question. If Quine is confident that a naturalized epistemology can answer the traditional question about knowledge, he must have some other reason for that confidence. He believes that skeptical doubts are scientific doubts, and he believes that in resolving those doubts we may make free use of all the scientific knowledge we possess. But if, as he allows, it is possible for the skeptic to argue by *reductio* to the conclusion that science is not known, then it cannot be that the second of those beliefs (that a naturalized epistemology is all we need) follows from the first.

Until the traditional philosophical question has been exposed as in some way illegitimate or incoherent there will always appear to be an intelligible question about human knowledge in general which, as I have argued, a naturalized epistemology cannot answer. And Quine himself seems committed at least to the coherence of that traditional question by his very conception of knowledge. If objective "input" from the world can always in general be isolated from everything we believe about the world as a result of that "input," it does not seem possible for Quine to expose and therefore defuse or get rid of the traditional question in the right way. The traditional bipartite view of knowledge leaves open the general possibility that the objective world is different from the way we take it to be, and so the question of how we know that that possibility does not obtain will always be in place. If I am right that naturalized epistemology alone cannot answer that question, then what is needed is a convincing repudiation of that alleged possibility or an exposure of its failure to give sense to the traditional philosophical question in such a way that naturalized epistemology cannot answer it. Only then would we be in a position to assert that naturalistic or scientific understanding of human knowledge will give us *everything there is to understand* about human knowledge.

Compare Quine's views with those of Hume, one of Quine's illustrious naturalistic predecessors. Hume certainly endorsed the naturalistic, scientific study of the origins of our beliefs. He too had the traditional conception of knowledge as a combination of an objective and a subjective factor. But he showed, as no one had shown before or since, the fatal consequences of that conception. It implies that we do not know anything about the world and have no more reason to believe one thing about it rather than another. For Hume that remains the real truth about our position, even though we can go on, if we like, to engage in "scientific" investigation and even to give "scientific" explanations of how we come to have the scientific beliefs that we have.[39] But for Hume that "scientific" account could never tell us the whole truth about our position; it is not all there is that can be said about how we get the knowledge we think we have. And the extra news, not covered by science or naturalized epistemology, is not good. For Quine the findings of naturalized epistemology are supposed to be not just the truth but the whole truth about human knowledge. There is supposed to be nothing left out. But if that is so, the general question to which Hume gave such a discouraging answer must make no sense. Science cannot answer it, and if science is all there is that is true, then the question must ask nothing, or at least not what it seems to.

What is needed, then, is some demonstration of the incoherence or illegitimacy of that question. If the operation of defusing that question were successful, the stage would be cleared for naturalized epistemology. That defusing operation would not show that we do know that the objective world is in fact the way we take it to be; so it would not imply that we do know in that way that there is an external world after all. Both skepticism and its apparent negation would have been set aside. But the task of exposing the traditional epistemological question and thereby guaranteeing that all intelligible questions about knowledge *can* be answered by naturalized epistemology alone is not itself part of naturalized epistemology. And it seems to me that it is in that task—in demonstrating that scientific investigation can give us everything we could intelligibly ask for—that the real epistemological progress would be made.[40]

Notes

1. W. V. Quine, *Word and Object* (Cambridge, Mass., 1960), p. 2.
2. *Ibid.*, p. 1.
3. *Ibid.*, p. 1.
4. W. V. Quine, *The Roots of Reference* (La Salle, Ill., 1974), p. 1.
5. Quine, *Word and Object*, p. 3.
6. Quine, *The Roots of Reference*, p. 2.
7. W. V. Quine, "Epistemology Naturalized," in *Ontological Relativity and Other Essays* (New York, 1969), p. 83.
8. Quine, *Word and Object*, p. 5.
9. Quine, *The Roots of Reference*, p. 4.
10. Quine, *Word and Object*, p. 22.
11. Quine, *The Roots of Reference*, p. 2.
12. Quine, *Word and Object*, p. 23.
13. *Ibid.*, p. 22.
14. W. V. Quine, "Two Dogmas of Empiricism," in *From a Logical Point of View* (Cambridge, Mass., 1953), p. 44.
15. Quine, *Word and Object*, p. 4.
16. *Ibid.*, p. 23.
17. Quine, "Epistemology Naturalized," p. 71.
18. *Ibid.*, p. 72.
19. *Ibid.*, pp. 75-76.
20. *Ibid.*, p. 76. It is not clear from this passage exactly how Quine understands the "doctrinal" question of "justifying our knowledge of nature in sensory terms." Throughout the essay he draws parallels between our knowledge of nature and mathematical knowledge, and perhaps that is why he tends to describe the problem of justifying our beliefs about the physical world as that of "deducing science from observations" or "strictly deriving the science of the external world from sensory evidence" (p. 75) or grounding science upon immediate experience "in a firmly logical way" (p. 74). That leaves it unclear whether he thinks that the "Humean predicament" is simply that of having no deductively sufficient justification for our beliefs about the world from our data, or the apparently much more serious plight of having no sensory justification at all, either deductive or non-deductive. I think Hume thought he had shown that we are in both "predicaments." But our being in the second does not obviously follow from our being in the first. In the essay Quine gives no reason for believing that we are in the second "predicament," and therefore no reason for abandoning the project of justifying our beliefs non-demonstratively or inductively on sensory grounds.
21. Quine, *The Roots of Reference*, p. 2.
22. W. V. Quine, "The Nature of Natural Knowledge," in *Mind and Language*, ed. S. Guttenplan (Oxford, 1975), p. 68.
23. Quine, *The Roots of Reference*, p. 3.
24. *Ibid.*, p. 3.
25. G. E. Moore, "Proof of an External World," in *Philosophical Papers* (London, 1959).
26. See R. Carnap, *The Logical Structure of the World and Pseudo-problems in Philosophy* (London, 1967), pp. 273-87, 325-34 and M. Schlick, "Positivism and Realism," in *Logical Positivism*, ed. A. J. Ayer. (Glencoe, Ill., 1959).
27. I have tried to illustrate the importance of some such distinction and the corresponding problems of understanding the "significance" of philosophical skepticism (with explicit consid-

eration of positivistic verificationism) in "The Significance of Scepticism" in *Transcendental Arguments and Science*, eds. P. Bieri, R. P. Horstmann, and L. Kruger (Dordrecht, 1979). The importance of Kant's distinction between the transcendental and the empirical is discussed in my "Kant and Scepticism," in *The Sceptical Tradition*, ed. M. F. Burnyeat (Berkeley, forthcoming).

28. The importance of Moore in this connection is best brought out in T. Clarke, "The Legacy of Skepticism." *The Journal of Philosophy* 69, no. 20 (1972):754-69.

29. Quine, "Epistemology Naturalized," pp. 82-83.

30. *Ibid.*, p. 83.

31. To say that a person's beliefs about the world transcend or are underdetermined by the sensory impacts that produce them could mean (i) it does not follow from the fact that he has received those impacts that he believes what he does about the world (his believing what he does is underdetermined) (ii) it does not follow from the fact that he has received those sensory impacts that what he believes about the world is true (the truth of his beliefs is underdetermined). The first appears to be a consequence of the general Humean point that when one event causes another it is still possible for the first to occur without the second. The second reading seems closer to Quine's intention. It appears to amount to the uncontroversial claim that truths about what actually happened at certain human sensory surfaces do not alone imply most other truths about the physical world. But this second reading would also have the consequence that the truth 'Impacts $I_1, I_2, \ldots$ occurred at sensory surfaces $S_1, S_2 \ldots$' is *not* underdetermined by those impacts, even though it is itself a statement about the physical world.

32. Quine, *Word and Object*, p. 22.

33. Accounts of knowledge or reasonable belief along these lines are now very popular. For some earlier examples, on which much of the subsequent discussion has been based, see, e.g., A. Goldman, "A Causal Theory of Knowing," *The Journal of Philosophy* 64, no. 12 (1967): 357-72; P. Unger, "Experience and Factual Knowledge," *The Journal of Philosophy* 64, no. 5 (1967):152-73; "An Analysis of Factual Knowledge," *The Journal of Philosophy* 65 (1968): 157-70; F. Dretske, "Conclusive Reasons," *Australasian Journal of Philosophy* 49, no. 1 (1971):1-22.

34. On Quine's view the origin of linguistic competence and cognitive development is to be found in language-learning; subjects are trained to behave linguistically in ways that come to conform to the general practice prevalent in their linguistic community. If we as experimenters were restricted solely to information about the subject's sensory impacts, we would not know what the general practices prevalent in his linguistic community were. We would have access to the *effects* of his linguistic community, since everything external that influences a person's speech does so through his sensory surfaces, and we have access to them. But those sensory effects presumably underdetermine every hypothesis about what causes them (in both of the two senses distinguished in note 31). So we could not begin to explain why the subject responds in one way rather than a thousand others compatible with the same impacts. We would have a multitude of his sensory impacts, but we would know nothing about what produced them. Our understanding of how and why our subject "posits" bodies and "projects" his physics from his "data" would therefore be at best extremely limited.

35. Quine, "Epistemology Naturalized," p. 83.

36. I say "at best" because, even in the restricted, third kind of situation we must rely on independent access at some time or other to the world that the subject's utterances are about if we are even to understand those utterances and thereby identify his beliefs about the world. I argue here that such independent access to the world is not available when we take the experimenter's attitude toward ourselves, so our position with respect to ourselves will be like that of the third kind of experimental situation only if understanding of the utterances is assumed in both cases.

37. Quine, *The Roots of Reference*, p. 3.

38. Quine, "The Nature of Natural Knowledge" p. 68.

39. I have tried to explain how the pursuit of scientific explanations of natural phenomena, including human behavior, can be incorporated within Hume's skepticism in my *Hume* (London, 1977), esp. chap. 10.

40. In parts of this paper I am repeating and elaborating suggestions to be found in slightly different form in my "The Signficance of Scepticism" (see note 27).

Reply to Stroud[1]

W. V. QUINE

Stroud raises a deep issue. I shall begin with the allusion to "the possibility that the world is completely different in general from the way our sensory impacts and our internal makeup lead us to think of it."[2] Let us view this possibility in the perspective of proxy functions and displaced ontologies.

Thus imagine an inclusive theory of the world, regimented in the framework of predicate logic. Let 'Fxy' stand for some open sentence that determines x uniquely for each value of 'y' and vice versa. Now where 'P' is a one-place predicate, reinterpret 'Pz' for each value of 'z' as '$(\exists y)(Fzy \,.\, Py)$'. Reinterpret every primitive one-place predicate in this way, and every primitive many-place predicate correspondingly. The structure of our theory of the world will remain unchanged. Even its links to observational evidence will remain undisturbed, for the observation sentences are conditioned holophrastically to stimulations, irrespective of any reshuffling of objective reference. Nothing detectable has happened. Save the structure and you save all.

Russell urged the all-importance of structure in his *Analysis of Matter,* and Ramsey made the point more rigorously with his Ramsey sentences. Russell and Ramsey were urging the indifference only of theoretical objects, as against observable ones. Once we take observation sentences holophrastically, however, reference and objects generally go theoretical. The indifference or inscrutability of onotology comes to apply across the board.

Consider how this bears on meaning. Words mean only as we learn to use them, and we learn to use them only as we observe their use by other speakers in observable circumstances. Those circumstances are largely verbal in turn: contexts and explanations. But it is the non-verbal circumstances of use, ultimately, that confer empirical content directly on parts of our language, and indirectly, through the linking of words to words, on other parts of our language. Our only access to these circumstances is through stimulations. But the relations of language to stimulations are unaffected by any shift of our ontology through proxy functions. Evidently then such shifts are indifferent to use, to meaning. The platitude that meaning determines reference goes by the board, along with the absoluteness of reference. The objects, or values of variables, serve only as nodes in a verbal network whose *termini a quis et ad quos* are observations, stimulatory occasions.

What then does our overall scientific theory really claim regarding the world? Only that it is somehow so structured as to assure the sequences of stimulation that our theory gives us to expect. More concrete demands are indifferent to our scientific theory itself, what with the freedom of proxy functions.

Our scientific theory can indeed go wrong, and precisely in the familiar way: through failure of predicted observation. But what if, happily and all unknown to us, we have achieved a theory that is conformable to every possible observation, past and future? In what sense could the world then be said to deviate from what the theory claims? Clearly in none, even if we can somehow make sense of the phrase 'every possible observation'.

In what way then do I see the Humean predicament as persisting? Only in the fallibility of prediction: the fallibility of induction and the hypothetico-deductive method in anticipating experience.

I have depicted a barren scene. The furniture of our world, the people and sticks and stones along with the electrons and molecules, have dwindled to manners of speaking. Any other purported objects would serve as well, and may as well be said already to be doing so.

So it would seem. Yet people, sticks, stones, electrons, and molecules are real indeed, on my view, and it is these and no dim proxies that science is all about. Now how is such robust realism to be reconciled with what we have just been through? The answer is naturalism: the recognition that it is within science itself, and not in some prior philosophy, that reality is properly to be identified and described.

What then of the semantical considerations that seemed to undermine all this? They concern questions not of reality but of method and evidence. They belong not to ontology but to the methodology of ontology, and thus to epistemology. And here still I recognize no first philosophy prior to science, but only a scientific study of relations between human animals and the rest of nature. Transcendental argument, or what purports to be first philosophy, tends generally to take on rather this status of immanent epistemology insofar as I succeed in making sense of it.

Stroud finds difficulty in reconciling my naturalistic stance with my concern with how we gain our knowledge of the world. We may stimulate a psychological subject and compare his resulting beliefs with the facts as we know them; this much Stroud grants, but he demurs at our projecting ourselves into the subject's place, since we no longer have the independent facts to compare with. My answer is that this projection must be seen not transcendentally but as a routine matter of analogies and causal hypotheses within our scientific theory. True, we must hedge the perhaps too stringent connotations of the verb 'know'; but such is fallibilism.

Thus, in keeping with my naturalism, I am reasoning within the overall scientific system rather than somehow above or beyond it. The same applies to my statement, quoted by Stroud, that "I am not accusing the sceptic of begging the question; he is quite within his rights in assuming science in order to refute science."[3] The skeptic repudiates science because it is vulnerable to illusion on its own showing; and my only criticism of the skeptic is that he is overreacting.

Experience might, tomorrow, take a turn that would justify the skeptic's doubts about external objects. Our success in predicting observations might fall off sharply, and concomitantly with this we might begin to be somewhat successful in basing predictions upon dreams or reveries. At that point we might reasonably doubt our theory of nature in even its broadest outlines. But our doubts would still be immanent, and of a piece with the scientific endeavor.

My attitude toward the project of a rational reconstruction of the world from sense data is similarly naturalistic. I do not regard the project as incoherent, though its motivation in some cases is confused. I see it as a project of positing a realm of entities intimately related to the stimulation of the sensory surfaces, and then, with help perhaps of an auxiliary realm of entities in set theory, contextually defining a language adequate to natural science. It is an attractive idea, for it would bring scientific discourse into a much more explicit and systematic relation to its observational checkpoints. My only reservation is that I am convinced, regretfully, that it cannot be done.

Notes

1. I am grateful to Burton Dreben for helpful discussion.
2. Barry Stroud, "The Significance of Naturalized Epistemology," this volume, p. 457.
3. W. V. Quine, "The Nature of Natural Knowledge," in *Mind and Language,* ed. S. Guttenplan (Oxford, 1975), p. 68.

The Metaphysic of Abstract Particulars

KEITH CAMPBELL

1. THE CONCEPTION OF PROPERTIES AS PARTICULAR

A classic tradition in first philosophy, descending from Plato and Aristotle, and recently reaffirmed by D. M. Armstrong,[1] proposes two equally essential, yet mutually exclusive, categories of reality: Substances (or Particulars), which are particular and concrete, and Properties (and Relations), which are universal and abstract. Material bodies are the most familiar examples of Concrete Particulars, and their characteristics, conceived of as repeatable entities common to many different objects, are paradigms of Abstract Universals.

Particular being's distinguishing mark is that it is exhausted in the one embodiment, or occasion, or example. For the realm of space, this restricts particulars to a single location at any one time. Particulars thus seem to enjoy a relatively unproblematic mode of being.

Universals, by contrast, are unrestricted in the plurality of different locations in space-time at which they may be wholly present. Altering the number of instances of a universal (*being a bee*, for example), increasing or decreasing it by millions, in no way either augments or diminishes the universal itself. In my opinion, the difficulty in comprehending how any item could enjoy this sort of reality has been the scandal which has motivated much implausible Nominalism in which, with varying degrees of candor, the existence of properties and relations is denied.

The scandal would disappear if properties were not really universal after all. In modern times, it was G. F. Stout who first explicitly made the proposal that properties and relations are as particular as the substances that they qualify.[2] Others have given the notion some countenance,[3] but its most wholehearted advocate, perhaps, has been D. C. Williams.[4] What are its merits?

In the first place, that a property should, in some sense, enjoy particular being, is not a contradiction in terms. The opposite of *Particular* is *Universal*, whereas the opposite of *Concrete* is *Abstract*. In this context, an item is abstract if it is got before the mind by an act of abstraction, that is, by concentrating attention on some, but not all, of what is presented. A complete material body, a shoe, ship, or lump of sealing wax, is concrete; all of what is where the shoe is belongs to the shoe—its color, texture, chemical composition, temperature, elasticity, and so on are all aspects or elements included in the being of the shoe. But these features or characteristics considered individually, e.g., the shoe's color or texture, are by comparison abstract.

The distinction between abstract and concrete is different from that between universal and particular, and logically independent of it. That some particulars as well as universals should be abstract, and that, specifically, cases or instances of properties should be particulars, is at least a formal possibility.

In the second place, it is plain that one way or another, properties must take on or meet particularity in their instances. Consider two pieces of red cloth. There are two pieces of cloth, *ex hypothesi.* Each is red. So there are two occurrences of redness. Let them be two occurrences of the very same shade of redness, so that difference in quality between them does not cloud the issue. We can show that there really are two pieces of cloth (and not, for example, that one is just a reflection of the other) by selective destruction—burn one, leaving the other unaffected. We can show that there really are two cases of redness in the same sort of way; dye one blue, leaving the other unaffected. In this case there remain two pieces of cloth. But there do *not* remain two cases of redness. So the cases of redness here are not to be identified with the pieces of cloth. They are a pair of somethings, distinct from the pair of pieces of cloth. A pair of what? The fact that there are two of them, each with its bounded location, shows that they are particulars. The fact that they are a pair of *rednesses* shows them to be qualitative in nature. The simplest thesis about them is that they are not the compound or intersection of two distinct categories, but are as they seem to reflection to be, items both abstract and particular. Williams dubs abstract particulars *tropes.*

The argument above is to the effect that tropes are required in any proper understanding of the nature of concrete particulars (in this case specimen material bodies, pieces of cloth) and that this becomes evident in the analysis of local qualitative change.

A third ground for admitting tropes in our ontology is to be found in the problem of universals itself. The problem of universals is the problem of determining the minimum ontological schedule adequate to account for the similarities between different things, or the recurrence of like qualities in different objects. Take a certain shade of red as an example. Many different items are the same color, this certain shade of red. There is a multiple occurrence involved. But what, exactly, is multiple? The *universal* quality, the shade of red, is common to all the cases but is not plural. On the other hand, the red *objects* are plural enough, but they are heterogeneous. Some are pieces of cloth, others bits of the skin of berries, others exotic leaves, dollops of paint, bits of the backs of dangerous spiders, and so on. There is no common recurrent substance.

What does recur, the only element that does recur, is the color. But it must be the color as a particular that is involved in the recurrence, for only particulars can be many in the way required for recurrence.

It is the existence of resembling tropes which poses the problem of universals. The accurate expression of that problem is: What, if anything, is common to a set of resembling tropes?

2. TROPES AS INDEPENDENT EXISTENCES

Williams claims more for tropes than just a place in our ontology; he claims a fundamental place. Tropes constitute, for him, "the very alphabet of being," the independent, primitive elements which in combination constitute the variegated and somewhat intelligible world in which we find ourselves.

To take this line, we must overcome a long-standing and deeply ingrained prejudice to the effect that *concrete* particulars, atoms or molecules or larger swarms, are the minimal beings logically capable of independent existence.

We are used to the idea that the redness of our piece of cloth, or Julius Caesar's baldness, if they are beings at all, are essentially dependent ones. Without Julius Caesar to support it, so the familiar idea runs, his baldness would be utterly forlorn. Without the cloth, no redness of the cloth. On this view, concrete particulars are the basic particulars. Tropes are at best parasitic.

Being used to an idea, of course, is not a sufficient recommendation for it. When it is conceded that, as a matter of fact, tropes tend to come in clusters and that a substantial collection of them, clinging together in a clump, is the normal minimum which we do in fact encounter, we have conceded all that this traditional point of view has a right to claim. The question at issue, however, is not what is in fact the ordinary minimum in what is "apt for being," but what that minimum is of metaphysical necessity. The least which could exist on its own may well be less than a whole man or a whole piece of cloth. It may be just a single trope or even a minimal part of a single trope.

And some aspects of experience encourage the view that abstract particulars are capable of independent existence. Consider the sky; it is, to appearance at least, an instance of color quite lacking the complexity of a concrete particular. The color bands in a rainbow seem to be tropes dissociated from any concrete particular.

All Williams requires here, of course, is that dissociated tropes be possible (capable of independent existence), not that they be actual. So the possibility of a Cheshire Cat face, as areas of color, or a massless, inert, impenetrable zone as a solidity trope, or free-floating sounds and smells, are sufficient to carry the point.

The way concrete particularity dissolves in the subatomic world, and in the case of black holes, suggests that dissociated tropes are not just possibilities but are actually to be encountered in this world.

On the view that tropes are the basic particulars, concrete particulars, the whole man and the whole piece of cloth, count as dependent realities. They are collections of co-located tropes, depending on these tropes as a fleet does upon its component ships.

3. THE ANALYSIS OF CAUSATION

D. Davidson has provided powerful reasons why some singular causal statements, like

The short circuit caused the fire,

are best interpreted as making reference to events.[5] Davidson's example is a specimen of an *event-event* singular causal claim.

But by no means all singular causal statements are of this type. Many involve *conditions* as terms in causal connections. For example:

Condition-event: The weakness of the cable caused the collapse of the bridge.

Event-condition: The firing of the auxiliary rocket produced the eccentricity in the satellite's orbit.

Condition-condition: The high temperature of the frying pan arises from its contact with the stove.

Now the conditions referred to in these examples, the cable's weakness, the orbit's eccentricity, the frying pan's temperature, are properties, but the particular cases of properties involved in particular causal transactions. It is the weakness of this particular cable, not weakness in general or the weakness of anything else, which is involved in the collapse of this bridge on this occasion. And it is not the cable's steeliness, rustiness, mass, magnetism, or temperature which is at all involved. To hold that the whole cable, as concrete particular, is the cause of the collapse is to introduce a mass of irrelevant characteristics.

The cause of the collapse is the weakness of this cable (and not any other), the whole weakness, and nothing but the weakness. It is a particular, a specific condition at a place and time: so it is an abstract particular. It is, in short, a trope.

Events, the other protagonists in singular causal transactions, are widely acknowledged to be particulars. They are plainly not ordinary concrete particulars.[6] They are, in my opinion, best viewed as trope-sequences, in which one condition gives way to others. Events, on this view, are changes in which tropes replace one another. This is a promising schema for many sorts of change.

Attempts to avert reference to tropes by use of *qua*-clauses do not succeed. If we affirm that

The cable *qua* weak caused the collapse

yet deny that

The cable *qua* steely caused the collapse,

then we are committed to the view that

The cable *qua* weak ≠ the cable *qua* steely.

So at least one of these terms refers to something other than the cable. What could it be referring to?—only the weakness (or steeliness) of the cable, that is, only to the trope.

The philosophy of cause calls for tropes. That on its own is virtually sufficient recommendation for a place in the ontological sun.

4. PERCEPTION AND EVALUATION

The introduction of tropes into our ontology gives us an extremely serviceable machinery for analyzing any situation in which specific *respects* of concrete particulars are involved.

In the philosophy of perception, tropes appear not only as terms of the causal relations involved but also, epistemically, as the immediate objects of perception. The difficulties involved in Direct Realism with material objects disappear. Notoriously, we do not see an entire cat, all there is to a cat, for a cat has a back not now perceived and an interior never perceived. The immediate object of vision cannot even be part of the front surface of the cat, for that front surface has a texture and temperature which are not visible, and a microscopic structure not perceptible by any means. So that when you look at a cat what you most directly see is neither a cat nor part of its front surface. This conclusion has, to say the least, encouraged Idealist claims that the immediate object of perception is of a mental nature, a percept or representation standing in some special relation to the cat.

In the trope philosophy, a Direct Realist theory of perception would hold that not cats, but tropes of cats, are what is seen, touched, and so on. The cat's shape and color, but not its temperature or the number of molecules it contains, are objects of vision. Some of the tropes belonging to the cat are perceptible, some not. On any one occasion, some of the perceptible ones are perceived, others are hidden. That is the way in which the senses are selectively sensitive; that is why there is no need for embarrassment in admitting that the senses can give us knowledge only of certain aspects of concrete particulars.

Evaluation is another field in which the admission of tropes does away with awkwardness. Concrete particulars can be simultaneously subject to conflicting evaluations—in different respects, of course. A wine's flavor can be admirable and its clarity execrable, a pole vaulter's strength be splendid and his manners ill. On a trope analysis, the immediate object of evaluation is the trope, so that strictly speaking, different objects are being evaluated when we consider the flavor and the clarity of the wine, and thus the incompatible evaluations give rise to no problem at all.

5. THE PROBLEM OF CONCRETE INDIVIDUALS

The problem of concrete individuals is the problem of how it is possible for many different qualities to belong to one and the same thing. To answer it is to give the constitution of a single individual. For convenience's sake, we tend to discuss the issue in terms of items of medium scale, such as books, chairs, or tables, although we know such objects are not really single units but assemblies of parts which are themselves also individuals. The question of the constitution of a single individual is, of course, quite distinct from the relationship between complex wholes and their simpler parts. To avoid confusion we might do better to use as an example some more plausible specimen of a single concrete individual, such as one corpuscle in classical Atomism. Our question is: what is it, in the reality of one corpuscle, in virtue of which it is one, single, complete, distinct individual?

In an ontology that recognizes properties and relations only as *universals*, no satisfactory solution to this question can be found. There are two ways of tackling it:
(i) A complete individual is the union of universal properties with some additional, particularizing reality. For Aristotelians, this will be the Prime Matter that qualities inform, for Lockeans the substratum in which qualities inhere. The common ground of objection to solutions of this type lies in their introduction of a somewhat which, because it lies beyond qualities, lies by its very nature beyond our explorations, describings, and imaginings, all of which are of necessity restricted to the qualities things have. We do well to postpone as long as possible the admission into our ontology of elements essentially elusive and opaque to the understanding.

To avoid such elements, we must deny that in the ontic structure of an individual is to be found any non-qualitative element. Which is precisely the course followed in the other main tradition:
(ii) A complete individual is no more than a Bundle of qualities, viz., all and only the qualities that, as we would ordinarily say, the thing has. In banishing "metaphysical" particularizers, such views are appealing to Empiricists, for as long as they can forget their Nominalism, which is, of course, incompatible with any Bundle theory.

Where the bundle is a bundle of universals, the very same repeatable item crops up in many different bundles (the same property occurs in many different instances). And herein lies the theory's downfall. For it is a necessary truth that each individual is distinct from each other individual. So each bundle must be different from every other bundle. Since the bundles contain nothing but qualities, there must be at least one qualitative difference between any two bundles. In short, this theory requires that the Identity of Indiscernibles be a necessary truth.

Unfortunately, the Identity of Indiscernibles is not a necessary truth. There are possible worlds in which it fails, ranging from very simple worlds with two uniform spheres in a non-absolute space to very complex ones, without temporal beginning or end, in which the same sequence of events is cyclically repeated, with non-identical indiscernibles occurring in the different cycles.

Bundle theories with elements that are universal qualities thus come to grief over the status of the Identity of Indiscernibles. But where the elements in the bundle are not repeatable universals but particular cases of qualities, not smoothness-in-general but the particular smoothness here, in this place, qualifying this particular tile, the situation is quite different. Now the elements in the bundles are tropes, and no matter how similar they are to one another, the smoothness trope in one tile is quite distinct from the smoothness trope in every other tile. So the bundles can never have any common elements, let alone coincide completely.

The question of the Identity of Indiscernibles becomes the question whether all the elements in one bundle match perfectly with all the elements in any other, which is, as it should be, an *a posteriori* question of contingent fact.

Tropes of different sorts can be *compresent* (present at the same place). In being compresent they, in common speech, "belong to the same thing." Taken together, the maximal sum of compresent tropes constitutes a complete being, a fully concrete particular. Each fully concrete individual is, of necessity, distinct from every other.

There is no need for any non-qualitative particularizer, nor any problem over the Identity of Indiscernibles. In the trope philosophy, the Problem of Individuals has an elegant solution.

A. Quinton recently proposed that an individual is the union of a group of qualities and a position, and D. M. Armstrong has endorsed a similar view.[7] If we take this as a version of the Lockean *substratum* strategy, it invites the criticism that it involves an *a priori* commitment to absolute space or space-time, anterior to the placing of qualities. To avoid such objectionable *a priori* cosmology, we must hold not that place and the quality present at that place are distinct beings, one the particularizer and the other a universal, but that quality-at-a-place is itself a single, particular, reality. And this second view is just the trope doctrine re-expressed.

6. THE PROBLEM OF UNIVERSALS

Tropes can be compresent; this makes possible a solution to the problem of individuals. Tropes can also resemble one another, more or less closely. Williams holds that this facilitates a solution to the problem of universals. I regret to report that I cannot fully share his optimism.

The Problem of Universals is the problem of how the same property can occur in any number of different instances. "The Problem of Universals" is not really a good name, since the principal issue is whether there *are* any universals; the problem is: what ontological structure, what array of real entities, is necessary and sufficient to account for the likenesses among different objects which ground the use on different occasions of the same general term, 'round', 'square', 'blue', 'black', or whatever. "The Problem of Resemblance" would thus be a better name; proposed solutions consist in theories of the nature of properties.

As with the problem of individuals, philosophical tradition exhibits an ominous unstable oscillation between unsatisfactory alternatives. Realism claims the existence of a new category of entities, not particular, not having any restricted location, literally completely present, the very same item, in each and every different circular object, or square one, or blue one, or whatever. Nominalism holds that roundness and squareness are no more than shadows cast by the human activity of classifying together, and applying the same description to, sundry distinct particular objects. The classic objection to Realism is Locke's *dictum* that all things that exist are only particulars. This amounts to the difficulty of believing in universal beings. The objection to Nominalism is its consequence that if there were no human race (or other living things), nothing would be like anything else.

Can a philosophy of abstract particulars be of any assistance? Williams claims that a property, such as smoothness, is a set of resembling tropes. Members of this set are instances of the property. Tile A's smoothness, tile B's smoothness, tile C's smoothness, insofar as they resemble one another, all belong to a set S. There are no *a priori* limits on how many members S should have, or how they should be distributed through space and time. So in this respect S behaves as a universal must. Moreover, since the members of S are particular smoothnesses, each of them is fully smooth, not merely partly smooth. This is again a condition which anything proposed as a universal must meet.

The closeness of resemblance between the tropes in a set can vary. These variations correspond to the different degrees to which different properties are specific. According to this view, Resemblance is taken as an unanalyzable primitive, and there are no non-particular realities beyond the sets of resembling tropes. So this view holds that there is *no* entity literally common to the resembling tropes; it is a version of Particularism.

Can we take Resemblance as a primitive? Resemblance between tropes, rather than between concrete particulars, avoids two classic objections to this line.

Objection 1. The Companionship Difficulty[8]

Attempts to construct a property as a Resemblance-Class of the items that "have the property" face this objection: there could be two *different* properties (say, *having a heart* and *having a kidney*) which, as a matter of fact, happen to be present in the very same objects. But if each property is no more than the Resemblance-Class containing all and only those objects, since these two different properties determine the same Resemblance-Class it will turn out that the 'two' properties are not different after all. The theory falsely identifies *having a heart* with *having a kidney*, and indeed any pair of co-extensive properties.

This problem cannot arise where the members of the Resemblance-Class are *tropes* rather than whole concrete particulars. Although the *animals* that have hearts coincide with the animals with kidneys, the instances of having a heart, as abstract particulars, are quite different items from the instances of having a kidney. The Resemblance-Classes for the two properties have no members in common, and there is no basis for the objectionable identification.

Objection 2. The Difficulty of Imperfect Community[9]

In constructing a Resemblance-Class, we cannot just select some object O and take all the objects that resemble O in some way or other. That would yield an utterly heterogeneous collection, with 'nothing in common', as we would intuitively put it.

To avoid saying that the members of the Resemblance-Class must all resemble O in the same respect, which introduces *respects* as Realistically conceived universals, we have to require that all the members of the Resemblance-Class must not only resemble O but must also resemble one another.

But although necessary, this restriction is not sufficient. For consider the case where

O_1 has features P Q R
O_2 has features Q R S
O_3 has features R S T
O_4 has features S T P

Each of these objects does resemble all the others. But they share no common property. This is the phenomenon of *imperfect community.* Family resemblance classes are examples. Not all resemblance classes pick out a genuine universal property. More precisely, this is the case where the members of the resemblance classes are objects with many different features.

The problem of imperfect community cannot arise where our resemblance sets are sets of tropes. For tropes, by their very nature and mode of differentiation, *can* only resemble in one respect. An instance of solidity, unlike a complete material object, does not resemble a host of different objects in a host of heterogeneous ways. The difficulty of imperfect community springs from the complexity of concrete particulars. The simplicity of tropes puts a stop to it.

Although the prospects for a resolution of the problem of universals through appeal to resemblances between tropes are better than those for resemblance between concrete particulars, it is by no means plain that this line succeeds.

The difficulty is that we have an answer to the question: What do two smooth tiles have in common, in virtue of which they are both smooth? They both contain a trope of smoothness; *matching* tropes occur in their makeup. But then we at once invite the question: What do two smooth tropes have in common, in virtue of which they match? And now we have no answer, or only answers that restate the situation: These tropes resemble, or are alike, in virtue of their nature, in virtue of what they are. This leaves us with no answer to the question: Why isn't the way a rough trope is, a ground for matching a smooth trope? We cannot say it is the wrong *sort* of thing. We must just say: because it isn't.

Now explanations must stop somewhere. But is this a satisfactory place to stop?

7. THE ROLE OF SPACE IN A FIRST PHILOSOPHY

The metaphysic of abstract particulars gives a central place to Space, or Space-Time, as the frame of the world. It is through *location* that tropes get their particularity. Further, they are identified, and distinguished from one another, by location. Further yet, the continuing identity over time of the tropes that can move is connected with a continuous track in space-time.

Still further, space (and time) are involved in *co-location,* or compresence, which is essential to the theory's account of concrete particulars. So the theory seems to be committed to the thesis that every reality is a spatio-temporal one.

This would make a clean sweep of transcendent gods, Thomist angels, Cartesian minds, Kantian noumena, and Berkeley's entire ontology. But that is too swift, too dismissive.

There is, in fact, a less drastic possibility open. That is, that to the extent that there can be non-spatial particulars, to that extent there must be some analogue of the locational order of space.[10] And in that case, there will be an analogue of location to serve as the principle of individuation for non-spatial abstract particulars.

To concede that there can be non-spatial particulars to the extent that they belong in an array analogous to space is generous enough toward such dubious items.

We are, however, not yet at the end of the special status of space. The geometric features of things, their form and volume, have a special role. Form and volume are not tropes like any others. Their presence in any particular sum of tropes is not an optional, contingent, matter. For the color, taste, solidity, salinity, and so on, which any thing has are essentially spread out. They exist, if they exist at all, *all over* a specific area or volume. They cannot be present except by being present in a formed volume. Tropes are, of their essence, regional. And this carries with it the essential presence of shape and size in any trope occurrence. The often-noticed fact that shape and size, like Siamese twins, are never found except together, is part of this special status of the geometrical features.

Color, solidity, strength are never found except as the-color-of-this-region, the-solidity-of-this-region, and so on. So wherever a trope is, there is formed volume. Conversely, shape and size are not genuinely found except in company with other characteristics. A mere region, a region whose boundaries mark no material distinction whatever, is only artificially a single and distinct being.

So the geometric features are doubly special; they are essential to ordinary tropes and in themselves insufficient to count as proper beings. Form and volume are therefore best considered not as tropes in their own right at all. Real tropes are qualities-of-a-formed-volume. The distinctions we can make between color, shape, and size are distinctions in thought to which correspond no distinctions in reality. A change in the size or shape of an occurrence of redness is not the association of the same red trope with different size and shape tropes, but the occurrence of an (at least partly) different trope of redness.

There is no straightforward correlation between distinct *descriptions* and distinct tropes. That predicates may not go hand-in-hand with tropes is important, for therein lies the possibility of reduction, exhibiting one trope as consisting in tropes which before the discovery of the reduction would have been considered "other" tropes. Reduction is the life and soul of any scientific cosmology. Reductions involving elements in familiar human-scale material bodies provide the best of explanations why tropes ordinarily occur in compresent bundles which cannot be dissociated and whose members resist independent manipulation.

8. THE PHILOSOPHY OF CHANGE AND MODERN COSMOLOGY

The admission of abstract particulars as the basic ontological category gives us a way into the philosophy of change. We all feel in our bones that there is a quite radical distinction to be made between the sorts of changes involved in becoming bald and the sorts involved in becoming a grandfather. The first sort are closer to home. They are intrinsic, whereas the others are in some way derivative, dependent, or secondary. If we content ourselves with an analysis of change in terms of the applicability of descriptions, however, the two sorts of change seem to be on a par.

We can do justice to the feeling in our bones by distinguishing changes in which different descriptions apply to O in virtue of a new trope situation at O itself, from changes in which the new descriptions apply as a consequence of a new trope situation elsewhere. Trope changes become the metaphysical base from which other sorts of change derive.

We can recognize three basic types of change into which tropes enter:

1. *Motions,* the shifting about of tropes which retain their identity. When a cricket ball moves from the bat to the boundary, it retains its identity, and the tropes that constitute it retain their identity also. Many *instances of relations,* of being so far, in such direction, from such and such, are involved. For all that has been said so far, these are tropes too. Many such enjoy a brief occurrence during any motion. Because there cannot be relations without terms, in a metaphysic that makes first-order tropes the terms of all relations, relational tropes must belong to a second, derivative order.

2. *Substitutions,* in which one, or more, trope passes away and others take its place. Burning is a classic case. The object consumed does not retain its identity. Its constituent tropes are no more. In their place are others which formerly had no existence.

3. *Variations.* An object gets harder or softer, warmer or cooler. With such qualities which admit of degree, I think we should allow that the same trope, determinable in character though determinate at any given point in time, is involved. Call an abstract element in a situation, extending over time, a *thread.* Variations are homogeneous threads; processes, such as burning, are heterogeneous ones.

The concept of a thread is very useful in ordering categories. Stability is represented by the most homogeneous threads of all. Variations in a quantity, as we have seen, involve no deep discontinuity; different parts of the thread are plainly instances of the same type of property. *Events* are of various sorts: a rise in temperature is a quantitative alteration along a homogeneous thread; an explosion terminates many threads and initiates many different ones. Events, processes, stabilities, and continuities are all explicable as variations in the pattern of presence of tropes. All these are categories constructable from the same basis in abstract particulars.

Attempts to relate these three kinds of change are of course a perfectly proper part of cosmology. Classical Atomism, for example, the very apotheosis of concrete particularism, involves the thesis that all three types of change resolve, on finer analysis, into motions, in particular the motions of corpuscles.

But Classical Atomism is false, and any type of atomism looks unpromising at the present time. The cosmology of General Relativity takes a holistic view of space-time. And it seems positively to call for a trope metaphysic and a break with concrete particularism. The distinction between "matter" and "space" is no longer absolute. All regions have, to some degree, those quantities which in sufficient measure constitute the matter of the objects among which we live and move and have our being.

The world is resolved into six quantities, whose values at each point specify the tensor for curved space-time at that point. Material bodies are zones of relatively high curvature.

The familiar concept of a complex, distinct, concrete individual dissolves. In its place we get the concept of quantities with values in regions. Such quantities, at particular locations, are dissociated abstract particulars, or tropes. Considered in their occurrence and variation across all space and all time, they are pandemic homogeneous threads.

The metaphysic of abstract particulars thus finds a vindication in providing the most suitable materials for the expression of contemporary cosmology.

Notes

1. D. M. Armstrong, *Universals and Scientific Realism* (Cambridge, 1978).
2. G. F. Stout, *The Nature of Universals and Propositions* (Oxford [British Academy Lecture], 1921).
3. G. E. L. Owen, "Inherence," *Phronesis* 10 (1965):97-108; N. Wolterstorff, "Qualities," *Philosophical Review* 69 (1960):183-200 and *On Universals* (Chicago, 1970). A. Quinton, "Objects and Events," *Mind* 87 (1979):197-214. J. Levinson, "The Particularisation of Attributes," *Australian Journal of Philosophy* 58 (1980):102-15. P. Butchvarov, *Being Qua Being* (Indiana, 1979), pp. 184-206, discusses but rejects the view.
4. D. C. Williams, "The Elements of Being," in *Principles of Empirical Realism* (Springfield, Ill., 1966).
5. D. Davidson, "Causal Relations," *The Journal of Philosophy* 64 (1967):691-703; "The Logical Form of Action Statements," in *Logic of Decision and Action*, ed. N. Rescher (Pittsburgh, 1966).
6. If Quine is right, they are four-dimensional concrete particulars whose boundaries are determined not by material discontinuities but by discontinuities in other respects, which we pre-theoretically describe as discontinuities in *activity*.
7. A. Quinton, *The Nature of Things*, part 1 (London, 1973); D. M. Armstrong, *Universals*, chap. 11.
8. See N. Goodman, *The Structure of Appearance*, 2nd ed. (Indianapolis, 1966), chap. 5.
9. See *ibid.*, chaps. 5 and 6.
10. Cf. P. F. Strawson, *Individuals* (London, 1959), chap. 2.

The Fallacy behind Fallacies

GERALD J. MASSEY

1. STATE OF THE SUBJECT

Discover its natural habitat and you learn much about an animal. The same holds for matters logical. Just by determining where it is dealt with you come to know a great deal about a topic. Take, for instance, fallacy. Rarities aside (even prothonotary warblers are sometimes sighted in Maine), you do not come across treatments of fallacy in journals or scholarly treatises or advanced textbooks. Rather, introductory textbooks, especially those that propound so-called *informal logic,* constitute their natural habitat. What, then, should this distributional fact about discussions of fallacy lead us to expect?

Let us begin with the obvious. Textbooks are parasitic upon journals and scholarly tomes, and properly so. Cut off from their natural source of nourishment, textbooks are likely to suffer from conceptual malnutrition. Some of its symptoms: aimless or directionless thinking, exaggerated fascination with taxonomies, and shoddy reasoning. Alas but not unexpectedly, textbook treatments of fallacy exhibit all three symptoms.

Consider, for example, aimless or directionless thinking. Chapters or units on fallacy contrast markedly with those on sentential logic or quantifiers or even syllogistics. However maladroit in other respects, treatments of these latter topics appear organized and unified. Why? Because a highly articulated, well-understood theory underpins them. But there is no theory to underpin or give structure to treatments of fallacy. Consequently these treatments appear as a hodgepodge or miscellany of "fallacies" individuated by historical accident and sometimes related only by possession of a common pejorative label.

A possible explanation suggests itself. Perhaps the science of fallacy has yet to emerge from its natural history phase. At this early stage progress consists largely in collecting specimens and organizing them in suggestive ways. Note how this explanation accounts in one swoop for the predilection (obsession) of informal logicians to add to the already thick catalogue of documented fallacies as well as for their preoccupation with classificatory schemes.

Richness of classification and poverty of theory are directly related. As evidence thereof, compare the taxonomic wealth of neo-Aristotelian logic with the classificatory austerity of the logic of sentence connectives and quantifiers. The myriad and intricate schemes for classifying fallacies suggest that there is little theory behind the science of fallacy. This suggestion misleads only by implying that there is any theory at all behind it. The unvarnished truth is this: *there is no theory of fallacy whatsoever!* I will return to this claim shortly.

The third symptom of conceptual malnutrition is shoddy reasoning. Many authors virtually identify fallacies with shoddy thinking, so at the very least you might expect them to eschew such thinking in their presentations. If so, you would be disappointed. For example, look at the treatment accorded the very first fallacy, "suppressed evidence," in Kahane's recent textbook on fallacies.[1] In the absence of theory, taxonomy governs the order of topics treated. Kahane divides fallacies, defined as arguments that *should not* persuade a rational person to accept their conclusions,[2] into two groups: those that are *fallacious even if valid* and those that are *fallacious because invalid*.[3] According to Kahane the fallacy of suppressed evidence falls into the first class. This surely suggests that some valid arguments embody this fallacy. As best I can make out from the text, the fallacy is supposed to consist in advancing reasons favorable to your conclusion while omitting those unfavorable to it. Now assume, not unreasonably, that these reasons take the form of premises. Then Kahane's presentation (not Kahane—he knows better) suggests that there is something wrong with deriving a conclusion deductively from premises that encapsulate some of your evidence when other evidence at your disposal renders the conclusion improbable. But as everyone knows, valid arguments remain valid no matter what other premises are added. That is, if some of it implies the conclusion, so does your total evidence. It is impossible, then, for a valid argument to instantiate the fallacy of suppressed evidence.

For more shoddy thinking about shoddy thinking, turn to the first set of exercises on fallacies in the fourth edition of Copi's widely used textbook. The second exercise, and the first for which no answer is supplied, asks the reader to identify the fallacies exhibited by the following argument of Duns Scotus and to explain how the argument commits them:

> To put it briefly, then, we can maintain that natural reason cannot prove that the resurrection is necessary, neither by way of *a priori* reasons such as those based on the notion of the intrinsic principle in man, nor by *a posteriori* arguments, for instance, by reason of some operation or perfection fitting to man. Hence we hold the resurrection to be certain on the basis of faith alone. (Duns Scotus. *Oxford Commentary on the Sentences of Peter Lombard*).[4]

Of the thirteen fallacies enumerated by Copi only two seem at all germane to Scotus's argument, viz, *ignoratio elenchi* and *argumentum ad ignorantiam*. One cannot be sure of this because no "answer" is furnished, but apparently Copi wants the reader to classify the argument as an *ignoratio elenchi* on the grounds that Scotus purports to derive that something is held certain by faith whereas he establishes only that the necessity of something cannot be shown by natural reason. But such an analysis does a grave disservice to the subtle teacher *(doctor subtilis)*. To evaluate anyone's argument we must first know what it really was. And to see what Scotus's argument really was we must look at the cited passage in context. What context? At least the work in which it appears, even better the whole Scotus's corpus.[5] This done, we find doctrines like these functioning as background assumptions:

(i) Something established by reason is certain only if necessary.

(ii) The propositions of faith are certain.

(iii) There are just two ways in which reason can establish the necessity of something, viz. *a priori* and *a posteriori*.

(iv) That Christ was resurrected is an article (proposition) of faith.

When background assumptions (i)-(iv) are made explicit, Scotus's passage is seen to embody a valid argument. To evaluate Scotus's argument as shoddy thinking is itself shoddy thinking. To wrench a passage from context and then damn it as a case of *ignoratio elenchi* reflects poorly on the evaluator, not on the argument.

In fairness to Copi I must acknowledge that the tortured English translation of Scotus's argument makes another interpretation possible albeit unlikely. Copi might have read the first sentence of Scotus's passage to mean that natural reason cannot prove that the resurrection is not necessary. Then he might have taken Scotus to infer from this that the resurrection is necessary, thereby committing the fallacy *argumentum ad ignorantiam*. Although this interpretation seems too farfetched to dwell upon any longer, Copi's treatment of the aforementioned fallacy warrants further attention.

Copi says that the fallacy *argumentum ad ignorantiam* is committed whenever one argues that something is true *because* it has not been proved false, or that it is false *because* it has not been proved true.[5] He then claims that all such arguments are fallacious except in courts of law where the legal principle of presumption of innocence renders them non-fallacious.[6] Here Copi confuses two concepts, *innocence* and *legal innocence*. The latter does not entail the former any more than *apparent mistake* entails *mistake*. Many legally innocent people are guilty of the charges on which they were exonerated. If fallacious anywhere, the inference from 'It has not been proved that x did y' to 'x did not do y' or 'x is innocent of y' is fallacious everywhere, courtrooms not excepted. Verdicts of innocence are not incantations that turn guilty people into innocent parties.

2. FORMAL FALLACIES

So-called *formal fallacies* appear to falsify my claim that there is no theory whatsoever behind treatments of fallacy.[7] Why? Because formal fallacies are rooted in inference patterns proscribed as invalid by logical theory. For example, the inference pattern or argument form (1)

(1) $p \supset q$
     q
     p

is rejected as invalid by truth-functional logic on the sensible ground that some instantiations of it have true premises but a false conclusion. The formal fallacy called *affirmation of the consequent* is defined relative to the invalid pattern (1). But exactly how?

A naive account might go like this. Argument form (1) is invalid, so any argument of that form is invalid. Hence any such argument will be said to commit the affirmation-of-the-consequent fallacy. This naive account gains plausibility from such textbook examples of affirmation of the consequent as (2).

(2) If Philadelphia is the capital of Pennsylvania, then Pittsburgh is not.
     Pittsburgh is not the capital of Pennsylvania.
     Philadelphia is the capital of Pennsylvania.

Argument (2) is clearly invalid (its premises are true but its conclusion is false). But is it invalid because it instantiates (1)? Surely not, for then any argument that instantiates (1) would be invalid. Yet (3),

(3) If something has been created by God, then everything has been created by God.
     Everything has been created by God.
     Something has been created by God.

an argument that instantiates (1), is valid. The naive account, therefore, must be wrong.

It is easy to see where the naive account goes astray. The cardinal principle that undergirds the application of formal logic to natural languages is (4).

(4) Arguments that instantiate valid argument forms are valid. (Principle of Logical Form)

In tandem with principle (5),

(5) Translations of valid arguments are valid, and translations of invalid arguments are invalid. (Translation Principle)

the principle of logical form enables one to show natural-language arguments valid thus. First, one translates the natural-language argument into a formal language like sentential logic. The translation principle guarantees that the natural-language argument and its formal translation stand or fall together with respect to validity. Then one inspects the form of the formal argument for validity. If it proves valid, the principle of logical form allows one to conclude that the original natural-language argument is valid.

The naive account of formal fallacy uncritically supposes that proofs of argument invalidity go like proofs of argument validity. That is, it supposes that one proves an argument invalid by showing that it instantiates some invalid argument form. This is a mistake, a very elementary one, yet so common as virtually to escape notice.

There are three mutually reinforcing sources of the mistake. The first is common practice. Philosophers, logicians, and their students routinely do pretend to convict arguments of invalidity by producing invalid forms that the arguments instantiate. Introductory textbooks aid and abet this pernicious practice. After each installment of theory, they proffer exercises that require the student to prove certain arguments invalid. How? By translating them (as fully as possible) into the formal language at hand and then showing that the theory just imbibed declares the form of the resulting argument invalid. The method *seems* to work but only because authors choose their examples judiciously, supplying only intuitively invalid arguments when they want a verdict of invalidity.[8] But what confusion must greet the industrious student who applies the method to exercises appended to later chapters! Intuitively valid arguments accredited as valid by the next theory installment turn out invalid! Only lethargy protects students from this trauma.

The second source of the mistake is a simple confusion. Most textbook authors take pains to distinguish argument forms from arguments but subsequently disregard their own distinction. For example, in an otherwise unusually rigorous book on informal logic, Fogelin becomes careless about the difference between arguments and argument forms at the point where he first mentions formal fallacies.[9] This carelessness causes him to endorse the fallacious method of showing invalidity discussed above. The endorsement takes the form of Fogelin's false claim that truth-table techniques constitute a *"decision procedure for determining the validity of every argument involving conjunction, disjunction, negation, and conditionals."*[10] Truth tables do provide a decision procedure for sentential argument-form validity; they do not constitute one for argument validity.

The third source of the mistake is uncritical application of the seductive principle (6).

(6) Valid arguments instantiate valid argument forms. (Converse Principle of Logical Form)

The converse principle of logical form gives teeth to the widely held thesis that argument validity is at bottom a matter of form. Still it does not bite so deeply as its adherents seem to believe. The converse principle does not circumscribe or specify the argument forms that underpin validity. Yet those who implicitly accept it act as if the principle guarantees that proper analysis of intuitively valid arguments will yield valid argument forms of some standard logical system, typically quantification theory. Hence, when close analysis fails to isolate such a form, they feel justified in certifying the argument invalid. Far from legitimating the fallacious method of showing arguments invalid, the converse principle of logical form confers on it only unmerited respectability.

3. THE ASYMMETRY THESIS

In his informative treatise on fallacy, Hamblin succinctly describes a *fallacious argument* as an argument that seems valid without being so.[11] It is with fallacies so defined that I will hereafter be concerned.

Note first that fallacious arguments are invalid. Hence a theory of fallacy presupposes a theory of invalidity. Therein lies the rub. But, as I claimed above and have argued for elsewhere, a theory of invalidity has yet to be developed.[12] It is not surprising, then, that treatments of fallacy eschew theory. There is no theory on which they could be based.

My claim about the non-existence of a theory of invalidity is so strong as to strike most philosophers as absurd or at least implausible. Everyone agrees that to show it has true premises but a false conclusion is to show that an argument is invalid. I call this *the trivial logic-indifferent method* of proving invalidity. This trivial method of showing invalidity is clearly independent of logical theory. Of course logical theory sometimes proves useful in the enterprise of establishing truth-value but that hardly makes this trivial method of showing invalidity a matter of logic. Physics is sometimes relevant to the determination of truth-value too, but no one would deny for this reason that the trivial method is indifferent to physical theory.[13]

Apart from the trivial logic-indifferent method, I claim, there is *no method whatsoever of establishing invalidity* that has theoretical legitimacy. To falsify this claim a single counter-instance would suffice. To date my critics have failed to produce any.

What positive evidence can be marshaled for my claim which Bencivenga has dubbed *the asymmetry thesis*[14] as a reminder that our ability to prove invalidity is markedly more circumscribed than our ability to prove validity? Suppose one accepts both the principle of logical form and its converse, i.e., principles (4) and (6). (My case becomes even stronger when the converse principle of logical form is rejected.) Then an argument is invalid if and only if there is no valid argument form that it instantiates. For the sake of argument I concede that one can recognize a correct translation of a natural-language argument into a formal language, thereby establishing that the argument instantiates a particular argument form. If such translation yields a valid argument form, the principle of logical form allows you to conclude that the original argument is valid. But, suppose it yields an invalid argument form? That fact alone entails nothing about the goodness of the original argument. Suppose further that every translation you can come up with into every formal language you know and respect yields an invalid argument form. What may you then infer about the invalidity of the original argument? Nothing! Why? *First*, someone more clever than you might have been able to come up with an ingenious translation that yields a valid argument form. *Second*, even if it were somehow impossible to get a valid argument form by translating the argument into any of the formal languages you know and respect, or even into any of the extant formal languages you would respect if you knew them, there might be hitherto undreamt of formal languages congenial to you such that translation into them would yield a valid argument form.

Let us look at these two considerations more closely. To appreciate that the first is not just a skeptic's quibble, consider arguments (7) and (8).

(7) John took a walk by the river.
   John took a walk.
(8) Tom, Dick, and Harry are partners.
   Tom and Harry are partners.

Davidson deserves credit for showing how to translate (7) into standard predicate logic in such a way as to get a valid argument form.[15] (Davidson's translation turns on quantification over events, something that some philosophers find objectionable, but that is another matter.) *Ante* Davidson, no one seemed able to supply such a translation, and so argument (7) was deemed invalid. To appease intuition which views the argument favorably, pre-Davidsonian philosophers regarded (7) as an enthymeme rendered valid by a suppressed premise relating the predicate 'took a walk by the river' to the logically unrelated predicate 'took a walk'. (I have discussed the disingenuousness and ultimate futility of this *enthymematic ploy* at length elsewhere.)[16]

Similarly, before 1940 philosophers judged argument (8) invalid, unless enthymematic, for want of a formal-language translation that yields a valid argument form. But when the combined talents of Leonard and Goodman produced such a translation into mereological predicate logic, they reversed their verdict.[17] Leonard and Goodman's ingenuity enabled philosophers to treat (8) as a robust argument that stands validly on its own feet rather than as an anemic enthymeme propped up by suppressed premises.

The above examples show that more than skeptical fancy underlies the concern that failure to furnish valid-form translations may reflect badly on the translators rather than on the natural-language arguments translated. But you might object that through my choice of examples I have stacked the deck against good logical sense. After all, my examples (7) and (8) represent intuitively good arguments. When such arguments are at issue, does not prudence dictate that failure to come up with valid-form translations should result at most in provisional findings of invalidity? On the other hand, when intuitively bad arguments like (9)

(9) If Harrisburg is the capital of Pennsylvania, then Pittsburgh is not.
   Pittsburgh is not the capital of Pennsylvania.
   Harrisburg is the capital of Pennsylvania.

are at issue, universal failure to find valid-form translations should count as conclusive evidence of their invalidity for anyone who has not succumbed to skepticism.

A bonafide *theory* of invalidity would offer a principled account of why universal failure to find a valid-form translation of (9) shows it invalid whereas exactly the same failure in the case of an intuitively valid argument warrants only suspension of judgment. The method of showing invalidity advocated in the preceding paragraph amounts to unprincipled appeal to intuition. An account of invalidity that decides particular cases by how intuition views them forfeits all rights to the title 'theory of invalidity'. There is nothing wrong with such appeal to intuition, but it must not be allowed to masquerade as theory.

The second consideration mentioned above rises out of the *apparently un-*

finished state of contemporary logic reflected in the fact that no philosophers would be so foolish as to claim that the family of formal languages they know and respect exhausts all possible systems that they would find congenial. This openendedness of logic suffices itself to ground the asymmetry thesis. For even if it could somehow be established that no translation of an argument into extant formal systems yields a valid argument form, how could one hope to prove the same result about all *possible* systems?

But one might object that all sciences are unfinished, and so any asymmetry to which the apparent unfinished state of logic gives rise must be replicated in all the other sciences. Indeed, the objection might be put this way: Because physics is unfinished, pronouncements about what things are physically impossible must be deemed provisional. Similarly, in view of its unfinished state, verdicts of invalidity handed down by contemporary logic are subject to reversal wrought by theoretical advance.

The foregoing objection incorporates several misconceptions. Chief among them is the belief that the asymmetry thesis amounts to nothing more than the empiricist caution not to chisel in granite the deliverances of even the most entrenched contemporary theories. But the asymmetry thesis does not attribute to invalidity verdicts the kind of provisionality demanded by second-order induction over the fates of past scientific claims. If invalidity verdicts suffered from only the general dubiety that infects all human judgments, validity and invalidity verdicts would enjoy perfect parity. But whereas logical theory underwrites validity verdicts, the case for invalidity verdicts (where the trivial logic-indifferent method is inapplicable) rests at bottom on intuitive judgments of invalidity altogether unsupported by theory.

A popular tune of the 1940s urges us to accentuate the positive and eliminate the negative. Applied to fallacy and invalidity, the advice is sound. For, does our general inability to prove invalidity hamstring us in any way, either in composing arguments ourselves or in assessing those of others? Not if we accentuate the positive. All of us try to advance good arguments. Validity, of course, is one element of the goodness sought. If we devise a seemingly good argument only to find its validity challenged, we can call upon logical theory which will usually establish its validity to everyone's satisfaction.

But suppose none of the arguments we devise for some proposition *p* strike us as valid. What then? Do we need a theory of invalidity to discredit them? By no means! That these arguments seem upon careful reflection to be invalid is reason enough to abandon them and to look elsewhere for a good argument for *p*. It is much the same with arguments propounded by others. When appropriate, we can invoke logical theory to validate those arguments that appear good to us. Those that upon close crutiny seem invalid are best set aside unless and until their composers or admirers supply cogent evidence of their validity. In short, the asymmetry inherent in showing validity and invalidity is exactly counterbalanced by a pragmatic asymmetry in burden of proof. Consequently, the asymmetry thesis does not generate any special difficulties for the practical use of logic.

4. FALLACIES, RULES, AND INFERENTIAL PRACTICE

It is customary among logicians to name formal fallacies after the logical rules they violate.[18] For instance, argument (10)

(10) All bachelors are rich.
 All unmarried adult males are rich.
 All unmarried adult males are bachelors.

is said to embody *the fallacy of undistributed middle term* because it violates the syllogistic rule that prescribes that the middle term be distributed at least once.

The aforesaid practice runs roughshod over the distinctions between arguments, argument forms, and their respective notions of validity. Note that as measured against the classical standard of argument validity, viz, joint impossibility of truth of premises with falsity of conclusion, (1) qualifies as a valid argument because its conclusion is necessarily true.[19] And since we have taken fallacies to be *invalid* arguments that seem valid, it follows that (10) is no fallacy at all. What is "fallacious" in the sense of being invalid is not (10) but rather argument form (11)

(11) All H are G
 All F are G
 All F are H

which (10) instantiates.

But suppose we take (11) to be a *rule of inference* rather than an argument form. (It is of course a *bad rule* because it sometimes authorizes a falsehood to be inferred from truths.) Suppose further that someone advanced argument (10) *by applying* rule (11) to its premises. Then we might sensibly speak of (10) as a fallacy, specifically as a fallacy of undistributed middle term, in the *new sense* of being an argument generated by application of invalid rules. It seems to me that just such an account lies behind many presentations of fallacies.

Note that a fallacy in this new sense need not be an invalid argument. Strictly speaking, what is denominated fallacious or defective is not the argument itself but the way it was constructed through application of rules. Even valid arguments like (3), (7), (8), and (10) will be fallacious if bad rules figured in their production.

This rule-based account of fallacy presupposes two things: that sense can be made of the notion of application of rules in inferential practice, and that the sense thus given enables one to ascertain which rules people have actually applied in composing particular arguments. In advance of someone's producing such accounts, one can only speculate about the shapes they are likely to assume. Here are my speculations.

The rules of reasoning that a person P accepts are reflected in P's inferential practice, i.e., in the arguments that P advances (the positive inferential corpus) as well as in the ones that P refuses to advance (the negative inferential corpus). That is, the rules P accepts constitute a theoretical explanation of P's total inferential behavior. Hence the rules actually accepted by P are determined by the best explanation of P's inferential behavior. For example (and with considerable simplification), if P's positive inferential corpus contains numerous cases that fit scheme (12)

(12) $p \supset q$
$\underline{p}$
q

while P's negative inferential corpus, when rectified for extraneous factors, contains virtually no cases that fit (12), we would say that P accepts *modus ponens*. Similarly, if we found that P's positive inferential corpus conforms to schema (1) whereas P's negative inferential corpus resists the same schema, we would say that P accepts the rule of *affirmation of the consequent*. But at this stage of human evolution it is unlikely that anyone accepts affirmation of the consequent. To accept affirmation of the consequent would amount not merely to a simple fallacy but to nearly certain suicide. Exposés of fallacies are not needed to eliminate affirmers of the consequent; evolutionary pruning does the job much more decisively.

But to know what rules P *accepts* is a long way from knowing what rules P *has actually applied* to construct a particular argument. Consider, for example, a person Q who accepts *modus ponens* and who advances (13).

(13) If Philadelphia is the capital of Pennsylvania, then Pittsburgh is not.
Philadelphia is the capital of Pennsylvania.
Pittsburgh is not the capital of Pennsylvania.

Mere instantiation of an accepted rule schema by an argument does not mean that Q applied the rule to construct the argument. There might be other rules in Q's rule repertoire (the rules Q accepts) that would yield exactly the same argument. Again, one must look to the best explanation, i.e., to the rules in Q's repertoire that most efficiently yield the given argument. In the example, it is likely that Q's rule repertoire uniquely fixes *modus ponens* as the rule Q applied to get (13). Probably such unique determination of rules applied is rare; typically, Q's rule repertoire would contain several comparably efficient routes to a given argument. (The matter is analogous to the annotation of a Fitch-style natural deduction. Typically, the same deduction can be annotated in several ways.)

Suppose now that Q advances (9). That Q must be alive to advance any argument virtually eliminates *affirmation of the consequent* as the rule Q applied to construct (9). Suppose further and realistically that Q's rule repertoire contains no route to the conclusion of (9) from its premises? Where, then, does (9) come from?

To answer the previous question we need a pathology. Let Δ be the subset of Q's positive inferential corpus that contains all and only those arguments in the corpus that cannot be accounted for by Q's rule repertoire. Again we look for a best explanation, this time for the simplest set of rules F that, in conjunction with Q's rule repertoire, generates Δ. Unlike those in Q's rule repertoire, the rules in F are not accepted by Q. Rather, they may be described as rules that Q occasionally employs but does not accept. Because the typical member of F is an invalid rule like affirmation of the consequent or denial of the antecedent, F may be called Q's *pathological repertoire*. (Similarly, the typical member of Q's rule repertoire is a valid rule like *modus ponens* or simplification.) We might even call the members of F *fallacies*.

In the end, then, we explain the arguments in Δ as fallacious, i.e., as arguments constructed by Q through application of fallacies. Which fallacies? Those belonging to the simplest and most direct route in F to the given argument. For example, the likeliest explanation makes (9) a case of Q's affirming the consequent, i.e., an argument generated by application of rule (1) which belongs to F.

A careless and forgetful reader might object that I have traveled a long and circuitous path to reach the same conclusion that someone who merely examined (9) in isolation would reach, viz, that (9) exhibits the fallacy of affirmation of the consequent by virtue of instantiating (1). The objection would make fallacy purely a matter of form, the fundamental mistake that I have tried to expose in the previous sections. Fallacy is rather a matter of the generative limitation of accepted rules which are in turn a matter of theoretical explanation of inferential practice. Fallacies, therefore, are perhaps of more interest to psychologists and psychiatrists than to logicians and philosophers. Indeed, a recent magazine article on psychotherapy enumerates ten "negative" ways of thinking that distort reality.[20] Among them are found four familiar textbook-variety fallacies. Perhaps the topic of fallacy has at last found its natural place.[21]

Notes

1. Howard Kahane, *Logic and Contemporary Rhetoric* (Belmont, Calif., 1971).
2. *Ibid.*, p. 1.
3. *Ibid.*, p. 4.
4. Cited in Irving Copi, *Introduction to Logic,* 4th ed. (New York, 1972), p. 87.
5. *Ibid.*, p. 76.
6. *Ibid.*, p. 77.
7. Curiously, none of the fallacies treated by Kahane are formal fallacies.
8. Most authors are altogether insensitive to the radical disability of the invalid-form method of showing argument invalidity. Copi, in his textbook already cited, is a happy but not wholly blameless exception. What Copi calls *refutation by logical analogy* (see pp. 268-75) is essentially the aforementioned discredited method. However, at each relevant juncture Copi appends a footnote to his account of refutation by logical analogy, the intent of which footnote is to restrict application of the method, in theory anyway, only to arguments for which it will yield the right verdict (see pp. 185, 268, and 338). These footnotes stipulate that refutation by logical analogy works only if certain conditions obtain, e.g., that the only logical relations that obtain among the unanalyzed statements be those asserted or implied by the premises. But as the establishment of these conditions is equivalent to the problem of showing arguments to be invalid, the footnotes do not circumvent the basic failing of the method, even in theory. In practice as well as in the body of the text, Copi ignores his own footnoted injunction.
9. Robert J. Fogelin, *Understanding Arguments: An Introduction to Informal Logic,* (New York, 1978), p. 132.
10. *Ibid.*, p. 134
11. C. L. Hamblin, *Fallacies* (London, 1970).
12. Gerald J. Massey, "Are there any Good Arguments that Bad Arguments Are Bad?" *Philosophy in Context* 4 (1975): 61-77 and "In Defense of the Asymmetry," *Supplement* to *Philosophy in Context* 4 (1975): 44-56.
13. This point seems to have been insufficiently appreciated by Bencivenga on p. 249 of his

recent criticism of my work. See Ermanno Bencivenga, "On Good and Bad Arguments," *Journal of Philosophical Logic* (1979): 247-59.

14. Bencivenga, "On Good and Bad Arguments," p. 249.

15. Donald Davidson, "The Logical Form of Action Sentences," in *The Logic of Decision and Action,* ed. Nicholas Rescher (Pittsburgh, 1968).

16. See the papers cited in note 12 as well as my "Tom, Dick, and Harry, and All the King's Men," *American Philosophical Quarterly* 13 (1976): 89-107.

17. Henry Leonard and Nelson Goodman, "The Calculus of Individuals and its Uses," *Journal of Symbolic Logic* 5 (1940): 45-56. Cf. my "Tom, Dick, and Harry," *passim.*

18. This nomenclature wholly succeeds only when the logical rules have been formulated in such a way that an argument form is invalid if and only if at least one rule is violated. Because formulations of syllogistic rules typically meet this condition, syllogistic fallacies get their names from the rule or rules violated. In his treatise already cited, Hamblin avers that unless the rules are so formulated that no more than one rule can be violated by a given argument form, the resulting classification of fallacies will be pointless (p. 201). He seems to think that fallacies are insufficiently individuated when a single argument form may embody several. But it is enough for the individuation of fallacies that the *sets* of forms embodying each fallacy be distinct. (Hamblin's treatment also suffers somewhat from failure to keep distinct argument validity and argument-form validity. For example, he asserts that syllogistic rules define the set of valid syllogistic arguments rather than the valid syllogistic argument forms.)

19. Relevance logicians, for example, would substitute a much more stringent standard of validity.

20. David D. Burns, M.D., "How to Break Out of your Bad Moods," *Self* (June 1980): 121-31.

21. In writing this paper I profited from discussions with Barbara Alpern and Robert Brandom.

A Proposed Solution to a Puzzle about Belief

RUTH BARCAN MARCUS

In "A Puzzle about Belief"[1] Saul Kripke discusses a predicament that is generated by the theory of direct reference for names taken in conjunction with a plausible disquotation principle relating belief to assent. His thesis is that "the puzzle *is* a puzzle." In this paper I will propose a solution (or partial solution). My proposal has ramifications which will be mentioned, but a more complete discussion of those ramifications will be postponed for a subsequent paper.

1. THE PUZZLE

The plausible disquotation principle is as follows:

> A. Let us assume throughout that all assent is sincere and reflective. If a normal English speaker assents to 'p' and 'p' is a sentence of English, then he believes that p.

In the theory of direct reference for names, the value of a name is fixed; that value just *is* the object to which it refers. But a speaker may assent to

1. Cicero was bald.

and seemingly coherently fail to assent to

2. Tully was bald.

and seemingly coherently assent to

3. Tully was not bald.

On principle A, if he assents to 1 and fails to assent to 2, then although it follows that he believes that Cicero was bald, it appears that it does not follow that he believes that Tully was bald. If he assents to 1 and 3, then he believes that Cicero was bald and he believes that Tully was not bald. Yet on the theory of direct reference, 1 and 2 have the *same* semantic content, and they are incompatible with 3.

How can a speaker seemingly coherently believe that Cicero was bald and, apparently, fail to believe that Tully was bald? How can someone, seemingly coherently, believe that Cicero was bald and believe that Tully was not bald? Does he or does he not believe that Cicero was bald?

Kripke sharpens the question with other examples. Consider a speaker who knows something about a pianist Paderewski. On the assumption that no musician would ever be a politician, he might, on learning from sources he takes to be reliable that some person Paderewski is a politician, assent to

   4. Paderewski is a politician.

and to

   5. Paderewski is not a politician.

Now whatever the speaker's knowledge or beliefs about musicians and about whether 'Paderewski' occurring in 4 names the same thing as the occurrence of 'Paderewski' in 5, on the theory of direct reference those occurences do *in fact* name the same thing. Does he or does he not believe that Paderewski is a politician?

The puzzle is brought into sharpest focus by using a bilingual example. Here a plausible principle of translation is also assumed.

   B. If a sentence of one language expresses a truth in that language, then any translation of it into another language also expresses a truth in that other language.

In the bilingual case Pierre, a native Frenchman, from what he has heard or read about the attractiveness of Londres, assents to

   6. Londres est jolie.

He emigrates to England where he takes up residence in a neighborhood in London which he finds ugly. There he learns English by exposure, without recourse to translation manuals, dictionaries, and the like. He now assents to

   7. London is not pretty.

From A and B it follows that he believes that London is not pretty and he believes that Londres is pretty. Since 'Londres' and 'London' have the same semantic value, the puzzle is, what does Pierre believe? He has used 'jolie' and 'pretty' appropriately. He has committed no logical blunders. He is not conceptually muddled. He can even produce perfectly coherent grounds of a familiar sort for assent to 6 and assent to 7. Nor does it appear that he abandoned a belief that London is pretty for a new belief that London is not pretty. He has not changed his mind about London. Kripke sees the puzzle as a paradox in that plausible and intuitively acceptable principles about assent, belief, translation, and naming may lead us to a baffling conclusion.

My attempt at a solution will focus on the disquotation principle A. I will not quarrel with the theory of direct reference for proper names. I advanced such a theory[2] before the detailed and subtle arguments of Kripke, Donnellan, Putnam, and others advanced its acceptance against entrenched views.

2. SOME REMARKS ABOUT DISQUOTATION AND DIRECT REFERENCE

The assumption in A, that a speaker is reflective, is supposed to dispose of those cases where someone might assent to a sentence that on *reflection* is seen to be conceptually or linguistically confused, and hence should not carry over into a belief. In such cases Kripke says, "No further information (beyond reflection) is required." His example, in which he attributes linguistic or conceptual confusion to someone who assents to 'Some doctors are not physicians', shows that something more must be said in such cases. The idiolect of a speaker who takes 'doctor' and 'physician' to be synonyms is different from the idiolect of one who does not take them to be synonyms (me for example). A lexical decision or a lexicon that normalizes the use of such nouns is information of a kind and required if we are to be able to communicate our beliefs. Such normalization of the language is therefore a condition that should be added to A. But that modification does not address the puzzle at hand. An encyclopedia, a biographical "dictionary," a "dictionary" of names and their variants are not *definitive* with respect to proper names — nor can there be a decision to "normalize" the use of proper names in an arbitrary way by agreeing on a lexical entry.[3] On the theory of direct reference, it is the case that for all normal speakers, *whatever their idiolect,* the semantic value of proper names remains fixed as compared with nouns like 'physician' and 'doctor' which may differ in use in different "idiolects." It is also the case that an encyclopedia, a biographical "dictionary," or a "dictionary" of names might, unbeknownst to *any* speaker, be mistaken in telling us two names name the same or different things. Imagine, for example, such a "dictionary" or encyclopedia prior to the discovery that Hesperus is Phosphorus. It might deny that 'Hesperus' and 'Phosphorus' were variant names of the same heavenly body. Or imagine an instance of "mistaken identity," for example, some variation on *Twelfth Night* modified to make the point, where it is believed that the expressions 'Cesario' and 'Sebastian' are names of the same person whereas Cesario and Sebastian are in fact not identical.

Nor is a translation manual, such as the one that tells us that 'Londres' and 'London' are intertranslatable, immune to those possibilities. Imagine that an English-speaking anthropologist Smith studies the original account of a journey of an explorer Jones, written in the quite distant past. Jones recorded his discovery of an island which he named 'Lebensville'. Subsequent to that journey, no one has attempted to locate Lebensville again, although accounts of the journey to Lebensville are included in historical texts as well as celebrated in song and story. Jones's log includes some description of the island. He also states that although there were ample signs of human habitation, his destination was elsewhere and he could not stay long enough to seek out the occupants. Smith sets out to find Lebensville. Using Jones's log he follows what he believes to be a correct route and comes upon an island that seems to fit Jones's description. He sets up camp and stays long enough to meet the occupants and learn their language. They call their island 'Glyph'. Smith returns home and prepares an English-Glyphian manual in which it is stated that 'Lebensville' and 'Glyph' are intertranslatable. But of course any such manual is mistaken.

If Pierre had prepared a translation manual, he would have claimed that 'London' and 'Londres' are *not* intertranslatable, and he would have been mistaken. The referent of a proper name on a given occasion of use is fixed by the language viewed as a historical institution evolving over time. I want to argue that if the object of a belief has as constituents the fixed values of proper names, then if the speaker assents to a sentence that is incompatible with that valuation, the assent does not carry over into a belief. A modification of the disquotation principle is required. But first some preliminaries.

3. ATTITUDES TOWARD STATES OF AFFAIRS

Knowing and believing have been characterized as "propositional attitudes." The vagaries of the many uses of 'proposition' have been a considerable source of epistemological confusion. There is a seemingly naive as well as much maligned view, to which I subscribe, Russell's for example, where knowing and believing are attitudes toward states of affairs (not necessarily actual), which may have individuals and attributes as constituents. The "propositional content" of a sentence on an occasion of use is (are) the (those) state(s) of affairs that would make that sentence true. States of affairs may be actual, not actual, possible, necessary, even impossible.[4]

Possible states of affairs are those which obtain in some world; in some structure. An impossible state of affairs obtains in no world or structure. Hence the "propositional content" of 'Tully is bald and Cicero is not bald' is not a possible state of affairs since it is not possible (metaphysically) that Tully be simultaneously bald and not bald in some one world or structure. Similarly for 'London is pretty and London is not pretty'. That there are impossible states of affairs conforms to common usage; but there are no worlds that include such impossible states.

We will take knowing and believing to be epistemological attitudes toward states of affairs (or if you like, propositional contents). It is generally held that if someone *knows* that p, then as contrasted with belief, p is the case in that epistemological subject's world. p obtains, p is actual, or, if we use "true" for propositional contents as well as sentences, p is true. A basis for that claim is the widely shared intuition that if someone claimed to know that p, he would say, on discovering that p did not obtain, was not actual in his world, was not, if you like, true, that he was *mistaken* in claiming to know that p. His clinging to his knowledge claim on the known falsity of p (on the knowledge that the state of affairs does not obtain) would be seen as a conceptual or linguistic confusion. Whether someone knows that p is therefore partly dependent on the way things *are*.

Suppose, *assuming the principle of translation B*, our bilingual Pierre claims also to *know* that London is pretty and claims to *know* that London is not pretty. If necessary conditions for knowing p are that p be believed and p be true, then there is a consequent puzzle about knowledge. If we cannot answer the question what does Pierre believe, how can we answer the question what does Pierre know?

The consequent puzzle about what Pierre knows *seems* less paradoxical for he cannot, whatever his beliefs, *know* that London is pretty and know that London

A PROPOSED SOLUTION TO A PUZZLE ABOUT BELIEF   505

is not pretty. But the question about knowledge retains inherited baffling features; for the puzzle about belief is that there are particular propositions which Pierre seems both to believe and not to believe, and, even if such a proposition were true, has the belief condition for knowing that p been fulfilled, i.e., does Pierre believe that p?

There is an intuition about belief which I have (as do others) but which is *not* so widely shared. That intuition suggests a modification of the disquotation principle. Suppose that someone were to claim that he believes Hesperus is not identical with Phosphorus or that Tully is not identical with Cicero, or that Londres is not the same as London where in those contexts of use the names of the "pairs" in question do, on the theory of direct reference, refer to the same thing. It is my (non post-hoc) intuition that on *discovery* that those identities hold, and consequently that the associated name pairs name the same thing, I would *not* say that I had *changed* my belief or acquired a new belief to replace the old, but that I was mistaken in claiming that I *had* those beliefs to begin with. After all, if I had believed that Tully is not identical with Cicero, I would have been believing that something is not the same as itself and I surely did not believe *that*, a blatant impossibility, so I was mistaken in claiming to *have* the belief. Nor am I insisting that I did not have *any* belief, but only that it was not the belief that Hesperus is not the same as Phosphorus, that Tully is not the same as Cicero, that Londres is not the same as London. Perhaps what I believed was that the thing named by the expression 'Hesperus' was different from the thing named by the expression 'Phosphorus' which eludes the puzzle. Russell and others at times suggested that those very descriptions are the preferred ones which should *always* be surrogates for ordinary proper names. But I am not urging that conclusion. Perhaps it is still something else that I believed; there are other alternatives. Perhaps I had no belief at all.

The analogy between this intuition about belief claims and the more universally accepted ones about knowledge is close. Just as a condition for knowing that p is that p obtains, so a condition for believing is

    C. If x believes that p, then possible p.

The link between belief and possibility also suggests a modification of the disquotation principle A as follows.

    D. Again assuming that assent is sincere and reflective, if (i) a normal English speaker assents to 'p' and (ii) 'p' is a sentence of English and (iii) *p is possible,* then he believes that p.

It follows from C and D given all the assumptions, that

    E. If a speaker assents to 'p,' then he believes that p if and only if p is possible.

I will leave open the question of the strength of the "if and only if" in E.

The additional condition in D captures some intuitions about the divergence of assent and belief. Consider the account of Pierre who before departing for England assented to 6, i.e., 'Londres est jolie'. The grounds for that assent were perfectly reasonable; he saw pictures, heard or read reports, and so on. Since it is possible that London is pretty, then in accordance with D Pierre believes that London is pretty. After emigrating to London and acquiring English he, on reasonable grounds, assents to 7, 'London is not pretty'. Given the possibility of such a state of affairs, i.e., London's not being pretty, it follows in accordance with D that Pierre believes that London is not pretty.

If Pierre is not conceptually or linguistically confused as we suppose he is not, given his assents to 6 and 7, and his bilingualism, he would also *assent* to

8. London is not pretty, and Londres is pretty.

and as a consequence (or presupposition) of his assent to 8, would assent to

9. London is not identical to Londres.

and

10. The expression 'London' and the expression 'Londres' name different things.

He would *not* assent to

11. Londres is not pretty.
12. London is pretty.
13. Londres is not pretty, and London is pretty.

Nor would he assent to the outright contradictions

14. London is not pretty, and London is pretty.
15. Londres est jolie et Londres n'est pas jolie.

In accordance with the modified disquotation principle, 9 does not carry over into a belief. It is at the root of our intuition that if someone were to discover an identity, he would say he was mistaken in claiming to believe that it did not obtain. If Pierre should discover that 'Londres' and 'London' name the same thing, he would say that he was mistaken in claiming that he believed that London and Londres are not the same, for how can something fail to be the same as itself?

Does assent to 10 go over into a belief? Since 10 is about expressions, it goes over into a belief. The expression 'London' has, for example, been used to name a city in Ontario. But what of 8, 'London is not pretty, and Londres is pretty'. We have seen on D that assent to each of the conjuncts goes over into a belief, but assent to 8 does not. If Pierre were to "learn" that 9 was false, i.e., that London was the same as Londres, he would if he shared my intuitions say he was mistaken in claiming, if he did so claim, that he believed that London is not pretty and Londres is pretty. For, 8, unlike 11 and 12, *is* sensitive to the identity of the values of the names. In 8, the possibility condition of D is not fulfilled. Nor is it suggested that *every* sentence containing two names for the same thing is sensitive to the identity of the values of those names. The sentence 'Tully is a Roman and Cicero is an orator', if assented to, could go over into a belief. Nor is it suggested that every sentence containing one or more occurrences of the same proper name, i.e., name with fixed semantic value, is *insensitive* to the value of the name. In the Paderewski example, 4 and 5 each go over into a belief but not an assent to 'Paderewski is a politician and Paderewski is not a politician'. Although the speaker here, if he is not conceptually or linguistically muddled, would also have to assent to 'The first occurrence of 'Paderewski' names something different from the second occurrence of 'Paderewski',' he would be in error and the conjunction, which designates an impossible state of affairs, does not carry over into a belief.

It is clear that on the above analysis, that belief, like possibility, does not always factor out of a conjunction. Now there are less puzzling counterexamples to the factoring principle of belief, and comparing the cases is illuminating. There is the lottery example in which some very large number of tickets have been sold to a_1, a_2, ... a_n, and although we might believe that for each a_i that a_i won't win, we do not believe that a_1 won't win and a_2 won't win ... and a_n won't win. In fact we believe the opposite. On the surface, the lottery case is not comparable with the case of Pierre, because the *assenting* would not be analogous. It is perhaps doubtful that we would assent to each of the conjuncts since assent is categorical and belief allows degrees.[5] But even if we assented to each of the conjuncts in the lottery case, we would, unlike Pierre who assented to 8, *not* assent to the conjunction. Still on the theory of direct reference and its consequences for epistemology, the cases are in some interesting respects comparable. In the lottery case *knowledge* of the impossibility of a state of affairs in which no one wins precludes assenting to the conjunction. In Pierre's case he is ignorant of the impossibility of a state of affairs that supports the conjunction. Hence, although he assents to 8, the associated belief cannot be ascribed. What accounts for his ignorance of that impossibility is his ignorance of many facts including the fact that 'Londres' and 'London' have the same semantic value.

The analysis brings into relief some of the distinctions between pure epistemological notions and those which hook into the world. Pierre, given his ignorance, assents to each of 6, 7, 8, 9, and 10 as well as their conjunction. He finds their conjunction *conceivable*. But conceivability is independent of metaphysical possibility. The state(s) of affairs that are the "propositional content" of such a conjunction is (are) not realizable in *any* world or structure. Therefore, however cogent Pierre's reasons for assent, they cannot justify belief. We see that the possibility condition has considerably weakened the connection between assent and belief by strengthening the connection between belief and "reality," i.e., possible worlds or structures.

Returning now to Kripke's question; does Pierre or does he not believe that London is pretty? There seem to be no grounds for denying either that Pierre believes London is pretty or that Pierre believes London is not pretty. Therefore, says Kripke,[6] "we must say that Pierre has *contradictory* beliefs. . . . But," he goes on, "there seem to be insuperable difficulties with this alternative as well. We may suppose that Pierre . . . is a leading philosopher and logician. He would *never* let contradictory beliefs pass. . . . He lacks information, not logical acumen. He cannot be convicted of inconsistency."

If we take seriously that the objects of beliefs are states of affairs, then for a speaker to believe that p he must be in a certain psychological and behavioral state relative to that state of affairs. He thinks, behaves, has dispositions to respond *as if* he believed that that state of affairs obtained. If he is a language user, if he is not reticent, and other normal conditions prevail, then, where he believes that p, among his dispositions are dispositions to assent to some sentences descriptive of that state of affairs and to dissent from some sentences that describe states of affairs incompatible with p. But something more must be added. Recall that Pierre under certain clear and predictable conditions will think and behave as if he believed that London was pretty. Under other clear and predictable conditions he will think and behave as if he believed that London was not pretty. Belief, then, relates a subject, a set of conditions, and a state of affairs. The conditions under which he believes that London is pretty include the ones under which he is also disposed to assent to 'Londres est jolie'. Among the conditions under which he believes that London is pretty are other beliefs he may have such as the belief that 'Londres' and 'London' name different cities, or the belief that the pretty pictures of London he saw in France were representative of the entire city, or his belief that the accounts of the beauty of London he heard prior to his emigration were true accounts, and so on. Similarly, the conditions under which he believes that London is not pretty include the ones which he assents to 'London is not pretty.'

In summary, on such an account we would say that under a given set of conditions Pierre believes that London is pretty, i.e., he thinks, behaves, has dispositions to respond *as if* he believed that state of affairs obtained. Under other conditions he believes that London is not pretty. Since London's being pretty cannot obtain and not obtain in the same world or structure, we say that his beliefs are incompatible, but he has those beliefs nevertheless. A knowledge of certain facts will lead Pierre to give up one of those beliefs. (The assumption of Kripke's paper is that prettiness is a property a thing has or does not have.) But although prior to such knowledge Pierre would have assented to 'Londres is pretty and London is not pretty', he would (should?) say on discovering the facts that it was a mistake to claim he had such a belief. If my intuitions here are correct, there is a rationalist principle that constrains what we count as a belief.

Of course Pierre would not report his beliefs using the *sentences* 'I believe that London is pretty', 'I believe that Londres is not pretty', but he has them nevertheless.

4. THE STRENGTHENED DISQUOTATION PRINCIPLE

Kripke considers additional elaborations on the puzzle about belief if we also assume the converse of A. It seems to me a wholly unacceptable principle, whether we so strengthen A or D or E. There are of course the indexical counterexamples in which, for instance, I may correctly report that Pierre believes that my native city is New York although Pierre is a native Parisian. Kripke excludes indexical belief claims, but the strengthened principle remains unacceptable.

Pierre believes that London is pretty, but he does not assent accordingly. Indeed the strengthened principle suggests that believing always entails assenting. Higher animals and infants seem clearly to have beliefs, however rudimentary. To deny higher animals beliefs is as absurd as Descartes's denying them pain. Therefore, even if we confine our epistemological subjects to normal language users, there is no reason to suppose that for every belief they have there is a sentence that "captures" the belief and to which they would assent.

5. SOME CONCLUDING REMARKS

It should be clear that there is an independent motivation for modifying the disquotation principle. The principle was strengthened not in response to the puzzles about belief but in response to intuitions about when we would say we were mistaken in claiming we had a belief as opposed to saying that we had discarded a belief.

The additional condition is strong and goes beyond puzzles about belief and proper names. If mathematical truths are necessary, then we cannot believe them false. We might *assent* to the negation of such a truth, but we would revise our judgement about *whether we had believed it* if its truth were disclosed to us. In accordance with the Kripke-Putnam theory about natural kind terms and the modified disquotation principle, *we* cannot believe that water is not H_2O. That is at the heart of the claim which seems so absurd; that if someone in a linguistic community assented to 'water is not H_2O' and if the state of affairs so described is a proper object of belief, i.e., a possible state of affairs, then he is not just a normal English speaker with a variant idolect, but not an English speaker at all. One could of course restrict the condition on possibility in D and E, but that is another long story.

Notes

1. In *Meaning and Use*, ed. A. Margalit (Dordrecht, 1979), pp. 234-83.

2. In "Modalities and Intensional Languages," *Synthese* 13 (1961):303-22, I propound a theory of direct reference for proper names as well as the principle of the necessity of identity. I say, on p. 310, that "this tag, a proper name, has no meaning. It simply tags." I mark some now widely accepted differences between standard uses of singular descriptions and proper names and claim that although one might discover empirically that the evening star is the morning star, it is nevertheless the case that if 'a' and 'b' are proper names of that star, then necessarily a = b. I also note that a description can come to be used purely referentially and say on p. 309, "it often happens, in a growing changing language that a descriptive phrase comes to be used as a proper name—an identifying tag—and the descriptive meaning is lost or ignored." I note that sometimes we use certain devices such as capitalization and dropping the definite article to mark the shift in use (a foreshadowing of Donnellan's "Reference and Definite Descriptions," *Philosophical Review* 75 [1966]:284-304).

In the discussion of that paper by Quine, Kripke, McCarthy, Follesdal, and Marcus in *Synthese* 14 (1962):132-43, I argue that the intension-extension duality for *all* terms is an unnecessary proliferation of entities. However, my suggestion, on p. 138, that the duality was motivated by "a passion for symmetry" seems in retrospect a bit of rhetorical hyperbole.

It is of some historical interest that in his "Comments," *Synthese* 13 (1961):327, Quine says "I see trouble anyway in the contrast between proper names and descriptions as Professor

Marcus draws it. Her paradigm for the assigning of proper names is tagging. We may tag the planet Venus some fine evening with the proper name 'Hesperus'. We may tag the same planet again some day before sunrise with the proper name 'Phosphorus'. When at last we discover we have tagged the same planet twice, our discovery is empirical. And not because the proper names were descriptions." Having put the matter so succinctly, Quine goes on to conclude, in the discussion, *Synthese* 14 (1962):142, "The distinction between proper names and descriptions is a red herring. So are tags." As it turned out, the theory of direct reference for proper names was a very stubborn red herring.

3. In the discussion mentioned in note 2, *Synthese* 14 (1962):142, I say, "We can and do attach more than one name to a single object. We are talking here of proper names . . . tags and not descriptions. Presumably if a single object has more than one tag, there would be a way of finding out such as having recourse to a dictionary or some analogous inquiry, which would resolve the question as to whether two tags denote the same thing." But of course as I now see, recourse to a "dictionary" is not a solution. Of course a "dictionary" of *abbreviations* is definitive. However, in an abbreviation we are not giving the object another name, but rather agreeing on a convention to use one expression in place of another.

4. The dominance of Fregen views in recent years, in which reference was always detoured through senses, meanings, thoughts, has obscured the fact that Russell's essential position has never been wholly abandoned by some philosophers. It has been subscribed to by R. Chisholm, "Events and Propositions," *Noûs* 4 (1970):15-24 and "States of Affairs Again," *Noûs* 5 (1971): 179; F. Fitch, "The Reality of Propositions," *Review of Metaphysics* 9 (1955):3-13 and "Propositions as the Only Realities," *American Philosophical Quarterly* 8 (1971):99-103. Alvin Plantinga's *The Nature of Necessity* (Oxford, 1976), is a systematic and elaborate effort to take propositions as states of affairs or something very much like them. True propositions are states of affairs that obtain in the actual world. Similarly for the pairs 'false' and 'does not obtain in the actual world', 'necessary' and 'obtains in all possible worlds' and 'impossible' and 'obtains in no possible world'. For Plantinga, a world is itself a state of affairs that is a maximal "conjunction" of states of affairs. "Adding" an additional state of affairs to such a structure would vitiate its worldhood—would make it impossible. I am not here defending the plausibility of that extension, but only noting an attempt to take states of affairs as basic.

If we take states of affairs as basic, a sentence like 'Tully is bald' is about Tully and baldness and not about the constituents of other sentences with which it is logically equivalent. But possible world semantics does not differentiate those "contents," and that creates the familiar difficulties of substitution of logical equivalents in the context of propositional attitude verbs. There is altogehter a Hegelian implausibility to possible world semantics. As in Tennyson's flower in the crannied wall; sentence, if I understood you, I would know all possible worlds.

A detailed and adequate semantics grounded in states of affairs has, until recently, not been developed. Some of David Kaplan's work including his unpublished Locke lectures are a move in that direction. Jon Barwise and John Perry's "The Situation Underground," unpublished, and their "Semantic Innocence and Uncompromising Situations," this volume, pp. 387-403, and Jon Barwise's "Scenes and Other Situations," unpublished, are full-fledged efforts.

5. There are further divergences between assent and belief, since assent seems categorical. I might assent to 'I have a pain' but not to 'I believe I have a pain', since the latter suggests the possibility that I might be mistaken. Similarly for my assent to 'Tully is bald or Tully is not bald'. But such considerations are not relevant here.

Since belief comes in degrees, degrees of belief will presumably be correlated with certain systematic variations in the subject's thoughts and behavior with respect to the relevant state of affairs under the relevant conditions. Betting behavior, for example. So under the conditions where Pierre assents to 'Londres est jolie' he would bet in its favor. Under the conditions where he assents to 'London is not pretty' he would bet in the latter's favor, although those states of affairs are incompatible. Since they are incompatible and he had placed both bets, the bets would cancel each other.

6. See footnote 1, p. 257.

Donnellan's Distinction[1]

MICHAEL DEVITT

Keith Donnellan has distinguished two uses of definite descriptions, "referential" and "attributive" (1966 and 1968). I take this to be a distinction between two *conventions*: descriptions are *ambiguous*; the truth conditions of statements containing descriptions vary according as the description is used referentially or attributively. So I take it that, if Donnellan is right, he has discovered a semantically significant distinction.

Donnellan's own view of the significance of his distinction is more equivocal, as Saul Kripke has pointed out (1979, pp. 7, 12-13; see also Donnellan 1979, pp. 41-42).[2] It will be convenient to overlook this here, interpreting Donnellan as claiming for the distinction what I have just claimed for it.

Kripke (1979)[3] has recently cast doubt on this claim: he doubts that descriptions are ambiguous and hence that Donnellan has discovered a semantically significant distinction. Kripke's main concern is not with this substantive question of the significance of the distinction; it is methodological. Donnellan's papers are partly a criticism of Russell's theory according to which, in Donnellan's terminology, descriptions can only be used attributively. Kripke's methodological conclusion is that "the considerations in Donnellan's paper, *by themselves*, do *not* refute Russell's theory" (p. 6). I agree (1974, pp. 193-94; 1981a, sec. 2.7). However, it is easy to think that the considerations in *Kripke's* paper undermine, even if they do not refute, the view that descriptions are ambiguous. Kripke himself encourages this thought on the substantive question: in his view the considerations in his paper make it "overwhelmingly probable" that the phenomena that interested Donnellan are not to be explained by an ambiguity in descriptions (pp. 21-22).

My aim in this paper is to describe a certain theoretical perspective which gives semantic significance to Donnellan's distinction and to show that, from this perspective, the above thought on the substantive question is mistaken: Kripke's paper should cast no serious doubt on the significance of Donnellan's distinction.

511

Ironically enough, this perspective was stimulated by Kripke's earlier suggestion of "causal" theories of reference (1972).

Aside from its criticisms of Donnellan, Kripke's paper contains some brief suggestions for an alternative account of Donnellan's phenomena from the point of view of a theory of speech acts (p. 15). John Searle has also offered an alternative along those lines, in much more detail, and including a criticism of Kripke's (1979). I shall not be concerned here with refuting these alternatives. However, my defense of Donnellan implies a criticism of them.

My procedure will be to abstract from Kripke's methodological discussion what Kripke seems to regard as arguments against Donnellan on the substantive issue, or what might reasonably be so regarded. I shall set out my theoretical perspective in the course of considering the first of these arguments.

1. KRIPKE ARGUMENT I: SMITH AND JONES

Kripke gives an example of the sort that suggested the distinction to Donnellan.

> Someone sees a woman with a man. Taking the man to be her husband, and observing his attitude to her, he says, "Her husband is kind to her." . . . Suppose the man is not her husband. Suppose he is her lover, to whom she has been driven precisely by her husband's cruelty (p. 7).

Consider the remark,

(1) Her husband is kind to her.

According to Donnellan (as we are interpreting him), 'her husband' in (1) is a referential use of the description and refers to the lover. Provided the lover is kind to the woman, (1) is true. According to Russell, of course, (1) is false. However successful Russell's theory is with attributive uses, Donnellan thinks it fails with these referential ones. Russell missed the fact that descriptions are ambiguous.

Kripke is struck by the similarity between this example and another involving names.

> Two people see Smith in the distance and mistake him for Jones. They have a brief colloquy: "What is Jones doing?" "Raking the leaves" (p. 14).

Let us suppose, for convenience, that the final remark here were

(2) Jones is raking the leaves.

The first argument on the substantive question that I abstract from Kripke's discussion (pp. 15-18) goes as follows. First, since we are not tempted to posit a special semantic ambiguity to explain 'Jones' in (2), why should we posit one to explain 'her husband' in (1)? Second, Kripke introduces a Gricean distinction between "speaker's reference" and "semantic reference" which he uses to explain both cases without any mention of Donnellan's distinction. Such a general explanation, postulating no ambiguity, is surely to be preferred to Donnellan's, applicable only to (1) and postulating an ambiguity.

What is Kripke's general explanation? He claims that the *semantic* referent of 'her husband' is the woman's husband and that of 'Jones' is Jones, so that *both (1) and (2) are false*. On the other hand, the *speaker's* referent with 'her husband' is the lover and that with 'Jones' is Smith, with the result that *what both speakers mean is true*. Each singular term has only one possible semantic referent (in the context): there is no (relevant) ambiguity. A speaker can mean something by a term other than its semantic referent, but that is a matter of "pragmatics," not "semantics"; and it arises as much for names as for descriptions.

To assess this explanation we need to look closely at the Gricean distinction and its application to (2). The notion of semantic reference is clear enough: it is *conventional* reference (p. 14). Further, it seems clear that Jones is the semantic referent of 'Jones', just as Kripke claims. And I have no doubt that in theorizing about language we need another notion, distinct from semantic reference, and along the lines of Kripke's notion of speaker's reference. The general problem is knowing precisely what notion we need. The particular problem here is understanding Kripke's notion.

In explaining his notion, Kripke first makes gestures toward Grice (pp. 13-15) and "a general pragmatic theory of speech acts" (p. 18). These gestures are insufficient for our purposes, however, because Griceans have had nothing to say about cases of confusion like (2). Second, Kripke offers, "tentatively," a definition:

> the speaker's referent of a designator [is] that object which the speaker wishes to talk about, on a given occasion, and believes fulfills the conditions for being the semantic referent of the designator (p. 15).

So Smith is the speaker's referent of 'Jones' in (2) because the speaker wishes to talk about him and believes he fulfills the conditions of being the semantic referent of 'Jones'.

One objectionable feature of this definition is that it requires a speaker to have a fairly sophisticated semantic theory before he can refer. How many people have given *any* thought to the conditions on reference? Set that aside.

The definition cries out for further explanation. In virtue of what is it *Smith* that the speaker of (2) "wishes to talk about" and has this semantic belief *of*? Kripke does not tell us. His general explanation, hence much of the force of his argument against Donnellan, *rests simply on the intuition* that it is Smith, an intuition that he expresses using a range of locutions: aside from those already mentioned he thinks, for example, that the speaker "meant" Smith and "intended to refer to" him. In the absence of an answer to our question, talk of Smith being the "speaker's referent" is just another way of putting ordinary intuitions about what the speaker "meant," and so on.

It is partly by seeking an explanation of these intuitions that I hope to save Donnellan's distinction from Kripke's argument. Nevertheless, as a point against Donnellan himself, the argument may seem fair enough as it stands. For, Donnellan's view that 'her husband' is a referential use picking out the lover rests ultimately on similar intuitions about what the speaker "meant," "had in mind," and so on.

Donnellan offered no theory to support this. So Kripke's point is that we have similar intuitions about 'Jones' and yet there is no ambiguity there.

I shall claim first that Kripke's intuitions about what the speaker of (2) meant are dubious; certainly they are insufficient to *settle* the matter against Donnellan (section 2). Second, I shall argue that when we seek an explanation of our intuitions about speaker's reference (section 3), and other related ones (section 4), Kripke's argument collapses (section 5).

2. INTUITIONS ABOUT SPEAKER'S REFERENCE

My intuitions about what the speaker of (2) meant are as follows. He did not straightforwardly mean Smith, as Kripke claims he did, but neither did he straightforwardly mean Jones. The belief the speaker expressed by (2) comes with two others, the true one that that man (pointing to Smith) is raking the leaves, and the false one that that man (pointing to Smith) is Jones. *The speaker is confusing two people.* As a result, we have no clear intuition that he meant one and not the other. There is no determinate matter of fact which he meant to refer to.

If this is right and yet the speaker of (1) meant the lover, as everyone seems to agree he did, then the two examples are not alike at the level of speaker's reference. Kripke's general explanation breaks down. (At one point, p. 25, note 26, Kripke seems to recognize this difference between the two cases, but he takes no account of its consequences for his argument.)

It may be objected that Kripke's intuitions about (2) are supported by the fact that the speaker would agree that he "referred to" *that man* (pointing to Smith). But, of course, he would also agree that he "referred to" Jones. If we have evidence of anything here it is that the speaker meant *more* than what he said,[4] a view that supports my intuitions rather than Kripke's.

Support for Kripke's intuitions may also be sought in the behavior of the speaker should he learn that it was not Jones but Smith before his eyes. It will be claimed that he would withdraw (2), saying instead, "Smith is raking the leaves." What relevance has this to the issue? The speaker has just learned something new and significant which has led him to *change his views*. What bearing has this on what he meant by (2)? At most it shows what is not in contention: that the speaker did not *simply* mean Jones. If what the speaker would say is to support Kripke's intuition that the speaker meant Smith, then it should be something he would say before discovering his error.

In this respect it is important to note that in all the standard Gricean cases of a speaker meaning something other than what he says — metaphor, irony, indirect speech acts, speaker in a foreign country — *the speaker is in a position at the time of utterance to confirm what he is said to mean.* So the Gricean intuitions about what he meant are well supported in those cases. This feature is conspicuously lacking here. So also is another feature of the standard cases: *an explanation of why he did not say what he is said to mean that does not undermine the claim that he does mean that.*[5]

Furthermore, it is worth noting that the speaker of (2) might not make the above replacement if he were to discover his error. Perhaps if he were to realize that the person was Smith and not Jones he would not believe the person was raking the leaves: "I can't imagine a slovenly person like Smith ever raking leaves. He must be doing something else." "Observation statements" like (2) are theory-laden.

What follows from this journey among intuitions? I rest nothing simply upon the accuracy of mine. However, I do claim that this discussion should throw doubt on Kripke's. And insofar as his intuitions are dubious, so also is his Argument I. For, a great deal of the plausibility of that argument comes from the claimed similarity of (1) and (2) at the level of speaker's reference, a claim that rests on nothing but these intuitions. If (1) and (2) are not similar at that level, perhaps they are not similar at the level of semantic reference either. Perhaps Donnellan is right after all.

To show that Kripke Argument I against Donnellan is weak is not, of course, to show that Donnellan is right about the semantic referent of 'her husband'. To make any progress with that question we have to move beyond the low-level intuitions we have explored in this section. We must seek their explanation.

3. THE EXPLANATION OF SPEAKER'S REFERENCE

In virtue of what does a speaker mean Smith or Jones? What would make either person "the object of thought"? I suggest answers in terms of causal chains of a certain sort; I call them "d-chains," short for "designating-chains" (1981a).[6]

Consider a *straightforward paradigmatic* use of the name 'Jones' in Jones' absence. We would say that the speaker "meant," "intended to refer to," etc., Jones. In virtue of what? Underlying his use of the name is a causal network stretching back through other people's uses and ultimately "grounded in" Jones in a face-to-face perceptual situation. This underlying network is made up of d-chains. The reason that Jones seems to have *something* to do with the speaker's meaning in uttering (2) is that a network of d-chains grounded in Jones underlies that utterance too. That is why he used the name 'Jones'. The reason that Smith also seems to have something to do with his meaning is that this situation is a perceptual one of just the sort to ground a network in Smith. D-chain networks are grounded in their objects not only at a baptism; they are multiply grounded. Confusions like the present one lead to a network being grounded in more than one object. Because there are d-chains to both Jones and Smith, I would say that neither was the speaker's referent but each was his *partial* referent (using a notion borrowed from Field [1973]).

That is my explanation of the intuitions about (2). What about (1)? Kripke claims that the speaker's referent of 'her husband' is the lover. How could a speaker mean the lover in using a description that does not uniquely describe that person? Once again I call on d-chains to explain this: it was his perception of the lover that prompted the remark; the remark was "grounded in" the lover. But in this case, unlike the earlier one, the other object, which Kripke claims is the semantic referent, is *not* causally linked to the utterance in an appropriate way. Here only one object, the lover, is a candidate for the speaker's referent (in my sense).

I have been careful in these remarks not to commit myself to the view that the lover *is* the speaker's referent in this case. I think that he is *if anyone is*. And I claim to explain the intuition that he is. Whether he is depends on the theoretical significance we attach to the failure of 'her husband' to describe the lover *at all:* not only is he not her unique husband, he is not her husband at all. I shall return to this (section 5).

I have already found Kripke's argument somewhat flimsy at the intuitive level (section 2). If the above theory of speaker's reference is correct, the argument is further weakened. According to the theory, (1) and (2) are not alike in speaker's reference, and Kripke is wrong about (2).

Despite these errors about speaker's reference, an important aspect of Kripke's argument remains. It is the suggestion that, with the help of a Gricean distinction, we can see that the semantic referent of 'her husband' is the husband. Although Kripke may be wrong about speaker's reference, thus weakening his argument against Donnellan, this suggestion may still seem sound. Indeed I agree with Kripke that the mere consideration of cases of confusion like (1) does not establish the semantic significance of Donnellan's distinction (though such cases suggested the distinction to Donnellan in the first place). We must look elsewhere. When we do, Kripke's argument collapses.

4. AN ARGUMENT FOR DONNELLAN'S DISTINCTION

We are to consider the claim that there is a "referential" convention for definite descriptions as well as the uncontroversial, Russellian, "attributive" convention. When first confronted with this claim, we have, it seems to me, two grounds for skepticism. First, we wonder how there *could* be a conventional way of identifying an object with a description that does not uniquely apply to it, that does not, in my usage, "denote" it. How is it possible to so identify an object? Second, we wonder why we should need to posit a second convention. It seems that the descriptions we use typically apply uniquely, thus identifying an object; at least they typically seem to *purport* to do this. Thus one convention seems enough.

The discussion in the previous section suggests a response to the first ground for skepticism. We saw there that a speaker can "mean," etc., a certain object in virtue of being causally linked to that object by a d-chain. Perhaps then there is a convention making use of d-chains to identify objects. Perhaps the referential use of descriptions is made possible by d-chains.

One reason for being favorably disposed toward this suggestion would be the existence of such a convention for other terms. I think there is one. It is plausible to think that deictic (non-cross-referential, non-anaphoric) demonstratives and personal pronouns involve such a convention. Words like 'this' and 'he' seem to depend for their reference on d-chains: their use is prompted by a causal link from the speaker to the object, a link created by perception of the object; the term refers to that object, and none other in the environment, because underlying it is a d-chain grounded in that object.

If we could now show that descriptions have a use that is like that of deictic demonstratives and pronouns, we would have a very good reason for believing in the suggested convention for descriptions. I think we can show this by considering "imperfect" definite descriptions like 'the table'.[7]

Kripke begins and ends his paper with the observation that these imperfect descriptions may favor Donnellan as against Russell (pp. 6, 22). I think they do. Kripke also mentions the temptation to assimilate such descriptions to the corresponding demonstratives, e.g., 'the table' to 'that table' (p. 22). We should give in to this temptation.

Imperfect descriptions are important because they *obviously* do not denote (apply uniquely to) an object. The Russellian response is to see them as elliptical. In my view it is more plausible to see them, in their normal use, as like demonstratives and personal pronouns. In that use, not only do they not denote, *they do not even purport to denote*. They are not uttered with the intention of applying uniquely, nor would their audience normally take them to have been uttered with that intention. *Denotation is irrelevant to determining their referent.*

We have here a response to the second ground for skepticism about there being a "referential" convention for definite descriptions. Contrary to what was supposed, many of the descriptions we use do not even purport to apply uniquely, for many of them are of the imperfect variety. So there may well be a need to posit a second convention to cope with these.

If imperfect descriptions are like demonstratives and pronouns, then, from my theoretical perspective, the crucial respect in which they are like them is in depending on d-chains for identifying reference. 'This' refers to an object in which the underlying d-chain is grounded; 'he' to a male in which the underlying d-chain is grounded; 'that table' to a table in which the underlying d-chain is grounded. Similarly (normally), 'the object', 'the male', and 'the table', respectively. (I am assuming for the moment that the semantic referent of 'that F' and 'the F' must be an F even though it need not be the one and only F; but see section 5). I suggest that this account is just as plausible for the descriptions as it is for the demonstratives and pronouns. And it is very plausible for the latter. All these terms share a mode of identifying reference that has nothing to do with denotation (unique application); call the mode "designation."

It is uncontroversial that "perfect" definite descriptions like 'her husband' (in our society) have a use depending on denotation for identifying reference, an "atributive" use. Presumably an imperfect description like 'the table' can have that use too. It would not *normally* be so used because it is *obvious* that it does not denote: only someone with crazy beliefs would so use it. So all descriptions have a use depending on denotation, and, I have just argued, imperfect ones have one depending on designation. Do perfect descriptions have that use too? If the imperfect ones do, it is hard to see a good reason for denying that the perfect ones do too. All descriptions lie on a spectrum of varying degrees of "descriptive content," with 'the object' at one end and 'her husband' at the other. ("Perfect" and "imperfect" are simply vague terms marking off the extremes.) There seems no basis for drawing a line on this spectrum beyond which designation cannot be relevant to determining reference.

The earlier discussion (section 3) gives a very good reason for supposing there is no such line. In explaining intuitions about what the speaker meant by 'her husband', I called on d-chains, the very same sort of causal link that is involved in designation. Given that such links to an object can exist when any description is used (whether perfect or imperfect), and that there is a conventional use of imperfect ones depending on those links, it would be surprising indeed if there were not a conventional use of all descriptions depending on them (even, I suspect, superlatives, though these are not on our spectrum). This convention depending on designation is Donnellan's referential use.

Donnellan is right (as we are interpreting him). There are two conventional ways of using 'the F'. We might attempt to express its meaning in its attributive use as "whatever is alone in being F"; this use depends on denotation for identifying reference. We might attempt to express its meaning in its referential use as "an F in mind" or, using my terminology, "a designated F"; this use depends on designation for identifying reference.

(Objection. "This account cannot be right because it explains the meaning of a referentially used description in terms of d-chains, something about which the ordinary speaker who has grasped the meaning of descriptions knows nothing." In my view the linguistic competence of ordinary speakers is a *skill* and does not consist in semantic propositional knowledge; it does not consist in his knowing *that* an expression means such and such (1981a, secs. 4.5-5.5). What I have offered above is part of a semantic theory. Ordinary ignorance of it is beside the point.)

In summary, the key steps in the argument for a semantically significant Donnellan's distinction are as follows: (i) the view that the reference of demonstratives is determined by a certain sort of causal link to objects; (ii) the view that, in their normal use, some descriptions (the imperfect ones) are like demonstratives in this respect; (iii) the view that intuitions that the speaker "meant," etc., a certain object in cases of confusion like (1) (an intuition shared by Kripke and Donnellan) are explained by the existence of a causal link of the above sort to the object.

Finally, I should like to mention a further argument for the significance of Donnellan's distinction: its bearing on the semantics of statements attributing propositional attitudes. Quine has distinguished two sorts of context here, "opaque" and "transparent," and has suggested that the "exportation" of a singular term involved in the inference from opaque to transparent is in general implicative. However, this leads to difficulties (the problem of 'the shortest spy'). In my view, the solution is that only referential terms may be exported. This is not the place to argue this (but see 1981a, chapters 9 and 10, and 1981b, part 2).

5. VERDICT ON THE HUSBAND AND LOVER

My verdict on the case of Jones and Smith is clear. Jones is the semantic referent of 'Jones' (section 1), and so (2) (in its semantic meaning) is false. However, what the speaker meant by 'Jones' was partially Smith and partially Jones (section 3), and so what the speaker meant is partially true and partially false.[8]

Part of the verdict on the case of the husband and lover is now also clear. The speaker of (1) was using the referential convention for the description 'her husband', and so whether, and what, the description denotes is irrelevant: no question of denotation arises for a referential description in determining either its semantic referent or its speaker's referent (section 4). So the properties of the husband have nothing to do with the truth value of (1) nor of what the speaker meant by (1). The only object whose properties *could* bear on truth values, and the only object that the speaker *could* mean, is the lover. And that is the explanation of Kripke's intuition that the speaker did mean the lover (section 3). *Did* the speaker mean the lover? *Does* the kindness of the lover make (1) true (in its semantic meaning)? More needs to be said on these questions.

In section 4 I assumed, in effect, that the lover was *not* the semantic referent of 'her husband'. The assumption in question was that the semantic referent of 'the F' used referentially must be an F.[9] If this is right, then whether 'F' applies to x is relevant to whether x is the semantic referent of 'the F' (referential). What my stand on Donnellan's distinction rules as irrelevant to this question is whether 'F' applies *uniquely* to, denotes, x. According to this assumption, then, the lover is not the semantic referent of 'her husband', even though he is linked to it by a d-chain, because he is not *a* husband of the woman. A successful referential use requires application as well as designation.

Is the assumption right? I am far from sure, though I tend to think it is. Our intuitions about these cases of mistake and confusion are not clear. Perhaps there is no determinate answer to the question. If our best theory explains such intuitions as we do have about these cases, I suspect we should be happy to let it settle the answer to the question at will.

Kripke mentions an example (pp. 7-8) that may seem to cast doubt on the assumption. A religious narrative refers to its main protaganist as "The Messiah." Whether or not that person was a messiah does not seem to affect the success of the term in referring to him. However, we can save the assumption in a plausible enough way by deeming the term here to be a *name;* in my view (with some qualifications that need not concern us) application is irrelevant to the reference of names. What this example does suggest is that there is no sharp line between referential descriptions, depending on application and designation, and names, depending only on designation. What starts as a description may turn into a name.

I am even less confident about speaker's reference. Certainly we can explain the intuition that the speaker of (1) meant the lover (in terms of d-chains). But whether this justifies introducing into our theory a notion that would make the lover "the speaker's referent" of 'her husband' is much less clear. We seem to need notions of speaker meaning that enable us to explain conventional meaning. It seems that conventional meaning must be built up in some way from common speaker meanings. Suppose my tentative assumption that application is relevant to the referential convention for 'the F' is right. How could that convention have become established if application were irrelevant to the term's speaker's reference?

Despite the uncertainties of this account of (1), I am firm on what matters to Kripke's argument. The idea that descriptions have a referential use *does* have a semantically significant role in explaining reference for (1): the woman's husband is irrelevant to the truth conditions of that sentence. It is appropriate to see descriptions as ambiguous despite the comparison of (1) with (2). Sensitivity to Gricean distinctions does not undermine the significance of Donnellan's distinction. Quite the contrary. Kripke's argument collapses.

6. KRIPKE ARGUMENT II: THE SPEAKER OF RUSSELL ENGLISH

The second argument we can abstract from Kripke's paper runs as follows. It is surely *possible* that people should speak a language in which the descriptions are used only in the Russellian attributive way. Let us then *stipulate* that a group of people do speak such a language based on English, "Russell English." The same phenomena that impressed Donnellan in speakers of English will also arise for this group. The group will be indistinguishable from English speakers. This makes plausible the suggestion that English *is* Russell English (pp. 16-17).

Suppose a speaker of Russell English is at a party and mistakenly thinks that someone is drinking champagne who is actually drinking sparkling water. The speaker wants to remark that the man is happy. According to Kripke he might say, "The man in the corner drinking champagne is happy tonight," and we would say that he was referring to the teetotaler. So we have the same sort of intuition about this case as we have about Donnellan's cases. Yet we have *stipulated* that this person speaks Russell English. Perhaps then the people in Donnellan's case speak Russell English after all.

Kripke's example shows vividly the need to seek an explanation of intuitions about what a person is referring to. What could be the basis for our view that the speaker was referring to the teetotaler? Kripke does not say. According to me, we must think that this is a referential use, arising out of perception of the object and relying on designation for identification. But then our view would be inconsistent with the stipulation that the speaker is using Russell English.

Russell English differs from English in that definite descriptions are not devices in it for the designational mode of identifying reference. However, other devices for that mode remain: demonstratives, pronouns, even names. So if the speaker has a particular object in mind (the teetotaler) and means to refer to him, he will use one of those devices, not a definite description like 'the man in the corner drinking champagne'. Speakers of Russell English will behave differently from speakers of English. Donnellan's phenomena could not arise in Russell English. Kripke's claim to the contrary can seem obvious only if we tacitly treat the speaker as if he were like us, able to use descriptions referentially; i.e., as if he spoke English.

7. KRIPKE ARGUMENT III: EXPECTATIONS OF AN UNAMBIGUOUS LANGUAGE

Kripke claims that if descriptions were really ambiguous in the way Donnellan claims, we would expect to find some languages that removed the ambiguity. Yet not only do we not know of any such language, we would be very surprised to find one (p. 19). This suggests that English is not ambiguous in that way.

I shall point out below why the ambiguity causes us little trouble in practice. If it does not cause much trouble, *should* we expect to find an unambiguous language? It seems likely that scope ambiguities are more irksome, yet would we expect to find a language that removed them? Further, it is not obvious to me that we *would* be surprised to find such an unambiguous language. I doubt that much can be built on our intuitions here.

The ambiguity causes little trouble in practice for the following reasons. First, most of the descriptions we use can be placed easily into one of two groups, "imperfect" and "perfect." Imperfect descriptions are ones that are unsuitable for attributive use because only someone with crazy beliefs would so use them: it is obvious that they do not denote. Perfect descriptions, on the other hand, are suitable for attributive use. They will almost always be complex, including a name or similar device; e.g., they will be of the form 'the F of a'. It is hard to denote otherwise. Second, when a description is used referentially, there is often an obvious candidate for being an object in mind, whereas when a description is used attributively there is often no such obvious candidate. Put these two reasons together and we can see why, for the vast majority of actual description tokens, it is obvious whether they are referential or attributive.

We would expect difficulty in two sorts of cases: (i) a perfect (or near perfect) description is used attributively where there is an obvious candidate for being an object the speaker has in mind; (ii) such a description is used referentially where there is no such candidate. In both these sorts of cases there are conversational practices that remove the difficulty.

Consider an example of (i). Suppose it is well known in a group that Tom suspects a certain person of Smith's murder. Tom's investigation of the crime has led him to the quite general belief, suspicions aside, that *whoever* murdered Smith must be insane. Should he wish to express this belief to the group there is an obligation on him not to say simply "Smith's murderer is insane," but something along the lines of "Smith's murderer, whoever he may be, is insane" or, better, "Whoever murdered Smith is insane." The first remark would be taken to "conversationally imply" that he was talking about his suspect in particular, i.e., using the description referentially.

Consider next an example of (ii). Suppose that, unbeknownst to a group, Tom has a suspect for Smith's murder with the name of 'Jones'. Tom is aware that there is speculation in the group that whoever murdered Smith is insane. Tom's observations of Jones and the murder scene have led him to the belief that Jones is insane. Should he wish to express this belief to the group, there is once again an obligation on him not to say simply, "Smith's murderer is insane," but something along the lines of, "The man I suspect of Smith's murder is insane." The first remark would be taken to "conversationally imply" that he was talking of whoever murdered Smith, i.e., using the description attributively.

In sum, for most descriptions in most contexts there is no danger of confusing referential and attributive uses. Where there is danger there are conversational practices to prevent confusion.

8. KRIPKE ARGUMENT IV: ANAPHORA

Consider the following dialogue:

  A. "Her husband is kind to her."
  B. "No he isn't. The man you're referring to isn't her husband."

Now, according to Donnellan, A's use of 'her husband' is referential, referring, if at all (see section 5 above), to the lover. Kripke claims that B's use of 'he' is anaphoric, depending for its reference on 'her husband'. Yet 'he' clearly refers to the husband. So 'her husband' must refer to the husband too; Donnellan is wrong (p. 21).

Kripke suggests one way out which he goes on to dismiss straightaway:

> it might be suggested that B uses 'he' as a pronoun of laziness for A's 'her husband', taken in the supposed referential sense. This move seems to be excluded, since B may well be in no position to use 'her husband' referentially. He may merely have heard that she is married to a cruel man (p. 27, note 34).

However, there is a further possibility which Kripke does not consider: that B's use of 'he' might be a pronoun of laziness for 'her husband' *taken attributively*, even though A's use of 'her husband' is referential. If this is possible, then of course Donnellan can explain the dialogue.

I know of no reason for denying this possibility out of hand. However it is hard to be confident it should be accepted. We need to know more about pronouns in general to be confident; we need to know more about anaphora and more about how much laziness is generally acceptable. Meanwhile I think it must be allowed that Kripke has pointed to something that may be an anomaly for Donnellan's account.

CONCLUSION

Aside from this possible anomaly, I have found nothing in Kripke's paper that should cast doubt on the semantic significance of Donnellan's distinction. I have indicated that Donnellan's distinction fits into a general theory of singular terms, a theory that has a place for Gricean distinctions of the sort Kripke thinks important. This is not the place to attempt to show that this theory can accommodate a wide range of phenomena, but I do claim that it can. An advantage of the theory's emphasis on causal chains grounded in objects is that it promises an answer to the old question, "How is language linked to the world?"

Notes

1. A draft of this paper was delivered at the University of Melbourne in July 1980. I am grateful for the comments it generated on that occasion and also indebted to David Armstrong, Keith Campbell, Greg Curry, and Kim Sterelny.
2. I was insensitive to this equivocation in my 1974 paper (pp. 190-96). So Bertolet is quite right to criticize that paper's interpretation of Donnellan (Bertolet, 1980, pp. 281-83).
3. All page reference to Kripke are to this 1979 paper.
4. So I think Searle has some intuitive support for his claim that cases like this should be seen as cases of indirect speech acts (1979, pp. 194-95). However, his treatment of such cases does not conform to this view. He thinks there is one "referential aspect" other than the one that the speaker employed (e.g., in this case *that man* and not *Jones*), which the speaker would fall back on, which he meant, and which determines the truth conditions of his statement (pp. 195-97). So the speaker does not mean something *more than*, but something *different from*, what he says.
5. Similar criticisms apply to Searle's similar claims about speaker meaning (1979, pp. 194-97).
6. The theory in this and the next two sections, part of a "causal" theory of names and other related terms, is set out in more detail in my recent book (1981a, particularly secs. 2.5-2.7, 5.4). An inadequate and partly mistaken version of the theory is to be found in my 1974 article. I have preferred the term 'designational' to Donnellan's 'referential' in these other writings.
7. Finding a suitable term for these descriptions is difficult. I prefer the term 'imperfect' to Kripke's 'improper' because such a definite description does not describe its referent perfectly, whereas there is nothing in the least improper about its use (or so I shall argue). 'Indefinite definite description' is infelicitous to say the least, and 'indefinite description' is reserved for the likes of 'a table'. We should be reluctant to call on 'incomplete' to help us out because of the role given it by Frege.
8. Note that (2) grounds 'Jones' in Smith (section 3) and so could be the start of a *new* convention (though it is unlikely it would be in this case); it could be the start of a reference *change* (Devitt, 1981a, sec. 5.4).
9. This assumption goes against what Searle (and doubtless many others) sees as a "crucial feature" of Donnellan's distinction (1979, p. 190). I do not think the feature is crucial, but if it is we must simply conclude that what I am here contemplating is the dropping of Donnellan's distinction in favor of a closely related one. I shall continue to write as if the feature were not crucial.

References

Bertolet, Rod, "The Semantic Significance of Donnellan's Distinction," *Philosophical Studies* 37 (1980):281-88.
Davidson, Donald, and Gilbert Harman, eds., *Semantics of Natural Language* (Dordrecht, 1972).
Devitt, Michael, "Singular Terms," *Journal of Philosophy* 71 (1974):183-205.
_____, *Designation* (New York, 1981a).
_____, "Critical Notice" of French, Uehling, and Wettstein 1979, *Australasian Journal of Philosophy* (1981b).
Donnellan, Keith S., "Reference and Definite Descriptions," *Philosophical Review* 75 (1966): 281-304.
_____, "Putting Humpty Dumpty Together Again," *Philosophical Review* 77 (1968):203-15.
_____, "Speaker Reference, Descriptions, and Anaphora," in French, Uehling and Wettstein 1979, pp. 28-44.

Field, Hartry H., "Theory Change and the Indeterminacy of Reference," *Journal of Philosophy* 70 (1973):462-81.
French, Peter A., Theodore E. Uehling, Jr., and Howard K. Wettstein, eds., *Contemporary Perspectives in the Philosophy of Language* (Minneapolis, 1979).
Kripke, Saul, "Naming and Necessity," in Davidson and Harman 1972, pp. 253-355, 763-69.
―――, "Speaker's Reference and Semantic Reference," in French, Uehling, and Wettstein 1979, pp. 6-27.
Searle, John R., "Referential and Attributive," *Monist* 61 (1979):190-208.

Contributors

Notes on Contributors

Diana F. Ackerman is Associate Professor of Philosophy at Brown University. She is currently writing *The Methodology of Philosophy*.

Sir A. J. Ayer is Professor at Wolfson College, Oxford University. Among his recent books are *Russell and Moore: The Analytical Heritage*; *Probability and Evidence*; *Bertrand Russell as a Philosopher*; and *The Central Questions of Philosophy*.

Renford Bambrough is President of St. John's College, Cambridge, and Sidgwick Lecturer in Philosophy, University of Cambridge. He is the author of *Reason, Truth, and God* and *Moral Scepticism and Moral Knowledge*. Since 1972 he has been Editor of *Philosophy*, the journal of the Royal Institute of Philosophy.

Jon Barwise is Professor of Philosophy at Stanford University. He is the author of *Admissible Sets and Structures* and the editor of *The Handbook of Mathematical Logic*.

Paul Benacerraf is Stuart Professor of Philosophy and Chairman of the Philosophy Department at Princeton University. His principal area of interest is the philosophy of mathematics, which he views as a microcosm in which many of the larger logical, metaphysical, and epistemological issues can be seen in particularly sharpened form.

Gustav Bergmann is Emeritus Professor of Philosophy and Psychology at the University of Iowa. Among his books are *The Metaphysics of Logical Positivism*; *Meaning and Existence*; *Logic and Reality*; and *Realism*.

Graham Bird is Sir Samuel Hall Professor of Philosophy and Head of the Philosophy Department at Manchester University. He is the author of *Kant's Theory of Knowledge*; *Philosophical Tasks*; and he has published articles in a number of philosophical journals.

Keith Campbell is Associate Professor of Philosophy at the University of Sydney. During 1979-80 he was President of the Australasian Association of Philosophy. He is the author of sixteen aritcles in philosophy and two books, *Body and Mind* and *Metaphysics, An Introduction*.

NOTES ON CONTRIBUTORS

Charles Chihara is Professor of Philosophy at the University of California, Berkeley. He is the author of *Ontology and the Vicious-Circle Principle* and numerous articles on such topics as the semantic paradoxes, the theory of types, Gödel's Platonism, the surprise examination paradox, and Wittgenstein's philosophy of mathematics.

Roderick M. Chisholm is Professor of Philosophy and Andrew W. Mellon Professor of the Humanities at Brown University. He is the author of *Perceiving: A Philosophical Study*; *Person and Object: A Metaphysical Study*; *The Theory of Knowledge*; and *The First Person: An Essay on Reference and Intentionality*. He has edited and translated works by Brentano and has authored many journal articles.

Michael Devitt is Senior Lecturer in Philosophy at the University of Sydney. He is the author of *Designations* and various articles in the philosophy of language. He is currently at work on a book called *Realism and Truth*.

Herbert Hochberg is Professor of Philosophy at the University of Texas at Austin. He is the author of *Thought, Fact, and Reference* and of a number of papers in metaphysics and the philosophy of language.

W. D. Hudson is Reader in Moral Philosophy at the University of Exeter, England. Among his more recent books are *A Philosophical Approach to Religion*; *Wittgenstein and Religious Belief*; and *A Century of Moral Philosophy*.

E. D. Klemke is Professor of Philosophy at Iowa State University. He has written extensively on foundational figures in contemporary philosophy.

Douglas Lackey is Associate Professor of Philosophy at Baruch College of the City University of New York. He has edited Russell's posthumous logic papers for the Bertrand Russell Estate and published a collection of these papers under the title *Essays in Analysis*.

Michael Lockwood is Lecturer in Philosophy at University College, Oxford. His publications include articles on philosophical logic, medical ethics, animal rights, and the philosophy of science.

Ruth Barcan Marcus is Hallek Professor of Philosophy at Yale University. She is the editor of *The Logical Enterprise* and the author of several journal articles.

Gerald J. Massey is Professor of Philosophy at the University of Pittsburgh. He is the author of *Understanding Symbolic Logic* and articles in logic and the philosophy of physical geometry.

Richard L. Mendelsohn is Assistant Professor of Philosophy at Herbert H. Lehman College of The City University of New York. He has written in the areas of philosophy of logic and philosophy of language.

J. M. Moravcsik is Professor of Philosophy at Stanford University. He is the author of *Understanding Language* and has published many articles and anthologies on the philosophy of language.

Terence D. Parsons is Professor of Philosophy at the University of California, Irvine. His recent book, *Nonexistent Objects*, was published by Yale University Press.

John Perry is Professor of Philosophy at Stanford University. During 1980-81 he is fellow at the Center for Advanced Study in the Behavioral Sciences and a National

Endowment for the Humanities Fellow. He has written a number of articles and tried to write a number of books.

W. V. Quine is Professor of Philosophy Emeritus at Harvard and past President of the American Philosophical Association and the Association for Symbolic Logic. His fourteen books include *A System of Logistic*; *Word and Object*; *Set Theory and Its Logic*; and *The Roots of Reference*.

Michael D. Resnik is Professor and Chairman of the Philosophy Department at the University of North Carolina, Chapel Hill. His *Frege and the Philosophy of Mathematics* has been recently published by Cornell University Press.

David H. Sanford is Professor of Philosophy at Duke University. He has published journal articles primarily in the areas of metaphysics, philosophical logic, and the theory of knowledge. His writings on the philosophy of perception include "The Primary of Objects of Perception" in *Mind*.

John R. Searle is Professor of Philosophy at the University of California, Berkeley. He is the author of *Speech Acts*; *The Campus War*; and *Expression and Meaning*.

Fred Sommers is the Harry A. Wolfson Professor of Philosophy at Brandeis University. He has published articles on formal ontology and logical theory. His most recent work is a book, *The Logical Syntax of Natural Language*, scheduled for publication in 1981 by Oxford University Press.

Barry Stroud is Professor of Philosophy at the University of California, Berkeley. He is the author of *Hume* and a number of papers on a variety of topics in the theory of knowledge and the history of modern philosophy.

Irving Thalberg is Professor of Philosophy at the University of Illinois, Chicago Circle. He has written *Enigmas of Agency* and *Perception, Emotion, and Action*, as well as many articles in epistemology, metaphysics, and social philosophy.

Zeno Vendler is Professor of Philosophy at the University of California, San Diego. He is the author of *Linguistics in Philosophy*; *Adjectives and Nominalizations*; and *Res Cogitans*.

Morris Weitz is the Richard Koret Professor of Philosophy at Brandeis University. He is the author of many articles on aesthetics and the philosophy of language. His latest book is *The Opening Mind: A Philosophical Study of Humanistic Concepts*.

A. R. White has been the Ferens Professor of Philosophy at the University of Hull since 1961. He is the author of many books, including *G. E. Moore: A Critical Exposition*; *Attention*; *The Philosophy of Mind*; *Truth*; and *Modal Thinking*. He is editor of *The Philosophy of Action*.